The Feat_
Ogre

For Morgan,
with love
— F. P.

To my dear
nephew Ambroise
— S. F.

Barefoot Books
294 Banbury Road
Oxford, OX2 7ED

Series Editor: Gina Nuttall
Text copyright © 2011 by Fran Parnell
Illustrations copyright © 2003 & 2011 by Sophie Fatus
The moral rights of Fran Parnell and Sophie Fatus have been asserted

First published in Great Britain by Barefoot Books, Ltd in 2011
This story is an abridged version of a chapter of
The Barefoot Book of Monsters, published in 2003
All rights reserved

Graphic design by Helen Chapman, West Yorkshire
Reproduction by B&P International, Hong Kong
Printed in China on 100% acid-free paper by Printplus, Ltd
This book was typeset in Chalkduster, Gilligan's Island and Sassoon Primary
The illustrations were prepared in acrylics

Sources:
Calvino, Italo. *Italian Folktales*. George Martin, Translator.
Harcourt, Brace, Jovanovich, Inc., New York, 1980.

Chopra, Jagmohan. *Folk Tales of Italy*.
Sterling Publishers Pvt, 1985.

ISBN 978-1-84686-561-9

British Cataloguing-in-Publication Data: a catalogue of
this book is available from the British Library

1 3 5 7 9 8 6 4 2

The Feathered Ogre

A Story from Italy

Retold by Fran Parnell • Illustrated by Sophie Fatus

Barefoot Books
Step inside a story

Contents

CHAPTER 1

AN
IMPOSSibLe TaSK

Long ago in a country far away,
the king was very sick. The royal doctor
came to his bedside. First, he made the
king say, 'Ahhh'.

Then, he counted the beats of the
king's heart. Finally, he shook his head.
'Only a magic feather from the
Ogre's back can cure you, Your Royal
Highness,' he said. All the noble knights
and ladies gasped. They were horrified.

The Feathered Ogre lived on an
island far to the north. Everyone in the
kingdom was afraid of him.

Every year he jumped into a boat
and came to the mainland. He captured
one hundred of the most tasty and
tender young men and women.

He took them back to his island and
stored them for food. One year he even
snatched the king's older daughter. She
had been visiting her aunt in the north.

Many brave men had tried to stop
the Ogre. Many set off to the Ogre's
den, but none had ever returned.

The very sick king sighed. It was a
huge sigh. Then he announced, 'I will give
a reward to whoever brings me a feather
from the Ogre's back.

'I will give him my beautiful younger daughter in marriage. I will also give him half of my kingdom.'

But in his heart, the king was sad. He did not believe it could be done. And, in their hearts, his people agreed with him. The journey was so frightening. It was utterly impossible to pluck a feather right from the evil Ogre's back.

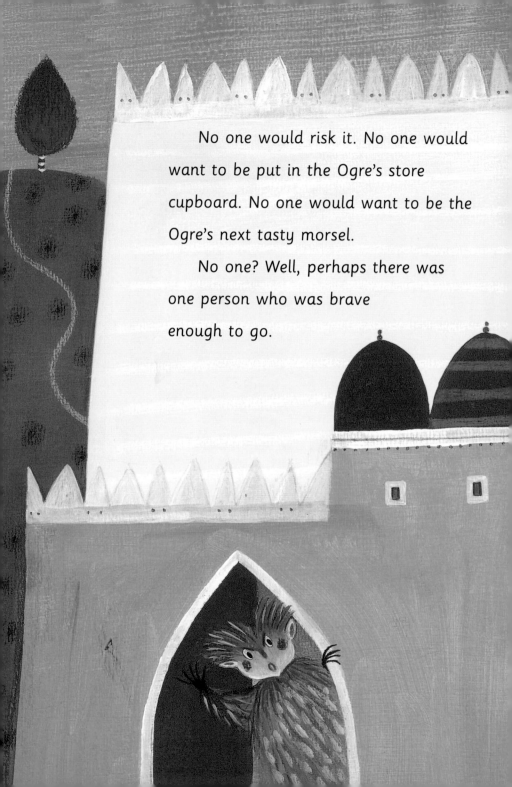

No one would risk it. No one would want to be put in the Ogre's store cupboard. No one would want to be the Ogre's next tasty morsel.

No one? Well, perhaps there was one person who was brave enough to go.

CHAPTER 2

A FrighteNiNg JourNey

Pírolo was one of the king's gardeners. He was the youngest one. But he was tired of weeding the royal potato patch. He was fed up with picking fat caterpillars off the royal cabbages.

When he heard about the reward, his eyes became dreamy. He longed for a wild adventure. He imagined half a kingdom of his own.

The only bad part was marrying the younger princess. She always made faces at him from the palace windows.

However, Pírolo decided to try and
get the feather. He threw down his
spade and found a strong walking stick.
Then he set off to the far north.

15

Pírolo travelled for many days. He went
uphill and he went downhill. He walked
through valleys where the grass was as soft
as silk and as green as a frog. He walked
over rocky cliffs where the rough stones were
as lumpy and twisted as a witch's nose.

Finally, he reached the shore at the end of the kingdom. In front of him was the sea.

Is there a boat anywhere?

And across the sea was the Feathered Ogre's island. Pírolo stood there and wondered how he might get across.

Suddenly he heard the splash
of oars and a person sighing. The
sighs were long and sad.

A rickety wooden boat was
drifting towards him over the
waves. In the boat sat the oldest
man that Pírolo had ever seen.

His face was as wrinkled as a raisin. He had a long white beard. The tip of it trailed over the side of the boat into the salty water. The boat reached the shore.

Hello, old man!

'Good day!' called Pírolo in a cheery voice. 'Will you row me over to the Feathered Ogre's island?'

The boatman looked at Pírolo with
tired eyes. Then he spoke to Pírolo
with a very tired voice. Pírolo thought
it was the weariest sound in the world.

'Traveller, I have rowed from shore
to shore for a thousand years. I am
worn out to my bones. The Feathered
Ogre has put a spell on me and I
cannot get out of this boat. So, sir,
it does not matter to me if there is a
passenger in it or not.'

Pírolo shook his head sadly at the boatman's gloomy tale. Then he jumped into the little boat.

CHAPTER 3

A Helping Hand

When they reached the island, the
boatman pointed to a huge wooden
door. It was set into the cliff nearby.
Pírolo took a deep breath. He knew
what he had to do. He marched bravely
across the sand and banged on the door
with his walking stick.

After a while, the door slowly
creaked open. Pírolo raised his stick
again. He was ready to give the Ogre a
bop on the nose. But it wasn't the ugly
Ogre standing behind the door.

Instead, it was a beautiful girl. She had bright blue eyes. She looked at Pírolo with a puzzled frown. 'You're not the Feathered Ogre!' she said. 'Who are you? Why are you here?'

Hello, I am a princess!

Pírolo explained everything to the girl. She was surprised. 'Why, the king is my father!' she said. 'That wicked old Ogre captured me last year when I was visiting my auntie. He didn't eat me because I offered to keep his cave spick and span for him.

'I helped the other people escape from him. I fed the Ogre mutton instead. Now I want to go home too.

'If you help me to find the
way, I will get a feather for you.'
Of course, Pírolo agreed.

I'll
help you

'Come into the cave and hide under the table,' said the princess. 'The Ogre will be back soon!'

Pírolo dived under the table just as the door flew open. The Feathered Ogre burst in.

CHAPTER 4

The Ogre's Secret

The Ogre looked horrible. He was scowling. His face was as scrunched as a rotten cabbage. 'Where is my supper?' he shouted.

'Here it is, Ogre dear,' said the princess. 'You munched the last man yesterday. So I have made delicious dumplings for you tonight.'

29

'Bah!' roared the Ogre. And he stuffed all of the dumplings into his mouth at once. 'Tomorrow I will catch more tasty human beings for my supper.' Then the Feathered Ogre wiped his chin on one feathery arm.

'Hah, hah, hah!' he sniggered.
'Every time I sit in the boat with that
old boatman, I laugh to myself. If only
he knew!' And he wiped a tear of
laughter from his eye.

'If only he knew what, Ogre dear?'
asked the princess.

'If only he knew how easy it is for him to escape from my magic! He could be as free as the air. All he has to do is give his passenger the oars to hold and then jump quickly out of the boat. The passenger would be stuck in his place instead.

32

'The passenger would be the
one rowing from shore to shore until
doomsday. Hah, hah, hah!'

Pírolo was listening carefully under
the table.

33

'Ogre dear, you look tired,'
murmured the princess thoughtfully.
'Why don't you have a little nap?'

'Mmmm,' said the Feathered Ogre
with a big yawn. 'That is a good idea.
I am tired out.' And he put his head
down on the table.

The girl stroked the Ogre's feathers and sang to him. Finally, he fell into a deep sleep and began to snore.

Now my father will get better!

The princess quickly pulled a magic feather from his back. She threw it under the table to Pírolo.

'Ow!' howled the Ogre, waking up.

'I've been stung!'

'There, there, Ogre dear,' the princess said softly. 'It was just a little spark from the fire that burned one of your pretty feathers. Go back to sleep.'

'Hmmm,' said the Ogre sleepily. He put his head back on the table. Soon he was snoring again.

'Quick!' whispered the princess to Pírolo. 'Now is our chance. RUN!'

CHAPTER 5

The Great Escape

Let's get out of here!

Pírolo and the princess held
hands and ran across the cave. They
opened the huge door and rushed
outside into the daylight. But the
door slammed shut with a loud bang.

As Pírolo and the princess ran
towards the boat, they heard the
Ogre wake up. 'Aaaargh!' the Ogre
raged angrily.

'Row, boatman, row!' cried
Pírolo as they flung themselves into
the boat. Behind them, the door of
the cave burst open and the Ogre
charged out.

'Come back!' shouted the Ogre. He hopped up and down in the sand.

But the boatman rowed as if the sea was on fire. At the other side, Pírolo and the princess jumped out safely.

We will be home soon.

I am so happy!

Then they told the boatman
how to escape from the spell. The
boatman smiled for the first time
in a thousand years!

Pírolo and the princess ran towards home. The princess clutched the precious feather in her hand. Uphill and downhill they dashed. Finally, they reached the palace.

42

The magic feather cured the king instantly. He was delighted to see his older daughter again. He even danced a jig around the throne room.

He kept his promise and gave Pírolo half of his kingdom. And he let Pírolo marry the older daughter instead of the younger one.

Everyone was happy!

Everyone? Well, everyone except for the wicked Feathered Ogre. While Pírolo and the princess were running home, the boatman rowed back to the island.

When he got there, the Ogre leaped into the boat with a roar. 'I will catch that nasty pair, you will see,' he shouted. 'Row faster!'

The Ogre was very angry. So he
did not notice the boatman smile.
The boatman said, 'Why don't you
take the oars? A mighty ogre like you
could row much faster than an old
man like me.'

45

The Ogre did not realise that
the boatman knew the secret.
The Ogre grabbed the oars and
sent the boat skimming over the
waves like a bird.

But before he could get out
at the other side, the boatman
jumped out of the boat into the
shallow water.

'Hah, hah, hah!' the
boatman laughed. He clicked his
heels in the air with delight.

'I'm free! I'm as free as the
air!' And he ran away over the
pebbly beach.

The Feathered Ogre howled in horror.
Pírolo and the princess heard it far away
in the palace. Now the Ogre was cursed
by his own spell. He had to row the boat
from shore to shore until doomsday. And,
as far as I know, he is still rowing!

Preface

Tourism continues to reach out in to space and time. Implicit within the trite phrase of 'tourism is the world's largest industry', it *appears* that everyone is either a tourist or a potential tourist, everywhere is someone's destination and no human activity is immune from the fleeting glimpses of transient eyes. Appearances, of course, can be deceptive.

Ironically, change, movement, development and growth are the norms that characterise a phenomenon that many still see as an opportunity to slow down, relax and do little. The new millennium will undoubtedly see more tourists, more tourism, more travel, more impacts, more to market, more to manage. Core human traits of creativity and curiosity, desires to consume and commune, along with the need to survive, remain as the fundamental, and often conflicting, drivers for this thing we label tourism. Tourism is an important subject of academic inquiry *precisely* because it is an extension of our humanity and the cultures we inhabit, and because of the rapidity of change and growth that now typifies it.

This series of six volumes arose out of a major international conference held at Sheffield Hallam University, UK, in September 2000. Organised by the Centre for Travel and Tourism, University of Northumbria and the Centre for Tourism Sheffield Hallam University, **Tourism 2000: Time for Celebration?** was designed to reflect on, evaluate and anticipate the growth and development of tourism from its roots in pilgrimage and exploration, to its present and future role as a vast and complex social and cultural activity, a diverse international industry, and a focus for academic discourse. The conference attracted tremendous interest from academics, policy makers and practitioners from across the world and in itself was a touristic experience. These books contain 173 of nearly 200 papers presented at the conference.

The importance of this series lies in its diversity as well as its dimensions. We believe it to be important that authors from differing disciplines, perspectives, nationalities and cultures are able to reflect on the many facets of tourism. With diversity, however, comes problems of categorisation and hard editorial decisions. We trust that in the main we have managed to produce a reasoned and manageable breakdown of papers.

The production of one book can generate a plethora of problems. Not surprisingly the production of six volumes involving so many contributors and from such a diversity of locations has not been without anguish. Differing interpretations of the word 'deadline' is a common source of editorial angst! Technology too, though we are indebted to it, has frequently been the object of derision – the email delivery failure, the server that is down, the lost file, the scrambled text, and the ever popular 'pressing the wrong button.'

Fortunately there are those amongst us that appear to take problems in their stride and who sail on through the waves of worry. Thanks must go to Richard Shipway for his help in chasing the most elusive of authors. Thanks also to Jill Pomfret for her help in the editing process and to Amanda Miller for her assistance. Central to this bout of thanks are the staff at Business Education Publishers Ltd (BEP), who have been down this road with us many times now and continue to deliver a service second to none. Without the professionalism, commitment and good humour of Andrea Murphy, Moira Page and everyone who has worked on this series at BEP, you would not be reading this.

Finally our thanks go, as ever, to all the contributors to the series. Reflections on International Tourism provides a home for over 200 researchers, thinkers, critics and practitioners from nearly forty countries who have been through the processes of contemplation and reflection – those precious intellectual spaces between doing and being.

The important thing that all our authors now offer us through the work contained in these pages, is an invitation for you, the reader, to engage in your own process of reflection.

Mike Robinson
Sheffield, 2000

Introduction

It would be hard to conceive of tourism without heritage. The same fascination exhibited by the Euro-elite, 'grand' tourists of the eighteenth and nineteenth centuries for the antique and the picturesque - physical symbols of social, political and economic change – has evolved into a powerful core feature of contemporary international tourism. The search for our own past, and that of 'others', continues. Short breaks to the cultural capitals of Europe in a 'done it – seen it' postmodern pastiche of the grand tour; long-haul, independent, emotional explorations of the temples of South East Asia; half-day token coach excursions from Mediterranean beach resorts to Roman amphitheatres and aqueducts; 3,000,000, largely secular visits per year to Westminster Abbey in London; 700,000, quasi religious visits per year to Elvis Presley's Graceland Mansion; and the contemplative emotive gazing upon the huts at Buchenwald concentration camp, are all valid examples of contemporary heritage tourism.

The tourism industry has long capitalised upon the public appeal of the past, its rootedness in, and across, cultures, its interpretative flexibility, its apparent capacity for perpetual re-invention, and the contagion of nostalgia. Historic sites, landscapes, museums, galleries and historically based attractions and entertainments are very much a part of the tourist experience. Unlike a favourable climate, all actual and potential destinations can draw upon some aspect of their heritage as a tourism resource.

Our pasts are continually being restored, reconstructed, packaged, interpreted and displayed, with varying degrees of sensitivity. Tourists are offered a wide choice of heritage 'products' ranging from 'natural' landscapes, built heritage sites not originally constructed for tourism purposes, those specifically designed to attract visitors, to rather more intangible festivals and events embodying 'living' cultural heritage. We can choose between numerous gradations from largely authentic historic sites to 'new improved' versions of the past. What we term 'heritage' is loose and elastic and increasingly the past is closer than we think, allowing more generations to connect with a heritage that they have actually lived through. Whilst some argue that vernacular housing once occupied by pop singers, and exhibitions of 1970's kitsch should be excluded from 'pure' heritage, the tourism industry and its economic development patrons have adopted a typically pragmatic approach. The amorphous nature of the term has only served to increase actual and potential tourist markets. Arguably tourism has exerted a democratising influence across the heritage sector, allowing new heritage forms to emerge and new audiences to develop.

Local heritage centres, locally owned and managed, drawing upon intimate relationships with local cultures and environments are proudly exhibited to visitors as expressions of community continuity, participation and civic pride. Increasingly in such cases the past has become the focus for economic regeneration and social revitalisation.

At national level too the tourism potential of a state's heritage resources (in some cases heritage may be the only resource) is seldom overlooked by governments and developers – both native and foreign. The way in which a nation's past is utilised and presented to visitors raises a host of issues relating to national and regional identities, socio-cultural participation in heritage designation, and the wider processes of economic and social restructuring and investment priorities.

Typologies of heritage, however semantically unfulfilling, together with hierarchies of its cultural and political importance, pervade policy making and academic discussion. Since the 1972 UNESCO 'Convention Concerning the Protection of the World Cultural and Natural Heritage', the concept of *world* heritage has emerged as an important element of tourism-heritage discourse. There are (at the time of writing) some 630 World Heritage Sites in 118 States. Through the very act of legitimate designation for protective purposes, many World Heritage Sites have been transformed into desirable and popular tourist destinations, and the pressures upon many have increased. Emphasis is therefore increasingly upon the management of tourism activity at such sites of international significance - a process that often sits more comfortably in the theoretical rather than the practical realm.

The underlying tension between the cultivated popularity of World Heritage Sites and the pressure that tourism can bring upon them is of course manifest across the full spectrum of heritage attractions. The economics of heritage preservation and protection frequently entails the forging of uneasy relationships with the tourism industry. Tourists to heritage sites can generate both direct and indirect income for site owners and managers, however, visitor pressures and the environmental and social impacts of tourism development activity raise issues of quality, authenticity, heritage integrity and long term sustainability. Anticipatory planning and research, together with effective management strategies, can assist in tackling such issues.

Numerous aspects of the practical management dimensions of tourism and heritage relations are covered in this volume. Examples of good practice fortunately emerge from the research that has been undertaken in the context of both world and local heritage. There is of course an immense need for further research into areas such as the valuation and pricing of heritage, mechanisms for community participation in the planning and management of heritage sites for tourism, physical and intellectual access to heritage and the development of 'new' heritages. Given the importance of tourism and the *de facto* deepening of our heritage resource base generation by generation, these research themes will not evaporate. Indeed, they open up a seam of deeper issues that are also tackled by the chapters that follow. Two inter-related issues are worthy of mention at this juncture.

First, as has been increasingly recognised over the years, the past is seldom value-neutral. Heritage does not exist independently of the social, cultural and environmental contexts that shape it. Physical manifestations of the past are duly symbolic of particular cultures and societies at particular times. The commodification of heritage for touristic consumption is in itself a cultural output. The processing and packaging of the past for tourists is selective and contentious. Akin to Heisenberg's dictum that in the process of examining an object or phenomenon we change it, as we seek to make our heritage accessible, popular, entertaining, educational, we are re-defining it - we are changing not necessarily what it is, but what it *means* to us in cultural terms. One view is that in its search for heritage 'products' the tourism industry is positively re-enforcing the importance we attach to the past. Another, and equally valid view, is that tourism is actively, and positively, challenging our relationships with the past.

This links to a second critical issue: that of ownership. Following George Orwell's observation from Nineteen Eighty Four of "who controls the past controls the future: who controls the present controls the past", it is clear the 'ownership' of heritage is an important issue that pervades the tourism-heritage debate. Changing our own heritage through, and for, tourism is one thing, changing the heritage of others for similar purposes is quite another. The concept of World Heritage is at once liberating and provocative in this respect. Notwithstanding the recognition of the need to preserve and protect important heritage sites, the question still remains of *who* are we protecting such sites for? In contrast to resource starved local communities and public authorities, it would seem that in terms of allowing or limiting access, the power to promote, to iconise, to develop, to buy and to sell, it is increasingly the tourism industry that owns and controls our heritage.

Tourism can be seen to validate acts of heritage appropriation and cultural imperialism. Certainly western, white, middle class conceptions of what heritage is, what it should be, and who it should be for are prevalent in the tourism industry. The cultural and artefactual heritages of local communities, indigenous and First Peoples appear to exist primarily for the entertainment and education of the passing tourist gaze. Ironically however, in some cases it is because of tourism that such heritages are being maintained and re-discovered.

The relationships that tourism shares with heritage are multi-layered, complex, emotive and appear at times to be annoyingly dominated by intractable issues. These features guarantee that policy and academic debate in this field will remain vigorous. Through their diverse insights into practical cases coupled with much needed theoretical explorations, the papers in this volume will make a significant contribution toward further understanding tourism - heritage relationships and will undoubtedly fuel further debate.

Reflections on International Tourism

Tourism and Heritage Relationships: Global, National and Local Perspectives

Table of Contents

Museum, monuments and tourism: The Nigerian example

M O Adesina

National Museum Calabar, Nigeria

Introduction

Tourism has been defined as the art of movement of persons or groups of people from one place to another for any reason but essentially for pleasure or in search of pleasure and entertainment. If in the course of movement the traveller crosses the international boundary and spends a minimum of 24 hours he becomes an international tourist, while a period of 96 hours qualifies him to be one within his own country (Gamely 1998). In both cases therefore any sojourner that stays shorter than the stipulated period may be technically classified as an excursionist.

Mats Epagoge (1985), in a paper presented at the public service lecture in Lagos, says that tourism in Nigeria dates back to the 15th century when in 1472, Lagos received her first visitors - the Portuguese. Historical accounts also tell us of the itinerant trans-Saharan caravans, and the old Kino merchants. With the advent of missionaries and colonial administrators, a steady stream of visitors came to what later became known as Nigeria.

This phenomenon, which started as a trickle grew in proportion over the centuries and gradually metamorphosed into what can be described as a deluge after our independence. This prompted the Nigerian Government in 1992 to establish the Nigerian Tourist Association (NTA) a quasi governmental agency that was charged with the responsibility for overseeing this novel phenomenon.

This background has greatly affected the development of the tourism industry, with successive governments giving it mere "lip service". That is governments have had a passive involvement in the development and promotion of tourism. The hypothesis also partly explains why government participation in tourism matters over these years leaves much to be desired as funds earmarked for the execution of tourism programmes are mismanaged. Due to the above and combination of factors tourism development has not taken a proper perspective.

Tourism demand is met by the concentrated effort of a wide range of tourist services. Together these services form the worlds largest and fastest growing industry. Because some of these services are crucial to the generation and satisfaction of tourist needs, while others play only a peripheral or supportive role, it is not easy to determine what constitute the tourism industry.

However, the tourism industry is supported by many services such as transport (air, land, sea) accommodation (hotels, guest houses, inns, motels) and sightseeing (festivals, physical formation, caves, beaches). All these constitute functional parts of the tourism industry without which it ceases to have any meaningful and justified existence.

The role of museums and monuments

Until very recently, the major concern of most of Africans Museums has been to preserve the Continent's cultural heritage with little attention paid to the way these institutions can contribute to economic development and improvement in social services.

The history of the museum has been variously traced by historians to either the period of Niobium, one of the last kings of Babylon in 666-538BC, a display of archaeological relics of an historic building. Others trace it to Mouseion of Alexandria founded by Ptolemy Philadelphus while yet others trace it to other classical traditions, such as Thesaurus as the temple of strong gifts to the gods or the palace art galleries the Pinakothekai. The wonder ram mere of the sixteenth and seventeenth centuries is often citied as the modern museums precursor.

In the western world, museums are seen as a celebration of science and colonial conquest. Museums in Nigeria were created for more political exigencies to arrest the wanton destruction of Nigerian antiques both by human and natural agencies, and to tell the whole world whom we are and what are past has been culturally. Whether in Nigeria or elsewhere museums serve a variety of useful purposes namely to preserve (both objects and information), to present (what is has preserved), to interpret (in different ways to different communities) and to stipulate study and research concerning what has been preserved.

As professional repositories of man's natural and cultural heritage, museums have become the firmly established treasure of all civilised societies. Today they are no longer considered to be mere repositories or agents for the preservation of a country's cultural heritage but rather a powerful instrument for the promotion of tourism. There has been a tremendous increase in museum visitors, covering the entire spectrum of the Nigerian public ranging from pre-school children to university students. Adults, both literate and illiterate, come to the museum on their own to gain knowledge and enjoyment.

Through exhibitions, museums highlight the similarities and the differences in Nigerian Culture and giving the visitors a good chance to compare and contrast the different cultures of the Nigerian people.

Some of these exhibits not only enhance self-pride but also help to close gaps that existed in history as if the people only started life when the Europeans came to West Africa. The Nok, Ife, Igbo Ukwu, Owo, and Benin Art, for example has placed Nigeria in the correct historical perspective as being amongst the most important culture in Africa.

Museums also cater for the research-minded academic who spends time perusing collections and archival materials. Thus, one finds in any museum a cross section of the public mixing and walking through the various galleries in a relaxed manner, learning about the cultural habits, achievement and development of the people and their history through visual arts.

Monuments, on the other hand, are usually relics such as building sites, column, statues etc. They can be described as the gapping icons or chain that link one generation to another and their potential cannot be over emphasised. The commission has identified over seventy monuments and sites as national monuments. Three of them have been recommended as part of UNESCO'S world heritage sites as being historically significant centres. These monuments are objects of special historic interest located in different parts of the country. Having listed these monuments in Nigeria, it is most appropriate to consider how they fit into the tourism world. As a historical relic there is need to preserve them and make them attractive to tourists in such a way that they can be seen and enjoyed for what they are.

We all know that preservation involves money and will readily agree that these days revenue allocation to museums is insufficient and erratic. Keeping museums and monuments in good condition becomes a difficult task. One of the reasons why the problems of museums and monuments appear to be so large is because in Nigeria the maintenance and running of these institutions is entirely the responsibility of the government. In Britain, for example, most museums operate independently while there are few national museums. In Nigeria, a separate organisation, the Ancient monument inspectorate, an arm of the public works department, is responsible for the maintenance and preservation of monuments.

If we agree that preservation is an important aspect of the museum work we should realise that display or exhibition is necessary if museums and monuments are to be of any benefit especially to the tourism world. Display is the basic means by which a museum communicates with the visitors but display alone is not enough. Objects must also be interpreted, implying more than a mere presentation of the objects and its associated facts is augmented by clear and accurate labelling and in the best of our museum, this is fully appreciated.

In the case of monuments the job of displaying is a bit easier. Take the case of the Old residency in Calabar and the old teacher training college in Katsina. Anyone who can perceive hardly needs to be told that they are traditional buildings. One only needs to know a little of the history behind them. The tourist guide or museum guide can usually provide this information on the spot as the case may be, supplementary to signpost affixed to the monuments.

The majority of our monuments, especially those located outside the city, have a problem of accessibility; the roads leading to them are not properly maintained, making it difficult to take tourists to them. The Kenya Museum and tourist agencies for example organise excursions for tourists who want to see various monuments and games sites, which are highly appreciated by tourists. A well-organised system of tourist management has yet to emerge that would ensure facilities for taking tourists round the various museums. A well-organised tour needs good facilities and good management. There is a need for good tourist travel agencies with a well-developed tourist guide that would organise tourist's travels that will guarantee comfort and efficiency.

Nigerian archaeologists and anthologist also have an important role to play in locating, managing and organising trips to the national monuments and sites. As professionals with wide knowledge about cultural sites and monuments they are in a better position to up-date these sites with required information and necessary facilities to make them attractive.

The potential benefits from the tourist industry are obvious but one can mention a few; Tourism brings in foreign exchange from visitors who come to visit our museum and monuments thereby increasing our revenue potentials. International tourism could also encourage the conservation of foreign exchange, which has been exported out by our nationals visiting other nations. It is not that one should not visit other nations but if we have a well developed tourist industry, our nationals might prefer to stay home and visit local sites rather than going on expensive tourist trips abroad.

Development of domestic tourism to international standard - the way forward

For a museum to serve the international tourism industry adequately an attempt should be made to interpret objects on display accurately, in order to leave its visitors as satisfied as possible. Tourists coming to Nigeria want to learn about Nigeria's cultural and natural heritage in its original and pure context. The emphasis therefore should be on improvement in display and interpretation. The museum display should be innovative and skilful to arouse the interest of the tourist. Only a well-constructed and informative display will ensure that the message gets across.

In order for Nigerian museums to attract international tourism it is important to continue to respect the principles on which they were founded although the focus of their display may shift from time to time. Our museums principles for example are founded on research, education, and exhibition and every attempt should be made to create a conducive atmosphere in which all visitors are welcome. A tourist will visit a museum to learn in an informal manner. The method of presentation should also take into consideration people's traditional setting and bear some relationship to the community they serve. This should form the basis of an exhibition. As this is the only sure way to attract tourists to spend more time digesting the display instead of allowing a situation in which he will quickly roam around the exhibition and then depart.

The geographical location of the museum and monuments is also important. The museum must be accessible to visitors, as tourists coming to Nigeria would like to learn about the country in the limited time available. While many of our museums are accessible the contrary is the case of our monuments, majority of which are located far away from the city and this explains the fewer visitors to them.

Our museums and monuments also lack modern communication facilities. Thus accurate information on them is inadequate and sometimes lacking. The situation is such that in some of our towns where museums are located communication facilities do not exist, thus resulting in the majority of people wishing to visit them staying away. In order to develop international tourism adequate communication facilities and information technology should be provided.

Museums should make an effort to attract visitors through special exhibitions on themes that relate to the people's way of life, thus making the tourists visit to our museums as successful and satisfying as possible. When all these are carefully taken care of, a museum with an active programme of activities is likely to receive revenue through related activities such as guided tours, photography, sale of souvenirs and donations towards such things as publications and mounting exhibitions.

Conclusion

It has been argued that the socio-economic well being of people is a pre-requisite for tourism appreciation and development; it's impossible for tourism to develop in a society that is riddled with hunger and poverty. A hungry man may only be concerned with the ways of 'filling' the stomach rather than listening to the rhetoric of promotion which may not make much sense to the individual. When the majority of the citizens can feed, shelter and clothe themselves, the message of domestic and international tourism development can then make an impact. If the people's basic needs are promptly satisfied, it could save time, which has been excessively spent in satisfying such needs, thereby creating room for leisure and tourism. It will afford time and opportunity to take trips to important cultural sites and monuments including the visit to museums. The present state of apathy, hopeless future and grinding poverty in Nigeria is not the best for the development of tourism.

References

Alagoa, E. J. I. Awe, B., (1972), (eds) Nigeria Antiquities special No. *African Notes* report of a symposium held at the institute of African Studies University of Ibadan 20-23 April.

All Amahan, (1991), Museum and tourism the example of Morocco ICOM. What museum for Africa? Heritage in the future ICOM.

Bassey, J. O. (1984), *Museum and Education* lecture notes centre for Museums Studies, Jos.

Beier, U. (1972), the preservation and protection of Nigeria Antiquities.

Francis, B. M. (1991), Museum and Tourism *what museum for Africa*? Hertiage in the future ICOM.

Foster, D. (1985), *Travel and Tourism Management*, London Macmillan Education Ltd.

Garba Gumel, (1988), Opening address at the 7th conference of the Archaeological Association of Nigeria, University of Port-Harcurt.

Hegarty, T. A. (1988), Economic and cultural development of tourism, a paper presented at the 2nd Nigerian International Tourism Ekpo 88, Kaduna.

Holloway, J. C. (1989), *The Business of Tourism*. Pitman, London.

Hyellahorda, E. S. *The Role of Tourism in the economic development of Gongola state* (unpublished) H. N.D Thesis Kaduna Polytechnic, Nigeria.

Provinical Museum and Galleries (1973), A report of a committee appointed by the paymaster General Department of Education and Science HMSO, London.

Museum (1978), Unesco Vol. xxxz Paris.

Towards a feedback relationship between tourism and cultural heritage in Nigeria

Olalekan Akinade

National Museum, Nigeria

Abstract

The availability of cultural and natural resource facilities the promotion of tourism world-wide. On the other hand, the management of cultural resources and related natural resources fall under the province of the museums at the global level.

The Nigerian Museum, as an industry or more appropriately, an institution, has witnessed more patronage in recent times because the international community and Nigerian public at large are gradually giving it a better recognition than before. The reason for this sudden change has been ascribed to the symbiotic relationship that exists between Tourism and Cultural Heritage.

The paper examines what the terms "Cultural Heritage" and "Tourism" mean to the fun-loving, business conscious and ever resilient humanity.

The inherent socio-political and economic values of the cultural heritage of Nigeria are highlighted. The unique roles of the various National Museums in the promotion of Cultural Tourism or Intellectual Tourism are also identified in a concise manner. As a corollary, the writer examines the place of Cultural Heritage in the struggle of Man for better up-liftment of his economy, structural and infrastructural development.

The intrinsic value of tourism from the point of view of promotional strategy and quality of packages for tourists is appraised in line with the prominence of Nigerian Cultural heritage and the National Commission for the Museums and Monuments which serves as the agency that manage the overall cultural resources of the nation.

The writer concludes that proper funding of the museum will enhance better management of tourism. Tourism promotion is acknowledged as a very good catalyst for the improvement of museum and management of Cultural Heritage. A cautionary not is given on the adverse effect of Tourism Promotion on the Heritage of Nation.

Cultural resources and establishment of museums

Nigeria is well endowed with diverse cultural resources in all the states of the Federation. The resources are historical, ethnographic and archaeological in nature. The scope of this paper will not cover a detailed study of the resources. However the resources include:

(a)   Cultural festivals, ceremonies and religious practices, e.g. Argungun Fishing Festival, (Kebbi State), Osun Festival (Osun State), Onunu Festival, Nsukka (Enugu State), wordhipping of deities e.g. Sango etc.;

(b)   Narration of oral traditions, folklore, poetry, music, traditional dance and modes of dressing;

(c)   Cultural properties e.g. Shrines and their contents, historical monuments, cultural landscapes (Sukur – Adamawa state), museums and national antiquities of ethnographic nature; and,

(d)   All archaeological sites, features and artefacts (i.e. archaeological heritage).

The locations of the resources necessitated the establishment of museums nation-wide. The available resources also determine the types of museum that are established in the respective areas. To date, the Federal Commission for museums and monuments has ensured that at least thirty out of thirty- six States have museums that will take custody of the different ethnic groups and localities. The patronage of the museums by tourists is usually determined by the type of the museum and in particular the nature of the exhibits on display.

In the past, the chance discoveries of archaeological objects and the need for the preservation of abandoned and condemned ethnographic materials facilitated the building of local museums at Esie (Kwara State), Ile-Ife (Osun State), Oron (Akwa Ibom State), Jos (Plateau State) and Benin (Edo State). On the whole, the onerous duties of Late Mr K. C. Murray and Late Mr. Bennard Fagg contributed to the establishment of museums in Nigeria in the Colonial period as well as the preservation of antiquities in general.

Tourism promotion and cultural heritage

The concepts of tourism embrace the following perceptions about tourism:

(a)   That tourism is the act of movement of people within or outside a country for the purposes of having leisure, cultural, educational, sporting and religious activities etc.;

(b)   That tourism is a mixing pot for people of different faith, cultures, races and social background (Andah, 1990);

(c)   Tourism is considered an industry dealing with travelling for recreation; and,

(d) Tourism is also seen as a recreation i.e. leisure activity and also as an economic activity (Appah, 1988:65)

Tourism could be defined as a service industry that provides opportunities for tourists to move from one place or county to another fir the purposes of relaxation, enjoyment, education and business. It can also be defined simply as a social and money-yielding industry that promotes awareness, guarantees relaxation, enjoyment, amusement, but requires the movement of people.

Efficient management, specialised skill and attractive package enhance tourism for tourists. Tourism promotion on the other hand requires efficient and workable road-network, availability of cultural and natural resources. Modern transportation facilities, structural facilities such as light, water, electricity and communication media etc. Contrasting climate resources, landscapes, landforms, vegetation and abundant Cultural resources and facilities.

Tourism enhances the promotion and propagation of cultural resource management as a whole and serves as a catalyst for the sustenance of museums. It serves as an avenue for generating revenue. The development of rural-urban areas and growth of communities are also facilitated by tourism. Tourism also promotes international trade and mutual co-existence through cross-cultural interaction and investment. Stimulation of the development of structures and infrastructures in the society is also made possible by tourism.

Tourism has been found to encourage intellectual awareness and social uprightness. More importantly tourism promotes the preservation, conversation and ethical use of archaeological resources for the research and other educational purposes.

On the basis of the destination of the tourists, two types of tourism can be identified namely International tourism (from one country to another) and domestic tourism (movement within the country). On the other hand, tourism can be group into two, based on the nature of the tourist centres and facilities available for sight seeing. In this regard, there are Eco-Tourism (requiring the use of natural resources) and Cultural or Intellectual tourism (that focuses mainly on the Cultural heritage of the country).

Tourism management can be perceived as the planning, organisation and implementation of all forms of arrangement for successful promotion of tourism. The strategy involves the use of attractive tourist package, preparation of tourist centres, availability of transportation facilities and decent accommodation.

Tourism as a dynamic entity is no longer seen solely as an opportunity for leisure, expression of wealth or affluence and a display of technological or architectural development. The current trends in the management of tourism include:

1. The use of tourism by most governments as a formidable contributor to the economic growth and a major foreign exchange earner for their countries. Tourism is a source of national income for countries such as Kenya, Tanzania, South Africa (in Africa), Barbados in the West Indies and Hawaii in the Pacific. In these countries, tourism contributes about 70% of the national revenue. In a

similar vein, in Mexico, in the Caribbean, tourism contributes to 15% of the annual foreign exchange (Onyige, 1998);

2. The most interesting trend now is, the attention given to cultural tourism at the international level, with a more popular term known as Intellectual Tourism. This type of tourism is being given prominence in Europe;

3. The use of sporting activities, religious programmes and academic workshops, congresses or international conferences, to lure tourists to various countries e.g. Mali, South Africa, Kenya, Saudi Arabia, Italy, USA etc.;

4. It is more fashionable today, to concentrate on environmental conversation and cultural resource management as catalyst for Tourism rather than placing too much emphasis on hotel management as a major focus. This new dispensation enhances the preservation of endangered floral and faunal species as well as the ever-threatened cultural property of human race;

5. It is now common, to see the state Governments in Nigeria rejuvenate their natural and cultural resources, as well as develop their rural areas in order to encourage tourism and foreign investments; and,

6. Intellectual and secondary schools as well as some tertiary institutions in Nigeria, as a matter of necessity.

In a recent review of tourism potential, key fundamental truths about tourism are highlighted as:

1. Tourism generates income by importing tourists rather than exporting its product;

2. Entertainment is provided by tourism, thereby making it possible for tourists to be consumers;

3. In tourism promotion, the private sector aspires for the greatest profit;

4. In most cases, tourism consumes quite a lot of resources and often competes with other industries in order to survive; and,

5. In a more basic perception, tourism is seen to be complex and sometimes beyond control.

Ecotourism Society defines Ecotourism as "travel to natural and cultural areas that conserve the environment and sustain the well-being of the people." This definition reflects the relationship between the environment and the culture(s) of the people. While the cultures of people sum up the cultural heritage of humanity, the Cultural Tourism thrives better in an atmosphere where there is no cultural disharmony it therefore depends on availability of well-endowed cultural resources.

Cultural Heritage could be defined as the inherited symbolic and non-symbolic aspects of people's ways of life. Where there is a well-harnessed cultural heritage, the existence of museums is facilitated. The museums on the other hand, serve as the repositories or custodians of either archaeological or products of historical past with their associated non-material values. Cultural heritage by implication attracts cultural tourism, creates job opportunities, cultural awareness, social and economic benefits.

The cultural heritage of Nigeria is characterised mostly by the material cultures of her people, who are of diverse ethnic groups and aspirations. The totality of the cultural heritage of Nigeria teaches a sense of pride, national consciousness and identity. It also reminds the people about the problems and prospects in the Nigerian environment as a cultural milieu. In a broad sense, the economy, technological know-how and artistic endowment are enshrouded in the nation's cultural heritage.

The Nigerian Cultural Heritage is typified most profoundly by the "Two Thousand Years of Nigerian Art Works" which summarises the history, ethnography and archaeology of Nigeria that serve as pointers to the prehistory of Nigeria. Beyond the scope of the ancient art works is the aspect of the prehistory of Nigeria revealed mainly by archaeological discoveries concerning the Early Stone Age, Middle Stone and Late(r) Stone Age of Man's occupation of Nigeria. The resources from various archaeological sites that attest to the survival of the Nigerian forebears during Stone Age also engender cultural tourism as a catch phrase.

Essence of cultural tourism

In Nigeria, the federal Ministry of Culture and Tourism has two major Organisations otherwise known as parastatals, that oversees the activities of both Culture and Tourism. The agencies are, the National Commission for museums and Monuments and the Nigerian Tourist Board respectively.

The National Commission for Museums and Monuments was established by Decree 77 of 1979 established the National Commission for Museums and Monuments. The responsibilities of the commission include the administration of National Museums, antiquities and Monuments; as well s establishing and maintaining national museums and other outlets for, or, in connection with, but not restricted only to antiquities, science and technology, warfare, African, Black and other antiquities, arts and crafts, architecture, natural history and educational services. The commission is empowered to be the sole accredited agency of the cultural heritage of Nigeria, especially the antiquities of Nigeria.

The Nigerian Tourist Board was established by Decree No. 54 of 1976. The Board is empowered to:

(i)   Provide advisory and information services;

(ii) Promote and undertake research in the field of tourism;

(iii) Grade and classify hotels in such a manner as may be prescribed;

(iv) Render financial assistance to the States in the field of tourism; and,

(v) Contribute to or reimburse expenditure incurred by any other person or organisation carrying on activity, which the board has the power to carry on.

In the case of the States of the Federation, the Decree empowers them to set up Tourism Committees whose functions are:

(a) To assist and advise the board on the implementation of the Decree;

(b) In consultation with the board to advise and carry out scheme aimed at encouraging Nigerians to visit the state;

(c) In consultation with the board, to carry any undertaking necessary for the promotion and development of a tourist industry of the state; and,

(d) To perform such other functions as may be designed to it by the board (Onyige, 1988).

Decree No. 54 of 1976 makes the existing structure for tourism development in Nigeria to be highly centralised. This makes it impossible for any independent action to be taken by the State Government, for the development of tourist resources and potential in the respective States of the Federation. In the past, this impediment apparently did not enhance rapid development of tourism in Nigeria. However, following the democratic nature of governance in the country, new trends towards a dynamic tourism promotion are emerging.

Tourism thrives in Nigeria because of the rich cultural heritage, tourist centres and the multi-ethnic nature of the population, etc. all of which facilities easy promotion of tourism as a whole. The national museums, monuments and the various archaeological sites provide facilities that stimulate tourists.

The Nigerian prehistory and the diverse ethnographic potentiality of the country found in nearly all geographical locations have prompted different researchers into cultures of the people. The most prominent aspect of the cultural heritage of Nigeria is the Two Thousand Years of ancient art works, which have featured in different international exhibitions in Europe and America as well as the Niger valley exhibitions, which have been moving form one country to another, amongst the countries through which river Niger passes West Africa.

The non-material aspect, which include poetry, folklore oral traditions dancing music and traditional wear etc. distinguish Nigerian in general and also give them national pride and identity. On the other hand the diverse material cultures of the people portray them as united in diversity. This rich aspect of the people's cultural heritage cannot be overemphasised, but it is appreciated when the opportunities are offered. The easiest way of getting in close touch with cultural heritage of Nigeria is the proper management of cultural tourism in the country.

The Nigerian prehistory is characterised by the activities of the Nigerian forebears in the Stone Age and Iron Age. There are archaeological sites on the Early Stone Age, Middle Stone Age, and the Late Stone Age, during which man did not have the means of writing in Nigeria, thus prompting reliance on archaeological discoveries and reliable oral traditions where they are available and applicable. Historical records and ethnographic researches have also added colours to the rich heritage of the people.

Archaeological sites on the activities of man during the Stone Age abound in the South East, South West, North Central, North East and North West in different nature and with different records that attest to the various environmental situations of the different periods. The means of survival of man consequently varied overtime. The notable archaeological sites in Nigeria include Iwo Eller, Rockshelter near Akure, Ondo State, Itaakpa Rockshelter at Iffe-Ijumu in Koki State, Taruga Iron Smelting site near Abuja, Federal Capital Territory. Ropp Rockshelter near Barkin Ladi, Plateau State, Dutsen Kongba Rockshelter Rukuba Plateau Sate and Saminaka Middle Stone Site, Kaduna State. Others are Nok site near Kwoi, Kaduna State, and Daima in Borno State etc. All the sites listed above revealed the activities of Man and the environmental situations in the Middle Stone Age, Late Stone Age and Iron Age.

The ancient arts of Nigeria dominate the material culture of man in Nigeria. They illustrate the artistic ingenuity of the Nigerian forebears as portrayed by the terracotta objects, (made of baked clay), bronze, brass, and soap stone sculptures, wooden objects, etc. The most notable ones of the series of corpus are the Nok terracotta objects, Igbo-Ukwu bronze objects, Ife terracotta and bronze objects. Others are the Benin bronze/brass and terracotta objects; Iwo and Tada sculptures in terracotta and bronze respectively.

The National Commission for Museums and Monuments has established different types of museums that display the various sculptures for the public in different location. The most outstanding of the museums are the National Museum, Jos in Plateau State, National Museum in Lagos in Lagos State, Kaduna Museum, Kaduna in Kaduna State, Owo Museum in Ondo State, Ife Museum, Ile – Ife in Osun State and Benin Museum, Benin City in Edo State. All theses museums have different exhibitions on the Two Thousand Years of Nigerian art works.

The Commission has also established three museums of national unity in Sokoto, Ibadan and Enugu. The galleries of these museums are still under construction. The most prominent of the local museums are Esie museum, Esie, Kwara State, Kano Museum Kano State, Ife Museum and Owo Museum. There are also museums of Colonial History at Aba, Abia State and the Old Residency, Calabar, Cross-River State. On the whole the location of these museums also have outstanding monuments, which are under the protection of the commission. Some of the outstanding ones are found in Plateau State, Bauchi State, Kano State, Borno State, Ogun State and Edo State.

On the basis of the available cultural resources in Nigeria and disposition of the Federal and State Government towards the promotion of tourism in the country, it can be clearly stated that the promotion of tourism in Nigeria has now assumed a new outlook which favours both tourists and the promoters. The Department of Tourism in the Federal Ministry of Culture and Tourism is also a driving force that ensures smooth conduct of affairs on tourism. The National Commission for Museums and Monuments on the other hand ensures that cultural tourism thrives because it sustains the existence of the Commission and encourages the different governments to be more interested in funding activities on cultures, so that tourists will visit the country as a whole and in return stimulate investments by foreign nationals in the different States of the Federation.

A critique of the relationship between tourism and cultural heritage

New trends in tourism have made it to become a more viable catalyst for the management of cultural resources in Nigeria. The enlisting of Sukur archaeological site, cultural landscape as a world heritage site is an example of how good preservation of cultural resources will attract tourists to a country. The status of Sukur will go a long way to drawing tourist to Borno State and also make the State Government and the Local Government in which the site is located to see to the regular maintenance of the site as well as the wish to promote cultural development in the state. There are other sites that are being considered for the World Heritage List.

In Nigeria today, both the Federal Government and State Governments are quite aware of the need to promote tourism as a means of generating revenue and also as a way of luring investors into the country. In the recent time the hosting of the World Youth Soccer Championship, tagged Nigeria '99 prompted the Federal Government to rehabilitate some of the national museums, monuments and other tourist centres. In the same vein, many State Governments such as Plateau, Borno, Edo, Oyo, Kaduna etc. have embarked on proper management of cultural resources, parks and other natural resources with a view to encouraging tourism promotion and also making tourists get acquainted with available resources that will facilitate investments in the States.

The relationship that exists is, that proper management of cultural resources serves as a catalyst for the promotion of tourism thus enhancing the thriving of cultural tourism. It is also realised that cultural tourism thrives in Nigeria, and as such governments are encouraged to fund activities on culture and tourism as a matter of priority.

The sad aspect of cultural tourism is that art lovers and dealers are becoming more desperate to buy antiquities of which there is a ready international market operated by syndicates. The juicy-nature of the prices of these ancient art works has made local people to plunder archaeological sites by digging them illegally for financial rewards. The Nok culture areas in Kaduna State, and Federal Capital Territory have been illegally dug-up in haphazard manner, in order to steal the Nok terracotta objects in the archaeological contexts and offer them for sale to illicit traffickers. The anthropomorphic ancient pottery of the Cross River area, especially Calabar has also been illegally excavated from the different archaeological sites in the metropolis.

There is also the sad stories of the looting of museums in Ile-Ife, Jos, Kaduna, Abeokuta, Esie, Makurdi etc. as well as local shrines for the priceless ancient art works of the people in the name of art-dealing. The illicit traffick in cultural property by the men of the underworld is a matter for concern to the government and people of Nigeria because of the loss of these irreplaceable art works, loss of lives and the dwindling of the cultural heritage of the country. Cultural tourism is identified as the major factor that invigorates the shady deals in ancient art works in Nigeria and perhaps in countries such as Senegal and Mali where similar incidents are rampant.

Conclusion

The consequences of unbridled cultural tourism promotion are too profound to be overlooked. This reality therefore calls for reappraisal of the development, operation and management of tourism as a whole, so as to protect and manage effectively the rich cultural heritage of Nigeria.

The recommendations towards this direction are:

1. Federal Government of Nigeria must empower both the Department of Tourism and the National Commission for Museums and Monuments to evolve ways cultural tourism can be promoted without its adverse effects on the cultural heritage of the country;

2. The need for proper funding of the activities of the two agencies cannot be over emphasised. The necessary facilities must be provided and maintained from time to time for positive results;

3. International tourists also need to be assured of the safety of their lives and property while in the country. Adequate incentives and encouragement must be given to the tourist regularly;

4. The United Nations and the UNESCO must wade into the issue of illicit traffick in cultural property with the utmost goal of putting an end to it; and,

5. The promotion of cultural tourism should not be seen as a misplaced venture but rather as an alternative means of generating revenue for the country and providing social services for humanity.

As the world is savouring the euphoria of the year 2000 the United Nations, (UN), the UNESCO and the Organisation of African Unity (OAU) must goad and encourage all the governments of the day, world-wide to place Culture and Tourism in the utmost priority of their policies and budgets. They are also to provide adequate financial provisions and necessary facilities for Tourism to survive and for the world cultural heritage to be properly harnessed and preserved. It is if, and only if, all these are done that humanity can celebrate in the year 2000.

References

Andah, B. W. (1990), Tourism as Cultural Resources: Introductory Comments. *Cultural Resource Management An African Dimension.* Andah, B. W. (Ed.) Ibadan; Owerri: Wisdom Publishers Limited.

Appah, H. O. (1990), Tourism in India – A Paradigm for the Development of the Tourism Industry in Rivers State. *Proceedings of the 7th Annual Conference of the Archaeological Association of Nigeria.* Nzewunwa, N. and Derefaka, A. (Eds).

Eyo, E. (1977), *Two thousand Years of Nigerian Art.*

Nzewunwa, N. (1988) Towards Tourism Development in Nigeria. Some global hints and queries. *Proceedings of the 7th Annual Conference of the Archaeological Association of Nigeria.* Nzewunwa, N. And Derefaka, A. (Eds.)

Ojo. R. A. (1998), The Role of Tourism in National Building. *Proceedings of the 7th Annual Conference of the Archaeological Association of Nigeria.* Nzewunwa, N. And Derefaka, A. (Eds.)

Onyige, P. U. (1988), Factors Limiting the Development of the Tourist industry in Nigeria. *Proceedings of the 7th Annual Conference of the Archaeological Association of Nigeria.* Nzewunwa, N. and Derefaka, A. (Eds.)

Industrial heritage tourism as a force for the regeneration of coalfield communities: A feasibility-desirability analysis

Rick Ball

Staffordshire University, UK

Introduction

The debate about Britain's coal industry – whether in the remnants of its productive guise, or the legacies of it's dismantling, is likely to continue for some time. This reflects the acute sensitivities that surround the demise of 'king coal', the impact on the localities and communities that supported it (Coalfields Task Force, 1998), and the need to generate an alternative, more diverse base for local economic development. Amongst the potentials for resurrecting the local economies and communities concerned, heritage-based and other tourism has been mooted and encouraged in the coalfields by a variety of agencies and funding regimes (Arwel Edwards and Coit, 1996; Ball and Metcalfe, 1995; Jansen Verbeke, 1999). Yet, in the rush to secure a brighter economic future for such areas, and in the quest to secure scarce regeneration funding, the notion of heritage-based tourism built around former coal communities, and coal-related attractions, has not been given the degree of critical assessment that it's seeming marginality might require, and that it's sceptics except.

In a sense, coalfield areas are, conventionally at least, amongst the least likely areas to develop tourism (Buckley and Witt, 1985). The provision of European and other resources and the requirement for appraisal and evaluation (Ball, 1998) has changed that, but the policy community has found it very difficult to generate a balanced and objective assessment. Talk of heated debates during the production of regional strategies or 'Programming documents' is perhaps testimony to such scepticism. At the centre of the debate are, as we shall argue, scepticisms over the feasibility and the tensions over the desirability of industrial heritage tourism.

Against a background of the growing resolve to deploy heritage as a foundation for economic regeneration (Ball and Stobart, 1996; Goodall, 1996), this paper discusses the rationale, pressures, processes, constraints and likely successes of tourism development in former coalmining localities. It contrasts the attitude and approach adopted in various European regions as a context foe evaluating the likely impacts of coalfield community tourism initiatives in the UK. In such terms, it touches on the critical success factors that might control its outcomes. It thus provides a contribution to the understanding of aspects of coal heritage tourism, focusing on the processes of heritage mobilisation and the real challenges and constraints that abound. These range from scepticism amongst some, to market and resource capacity limitations of what some view as marginal tourist attraction systems in coalfield locations.

The paper argues that, with careful nurturing, sound strategic development, and a realistic and not overoptimistic idea of attainable outputs, there is a positive role for tourism in the former coal communities. However, it also assesses the effects of limited market information and poor imagery. It then traces the lessons of success and failure that might be drawn from available policy histories. This comparative approach uses example's which include notable development, such as the Chatterley Whitfield colliery site in North Staffordshire, the coal-heritage developments in Germany's Emscher Landscape Park, and the parallel developments in the brown coal regions of Saxony, but also some of the smaller, less visible projects that are scattered around the UK and other European coalfield areas. The basis for part of the paper derives from the experience of embryo coal heritage attractions in the UK West Midlands in their quest to legitimise, secure financial and other support and, above all, succeed as sustainable businesses.

Coalfield regeneration, tourism and the industrial heritage bandwagon

The context

The spate of closures typifying UK coalfields in the 1980s and 1990s marked the culmination of a relatively (Ball, 1998). What have appeared to be rather entrenched social and economic problems of law attainment, social deprivation, and economic demise, were, as a consequence, brought into even shaper focus.

The reaction and response has been for the national, regional and local regeneration machine to move into action, seeking to inject catalysts for recovery, and to create new or expanded business opportunities. Parallel to all this, and in effect at the heart of the regeneration challenge, has been the intent to support community development and, by definition, to support the survival of the former mining communities in both social and built form.

Heritage and the survival motive

Clearly, issues of heritage are strongly entwined with the survival motive. Not surprising, amongst the tranche of potential action, tourism has been viewed as a likely candidate. The sequence of colliery closures has run parallel with an emerging commitment to, and recognition of heritage as a regenerative force (see BURA, 1996; English Heritage, 2000). As a consequence, in the UK the industrial heritage tourism bandwagon finally reached these rather marginal spaces from the 1980s onwards (see Buckley and Witt, 1985; Ball and Stobart, 1996).

If heritage-based regeneration is a challenge in general, it is even more of a challenge in the former coal producing areas. There are major development costs associated with developing and maintaining colliery and related attractions, and potential markets are modest. More than that, the failure to recognise the critical success ingredients in maintaining and sustaining such attractions has been major limitation (Barratt, 1999). That said, matters are changing, and a much more realistic view seems to have been engendered. Indeed, there are examples of what appear to be relatively successful mining attractions in coalfield regions such as the East of Scotland, and the Rhondda Valley (Ball, 2000). In the conventional traditions of research, that prompts the question of why are they successful?

From documentation to understanding

The research challenges relating to coal heritage tourism involve three sets of linked questions, context and understanding, feasibility and desirability, and process and outcome. Thus, why is coal heritage tourism important and why has it been favoured and developed? Is it feasible, and, if so, is it desirable – who benefits? What are the possible processes of feasibility enhancement and the outcomes involved? Moreover, is it possible to learn from past experiences, especially those from areas – and cultures of regeneration – outside of the UK? These issues are addressed in sections, 3, 4 and 5, which follow.

The emerging importance of coal heritage tourism as a regeneration initiative

In order to understand and thus contextualise the growing interest in, and emergence of coal heritage as a potential tourist attraction in the UK, we need to review some key factors. These include its sensitivity to contemporary debates about regeneration, the influence of available funding streams, and the existence of alternatives. Moreover, we perhaps need to set development with regard to coal heritage and colliery-based experiences, into the wider context of tourism as regeneration.

More specifically, a tourism-led and supported focus in coalfield economic regeneration is based on what appears to be a number of premises:

- The controversy and conflict over colliery closures in 1997 generated a high level of publicity, and, in a sense, created the conditions under which former collieries became politically charged attractions; the very sensitivities that surrounded the closure programme generated a wider interest; as such, using the 'heritage' is an option that seems sensible;

- There has been a general recognition of the potential foe industrial heritage tourism development by a range of industries (see Robinson, 1999); and it appears that this recognition has spilled over into the public domain, influencing policy makers at all scales (see Ball, Bull, Church and Tyler, 1999);

- The harnessing of 'heritage' has become popular with local authorities, not least of all in the benefits linked to place image and marketing; associated with that;

- Industrial heritage as a regenerative force has been linked to European funding motives; there is the huge impetus that has come from urban and regional policy, and in particular, the targeting of European Structural Funds on restructuring areas such as the coalfields; this has generated substantial European funding from Objective 2 and RECHAR via ERDF and ESF (see Ball, 1998 on the RECHAR II Programme);

- Mobilising heritage has been seen as a catalyst for the 'refurbishment turn' in the industrial buildings arena (Ball, 1999); if the 'value' of a building is associated with heritage as much as use value, then it may be retained; that gives the coal heritage tourism idea an added boost;

- There is also the catalyst of apparent success elsewhere; coalfield area regeneration approaches in parts of the European arena have successfully nurtured the heritage element, either as part of the wider effort (see Muller, 1999; and KVR, 1997 on the Route der industriekultur), through the entry regional development strategies (Jansen-Verbeke, 1999).

In general then, there appears to have been a tentative resurgence of interest in industrial heritage developments built around coalfield experiences, hitherto the poor cousin of the heritage arena.

Whilst there has been a resurgence of interest in using rather than dismantling the community and built environment structures of colliery remnants, there is a great complexity to this whole scene. For a start, there is a suggestion that the new enthusiasm is not matched with a real understanding of either the feasibility or the desirability of such developments. Beyond that, and as we shall note later, there are sensitivities and tensions between the motives and objectives of commercial and preservationist interests.

The outstanding research questions relate to issues. Thus, to what extent is the notion of heritage tourism-led regeneration a myth, or is it a real opportunity for diversification without losing the community character? In a wider sense, is it possible to almost any type of industrial infrastructure, and, if so, what lessons are to be learned? Does geography still matter here? The geographical perspective is generally vital for an understanding of the tourism industry, because whatever attractions offer accessibility is nearly always a success or failure factor. Does that still apply to coal heritage tourism, and, if so, what are the chances of durable success? How should success be measured-does it require hard outputs or is an improvement in the image and vitality of coal communities in itself adequate? Just hoe viable are coalfield features and scenarios as tourist attractions?

Heritage as tourism: Issues of feasibility and desirability in the coalfield areas

Against a background of resource led encouragement, we have argued that the debate about coal heritage tourism is related to two key, interdependent issues – feasibility and desirability. In other words, is it possible to develop a visitor attraction element around coal heritage? If so, is it desirable in the regeneration 'benefits' that it creates?

The feasibility – desirability context – issues of celebration and subservience

The questions of feasibility and desirability are vitally important, interconnected issues. Heritage developments based around coal-mining are virtually always controversial in what they are seen to be able to create, and also for what they do not deliver. Until recently at least, the coalfields would have been amongst the most 'unlikely' areas for tourism development, but new thinking is gradually eroding such attitudes. Nevertheless, we are left with the questions of scale and potential – and a need to confront questions such as just how many visitors does it need to make tourism a success?

Matters may have changed through funding, new fashions in attraction development, or the perceived success of others, but scepticism still prevails. Apparent scepticism is sometimes revealed, perhaps inadvertently. For example, an article in *The Guardian* entitled 'beyond the pits' runs with a sub-heading that 'it's not all smoke and slag heaps in the north east' and a sub-text that industrial heritage is not attractive (Cook, 2000, p.10). Even in Germany's Ruhrgebiet, where industrial heritage appears to be more overtly and genuinely celebrated, scepticism occurs in tourism marketing discourse. For example, the Essen City Web site recognises the value of retaining and displaying coal (and other) heritage in the 'Emscherzone' where it is still possible to find 'some similarity to the old images of Essen', but reveals the subservience of industrial heritage by going on to state that 'south of the city, however, astonishes the visitors with scenic harmony that is unparalleled' (Essen City Web site, 1999).

Feasibility issues are also important, as there is a clear link to desirability. If an initiative appears to be feasible it just might gain popularity as a regeneration device. In the following section, we briefly discuss the desirability issue, before focusing more fully on the vital question of feasibility.

Coal heritage tourism initiatives – assessing the desirability factor

Following years of neglect, and in the wake of the topsy - turvy worlds of global energy markets, and the vagaries of political sensitivity, coalfield communities, and the politicians and agencies that serve them, are longstanding sceptics over the course, style and even the fact of regeneration.

The question of what might be delivered is a key consideration in the arena of coal-based heritage development. Just what will be created, who will benefit and in what ways? Is a visitor attraction what communities really need or want, are there alternatives, and just what it will offer?

Earlier we accounted for the growing interest in coalfield heritage that has been based on recognised benefits, especially in the face of limited alternatives. The European level response seems to have been that using the 'heritage' is an option that seems sensible. Indeed, we have recorded recognition of its potential by industry and business, and the popularity of 'heritage' with local authorities.

Nevertheless, we are left with the questions of what does it actually create, and more important, the fear that it has been developed through over enthusiastic expectation, and in ways that will be difficult to sustain.

There is a general recognition that tourism is valuable as a regeneration device. It creates appropriate jobs in areas that need them, it provides a new positive image for places, helps nurture new businesses, possibly saves buildings, and fits in with other regeneration should provide a major stimulant to ailing destabilised communities, and with careful, strategic management, may become a sustainable pivot of new, regeneration area economies.

Whilst there are sceptics, the more overt criticisms of coal heritage developments concerns the quality, volume, and management of the attractions (Barratt, 1999), and not so much the fact of heritage tourism-based development. Feasibility is at the centre of this debate.

Addressing the feasibility issue

Feasibility is perhaps the key aspect. If it is feasible, it is easier to 'market' as a potential regeneration force. Unfortunately, it is easier to display the constraints than the possible with coal heritage-based tourism. That said, and as we will argue in section 5, there are ways forward, and, in any case, the evaluation of tourism initiatives does not always encompass all of its true outcomes.

The typical constraints associated with the attempt to develop coal-based heritage locations are as follows:

- Aside from those directly involved in the industry, coal is not an obviously attractive attraction base;

- The market for visiting heritage attractions is globally large but locally diffuse; accessibility to population is a key factor and many coalfield locations are either not central or not accessible to an appropriately large potential visitor base;

- Whilst much has been done to nurture interesting attractions in various UK coalfield areas, coal heritage lacks a general uniqueness and there are often alternative or interviewing opportunities for the tourist;

- The educational market is important, if not crucial, but it is low spending segment and the impetus for the development in the first place is jobs and spends;

- To a degree, and unsurprisingly, coal heritage developments tend to be supported on emotional rather than economic bases, and linked to that;

- They have sometimes been initiated and controlled by local voluntary, groups who lack marketing experience and financial support; significantly,

- Many local authorities and other agencies in the coalfield areas do not have great experience of nurturing coal-related attractions or experiences; as a consequence,

- Engaging in initiatives to stimulate tourism in this way represents a new, and relatively untried departure that is not always welcome in local authorities that are sensitive to success and failure in regeneration initiatives.

Against the constraints, there are possible positives, particularly connecting with essentially local enthusiasm, available resources, and innovative design, representation or management. Indeed, there are examples of sustained coal heritage developments in the UK, the Rhondda Heritage Park for example, or examples in other parts of Europe, in the Emscherzone in North-Rhine Westphalia, that appear to be performing relatively well.

Perhaps the important point is that feasibility may not only be constrained but also induced by the particular incidence and operational effect of these factors. Success or failure will not only result from the quality, location and scale of the attraction, but will also be a function of the degree of innovativeness in attraction development, the existence or otherwise of local policy support, as well as attitudes to coal heritage tourism, and the incidence of 'champions', whether amongst local authorities, voluntary or community groups, or private sector interests. That said, whilst it may be possible to encourage large existing firms to marginally diversify towards heritage attractions, such as with the brewery, glass, or ceramics industries (Robinson, 1999), there is no substantial base remaining in the coal sector.

Beyond all this, there are deeper debates, sensitivities and tensions.

Feasibility and desirability are key issues, but the question of what alternatives needs to be addressed. As a general point how else can the legacy of the coalfield be harnessed in positive ways that generate economic opportunities and fresh images, and if there are ways, are they potentially as effective? Just what else is there?

More than that, there is no reason why lessons cannot be learned, and new ideas developed. Learning to do it better, through training, careful development, or commitment, is vital in any regeneration process, and there may be lessons for UK coalfield regions from elsewhere. As such, in the following section, we focus on processes of enhancement, maximising the chances of success with coal heritage tourism.

Exploring processes of enhancement through comparative analysis – towards the coal heritage learning region

How might the feasibility of developing coal heritage tourism be enhanced, and with what suite of policies?

A vital issue is clearly how to manage, sustain and develop coal heritage tourism activities. In this final substantive section we focus on the process of enhancing the chances of successful coal heritage based tourism development and the potential outcomes of such initiatives – not least of all because that will provide signals and direction for the policy and planning machine. This generates challenges such as what makes a successful coal heritage attraction? In fashionable language, what are the critical success factors and is it possible to pin them down? What is the process of transaction from redundancy to heritage attraction – what factors are involved?

On the basis of our preceding analysis, we might say that it is linked to a series of local factors and actions as follows:

- The 'strength' of an attraction – the costs of its development; its marketability and its competitive situation;

- Local support, and the constraints on successful implementation of ideas – in terms of the costs, and the willingness of owners, the local population, and the local authority;

- The existences of support funding, and innovative policies;

- The ability of project initiators to effect change in attitudes to the heritage use of former colliery sites;

- Issues in the 'local' – which include refurbishment needs, the condition and status of built fabric, and whether buildings are 'listed', 'scheduled' or preserved in some other legal stricture; and,

- Whether there is local support or antagonism.

At this stage of discussion, some examples might be useful. Given limitations on space, we set out some background on typical UK industrial area and its tourism initiatives. We then contrast and compare its experiences with a contrasting regeneration environment.

Moving towards coal heritage tourism as a part of a wider heritage thrust – the North Staffordshire region

North Staffordshire is a restructuring area economy historically typified by coal mining, ceramics, steel - making and other manufactures. As such, it represents a valuable laboratory with which to test and judge heritage potentials. Whilst tourism has been recognised as an area of growth and potential in general (Ball and Metcalfe, 1995), it is in the industrial environment where the increased recognition of tourism strategies in such areas has both precipitated and required the greatest attitudinal change on the part of local political interests. Changing the culture of the manufacturing or mining base is a difficult process, part of the wider challenge facing all industrial areas that aspire to develop a tourism base. This includes the following limitations:

- The lack of a strong and experienced culture of hospitality, at least to market standards;

- Underdeveloped expertise within local authorities in the short-term;

- An inability to realise the potential of tourism on the part of some groups within the locality – the scepticism factor in the light of the unattractive image which is thought to deter tourists;

- Past failures, although these may be counter balanced by the successes of others.

As with local economic regeneration policy in general, the major differentiating factor between places is the activeness, indeed proactiveness of the responsible agencies. Similar to the process of engagement in the local economic policy (Sellgren, 1991), the gradual involvement of localities in heritage tourism probably reflects the incidence of decline that confronted them, with a few pioneers such as Bradford (Buckley and Witt, 1985) leading the way.

In terms of tourism potential, the Stoke-on-Trent area is typical of an industrial urban environment. There has been a long tradition of pottery heritage with developments such as those at the Gladstone Pottery Museum from the early 1970s, and others. However, most of the early heritage attractions were developed and maintained as adjuncts to the core manufacturing business, or as devices for saving local heritage buildings. This was reflected in the policy infrastructure. Even when the 1986 National Garden Festival was under development, the City of Stoke-on-Trent maintained only a part-time tourism officer who doubled as economic development manager!

As elsewhere, conditions have changed in places like Stoke-on-Trent. From the late 1980s onwards, it has considerably increased its commitment to tourism (and to economic development). The motive came through the regeneration challenge and the search for alternative economic activities in the face of ceramic industry labour shedding and more recently, the coal closures.

Beyond the restraints of the business culture, coalfield industrial areas such as this are confronted with attraction limitations and deficiencies. There are often plenty of marketable attractions, but they tend to be small scale, generating only a modest visitor base. For example, the plan to develop a heritage attraction on the basis of an existing drift mine at Apedale in Newcastle-under-Lyme (Apedale Mining Heritage Centre Business Plan, 1999) is likely to be constrained by such forces and needs to find ways of generating larger markets (see Ball and Stobart, 1996; Stobart and Ball, 1998).

In contrast, large attractions in coal heritage have proved problematical, controversial and politically sensitive. Indeed, there have been failures and this is perhaps the most prominent part of the area's coal heritage experience. The Chatterley Whitfield colliery site – in terms of retained buildings, with 28 Listed or Scheduled certainly one of the best preserved examples of a working colliery (English Heritage, 1999), was developed as a coal museum. It acquired the British Coal collection, but failed to secure enough revenue and/or funding support to retain its activities. It opened in 1978, but after a mix of success and failures in terms of visitor's numbers and related activities, closed in 1993. It had suffered from the closure of its unique underground experience when an adjacent colliery that pumped water from Chatterley Whitfield also closed, began to lose out to the growing array of mining experience elsewhere as the coal industry contracted, and proved difficult in terms of its inaccessible location. It may be that future Lottery funding might change the cost position, although the idea of the site solely as a heritage tourism location has been long since jettisoned (see Stoke-on-Trent City Council, 1998).

With a strong hint of irony, it has been increasingly recognised that industrial heritage features are potentially viable as tourist attractions if they are able to promote quality and if they are accessible. Perhaps on its belief, the Stoke-on-Trent area now boasts an array of industrial museums, visitor centres and linked attractions, and it has begun to develop business tourism. In effect, it offers a combination of attractive business and conference tourism, and the less comfortable heritage attractions with other more fashionable locations, such as the Peak District recreational potential and Alton Towers. It has been able to successfully market, in conjunction with Staffordshire Tourism, a short-breaks element.

Whether this industrial area will be able to maintain and enhance its tourism development impetus is the central question. Certainly, coal is only likely to be part of the scene. There is only a minute for heritage attractions, but there are well-known names such as Wedgwood, and Royal Doulton. These are international household names – icons of quality, and are able to attract overseas as well as domestic tourists. Many of these pottery firms have invested in enhanced visitor facilities over the last few years; for example, Wedgwood has a £6m redevelopment of its visitor centre complex due to commence in late 1999.

The area was further stimulated from the mid-1990s when it began to receive European funding through Objective 2 and/or RECHAR status for parts of North Staffordshire, as well as receiving Urban Pilot Project funding. A variety of tourism projects – including the development of the cultural quarter in Hanley, Gladstone Pottery Museum, and Apedale Mining Heritage Centre – have received support. This is reflective of the initial stimulus – the regeneration catalyst, an influence that has unlocked the potential of local cultural heritage. This, together with the lurking and convert influence of the sustainability debate, and the disputably clean and friendly image of tourism, has been a major element in raising the prominence of tourism policy and planning in this industrial environment.

Whilst the area has a poor image, limited tourist infrastructure, and a modest accommodation base (Heart of England Tourist Board/Stoke-on-Trent City Council, 1997), the key to a successful future development of tourism in an old industrial area such as Stoke-on-Trent resides in actions, resources and competition. Innovative local officers, a willingness to commit resources, together with support from outside agencies – regional-national-European – will condition future development. That said, the area struggles to shake off its industrial image, and to secure large visitor numbers. The most recent visitor survey estimates almost 2 million visitors per annum, but this includes a large proportion of sub-regional shoppers. Individual attractions struggle to increase visitor numbers beyond 40,000, and it is only Wedgwood that, so far, has been able to expand into the higher echelons. The typical problems of older industrial areas aspiring to tourism developments are that whilst they may have enhanced commitment for it, many other places have gone through the same process of attempted diversification. The competition between such places is substantial (Ball and Stobart, 1998; Hall, 1993) and that inherently geographical feature remains the ultimate challenge for them all.

On the face of it, this would be an obvious place to nurture a coal heritage tourism sector. However, this is an example that demonstrates the limitations, perceived and otherwise, of nurturing tourism in old industrial areas such as those around coalfield communities. Some substantial change in the culture of regeneration needs to occur.

What has been learned so far, and are there more lessons to be learned? It seems that feasibility may well be enhanced if marginal attractions are combined into a package of mixed attractions. This is becoming apparent in some UK environments, not least of all because it has been tried and tested in other regeneration environments such as Ruhrgebiet in Germany

Borrowing from others – how to be effective with tourism initiatives: some observations

Given the limitations on coal and other heritage development in areas such as North Staffordshire, how night feasibility be enhanced? That requires a consideration of how we improve regeneration policy.

The regeneration learning process works through the identification and application of ideas, some of which might be original but most of which are applications of existing practice. In such terms, perhaps the way forward is to learn from the experiences of others. Exchange of Experience activities have been encouraged by the European Commission through its various Structural Fund initiatives, in the UK particularly through Objective 2 and Community Initiatives such as REDHAR. From these, numerous insights are available. In the case of coal heritage development, an exchange of experience project in the West Midlands that has involved working visits to North Rhine Westphalia and Saxony, as well as Midlothian and Rhondda Cyon Taff (see Ball, 2000) has generated some fascinating insights into the subject.

Although they are subject to vagaries of fluctuating interest, both the Scottish Mining Museum, and Rhondda Heritage Park, have been moderately successful in sustaining a visitor demand (Ball, 2000). The ingredients seem to be local enthusiasm, the existence of a charismatic and/or innovative Director and team, the ability to link developments to wider refurbishment, planning and regeneration initiatives, and support from the local state. Beyond that, the scale and quality of attraction and the accessibility are important factors. In Rhondda, there is an enduring issue over competition with Big Pit, just a few miles to the South East. Smaller attractions are likely to suffer even more, and it is this scale of facility that is most numerous in the general array of potential attractions. As such, surmounting the constraints of smallness is the vital factor.

In Germany's North Rhine Westphalia (NRW), the regeneration effort has been substantial and sustained. The heritage factor is an important part of the scene. Coal-based heritage developments, partly fostering tourism but with wider objectives, and although in their early stages, reflect heritage as celebration. In contrast to many UK experiences, developments are typified by:

- The tendency to take a more holistic view of regeneration sites and processes; as well as,

- Engaging the local community and heritage groups from the outset;

- A confidence in nurturing and developing major colliery sites, a larger and more adventurous scale of attractions; linked to this,

- A more generous allocation of resources to preserve and enhance rather than demolish, and a willingness to selectively retain, in a way that has been gradually becoming evident in the UK (see Ball, 1999);

- An attitude of celebration rather than concealment, with an innovative use of colliery infrastructure and less likelihood of dismantling without a consideration of alternative uses;

- The development of mixed-uses and mixed attractions at sites, with for example, an array of tourist and non-tourist uses of major sites (see, for example, Muller, 1999); usually involving,

- New ideas in attraction system development with a quest for uniqueness and the large scale interconnection of attractions in order to generate a viable attraction system.

An excellent example of the commitment to heritage, involving coal and linked industrial attractions, is the Route der industruekultur (KVR, 1999), the Ruhr District Association of Communities. This is an agency which covers the main settlements in the area, and a total population of around 5.5million spread over 4,434 sq.kms, 116kms from east to west and 67kms from north to south.

From its earlier, and original regional basis as an association of coal districts in the 1920s, KVR has developed and maintained its involvement in land-use, planning and promotion, with a continuing commitment towards coal communities. It is early days with this initiative, so early in fact, that they don't seem to have settled on an English translation. Some refer to the Route of industrial culture, others to the Route of industrial heritage, although the latter seems likely.

Figure 1   The route der industriekultur

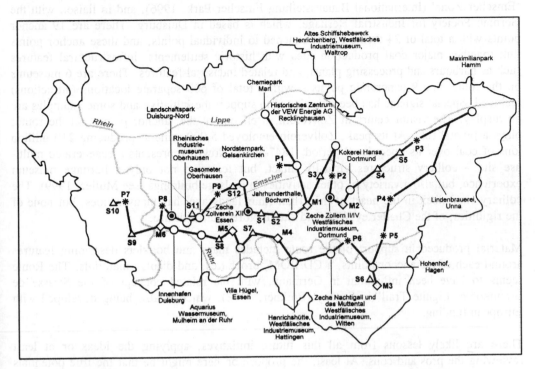

O   **Anchor point**

◉   **Anchor point with Visitors Centre**

◇   **Museums - technology & social history**

M1   Deutsches Bergbau-Museum, Bochum
M2   Deutsche Arbeitsschutzausstellung, Dortmund
M3   Westfälisches Freilichtmuseum Hagen,
         Landesmuseum für Handwerk und Technik
M4   Eisenbahnmuseum, Bochum-Dahlhausen
M5   Ruhrlandmuseum, Essen
M6   Museum der Deutschen Binnenschiffahrt, Duisburg

✳   **Industrial landscape panoramas**

P1   Halde Hoppenbruch, Herten
P2   Halde Schwerin, Castrop-Rauxel
P3   Halde Grosses Holz, Bergkamen
P4   Fernsehturm "Florian", Dortmund
P5   Hohensyburg, Dortmund
P6   Berger-Denkmal auf dem Hohenstein, Witten
P7   Halde Pattberg, Moers
P8   Alsumer Berg, Duisburg
P9   Tetraeder, Bottrop

△   **Housing & communities**

S1   Flöz Dickebank, Gelsenkirchen-Ückendorf
S2   Dahlhauser Heide, Bochum-Hordel
S3   Teutoburgia, Herne-Börnig
S4   Alte Kolonie Eving, Dortmund
S5   Ziethenstrasse, Lünen
S6   Lange Riege, Hagen-Eilpe
S7   Altenhof II, Essen
S8   Margarethenhöhe, Essen
S9   Rheinpreussen, Duisburg-Homberg
S10   Alt-Siedlung Friedrich-Heinrich, Kamp-Lintfort
S11   Eisenheim, Oberhausen
S12   Gartenstadt Welheim, Bottrop

The 400km route (Figure 1) has been developed within the Internationale Bauausstellung Emscher Park (IBA), the international building exhibition in what is referred to as the 'Emscher Zone' (International Bauausstellung Emscher Park, 1996), and in liaison with the German Society for Industrial Heritage, which is based in Duisburg. There are 19 anchor points with a total of 24 theme routes attached to individual points, and these anchor points link together major coal production sites with historic settlements, infrastructural features such as harbours and processing plants, and related industrial features. There are 6 museums on the route, and 9 panoramic points – with a total of 600 separate locations (attractions) included. Special signage has been developed to support the initiative and some examples are on display. The visitor centre at Zollverein, itself one of the 'anchor points' on the route, plays a pivotal role. At its peak, Zollverein employed 5,000 miners, producing 210 million tons of coal over its operational period, 1847-1996. Now it represents a regenerated multi-use site – colliery structures virtually intact, but featuring not only a heritage museum experience, but also a variety of other activities in its large buildings (see Muller, 1999). The colliery site, albeit in the heart of the urban Rhur landscape, has many echoes, but none of the rigidities, of the Chatterley Whitfield site in North Staffordshire.

Material produced in support of the route includes maps and booklets describing features around each of the anchor points, a CD ROM, brochures, and display materials. The Route seems to have been influential in Germany, with the related concept of the Strasse de Braunkohle 'Lignite Trail' in Saxony (Berkner, 1998), which is also being developed with European funding.

There are likely lessons from all this future initiatives, applying the ideas or at least reviewing the pros and cons. At least, the proposition here might be that the true potentials for coal heritage tourism reside in the notion of multi-use (attraction) approach, or a mixed-market strategy. This might correspond to potentials, in terms of regeneration generalities, and in terms of specific opportunities (such as using a former colliery building, and/or building an attraction around coal heritage).

Conclusions and reflections

The world of heritage, tourism and regeneration is full of tensions and sensitivities and even links through to subsidisation and public-private competition.

In the German culture of regeneration, we find innumerable good ideas and a strength of support for industrial heritage that is only now being generated in the UK. Of course, developments are yet to be tested – and in any case, what criteria should be deployed? There is a tendency for assessment to be in terms of difficult to achieve (and even verify) targets such as the 'number of overnight stayers induced' by a project. There may be a need to take a wider, more considered view of the heritage retention and the long-term achievements in the search for a 'quick fix'.

The government machine has recently 'revisited' the problems of coalfield regeneration and is taking a wider, fuller and longer-term view. That said, it is evident the tourism and heritage focus in this regime has been relegated to a lesser, yet still existent, position. For example, the 1998 Report of the coalfields Taskforce includes only three references to tourism, two of which are focused on supporting the National Mining Museum at Wakefield (Coalfields Task Force, 1998).

That rather accords with the view of industry professionals. For example, Barratt (1999) is sceptical, not about heritage potential but about the business sensibility and management quality of existing and developing attractions. He considers the relatively 'easy' funding conditions to be very much a 'mixed blessing', leading to non-commercial viability and ultimate failure. A case in point would be the £50 million, Millennium Lottery funded Earth Centre in Doncaster. This is cited in the media as a faltering project that has struggled to get anywhere near its target visitor base. Barratt would argue that it lacks a clear brand and that it is probably not in a suitable location (Barratt, 1999).

What are the implications of all of this? It may be that the policy and funding machine should focus only on commercial viable attractions – in effect, invoking a centralisation strategy. The question is still how does that accord with the wider remit for heritage? Consequently, a tension emerges between the heritage preservationist lobby and those with a stronger and stricter commercial edge and requirement. Perhaps the government review initiated in February 2000 (English Heritage, 2000), and partly focused on heritage and economic development, will help to rectify matters.

Tourism is definitely on the regeneration agenda in wider spheres. For example, the European Commission in their guidelines for co-ordinating the Structural Funds programmes over the 2000-2006 period with the Cohesion Fund, make a deliberate reference to tourism and culture as advantageous and needing to be supported (European Commission, 1999, p.25). As such, it seems certain that coal heritage tourism is destined to be a matter of 'potential rather than pretender'.

Debates are still ongoing, and there are seemingly more sceptics than advocates. That gives an even greater sense of centre stage to the questions of feasibility-desirability. The importance of learning for regeneration (Ball,1999) and flexible strategies is evident. As the debate pans out, these are likely to be the critical success factors in any sustainable tourism based on coal heritage.

Chaos and confusion still surround strategic thinking as regards coal heritage developments. Whilst it may be that the poor cousin fights back, with the resurgence of interest in industrial heritage tourism as a force for the regeneration and reassertion of community in the coalfield locations and tourism, both the feasibility and the desirability have yet to be fully and unequivocally debated.

References

Arwel Edwards, J. and Llurdes I Coit, J. C. (1996), Mines and quarries: industrial heritage tourism, *Annals of Tourism Research*, 23 (2): 341-363.

Apedale Mining Heritage Centre (1999), *Business Plan*, Apedale, Newcastle-under-Lyme.

Ashworth, G. (1996), Heritage and tourists: a simple relationship but a complex management problem, Paper presented at RGS conference on heritage tourism, RGS, London, October.

Ball, R. M. (1998), RECHAR II in the West Midlands: the anatomy of a Community Initiative, *Local Economy*, 12 (3): 335-361.

Ball, R. M. (1999), Developers, regeneration and sustainability in the re-use of vacant industrial buildings, *Building Research and Information*, 27 (3): 1-9.

Ball, R. M. (2000), Learning for Regeneration: reflections at the interim stage, Keynote Lecture, West Midlands RECHAR II Exchange of Experience Project, Interim Dissemination Conference, Staffordshire University, Lichfield, 4th February.

Ball, R. M., Bull, C., Church, A., and Tyler, D. (1999), Public policy responses to tourism, paper presented at the Geography of British Tourism Conference, University of Exeter, September.

Ball, R. M. and Metcalfe, M. (1995), Tourism development at the margins: pits, pots and potential in the Potteries locality, in tourism in Europe – the 1992 Conference, Durham.

Ball, R. M. and Stobart, J. (1996), Promoting the industrial heritage dimension in Midlands tourism: a critical analysis of local policy attitudes and approaches, Chapter 2 of Robinson, M.;N. and Callaghan, P. (eds) *Managing Cultural Resources for the Tourist*, Business Education Publishers, Durham.

Ball, R. M. and Stobart, J. (1998), Local authorities, tourism and competition, *Local Economy,* 12 (3): 342-353.

Barratt, M. (1999), Tourism and the regeneration process – a perspective on Wedgwood from the private sector, Paper presented at the Regional Studies Association Conference on 'Tourism, heritage and the sustainable region; from degeneration to regeneration', Staffordshire University, Stoke-on-Trent, November.

Berkner, A. (1998), *Projekt Mitteldeutsche Braunkohlenstrasse*, Dachverein Mitteldeutsche Strasse der Braunkhole e. V, Espenhain.

Buckley, P. and Witt, S. (1985), Tourism in difficult areas I: case studies of Bradford, Bristol, Glasgow and Hamm, *Tourism Management*, 6 (3): 205-213.

British Urban Regeneration Association. (1996), *Visitor Cities: Museum and Heritage Projects as Catalysts for Urban Regeneration*. BURA, London.

Charlton, C., Essex, S. (1996), The involvement of District Councils in tourism in England and Wales, *Geoforum*, 27 (2): 175-192.

Coalfields Task Force (1998), *Making the Difference: a new start for England's coalfield communities*, The Coalfield Task Report, June.

Cook, S. (2000), Northumbria: Beyond the pits, *The Guardian*, 8th January, p10.

English Heritage. (1999), Chatterley Whitfield Colliery, Papers provided for a Board members visit, May.

English Heritage. (2000), Government's review of policies relating to the historic environment, Invitation to participate, English Heritage, London, February.

Essen Web Site (1999), Introduction to tourism in Essen, http://www.essen.de European Commission (1999) *The Structural Funds and their co-ordination within the Cohesion Fund: Guidelines for programmes in the period 2000-2006,* European Union, Regional Policy, Communication, Brussels.

Gale, A. (1994), *Fuel for thought: the status and future of coal-mining collections in North East museums,* North of England Museums Service.

Goodall, B.(1987), Tourism and regional development, *Built Environment,* 13 (2): 69-72.

Goodall, B (1996), The future for heritage tourism: prospects and pitfalls, Paper presented at RGS conference on heritage tourism, RGS, London Board Worcester.

Heart of England Tourist Board/Stoke-on-Trent City Council. (1997), *A Tourism Strategy for Stoke-on-Trent,* May.

Heart of England Tourist Board. (1998), *Visitor Focus: Growing Prosperity in the Heart of England through Tourism, 1998-2003,* Heart of England Tourist Board, Worcester.

Hudson, R, and Townsend, A. (1992), Tourism employment and policy choices for local government, chapter 4, of Propml, W. and Lavery, P. (eds) *Tourism in Europe: Structures and Developments,* CAB International, Wallingford.

IBA (Internationale Bauausstellung) Emscher Park.(1996), *The Emscher Park International Building Exhibition: an Institution of the State of North-Rhine Westphalia,* IBA Emscher Park, Gelsenkirchen.

Jasen-Verbeke, M. (1999), Industrial heritage: a nexus for sustainable tourism development, *Tourism Geographies,* 1 (1): 70-85.

Kommunalverband Ruhregebiet (KVR)(1997), *Route der Industriekultur: Tourismus im Ruhrgebiet,* Projekt – Info, KVR, Ateilung Planung in Zusammenarbeit mit der Deutschen Gesellschaft fur Industriekultur, Essen, June.

Muller, K. (Ed) (1999), *Zollverein: a symbol of structural transformations,* Stiftung Zollverein, Essen.

Robinson, M. (1999), Tourism development in deindustrialising centres of the UK: change, culture and conflict, Chapter 6 of Robinson, M. and Boniface, P. (eds) *Tourism and Cultural Conflicts,* CAB International.

Sellgren, J. (1991), The changing nature of economic development activities: a longitudinal analysis on local authorities in Britain, *Environment and Planning C,* 9,pp.341-362.

Stobart, J. and Ball, R. M.(1998), Tourism and local economic development: beyond the conventional view, *Local Economy,* 13 (2): 228-238.

Stoke-on-Trent City Council, (1995), *Tourism Strategy, 1995-1997,* Stoke-on-Trent.

Stoke-on-Trent City Council, (1998), Chatterley Whitfield Conference Proceedings, Potteries Museum, Hanley.

Gastronomy, the neglected heritage

Alicia Bernard and Patricia Dominguez

Universidad de las Americas-Puebla, Mexico

Abstract

This paper explains the development of art and gastronomy routes to promote urban tourism in a sample of colonial cities which are UNESCO World Heritage Sites. As an example, routes developed for Mexico City, Puebla and Oaxaca are presented. The search for new and more interesting products has led to the rediscovery of cultural tourism with all of its aspects. However, an aspect that reflects the ancestral customs, history, geography, daily life, religion, economic and social development of a region has not been fully explored: gastronomy. This paper offers suggestions to integrate gastronomy to the cultural tourist product, as a way to fully explore heritage sites.

Introduction

The tourism industry has been forced to broaden its options to respond to the increasing demands of more sophisticated tourists. Hence, in recent years there has been a rediscovery of the importance of cultural tourism in its multiple stages. Nevertheless, there is a stage that carries by itself ancient customs, history, geography, religion, economy and social life that has not been profoundly studied: gastronomy.

Cultural tourism

The international tourism market is changing. The increase in purchasing ability, greater availability of leisure time, as well as social and democratic changes in the developed countries, have been modified travellers demands creating a substantially different market in the 90s in comparison to the one in the 70s. The outcome of these social changes translates into a larger variety of tourists regarding type, needs and patterns (Martin and Mason, quoted by Weiler and Hall, 1992). The tourist market is more segmented and specialised in the development of new leisure and tourism styles. (Weiler and Hall, 1992). Nevertheless, the limited number of studies on specialisation within the tourist market reflects the difficulties found while attempting to classify tourists on a basis of motivation. The profile for the tourist with special interests is very limited.

Generally, these tourists belong to the allocentric category according to Plog's psycographic classification (quoted by Weiler and Hall, 1992). An allocentric person is one whose interest patterns are focused on varied activities. Such a person is outgoing and self-confident and is characterised by being adventurous and willing to reach out and experiment. For the allocentric personality, travelling becomes a way to express inquisitiveness and to satisfy curiosity (McIntosh and Goelder, 1990).

Culture, heritage, and the arts have long contributed to the appeal of tourist destinations. However, in recent years, culture has been rediscovered as an important marketing tool to attract those travellers with a special interest in heritage and arts. Throughout the world, museums, art galleries, heritage sites, historic landmarks, archaeological sites, and festivals have become major tourist attractions. Rather than just being peripheral or secondary attractions, arts and heritage are increasingly becoming major catalysts in the whole travelling experience (Zeppel and Hall, quoted by Weiler and Hall, 1992).

Gastronomy and UNESCO world heritage

UNESCO's mission is and has been to promote understanding through the intercultural bonds among cultures. To achieve this contact with historic, monumental, and natural heritage becomes a cognitive experience and a source of spiritual uplifting. According to these goals, UNESCO sponsored in 1996 Havana, Cuba, the International meeting on Cultural Tourism in Latin America and the Caribbean. The meeting's purpose was to be a discussion forum which would spring like, De Angeli and Gironella from Mexico, and Olaya from Colombia, among others, presented papers on food and gastronomy, which set the tone for the main topic for UNESCO's meeting: Gastronomy. In October 1999, this event took place in Puebla, Mexico. A baroque city, whose art was transmitted from the cuisine of convents during the colonial era, when baroque dishes were created. These dishes are still considered masterpieces of Mexican cuisine. This international organisation that has the maximum creditability in cultural studies, is giving gastronomy the importance that it deserves.

Nevertheless, gastronomy has not been considered for its real potential, nor exploited conveniently as a tourism resource. Even the references that mention this important cultural expression as a tourist resource are scarce and contained within the cultural tourism frame.

Few countries have the honour or the privilege to have as many UNESCO World Heritage sites as Mexico. In fact, there are twenty sites (www.UNESCO.org/feb.2000). Most of them are joint masterpieces by nature and mankind that showcase the country's extraordinary wealth.

This paper selects three colonial cities, Mexico City's historic centre (UNESCO, 1987), Puebla de Los Angeles (UNESCO, 1987), and Oaxaca de Juarenz (UNESCO, 1987) to analyse their gastronomy. Mexico's gastronomy is based on Prehispanic ingredients, corn, chilli and beans. For example, in Mexico City, the remains of the Aztec culture, the colonial era and modern urbanisation are gathered. Gastronomy is represented by many states of the country. Besides a foreign presence introduced at different stages but particularly at the time of the reign of Maximillian and Carlota (1864-67). Among the gastronomical diversity offered by the city, are restaurants offering authentic pre-Hispanic cuisine, local and regional

Mexican food, Mexican nouvelle cuisine and international cuisine. Puebla, the first Spanish city on the American Continent is famous for its baroque cuisine born in the convents during the sixteenth and seventeenth centuries. Some dishes created there still hold their own identity in the Mexican gastronomy.

Oaxca is characterised by a huge variety of dishes with a definite flavour. Insects, small animals, cacti, native vegetables and herbs constitute the main ingredients in many dishes. Famous among its alcoholic beverages are mescal, pluque and tepache. In each of the selected cities, the blending of culinary traditions developed distinct characteristics, integrating available ingredients and including cultural features of the local inhabitants.

Mexican cuisine, historical background

During the sixteenth century, the immediate contact between such different cultures awoke a feeling of rage among the indigenous and the Spanish but also an enormous curiosity. Proofs of this are the testimonies of the great reporters of the Conquest of Mexico. In those testimonies the aboriginal customs are described in detail.

There was certainly an urge to establish, in some way, a routine in daily life. To cover the great emptiness left behind by the Conquest war. Pursuing the purpose to recover their habits, one would discover that everything had changed. The Spanish were in an unknown land and not capable of consuming the products bred by the aborigines. There was a need to fulfil the new-born colonies with wheat, oil, wine and the basic ingredients of their religious and culinary traditions. There was also the need to attract domestic animals that would provide them with meat, another important product. "Questioning those who lived in Europe during that time Sonia Corcuera says, "A common food element is found: a craving for meat and the necessity of bread". On the other hand, in Mexico, meat was rarely consumed; most nutrients came from fruits.

Undoubtedly, necessity broke through the original resistance of some and others benefited from the acceptance of foreign food. Nevertheless, at the same time, Mexicans and Spaniards held faithfully to their culinary traditions. An affirmation process of what they already had taken place, and also developed the acceptance of the new products. The descriptions of Fray Bernardio de Sahagun and Bernal del Castillo remain as a testimony of this process. The first one tells about "the food used by the Aztec Lords", where we learned that they ate a wide variety of tortillas, plain or bean tamales, pots with chiles, tomatoes and smashed pumpkin seeds called pipian, birds, fish, frogs, tadpoles, ants with wings and agave worms, grasshoppers and shrimp, fruits such as plums, zapotes, and anonas, tree roots, batatas, green leaves, mazamorres and thick beverages made from chilli and honey.

Bernal Diaz del Castillo describes the first banquet by Hernan Cortes in Coyoacan to celebrate the triumph over Tenochititlan hogs and wine were brought in. The same reporter tells the story of the banquet that the first viceroy Con Antonio de Mendoza and the conqueror Hernan Cortes, Marquis of the Valley of Oaxaca, gave in 1538 to celebrate the peace treaty among France and Spain. They served salads, olives, radishes, cheese, turnips, garbanzo beans, all sorts of meat and birds, in turnovers, cakes, and casseroles. The dishes were "pure delicacy", pepitoria, royal torte and escabeche. Desserts were mazapanes, almonds, confites, acitron and fruits. The gold and silver cups were filled with white and red wine, sherry and cacao. In this banquet, turkey and cacao were combined with other products of the Spanish cuisine.

This food product exchange worked both ways, the affirmation of traditions and the acceptance of new food products is what Mexican cuisine is based upon.

Once the conquest was over and the colonisation process was initiated, neither of the groups forgot their traditions regarding food. But the trend to merge and innovate, natural in the kitchen, starts to combine strange elements of both cultures to give birth to excellent and exquisite dishes.

New harvesting and production forms, domestic animals to be eaten and to transport, new abilities and industries. They all contributed to create a new family and society. The nuns and monks at the convents, the cooks at the dining rooms, and the housewives at the homes that were established were all innovating. They rehearsed and produced new dishes, using the local natural products with exclusive particularities that integrated the heterogeneity and plurality of an incipient national cuisine. However, the gestation of the great Mexican dishes had to wait for the convents, the palaces and the haciendas that could benefit and shelter the baroque productions of the New Spain.

Three cities, three cuisine

Mexico City

Mexico city raises majestically on top of Tenochtitlan's ruins. Founders and inhabitants of Tenochtitlan adopted their traditions from Mesoamerican cultures and through tribute from their subjugated neighbours they become wealthy. With shipments of fish from the Caribbean, Tenochtitlan could enlarge its regular meals. It also improved its harvest through the use of floating gardens known as chipanpas'. Powerful and rich inhabitants were able to enjoy all these benefits therefore becoming pioneers in the development of the art of cooking.

Daily meals for these old Mexicas around the Colonial period, consisted of a wide variety of food stuff. Corn, beans, and chile (hot pepper) were the main products in their diet. Amaranto, a small popped seed, was another important ingredient. Corn was used to prepare tortillas (the Mexican bread), tamales, and atole (thick and sweet beverages normally drank hot) that nowadays are still being prepared by numerous Mexican families, with very little change in their traditional preparation. Among the protein sources of animal protein were turkeys and dogs. Wild animals including deer, armadillo, rabbit, owl, pecari, and tlacuache were hunted, and were consumed also. Aquatic fowls, fish, and seafood besides small snakes, frogs, ajolotes, shrimp, and insects were other options. Fruits consumed those days were mamey, zapote, pineapple, chirimoya, avacado, pitaya, tuna, plum, and guava. Beverages made with chia water and many recipes containing cacao with honey were very popular. The main drink for ritual purposes was pulque, a fermented beverage made from the agave (SEP, INAH, 1988).

Through history we know that Moctezuma II, the emperor received a vast varitey of meals every day, with up to hundred different dishes some days. He was served poultry dishes, tropical fruits, exotic beverages, and ice cream prepared with melted snow from the volcanoes Iztaccihuatl and Popocatepetl. As well as delicious fish dishes. Like the Huachinango kind, brought specially for the emperor every day by fast messengers. These messengers had to travel sometimes more than 400 kilometers just to please the emperor.

With the conquest, many European ingredients were added to the Mexicans' diet. So were kitchen tools, and cooking techniques that enriched and modified the already existing cuisine. In the nineteenth century, Mexico became an independent country, and expressed its admiration for the French ideas and cuisine. Even when the politic-gastronomic relationships between these two countries were not totally satisfactory. In 1838 "the cake's war" broke out due to commercial pressure and military activity from France.

Wealthy families adopted a fancy life style. It was then French cuisine emerged and was present in some restaurants and hotels with dishes like aspic, bouillabaisse, brioche, chaufroids, croquenbuche, foiegras, fumet, hors d'oeurve, profiteroles, soufflé, and sauces like béchamel, financiere, maitre d'hotel, revigote, and veloute.

Some cook books from last century show how it was taught to society. These books include also Italian, Spanish, and English styles stressing the fact that these recipes were adapted to the Mexican taste. This fact supports the theory that the foreign cooking style was modified by traditional Mexican Cuisine (Stoopen, 1998).

After the Reveloution, at the beginning of the 20th century, high Mexican cuisine starts developing. Since the 1940s, with the growth of tourism and the construction of the Mexico City – Acapulco's highway internationalisation of the country was initiated . Even the Hollywood industry contributed to expand Mexican cuisine's fame with movies like: La noche de la iguana. Nowadays Mexico city with population of more than 20 millions inhabitants, offers unimaginable options for the tourist interested in culture, ruins, museums from the colonial to the modern period, and many restaurants with a wide range of options between national and international cuisine. Without forgetting the great experience that visiting a Mexican market represents. These markets represent real food libraries where the diversity and richness of the country shows up.

Puebla

The State of Puebla has numerous types of ecosystems with fertile valleys surrounded by lakes where a lot of crops are harvested as well as fruits, vegetables, aromatic herbs, and flowers.

Puebla also has a huge diversity of domestic and wild animals. All these priviledges and characteristics make Puebla a land easy to be adapted to many foreign species such as wheat. Since colonial times, the baking industry started to develop fast and represented a creative and large industry.

The list of different and exquisite options that Puebla offers includes dishes and appetisers such as: pipianes rojo and verde (green and red chile-based sauce), mole de espinazo de chivos (meat from the back of a goat), tinga (chicken or beef mixed with onions, tomatoes and chives), chalupas (fried tortillas with chile sauce and onions), chanclas (fried tortillas filled with refried beans covered with chille sauce and cheese), pelonas (deep fried bread with chile sauce filled with beef), molotes (deep fried kind of tortilla filled with different stuff), cemitas (hamburger alike), tlacoyos (tortilla filled with refried beans), etc. Huitlacoches (a kind of fungus produced by the corn), gusanos de maguey (worm from the agave plant), and escamoles (ant's eggs) constitute other very exquisite and representative Pueblan dishes. The mole de olla con Verduras (beef broth with vegetables), mole de ladrillo can carne de res (beef broth), mole prieto, chipozonte de pollo von hongos (Chicken and mushroom), texmole de chito and much more can be added to this list. A very exotic dish that combines meat, fruit, species, sweets, spicy, bitter and salty ingredients is the manchamanteles (Benitez Muro, 1999).

Some particular dishes even have a story and a place of invention. Mole poblano, a mix between spices, chiles and chocolate used as a sauce, for instance was invented in the Dominican's Convent. Chiles en Nogada (stuffed chile covered with nut's sauce), a delicious dish, was cooked for the first time in Santa Monica's Convent (Gutierrez, 1998).

Another very famous industry in Puebla is the candy industry. It started to become relevant in the sixteenth and seventeenth centuries. In mentioning the seventeenth century in New Spain it is obligatory to mention Sor Juana Ines se la Cruz. She was an important writer of the divine and human. In addition to her meditation regarding chemical properties of the ingredients, she also put together about forty recipes from convents. Celestial names from the Baroque style were given to some desserts like: bishop's tears, aleluyas, gorja de angel, and Santa Clara cookies.

The cooking rituals performed with devotion by ancestors are getting lost. A long time ago it was a main tradition for grandmothers to teach their granddaughters how to prepare home made candies. Now industrial processes dominate candy elaboration. Santa Clara street is a place where visitors can buy typical Pueblan candies at the same time as they enjoy the great view of Puebla's downtown. This street offers Santa Clara cookies, marina de nuez (nuts' candy), bocado de coco y pina (pineapple and coconut candy), mustachon de pepita con canela (pumpkin seed and cinnamon candy), mustachon de leche con canela (milk and cinnamon candy), ciruelas rellanas de almendras (plums stuffed with almonds), datil relleno de nuez, besitos de almendra (sweet almonds), trufas de nuez y chocolate (chocolate and nuts truffle), maragaritas de pinon, mueganos (sweet little piece of bread), jamoncillos, mazapanes, polvorones and the famous camotes (sweet potato candy) among others.

Puebla's cuisine has its own identity and some of its dishes and candies can be viewed as one of the most important and representative variants of Mexican gastronomy.

Oaxaca

Land of seven regions, seven ethnic groups, seven moles (sauces), Oaxaca keeps alive the cooking tradition started in prehispanic times. It is possible even in these days to see the use of old kitchen tools such as the Metate (big rectangular stones used to grind seeds) and the comal (a kind of pan in tray shape used to heat up or make tortilla). The indigenous comal is normally set over three round stones known as tlecuil. These tools have a peculiar angle o inclination and required that the woman who is using them bend on her knees. This position represents the fact the woman has to be obedient.

Oaxaca has moles and several sauces to be used over meat, seafood, tamales, etc. The different kind of cheeses can be fried and served with epazote sauce, or eaten as a snack with gusanos (worm from the cactus), chapulines (crickets), or homigas chicatanas (ants). Tortillas are used like bread, they are eaten with almost any dish or to prepare chilaquiles, quesadillas, empanadas, memelas, picadas, gorditas, tocas, and molotes. Very popular are the tlayudas (huge shell round tortilla) and tamales of black mole wrapped in banana leaves. The main meal is done between two and three o'clock. It may start with a soup of garanzo, frijol (beans), guias de calabazas (pumpkin shoots), nopales (cooked cactus), coles, elotes (corn), or with chicken broth. Main dishes are divided into two groups: native and Spanish dishes. Some native dishes emphasise different kinds of meats with chile sauce, spices, and aromatic herbs. Spanish ones, on the other hand, include ingredients such as olives, almonds, tomato sauce, garlic, and onions.

With regard to desserts, charamuscas, conduminos, palanquetas, pepitorias, chilacayotas, empanada de Corpus, turrones, mamones, gaznates, and the famous water-based ice cream of different fruits, burned milk with pickle pear, and sorbets represent good option for visitors. As Oaxaca is one of the most important producers of cacao it is not surprising that hot chocolate is one of the favourite beverages of its inhabitants. The best way to enjoy a good hot chocolate in Oaxaca is by having some sweet bread at the same time. This hot chocolate can be made with milk or water and mixed with corn to have atole, champurrado y chocolate atole. All these are hot drinks. Another important figure in the list of drinks is the alcoholic beverage called tepache, which is a fermented pineapple drink. The tejate and home made flavoured sodas (horchata, zapote, ciruela, and other fruits) are other options too. It is said that a good meal must be finished with a mescal shot served in a black clay wine cup.

Purpose of the study

The project intends to generate tourism routes in several States that integrate diverse cultural attractions, with a special emphasis on the local gastronomy. In this paper, touristic routes in three colonial cities, which are UNESCO World Heritage Sites (1987, 1989), are presented.

Methodology

(a) A database was generated of all the tourist, cultural and gastronomical attractions of the selected cities.

(b) A map was prepared to show all the important attractions.

(c) Routes were designed combining art and gastronomy, as well as other aspects of interest to potential visitors.

(d) On-site visits were carried out in order to verify the feasibility of the circuits in terms of the time frame and availability of the type of restaurants according to the main theme of the route.

(e) The circuits were judged by a panel of 10 experts. The panel consisted of senior staff members of travel agencies in Mexico City, Puebla and Oaxaca.

Assessment instrument

The following questionnaire of semi-structured questions was applied through interviews:

- Do you think there could be tourists interested in art and gastronomy circuits?

- Do you consider that the proposed circuits are of interest?

- What type of market segment could be interested in the proposed circuits?

- What kind of promotion efforts do you think would be adequate for this proposal?

Results

Because of space limitations, the routes are presented in an abbreviated form, pointing out only the most important aspects. In the original paper, extended information is included not only about the cities studied but also about their corresponding State. There is also detailed information on the local gastronomy.

Mexico City – route of palaces

Since the XVI century, a lot a palaces have been built in order to host novohispanic royalty. There are samples of different styles in these building such as renacentric, baroque, neoclassic, due to the period of its construction. The City of Palaces, as addressed by the German scientist Von Humbolt (nineteenth century), still keeps some of these valuable buildings which are now used as museums or as government offices.

Remarkable Mexican muralists left part of their art in these palaces. Diego Rivera in the National Palace, Rufino Tamayo in the Archbishop Palace and Jose Clemente Orozco in the Marquez del Valle de Orizaba Palace. The Condes de Samaniego Palace, The National Palace, and the Archbishop Palace were built over Aztec ruins which are still visible.

In this route 10 places and a castle are visited. It will take two days (Maiz M,1997).

Day 1	Day 2
Mexico City Museum National Palace Archbishop Palace Inquisition Palace Iturbide Palace	Marques del Valle de Orizaba Palace (Tiles House) Fines Arts Palace Palacio de Correos Mining Palace Art National Museum Chapultepec Castle

Gastronomy: As the visitor enjoys the trip, some prehispanic-food restaurants will be found. These restaurants offer authentic Mexican food as well as international cuisine.

Puebla, Baroque City

For this route, some buildings from the XVII century have been selected. These buildings are richly ornamented with Talavera tiles, and others, like the Rosario's Chapel with gold. The Biblioteca Palafoxiana (Palafoxiana library) with 4300 books is the most important one of this period. This library has many books written in romance languages, some in Nahuatl and just few in Spanish. This route includes two museums. The Andres Bello Museum with fifteen rooms and a huge collection of talavera, copper, glass, and religious objects and the Alfenique house, from the XVIII century. The churches and museums house important art pieces from the Colonial period. The market E1 Parian, offers its visitors a wide variety of handicrafts and good prices.

> Santo Domingo Church and Rosario's Chapel
> Jose Luis Bello Museum
> Concordina Church and the tiles' courtyard
> Palafoxian Library
> Parian Market
> Alfenique House
> San Francisco Church

In this tour around the historic downtown, the visitor will have the opportunity to enjoy an authentic baroque meal at typical small restaurants (Gutierrez F., 1998)

Oaxaca: Prehispanic - colonial route

The city was founded in 1521. It has many attractions, for this tour religious architecture from the XVII and XVIII centuries have been selected. Some examples are Santo Domingo de Guzman Temple and the Rosario's chapel. The trip may be complemented with a visit to the archaeological site of Monte Alban which is just ten kilometres from the city. Very interesting festivities and celebrations are also indicated.

Rufino Tamayo Museum
Santo Domingo de Guzman Temple
Rosario's Chapel next to the Santo Domingo de Guzman temple
Regional Museum of Oaxaca- Ex Convento de Santo Domingo de Guzman
Oaxaca's Cathedral, Siglo XVII y XVIII. A clock from 1752 still working, and an organ
Italian tiles are important pieces to see in the cathedral.
Macedonio Alcala Theatre, siglo XX

Handicrafts

Textiles, ceramics in black clay, works made of palms, straw, leather, masks, machetes, and hand knifes.

Gastronomy

All dishes mentioned in this study to find any restaurants or markets in the area.

Festivities and celebrations

The Guelagetza, folkloric party where all Oaxaca ethnic groups participate.
The party of Soledad, December 18th
The noche de los rabanos or night of radishes: December 23rd where different figures, made in radishes are presented in contest.
Christmas in Oaxaca (Munoz R, 1997)

Final Considerations

According to the results of the study, it can be concluded that the art and gastronomy routes of the three cities are a viable option. They hold great potential for the increasing number of travellers interested in cultural tourism, both of national and international origin.

This great gastronomical diversity constitutes an area of great richness. Sadly, it has remained widely unexplored. As an important cultural resource it can and should be integrated into the tourist products that different regions offer. It seems only natural to take advantage of the regions gastronomical resources, combining them with its artistic legacy, and natural heritage, and offer it to tourists seeking new and more fulfilling travel experiences. Furthermore, by helping preserve ancient traditions and ways of life, many times expressed through food and preparation, and promoting the use of local products for ingredients, this kind of tourism can definitely be viewed as sustainable. Finally, according to Lambert Ortiz's observation (quoted by Leonard, 1968): "Those who explore the cuisine of Latin America must have something of a botanist, an historian, an archaeologist, a traveller, detective and overall be a persistent eater".

References

Benitez Muro, A. (1996), *La Cocina Mexicana a traves de los siglos. Tradiciones regionales*. Editorial Clio y Fundacion Herdez, Mexico.

Gutierrez Folrencia, P. (1997), Rutas de arte y gastronomic de la ciudad de Puebla. Depto de Hoteleria. Universidad de las Americas, Puebla, Mexico.Tesis sin Publicar.

Leonard, J. (1968), *Latin American Cooking*. Time-Life Books, New York, USA.

Maiz Magallon, M. (1997), *Rutas de arte y gastronomia de la cuidad de Mexico*. Depto de Hoteleria. Universidad de las Americas, Puebla, Mexico. Tesis sin publicar.

McIntosh, R. and Goeldner, C. (1990), *Tourism, Principles, Practices, Philosophies*. Wiley, USA.

Munoz Rugerio, G. (1997), *Promocian del Estado de Oaxaca a traves de su arte, gastronomia y recuros naturals*. Depto de Hoteleria. Universidad de las Americas, Puebla Mexico. Tesis sin publicar.

SEP, INAH (1988), *Atlas Cultural de Mexico* – Gastronomia Editorial Planeta, Mexico.

Stoopen, M (1998), *El universo de la cocina mecicana*. Fomento Cultural Banamex A.C. Mexico.

UNESCO (1996), *Turismo Cultural en America Latinsa y el Caribe*. Ferrari Grafiche S.P.A, Hadana, Cuba.

UNESCO World Heritage (Feb.2000), Mexico. www.UNESCO.org/.

Weile, B. and Hall, C. (1992), *Special Interest Tourism* Belhaven Press, London.

The political and socio-cultural relations of world heritage in Garajonay National Park, La Gomera

Raoul V Bianchi

University of North London, UK

Jonay Izquierdo Trujillo, Beatríz Martín de la Rosa and Agustín Santana Talavera

Universidad de La Laguna, Tenerife

Abstract

The designation of World Heritage Sites has become an increasingly important component of national and international conservation policies, in conjunction with the consumerist ideologies of governments wishing to promote tourism. Garajonay National Park was the fourth national park to be created in the Canary Islands (in 1981),and the first World Heritage Site in the region, ratified by UNESCO in 1986. This paper examines the processes of transformation of this 'natural' landscape from agrarian resource to natural *heritage*, and tourism product. It traces the contours of conflict which have arisen in the context of the political regulation and institutionalisation of nature conservation, and the increasing pressures to exploit its tourist potential. A number of antagonisms emerge in the context of competing conceptions of place and culture implicated in both local heritage and global discourses of world heritage; the relations of participation and custodianship/conservation of the environment; and questions of political economy linked to rural tourism development and socio-economic regeneration.

Introduction

This paper reflects upon some of the preliminary results of an anthropological investigation into the processes, discourses and conflicts which have emerged in the context of the declaration of Garajonay National Park in La Gomera (Canary Islands) as a World Heritage Site (WHS). The principal focus is on the interplay between the institutions of (natural heritage) conservation, local inhabitants and tourism and the contrasting discourses and values of place which construct and reproduce this 'heritage landscape'. In this brief review it is possible only to highlight some of the antagonisms which have emerged in connection to contrasting meaning and value of landscape. These tensions encompass, the relationship between the institutionalised norms and practices of conservation and the cultural value of landscape, as well as between the different agencies implicated in the use and exploitation of natural resources, particularly where the conflicting interests of conservation, tourism and local livelihoods are concerned.

From the outset it should be stressed that we are dealing with a particularly unique world heritage landscape, although this does not of course preclude parallels with other sites. Not only does the geographical situation of Garajonay National Park in the middle of the island (encompassing nearly 10% of its land mass) implicate the majority of the island's population in many of the issues to be discussed here, La Gomera itself is situated in the midst of one of the most heavy concentrations of tourism resort areas in the world.[1] Furthermore, prior to its inscription in the World Heritage list in 1986, the laurel cloud forest known to most local inhabitants as *el monte* or *monteverde*, literally "mountain" or "green mountain" (more on this later), had already been granted the highest protective status that could be given to the natural environment, that is, a National Park (1981). Indeed, if we include natural areas which are protected by regional laws, approximately one third of the island is protected by some degree of conservation legislation (see Mora Morales 1995). Finally, but perhaps most significantly, the traditional agrarian activities of the population settlements situated around the edge of the Park had already been severely restricted by municipal governments in the 1940s and their population depleted by emigration. Notwithstanding the sense of loss felt by many inhabitants towards *el monte*, the terrain of conflict has shifted towards conservation and tourism rather than agriculture.

Geographical and natural characteristics

The island of La Gomera (378 sq. kms) is one of seven islands in the Canary Island archipelago which are situated in the Macaronesian Atlantic, approximately 1000kms south of the Iberian peninsula and 100kms west of the African coastline. The particular geological and climactic features of the island of La Gomera have given rise to one of the most unique and spectacular landscapes in the Canary Island archipelago. The island is made up predominantly of ancient basaltic block which has remained unaltered by volcanic eruptions for approximately 2 million years. As a result, wind and water erosion has left a uniquely denuded landscape punctuated by volcanic dykes and domes (*roques*), as well as a series of deeply eroded valleys (*barrancos*) which radiate outwards from the central plateau or *meseta*. Moreover, the valley walls are characterised by spectacular terraced landscapes, which stand as a monument to the intellectual and physical efforts of the local population to overcome the constraints of geography in order to make a living.

The island's vegetation cover is closely determined by its geographical location and topography. The windward side of the island faces the north-east Atlantic trade winds which give rise to the extensive cloud cover and moisture upon which the sub-tropical laurel forest survives. The island's vegetation consists of a variety of different endemic species, including heath-moorland, savin, pine, palm and xerophyte vegetation. However, the most salient feature, and indeed, the principal *raison d'être* for the Park itself, are the various species of laurel (*laurisilva canaria*) which occupy 6,000 hectares of the island's land mass. The laurel forest, which constitutes the largest remaining example of its kind and once covered large expanses of the Mediterranean during the tertiary period (3 million years ago), is situated on the central plateau which then drops sharply towards the radial valleys at the point where the forest cover begins to thin out, known locally as "la sita del monte" (Fernández López 1998: 33).

The National Park encompasses 3,984 hectares of laurel forest except for a natural clearing in the centre known as *La Laguna Grande*. It is in fact made up of six public forests which belong to six distinct municipal districts: Agulo (770ha), Alajeró (250ha), Hermigua (1,024ha), San Sebastián (290ha), Valle Gran Rey (350ha) and Vallehermoso (1,300ha). Although there are no population settlements inside the Park itself a number of agrarian settlements (*caseríos*) situated at the heads of the steep ravines where natural springs emerge from the groundwater (El Cedro) and around the southern perimeter of the Park, (Chipude, El Cercado, las Hayas), have been included in a peripheral exclusion zone known as the *zona periférica de protección*. Given their traditional involvement in subsistence agriculture and pastoralism, activities both of which were closely tied to the forest eco-system, these populations have traditionally had a deeper social and cultural relationship to *el monte,* a fact which lies at the heart of some of the problems encountered in the Park and World Heritage declaration process.

Garajonay and *"el monteverde"*: The historical context

From the outset, it should be emphasised that Garajonay is a complex historical landscape whose characteristics owe as much to the island's natural ecological processes, as it does to the historical economic and cultural activities of the local inhabitants who have historically resided on the edge of the Park but inside *el monte*. Indeed this distinction between institutional and cultural boundaries of place illustrates the fact that Garajonay also represents a series of cultural landscapes constituted out of the historical struggles between various centralised authorities and resident peasant communities to resist the appropriation of *el monte* and ensure access to the natural, cultural and economic resources it has historically provided for them. Broadly speaking the evolution of human intervention into the forest landscape can be divided into six distinct phases:

1. Precolonial (prior to the Spanish conquest in the 15th C.)

2. Colonial (*señorial*): 15th-19th C.

3. Postcolonial or transition phase (1850s-1960s)

4. Centralised planning (*consorcios*): 1960s-1974

5. National Park declaration period (1974 -1986)

6. Consolidation phase: World Heritage and tourism product, (1986 - present).

Prior to the arrival of the Spanish *conquistadores* in the 15th century, La Gomera was inhabited by the ancient gomeros who were split into four different clans or tribes. The forest, and particularly its highest point, el Alto de Garajonay (1,487m), after which the park is named, was a place of spiritual worship for these ancient gomeros as were many elevated areas and rocky promontories throughout the archipelago (Fernández y Paredes 1996: 328). After the Spanish conquest, the island was ruled by feudal lords (*Condes de la Gomera*) who forcibly removed the gomeros from their lands and set about clearing territory for cultivation and cutting down parts of the forest in order to provide building materials, agricultural tools and fuel for the sugar mills. During the 15th to 19th centuries the regulation and exploitation of the resources (*aprovechamientos*) on *el monte* was controlled by the feudal lords, until the rise of liberalism and the dissolution of aristocratic privileges led to the transfer of this territory into the hands of the six municipal governments, created in the mid-19th century. Until the creation of the national park, these took over responsibility for the management and regulation of agrarian and conservation activities in the forest.

Over the course of the 19th and 20th centuries increasing degradation of the forest environment, particularly due to grazing, provided the impetus for increasing restrictions on the use and exploitation of the forest. In 1944 the municipal council of Hermigua became the first institution to restrict grazing inside the forest. Others councils promptly followed suit, however some pockets of clandestine grazing (and still do) continued into the 1970s. Further restrictions were to follow, including in 1964, the prohibition of tree-felling and in 1974 the prohibition of dead wood and leaf collection, until 1981 by which time all six municipal councils had banned grazing. The conflict between grazing, sedentary agriculture and conservation is not of course restricted to la Gomera, moreover, its significance goes right to the heart of the conflict over the custodianship and exploitation of agrarian resources across Spain. However, it is relevant that here the control of *el monte* passed directly from the feudal lords to the legally-enshrined custodianship of the municipal governments. Thus, unlike ecclesiastical and feudal lands in other parts of the Canary Islands (and indeed Spain as a whole), this territory was not put up for sale during the disentailments of the 19th century, but rather declared *montes publicos* (public territories).

According to, Virgilio Brito, a council official in the municipality of Hermigua during this period (Brito 1995), the principal motivation of the local councils were purely conservationist and were intended to stem the environmental degradation caused by traditional agrarian activities. Although it is impossible to be certain, it is also likely there may have been other rationales in-keeping with the economic and political environment of the time. On the one hand, moves to protect the natural environment are congruent with the prevailing nationalist ideology of Franco's regime, which envisaged nature as emblematic of the purest values of *la patria*, or national identity. Indeed it was not uncommon for the regime to glorify the values of nature (and peasant life) in contrast to the vices of modernism associated with urban life (Behar 1986: 1986). Conversely, growing demand for labour on the expanding export plantations in the lowland valleys in the 1950s, may have led landowners to exert pressure on the council to restrict grazing on *el monte,* which would have forced upland inhabitants to move down towards the lowland areas in search of work. Although these may not have been clear causative factors, the fact that many of the inhabitants of working class neighbourhoods in the valley of Hermigua (one of the principal areas of banana cultivation) are originally from the upland mountain areas, suggested that there may be some truth in these assertions. Furthermore, it is indeed ironic, as recognised by Brito himself, that many amongst the land-owning and political classes themselves grazed their goatherds on *el monte* at the same time that the council was beginning to enforce restrictions on agrarian activities (Brito 1995).

During the 1960s attempts by the state bureaucracies to protect the natural environment continued, this time under the auspices of an agreement between the central government and local councils, known as *consorcios*, to regenerate the denuded forest cover through the introduction of a species of pine from the Iberian peninsula into degraded areas. These pines were, however, ill-suited to the insular eco-system, thus leading to a deterioration of the island's water table. Moreover, this policy was seen by many islanders, as another example of the ignorance and disregard the Spanish central government (at that time controlled by the Franco dictatorship) had for local customs and knowledge. Indeed ICONA (*Instituto Nacional para la Conservación de la Naturaleza*), which was until its dissolution in 1995 the principal central government agency (affiliated to the Ministry of Agriculture, Fisheries and Food) responsible for all matters environmental and conservation management, earned the reputation as the "*Institute for the Destruction of Nature*" due to such disastrous reforestation policies (Gibson 1992: 111).

Progressive restriction on the use of traditional resources on *el monte* by the state thus took place over several decades. However, agrarian decline also played its part in the abandonment of the *medianías* (upland areas) and emigration. Since the 1950s the population of La Gomera has dropped from around 30,000 to its current level of approximately 17,000 (Cabildo Insular de La Gomera 1997). Between 1961 and 1980, nearly 17,000 inhabitants emigrated to the neighbouring island of Tenerife alone (Gómez Sal et al. 1987: 172) in search of employment in construction and tourism. Despite the decline of the forest cover on *el monte* over the centuries, it is remarkable how much of it had indeed remained intact prior to the advent of the National Park. Angel Fernández, the current director of the National Park, points out that this is due to the positive legacy of centralised control (even the feudal lords prohibited tree felling in some areas). However, it is often reiterated by state officials that the conservation of the forest has benefited largely from the careful, almost communal exploitation of its resources by generations of ordinary Gomero farmers and pastoralists who recognised the importance of the forest for their economic survival (Fernández López 1992, 1999).[2] Yet, despite the recognition of the Gomeros' mindful custodianship of *el monte* and the laurel forest, this rhetoric is often not matched by the political and institutional reality which serves to further restrict and define the appropriate use to which *el monte* should be devoted, thus alienating the local population further from their historical link to this natural-cultural landscape. Indeed, it can be said, that the discourses of heritage, conservation and tourism which are linked together in this historic natural-cultural landscape, have been shaped by the ongoing tension between centralised power and local autonomy, an omnipresent theme in Spanish political and social history.

Garajonay: From National Park to World Heritage Site

The declaration of National Parks in Spain was initially restricted to isolated 'wilderness' areas, as exemplified by Ordesa (1918) and Aigües Tortes (1955) in the High Pyrenees, Coto Doñana (1969), and the four volcanic peaks in the Canary Islands, Teide on Tenerife (1954), La Caldera du Taburiente on the island of La Palma (1954), Timanfaya on Lanzarote (1974), and most recently, Garajonay (1981). On the one hand these areas were seen as empty 'wildernesses' in which human activity was minimal if not altogether absent, thus ignoring the social forces which had often forged these landscapes, and on the other, it is notable that these same principles of nature conservation were not initially extended to more "humanised landscapes" (Morris 1992). Thus, nature preservation under Franco reflected the authoritarian and centralised nature of policy-making during this period, but whose high-minded ideals were simultaneously contradicted by the modernisation impulses to which the rest of the Spanish territory was subject, particularly the coastal and island areas, as a result of the capitalist growth model promulgated by the regime itself from the late 1950s onwards (Jurdao 1990: 124)

The period during which Garajonay was accorded the protective status of a National Park was a time of turbulent political upheaval and rapid socio-economic change, precipitated by the transition to democracy and the renewed expansion of large-scale tourism development in the 1980s. The dawn of the new democratic era saw the creation of the state environmental agency ICONA in 1971, and four years later the Law of Natural Spaces (*Ley 15/1975*) was passed by the Spanish parliament, which declared a range of parks with distinctive protective status, in tandem with a framework which was to allow for different levels of administrative control over these areas, from state to local level (Morris 1992: 24). Moreover, the constitutional responsibility of the state to uphold the environmental quality of life was enshrined in Article 45 of the 1978 Spanish Constitution. Subsequent integration of Spain into the European Community in 1986 added further impetus to environmental protection, as national legislation had to be adapted to European environmental regulations as well as the fact that numerous European structural funds have been channelled towards nature conservation and environmental protection (Esteban Alonso y López López 1989).

The transition to democracy precipitated the (re)emergence of submerged regional identities as many powers were transferred to the new tier of autonomous governments at a regional level. Not only did this increase *de jure* political jurisdiction over environmental affairs in the regions - Article 148 of the constitution makes reference to the fact that regional governments should assume responsibility for environmental management (Esteban Alonso y López López 1989: 66) - but it also had the effect of galvanising widespread local concern for regional landscapes and cultures (Morris 1992). Although there is little evidence of the emergence of widespread ecological activism in relation to the protection of *el monte* at this time in la Gomera, Fernández does suggest that the Canary Islands were pioneers of sorts with regard to matters of conservation due to the uniqueness of the insular eco-systems and high number of endemic species present in the archipelago (Fernández López 1999). Thus by the mid-1970s a catalogue of protected species had already been carried out, leading a few years later to the creation of a network of protected spaces (*Red de Espacios Naturales*).

Externally, an important stimulus to the creation of a national park came from the international scientific community.[3] The laurel forest on La Gomera had been well known amongst numerous naturalists, botanists geologists many years prior to regional political interest in the protection of this landscape (Sánchez 1995: 20). Explicit political recognition of the intrinsic scientific-ecological value of *el monte* was, however, triggered by the a report compiled in the late 1960s, by a group of Swiss scientists from the University o: Zurich, urging the island government (*Cabildo*) to take measures to protect this unique natural environment (Sánchez 1995: 20). At the same time several key figures within the provincial forest services in Tenerife, which at that time had jurisdiction for environmental conservation on La Gomera, also began to formulate plans to make a bid for national park status. Having recently participated in numerous seminars in the United States in order to celebrate the one hundredth anniversary of the establishment of Yellowstone National Park, a formal request was put forward to ICONA in 1974 for the creation of Garajonay National Park. Despite some initial trepidation from municipal governments upon whose territory the proposed Park was situated, principally regarding access to water, the proposal was on the whole supported by both the six municipal councils and the island government (Fernández and Paredes 1996: 338). Not surprisingly, given La Gomera's traditional economic and political subordination to Tenerife, the potential touristic importance of the Park was already being recognised at the outset (Fernández and Paredes 1996: 340).

Given the particular timing of this process, the declaration of the National Park was not confirmed until some years later, in 1981. Not long afterwards Spain formally ratified the World Convention (1982) and the regional conservation authorities and ICONA, led by the key instigator of the National Park, began to prepare a bid to inscribe Garajonay National Park in the World Heritage List. In 1986 their efforts paid off, backed by two favourable IUCN reports, Garajonay National Park became the first WHS to be declared in the Canary Islands, and the first natural landscape in Spain to be incorporated into the World Heritage List. In terms of its impact on the local populations, it should be emphasised that the declaration of the WHS merely consolidated the processes which had been set in motion as a result of the declaration of Garajonay National Park. Consequently, they are not often explicitly distinguished in the minds of local people. Although, for many it is evident that, whatever the terminology employed, the 'national park' constitutes a metaphor for the involvement of external agencies in island cultural, economic and environmental affairs, which are the emphasis of the last section of this paper.

World heritage and local patrimony

Despite the absence of overt conflict between pastoralists, agriculturists and conservation authorities which has plagued other areas, such as *Coto Doñana* National Park in Andalusia (Crain 1996), there are a number of submerged tensions and latent conflicts below the overt relations of conservation. These tensions have emerged within the context of the relations between conservation, tourism, and local socio-cultural connections to this landscape, which are constituted by contrasting discourses of place in relation to the use to which *el monte* and its resources should be devoted. According to the IUCN, the intrinsic conservation value of Garajonay rests upon the inherent ecological characteristics of the ancient laurel forest, which represents:

> *one of the largest continuous areas of laurisilva forest, a habitat that has almost disappeared from southern Europe and North Africa. Almost half of the remaining forest in the Canary Islands is included in the park. In spite of being biologically diverse, a large proportion of the fauna (50%) are endemic, and many species are considered to be nationally threatened.* (http://www.wcmc.org.uk//protected_areas/data/wh/garajona.html, consulted 30/11/99).

The restrictive regulatory framework put in place by the Park Law clearly reflects a vision of nature as a pristine wilderness in which the traces of human intervention are absent (or should be removed). The principal regulatory basis of conservation is enshrined in the National Park Law (*Ley 3/1981, 25 de marzo*) thus prohibits any alteration of the forest eco-system whatsoever, but more significantly, restricts any form of construction, other than that which is in the "public interest" in the *zona periférica de protección* (*article 4, Ley 3/1981*). Many of the residents in this exclusion zone (approximately 1,200 inhabitants), argue that their livelihoods have been severely damaged by these restrictions, particularly with regard to the construction of housing. The increased complexity of the planning framework, as well as traditional resistance to bureaucratic institutions amongst local communities, has resulted hostility towards the Park, manifest in a proliferation of illegal construction in the *zona periférica,* and in extreme cases, setting fire to certain parts of the Park and peripheral zone. Responsibility for interpreting the precise definition of the "public interest" lies with the park council (*patronato*) which meets to consider planning applications before they are approved by the planning department of the regional government, a responsibility which now lies with the island government. Although it only performs a consultative role, the *patronato* has tried to interpret the law in as benign a manner as possible (in effect contravening it), in order to accommodate local concerns, and ultimately, avoid direct hostility towards the Park which is often exploited by populist local councils.

These tensions go straight to the heart of the wider debate between the landscape as an expression of the cultural values of its inhabitants and biocentric attitudes towards nature which "insist on the inherent worth of the natural environment, maintaining that man has no special rights to exploit nature..." (Saarinen 1998: 30). Although inscription into the World Heritage List did not have any ramifications for the legal status of the Park, it reinforced the legitimacy of the intrinsic *ecological* value of the forest, over and above either local discourses which emphasise the cultural value of *el monte*, or indeed, against the more mercenary approach to nature exemplified by commercial (tourism) interests who envisage the Park primarily as a green tourism product:

> *El hecho de que este es un patrimonio mundial nos sirve a los gestuarios de cuidarlo. Tenemos que dar respuesta ante organsimos internacionales y esto es una bandera ques se utiliza, o sea que es para mi el punto más importante. Posiblemente para el político local el importante sea la marca de calidad. Para nosotros [...] sirve un poco para garantizar la conservación.* (Fernández López 1999)[4]

World Heritage status thus reinforces the legitimacy of (external-national) state intervention into the landscape. However, many of those involved in nature conservation themselves concede that the Park Law is too restrictive and that these restrictions are damaging not only to the public image of the National Park, but also to the opportunities for the long-term sustainable development of these peripheral communities. Nevertheless, they suggest that such a restrictive regulatory framework is partly justified by the fact that emigration and agrarian decline had already led to a substantial decline in the resident population in these communities, and that furthermore, few of the existing inhabitants were still engaged in traditional agrarian pursuits.[5] There has indeed been a decline in agriculture, particularly in the upland areas, and the windward municipalities which are still more dependent on agriculture (Cabildo Insular 1997: 83-87). This has resulted in a significant generational shift with regard to the value of *el monte* amongst the younger population, and accordingly, the growth of a more environmentalist conception of *el monte* amongst this segment of the population. However, according to Isidro Ortíz, artisan, agriculturist and inhabitant of the mountain village of Chipude with a deep-seated knowledge of *el monte*, it has also had the effect of precipitating a deeper rupture between the urban-metropolitan values associated with the arrival of tourism, and the cultural values linked to *el monte* and traditional modes of environmental custodianship (Ortíz 1999).

Thus, while the Park has witnessed few overt conflicts between environmental conservation and local communities, on a scale seen elsewhere, the Park has in many ways become a metaphor for state 'interference' in local affairs particularly amongst elderly residents with some past connection to the agrarian livelihood of the forest. A significant reason for this descends from the particular historical context within which *el monte* was turned into a National Park and inscribed into the World Heritage list. Although the role of the Gomeros in protecting 'their' mountain/forest is constantly evoked by conservation officials, according to Isidro Ortíz, all but the most cursory lip service was paid to local involvement, a point confirmed by the mayor of Agulo at that time, who claimed that he was never once required to call a meeting of the council in order to discuss their opinions regarding the creation of the Park (Almenara 1999).

The legacy of political and ideological repression from the dictatorship was manifest in a poorly developed civil society with the result that it was still customary to passively submit to policies for change instigated 'from above' (cf. Waldren 1998). Principal responsibility was thus to family, village and nation, reinforcing a vertical hierarchy of social relations in which collective solidarities and abstract notions of citizenship were largely absent, more so amongst poor agrarian communities (Montero 1995). This comment from Isidro Ortíz describes the political context of the time:

> *Recién salidos de un sistema totalitario, tenía el pueblo entonces aquí ni noción ni idea de lo que podía ser una manifestación, de efecto que podía tener, de los peligros que encerraba también tenía temor. El pueblo no se manifestó en aquel tiempo yo creo que por eso, porque por ganas muchos las tenían, [...] El sólo hecho de decir "mire usted me lo está diciendo, pero yo no lo creo" eso ya era muy grande. ¡Cómo se lo iba a decir una persona al gobernador! Eso ya era decir ¡caramba, que valiente fue fulano que se atrevió!* (Isidro Ortíz, 1999).[6]

Despite the fact that since 1995 ICONA has transferred its responsibility for the management of National Parks to the *Organismo Autónomo de Parques Nacionales* in the Ministry of Environment, many inhabitants still refer to ICONA as a metaphor of authority or 'surveillance'. Indeed some rangers are reluctant to denounce people for infringing park regulations given that their allegiance to friends and neighbours remains stronger than their notions of responsibility as citizens and/or the objective custodians of nature. It is clear from the interviews with inhabitants in the peripheral areas, that in some cases earlier hostility for the restriction of traditional agrarian activities on *el monte* has been transferred onto the state authorities responsible for the National Park. Moreover, although regional and island governments have been granted increased autonomy in environmental matters (although responsibility for the Park still lies with the central government) the devolution of powers has to some extent also led to a certain degree of confusion and exacerbated intra-island political rivalries, thus vindicating Hall's view that:

> *The tension between the global and local, between different conceptions of use and value, operating within the context of the Convention has probably been seen more in federal systems.* (Hall 2000: 123)

Despite current attempts to relax some of the restrictions on building and development in the *zona periférica*, the fact remains that many inhabitants feel disenfranchised from the day-to-day running of the Park. Even, as suggested by Fernández, that the perception of state interference and restrictive planning amongst local inhabitants is exaggerated, it will be difficult task to establish the identity of the Park authorities as a benevolent force in the mind of the older inhabitants of the park periphery, orientated to local interests, given the historical events-context which surround its creation. More specifically, any amendment to this legal dimension can do little to redress the sense of cultural loss experienced by those who feel the forest been lost forever as a living landscape. Increasingly, in the Canary Islands as elsewhere in Spain, concern for the environment is linked to demands for local territorial and regional autonomy (Morris 1996: 83). Although this is often exploited by regional nationalist political parties in a rather populist manner, the growth of regional autonomies has seen a number of local non-governmental organisations committed to reinforcing the links between historical landscapes and cultural identity. Many archaeological sites, some of them outside the Park such as the cave of *Aguajedum,* (the place where the indigenous gomeros are said to have killed one of the ruling nobles in 1488), but inside the Park also, such as the *Alto de Garajonay,*[7] are associated with key events in la Gomera's history which have helped to shape their cultural identity. Various ecological-cultural organisations on the island, which themselves adopt indigenous names (e.g. *Tagaragunche),* have become key agents in a growing debate concerning demands for local autonomy in relation to the preservation of la Gomera's natural-cultural heritage whose resonance is clearly articulated by this statement:

> *consideramos la reconquista de nuestro monte como vital para el progreso económico y social de los Gomeros.* (Morales Cano 1998)[8]

Although the disappearance of the traditional agrarian economy of *el monte* has meant that younger generations of Gomeros will no longer experience the cultural attachment to the forest as did their parents and grand-parents, the antagonisms discussed above have by no means been dissolved. Moreover, new antagonisms, for example, between the demands of nature conservation and the pressures for urbanisation of rural areas from agents of tourism development, may become increasingly salient

World heritage, nature conservation and tourism

It is perhaps inevitable, particularly given La Gomera's proximity to Tenerife, that it should increasingly be seen as one of the central tourism products which *differentiates* La Gomera from the other islands. Nature conservation and rural tourism are seen by the various different authorities as the cornerstones of an alternative economic development model which will enable La Gomera to avoid the large-scale tourism growth model which has so damaged cultural and ecological environments in other parts of the archipelago. Both La Gomera's proximity to Tenerife and the recent inauguration of the new airport, in tandem with the concerted attempts to capitalise on images of a pristine rural landscape to attract tourists, are the very forces which serve to reinforce the market-driven logic of tourism development which is introducing new speculative pressures into the rural landscape. For example, abandoned rural dwellings in the medianías are increasingly being rehabilitated by returnee migrants and foreign residents, as well as becoming incorporated into the rural tourism portfolios of international tour operators.

For the island tourism authorities the world heritage status of Garajonay National Park is seen as a mark of quality, a point reiterated by the tourism minister for the island who referred to it in the anodyne manner typical of political discourse, as the "jewel" of the island (González 1999). Tour operators specialising in walking tours suggest that La Gomera enables you to "take a break from life in southern Tenerife" (which indicates a degree of incompatibility with the authorities desire for an exclusive tourism model), but more significantly, often advertise the destination as a "World Heritage Island" (http://www.walking.demon.co.uk/lag.htm, 01/09/99). Garajonay has thus become inextricably woven into the commercial imperatives of the tourism industry and the desire for local politicians to promote a 'sustainable' tourism policy for the island, a situation which is to some extent undermined rather than resolved by the emphasis on its outstanding natural beauty.

Thus, in spite of the antagonisms between the demands of nature conservation and pressures to exploit the touristic potential of La Gomera's rural landscape, the transformation of *el monte* into a National Park and WHS also, however, underlines the close connection between conservation and consumption. Not only does the prestige value of a world heritage sites act as a magnet for tourists (cf. Shackley (1998) it also reflects how conservationist and consumerist versions of place may over-lap within the context of the construction of heritage tourism products (Daniels 1992: 312). Garajonay National Park can thus also be seen as a new commodity which dove-tails neatly with the 'new' paradigms of consumption in which tourists have become increasingly interested in nature as 'entertainment' without being unduly concerned with its preservation (Honey 1999). Furthermore, due to the rapid expansion of tourism and the fact that the majority of la Gomera's population now lives in the coastal areas, particularly San Sebastián and the burgeoning tourism resort areas of Valle Gran Rey and Playa Santiago, for all but the remaining residents of the mountain villages, *el monte*, has become a space to be passed through (on the way to La Laguna Grande or to the southern beaches) rather than gazed at in its own right, much less a marker of cultural identity.

Prior to the construction of the principal highway which traverses the Park (built before the Park was created), travel into the forest and around the island involved an arduous journey of several hours around a narrow and winding road from San Sebastián, through the villages on the windward face, and over the plateau above Vallehermoso down to Valle Gran Rey. The development of the Park and its associated infrastructure, in particular the construction of roads and the establishment of a regular ferry service between San Sebastián and Tenerife in 1974), has transformed the existing relations between time, space and nature, formerly embedded in and structured by the demands and rigours of the traditional agrarian economy. Not only have the roads, sign-posting, viewpoints and rural trails, denoting fixed points of 'tourist interest/value', been improved in order to enhance the visitor experience of the forest, but the Park itself acts as an intersection between different communities, resorts and environments given its location at the centre of the island. Apart from serious hikers, a substantial proportion of tourists (a large percentage of whom are day trippers from Tenerife) 'experience' the Park through the windows of vehicular cocoons, whether rental cars, jeep safaris or large tour buses, which are disgorged daily from the ferries which arrive several times a day from Tenerife.

The transformation of *el monte* into a space of tourist consumption has thus also reinforced a distinct iconography of landscape where time appears to stands still, that is, into "monumental time" (cf. Herzfeld 1991). In this respect the diverse *caseríos* and forest landscapes that made up the distinct cultures of *el monte* have been reconstituted and presented as a relic of times gone by. Indeed, conversations with tourists revealed a predominantly archaic notion of local culture rooted in images of its noble peasant past and Spanish heritage linked to the conquest (La Gomera is famous for being Columbus's last stopping off point prior to sailing towards the Americas). Tourists experience the Park as a tableau upon which they project notions of a 'green idyll' uncontaminated by the degrading forces of mass tourism. Their emphasise on the 'tranquility' and natural beauty of the forest coincides with the biocentric-humanist view of nature (cf. Saarinen 1998) reflected in the Park, whose rationale, amongst others, is to enable tourists to get as close to nature as possible through a combination of aesthetic and educative experiences, by maintaining it as a pristine wilderness (Fernández López 1999). This is in stark contrast to the inhabitants of the villages in the peripheral areas, who point to the fact that *el monte* has literally been emptied of life (shepherds' whistles, goats etc..) and re-configured to meet the needs of tourists (Ortíz 1999). One could perhaps argue, therefore, that the consolidation of the Park as a central tourism product has distanced the visitor from contact with the host population, and arguably, nature.

In spite of the problems discussed above, many, even those in the upland villages, concede that the creation of the National Park has brought some benefit to La Gomera. Not least it has demonstrated to outsiders, if only at the level of rhetoric, the historical role performed by ordinary Gomeros in the preservation of *el monte*, in contrast to the other islands where *laurisilva* has all but disappeared. Yet, the significance of the park as a World Heritage Site is not well articulated at either the politico-institutional level, nor at the level of 'lived experience' within local populations. This perhaps reflects the ambiguous nature of the world heritage programme itself: whose self-professed aims are, on the one hand, to highlight specific natural [and cultural/architectural] landscapes which "need to be preserved as part of the world heritage of mankind [sic] as a whole..."(preamble to the World Heritage Convention, cited in Suter 1991: 8), while on the other, concerned with the distinguishing symbolic properties which pertain to the history of that particular place and its inhabitants.

Conclusion

The historical transformation of *el monteverde* has been historically defined by the struggle over competing uses and contrasting discourses of place, through which its geographical and cultural features have been shaped. Most notable of these tensions has been the continuous conflict between centralised control, initially represented by the feudal lords but also reflected in the role of the central government administration in the management of the

National Park, and local custodianship of *el monteverde*. Arguably, the natural environment within the park is now better protected and better managed than ever, although local inhabitants continue to dispute this (e.g. Ortíz 1999). Above all it has become *universally* valued for its inherent ecological worth, as well as the historic contribution to its preservation made by its inhabitants, thanks to the UNESCO declaration. However, if *world heritage* is to mean more than simply another protected landscape, whether cultural, architectural or natural, then Garajonay National Park has yet to fulfil its promise. It has failed to adequately incorporate a tradition of environmental custodianship handed down through generations of Gomera's inhabitants, albeit one that has largely disappeared. But more significantly perhaps, it has also failed to embed itself at the level of insular cultural identity, in all its contradictory manifestations, beyond its merely utilitarian or humanistic value as a touristic resource. Garajonay is today ecologically rich, yet culturally barren.

Yet it should also be recognised that the creation of the National Park and its incorporation into the world heritage list, occurred in a relatively peaceful and uncontested manner. However, as the comments by Ortíz demonstrate, this has much to do with the social and political environment of the time during which the National Park was created, which left a legacy of repression and centralised control that had not altogether disappeared even by the time the Park became incorporated into the World Heritage list. Arguably it is also due to the fact that the Park constitutes an explicit recognition, albeit slight, of the role of La Gomera's inhabitants in the preservation of *el monte* over the centuries. Garajonay has become a symbol of La Gomera's uniqueness in the context of continuous large-scale tourism development which has degraded eco-systems and led to a sense of cultural dislocation in many parts of the archipelago. In time, Garajonay may well come to symbolise the ability of Gomeros to embrace the demands of modernity and globalisation whilst at the same time reinforce a sense of their own identity as distinct from the other islands, whose inhabitants have traditionally looked down upon their 'backward' neighbours.

Acknowledgements

The authors wish to express their gratitude to the Garajonay National Park authorities and Angel Fernández López in particular, for their assistance and cooperation with this research project.

Endnotes

1. The Canary Islands plays host to around 10 million tourists each year, while la Gomera receives approximately 600,000 visitors per year, of which most if not all pass through the park at some point (Fernández López, *La Isla*, 3 septiembre 1999).

2. According to Fernández López (1992: 62) the forest provides up to 70% of the islands water supply.

3. Interest in the Spanish 'wilderness' amongst north European scientists is highlighted by the role of British naturalists who demonstrated the importance of the Coto Doñana for migratory birds (Crain 1996: 31).

4.   The fact that this is a world heritage site assists us, the managers, in its protection. We are answerable to international organisations and this is a form of benchmark that is used, thus for me it is the most important aspect. Possibly for local politicians the most important factor is the mark of quality. For us [...] it helps to guarantee conservation. (all translations, R. V. Bianchi)

5.   La Palmita, a small hamlet or caserío adjacent to the north perimeter of the National Park, used to have two schools each with about 35-40 pupils, both of which have since closed down for lack of pupils. (Herrera 1999).

6.   Having recently come out from a totalitarian system, people had little notion or idea of a protest, the effect it could have, they also feared the risk it involved. That's the reason why I think no one spoke out at that time, because it wasn't for lack of desire, of which there was a great deal,[...] The mere fact of saying "look sir, I do not believe what you are saying" was brave enough in itself. How was someone to say this to a governor ! That would be worthy of the remark "what a brave man he is who attempts to do this"!

7.   After the creation of the national park, an ancient tagoror (stone circles which served as political meeting points for the ancient gomeros) was removed from this spot and replaced by a viewpoint, from where tourists can look across the central plateau and see up to four of the other Canary Islands.

8.   We consider the reconquest of our mountain as fundamental to the economic and social progress of the Gomero people.

Interviews

Almenara, T. (1999), Former mayor of Agulo. Interview (J. Izquierdo and B. Martín), 6th September, Agulo.

Brito, V. (1995), Former Secretary of the Hermigua municipal council. Interview (Angel Fernández López).

Fernández López, A. B (1999), Director, Garajonay National Park. Interview (R.V. Bianchi), 8th September, Head Office, Parque Nacional de Garajonay, San Sebastian de La Gomera.

González, Nieves (1999), Minister for Tourism, Cabildo Insular de La Gomera. Interview (R. V. Bianchi), 13th September, Cabildo Insular.

González, José Miguel (2000), Former Director of ICONA, Tenerife Province, and principal instigator of Garajonay National Park. Interview (Agustín Santana), 29th March, Ayuntamiento de La Laguna, Tenerife.

Herrera, Antonio (1999), Former mayor of Agulo (1983-87). Interview (B. Martín), 7th September, Agulo.

Ortíz, Isidro (1999), Artisan and agriculturist, and *silbo* (traditional whistle language) monitor. Interview (J. Izquierdo and R. V. Bianchi), 12th September, Chipude.

References

Anon. (1985), Memoria Justficativa para la Declaración *del Sitio de Patrimonio de la Humanidad,* Ministro de Asuntos Exteriores de España, Madrid.

Behar, R. (1986), *The Presence of Past in a Spanish Village*, Princeton University Press, New Jersey.

Cabildo Insular de la Gomera (1997), *Estudio Socioeconómico de la Isla de la Gomera y Bases para un Plan Estratégico.* Excmo. Cabildo Insular de la Gomera.

Morales Cano, A. (1998), Devolución del monte a sus proprietarios históricos. *Eseken,* No. 6, p.13.

Carr, R. (1982), *Spain: 1808-1975,* Oxford University Press, Oxford.

Crain, M. (1996), Contested territories: the politics of touristic development at the shrine of El Rocío in southwestern Andalusia, in Boissevain, J. (Ed.) *Coping with Tourists: European Reactions to Mass Tourism*, Berghahn, Oxford, pp. 27-55.

Daniels, S. (1992), Place and the geographical imagination. *Geography*, 77, pp. 310-322.

Esteban Alonso, A. and A. López López (1989), Environmental policy, in Almarcho Barbado (Ed.) *Spain and EC Membership Evaluated,* Pinter, London, pp. 60-68.

Fernández López, A. B. (1992), La laurisilva canaria, un ecosistema fragil y amenazado. *Montes,* No. 30, pp. 59-67.

Fernández López, A. B. (1998), Garajonay: una selva nublada a las puertas del desierto, *Biológica*, No. 24 (septiembre), pp. 31-40.

Fernández, J. y R. Paredes Regel (1996), *Los Parques Nacionales Españoles: Una Aproximación Histórica.* Organismo Autónomo de Parques Nacionales, Madrid.

Gibson, I. (1992), *Spain: Fire in the Blood,* Faber and Faber, London.

Gómez Sal, Marín, C. and C. Mendaro (1987), Conserving and developing the valuable human landscape of La Gomera, Canary Islands. *Ekistics*, 323/324, pp. 170-175.

Hall, C. M. (2000), *Tourism Planning: Policies, Processes and Relationships*, Harlow, Prentice Hall.

Herzfeld, M. (1991), *A Place in History: Social and Monumental Time in a Cretan Town*, Princeton University Press, New Jersey.

Honey, M. (1999), *Ecotourism and Sustainable Development: Who Owns Paradise?* Island Press.

Jurdao, F. (1990), *España en Venta*, Ediciones Endymion, Madrid.

Montero, R. (1995), Political transition and cultural democracy: coping with the speed of change, in Graham, H. and Labanyi, J. (Eds.) *Spanish Cultural Stdies: an Introduction*, Oxford University Press, Oxford, pp. 315-320.

Mora Morales, M. (1995), *Los Espacios Naturales de La Gomera*. Editorial Globo, La Laguna (Tenerife).

Morris, A. S. (1992), A sea change in Spanish conservation, with illustrations from Gerona province. *ACIS (Association for Contemporary Iberian Studies)*, 5, (2), pp. 23-30.

Saarinen, J. (1998), Wilderness, tourism development, and sustainability: wilderness attitudes and place ethics. *USDA Forest Service Proceedings RMRS-P-4*, pp. 29-34.

Sánchez, I. (1995), Garajonay: Parque Nacional. In Pérez de Paz, P. L. (Ed.) *Parque Nacional de Garajonay: Patrimonio Mundial*. Madrid: ICONA, pp. 19-27.

Shackley, M. (1998) Introduction - world cultural heritage sites, in Shackley, M. (Ed.) *Visitor Management: Case Studies from World Heritage Sites*. Butterworth Heinemann, Oxford, pp. 1-9.

Suter, K. D. (1991), The UNESCO World Heritage Convention. *Environment and Planning Law Journal*, 8 (1): 4-15.

Waldren, J. (1998), The road to ruin: the politics of development in the Balearic Islands, in Abram, S. and Waldren, J. (Eds.) *Anthropological Perspectives on Local Development*, Routledge, London, pp. 120-140.

Tourism and world heritage sites: The Newfoundland experience

Lanita Carter

Memorial University of Newfoundland

Lee Jolliffe

University of Prince Edward Island

Tom Baum

University of Strathclyde

Abstract

As the oldest settled area of North America, part of Newfoundland, Canada's attraction for tourism is found in its history, culture and heritage sites. Among these sites the province's two World Heritage Sites have a pivotal role to play in the development of heritage for tourism. This paper profiles the relationship of these sites to heritage tourism in the province. It builds on previous research on cultural tourism in the peripheral islands of the North Atlantic that included Newfoundland. Using a set of critical success factors for the delivery of such tourism derived from this research an analysis is presented of the relationship of Newfoundland's World Heritage Sites to the province's tourism offerings.

Introduction

The concepts of culture and heritage are closely related to the development of tourism. Particularly in areas of economic decline, history is recognised as a resource that can be utilised in the creation of local heritage tourism products, destined for broader consumption. This trend is evident in the peripheral islands of the North Atlantic, such as Newfoundland (Jolliffe and Baum, 1999) where history transformed into heritage is recognised as a centrepiece of the overall tourism product (Carter, 1999).

One of the cultural attractions for tourism in the province of Newfoundland and Labrador is the numerous historic sites of this oldest settled area of North America. Foremost among these sites are the province's two World Heritage Sites, Gros Morne National Park and L'Anse aux Meadows National Historic Park. Tourism in Newfoundland is recognised to be in a developmental stage (Baum, 1999) and the province's World Heritage Sites have a key role to play in the formation of heritage tourism products and experiences.

This paper examines the role of these World Heritage Sites in the development of heritage as a tourism product in Newfoundland. This examination is divided into four main sections. First, the concepts of heritage, world heritage and heritage tourism are discussed. Second, the use of heritage in Newfoundland's tourism product is examined. Third, the province's World Heritage sites are profiled and their role in developing heritage tourism noted. Fourth, the relationship of these sites to heritage tourism is reviewed in the context of a set of previously proposed principles for cultural tourism development (Jolliffe and Baum, 1999) incorporating the concept of critical success factors in the evolution of heritage projects in Newfoundland (Carter, 1999). The paper takes a product approach to tourism, viewing history, heritage, world heritage and the sites that represent these themes as resources for tourism products, examining their development in an environment influenced by social, economic and political factors.

Heritage tourism

The concept of heritage denotes something inherited from the past. This cultural heritage is often based on material objects or remains of the past that become invested with values when heritage status qualities are attributed to them (Sletvold, 1996; Robb, 1998). In this process, history is commodified and transformed into heritage. Hewison (1987) views the emergence of the heritage industry as the production of commodities. As noted by Richards (1996b) he further observes in this process the use of heritage attractions for political and economic goals. The concept of world heritage encompasses heritage sites acknowledged to be of universal value, however the designation of each site is dependent on national concepts of heritage (Ratz and Puczko, 1999). The sites are recognised as symbols of national culture and character (Shackley, 1998). Infused with the value of national and world heritage many of these sites are major attractions in their country or region.

Heritage is found in many forms and a range of cultural and heritage aspects of each place attract the tourist. This includes historic sites, museums and galleries, cultural festivals and special celebrations (CTC, 1997). Tourism related to these cultural components represents a growing attraction in both domestic and international tourism. The Canadian Tourism Commission (1997) estimates that cultural tourism is growing at a rate of fifteen percent annually. Richards (1996b) identifies heritage tourism as being a part of the broader category of cultural tourism.

Prentice (1993) notes that the promotion of an area's heritage resources often form a part of local economic redevelopment initiatives. In areas where traditional economic activities are in decline heritage has thus been acknowledged as a resource for economic development and regeneration through tourism (Richards, 1996a; Jolliffe and Baum, 1999). The issue of developing history for tourism consequently finds its way onto the economic development agendas of these peripheral areas. One aspect in the nurturing of the resulting heritage tourism is the development of heritage attractions (Richards, 1996b). Historic sites, both natural and cultural are thus recognised as a one of the cultural resources for heritage tourism. A unique resource in the growth of such tourism are the sites on the World Heritage List, designated as unique sites of outstanding universal value (Shackley, 1998).

These sites, both natural and cultural, designated under UNESCO's 1972 World Heritage Convention represent unique aspects of world heritage. National governments submit nominations to the World Heritage Committee of cultural and natural properties of outstanding universal value that may benefit from designation. Potential sites must conform to guidelines regarding universal value, which differ for natural sites and cultural sites. There are two categories for cultural sites: that of monuments groups of buildings and individual sites and that of groups of urban buildings. Potential sites must also meet tests of authenticity in design, material, workmanship or setting, and in the case of cultural landscapes, distinctive character and components (Shackley, 1998).

Once conferred, the designation denotes a site as a World Heritage Site. This listing is perceived to attract visitors and thus increase tourist visitation (Shackley, 1998). The original purpose of designation was to assist with the management and preservation of these sites, however because of increased visitation sites are now also concerned with visitor management, maintaining the quality of the visitor experience and the impact that visitors have on fragile environments (Shackley, 1998). The World Heritage Sites List recognises two sites in Newfoundland, Gros Morne National Park, a natural site designated in 1987 and L'Anse Meadows National Historic Park, a cultural site designated in 1972.

Heritage tourism in Newfoundland

The province of Newfoundland and Labrador, situated on Canada's extreme East Coast, is one of the earliest settled areas of North America. Although Newfoundland did not become part of Canada until 1949 it has a long and colourful history. For centuries fishing boats have left Newfoundland ports heading for the rich cod fishing grounds of the Grand Banks.

Today, over forty per cent of the population of 580,100 (1996) reside in fishing villages along the rugged coastline, that includes many sheltered harbours and large bays. The interior of the main island of Newfoundland is made up of forests and rivers. The economy of the island has traditionally been based on the fishery, forestry and mining.

However, with the downturn in the cod fishery (Baum, 1999a) the island has adopted tourism as an economic development strategy. In this milieu history has become a resource to be transformed into heritage products, attractions and experiences. As such heritage projects in Newfoundland are subject to both political and economic influences.

An earlier analysis of the strengths for tourism development (Gunn, 1994) recognised that the province has the natural, cultural and human resources for the growth of tourism. The needs or opportunities for development recognised by Gunn included the protection of the tourism resource, the establishment of major attraction complexes, the improvement of the provision of information, the improvement of transportation, the integration of economic resource programs and the establishment of new tourism entities. The province, through its Tourism Development Strategy (1995) and its subsequent Product Market Match Study

(1996) has adopted a strategic approach to developing tourism and has made progress in addressing these issues.

Gunn also (1994) recognised the province as rich in cultural resources such as: prehistoric sites, historic sites and structures, legends, lore, crafts, life styles, architecture, fishing villages, and business and trade centres. In the case of historic sites, their subsequent emergence as heritage attractions has been driven by the initiatives of federal, provincial and community groups (Carter, 1999). As discussed by Getz (1995) the province has also utilised festivals and events, often in conjunction with historic sites to market the island as a destination and to increase its competitiveness. This is evident in the organisation of events such as Cabot 500 (1996) and Viking 2000 that transform sites into products, providing heritage experiences for tourists.

Culture and heritage are acknowledged as major motivating factors for the traditional touring market to the island (EPG, 1996). With annual tourism arrivals estimated at 330,000 (1997) the opportunity for increased tourism arrivals (Baum 1999a, 1999b) may be realised in part by the offering of products and experiences that reflect the culture and heritage of the province. To some extent heritage has been used to differentiate the Newfoundland and Labrador destination from others, as reflected in the marketing slogan, "A World of Difference" (Overton, 1996).

Regional tourism associations increasingly play a role in developing heritage experiences for tourism in the province. This is evidenced by the efforts of groups such as the Viking Trail Tourism Association, whose interpretive activities in relation to L'Anse aux Meadows National Historic Park are profiled in this paper. Local communities have also become directly involved in developing heritage for tourism as reflected by the case of the Baccalieu Trail (Jolliffe and Baum, 2000) and other regional heritage initiatives.

That heritage has long been recognised as a resource for the development of the tourism product in Newfoundland is reflected by the creation by the federal government of Canada of national parks in the province, which had economic development objectives (Bella, 1987; Overton, 1996). For example, Gros Morne National Park created in 1970 was expected to increase year round income from tourism for residents of this rural area of Newfoundland (Bella, 1987). At the time this park was also recognised to have potential as a World Heritage Site.

The contemporary heritage tourism product of the province includes a wide variety of festivals and events, theatrical re-enactments, historic sites and theme trails (Jolliffe and Baum, 2000). For example, in Trinity, the Newfounde Land Pageant, a dramatic presentation of local history presented in situ, has transformed this small fishing port into a destination with a unique heritage product to offer. In Bell Island, a series of outdoor murals highlighting the historic iron ore industry has contributed to attracting the tourist and the touring market interested in heritage. On the Bay de Verde Peninsula a local heritage corporation has created the Baccalieu Trail. On their own, these heritage products may not have a high enough profile to attract heritage tourists to Newfoundland. However, these products contribute to the heritage experience that the tourist receives and play a role in attracting tourists into the outlying areas.

The province's two World Heritage Sites, Gros Morne and L'Anse aux Meadows are recognised as among the most market ready products in Atlantic Canada (CTC, 1997). The 1996 Product Market Match Study conducted for the provincial department of tourism identified the UNESCO World Heritage Sites as one of the most important tourist appeals (EPG, 1996). It observed that while these sites are attractive on their own they are also the location for many of the activities, such as hiking, nature study, bird watching, archaeology, heritage and historic that make up the Newfoundland tourism product.

While reviewing the existing World Heritage Sites in the province of Newfoundland and Labrador it is of note that the Parks Canada Red Point site in Labrador is currently an applicant for designation. The addition of this third World Heritage Site, acknowledged as the whaling capital of the world in the 1500's and referred to as the first industrial site in North America (Canadian Heritage, 1999), will create an even stronger and more marketable tourism attraction focus for the western coast of Newfoundland and neighbouring Labrador.

Government policies have highlighted the promotion and use of the province's cultural resources for tourism development. This was evident in both the government's Strategic Economic Plan (1992) and the complimentary Tourism, Culture and Recreation Plan (1995-1996). Heritage and culture has thus become the centrepiece of the overall tourism product offered in Newfoundland and Labrador (Carter, 1999).

The world heritage sites in Newfoundland

Newfoundland's World Heritage Sites are both operated by Canadian Heritage/Parks Canada within the federal government's network of National Parks and National Historic Sites. This is part of the federal agency's mandate of presenting Canadian heritage for the benefit and enjoyment of all Canadians. The Newfoundland sites represent both a natural and a cultural World Heritage Site. Located on the western coast of the island of Newfoundland within the Viking Trail tourism region the sites functions as a strong anchor attractions for the region (Gunn, 1994). The sites and the Viking Trail form what Debdahl (1999) refers to as flagship attractions for this peripheral area and provide a central focus for the tourism marketing efforts of the province.

L'Anse aux Meadows National Historic Park

This thousand year old Viking settlement is North America's only designated Norse settlement. The site was discovered in 1960 by a Norwegian team looking for Vineland. It was excavated between 1973 and 1977 (Taylor, 1990). As Sletvold (1996) notes any authentic resource for Viking attraction development is solely archaeological and development beyond archaeology is based on interpretation of findings. In the case of L'Anse aux Meadows a replica was built of one of the Viking houses excavated and the site was developed by the federal government of Canada as a National Historic Park (Taylor, 1990).

As the location of the first European settlement in North America the site now ranks among the world's most important archaeological properties. Because of this significance L'Anse aux Meadows was designated as a World Heritage Site by UNESCO under the cultural category in 1972. The designation criteria recognised the site as bearing a unique or at least exceptional testimony to a civilisation that has disappeared.

Today through interpretive programmes the site offers visitors the opportunity to learn what life might have been like in this new world Viking settlement 1000 years ago (Canadian Heritage, 1999). Reconstructed Viking huts provide a background to the site's Encampment Program that includes consumed interpreters living the way the Vikings would have lived. The encampment depicts life in a seasonal camp similar to that established at L'Anse Aux Meadows, with animators using a first person approach as they interpret lifestyles and technologies from the era, including demonstrations in Viking ship construction, iron processing, domestic tasks, trade and the sagas (Canadian Heritage, 1999).

Gros Morne National Park

The federal government of Canada created this National Park in 1970. It was developed specifically to attract tourists and Bella (1987) refers to the emphasis in park establishment being on profit rather than preservation. Those dependent on fishing in the coastal communities within the proposed park initially opposed the development which was expected to increase incomes through tourism (Bella, 1987). However, it was subsequently recognised that the park contributed to decreasing the unemployment rate in the area.

The initial size of the park was 775 square kilometres (Bella, 1987). Today, Gros Morne National Park encompasses 1,805 square kilometres (Canadian Heritage, 1999). It was designated by UNESCO as a World Heritage Site in 1987 as an outstanding example representing major stages of the earth's history. The site has scenic beauty and unique geology that includes mountainous terrain, landlocked fjord lakes, picturesque valleys, majestic waterfalls and coastal seascapes (Canadian Heritage, 1999). The park represents hundreds of years of human history and over 500 years of geological history. The Tablelands is a rare piece of the earth's mantle and one of the most geographically significant areas in the world.

The site offers a wide variety of experiences for visitors, including hiking, walking, kayaking, camping, boat tours, sightseeing, wildlife and bird watching and live theatre. Interpretation programming is an important aspect of the operation of the park. In 2000 a new purpose built Discovery Centre will open. The new facility will feature a multi-media theatre with seating for one hundred and twenty, interactive and educational exhibits, a three dimensional model of the park and its features, a fossil room and mini theatre, a time wall with rock specimens, a folk art display, native plant gardens, a reception and information lobby and a gift shop.

Critical success factors for heritage tourism

Previous research on cultural tourism in the North Atlantic Islands of Newfoundland, Prince Edward Island, the Western Isles and the Isle of Skye identified principles common to the development of cultural and heritage tourism (Jolliffe and Baum, 1999). These principles were derived from a review of the literature on cultural and heritage tourism as well as from a product analysis undertaken in the form of case studies of cultural tourism offerings in the four islands. These factors are presented here (Table 1) and reviewed in the context of Newfoundland's World Heritage Sites. Highlighted as critical success factors for heritage projects, as presented by Carter (1999) they provide a framework for examining the role of the sites in the development of heritage tourism in Newfoundland and Labrador.

Table 1   Critical Success Factors for Heritage Tourism
(Based on Five Principles for Cultural Tourism Development, Jolliffe and Baum, 1999)

1.   A Community Based Approach to Heritage Tourism
2.   Management of Heritage Tourism
3.   Establishing Standards for Heritage Tourism
4.   Recognising the Benefits of Heritage Tourism
5.   Overcoming the Barriers to Heritage Tourism

A community based approach to heritage tourism

In an ideal sense, heritage tourism begins with the community, and what Murphy (1985) describes as a community based model for tourism development. In this model individual communities take control of the process, setting their own goals and planning accordingly with the result being the "community tourism product". However, in the case of Gros Morne and L'Anse aux Meadows the early development of the two parks was influenced by economic development objectives of both the federal (Bella, 1987; Taylor, 1990) and provincial (Overton, 1996) governments. While this approach initially received some community opposition as in the case of Gros Morne (Bella, 1987) elements of the community tourism product process are now evident. An example is found in the partnering between government, the community and heritage sites in the planning of the Viking Tourism Trail (Gunn, 1994) which connects the two sites and in recent heritage product development of the Viking Encampment (Canadian Heritage, 1999).

Management of heritage tourism

The previous study (Jolliffe and Baum, 1999) recognised management as a key factor in the offering of heritage tourism products in North Atlantic islands. This was outlined as including planning, partnering, developing people, promoting and caring for visitors. Parks Canada plans for and partners in the marketing of the sites, working closely with the provincial Department of Tourism, Culture and Recreation and with the regional tourism association, the Viking Trail.

In the case of the Newfoundland sites under the management of Parks Canada there is a strong focus on interpreting the sites for visitors and caring for their needs. This is reflected by the visitor satisfaction surveys that are carried out annually for each site (Canadian Heritage, 1998a, 1998b, 1998c). The issue of visitor management to influence the activities of tourists was noted in the previous study (Jolliffe and Baum, 2000) with the main benefits being increasing the length of stay in an area, and dispersing visitors into outlying areas. Visitor management is of concern to the managers of World Heritage Sites (Shackley, 1998) particularly as it relates to the control of visitation to fragile environments. In the case of the Newfoundland World Heritage Sites the parks have contributed to visitor stays and the dispersal of visitors. The managers of the parks have taken a responsible and proactive approach to visitor management; for example at Gros Morne, a range of activities is provided, dispersing visitors into outlying areas, thus serving as a tool for the management of visitation.

Establishing standards for heritage tourism

Previous research determined that a component of establishing standards for heritage tourism is integrity in the form of the authenticity of the story (Jolliffe and Baum, 1999). In the case of the UNESCO World Heritage sites profiled here the designation of the sites has authenticated the story that the sites represent. Managers of the sites see this as one of the main benefits of designation (Lough and Hall, 1999). The sites thus benefit from the value bestowed upon World Heritage Sites (Shackley, 1998). The value of designation to tourism may thus be viewed in terms of the validation of history, and the transformation of history into heritage, discussed earlier in this paper.

A further aspect inherent in establishing standards is that of innovativeness and freshness of product. The managers of Newfoundland's World Heritage Sites endeavour to continually upgrade the services provided at their sites. Interpretive techniques and media are employed to enhance the visitor experience. This is reflected by the annual surveys of visitor satisfaction (Canadian Heritage, 1998a, 1998b, 1998c) and by the development of new products and services, such as the Discovery Centre at Gros Morne.

Jolliffe and Baum (1999) note that quality, both in terms of authenticity and standard of presentation is a key issue relating to the market readiness of the cultural tourism product. In the area of quality the sites are recognised by tourism and culture researchers as being market ready (CTC, 1997; EPG, 1996, Carter, 1999). During the roundtable discussions on cultural tourism conducted by the Canadian Tourism Commission the sites were acknowledged as the most market ready product in the Atlantic region (CTC, 1997). The prerequisites of quality, authenticity and standard of presentation in the development of heritage tourism are thus present in the Gros Morne and L'Anse aux Meadows sites.

Recognising the benefits of heritage tourism

Researchers recognise that cultural and heritage tourism has a number of positive impacts (Richards, 1996; Lord, 1993, Jolliffe and Baum, 1999) on both local communities and on the development of tourism. For the host community heritage projects can contribute to improving the quality of life of local inhabitants. This trend is evident in terms of the local employment and improved infrastructure offered by the development of the two World Heritage Sites in Newfoundland.

It has also been noted that heritage projects can be designed to meet the development objectives of tourism (Jolliffe and Baum, 1999). The development process for Gros Morne has illustrated how government uses heritage sites for community economic redevelopment. Robb (1996) has noted that mutual benefits for heritage and tourism can be derived from the sustainable development of World Heritage Sites. The Newfoundland World Heritage Sites that balance site preservation aims and objectives with services for visitors illustrate that the preservation objectives of cultural organisations can be met by heritage projects.

Overcoming the barriers to heritage tourism

A common barrier to the development of heritage tourism is recognised as a lack of communication among the heritage and tourism sectors and limited resources for development (Lord, 1997). The active participation and stewardship by the federal government of the two Newfoundland sites has ensured that resources have been available for development. In the case of Newfoundland's World Heritage Sites there appears to be a good level of communication and co-operation between the various levels of government responsible for the preservation, management and promotion of the sites and the local tourism association. Residents in the area recognise the presence of these national sites as a benefit in attracting tourists and visitation to their area (Rural Dialogue, 1998).

Partnership is seen as important to overcoming some of the barriers that can impede the development of heritage tourism (Jolliffe and Baum, 1999). An example is the Viking Encampment that takes place at the L'Anse aux Meadows national Historic Site daily from early June to early October (Canadian Heritage, 1999). This is a partnership project of the Viking Trail Tourism Association and Parks Canada. In 1997, the Viking Encampment program was named winner of the province's top cultural tourism award. In 1999, Attractions Canada named the program the best international tourism product in Newfoundland and Labrador.

Conclusions

This paper has served to introduce and explore the relationship of Newfoundland's natural and cultural World Heritage Sites to the developing area of heritage tourism. There is ample opportunity for further research, supported by field work that explores the perceptions of the site managers, the provincial tourism destination organisation and the local tourism associations of the role that the sites play in heritage tourism in the province. The authors have outlined some of the concerns for this research approach in a recent research note (Carter, Jolliffe and Baum, 2000).

In this paper the role of World Heritage Sites in the emergence of heritage tourism has been examined using the sites of the province of Newfoundland as a case study. Heritage has been clearly identified as a centrepiece of the tourism product of the province and the designated World Heritage Sites are the flagship attractions of that centrepiece. An examination of the development of these sites demonstrates the benefits of site designation to tourism, in authenticating the value of the sites as representative of world heritage, offering a focus as visitor attractions for their destination and region.

A number of critical success factors in the development of heritage tourism have been examined in relation to Newfoundland's World Heritage Sites. Based on this assessment, these factors have been revised in the context of these sites and their involvement in heritage tourism (Table 2).

Table 2   Critical Success Factors for Heritage Tourism through World Heritage Sites
(Based on Five Principles for Cultural Tourism Development, Jolliffe and Baum, 1999)

1.   A Community Economic Development Approach to Heritage Tourism
2.   Visitor Management for Heritage Tourism
3.   Operating Standards for Heritage Tourism
4.   Improving Local Communities through Heritage Tourism
5.   Partnering for Heritage Tourism

It has been found that the development of the sites has been primarily government and economic development driven, rather than driven by community goals demonstrated by some of the smaller heritage projects examined in previous research (Jolliffe and Baum, 1999). It is thus observed that while heritage projects have critical success factors in common the scale of heritage attractions (for example; size) and the level of recognition of that heritage (for example; local, regional, national, global) effects the nature of the factors for success.

In the case of the World Heritage Sites visitor management has been identified as central to the delivery of heritage tourism products and experiences through the sites. The sites have developed both natural and cultural elements, identified as having universal value and operate with standards consistent with that expected for the delivery of heritage tourism through World Heritage Sites. Both sites have been developed within a community economic context and while these developments have not been community generated they nonetheless allow for the improvement of communities through heritage tourism. The element of partnering is evident in improving and extending the level of programming and products for visitor services at the parks, as with the case of the Viking Re-enactment at L'Anse aux Meadows.

The relationship of Newfoundland's World Heritage sites to the development of heritage tourism in the province is thus complex. It is a relationship that has been influenced by social, political and economic agendas, at the global, national, provincial and local levels. The critical success of these sites in acting as anchor and flagship attractions for the province is closely related to their status as World Heritage Sites and the related values of authenticity that accompany the designation. This status also brings with it an expectation of quality, in terms of the management, preservation and interpretation of the sites.

In conclusion, the role of the World Heritage Sites in the development of the Newfoundland tourism product is clearly critical and influential, directly contributing to the centrality of heritage and culture within this product offering. It is a relationship worthy of further research, supported by field research eliciting the participation of the key partners in the development and representation of Newfoundland's world heritage as a heritage tourism product.

References

Baum, Tom (1999), "The Decline of the Traditional North Atlantic Fisheries and Tourism's Response: the Case of Iceland and Newfoundland", *Current Issues in Tourism Research*, 2 (1), 47 - 67.

Bella, Leslie (1987), *Parks for Profit*, Montreal; Harvest House Limited.

Canadian Heritage/Parks Canada (1998a), L'Anse aux Meadows National Historic Site, Visitor Satisfaction Survey - Entrance, St. John's: Parks Canada.

Canadian Heritage/Parks Canada (1998b), Gros Morne National Park, Visitor Satisfaction Survey - Park Entrance, St. John's: Parks Canada.

Canadian Heritage/Parks Canada (1998b), Gros Morne National Park, Visitor Satisfaction Survey - Interpretative Activities, St. John's: Parks Canada

Canadian Heritage/Parks Canada (1999), Press Kit - Travel Notes from Parks Canada, Newfoundland and Labrador, St. John's.

Canadian Tourism Commission (1997), *Fulfilling the Promise: A Report on Regional Round Tables on Cultural and Heritage Tourism*, Ottawa.

Carter, Lanita (1999), "Defining Critical Success Factors for Community Based Heritage Tourism Projects," Unpublished Project Proposal, Memorial University, St. John's, Newfoundland.

Carter, Lanita, Jolliffe, Lee and Baum, Tom (1999), "Heritage Tourism and World Heritage Sites: The Case of Newfoundland," Unpublished Research Note.

Drost, Anne (1996), "Developing Sustainable Tourism for World Heritage Sites," *Annals of Tourism Research*, 23 (2), pp. 479 - 484.

Dybedal, Peter (1998), *Theme Parks as Flagship Attractions in Peripheral Areas*, Denmark: Bornholms Forkinsgentre.

Economic Planning Group of Canada (1996), *Product Market Match Study*, St John's: Department of Tourism, Culture and Recreation, Government of Newfoundland and Labrador.

Getz, Donald (1995), "Island Competitiveness Through Festivals and Events: the Case of Newfoundland," in Conlin, Michael V. and Baum, Tom (eds.), *Island Tourism: Principles and Practices*, Chichester: Wiley, pp.149 - 165.

Gunn, Clare, A. (1995), *An Assessment of Tourism Potential in Newfoundland and Labrador with Recommendations for a Planned Approach to Tourism Development*. Conference Proceedings, Tourism Planning and Development Workshops, Saint John's, September 1994.

Hewison, R. (1987), *The Heritage Industry: Britain in a Climate of Decline*, London: Methuen.

Jolliffe, Lee and Baum, Tom (1999), "An Agenda for Cultural Tourism on the Periphery: The Case of Four North Atlantic Islands," Paper Presented at CHME Conference, University of Surrey.

Jolliffe, Lee and Baum, Tom (2000), *Directions in Cultural Tourism: The Case of Four North Atlantic Islands*, Charlottetown: Institute of Island Studies, forthcoming.

Lord Cultural Resources Planning and Management Inc. (1993), *The Cultural Tourism Handbook*, Toronto: Government of Ontario.

Lough, Dave and Hall, Edna (1999), Interview with Lee Jolliffe, October 19, St. John's, Newfoundland: Canadian Heritage/Parks Canada.

Murphy, P. (1985), *Tourism: A Community Approach*, New York: Methuen.

Overton, James (1996), *Making a World of Difference; Essays on Tourism, Culture and Development*, St. Johns: Institute of Social and Economic Research, Memorial University.

Prentice, Richard (1993), *Tourism and Heritage Attractions*, London: Routledge.

Ratz, Tamara and Puczko, Laszlo (1999), "A World Heritage Industry? Tourism at Hungarian World Heritage Sites," presented at the Cross Gazes at the Heritage Concept Worldwide at the End of the 20th Century Symposium, October, 1999, Sorbonne, Paris.

Richards, Greg, ed. (1996a), *Cultural Tourism in Europe*, Wallingford: CAB International.

Richards, Greg (1996b), "Production and Consumption of European Cultural Tourism," *Annals of Tourism Research*, Vol 23, No. 2, pp. 261 - 283.

Robb, J.G. (1998), "Tourism & Legends: Archaeology of Heritage," *Annals of Tourism Research*, 25 (3), pp. 579-596.

Rural Dialogue (1998), "Rural Canadians Speak Out: Summary of Deer Lake Input," May 28, 1998. Ottawa: Government of Canada (http:/www.gc.ca/workshop/deerla).

Shackley, Myra (1998), *Visitor Management: Cases from World Heritage Sites*, Oxford: Butterworth Heinmann.

Sletvold, Ola (1996), "Viking Heritage: Contexts and Commodification", in Tourism and Culture: Image, Identity and Marketing, Tourism and Culture Towards the 21st Century Conference Proceedings, Sunderland: Business Educational Publishers, pp. 217 - 230.

Strategic Economic Plan (1992), St. John's: Government of Newfoundland and Labrador.

Taylor, C. J. (1990), *Negotiating the Past: The Making of Canada's National Historic Parks and Sites*, Montreal & Kingston: McGill-Queen's University Press.

Tourism, Culture and Recreation, 1995-1996 Plan (1995), Newfoundland and Labrador, St. John's: Department of Culture and Recreation.

World heritage sites and tourism: A case study of the Elephanta Island, Mumbai, India

Ilika Chakravarty

Indian Institute of Technology, India

Introduction

The World Heritage Convention of 1972 distinguished between the concepts of *cultural* and *natural* heritage. The concept of *cultural landscape* emerged subsequently, suggesting an integration between nature and culture. The perspective of *heritage* and its preservation in the context of cultural landscape by enlisting participation of the resident community has gained much importance in the recent times. The growth of tourism and the commoditisation of heritage have become a subject matter of considerable controversy with the economics of tourism conflicting with the natural and cultural aspects of heritage. *Preservation* is central to heritage building. The world wide objective of cultural heritage building is to identify, protect and preserve a monument, building or sites of historical, aesthetic, archaeological, scientific, or anthropological importance.

Prior to the declaration and inclusion of a national heritage in the list of World Heritage Sites (providing for shared international responsibility and financial support from the World Heritage fund) an assurance is sought from the national Government to ensure its protection from an activity inimical to conservation. The United Nations Educational Scientific and Cultural Organisation's (UNESCO) World Heritage Committee upon receiving assurance from India included the 6th century Elephanta island caves (officially known as Gharapuri), as a World Heritage Site in 1987. Incidentally, Elephanta island is Mumbai's only world heritage.

We have for the longest time neglected out heritage almost afraid it would seem to cherish their magnificence. Historians offer many reasons for this neglect - poverty, lack of education, a fear of being seen as elitist and a view of the world that tolerates decay as a part of the cycle. However, with expectations of the tourism industry being the biggest growth sector in the new millennia, attitudes are changing. We are at last beginning to recognize that our monuments are potential economic assets and that our great cultural heritage deserves attention.

Within an emerging context from concern, an assessment of Elephanta and the condition of its inhabitants have gained much importance. The two perspectives which emerge in this context are as follows: (a) the cultural-pilgrim oriented content of heritage preservation which discourages the pure tourist attraction of the site and prescribes for the promotion and development of an alternative site for tourist attraction (Jayakar, 1997), and, (b) the synthesis of tourism, heritage preservation and the interests of the host community (Young, 1997). Although these perspectives suggest alternative policy approaches, nonetheless, the single and primary objective of heritage preservation have been emphasised by either. As a spin off from this concern, a sociological investigation focusing on the economy, social structure and livelihood of the islanders becomes essential towards an analysis on the implications for heritage conservation.

Objectives of the study

The objectives of the study are as follows:

(i)   to provide a brief profile on the Elephanta caves and the island;

(ii)   to present an assessment of the social structure and living conditions of the islanders and their implications towards tourism and heritage management;

(iii) to outline the ongoing development efforts by the Government and local bodies in Elephanta;

(iv)   to review the willingness of the islanders towards participation in community development programs; and,

(v)   to suggest policy prescriptions for the betterment of the island and its residents.

Organisation of the study

The paper has been organised into six sections. Following the introduction, Section 1 will provide a brief profile on the Elephanta caves and island. Section 2 will highlight upon the social structure of the Elephanta community. Section 3 will discuss issues related to the social structure and living conditions of the islanders and their implications towards tourism and heritage preservation. Section 4 will provide some insights on the efforts of the ongoing development work at Elephanta under Government initiative and involvement of local bodies (as the INTACH). Section 5 will look into the willingness of the islanders towards participation in community development programs. Section 6 will suggest policy prescriptions for the development of Elephanta.

Methodology

The study has depended primarily upon the analysis of 125 household data (Rajbunder-65, Sethbunder-38, Morabunder-22) based upon the primary field work conducted by the Tata Institute of Social Sciences (TISS) in its socio-economic survey of Elephanta island in 1998.

The survey involved individual unstructured questionnaire interviews with the household heads supplemented with additional information generated through meetings and group discussions with the *Sarpanch* (village head) and members of the local community groups in the island. This study which is essentially exploratory in nature with substantially endeavour towards highlighting upon the impacts of tourism on Elephanta and in evolving a relationship between tourism, livelihood issues and heritage preservation.

A brief profile of the Elephanta Caves and Island

Elephanta is situated in the upper reaches of the Mumbai harbour (9 nautical miles from the Gateway of India/Apollo Bunder) in the Arabian sea. The island derives its name from the Portuguese who found a great monolithic stone elephant (eventually removed by Britishers to mainland Mumbai) where they landed and named it *'a ilha do Elephanta'*, (the island of the Elephant) in the 16th century.

Elephanta is one of the greatest monuments in sculpture and an important cultural and historic destination. It represents the only island caves in the world which are home to some of the most magnificent *Shaivaite* (the cult of Shiva), rock-cut sculptures in the country. Elephanta is equivalent to many as Mount *Kailasha*- the glorious abode of Shiva, where they come to purify and meditate. The grand cave has three entrances and one contains some magnificent sculptural panels, grandiose both in concept and size. In the grand column hall, the *shivalingam* stands in a shrine guarded by *dwarpalas* (gatekeepers) on its four entrances. The panels depicting Shiva's awesome eternal presence are depicted in forms as varied as - *Nataraja* (Shiva - the cosmic dancer), *Gangadhara* (Shiva receiving the descending Ganges), *Ravana Anugraha*, (Shiva crushing *Ravana* as he tries to lift Mount *Kailasha*), *Andhakari* (Shiva impaling the demon *Andhaka* with his trident) and *Kalyanasundara* (Shiva the gentle God with his beautiful consort). According to eminent art historian Professor Pramod Chandra, Elephanta is "perhaps the most significant early Hindu monument in India". However, it is the famous twenty feet panel depicting the triple faced bust of Shiva- the *Mahesh Murti* (erroneously called the *Trimurti*) lying within the inner recesses of the cave which is a masterpiece of Indian sculptural art. The three faces emerging out of darkness show Shiva as a Destroyer (left), Creator (right) and the pensive Preserver (centre). Rightly enough scholars like Andre Malraux referred to it as 'the world's greatest stone sculpture'.

In the absence of authentic historical records about the origin and past habitats of Elephanta, fanciful guesses have been made about the same. However, the Portuguese occupance of Elephanta has been widely accepted. References to British colonisation have also been found in the literature on Elephanta. The island was also home to the Buddhist settlements in the early years. The present relics of a Buddhist *stupa* (burial mound) whose antiquity has been traced to the 3rd century B.C. substantiate the view. In the 12th century, when it was known as *'Puri'* (Fortress City), Elephanta was a prosperous Mauryan port and capital of a coastal kingdom. Throughout its long and nondescript history, it acquired prominence following the excavation of the ancient rock-cut architecture when Brahmanism was on the rise in India. This eventually attracted the attention of scholars and travellers to give Elephanta its fame as 'the Goddess of fortune of the Western Coast'. Presently, the caves top the itinerary of the Mumbai bound domestic and international tourists. Approximately 1,000 people visit the caves each day with the numbers increasing on weekends. Elephanta draws about 10 lakh visitors each year, of which 6 lakh are casual picnickers who do not visit the caves but come for sheer enjoyment.

Situated in the Uran *tehsil* of the Raigarh district of Maharashtra, Elephanta is home to three villages: Sethbunder, Rajbunder and Mora Bunder with a population of an approximately 1,200 people residing in 144 households. Sethbunder is located on the foothills of Elephanta at the entrance of the jetty where the ferries anchor. Rajbunder is located south of the main hills housing the caves and Morabunder along the coastline at the further end, houses the old piers and the remains of a large *stupa* and temple relics (Map 1). While Sethbunder houses the more affluent societies in the island, Rajbunder has the bulk of its infrastructural set up. Accessibility of Morabunder to the first two hamlets is possible only during low tide. In the north east end of Elephanta, lies the Jawaharlal Nehru Port Trust (JNPT).

Map 1   Location and profile of the Elephanta Island

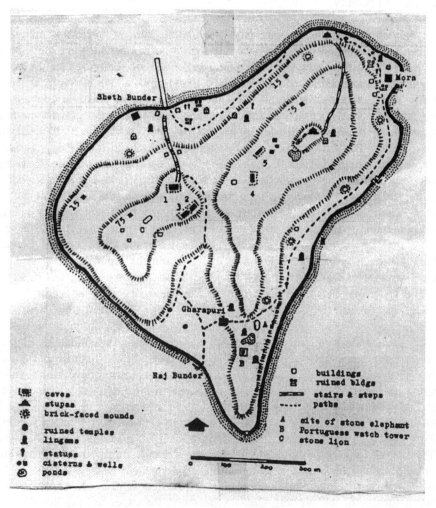

Source: Kail, O., (1984), pp.2

Different Government departments look after different areas of the 247 hectares of land in Elephanta. The caves and monuments are under the jurisdiction of the Archeological Survey of India (ASI). Tourism promotion in Elephnata is handled by the Maharashtra Tourism Development Corporation (MTDC). The forest lands are under the jurisdiction of the Forest Department while the Port Authority manages the jetty and the minor Ports Authority licenses the boats. The Collector of Raigad and the village *Panchayat* review the overall development of Elephanta.

Social structure of the Elephanta community

One of the earliest efforts in understanding the socio-economic profile of the Elephanta islanders was touched upon by the Bombay Natural History Society (BNHS) in its study on the coastal eco-system (Deshmukh, 1997). The social composition of the islanders reveals the following facets.

Elephanta registered a negative population growth and overall decline in sex ratio during 1981-1991. This was attributed largely to lower rates of natural growth, death and out-migration by the male members for employment and education. Most of the population is in the age group of 15-44 year although youth (15-29 years) constitute the single largest group. The average household size of the three villages is five and most families are of the nuclear type. The economic conditions of the islanders reveal the importance of tourism induced activities in terms of occupation, income and overall economic development. As per the estimated poverty line for rural Maharashtra (based on the monthly per capita expenditure figure for 1993-94 which was Rs. 194.69), more than 90 per cent of the households in Elephanta were above the absolute poverty level (Sengupta, 1998).

Although the livelihood of the islanders is derived from as many as thirty different occupations, in the absence of local resources for sustenance, the impact of tourism seems embedded as the principal instrument for labour division and income pooling activities for most households in all three hamlets. Almost 57 per cent of the total working population in the island earn from tourism related occupations (such as hawkers, hotel/restaurant owners-workers, ferry service), etc. Among the non-tourist based occupations, agricultural activities dominate within petty parcels of land. Fishing is dominant among the *Kolis* who are the traditional island community in the State. Many islanders also earn their living as agricultural laborers (Table 1)

Table 1 **Household members by tourist and non-tourist-based primary occupations**

	Rajbunder	Shethbunder	Morabunder	Total (Row) Per cent
Tourist Based	60.2 (71)	64.0 (48)	31.4 (11)	(No.) 57.0 (130)
Non-Tourist Based	39.8 (47)	36.0 (27)	68.6 (24)	43.0 (98)
Total	100.0 (118)	100.0 (75)	100.0 (35)	100.0 (228)

Source: Sengupta, C. (1998), pp. 8.

The facilities of social infrastructure which enhance human capital (as education, health, etc.), are largely inadequate in Elephanta. About 82 per cent of the population are literate with 54 per cent having qualified till middle school. Elephanta is also devoid of skilled individuals (only 2 per cent of the working population are skilled and these include a carpenter, electrician, photographer and painter (Sengupta, 1998).

In terms of caste, tribe and ethnic characteristics (as language, religion, etc.), Elephanta is a fairly homogenous society. The *Agra, Koli and Maratha* castes dominate the hamlets of Rajbunder, Sethbunder and Morabunder respectively. An interesting aspect of the cultural identity of most islanders finds expression through their spiritual desires and belief in the *Swadhyaya* cult which upholds the cultural and spiritual upliftment of individuals by promoting brotherhood among the 'children of God'. All caste members visit the four Hindu temples in the island and participate in community festivals. With four active political groups in the island (Shiv Sena, Bharatiya Janata Party, Congress and Setkari Kamgar Paksha with communist leanings) Elephanta represents a small community caught in the web of intricate political dynamics. An interesting aspect of the *Panchayat* is of women's participation in local Government. The political economy of Elephanta is inextricably linked with the unequal access to resources generated by tourism. The view of most islanders suggested that they wanted development of the island not as an alternative to tourism, but as a reasonable share in the existing tourist business in Elephanta.

Living conditions of the islanders and its implications towards tourism and heritage preservation

Several civic problems have crippled community infrastructural development in Elephanta island. There is a severe shortage as regards the availability of clean drinking water as also as regards the hardships involved in obtaining the same. Most wells, the only source of potable water, are located at distances from household premises and pose tremendous difficulties to women as regards storage and collection. Water is also collected from a cistern situated in the right side of the main cave. In the absence of water, the islanders have been unable to commence agricultural activities. Past commitments of the Mumbai Metropolitan Region Development Authority (MMRDA) in repairing the cracked water tank feeding Elephanta has not yet seen reality.

The islanders suffer from a grossly inadequate and permanent electricity supply. Electricity supplied by the MTDC run diesel generators is available daily from 7 P.M. to 10.30 P.M at an average cost of Rs. 55 per month per household. This however is limited to only two of the three hamlets, after which the island plunges into complete darkness. Street lighting is absent and the islanders have to manage with lanterns and torches for outings after 11 P.M. The solar energy arrangement by the Government at Morabunder is almost non-functional with only a few batteries in the solar panels in working condition. Many have expressed sleeping difficulties without fans particularly in summer when it is warm inside. The JNPT capability in supplying uninterrupted electricity supply through an underwater cable to Elephanta has also remained unutilised.

Education facilities for the community in the island have also been largely inadequate. There are no regular teachers in the school and those from Uran refuse to come here. There is only one Government aided primary school up to the 7th standard (with an enrolment of 100 children) run by two teachers. There is also one secondary school run by the private Konkan Education Society with five teachers. A *Balwadi* (children's school) is run by the *Panchayat*. Health facilities in Elephanta are grossly inadequate. The single first aid centre which is restricted to a doctor with a Diploma in Homeopathy (DHMS) visiting the island twice a week. Uran and Mumbai are the two options for regular treatment and emergency cases. The absence of safe drinking water has been responsible for water borne diseases (as diarrhea, dysentery, malaria, etc). In the absence of an adequate drainage and sanitation set up more than 90 per cent of the men, women and children use open spaces for defecation. A few make use of the awkwardly located and badly maintained *Sulabh Sauchalaya* (toilet complex) devoid of running water. Most of the domestic wastes are dumped in places convenient to the households. Inadequate postal and communication facilities, is yet another problem affecting the living condition of the islanders.

In response to the question of what were the major problems facing them, the answers from the respondents were not related to unemployment or poverty issues (as is the case in most Indian rural settings). Overwhelming responses were towards inadequate physical and social infrastructure which priority wise included electricity, piped water supply, hospital, toilet, proper roads, proper school, market (there is one post office and a ration shop, but no market), telecommunications and the monkey menace.

The poorly managed tourist facilities in Elephanta have been responsible considerably in being the prime deterrent towards foreign tourist flow. The ferries are in a pitiable condition causing much inconvenience to many. Accommodation facilities are absent for those wishing to stay overnight. The pavilion and benches for visitors is also in a bad condition. There are no arrangements for lights as regards photography and permission for the same (inside the cave temple) have to be obtained from the ASI. Government initiatives in Elephanta's development have so far met with little success The ASI Superintending Archeologist its stationed at Aurangabad has largely failed in bringing about positive development in the island. The MTDC with its limited resources and manpower has also failed in ensuring proper functioning of tourist facilities in the island.

In addition, several negative environmental impacts of tourism have also made their presence strongly felt in Elephanta. The island is under severe threat from the dangers of defilement and erosion. Much of this has off late been an outcome of the unregulated tourism development accompanied by industrial growth in the neighboring areas. This has resulted in vulnerability existing in many fronts. Over the years, the island has been exposed to a great deal of stress being located as it, is in midst of the country's most busy harbour- the JNPT. With its current pace of expansion, its domain of operations are likely to expand even further. The JNPT has received final clearance from the Ministry of Environment and Forests for constructing a marine storage terminal for varied toxic hazardous chemicals on 200 hectares of reclaimed land at Uran, at proximity to Elephanta. Such operations can have serious impacts on Elephanta and its protected monuments. Incidentally, the ASI prohibits such developments from occurring within a 1 km. radius of a protected monument and the Ministry of Environment prohibits such activities within a 5 kms. radius. Besides, chemical hazard, Elephanta's proximity to Trombay, wherein lies India's most modern atomic reactor has also made it prone to environmental threats.

Destabilisation of the regional land mass though subsidence and formation of cracks in the monuments as a result of the JNPT's under water blasting and dredging activities have added to the environmental problems. The GSI and ASI need to be aware of its grave consequences. Elephanta being located on the tectonic fault line is increasingly susceptible to natural disasters in the form of earthquakes to the intensity of 6 or 7 on the Richter scale.

Pollution caused by port activities is another environmental threat for the island. Oil spills, emptying of bilge by ships, flotsam from ship breaking activities at Darukhana, etc., have contaminated the sea waters and affected considerably the tropical tidal mangrove species - the 'lungs of the sea' (due to their oxygenation capacity in water). Fuel wood requirements of the islanders, eco-vandals and horticulturists supplying flowers to Mumbai's booming populace of florists (which require he mangroves as twigs), non-enforcement of environmental protection laws, straying buffaloes, etc., have all contributed in causing further depletion. Many rare mangrove species (as the *Sonneratia caseoloris)*, valued highly by botanists have off-late completely disappeared from their once sizeable concentration around Elephanta. Besides increasing the levels of chemical toxins in sea water such an activity has affected considerably affected the local ecosystem through the loss of valuable marine flora and fauna.

Soil erosion and the increasing loss of sea shore land through sea water invasion was of concern to most islanders and many pleaded for improvement and repairing of the bunds. For the Elephanta community, firewood is the second necessity after kerosene. As both these represent low quality fuels, indoor pollution is presumably high. No major incidence of tree felling was reported by the islanders. The growing garbage (mostly plastic litter) problem on Elephanta has also been rather acute in the recent years. Unfortunately, very few islanders are unaware of the negative consequences associated with the same. In addition there are problems related to tourist overcrowding and noise.

Developmental work at Elephanta

Government initiatives

Interestingly, while the islanders have developed their own coping mechanism to tackle daily problems, the Government response has been far from satisfactory. In the area of power supply, State interventions have not moved beyond discussions. The feasibility of laying underwater cables from JNPT for permanent power supply under the initiative of the Maharashtra State Electricity Board (MSEB) and the Port Authority have been abandoned due to the prohibitively high costs involved in the project. In Rajbunder, the dam built by the Maharashtra State Sewerage and Water Supply Board lies practically defunct due to serious leakage and seepage problems. Proposals for an underwater pipeline from Nhava Sheva to the nearest hamlet of Morabunder for water supply to Elephanta, have also unfortunately, till date remained on paper. The only concrete initiative of the State was in solar energy provision to Morabunder under the initiative of the Maharashtra Energy Development Authority. However this project too appears almost dead with old batteries not being replaced regularly.

Moreover, ad hoc decisions of local chieftains and disconnected Government Departments have resulted in crowding and unruly development of Elephanta. The unnecessary construction of the new jetty in the existence of a perfectly adequate low tide natural harbour at the rear end of Elephanta (as per nautical records), is an ignominious attempt in developing tourist facilities on the sylvan island. Besides being an aesthetic eyesore, it has acted as a sieve to the garbage floating in the sea and destroyed much of the mangrove ecosystem. The MTDC run toy train, intended in transporting tourists from the jetty to the foot of the steps leading to the monument, has been perceived by many as the first step towards a pattern of 'Disney land development' in Elephanta. Although, the operation was initially shelved following local protest, the project was subsequently revived and exists presently as an unviable enterprise. In the dearth of entertainment and education facilities for visitors to Elephanta, the State Forest Department had proposed an amusement park-cum-animal safari on a seventeen acre plot in Rajbunder. The project was however dismantled following protests from environmentalists demanding the preservation of religious sanctity associated with the site. Proposals for developing a pagoda and a thirty-bed dormitory for tourists were also rejected by local residents.

Presently, the Government proposes to start a nursery for the ornamental and medicinal plants found in the island. Proposals for the creation of a Nature Interpretation Centre focusing upon wildlife and marine ecology of the region are also being thought of. One can be optimistic that funds will be available for these projects.

Initiative of the local bodies - activities of theIntach

Although several Government agencies have been involved towards the development of Elephanta, there has been little bureaucratic coordination existing between them. Hence, nobody had been actively following a development policy to protect the monument from rapacious development, as well as to promote the interests and welfare of the islanders without sacrificing the island and the caves. Besides, in the risk to redeem past neglect and to cash in on the increasing tourist trade, inappropriate and gimmicky solutions have often been applied with little impact.

With respect to Non Government Organisation's (NGO's), the activities of the Indian National Trust for Art and Cultural Heritage (INTACH), Greater Mumbai Chapter, as a catalyst between the various Government organizations and the islanders has been commendable. INTACH 's concern has been towards encouraging a heritage and environ friendly approach to development through community involvement. According to INTACH Convenor, 'We are just not concerned about the stone, the site and the museum. They will be there and INTACH wishes to emphasize that its whole approach is people oriented'. The varied facets being looked into by INTACH include the following: (a) site management, (b) visitor management, (c) infrastructure development, (d) environmental regeneration, (e) economic sustainability, (f) socio-cultural development, and, (g) comprehensive management plan. Their salient features may be briefly outlined briefly as follows:

(a) Site management

- March, 1997 – Two day international seminar on 'Elephanta Caves- Management of a World Heritage Site'.

- January, 1998 - TISS commissioned to prepare a comprehensive survey of the socio-economic condition of the Elephanta community as a background towards implementing planned strategies for promoting their overall development.

- November, 1998- A week long Site Management Workshop involving various Government organisations, citizen's groups and community residents engaged directly in tourism promotion, heritage conservation and site management activities for the development of Elephanta.

- Formulation of a multi-pronged Visitor Management Plan for Elephanta (at the behest of the long standing requirement of the UNESCO and financial support from them) for the upgradation of visitor amenities and generation of heritage awareness.

- April, 1999- Restoration of the dilapidated ASI custodian's cottage by resorting to the highest conservation standards as a Site Museum and Visitor Information Centre through UNESCO funding and ASI support. The museum dedicated to the history of Elephanta showcases exhibits pertaining to the rock-cut architecture of the Elephanta sculptures and other Buddhist monuments. Some details on the legacy of the cave architecture in Mumbai and Maharashtra and in the other World Heritage Sites in the country have also been presented.

- November, 1999- Organisation of a benefit program – *'Kalchakra – Time Past, Time Future'* (featuring classical music, dance performance and an auction of art works and sculptures by eminent classical and contemporary painters) towards resource generation for the ongoing restoration, community development and site management work in Elephanta.

(b) Visitor management

- Refurbishing the ticket booth and entrance leading to the site.

- Construction of a storage at the ticket booth for items (as picnic baskets, musical instruments, radios, etc.), which are to be discouraged into the caves.

- Creation of an alternative recreation space and its conversion into a small garden for picnickers.

- Redesigning and construction of temporary stalls using natural materials for a simple and attractive appeal.

- Design and display of appropriate and prominent signage for tourist information.

(c) Infrastructure development

- Collaboration with the MMRDA for attending to the water and electricity shortage.

- Repair of jetty and improvement of boat conditions in collaboration with the MTDC and Port Trust.

- Clearance of garbage by recommending to the Ministry of Environment and ASI for banning all plastic bottles and packets from the World Heritage Site.

(d) Environmental sustainability

- Mangrove rehabilitation with assistance from the BNHS and financial support from the Vasant J. Seth Memorial Foundation.

- Action against JNPT's toxic chemical storage terminal plant and the Government proposal of put one leg of the eight lane Sewri-Nhava Sheva link on Elephanta.

- Proposal for banning eatables within the cave premises for reducing the ubiquitous monkey population whose presence has posed a serious threat alike to tourists and residents.

(e) Economic sustainability

- Addressing livelihood issues through employment and income generation programs for the youth and women of the resident community in collaboration with Project Mainstream, an NGO.

(f) Socio-cultural development

- Plans in augmenting the rudimentary education and negligible health facilities existing on the island in collaboration with other relevant NGO's.

(g) Comprehensive management plan

- Preparation of a long term comprehensive management plan for monitoring overall development activities in Elephanta under the aegis of the MMRDA and comprising of eighteen members from varied fields. Findings of the same are to be presented to a High Powered Committee (formed by the Chief Minister with the MMRDA Commissioner as Chairman in January, 1999).

Public participation in community development programs

The tourist element in heritage has always spawned contradictions. The debate as to whether heritage should be protected *for* tourism or *from* tourism has thus far remained inconclusive. While tourism has been economically beneficial to the State and the community concerned, concerns over the environmental impacts of tourism and its effects on the sanctity of the heritage site can no longer be ignored.

One of the propositions in preserving Elephanta's heritage rests in making the place completely pilgrim oriented by shifting tourists to alternative sites. However, with limited internal economic support, the influence of tourism on the livelihood pattern of most islanders is likely to intensify in the future, even in the lack of basic facilities. The tourist element may further complicate the pilgrim element of heritage in the coming years. A viable alternative lies in empowering the local community towards heritage preservation and community development through programs as afforestation, garbage disposal, cultural activities, etc. However, its scope becomes limited if the basic necessities of the islanders remain unattended.

Although most islanders seemed aware of the heritage value associated with the caves and of the myriad problems affecting the island, a social and moral responsibility for redeeming them seemed largely absent. Besides, their perceptions were not based on a clear vision but viewed as a part of the general issues resulting from the absence of adequate tourist facilities.

The problems associated with garbage and littering were little appreciated by as many as 71 per cent of the respondents. Instead, most respondents suggested improvements in tourists facilities which included- reduction in ferry rates, cycle rickshaws on the jetty, electricity, water supply, toilet blocks, guest houses, attractive landscape and gardens, etc. Suggestion for the construction of a bridge between Mumbai and Elephanta by one respondent reflects the livelihood-tourism equation in the community's perception of the island's development (Sengupta, 1998).

More than 70 per cent of the respondents expressed their willingness towards participation as volunters in community development programs for the benefit of the island and themselves. For those who answered negatively, time factor was the major constraint. As many as 71 per cent of the respondents stated that they were willing to accept jobs as security guards and as local language guides (Hindi, Marathi, Gujarati, etc.), for directing the domestic tourists (Sengupta, 1998).

The specific issue of community participation, was also viewed by many as a two-way progress. Although many islanders agreed to the MTDC's annual Elephanta Dance and Music Festival as being a cosmetic facelift for the island with some temporary economic gains, many complained in failing to culturally internalise the joys associated with the festival. The alienation of the *gonwallas* (villagers) by the MTDC from participation as organizers of the festival is an evidence of the Government's bureaucratic hold over the island in culturally distancing the local community. However, INTACH's initiatives towards involving active participation from the local communities were appreciated by most islanders.

With this amount of investigation, one cannot say with certainty that there is a symbiotic relationship between heritage preservation and the interests of the local community, or, what factors are promoting or inhibiting this relationship, if at all it exists. Further research on Elephanta will seek to provide answers to many of these issues. However, in the absence of a sound social infrastructure the need for heritage preservation would be little appreciated by the islanders.

Policy prescriptions for development of Elephanta

In order to protect the Elephanta World Heritage Site and improve the living conditions of its residents, there is an urgent need for the formulation of an all comprehensive multi-pronged management plan, which could take into consideration, policies for community development, infrastructure, environment and heritage preservation by involving the various agencies and resident participation in development.

The preservation and conservation of the Elephanta caves being of prime consideration for the ASI, efforts should be made towards their conservation through the use of new composite materials, (apart from cement as in the past) which may be more appropriate given the environmental stress the caves are subject to. The barricade to the site's periphery and tourist benches need repairing and maintenance. Presently, only the central *Maheshmurti* sculpture in the caves has a railing. Mobile railings should be placed in front of the sculptures to prevent people from touching, clinging and even climbing on the sculptures. In order to prevent the visitors from moving around the caves in an adhoc manner and even in playing games and picnicking inside them, efforts should be adopted to control their movement by hiring the services of trained security guards vigilant in controlling visitor movement and conduct.

The tourist guides should follow a fixed plan of movement when taking visitors around the caves. In order to help the ASI staff in monitor visitor traffic, especially on crowded weekends, the old entrance to the main cave could be used as the entry and the new present entrance as the exit. For preventing garbage accumulation inside the caves, food, drinks and cigarettes should be prohibited and garbage receptacles should be provided at the entrance to the caves at reasonable distances. Regular monitoring of cracks in the monuments and controlling water seepage in the caves could save the monuments from further degradation. Excavation and restoration of other archeological sites on the island (as the Buddhist *stupa* and ancient submerged Portuguese lighthouse) should be endeavored by the ASI. Perhaps, a buffer zone could be maintained around the archeological sites.

As regards generating revenues for restoration and site management works, the ASI could charge a dollar entry fee for the foreign tourists visiting the caves (as is the norm in many other World Heritage Sites). For earning extra revenues, the ASI could sell separate tickets for the use of still and video cameras. The old ticket counter could be converted into a small ASI stall selling visitor amenities (as mineral water, cold drinks, camera films, etc.), in keeping with the architecture of the site museum and an alternative could be developed elsewhere. The ASI as an appropriate agency could also put together a comprehensive photo documentation of the site.

Given the alarming levels of pollution within and around Elephanta and the unprecedented pressures it is subject to, perhaps, a trapezoid could be created for the region around Elephanta (as the Taj Mahal, Agra) followed by its declaration as an environmentally sensitive zone. Currently, a 1 km. radius around Elephanta lies within the protected zone and this should be expanded further for checking unregulated industrial development. Preparation of a hazard management plan could help in an assessment and appropriate management of the environmental threat to the caves and the island. Measures should also be expedited to clean up and control oil spills from ships plying around the Elephanta region. For reviving mangroves in the island, inlets could be provided beneath the jetty to allow free passage of sea water. The Maharashtra Environment and Forest Department should enforce mangrove protection laws and launch plantation programs along the peripheral area involving corporate support. In face of the regions dwindling greenery, a special project could also be launched for greening the defunct old quarry as a nature park and the forty acres of barren tract around it for removing an aesthetic eyesore besides creating a healthy new habitat for Elephanta's flora and fauna. In addition, all latter day constructions in the island should use eco-friendly building materials (tiles, wood, corrugated iron, etc.), and colors for blending with the natural setting.

Alternative ways of employing the villagers engaged in petty trade should be thought of, especially during the monsoon months of the year when the economy is closed to tourist trade. Perhaps, local skills and training could be imparted to women in home based industries (as incense sticks, candles, soaps, etc), with support from the *Khadi* and Village Industries Commission (KVIC). Tree growing co-operatives could be developed as another viable alternative for engaging the islanders in an environmentally sustainable endeavour and benefiting them economically through the sale of forest produce. The MTDC could impart training to islanders as tourist guides. Organising a banking co-operative for the availability of micro-credit and soft loans for business development could also be thought of.

For improving the island's educational facilities, a teacher's training program could be started for the primary and secondary levels. Likewise, a nursing program could be started with Red Cross support for benefiting those interested in obtaining professional Immunization programs, spraying for tacking mosquitoes, conducting health camps, etc., could be some of efforts to start with. Likewise, expansion of local awareness about the site and its history through a workshop for the community and site managers could also be arranged.

For the publicity and promotion of the Elephanta islands among the up market foreign clientele, Elephanta should be featured better in the elaborate city guides produced by most luxury hotels in Mumbai city. Incidentally, Elephanta is mentioned mostly as a side attraction and neither does it feature prominently the itinerary of the local tour conductors.

For making the boat ride to Elephanta an enjoyable, comfortable and safe experience, the tourist boat need to follow better standards punctuality, security and maintenance. The boat owners could be better organized and perhaps provided with low interest loans for improving and repairing the boats. The MTDC could be instrumental in collaborating with the Government's financial agencies for securing such loans. The boats could also be provided with folding plans so that the passenger can board and descend from them at ease. For tourist information, a short film on Elephanta could be shown during the one hour journey on boat and ASI literature on the site could also be sold. The boat timings could also be altered so that they leave early from the Gateway and give the tourist greater chances of savoring the beauty of the island's environs at ease.

For avoiding picnicking in the vicinity of the caves, peripheral sites and alternate destinations should be explored. Besides diverting tourist pressures from the ancient monument it could also lessen disturbances to the serenity and sanctity associated with the site. Uran, Nhava Sheva, Alibagh, etc., with their natural and cultural attractions could be viable alternatives for casual picnickers visiting Elephanta. However, the endeavor may find little initial support from most islanders whose interests in protecting their livelihood rights from tourism related activities may dominate over the needs for heritage conservation.

For checking the proliferation of unauthorized stalls along the steps leading to the caves, strict legal action should be adopted by the ASI. Commercial activities along the jetty should also be prohibited. For the improvement of stall get-ups, the tattered awnings should be immediately repaired and their designing improved though the use of eco-friendly construction materials. Their sizes could also be fixed so that they do not encroach on the steps besides obstructing the line of vision. Product diversification could also be looked into.

In the absence of hygienic food facilities, a small restaurant selling authentic local cuisine could be started. This could benefit the tourists and islanders through employment and monetary gains. As for water facilities in the toilet, perhaps plastic pipes could be laid to carry untreated sea water inside.

In order to tackle monkey menace in the island, some of their lot could be relocated as in the other national parks of Maharashtra. If this proves cumbersome, another alternative could be in working out a method for their birth control in association with the BNHS and the zoo authorities.

The existing conditions of the Elephanta World Heritage Site leave much to be desired and achieved for their improvement and management. If treated with care and respect, Elephanta could prove to be an example to the world of a collective endeavour towards heritage preservation and sustainable tourism development.

References

Deshmukh, S. (1997), *'Eco-development of the Mumbai Coast: Community based conservation and regeneration of mangrove forests: A Case Study'*, The Regional Center, National Afforestation and Eco-development Board, Ministry of Environment and Forest, Government of India, New Delhi.

INTACH (1999), *'Green Signal',* Amanat, Vol. 1, No. 3, (Jan.), Indian National Trust for Art and Cultural Heritage, Greater Mumbai Chapter, Mumbai, pp. 4.

INTACH (1999), *'Kalchakra- Time Past, Time Future: A Benefit Event for the Elephanta Project',* Indian National Trust for Art and Cultural Heritage, Greater Mumbai Chapter, Mumbai.

INTACH (1999), *'Visitor Management Plan for the Elephanta Island',* Indian National Trust for Art and Cultural Heritage, Greater Mumbai Chapter, Mumbai.

INTACH (1999), *'Proposed Adaptive Reuse and Repairs of the Existing ASI Cottage to a Site and Museum at Elephanta Island,* Vikas Dilawari - Conservation Architect for the Archeological Survey of India (ASI), Indian National Trust for Art and Cultural Heritage, Greater Mumbai Chapter, Mumbai.

Jayakar, P. (1997), Inaugural Address, Seminar on Elephanta Caves- Management of a World Heritage Site, (1st Mar.), Mumbai.

Kail, O. (1984), Elephanta- The Island of Mystery, D.B. Taraporewala Sons and Co. Private Limited, Mumbai.

Khanna A. (1999), *'Elephanta Site Management: Down to brasstackst'*, Amanat, Vol. 1, No. 3., (Jan.), Indian National Trust for Art and Cultural Heritage, Greater Mumbai Chapter, Mumbai, pp.10-11.

Khanna, A. (1999), *'Elephanta Site Museum-Value the Past'*, Amanat, Vol. 1, No. 4., (Dec.), Indian National Trust for Art and Cultural Heritage, Greater Mumbai Chapter, Mumbai, pp.16.

Mehta, T. (1998), *'Elephanta: INTACH Initiatives towards Appropriate Management'*, Amanat, Vol. 1, No. 1, (Mar.), Indian National Trust for Art and Cultural Heritage, Greater Mumbai Chapter, Mumbai, pp. 1-3.

MTDC (1996), *'In Praise of Shiva- Elephanta'*, Maharashtra Tourism Development Corporation, Mumbai.

Sengupta, C. (1998), *Elephanta Island-Heritage and Livelihood*, Report prepared for the Indian National Trust for Art and Cultural Heritage (INTACH), Mumbai, Tata Institute of Social Sciences (TISS), August, Mumbai.

TOI News Service (1998), *'Rare mangrove species are vanishing from Elephanta'*, Gunvanthi Balaram, The Times of India, (18th Nov.), Mumbai.

TOI News Service (1998), *'Elephanta Park Plan Displays Heritage Lovers'*, Gunvanthi Balaram, The Times of India (19th Nov.), Mumbai.

TOI News Service (1998), *'Lack of Amenities and alienation upset Elephanta cave residents'*, Gunvanthi Balaram, The Times of India, (20th Nov.), Mumbai.

TOI News Service, (1998), *'UNESCO gives ASI $25,000 to upgrade facilities at Elephanta'*, Gunvanthi Balaram, The Times of India, (22nd Nov.), Mumbai.

Young, C. (1997), *'On the Experience of Managing a World Heritage Site'*, Paper presented in the Seminar on Elephanta Caves- Management of a World Heritage Site, (1st Mar.), Mumbai.

Tourism representations and non-representative geographies: Making relationships between tourism and heritage active

David Crouch

Derby and Karlstad Universities, UK

Abstract

In this paper I make a series of arguments concerning the relationship between tourism practices and practices of people living in areas that are the object of tourism interest. In particular my focus is the way in which both 'sides' encounter – and construct - both one another and the environment. I develop this argument through one example of constructing a representation of the local culture and environment in which it operates. The author was involved directly in creating this representation, and this involvement is considered problematically. Whilst no issues are resolved, as such, within this paper, I explore some additional ways in which the encounter between 'tourists' and hosts' may be understood, represented, and critically argue the possibility of making the encounters of more mutual value.

Introduction

It is of course the case that considerable efforts have been, and continue to be made, in animating tourism sites so that they become more interesting to the tourist. This has been especially the achievement of tourist sites as diverse as theme parks and museums. However, there may be considerable scope for developing this 'animation' in other spheres of tourism activity. The particular concern of this paper is the 'lived heritage' of places that are the livelihoods and residences of people today that have a character shaped today and by previous culture with which the people there today may or may not share inheritance.

The intention here is not to convert peoples lives and the places they create in their cultural activity into something else for the purpose of tourism 'success', as objects of display. Nor is it to pursue a familiar line of argument that considers, presents and develops cultures and places as 'products' in terms of tourism definitions. Instead, the intention here is to explore relations between tourists and 'hosts'. Ways in which tourism is involved in making representations become a crucial component in these relations. In developing a discussion around the representation of place and culture the role of the cultural mediator, perhaps one of the constructors of representations, is important. In this paper I consider tourism as a process rather than product, wherein that process the tourism professional is one component. I am concerned to provoke further reflection on the content and practice of tourism and the role of tourism mediators. Moreover, these are considered in relation to the inevitably changing content of the lives of people who may, for want of a better expression, find their environment and their cultures the object of tourism. 'Representations' of places and cultures in tourism are often understood to occlude rather than assist mutual understanding as those representations seek to maximise other objectives, such as visitor numbers, profit and so one (Selwyn 1996, Urry 1990).

It is frequently the case that tourist places ('destinations' suggests a specific site set apart from other activities) are already someone else's lives and livelihood and environment, setting of human relations, values, meanings. These features can be appropriated, in tourism language, as the object of tourism representations (Hughes 1992, 1998). However, it is insufficient to argue that the tourist merely 'reads' inscriptions of places and cultures delivered by tourism mediators, as Rojek and Urry have rightly problematised (1997). In this paper I argue further that tourism is something that people 'do'; in terms of an active practice of a number of things. These things include grasping the world around them, making sense of and refiguring their lives, meanings and relationships. Furthermore that 'making sense' includes grasping the way in which 'nature', other peoples and also environments both work and relate to their own lives, to what they feel and know. In view of this we tourism emerges as a much more inclusive activity. Perhaps ironically, I choose not to pursue already well-considered ground concerning the limits, and deformations, of representation in tourism (Selwyn 1996) Instead, I discuss representations in relation to 'practices'.

In recent years considerable advances have been made in terms of understanding tourism in terms of its human, cultural and social content and process Crang 1996, 1997, 1999, Urry 1900, Game 1990, Warren 1991, Rojek and Urry 1997, Cloke 1995, Lash and Urry 1994, Wearing and Wearing 1996, Crouch ed 1999. An increasingly important part of this has been the grasp of tourism as a process of reflexivity, of making sense of the word, the self, and human relations. Indeed Lash and Urry argue that tourism/leisure (note) is one of the more significant practices of contemporary culture through which people are reflexive, i.e. making sense of their lives, refiguring and re-thinking their identities (Lash and Urry 1994). This is not, however, a practice of resolution, but can unsettle, rework, provoke. As in other fields of popular culture, it is no longer adequate to consider leisure and tourism sites as essentially 'constructed' in representations by cultural mediators, but as spaces and sites constructed in their experience, using a kaleidoscope of influences in their shaping (Wall, 2000; Crouch 2000).

One aspect of the ways in which places and cultures are represented is the emphasis in making representations as promoting consumer products. This is obviously wholly legitimate in terms of sites solely developed for tourism, theme parks, heritage interpretation centres perhaps, hotels and marinas. However, this becomes more problematic if the 'site' being promoted, or indeed included in the promotion, is also someone else's livelihood (away from tourism), a place or culture valued in terms much more widely, or different altogether from, tourism. In that sense tourism becomes almost 'parasitic' of what is 'already there'. The alternative may be not to omit its content from the tourism promotion and representation of the place/culture but to re-think the ways in which that representation may be made.

Making different kinds of representation as implied in these comments may learn a great deal from also understanding more fully the complex ways in which tourism is practised. In short, tourism representation tends to have a limited language: sites that are the object of the gaze (someone else's culture, 'distinctive' landscapes) or for example of special pursuits (white water rafting). 'Alternative', complementary content and means of representation may require a different perspective from seeing tourism as concerned with the consumption, especially by the gaze, of particular objects (people's lives, cultures, environments).

There is, it is argued, potential ground for exploring the complex dimensions of tourism practice and considering in a complementary way the potential ground for relating representations and the content of those representations in terms of peoples lives and the environments they use, celebrate, endure. As an encounter, tourism occurs between several things. It occurs between people, between people and space, amongst people as socialised and embodied subjects, and in contexts with which tourism is available. The encounter is also between expectations, experience, desire and so on. Aspects of the encounter are, then, actively contextualised (in a social and cultural way Bourdieu 1984; Young 1990) *and* practised by active human subjects.

There is a tendency to investigate and interpret what people do in tourism in relation to their preferences for one site or the other, understanding them as consumers in a fairly narrow sense. More critical debate on 'consumers' in the wider sense (notably in terms of shopping practices) has provoked a more fundamental rethinking of practice (Jackson 1999). Practice emerges as something much more active, complex, and in ways of multiple encounters rather than object-reading relationships. Indeed, the word 'practice' *centres* this complexity of what is happening.

Of particular interest for enlarging the content and complementing consumer-interpretations of tourism promotion is the recent multi-disciplinary interesting what is called *embodiment*. In summary, facets of embodiment open up some of the more complex, nuanced but also probably prevailing ways in which tourists come to know places and cultures. This is to enlarge the interpretation of tourism from the gaze with its emphasis on the spectacle to acknowledge more features of bodily encounter. In a way these are already implicitly acknowledged in the appeal to the sensuous, indeed sensual, dimension of lying on a hot beach, or 'bracing' the elements in skiing, white water rafting or walking along Skegness beach (a very 'British', indeed 'English' reference) (Cloke 1998).

Summarily, facets of embodiment include the multi-sensual rather than essentially visual way in which we encounter space (culture, environment and other content). However, acknowledging embodiment is to do more than recognise 'more than seeing'. (Indeed vision is more complex than the prevailing idea of the gaze suggests (Urry 1995). Space is all around us, therefore the body is alert and grasping a sense of the world in its multi-dimensionality. *Embodying* space and objects and other people in that space also concerns being expressive, moving around or even lying down. Moreover the individual, in embodying the space and its content is significantly social, and relates to that space through the presence, or absence, of other human beings and their activities. A further fascinating element in the grasp of embodiment is that the individual imagines, plays with places, spaces and their content, subjectively, on her own terms, refiguring them. Of course none of these 'elements' of embodiment works in isolation, and crucially they work, or rather are worked, by the individual person in combination, chaotically, working some semblance of relationship rather than order into all these influences and ways of grasping the world. The world is indeed not 'grasped' as a unified existence but in a kaleidoscope. That kaleidoscope changes, and memory is drawn upon unsteadily as different events occur, or are sensed. (Crouch 1999, Crouch 2000a). This process happens in flows through which the tourist, individual *makes sense* of the world.

Moreover the tourist as 'making sense' of the world is different from the idea of how we sense the world around us, important though the sensuous dynamic of practice is. The complexity of embodiment provokes a 'feeling of doing' that contributes to a practical knowledge, a way of grasping the intimacies and complexities of the world.

Through this complexity of experience, or rather practice, our grasp of the world and our identities and relations with it, our everyday practical ontology is enriched. (Shotter 1993). Moreover, the lives, the cultures, the environments of people living in heritage locations, their lives and their products also the content of heritage tourism, are also uneven, practised, refigured, rather than fixed (Crouch and Matless 1996).

This 'embodying' of the world is related to the several cultural contexts of the tourist, as gendered and so on, and as influenced but not structured by the contexts, that include representations, through which she arrives at the site (for example, see Aitchison 1999). Indeed, these contexts *alone* may immediately set the tourist 'apart' from the 'toured'. However, a key point concerning embodiment is that it includes ways in which both the tourist and the toured grasp their world that at least unsettles, maybe even cuts through, the constraints of 'fundamental' cultural contexts and the values through which the individual reflects on life and values its different components. Indeed the values on which the tourist as crude 'consumer' values and relates to places may not be the same as the individual embodying the world and working a whole complexity of attitudes and values may do so. Tourist reflexivity becomes constituted of more than representation, detachment and memory. Reflexivity emerges not only as a mental but also embodied process. Crang has argued the much more complex bodily and value-related significance of photographs (1997, 1999). Similarly we may argue that the numerous facets of tourism spaces and ways in which they are practiced unsettle the content and relationships of the tourist 'consumer', unsettle the tourist as detached hedonist or seeker after the sacred (Tresidder 1999) (indeed sacred can mean as much self-discovery as a yearning to discover 'the other'). It may be that this more inclusive way of encountering the world provides more active relationships and practical knowledge between tourist and 'toured' places and cultures and people than is usually envisaged.

I return to consider a little more explicitly the theoretical context of embodiment through a discussion and interpretation of one project, subject of the next section of this paper. In summary, we identify people bringing a complexity of things to tourism practice; we grasp the active practice of living heritage is something that is cultural in the contemporary sense of being practised. In the next section I consider, though one example, possibilities for making representation of tourism heritage sites more a mutually communicative act. I explore ways in which these two dimensions, both of them active, may have a potential for making this activity more available to the tourist. It is argued that there are potential 'spin-offs' in terms of heritage 'interpretation' and sustainability. The project is an experimental UK-based exercise in constructing interpretation and representation of culture and space. This discussion is built around the experience of the author in a project called People of the Hills.

The experiment in People of the Hills

The project People of the Hills is a continuing project to re-interpret culture and place. The 'hills' and the 'people' are situated in north-east England. The north-east of England's official agencies romantically- and powerfully- promotes itself in the tourist literature as 'Land of the Prince Bishops' (Grassick and Crouch 1999). Whilst this satisfies on grounds of exotic reference and at least partly constructed history, it renders place and environment in a time-capsule. The centuries-gone landowners share the story with unusual and often colourful flowering plant species, always beautifully executed in photographs. Our reservations with this narrative touch two grounds. First, the presentation of a place, visited and toured in contemporary times, as a place whose history of human-land engagement ended centuries ago. Second, that making flora exotic turns them into spectacle and except for a few persistent visitors, an unrealised feature of the visit. Indeed, some 'ecological' people would welcome the difficulty of most people discovering them, although ironically their beauty is used to attract.

In 1994 with a professional photographer I set off on a journey to develop another narrative of this place using the confinement and limitations of words and pictures. We have not completely resolved the dilemmas of rendering content and character, but we offer aspects of a project as pointers towards making better *connections:* between what the place is and whose place it is; peoples lives and visitors' experience; the content of environments and the way people come to know them. How do tourists and those who live and work longer in a place relate in terms of their encounter with ecology; is it possible to make environments available to a wide audience and to include in that communication intimations of nuances and textures that are the content of places?

We attempted a creative encounter between us as 'writers' and people who provide, and indeed influence. A bank of words and pictures (from 5,000 in all) was developed erratically over four years, to give time to develop rapport with people and to develop our approach to the stories and places and how people 'know' them. These images form the main content of the project. Richard has experience in the documentary photography tradition and its creative interpretation of reality (maligned by some postmodernists for its reality claims, i.e. that 'no reality exists'). David researches the content and felt value of places in peoples lives through enquiry into what they do, feel, grasp, by making long, deep interviews in empathy with the subjects; he made a documentary and wrote an 'alternative heritage trail' - of allotment sites (Crouch 1992). Our 'subjects' are groups of people and the places they know and value: small-holders, factory workers, children changing school, people who regularly rent caravans in the Dale, other people working in cement mining. We talked with them, got to know them, talked over the content of what we collected with them. Richard photographed them. The first result is a text, of about eighty pages, over sixty photographs, in colour, and a brief text. We juxtapose things people say about their lives and the place with photographs of people doing things and moving around or contemplating the place.

The 'ownership' of the story or representation is of central importance in trying to communicate meaning and experience. The authors of any representation, and ours is no exception, hold tremendous power in conveying the content and value of heritage sites. In developing this story with close interaction with the people who are its subject we sought at least to disrupt the location of its 'ownership' (Crouch 2000b).

We seek to engage tourists in these stories. We leave the car behind and walk through the disused quarries that turned F- into the village it is today. We walk west, up and along the River Wear, out of the village on the old railway line, past or through a number of caravan sites that straddle the river's edge and provide a very popular means of getting to know the Dale. In the following, in addition to the italicisation of quotes collected in the fieldwork, passages from the text of people of the Hills are italicised, to incorporate them in the text but to retain them as part of the content being discussed.

People talk about taking a kettle to unfreeze frozen pipes, and about their uncertain relationship with the finances of tourism, converting barns with grants. In such apparently 'ordinary' means of grasping a feel for a place we can be surprised:

> *"Caravanning and cycling make me smile inside. Here in the morning you open the door and feel you're breathing air into your living. People come down to the stream and stand and watch life go by. It's amazing how you can have such pleasure from something like that."*

This is a long way from 'proper' knowledge about ecology, but we argue that this is closer to a feeling of human relationship, care and love for a slice of environment often overlooked in the familiar special species listing and cameo portraits of special places and awe-inspiring 'views' that tend to be used to present places, environments and their ecology.

We have tried to bring to life environments through human encounter, as tourist, as mineworker, as farmworker, as mother taking children to the leisure centre and school. Photographs include the upper valley Silver Band stepping on the stones across the river, a farmer repairing a stone wall with his son, a woman looking across a field, a girl running against the wind in an open landscape above the valley. These are not 'nature' captured in nostalgic portrayals or pretty, and some are awkward and gritty, reflecting the fuller experience of environment. It becomes possible for 'visitors' (sic) to share their grasp of the place with the characters in the stories, to encounter their lives and values. It was important in this project to strain to achieve an approach in making sense of the place that opens the visitors' feelings and attitudes to a care for the place and the environment, the culture and its nature, something sustainable.

What is interesting in this instance is not so much the precision of the route but the narratives that a journey such as this invokes. It is the narrative that emerges in the voices and images... partly to entertain, partly to assist a mutual identity for the whole that people are visiting, reinstating the environment in place that is a relationship between present and previous human activity, so that they may come back, curious to find out more. (all parentheses are quotes from Grassick and Crouch, People of the Hills) Of course content in tourism representations cannot be rendered as 'ordinary', because the knack is to make places interesting and people curious. We have tried to mix this with a sense of care and curiosity.

We make *encounters* with places rather than flat-views and 'landscapes' detached and disembodied of lives. This happens through multi-sensual, complexly sensual feelings, being surrounded or engulfed by space, not as a landscape-as-framed, perspective picture, but as a multiplicity of fractured planes both visual and received in touch, sound. *To be a visitor to the Dales can be a complex experience... Our aim is to produce a 'picture', rather a 'feel' of the area that incorporates traditionally recognised places of interest to the visitor with places that have major local significance, as well as elements of the life and place that have attracted us.* We try and encounter the ways people *feel* about this particular place by nudging more closely together the way that people living and working there- and the 'tourists'- do so, that we argue is closer in any case than is usually understood in 'expert' discourses and content. In their everyday lives people grasp value in 'natural' features (Crouch 1996). Indeed painters don't 'know' places necessarily as 'pictures'. 'I found an ease... I found that things were happening, that flowers looking at me were actually happening.... The road as I went back into town was hedged either side, but the sea was on one side, .. blowing up over their hedge and all the small grasses were moving, .. with a curious blowing, twisting action.' This is being surrounded by space, knowing environments with two feet (Crouch and Toogood 1999).

Enabling tourist practices and heritage to engage

Our concern is less with a 'sense' of environment and more with how we 'make sense' of environments and how this may be communicated, to engage the visitor in active bodily experience, or rather encounter, with this heritage. If the visitor in any case engages in this way, why should things like a guide book have a place? Whilst the guide book is always merely one resource to be used 'at will', it has the potential to influence, particularly if it working with the tourist's own experience.

By engaging with the experience, practices and concerns of 'the people of the hills we suggest that there can be opportunities for greater flow between the lives and knowledges of the tourist and those whose lives form the content of much tourist practice. Tourist practice, then, includes the experience, values, knowledge of places founded through the way we move about, know a place, as much with two feet as two eyes; through actions, running about, metaphorically and perhaps practically picking things up and throwing them. Of course, sensuousness is important, and so is human sensuality in the way we move through place, often together, and enjoy. It is likely to be only researchers who go alone. Environment is not only hugely produced in human relation but it is enjoyed, or endured, through it. And that encounter with 'environment' and its ecology is hugely expressive, as the pictures indicate, in letting ourselves go, in enjoying space itself. It is also poetic.

Thus places, environments become of value, as we become something more ourselves. We know a place/culture and come to know people in many different ways. Our grasp of environment and other people's lives is potentially practised at a human scale and in empathy and understanding that is frequently absent from the style and content of the brochure. Indeed he brochure is barely identifiable in the practice/knowledge of tourism. It provides merely one resource on which the tourist may draw. The brochure may help to prompt of to provoke, but is likely to be of little more influence, as they are drawn into a wider cultural practice (Game 1991). The brochure is there to be forgotten. Of course other dimensions of cultural context and content are important, but deserve to be understood in a more complex interplay of ontological knowledge, of practised, lay geography.

We may argue that much more interesting than the brochure – even the experimental one discussed in this paper – is what people do, as has been argued throughout this paper. It is argued, however, that the approach tried in the People of the Hills project provokes more directions of encounter than necessarily occurs in most forms of representation for tourists. More crucially, the knowledge that people make in doing tourism, we suggest, provides an enormously valuable resource for developing more positive meanings and values about places, environments, and other people. It is interesting that Myers and Macnaghten identify language as a major dilemma for policy makers (1998). In their terms the crucial issue is that people figure, in their case, environment in terms of everyday knowledge and encounters and feeling, rather than through the kind of language that 'experts' and other environmental and cultural mediators utilise, or rely upon. Policies seeking to shift tourism into something more sustainable need to develop a language that can be used in representations that can work from the everyday knowledge that people use and resonate with the processes through which they make that knowledge. The conceptual and marketing use of commodity, consumption and product (sic) mystify what tourism in contemporary society means. Working from lay practices and knowledge and familiar places, sustainability emerges as something more sustainable. In the case of communication over tourism – in representations, in brochures, in promotion, there is perhaps a parallel dilemma at work. In sketching out the process of tourism practices and the significance of embodied 'feeling' we have sought also to get more points of entry and of departure for the individual, refiguring the content of the brochure thru their own experience.

Much of this embodied encounter happens in ways that incorporate 'non-commodity values'. This is Gorz expression for the ways in which individuals relate to the world, to other people and to each other not as 'consumers' but as rounded people, exercising love and care, tenderness (1984). Of course things are more complicated than this, but they are also more complicated than the consumer-market relations in which tourism tends to be debated, and delivered.

Understanding 'heritage' in terms of these everyday lay geographies directs attention to the tourist representation and practice of everyday life and their inter-relation. This relation becomes less a debate about authenticity than about empowerment and identity; about the 'ownership' of representational/promotional content.

A rigorous approach to looking after environment requires a human grasp of what places mean and how we make sense of them. Unsurprisingly most environment-oriented efforts miss where people, or rather where 'we' come in, and yet ironically most knowledge about environment is as lay people, through lay, everyday practice (Crouch 1999). Particular species and wilderness become engaged in our own practice from and thru what we do. We 'know' a place through our bodily and poetic encounter with it (Crouch 1999a), as our own popular culture in what we do and value (Crouch 1992a). Practices and their knowledge offer rich resources for popular rather than elite or formal care for the environment, more chances for engagement between these different, if sometimes complementary concerns. In tourism and its representation and in extending grater care in tourism practices communicating understanding is important. We have argued that this can be re-thought through a closer relation of tourist knowledge and what goes into information for tourists.

Our small book and its trails, its words and pictures, are merely there as ephemeral notes, like any guide to be crumpled and torn as we each make our *own* sense of what places are about. The lessons of producing this book are greater than the value of its content. *Indeed, getting to know a place is getting a feel for a place, both a kaleidoscope and a patina, not a perspective or a picture. The place surrounds you, the senses are aware and alert, perhaps relaxed, perhaps sweating in effort, in a rush. You have completed a discovery of time and place, of many different lives and lifestyles, families and histories that make this place.. of the way this environment, like others, is made by people's lives, and continues to be so.* To be a tourist is, like being anyone, a chance to explore, to feel and to know, to touch and to smell, laugh, stumble and feel exhilarated. It is through these, as many more mundane and everyday experiences, that environment becomes meaning, and care.

Story

When we are doing tourism we find ourselves in a place. This place might be a beach, a historic site, a park, mountain range, the inside of a club, on a raft in a river valley, a pub. We may be aware of people around us. We feel the ground, recall the brochure, the advertisements, the reports of what people do in places like this. We talk over what happened the pervious day. We turn round, touch a friend, sit on the ground. There is an atmosphere in the place. There may be effort felt in what we are doing in the way we move our body, work out a friendly encounter. We pretend, imagine, discover a sensuality and a texture in ourselves we had forgotten or hoped for, or we may feel frustrated. We think over where we have come from and how far we have come and where else we desire to go. We negotiate an awkward slope. We make little judgements, reflexively we talk things over, mixing and re-mixing all of these impulses and desires. There are particular things in this place, another encounter, recent memories of similar places and what we did there. We bend to adjust our clothing and notice that the view has changed, the cliff, the water surface, the group standing nearby, the edges of the caravan site have changed.

This brief story includes a number of components of embodiment. In this story there are at least two spaces. We may call these spaces of practice. Close-up there is a surrounding space that we touch, perhaps with both feet, smell, in which we meet people. Far off there may be a distant view. Nearby there may be a foreshortened space in terms of a spectacle. However there is always, almost always, the 'close up' space where we sit, shuffle to view an event, mingle amongst people, share a story, move through. In the 'far off' there may be a view through a window. Spaces reached only in vision.

Of course the space grasped immediately around the body and the one reached only in vision are not separate. They interact, we interact them in the sense that we acknowledge them together and in relation. The individual in body and thought turns, momentarily makes another grasp of what is around and moves on. Through this process we construct a kaleidoscope of events and artefacts in a subjective way, through points of reference and desire that collide reference and desire conveyed and made meaningful by a feeling and an imagination. Materiality and metaphor collide, as Radley puts it:

> '...these memories are part of culture and depend, in various ways, upon the physical setting for how people remember the course of events leading up to the present. It is not just that individuals remember specific things, or are reminded of the past by particular objects figured against a background of a shared discussion of the past. Artefacts and the fabricated environment are also there as a tangible expression of the basis from which one remembers, the material aspect of the setting which justifies the memories so constructed.' (1990).

Memory and meaning merge. Practice informs the way we negotiate meaning (Crouch 1997; 1998).

Conclusions

This chapter does not claim to resolve the programme it considers. Instead it problematises both the production of representations and the ways in which tourism is practised, and therefore problematises the position of 'heritage' in relation to both.

As evidently discussed throughout this chapter Reps cant simply make more active but can open possibilities for the tourist, who may also identify and grasp more readily the possibilities.

It is increasingly familiar, for example, that in policies on environment sustainability the language through which policy is conveyed, or attempted to convey, is widely different from that grasped in their everyday world by people 'at large' (Myers and Macnaghten 1998). In what we have attempted to do we claim to suggest alternative language, in terms of both visual and written content. In that sense there is perhaps a little insight here into the potential for using representations to open up reflection and understanding rather than simply offer 'set piece' of 'heritage'. What is heritage is a little unsettled by this approach. Moreover, the debate concerning the potential for appropriating heritage through tourism representations, promotions and uses becomes something different. The issue of 'heritage' in examples such as that chosen for the People of the Hills shifts focus from authenticity to ownership and empowerment. The content, and ideally the form of representation can be worked through the ownership of those (whose environment and culture is) portrayed. It may, we argue, be possible to use heritage representations to empower, partly by creating debate. Bringing together the, or perhaps one, reality of tourism and everyday life both as process, and heritage as process, makes it slightly more possible to achieve an active engagement between these two aspects of contemporary heritage in process.

References

Aitchison, C. (1999), Heritage and nationalism gender and the performance of power in Crouch D ed. *Leisure/tourism geographies*. Routledge London :59-73.

Bourdieu, P. (1984) *Distinction: a social critique of the judgement of taste* Routledge London.

Cloke, P. Perkins, H. (1998), Cracking the Canyon with the awesome foursome representations and adventure tourism in New Zealand. *Environment and Planning D: society and Space* 16:185-218.

Crang, M. (1999), Knowing, tourism and the practice of vision, in Crouch D. ed. op cit.: 238-256.

Crouch, D. (2000), Introduction, Popular culture and cultural texts, in Cook I et al. Eds. *Cultural Turns, Geographical Turns*. Longman London: 69-74.

Crouch, D. (2000a), *Leisure Studies*.

Crouch, D. (2000b), Focus of the people, *Tourism Concern* 34. Pp12-13.

Crouch, D. ed (1999), *Leisure/Tourism Geographies*, Routledge. London.

Crouch, D. (1999a), The Intimacy and Expansion of Space, in Crouch D. ed.: 257-276.

Crouch, D. and Toogood, M. (1999), Everyday Abstraction; geographical knowledge in the art of Peter Lanyon, *Ecumene*. 6.1:72-89.

Crouch, D. (1998), The Street in the making of popular geographical knowledge. In Fyfe N. *Images of the Street*. Routledge London.

Crouch, (D) (1997), Leisure practices and geographical knowledge, in Milbourne P (ed) *Revealing rural others*. Cassell. London.

Crouch, D. and Matless, D. (1996), Refiguring Geography: the Parish Maps of Common Ground, *Transactions of the Institute of British Geographers*.

Crouch, D. (1992a), *The Allotment; a viewers' guide*. Channel Four Books. London.

Game, A. (1990), Undoing Sociology Open University Press Buckingham.

Gorz, A. (1984), Paths to Paradise Pluto London.

Grassick, R. and Crouch, D. (1999), People of the Hills published courtesy Amber Films Newcastle *Sections in italics are taken from the work People of the Hills.*

Hughes, G. (1992), *Leisure Studies*.

Hughes, G. (1998), in Ringer G. *Destinations,* Routledge, London.

Lash, S. and Urry, J. (1994), Economies of signs and space, Sage, London.

Myers, G. and Macnaghten, P. (1998), Rhetoric of Environmental Sustainability *Environment and Planning D: Society and Space.*

Radley, A. (1990), Artefacts, memory and a sense of the past, in D. Middleton and D. Edwards *Collective Remembering,* Sage London.

Rojek, C. and Urry, J. (1997), *Touring Cultures* Routledge. London.

Selwyn, T. (1996), *Tourist Myths.* Wiley, London.

Shotter, J. (1993), *The Cultural politics of Everyday Life* Open University Press.

Tresidder, R. (1999), Tourism and sacred landscapes, in Crouch D. op cit.

Urry, J. (1990), *The Tourist Gaze,* Sage, London.

Urry, J. (1995), *Consuming Places*, Routledge, London.

Wall, M. (2000), in Cook I et al eds. op cit. *The popular and geography: music and racialised identities in Aotearoa/New Zealand*, in Cook I et al eds. op cit.

Warren, S. 'This heaven gives me migraine': the problems and possibilities of landscapes of leisure, in Duncan J et al eds. (1993), *place/culture/representation,* Routledge, London.

Wearing, B. and Wearing, S. (1996), Refocusing the tourist experience: the flaneur and the choraster *Leisure Studies*15:229-243.

Young, I. M. (1990), *Throwing like a girl,* Indiana University Press, Indiana.

**Rich Grassick, professional photographer and film-maker, Amber Films, Newcastle.

Dismantling a community's heritage "heritage tourism: Conflict, inequality, and a search for social justice in the age of globalisation"

Rami Farouk Daher

Jordan University of Science and Technology, Jordan

Introduction: The nature of conflict in the heritage tourism industry "stakeholders' zones of conflict"

The definition of the cultural heritage is a continuous process during which new meaning and values are always being discovered. Consequently different types of cultural resources are therefore incorporated into the realm of cultural heritage. This dynamic concept of heritage significance dictates a continuous re-evaluation of cultural sites management approaches and strategies within heritage conservation/tourism endeavours. The International Cultural Tourism Charter (ICOMOS, 1998), which focuses on managing tourism at places of heritage significance, considers heritage to be a broad concept including the natural as well as the cultural environment. "It encompasses landscapes, historic places, sites and built environments, as well as bio-diversity, collections, past and continuing cultural experience."

Tourism is becoming an increasingly global and complex phenomenon, with political, economic, social, cultural, environmental, and educational dimensions. Robinson (1998, 31) considers tourism to be the "largest of multi-national activities." Borley (1994, 4) defines cultural tourism as that "activity which enables people to explore or experience the different way of life of other people, reflecting social customs, religious traditions, natural and built heritage, and the ideas of a wide cultural heritage which may be unfamiliar" to the tourist promoting cultural understanding and literacy. Jamieson (1998, *65)* defines heritage tourism as "travel concerned with experiencing the visual and performing arts, heritage buildings, areas, landscapes, and special lifestyles, values, traditions, and events."

This paper is concerned with conflicts inherent within heritage tourism processes and mechanisms in this age of globalisation. The paper critically analyses the dynamics and be distribution of benefits among the different stakeholders (e.g., the host community, he industry, the state, foreign aid, heritage itself, scholars, and the community at large) involved in the heritage tourism industry. The paper will concentrate, specifically, on the conflict between the host community and the heritage tourism industry itself within the context of a third world country *(Jordan)*. It aims to present a theoretical framework through which the significant issues (e.g., community development throughout heritage tourism projects, commodification of historic environments, foreign aid-led projects, exploitation of heritage, levels of host community participation) are analysed and discussed. Each of the consequential and critical issues raised could form an engaging argument for future exploration.[1]

Even through heritage tourism has various cultural and economic benefits, especially for a struggling economy such as in Jordan, it still induces remarkable adverse impacts on the historic environments and the lives of people associated with them dismantling vital and significant links between the cultural heritage and its respective host-communities. It is true that tourism can create employment opportunities, generate foreign exchange revenues, and spread peace and cultural understanding; but still, "the processes by which tourists experience culture, and the way culture is utilised by the tourism industry and host communities, are increasingly characterised by conflict" (Robinson, 1999a, 1-2). In several parts of the world, primarily in third world countries; tourism is known to have caused gentrification, breaking down of social and economic structures, social disintegration of family values, varying degrees of environmental degradation, and deterioration of historic and cultural settings due exploitation practices and commodification of historic environments. The myth of tourism having the ability to generate conflict-free cultural harmony and understanding is largely "a residual attitude derived from the romantic (and elitist) traditions of travel in the 18th and 19th centuries" which were dominated by an Euro-centric moralistic tradition and ideology (Robinson, 1999a, 2-3).

Metalka (1986) defines demonstration effect as the tendency for a more economically primitive culture to imitate the behaviour patterns of a more complex nature and to incorporate the learnt behaviour into one's own lifestyle. When applied to tourism, the demonstration effect can bring about changes in attitude, values, and behaviour. This was the case in many countries in South West Asia (Smith 1989), especially in Thailand, where tourism lead to the break down of religious, cultural, and social values (e.g., women and children engaging in prostitution). One of the world's most disturbing global phenomena is what architectural critic Ada Louise Huxable has dubbed "commodification." As defined by Huxtable, this increasingly common phenomenon (Brink, 1998,61) turns authentic cultural expressions, of which the cultural heritage is but one, into commodities for commercial consumption and excessive capital accumulation. In this age of globalisation culture is becoming this increasingly paradoxical commodity it is sheep, yet important and subject to exploitation and a victim of consumerism. Robinson (1998, 31) illustrates how conflict is not solely attributed to cultural differences between tourists and host communities, but might arise also from the different "legitimated" processes of manufacturing heritage and tradition and consuming or commodifying culture.

> *It is not that conflict situations arise solely from inherent cultural differences;*
> *they also derive from the processes involved in the construction, accentuation,*
> *and promotion of cultural identities. The logic of consumptive behaviour drives*
> *these processes and creates "otherness" as a necessary precondition for tourist*
> *encounters. The tourism industry legitimates the manufacture of heritage and*

tradition, and is at the same time, legitimised by our attempts to manage and maintain difference. (Robinson, 1998,31)

Patin (1999, 35) states that one of the major serious adverse impacts of heritage tourism is the excessive exploitation of sites by the tourism industry disturbing host communities life-styles and socio-cultural modes and destroying the authenticity and significance of their heritage. In fact, tourism is a global phenomenon with a "globalising influence which can initiate dramatic and irreversible changes within the cultures of host communities." (Robinson, 1999b, 22). Conflicts within the tourism industry might arise from how certain empowered stakeholder, and through processes of late capitalism (e.g., investor, hotel developer, big money, the State as promoters and regulators, foreign aid agencies) exploits a certain locale or even the marginalised stakeholders (e.g., living cultures and communities). Such marginalised stakeholders are not equipped with the proper tools for resisting exploitation; they also do not receive a fair share of revenues from heritage tourism projects (Figure 1).

Figure 1   Stakeholders' Zones of Conflict in Heritage Tourism Endeavours

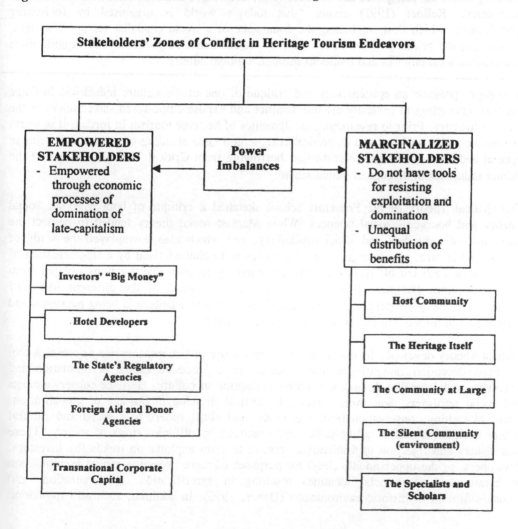

On the other hand, the world is also witnessing an increasing number of heritage or cultural tourists in this age of globalisation as oppose to the banal tourist seeking sunny beaches of the 1970s. This reflects a popularity of new modes of post-modern consumerism and consumption of which "culture" ranks first (Robinson, 1999a, 4 and Keller, 1996, 15). But unfortunately, a high proportion of the income generated by tourism in the developing world (like Jordan) does not remain in those countries but returns to the big tourism corporations and large financial institutions of the more developed world.

A critical theory of culture industries in the age of globalisation

It is a well-known fact that globalisation is plaguing local cultures and identities. Industrial capitalism has been replaced with financial capitalism; abolishing time and space and emphasising excessive capital accumulation at the expense of social justice and genuine cultural continuity. Such alarming political and socio-economic changes triggered critical thinking within all disciplines and sciences (e.g., sociology, anthropology, architecture, and economics). Kellner (1997) argues "that today's world is organised by increasing globalisation, which is strengthening the dominance of a world capitalist economic system, supplanting the primacy of the nation state by transnational corporations and organisations and eroding local cultures and traditions through a global culture."

This paper presents an epistemology and critique of one of the culture industries: heritage tourism, attempting to critically disclose conflict and expose empowered stakeholders in the tourism industry. Prior to researching the dynamics of heritage tourism in Jordan, it is worth presenting a philosophical and theoretical critique and understanding of culture industries in general and heritage tourism in particular, borrowing from Critical Theory's critique of the culture industries in this age of globalisation[2]

The Critical Theory of the Frankfurt School sketched a critique of both Marxian Social Theory and bourgeois social sciences. While Marxist social theory tended to neglect the dimension of individual and social psychology, and which also downplayed the study of culture and leisure; also bourgeois social sciences were characterised by a fragmentation of the sciences, each cut off from the other and pursuing its own investigations isolated from other disciplines (Kellner, 1996). Critical Theory is critical of the different forms of consumption that were generated within late capitalism where culture is being packaged and consumed and forced into cycles of capital accumulation.[3]

Critical Theory developed its own critique of the culture industries, they were seen as a tool for mass deception camouflaging objectives of mere excessive capital accumulation and obscuring social conflict through the commercialisation of culture. Heritage conservationists and social reformers, who were affected by critical thinking in the age of globalisation, aimed at shifting conservation from a technical and elitist sphere to a social and cultural sphere institutionalised in public policy and practiced by different strata of society. There was dismay and rejection *of fashionable* heritage tourism exploitation trends (by investors, developers, or the upper middle class) for purposes of mere excessive capital accumulation or creation of new social identities resulting in gentrification, musuemization, and commodification of historic environments (Daher, 1999). In addition, such an exploitation stirs up and provokes feelings of alienation and disassociation between the cultural heritage and local communities. According to Horkheimer and Adorno (1972), such fashionable cultural industries tend to be means for mass deception, which influenced and manipulated the public into accepting the current) organisations of society. Such cultural and heritage industries used the past and the heritage coupled with entertainment to "sugarcoat oppression while eroding cultural standards" and local identities.

In its critique of the commercialisation of culture, Critical Theory indicated that the culture industries are increasingly lacking substance where dominance of image and effects prevails. "The development of the culture industry has led to the predominance of he effect, the obvious touch, and the technical detail over the work itself, which once expressed an idea, but was liquidated together with the idea." In addition, Critical Theory critiques this association between culture and entertainment for purposes of capital accumulation not only because it leads to a depravation of culture, but inevitably to an intellectualisation of amusement." (Horkheimer and Adorno, 1972) The previous discussion and critique of the culture industries can be applied, to a certain extend, to the popular consumption of heritage and the unequal distribution of profits evident in the heritage tourism industry in Jordan orchestrated today by investors who adhere to cycles if late capitalism and consumerism.

Heritage tourism in Jordan: The myth of "equitable sustainable development

The cultural heritage in Jordan plays a significant role in the development of the tourism sector. "In 1996, the tourism sector provided more than JD 770 million or a little more than 11% of the GDP of Jordan. The tourism sector has been defined in 1995 as Jordan's number one foreign exchange earner" (JICA, 1994). Due to its rich ancient, classical, and modern history, the majority of tourists coming to Jordan (about 93%) seek distinguished cultural experience where Jordan has been chosen as their destination for its history and social make-up of the Jordanian society. Yet tourist products and services in Jordan (e.g., museums, visitor centres, and sue management and interpretation) were given a "poor" or "fair" rating by about 40% of tourist. One reason is that tourist products in Jordan suffer from over emphasis on antiquities and a below standard level f service and facility provision (Daher, 1999). Another reason could be attributed to the unplanned and over exaggerated development in hotel construction ignoring other types of tourism services such as good cultural site management. It has been estimated that only 0.3% of the income generated by the sites finds its way back to the sites and is spent n conservation, community development, and site presentation and interpretation (IICA, 1994). In many economically struggling countries of the world, the revenue from heritage tourism sites seldom returns to the site itself. Worse, such revenues are usually spent on " the building of tourist facilities, especially hotels, whose poor location and mediocre design seriously harm the quality and authenticity of cultural landscapes" (Patin, 1999, 36).

In addition, the modem culturally-life heritage of Jordan, dating to the last 200 years of Jordan's history, is marginalised in favour of major ancient or classical popular attractions such as Petra and Jerash. Whenever this heritage becomes the subject of development, investors induce a heritage tourism paradigm regardless of its suitability in all the diverse sites and contexts of Jordan; and with no proper consideration to issues of community development, conservation, and cultural site projection and presentation.

Dismantling heritage, commodifying historic environments

In Jordan, one can easily sense, based on an inquisitive and explorative research targeting several heritage tourism endeavours, an alarming trend prevailing in the heritage tourism industry. Tourism is being considered as the only development mode associated with such heritage conservation projects, in many cases this compelled and induced link between tourism and heritage conservation is working against a particular site or its respective community. Such projects follow an approach "in which heritage is viewed as a means for capital accumulation, and according to which each heritage site is treated as a commodity. This trend is being encouraged by wealthy investors who have tried to gain legitimacy through association with architects, archaeologists, and conservationists" (Daher, 1999, 34). This commodification of the recent past at the expense of the local community dismantles vital and basic relationships that exists between the heritage and its associated community leading to gentrification, disassociation, alienation, and despair. The following are brief narratives of several projects that are connected with heritage conservation/tourism. Such narratives will shed light on issues of conflict, social injustice, dependency on deterministic modes of development, and inappropriate funding mechanisms. These issues prevail, in varying degrees, in most of the selected projects:

- *Kan Zaman:* Originally the historic estate of the *Abu Jaber* family dating to the 19th century, located in *Al Yadoudah,* outside of Amman. The complex consists of several structures and outdoor spaces that occupy an approximate area of 10 donoms. The site has been adapted into a traditional coffee shop/restaurant with provisions for craft shops. The project constitutes one of the first projects to adopt such approaches in Jordan The design did not follow any guidelines for adaptive reuse or rehabilitation resulting in the commodification of the historic environment. But being a private property, the project did not exert an adverse effect on the local community.

- The *Bani Hamida* Project: located in southern Madaba, the project was intended to help the local women of *Bani Hamida* improve living conditions through production of crafts (mainly traditional carpets) for tourists. The project was geared into an elitist activity were most of the benefits find their way back into the organising body or investors rather than the community itself A traditional house in Amman from the early 1920s was adapted into the marketing centre catering for tourists and the rich and affluent society of Amman. The traditional crafts, a deterministic mode of development, becomes an end for itself; rather than a starting point for other modes of community development (e.g., agriculture, light industries). The Municipality of *Bani Hamida* is currently in dept and is asking the government for rescheduling of the dept and for land reformation in a last attempt to prevent immigration from the village to nearby urban centres. The project is completely owned by the investor where the local women are only engaged as workers for minimum wages.

- *Books @ Café:* In other projects related to tourism in Jordan (Daher, 1999), the architectural heritage has become a means for social differentiation and the production of a new social identity for the upper-middle class. The geographic constitution of such gentrified or conserved areas, such as *Books @ Café:* an internet coffee shop located in an adapted early 1930s house, is crucial to the production of such new identities, which usually centre around urban-living and the consumption of high-class cultural products (e.g., alternative music, arts and crafts). Despite its high-minded intentions, the *Books @ Café* constitutes an intrusion into this traditional calm residential neighbourhood of Amman, producing alienation and discomfort among the local community and creating a "schizophrenic difference" between the environments inside and outside the cafe, intensifying the separation between the neighbourhood and its architectural heritage.

- *Darat al Funun* (House for the Arts): One of very few examples where such projects exert a successful relationship between the different stakeholders (the State, project funding agency, scholars, and the local community). The project represents an adaptive reuse of a complex containing early 20th century houses of Amman into an art and cultural centre by the *Shuman Foundation* in 1993. The Project allowed a panoply of cultural events and historical layers (ancient, Roman, Byzantine, and early 20th Century) to coexist. The Project has attempted to "connect with the community both physically, through its architecture and overall layout within the neighbourhood, and spiritually, through its transparency and accessibility" (Daher, 1999, 35-36). It also rejected the current trend towards museumization of the cultural heritage, aspiring instead to allow cultural heritage the opportunity to evolve and regenerate.

- *Taybet Zaman* Tourist Village: Originally a rural village in the southern parts of Jordan (near Petra) became a gentrified environment that has been rented from its inhabitants by *Jordan Tourism Investments* on the basis of a long-term contract (about 30 years). "The village was then transformed into a luxurious tourist attraction, and many of the former villagers where offered low income jobs in the new development as cleaning and custodial work"(Daher 1999, 35). The village is being packaged and sold to the tourists in a fashion where the tourist deals with the values and imagery of the distant past rather than the dynamics and realities of the present.[4]

- *Iraq al Amir:* A rural development project in the area of *Wadi Assir,* organised by *Noor al Hussein foundation (NHF)* and based on the adaptation of small historic rural villages for tourism and community development. Originally the project aimed at comprehensive development (e.g., environment and health awareness, agriculture), but gradually, the project concentrated on tourism development only especially after the romantic adaptation of rural houses into shops for traditional crafts for tourists. Again, the local women are engaged as workers for minimum wages in a business run by NHF. Now, the local community is demanding the provision of other facilities in the village such as hairdresser, nursery, butcher, and also the consideration of other development options besides tourism since tourism revenues are seasonal and minimal (most of the revenues are kept within organising bodies and investors).

- *Umm Qais* Tourist Village: *Umm Qais,* is an Ottoman village from the last century in northern Jordan which was built on the ruins of ancient Gadara (Roman City). The Village underwent a series of battles and conflicts over the rights of its development. In the late 1970s and through the late 1980s the local community was evacuated and was put in standardised housing units unfit for village *life* and an agricultural community in order to conduct archeaological excavations of ancient Gadara leaving the village heritage to fall into neglect and despair. The evacuation dismantled this vital relationship between the village and its local community. Even though some of the courtyard houses in the village were conserved and adapted, by a wealthy investor, into tourist facilities (e.g., archaeological museum, rest-house and Italian restaurant), the local community was marginalised and never was engaged in the tourism development. The government is planning to sell the whole village for the same investor to turn it into a 5-star hotel for tourists. What is interesting today, is the collaboration between previous enemies (the local community, archaeologists), against the wealthy investors and processes of capital accumulation.

- *Dana* Nature Reserve: The historic village of Dana and surrounding nature areas were designated as a Nature Reserve by the Royal Society for the Conservation of Nature (RSCN). The RSCN started by regulating grazing lands and restoring the historic village, engaging the local community in the production of traditional and agricultural crafts. Recently, the *Dana* Nature Reserve is turning into a profitable business for the organisers of the project where local involvement is superficial and is limited only to cheap labour and few managerial positions. Complaints from the local community stated that the "investors" reduced grazing land, and kept the revenues of tourism (promises of giving back 50% of revenues to the local community were not met). Only parts of the houses were restored, the fruit-drying factory buys fruits for minimal prices from the locals and the same applies to the oregano harvest which is sold in Amman for tourists at expensive rates. The RSCN is enjoying a free access to the water supply and is buying large areas of land around the Reserve as a mean for more control. The non-governmental organisation (RSCN) is being viewed by many as a greedy investor whose main objective is capital accumulation, where nature projection, community development, and heritage conservation become a by product, a second priority, when affordable.

- Jordan Sustainable Tourism Development Project: This project, which began in 1995, has been funded by USAID, where a lengthy process led to the selection and design of tourist site management plans for 6 locations in Jordan (e.g., Amman Citadel, Umm Qais, Madaba, Petra). The institutional contractor was *Chemonics* International Inc. of Washington D. C. (a consulting firm from the donor country) together with local contractors. Most of the foreign aid was wasted on holding meetings and design reviews and on unnecessary funding dynamics and mechanisms. Eventually, the project was aborted at the end of the design stage, Jordan benefited nothing with the exception of increasing foreign dept and a blind dependency on foreign aid projects.

- *Qastal* Development and Conservation Project: Qastal, an archaeological and heritage site within a thriving modern community is located 25km south of Amman. The site contains not only an Ummayyad Palace, Mosque; *and* necropolis; but also an abandoned water infrastructure of cisterns and canals, which could be of valuable source for the community. The cultural heritage in the site also includes buildings from Ottoman and even more recent periods of history some in ruin, and some has been abandoned by the community. The project aimed not only at site protection, conservation and presentation; but also at community development and environmental protection through water harvesting and landscaping. Fund raising, from the start, was community based trying to engage the local community not only as cheap labour but also as partners in the project, taking a risk since the beginning as owners and operators of new flourishing businesses are supposed to be run by local investments from *Qastal*.

The listed projects represent a representative sample of the overall projects within the realm of heritage tourism. The following observations regarding the nature and processes of heritage tourism projects in Jordan are based on realities of the listed projects:

- Most heritage tourism and conservation projects claim community development as one of their objectives; in reality they result in *dormant* and *drugged* local communities who become addicted to deterministic modes of development (e.g., the banal overemphasis on traditional crafts as if they were the only mean for development). Wealthy investors who prioritise profit and capital accumulation usually operate such developments. Thus, local communities substitute long term with short-term economic stability.

- The cultural' heritage is being exploited by greedy investors and is valued only for its opportunistic developmental value, many projects end up commodifying and museumizing the heritage at the expense of vital relationships between the cultural heritage and its associated host community. Revenues from such development projects never find their way back to the site or to the community; instead, they pour into the pockets of wealthy investors or organising bodies.

- There is a blind dependency on foreign aid funded projects, very few projects are initiated out of governmental concern or with local fluiding mechanisms and efforts. Still many projects are never executed, they remain reports on the shelves of governmental agencies and institutions while foreign dept increases.

- Most heritage tourism projects tend to dwell in the past by freezing people's lives and promoting a reconstructed image of the lives of the host community that is appealing to tourists. Very few projects attempt to sustain a living environment, most projects end up musuemizing and commodifying historic environments, and denying the host communities and sites the rights to evolve and maintain a modern life.

- Very few projects (e.g., Qastal and Darat al Funun) exemplify success partnerships between the different stakeholders within the tourism industry.

Daher (1999,34) argues that the current approach to heritage tourism in Jordan continues to empower certain interests, and privilege certain pasts, above others. In particular, the local community has been marginalised and dis-empowered. Most investors or NGO development groups claim their projects will aid the community at large through heritage or eco-tourism developments by providing job opportunities for local residents. But such claims must be seen as a camouflage for their primary goal, flexible capital accumulation and monopoly control over the heritage resource. By hiring the local community at sweatshop" rates, tourist investment companies are further able to eliminate all potential competition from small businesses or local projects. In seeking such monopoly control, tourist investment companies "act as feudal landlords in heritage-conservationl/tourism and community development clothing."

Foreign aid: The legitimating ideology of domination

In Jordan, it is true that foreign aid had assisted and played a major and important role in financing the tourism development sector; yet, this does not automatically mean that foreign aid is a power-free enterprise. It is true that foreign aid supports Jordan's attempts for development, like many other countries in the region as well, but there is a price that Jordan and Jordanians have to pay in return. Foreign aid has to be re-evaluated and assessed not by using traditional and conventional project-evaluation methodologies but by "linking macro level international interests (aid agendas, geo-strategic objectives) with micro-level grass root variables" (Zetter and Hams, 1998, 185).

Funding conditions together with World Trade Organisation (WTO) restrictions open the markets of a certain country to the world restraint or limitation. They encourage privatisation, opening the financial markets or stock exchange to the world, and impose Western late-capitalist ideologies while diminishing the authority of the state, which becomes another institution among many. In many of the 3rd world countries, aid is conditioned with the adoption of Western late-capitalist mechanisms and ideologies[5] (e.g., secularism, accepting democracy at face value, family planning, privatisation of vital sectors, pluralism, supporting fragmentation policies of the State and of society, women rights). Many fear and view this politicised and conditioned funding as a mean for cultural, economic, and political domination or a camouflage for dilution of values and national/regional sovereignty. The recent failure of the WTO summit at Seattle, Washington and the popular rejection of globalisation by trade and labour unions from both First World and Third World countries is a clear indication that such fears and views have high credibility (Hornblower, 1999, and Gupte, 1999).

Kellner (1997) states that globalisation "could serve as a cover to neutralise the horrors of colonialism and could be part of a discourse of neo-imperialism that serves to obscure the continuing exploitation of much of the world by a few superpowers and giant transnational corporations, thus cloaking some of the more barbaric and destructive aspects of contemporary development." Contemporary theoreticians view foreign aid, structured within the forces of late capitalism and formal economies, as a mean for economic and social domination replacing the traditional 19th century modes of domination (colonisation and imperialism). Critical Theory can be adopted to critique and deconstruct foreign aid in this age of globalisation because it provides a platform for socio-historical inquiry and investigation or its origins, transformation, rhetoric, and processes going beyond traditional philosophical analysis (McCarthy, 1994).

The rhetoric of foreign aid uses the dogma of banal liberalism (e.g., community development, helping communities help themselves, equal opportunity, secularism and democracy, women's rights, public participation) to sugarcoat and disguise forces of global and economic domination, encouraging a gradual blind dependency on donor agencies and slaying local initiatives. This critique of foreign aid is based on first, the structure and politicised nature of the aid money. Second, aid money expenditure mechanisms and rationales. And third, foreign aid rhetoric and dogma of banal liberalism (Figure 2). In the case of Jordan for example, foreign aid originated primarily from the World Bank, but from other sources as well such as USAID, Canadian International Development Agency (CIDA), Japanese International Co-operation Association (JICA), and many other donor agencies. During the fist half of the 1990s decade, foreign aid through the World Bank, was geared into the areas of privatisation (primarily the telecommunication sector, power and mineral resources). The legitimating ideology was to increase the efficiency and performance of such sectors (World Bank, 1995, 138, 133, 152*)*. In addition, several projects that were targeting the heritage tourism sector were terminated (e.g., USAID funded Jordan Sustainable Tourism Development Project) without implementation but with great expenditure of the aid money on foreign consultations, research and design, and tendering mechanisms[6]. Such projects ended up as reports on the shelves that have increased Jordan foreign dept and dependency on foreign aid. The government of Jordan rarely supports heritage tourism or conservation projects. Such endeavours have to depend on donor agencies with imported funding mechanisms and cultural site management policies presenting obstacles for sustainability of such projects once aid money is terminated or projects are handed onto the local government. In addition, usually, foreign aid money has to be spent swiftly to meet deadlines creating insignificant time for proper tendering processes, research, and development prior to initiating a project.

Figure 2   Deconstructing Foreign Aid (a socio-historical, political, and economic critique)

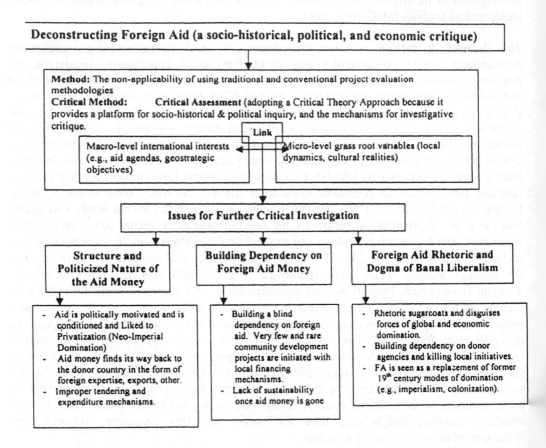

It has been proven, by the success of very few projects in heritage tourism (e.g., Qastal, Darat al Funun) that instead of "shopping" for development projects once aid money is suddenly available; it is more efficient for aid money to support already-existing projects. Such projects would have emerged from the local dynamics of development using local financing mechanisms, and better sustainability approaches. Besides, most of the external pressures on the State (by donor agencies) to engage in public. participatory approaches is translated into banal attempts to satisfy funding requirements and not out of a genuine believe in such approaches by the State and its different implementation agencies. Usually, such ideas for social equality are met with constrains by the extent to which external agendas fit domestic needs and priorities through which the state unsuccessfully works as a mediator between external and domestic interests and priorities (Zetter and Harnza, 1998).

International Heritage Tourism Charters and National Policies: "The widening gap between the glittering rhetoric and the dark reality"

In an attempt to establish principles to govern such a fragile and Sensitive relationship between the host communities, the cultural heritage, and tourism investments and projects; The International Council on Monuments and Sites (ICOMOS) has recently been moulding an International Cultural Tourism Charter (ICTC). The ICTC focuses on managing tourism at places of cultural significance, it prioritises conservation, presentation, and interpretation in addition to proper management of cultural sites appropriated for tourism especially at a time of increasing globalisation and escalating social injustice and conflict between different stakeholders within the tourism Industry (ICOMOS, 1998). The Charter focuses on the dynamic interaction between tourism and cultural heritage. Its objectives include facilitating and encouraging those involved with heritage conservation/tourism and management to make the significance of sites accessible to the host community and tourists alike and respecting and enhancing the heritage and living cultures of host communities. In addition, the Charter focuses on encouraging a dialogue between conservationists, scholars, and the tourism industry about the nature of the cultural places and their relationships with respective host communities. Unfortunately, realities of conflict and power dynamics between different stakeholders within the heritage tourism industry, especially in third world countries like Jordan, makes it extremely difficult to even come closer to meeting any of these objectives.

For example, Principle Four of the Charter stresses that "host communities and indigenous people should be involved in planning for conservation and tourism." Principle Five emphasises that "tourism and conservation activities should benefit the host community." The Charter further stresses that a significant proportion of the revenues derived from tourist investments and programs in heritage locations should be allocated to the conservation and interpretation of those places. Furthermore, the Charter demanded tourism projects, activities, and developments to minimise adverse effects on the cultural heritage and the life-styles of local host communities

At the national scale of Jordan, the new millennium triggered the Ministry of Tourism and Antiquities (MOTA) to start thinking seriously about its tourism strategies. The rhetoric and objectives of the Strategy are assuring. The Mission Statement for 1999-2000 is "Sustainable Tourism Development Towards Economic Prosperity." Tourism objectives include developing an advanced tourism industry utilising its competitive advantages, developing archaeological and tourism sites and resources to enhance the tourism product, expanding the role of the private sector, and upgrading the quality of tourism services to the highest international standards (Ministry of Tourism and Antiquities, 1999). In reality, when it comes to implementation, very few of these objectives are actually achieved. In addition, local strategies overemphasise the economic dimension of tourism, through overemphasis on large-scale projects funded from abroad as indicated previously, considering Jordan's cultural resources primarily for their money-generating potentials (Daher 1999,43). Such an emphasis, however, tends to negate the very *raison d'être* of cultural tourism, for when culture is exclusively viewed from a demand/supply perspective, it is reduced to a packaged experience. True cultural tourism on the other hand, is "a socio-culturally embodied phenomenon with diverse dimensions and untold influences of which economics is but one"

(Jafari, 1996). In Jordan, the heritage tourism industry should be emancipated from its present economic emphasis so it can begin exploring alternative value systems and paradigms.

Conclusions: A critical/phenomenological theory of community development in the age of globalisation

Gradually, with increasing globalisation, the past has been victimised by continuous museumization and commodification of the cultural heritage. Our cultural landscapes appear to have rich living histories, but unfortunately, they are increasingly becoming histories of artefacts and building forms rather thin genuine ways of life (Jacobs, 1992). This will result in creating a schizophrenic separation between the contemporary individual and his or her cultural heritage. This commercialisation of culture and commodification of historic environments increasingly lead to global cultural - homogenisation resulting in a loss of cultural difference.

The nature of this cultural commodification within the realm of late capitalism and consumerism within the heritage tourism industry in Jordan is occurring either directly or indirectly. Direct commodification is manifested in the production of replicas of cultural artefacts and heritage leading to de-symbolised environments cut from the lives of citizens. Indirect commodification of heritage and culture is harder to recognise because, often, it is sugarcoated with entertainment and liberal slogans of heritage conservation and community development, but still it takes place at various levels (Figure 3):

1. Commodification of the lives of host-communities: manifested in exploitation and increasing dependence on the tourism industry, which is orchestrated by excessive capital accumulation and deterministic modes of development Such commodifications freeze the lives of the host communities by conforming it to reconstructed life styles from the past that satisfies tourist expectations and marginalizes the present day modern life. These produces dormant and drugged societies that. are living in the past and that are unable to develop tools for modernisation.

2. Commodification of the Historic Environments: manifested in the museumization of environments that are voided from the lives of their respective communities. Vital and critical links between such historic environments and heritage and the living community are being dismantled.

In Jordan, the living past, which could be a valuable source of inspiration, is being replaced with staged, beautifully wrapped, and essentially fake environments. And cultural landscapes with rich living histories are becoming mere displays of artefacts and building forms without the support of a genuine way of life Such trends will eventually result in a schizophrenic separation between the contemporary inhabitants of such places and their cultural heritage.
(Daher, 1999,44)

Figure 3   Nature and Extent of Cultural Commodification in the Heritage Tourism Industry

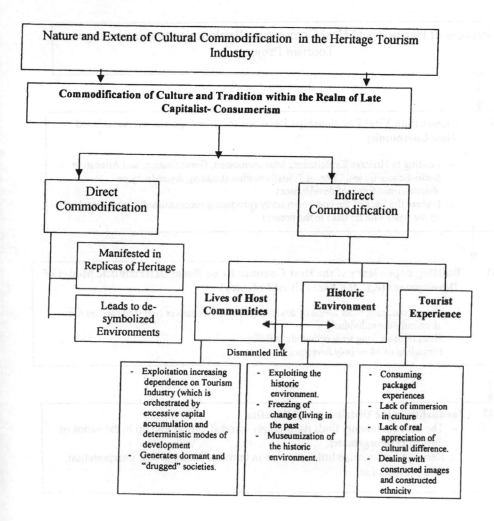

3.   Commodification of the Tourist Experience: more tourists are confronting "packaged experiences" where they find themselves dealing with "constructed images" and ethnicity of the past This results in a lack of immersion in culture and a lack of appreciation of cultural difference, presumably the essence cultural tourism.

The previously discussed cultural and socio-economic transformation within heritage tourism projects (e.g., gentrification, exploitation, commodification alienation) dismantle vital links between the cultural heritage and its respective host communities. This process of cultural and economic exploitation within many of the heritage tourism projects starts with (Figure 4):

Figure 4   Process of Heritage and Host Community Exploitation within Heritage Tourism Projects

```
┌──────────────────────────────────────────────────────────────────────┐
│        Process of Heritage and Host Community Exploitation within Heritage │
│                          Tourism Projects                              │
└──────────────────────────────────────────────────────────────────────┘
                                │
                                ▼
┌──────────────────────────────────────────────────────────────────────┐
│  I.    Dismantling Vital Relationships Between the Heritage and its Associated │
│        Host Community                                                   │
│                                                                         │
│        -  Leading to Heritage Exploitation, Musuemization, Gentrification, and Alienation. │
│        -  Socio-Economic and Cultural Transformation (building dependency on │
│           deterministic forms of development                            │
│        -  Freezes the lives of the host community (producing reconstructed images that dwell │
│           in the past) with no links to the present                     │
└──────────────────────────────────────────────────────────────────────┘
                                │
                                ▼
┌──────────────────────────────────────────────────────────────────────┐
│  II.   Building dependency of the Host Community on Banal Deterministic Modes of │
│        Development (e.g., the Banal Craft Industry)                     │
│                                                                         │
│        -  Not encouraging other forms of developments and initiatives (induced choices that │
│           dismantle the individual)                                     │
│        -  Short term vs. long term economic stability                   │
│        -  Prevailing of Monopoly Investors.                             │
└──────────────────────────────────────────────────────────────────────┘
                                │
                                ▼
┌──────────────────────────────────────────────────────────────────────┐
│  III.  Inequality in the Distribution of Benefits                       │
│        -  The host community finds itself empty-handed, profits end up in the hands of │
│           investors or organizers.                                      │
│        -  Heritage sites receive little attention in terms of conservation, interpretation, │
│           and presentation.                                             │
└──────────────────────────────────────────────────────────────────────┘
```

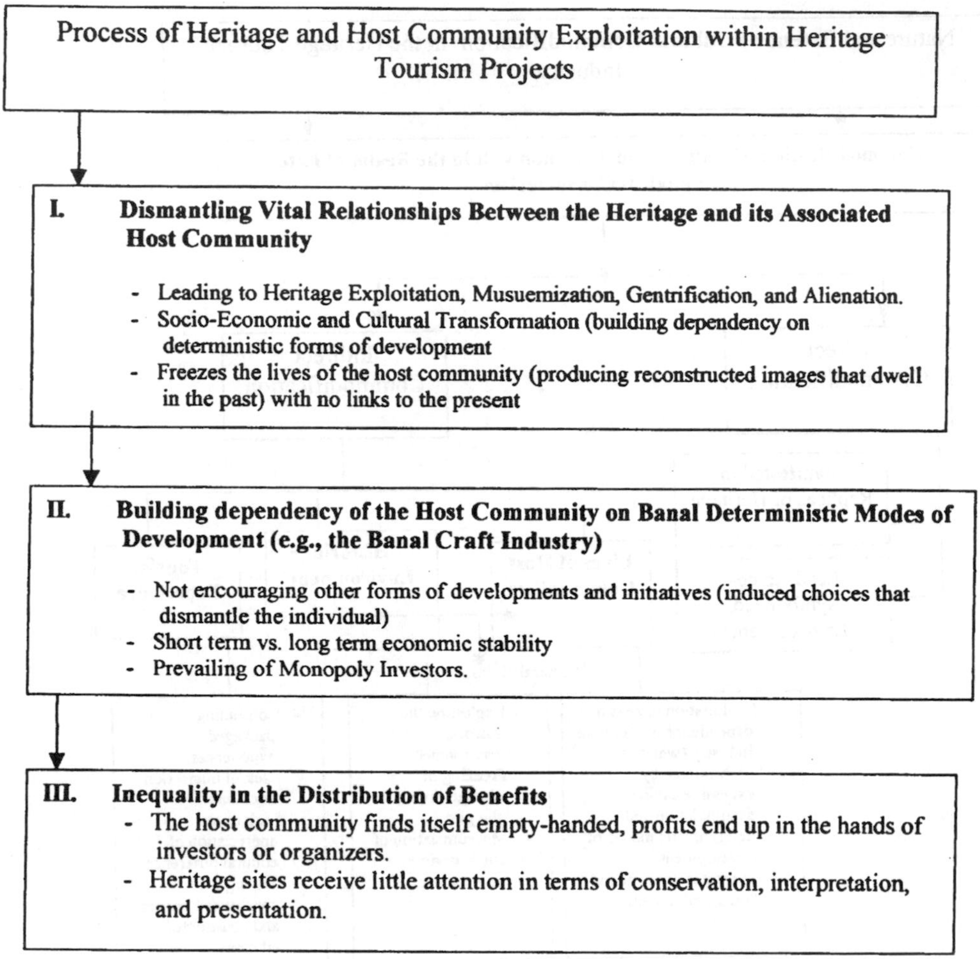

1. Dismantling of vital relationships between the heritage and its associated host-community: leading to heritage museumization and exploitation, different levels of gentrification of the host-community, and freezing of the lives of the host-community.

2. Building dependency of the host-community on banal and deterministic modes of development (e.g., the banal craft industry). Lack of encouragement of other forms and developments and initiatives and depending primarily on induced choices orchestrated by monopoly investors.

3. Inequality in the Distribution of Benefits from Heritage Tourism: The host community finds itself empty handed, most of the profits end up in the hands of investors or multinational corporations. The heritage sites even receive little

attention in terms of conservation, protection, and interpretation in comparison to the revenues they generated in the first place. This is due to the fact that most of the times, key players in the tourism industry are "often outsiders to the cultures and communities they impinge upon, so causing a potential source of friction" (Boniface, 1998,288).

A critical/phenomenological approach presents a pragmatic but critical framework, that; not only provokes the individual into rejecting such deterministic modes of development in heritage tourism; but also regulates the power relations between the different stakeholders within the heritage tourism industry avoiding conflict, heritage commodification, and host community exploitation.

> *Critical thinking is the function neither of the isolated individual nor of a sum-total of individuals. Its subject is rather a definite individual in his real relation to other individuals and groups, in his conflict with a particular class, and, finally, in the resultant web of relationships with the social totality and with nature.* (Horkheimer, 1972, 210-2 11)

Abdelhalim (1988, 11) stated that "conditions, values, or mechanisms of globalisation make it impossible to produce good environment, empower or sustain local communities and their resources (including indigenous architecture, arts and crafts) have been systematically dismantled to be appropriated as newly created settings and artefacts for a new class of tourists and global elite." To counteract the forces of globalisation within community development, Abdelhalim (1998) suggests providing an alternative mode to current trends in development that depends on community-based approaches. Such approaches do not conform to late-capitalism cycles of excessive capital accumulation. In addition, they aim to free the community and the individual from an addiction of deterministic development. How can such community-based approaches become reality in this age of globalisation, politicised foreign aid, fierce competition, and economic difficulties? This critica1/phenomenological theory proposes a solution through the formation of sub-cultures of resistance, that form a serious and educated opposition, at the scale of the individual and society as will be elaborated in details in the next two section of this paper (Figure 5).

Figure 5   A Critical/Phenomenoligical Theory of Community Development in the Age of Globalisation

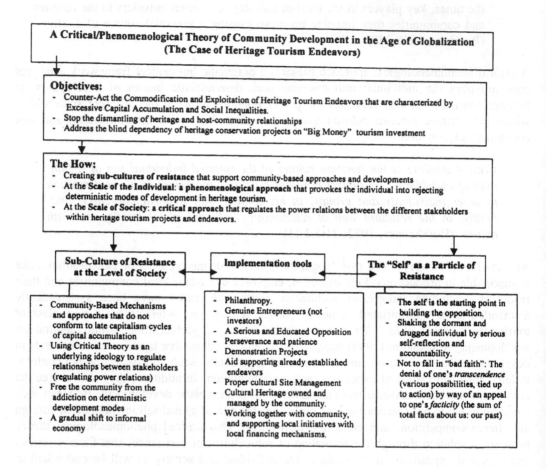

The "self" as an active particle of resistance "resisting the totally administered "one-dimensional" society"

The Frankfurt School became best known for its theories of "the totally administered society" or better known as the "one-dimensional society" which theorised the increasing power of capitalism over all aspects of social life. New forms of technology, new modes of organising production and consumption, new configurations of class, and new methods of social control were producing a "one-dimensional" society without opposition (Horkheimer and Adorno, 1972). When realising that this "one-dimensional and totally administered society" is shifting from a state-administered to a global transnational corporations-administered society orchestrated by mere economic rationales and ideologies; the need for an opposition becomes even more urgent in this age of globalisation. One apparent form of social control and domination practiced by such "big money corporations and funding agencies, is the induced and deterministic mode of development manifested in many heritage conservation/tourism projects in third world countries. This signifies *the end of the individual* and the end of subjectivity in favour of a mundane and prosaic objectivity in society.

In promoting community-based approaches in heritage tourism, the "self' should be the starting point to build the opposition against globalisation and deterministic modes of development Provoking the individual can be achieved by adopting a phenomenological approach to self-consciousness, influenced by Jean-Paul Sartre, that shakes the *dormant* and *drugged* individual by serious self-reflection, assessment, and accountability (Solomon, 1988, 181-183). Sartre distinguishes between two aspects of human condition; *facticity* (one's past: the sum total of facts about us and the situations in which we have been thrown), and *transcendence* (our various possibilities and potentials which are not just an act of imagination but that are tied up to action). Sartre links his concepts *of facticity* and *transcendence* in a most sophisticated philosophical conception that he labels *bad Faith* (the denial of one's *transcendence* by way of an appeal to *one's facticity)*. *"Bad Faith* is not just a tendency to fall back into the routines of everyday life, but is nothing less than a betrayal of one's self, a lie in which one deceives oneself about oneself. The most prevalent example of bad faith is the denial of one's freedom in the form of an excuse, typically beginning with "I couldn't help it" (Solomon, 1988, 181-183).

When applied to community development within heritage tourism projects; the marginalised individual lacking economic and social means to resist control by the empowered investors, should not use such a reality to fall victim and surrender to such deterministic modes of development and choices that are imposed on the community. Implementation tools to provoke the individual rests on educating a serious opposition within the host community helping it to realise that there are other modes of development and funding mechanisms that insure the retaining of the heritage in the hands of the host community. Then, the individual has to play an active and serious role in the development of the community where he or she is expected to take a risk, financially and socially with the help of educated philanthropists and entrepreneurs who can start to finance endeavours that can serve as demonstration projects for the future.

Sub-culture of resistance at the scale of society "informal, and community-based mechanisms"

The proposed critical/phenomenological theory proposes the formation of sub-cultures of resistance that forms a serious and educated opposition, also at the scale of society. The society should depend on community-based approaches and funding mechanisms that emerge from the local community's concept of development to resist the socio-economic and cultural control by global powers and late capitalist investors. Such approaches do not conform to late-capitalism cycles of excessive capital accumulation.

In sketching what alternatives does a community have in terms of funding options and development approaches; Abdelhalim (1998) presented three alternatives for the community. The first alternative proposes that the community should stay outside formal economies of globalisation, and depend primarily on informal financing mechanisms. This alternative is extremely difficult for the community to apply because it is difficult to disassociate entirely and all of a sudden from current formal economies missing on significant opportunities of funding. Alternative two calls on the community to embrace globalisation and late-capitalist consumption patterns. This option would create a passive community that surrenders to the forces of globalisation diluting identity, local culture, and a sense of belonging to a shared place. The third alternative, which is pragmatic and rationale, proposes a gradual shift to informal economy where the community is critical of funding mechanisms and deterministic development options. The community here accepts but re-adapts updated financial processes where resources of the community are owned and managed or co-managed by the community. Financing mechanisms are compatible with market economies, yet they reject exploitation of the cultural heritage and local community.

The proposed critical/phenomenological theory of community development within heritage tourism projects uses Critical Theory to regulate power relationships between the different stakeholders (e.g., local community, cultural heritage, the regulating authorities, funding agencies, empowered investors and corporations) in this gradual shift to the informal economy. The shift will not be easy at first, but with the help of philanthropist and entrepreneurs who might help fund well-designed heritage tourism/community development projects, the community at large, and also financing institutions will start to accept and even encourage such community-based approaches. *Place marketing* and processes of heritage conservation/tourism are currently being subject to global market economy and mechanisms leading, in most of the times, to exploitation of heritage and social injustice. The proposed formation of sub-cultures of resistance could slowdown the influx of such global hegemony and deterministic development Tiesdell (1996, 75) also emphasised the provision of local financing mechanisms that emerge from the local dynamics and contexts (e.g., philanthropists, tax incentives, revolving local funds and trusts, and low coast loans to entrepreneurs)

The cultural heritage of a particular region should be seen as a source of inspiration for future generations and as a mean for resisting globalisation and commodification of the built and social environments. Proper heritage conservation has been seen, by many sociologists, anthropologists, and geographers as a counter-force to cycles of capital accumulation expressed in many new developments. Frampton (1992) argues that society should depend on particular characters in any region to resist popular commodification of the built environment and social life. The region becomes the place of resistance against late capitalism and flexible accumulation Regional form becomes the instrument for that resistance when not only the architectural form, setting, and structures are conserved, but also the technologies and the know-how as well.

Forming an opposition that is serious and educated is essential to a successful implementation of such community-based approaches and gradual transformation to an informal economy. It is true that the host community might have knowledge of its exploitation and wretchedness; yet, its fragmentation and the fact that many of its members are uneducated will increase the chances of the host community falling victim to exploitative development schemes. Such schemes use glittering slogans of heritage conservation and community-development as a bait to camouflage oppression, heritage exploitation, and domination of society.

Jordan has not been able, yet, to establish itself as a prime tourism destination encountering severe competition from other significant tourist destinations like Egypt or Israel. Tourism to

Jordan, most of the times, is part of a package deal that includes Egypt, Syria, or Israel. The duration of stay in Jordan for tourists averages to about *1.5* days at the maximum. Even worse, the tourism market in Jordan is currently shocked by the inactive and sluggish season. This disaffirms previous predication by government officials and investors for a prosperous tourism decade that will change the economic reality of the whole country. Daher (1999) argues that if heritage tourism is to be endorsed as a major component of a national economy, a dynamic and balanced interaction should be maintained between the cultural heritage, host communities, and tourist industry investments. In addition, heritage tourism should be considered as one of the tools for community development in conjunction with other development alternatives (e.g., agriculture, industry, capacity building) within heritage tourism endeavours.

Principle Four of the International Cultural Tourism Charter (ICTC) encourages the involvement of the host communities in planning and managing conservation and tourism projects (ICOMOS, 1998). "One essential element in improving the encounter between tourists and local populations lies in the participation in and, ultimately, the control over the protection and management of sites by the local people themselves, as well as their sharing in the profits which derive from tourism" (Barre, 1996,8). There are different levels through which public participation is encouraged and implemented. It begins by adopting basis participatory approaches of sharing information, consultation or deciding together. Nevertheless, progressive levels of public participation and engaging the local community my depend on genuinely acting together or better yet supporting independent and community-based initiatives. Such independent initiatives might form the nucleus for subcultures of resistance that might be able to resist globalisation in general and the commodification of the host community and cultural heritage in particular.

Endnotes

1. This paper is presenting a theoretical framework depending not on a single case study approach but on a critical juxtaposition of various heritage tourism projects from Jordan. The author had the opportunity to work on some of the listed heritage tourism endeavours such as projects in Umm Qais, Salt, Jerash, Qastal, Kerak, and Amman.

2. The Critical Theory was initiated by the *Institute of Social Research, which* was established in Germany by scholars like Max Horkheimer and Theodore Adorno, as the first Marxist-oriented research centre affiliated with a major German University during the 192Os. Known as the Frankfurt School; the Institute aimed at developing a *supra-disciplinary* social theory which could serve as an instrument for social transformation. A synthesis of philosophy, social theory and research and the sciences characterised this new theory. Its objectives were to address human needs and eliminate suffering by promoting critical activity within a serious and educated opposition which is anti-globalisation, anti excessive capital accumulation, and commodification of the environment. The Critical Theory of the Frankfurt School during the second half of the 20th century continued to present a critique of late capitalism's processes of capital accumulation and mechanisms of social domination. The Critical Theory combines perspectives drawn from political economy, sociology, cultural theory, philosophy, anthropology, and history; thus avoiding the deficiencies of the traditional academic division of sciences and labour. Here individuals from various disciplines work together

collectively to sketch social critical theory that would form the basis for social and cultural change (Bronner, and Kellner, 1994).

3. The crisis of late capitalism was seen as the conflict between the ideology of bourgeois individualism and the reality of the concentration of power in the hands of a few large corporations, the military, and the government which they controlled. Since the myth of popular participation was a necessary presupposition of corporate domination, the politics of confrontation were employed to expose the existence of a power nexus which was essentially unresponsive to popular needs. (Horkheimer, 1972, XI).

4. A similar project is under construction at a near by location: Khirbet al Nawafleh.

5. In Jordan for example, there is an abundance of funding available for issues and projects that are tackling women studies, minorities, secular programs, liberal programs, and family planning; yet, funding is really scarce in other development issues such as community development, heritage conservation, and the environment.

6. In Egypt, for example, in addition to the fact that aid is conditioned with privatisation, Washington gets back a great deal of its aid in the form of money spent on foreign exports (e g, 26000 getting back 35% of aid money within the last two decades) and on importing heavy industrial machinery and equipment.

References

Abdeihamlim, A. (1998), Architecture, Community and Culture in the Context of Globalisation: An Argument Against Globalisation, *Traditional Dwellings and Settlement Review*, X, (1), pp 11.

Barre, H. (1996), General Introduction to the Debates, in UNESCO/AJEST Proceedings of Round Table, *Culture, Tourism, Development: Critical issues for the XXIst Century,* UNESCO/AIEST, Paris, pp.5-13.

Boniface, P. (1999), Tourism and Cultures: Consensus in the Making?, in Robinson, M. and Boniface, P. (Editors), *Tourism and Cultural Conflicts,* CABI Publishing, Oxon, UK, pp.287-307.

Borley, L. (1994), Cultural Diversity in a Changing Europe, in Fladmark, J, (Editor), *Cultural Tourism,* Donhead Publishing Ltd., London, pp.3-13.

Brink, P. (1998), Heritage Tourism in the U. S. A: Grassroots Efforts to Combine Preservation and Tourism, *APT Bulletin: The Journal of Preservation Technology, XXIX,* (34), pp. 59-63.

Bronner, S. and Kellner, D. (1989), *Critical Theory and Society: A Reader,* Routledge, New York.

Daher, R. (1999), Gentrification and the Politics of Power, Capital, and Culture in an Emerging Jordanian Heritage Industry, *Traditional Dwellings and Settlement Review*, X, (II), pp.33-47.

Frampton, K. (1992), *Modern Architecture: A Critical History*, Thames and Hudson, London.

Gupte, P. (1999), Whose Cause Is It, Anyway?, *Newsweek*, December 6.

Horkheimer, M. (1972), *Critical Theory*, Herder and Herder, New York.

Horkheimer, M., and Adorno, T. (1972), *Dialectic of Enlightenment*, Herder and Herder, New York.

Hornblower, M. (1999), The Battle in Seattle *Time*, December 6.

Jacobs, J. (1992), Cultures of the Past and Urban Transformation: The Spitalfields Market Redevelopment in East London, in Kay, R. and Gale, R. (Editors), *Inventing Places: Studies in Cultural Geography*, Longman Cheshire, Melbourne, pp. 194-214.

Jafari, J. (1996), Tourism and Culture: an inquiry into paradoxes, in UNESCO/AIEST Proceedings of Round Table, *Culture, Tourism, Development: Critical Issues for the XXIst Century*, UNESCO/AIEST, Paris, pp. 43-48.

Jamieson, Walter. (1998), Cultural Heritage Tourism Planning and Development: Defining the Field and Its Challenges, *APT Bulletin: The Journal of Preservation Technology*, XXIX, (3-4), pp. 65-69.

JICA, (1994), Study of the Tourism Development Plan in the Hashemite Kingdom of Jordan, (Study Report), Prepared by the Japanese International Development Agency.

ICOMOS, (1998), Eighth Draft of the International Cultural Tourism Charter: Managing Tourism at Places of Cultural Significance, *US/ICOMOS Newsletter*, (6): November/December.

Kellner, D. (1996), Critical Theory and the Crisis of Social Theory, (Internet Article), http:llwww.uta.edu/hunm/illuminations/kell.html.

Kellner, D. (1997), Globalisation and the Post-modern Turn, (Internet Article): http:/www. gseis.ucla.edu/courses/ed253a/dk/globpm.html.

Keller, P. (1996), General Trends in Tourism Today, in UNESCO/AIEST Proceedings of Round Table, *Culture, Tourism, Development: Critical Issues for the XXIst Century*, UNESCO/AIEST, Paris, pp.13-16.

McCarthy, T. (1994), The Critique of Impure Reason: Foucault and the Frankfurt School, in Kelly, M., (Editor), *Critique and Power: Recasting the Foucault/Habermas Debate*, The MIT Press, Cambridge.

Metalka, C. (1986), *The Dictionary of Tourism,* Merton House, Wheaton.

Ministry of Tourism (1999), Synopsis of Tourism Strategy, Ministry of Tourism and Antiquities of Jordan (unpublished report).

Patin, V. (1999), Will Market Forces Rule?, *The UNESCO Courier,* July/August, pp.35-36.

Robinson, M. (1998), Tourism Encounters: Inter-and Intracultural Conflicts and the World's Largest Industry, *Traditional Dwellings and Settlement Review*, X, (1), pp.31.

Robinson, M. (1999a), Cultural Conflict in Tourism: Inevitability and Inequality, in Robinson, M. and Boniface, P. (Editors), *Tourism and Cultural Conflicts,* CABI Publishing, Oxon, UK, pp.1-33.

Robinson, M. (1999b), Is Cultural Tourism on the Right Track?, *The UNESCO Courier,* July/August, pp.22-23.

Smith, V. (1989), Introduction, in Smith, V. (Editor), *Hosts and Guests: The Anthropology of Tourism,* University of Philadelphia Press, Philadelphia.

Solomon, R. (1988), *Continental Philosophy Since 1750: The Rise and Fall of the Self,* Oxford University Press, New York.

Tiesdell, S. Oc. T. and Heath, T. (1996), *Revitalising Historic Urban Quarters,* Butterworth-Heinemann, Oxford.

World Bank, (1995), *The World Bank Annual Report 1994,* World Bank, Washington, D.C.

Zetter, R. and Hamza, M. (1998), Egypt: The State, Foreign Aid and Community Participation in Urban Shelter Projects, *International Planning Studies*, 3 (2): 185-205.

Cost benefit analysis of tourism projects: Some consideration of the key issues analysed through a case study of a unique heritage project in the West of Ireland[1]

Donal A Dineen and Mary Walsh

University of Limerick, Ireland

Introduction

The process of carrying out economic appraisals of tourism projects gained considerable attention in Ireland during the period of substantial investment in tourism from 1989-99. This coincided with the period of major EU transfers and matching public sector investment in the Irish tourism sector such that a total of IR£1bn was invested in various forms of tourism product developments, new visitor facilities and training enhancements over the decade. The international tourism sector in Ireland attracted almost 6m. overseas visitors in 1999 who contributed IR£2.4 billion in foreign exchange earnings. Though the tourism sector has not led the 'roar' of the Celtic Tiger in recent years it has managed, however, to maintain a significant share of the economy's GNP (c. 6% in 1997-8) and to continue its role as an important employer (c. 8% of the total at work in 1998).

The development of project appraisals (most notably cost-benefit analysis) of major investments, at the insistence of the EU Commission and by extension the Irish Government, was not undertaken with the same rigour for many smaller projects. This has meant that many projects have gone ahead without subjecting them to the rigour of a prior economic appraisal which might at least have indicated some potential exposure of the public sector's investment in these projects. Project promoters may not have been keen to engage in such exercises especially where they are motivated by community and political factors to drive specific initiatives forward. A negative economic appraisal might simply drive the initiatives to ground. The result of this from a public policy perspective is that many projects are undertaken which may add very little, if any, net economic benefits to the economy, particularly when deadweight and displacement impacts are taken into account.[2] This paper is an attempt to apply cost-benefit analysis techniques to a particular tourism heritage project

– the Jeanie Johnston - which is being developed in Tralee, Co. Kerry. The paper is structured as follows: first, a brief overview of the changing tourism trends in Ireland is presented and set in the context of the investment programmes driven under the two EU Operational Programmes for Tourism (1989-93 and 1994-99); second, some of the concepts and issues which are relevant to undertaking cost-benefit appraisals and evaluations of tourism projects are examined: third, the Jeanie Johnston case study is presented and the core principles of cost-benefit analysis applied to an appraisal of this unique project; the final section presents a number of conclusions.

Overview of Irish tourism trends

The tourism sector in the Republic of Ireland has shown phenomenal growth since 1986 measured both in terms of the increased numbers of overseas visitors to the country and the revenue receipts from these visitors. Growth rates have easily outpaced those of other European country destinations for most of this period. Employment in the sector has expanded more or less on a pro-rata basis as productivity gains have been limited in much of this labour intensive sector of the economy.

Growth in international tourist numbers to Ireland

Figure 1 shows the trend in tourist arrivals for the period, 1968 to 1997 which highlights the contrast between the period up to 1986 and the subsequent expansion in visitor numbers.

Figure 1   Overseas and out-of-state* tourist arrivals to Ireland, 1968-99

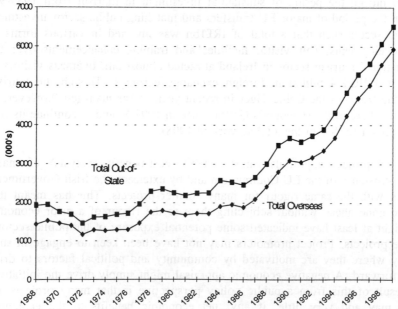

*Out-of-state includes visitors from Northern Ireland in addition to overseas visitors
Source: Derived from Bord Failte, Tourism Facts, 1968-99 (various issues)

Set in a comparative European context since 1986, Ireland has easily outpaced the growth in international tourists to the main destination countries on the continent (and to Britain). While overall international tourism to Europe increased by one per cent in 1999 (WTO , 2000), the corresponding growth rate to Ireland was 7.4 per cent – the second highest growth rate in the broader European region after Spain (+ 8.8%). Since 1987, Ireland has been steadily increasing its share of international arrivals to Europe from 1.1 to 1.7 per cent in 1999 (though Europe's share of world tourism arrivals has been falling steadily since the 1960s).

Growth in international tourism revenues

Revenue receipts from foreign visitors to Ireland showed a steady improvement in real terms from 1986-91and from 1993 onwards (Table 1). Annual real revenue growth was in double digits for seven of the fourteen years shown and the annual average growth rate was 9.6 per cent over the 1986-97 interval, an impressive figure given that total international tourism revenue growth was less than 5 per cent annually during this time.

The rate of revenue increase has slowed down considerably in 1998 and 1999, to below half the rates sustained over the 1993-7 period. Given that visitor numbers have continued to expand at a faster rate, it appears that average yields from overseas tourists to Ireland are beginning to decline.

Table 1   Real tourism revenue from overseas visitors to Ireland, 1986-99*

Year	IR£million♣	% Change (on previous year)
1986	577.5	-8.4
1987	647.1	+ 12.1
1988	746.1	+ 15.3
1989	829.8	+ 11.2
1990	929.3	+ 12.0
1991	969.7	+ 4.3
1992	953.9	-1.6
1993	1096.4	+ 14.9
1994	1178.2	+ 7.5
1995	1326.5	+ 12.6
1996	1471.0	+ 10.9
1997	1588.6	+ 8.0
1998	1664.5	+ 4.7
1999	1745.9	+ 4.9

*Total Expenditure by overseas visitors to Ireland, excluding international fare payments in getting to and from Ireland
♣ in constant 1997 prices

Source: Derived from Bord Failte, Tourism Facts (various years)

The above impressive trends in the Irish tourism sector translate into equally impressive income and employment generation outcomes. Tourism output comprised 6.4 per cent of GNP in 1997 while total employment dependent on tourism also expanded since 1986, rising from 45,700 (4.2 per cent of total employment) to 111,800 in 1997 (8.4 per cent of the total)[3].

Operational programmes for tourism, 1989-99

Substantial investment in tourist product development was a feature of the two Operational Programmes (OP) for Tourism, 1989-93 and 1994-99, which provided unprecedented sums of EU and Irish Government finance as part of the support for peripheral regions of the Community to bring living standards closer to the EU average level.[4] Over IR£1billion was spent on the total programme, co-funded by the Irish government, the EU Commission and the private sector, with over two-thirds spent on product development including the largely public sector funded natural and cultural tourism products. While Ireland had tremendous benefits as a tourist destination in terms of her natural beauty, it seriously lacked the matching product developments to enhance the visitor experience and provide greater variety for tourists. In the second Operational Programme, 1994-9, a key objective of the expenditure under the natural and cultural tourism sub-programme was to make cultural assets more accessible to tourists by enhancing the quality of presentation and interpretative facilities. While these represented the bulk of the funds, a number of complementary sources of funds were also available usually part-financed by the EU e.g., LEADER, INTERREG, International Fund for Ireland, EU Peace Fund and other sectorally based Operational Programmes.

The Jeanie Johnston project falls under the cultural tourism sub-programme and represents a unique example of a publicly-led and community-driven partnership with strong corporate sponsorship. Given the significant investment of public funds in a range of projects, it was not surprising that the EU became much more interested in ensuring good value for money in the second OP and insisted on economic appraisal studies for large projects[5] and recommended them for smaller projects.

Cost-benefit analysis of tourism projects: concepts and issues

The application of cost-benefit analysis to tourism projects is no different in principle from its application to other projects involving public sector spending. The core question is the same: is the project likely to generate net economic benefits for the economy? While broader macroeconomic characteristics can influence the measurement of specific costs, (e.g. the shadow price of labour in a full-employment compared with an underemployment scenario) the approach is essentially microeconomic and localised. One practical difference that is unique to tourism, as opposed to, for example, appraising a power plant investment, is the emphasis on the expenditure incurred by tourists during their visit to the area in which the project is located and the possible influence of the project on their reason for visit, length of stay and/ or level of expenditure. These associated expenditure benefits can have a crucial bearing on the ultimate economic impact of the investment.

Financial appraisal

The financial appraisal of the project is the first stage in the process in which the future net revenue receipts are discounted back to their present values and compared with the capital expenditures incurred in the initial stages and the net present value (NPV) is determined.[6] While appraisal and evaluation are used interchangeably, the former strictly refers to *ex-ante* analyses in which alternative uses of the funds can be considered while the latter refer to *ex-post* analyses the results of which may influence future public policy decisions.[7] Interim evaluations can do both, of course, but rarely lead to the abandoning of projects especially since sunken costs cannot easily be recovered. The present case study is written in an interim phase of the *Jeanie Johnston* project whereby a replica ship is almost constructed (Feb 2000), and significant costs have been incurred already, while revenue flows to any significant extent have yet to materialise. While revenue projections and cost estimates should carry an appropriate risk factor, the discount rate chosen is 5 per cent real rate of return, suggesting that if the project cannot generate this return there is a better alternative economic return available on the use of these funds whether in health, education or road investments (for example) or even in repaying the national debt.[8] The time period chosen for a return on the investment is 20 years, after which time the ship is assumed to have some positive salvage value.

Revenues

Critical issues in relation to revenue projections include the level of displacement from other tourist projects in the area, the mix of domestic and overseas tourists, the extent to which the existence of this facility is the main reason for visiting the area or for extending the length of stay of overseas tourists. The income impact of the project is what is important in this analysis and this takes into account the multiplier values of the direct tourism spend at the facility, indirect purchases from other business suppliers and induced spending arising from the incomes derived by those employed on the project or in those enterprises supplying goods and services to the project.

Displacement

Displacement is difficult to measure with any great degree of accuracy particularly without some hard data based on tourist expenditure patterns or survey evidence. It is important to define the geographical boundaries of the 'impact' area at the outset. Displacement can be influenced also by the degree of similarity or complementarity between projects in an area. From the point of view of the financial feasibility of the project, it may well be the case that this is positive only because business turnover is reduced in a range of other tourist attractions in the area (or at the expense of reductions in spending on other 'leisure' goods). The argument has been made that additional attractions can lead to additional spending by tourists simply because they do not always operate on tight fixed budgets but may over-spend simply because of the opportunities that present themselves during a holiday. For overseas tourists such spending at the Jeanie Johnston facility would be truly 'additional' while for domestic tourists could be considered to be displacement from other spending in the economy and thus not really 'additional'. The only qualification to the latter arises where domestic tourist spending is a substitute for foreign holiday spending and is thus a form of import substitution that has a similar impact to overseas holiday spending in Ireland.

Additional (associated) spending

Spending by domestic tourists is considered to be displacement of spending elsewhere in the economy though could be of net benefit to a narrowly defined geographical area. We can identify two possible forms of additional spending arising from the new project:

1. spending by additional overseas tourists who have come to the area because of the project, and

2. spending by those overseas tourists who have extended their stay in the area because of the project.

Multiplier values may be used to convert the additional spending into income or GNP, using the most recent estimates of Deane and Henry (1993) and a later update. The expenditures at the facility are included in the additional spending of the above categories and hence should not be double-counted in arriving at the income effects arising from the additional spend. The issue of scale economies in an area should not be ignored – the fact that there is an emerging "cluster" of tourist related businesses and attractions in an area can itself be a reason for encouraging more visitors, rather than this being attributed to a single facility; it can be a driving force also for local tourism interests, anxious to expand their tourism base to an appropriate scale.[9]

Prices

Prices may overstate the marginal benefits of projects in some instances where, for example, monopoly pricing practices are in operation. While there may be some instances of this in the case of the 'bundle' of tourism products and services expenditure (or of indirect spending on (say) electricity charges), there is limited evidence to indicate that prices are distorted in the industry on a systematic basis. Hence we can conclude that prices accurately reflect the marginal benefits associated with this project.

Intangible benefits

There are some intangible benefits or positive externalities which the development of some facilities can bestow on an area but which are difficult to measure. A community may take some pride in the new facility as it makes the town a more attractive place to visit and can develop as an icon or symbol of status. The development of a museum in an area can be of direct benefit to visitors to the museum but also has an 'option' value for residents. They may be prepared to make a contribution to the museum based on the value they place on the option of visiting it, though they may never actually do so.

Costs

The central issue on the cost side is the appropriate measure of costs to use and the extent to which the market prices paid reflect the true social opportunity costs of the resources used, especially labour. In a situation where there is considerable unemployment, labour hired at market wage costs may have a much lower opportunity cost or 'shadow wage' applied to it. Honohan, writing in 1986 when unemployment rates were quadruple present rates in the

Irish economy, suggested a realistic shadow price for labour at 50 to 75 per cent of the market price – which was three to four times what was often used. In the year 2000, with the buoyancy in the Irish economy and the tightness of the labour market, it can be argued that the shadow wage should be 25 to 50 per cent more than the market wage, to compensate for the opportunity cost of that labour in alternative employment and the extra pressure on house prices and other infrastructure caused by the influx of labour to an area. It would seem at the very least that the shadow wage should not be below the market wage though there is no consensus on what the appropriate value should be.

Other costs, such as bought in supplies, purchases of goods and services and materials purchased are included in the calculations at their market prices as it is assumed that these reflect the true opportunity costs of the resources used or goods/ services purchased.

Intangible costs

Paralleling the intangible benefits derived from the project there may also be intangible costs or negative externalities which arise. A particularly attractive project may be located in a relatively inaccessible area and thus give rise to serious traffic congestion costs for other road users, many of them local residents who may have no interest in the project. Additional car users on Irish roads such as those hired or owned by overseas tourists are likely to increase the costs to road users in general and may contribute to higher accident rates. Tourists can add to congestion costs in smaller towns and add to the costs of providing refuse collection services, and may also put pressure on sewerage and related facilities. While some of these negative externalities may be measured, it is frequently the case that they can only be identified and listed as part of the intangible costs of a marginal tourism project.[10]

Deadweight

Deadweight measures the amount of public funds used to support a project over and above the amount necessary for it to go ahead. It is only an issue in the cost-benefit analysis to the extent that the cost of public support for a project is greater than it ought to be and a different public/ private mix of funding could be achieved. Ideally the state should only support marginal projects where it can be demonstrated that the amount of state funding is just necessary to bring the project into being.[11] It may not always be possible to determine precisely the amount of this funding – it can depend critically on the alternative sources of funding available to the promoters and/ or on their capacity to maximise the public sector contribution to a project which thus minimises their own contribution.

Clearly the amount of public sector contribution (which can be from a variety of sources and take on a number of forms) determines the state's exposure to the project. The cost-benefit analysis proceeds on the basis of the *total cost* of the project, and not just on the basis of the public sector contribution. Using a five per cent real return as a benchmark figure it may be possible to establish (retrospectively) the extent of deadweight in some projects.[12]

Jeanie Johnston Project

The Irish Famine of 1845-7 gave rise to the first wave of mass emigration from Ireland to North America. A number of ships were used to transport the emigrants from Ireland, among them the Jeanie Johnston. This ship was built in Quebec, Canada in 1847 and constructed of timber. Its original port of registry was Tralee, Co. Kerry. The ship sailed from 1848 to 1854 on the North Atlantic with regular calls at Quebec, Baltimore (US) Tralee, Belfast and Liverpool.

Conditions of voyage for emigrants were, to say the least, highly unpleasant - emigrants were heavily dependent on what was available, being "the poorest and most destitute of people" while ship owners were concerned with the profitability of the transport service they were providing, without any Government subsidy.

The project in Tralee centres on the construction of a full-scale replica of the original Jeanie Johnston ship. Once constructed it is planned to bring it on a transatlantic voyage visiting a number of North American ports over several months in the year 2000 and possibly some in Northern Ireland, the UK and in Ireland. Upon its return to Tralee it will be berthed there alongside the Blennerville Windmill (from where the original Jeanie Johnston set sail on its westbound Atlantic routes). The main purpose is to have the ship available for "operating in museum mode in conjunction with the Windmill and an improved Emigration display". An unusual feature for this museum ship is that it will have made the initial voyage across the ocean before going into 'service', a feature which will add to its authenticity.

Costs and revenues

There are three distinct phases of the project which have varying cost and revenue implications:

Phase 1 (1996 - May, 2000): Construction stage of the Jeanie Johnston and new associated buildings, during which costs (revenue outflows) will be incurred with some offsetting revenue inflows paid through admission charges by those visiting the 'Visitor Shipyard';[13]

Phase 2 (May, 2000- Dec, 2000): Transatlantic voyage and visits to ports in the US and Canada, which will involve substantial operating costs offset by some revenue flows and corporate sponsorship; plans are in train to take in ports in Northern Ireland, Mainland Britain and the Republic of Ireland on the return phase of the journey thus delaying the arrival in Tralee by about five months;

Phase 3 (Jan, 2001 -): Museum ship, anchored off Blennerville, Tralee in which the annual operating costs are offset by revenues generated from both domestic and foreign tourists visiting the attraction.

The construction phase of the ship took about three and a half years and involved the employment of an average of 55 ship-building trainees, funded by the Irish Government's Employment and Training Authority, FAS (IR£900,000) and the International Fund for Ireland (IFI) (IR£200,000)[14]. In addition to these labour subsidies, the ship construction costs, the site acquisition costs and the building work costs added up to approximately IR£5m., over the period from the commencement of construction to April, 2000. The only offsetting revenues during Phase 1 were the admission charges to the visitor shipyard (50,000 in 1999) and some miscellaneous revenue flows (total of IR£100,000) which were more than offset by the operating costs of IR£400,000 over the same period. Table 2 summarises the costs and revenues associated with Phase 1.

Table 2   Costs and revenues in phase 1 of the Jeanie Johnston project, 1998-9

	1998 IR£000s	1999* IR£000s
Capital costs		
Shipworks	1,500	2,000
Building works	500	1,000
FAS/IFI trainees	400	700
Total capital costs	2,400	3,700
Operating costs	100	300
Revenues received	0	100

*to Apr 2000
Source: Derived from Jeanie Johnston project sources

The voyage phase of the project is potentially the most lucrative from a commercial point of view though will impact little on the local tourism economy in Tralee. The visitor centre will remain open during the voyage and daily satellite transmissions from the ship to the visitor centre, by courtesy of Eircom (telecommunications company), reflects the innovative approach of the promoters to revenue generation opportunities during this phase. Voyage costs are estimated at IR£0.9m., while the anticipated revenue flows amount to IR£2.5m; public sector supports of IR£250,000 are included as costs. These revenue flows come from a variety of sources such as the sale of berths on the trans-Atlantic crossing and between north American ports, admission charges and merchandise sales in various ports and corporate breakfasts, cocktails and dinners while in port. Table 3 shows the revenue and cost estimates for the voyage duration, including cost/ revenue flows at the shipyard site/ visitor centre in Tralee.

Table 3   Costs and revenues during the voyage phase of the Jeanie Johnston project, year 2000

Voyage items	IR£000s
Voyage costs	900
Voyage revenues (incl. sale of berths to Irish corporates)	2,370
Voyage public sector subventions	250
Visitor centre items	
Overhead costs	100
Visitor centre revenues	60

Source: As for Table 2.

The final phase of the project relates to the dry-docking of the returned ship to Tralee and its use as a museum centre, for tourists and residents alike. Operating costs will clearly be scaled down at this stage (from voyage levels) and the key factor determining viability will be the success of the promoters in generating a sufficient revenue flow to adequately cover the continuing costs of operating the museum ship and associated activities (shop, restaurant, visitor centre). There may be other more innovative ways of generating revenue e.g. hosting corporate events, rent for film-making and so on which could augment the gross trading revenues. Trading costs for the year 2001 are projected at IR£300,000, which are assumed to continue at the same level in real terms for the following 17 years, in the absence of any alternative information that these costs would rise or fall relative to the general price level.

The fixed assets of the company (comprising the ship, buildings and equipment and the site) are deemed to be worth IR£5m. when fully completed. While this will underpin the borrowings associated with the project, its assumed salvage value in 2018 of a similar amount (in real terms) is included in the appraisal calculations.

The only other variable which needs to be estimated for the period from 2001 onwards is the revenue flow. This is a function of the projected number of visitors and their average spend at the site. It is assumed that 100,000 visitors will visit in 2001, buoyed up by the initial curiosity value and generate an average admission charge of IR£3 per visitor. Additional spend of IR£3 between the shop and the restaurant is deemed to lead to a gross margin or contribution of 70p per visitor. It is further assumed that while visitor numbers will fall back to 80,000 for each of the following two years, the long-term trend growth in tourism numbers of 5 per cent per annum will apply from 2004 to 2018. Average admission charges are assumed to remain constant in real terms over the same period. Table 4 summarises phase 3 outcomes based on the foregoing.

Commercial appraisal

We are now in a position to carry out a commercial appraisal of the project, taking into account the outlays and returns for all three phases of the project. The discount rate used is 5 per cent, based on the usual rate used for public sector projects; the implication here is that if the project cannot earn a real rate of return of at least 5 per cent, the resources could be better used on alternative public investments or even to reduce the national debt.

The costs and benefits are narrowly interpreted here as the capital and running costs of the project compared with the revenue flows generated. While the project promoters managed to raise both public and private sector funds to cover much of the initial capital outlays, and also benefited from the labour subsidies provided by FAS and the IFI, these capital and labour resource costs are included in appraising the commercial feasibility of the project.[15] The net present value is estimated to be – IR£1.87m. and the associated internal rate of return is 2.2 per cent, well below the returns required for commercial viability.

Table 4   Projected costs and revenues for phase 3 of the Jeanie Johnston project, 2001 to 2018

	Total costs	Visitor numbers	Visitor revenues	Shop gross margin	Restaurant gross margin	Total revenues
	IR£000s	000s	IR£000s	IR£000s	IR£000s	IR£000s
2001	300.0	100.0	300.0	40.0	30.0	370.0
2002	300.0	80.0	240.0	32.0	24.0	296.0
2003	300.0	80.0	240.0	32.0	24.0	296.0
2004	300.0	84.0	252.0	33.6	25.2	310.8
2005	300.0	88.2	264.6	35.3	26.5	326.3
2006	300.0	92.6	277.8	37.0	27.8	342.7
2007	300.0	101.9	326.0	40.7	30.6	397.3
2008	300.0	107.0	320.9	42.8	32.1	395.8
2009	300.0	112.3	336.9	44.9	33.7	415.6
2010	300.0	117.9	353.8	47.2	35.4	436.3
2011	300.0	126.8	405.7	50.7	38.0	494.4
2012	300.0	133.1	399.3	53.2	39.9	492.5
2013	300.0	139.8	419.3	55.9	41.9	517.1
2014	300.0	146.8	440.3	58.7	44.0	543.0
2015	300.0	154.1	462.3	61.6	46.2	570.1
2016	300.0	161.8	485.4	64.7	48.5	598.7
2017	300.0	169.9	509.7	68.0	51.0	628.6
2018	300.0	178.4	535.1	71.4	53.5	660.0

Source: As for Table 2.

In a purely private sector project, all the public sector grants would be seen simply as an opportunity to reduce the net investment by the private sector operator and the NPV would then be estimated on the basis of the smaller net investment outlay. In this case, if the private sector funds and donations only are used as the basic investment, the overall investment "seeking" a return would reduce by IR£2.9m. to give an NPV of IR£0.84m. and an internal rate of return of 7 per cent, ensuring a viable project. However, in taking a public sector perspective, it is more appropriate and usual to include the total investment of both public and private funds.

Economic appraisal

Even though the commercial viability of the project is in doubt, a cost-benefit analysis which takes account of the broader economic (and social) impact of the project on the wider community might suggest otherwise. Some of these costs and benefits are measurable while others are not, especially the externalities associated with the project. A similar set of costs may be used for the economic appraisal if we can assume that prices paid for various inputs reflect the true opportunity costs of these inputs.

The one case where there is some doubt on this relates to the wage rates paid for labour, brought in for the construction phase of the project in particular.[16] Since these might otherwise be unemployed (having been recruited from unemployed personnel in the first instance) it could be naively argued that their opportunity cost is zero; however, they would be unlikely to be unemployed for the duration of the project especially given the tightness of the labour market. Given that unemployment rates are higher than average in the Tralee area and that there is limited if growing pressure on the infrastructure, a shadow wage of 50 per cent for the FAS/ IFI funded workers is assumed. This reduces the 'cost' of this input to IR£550,000 in the first two years of the project. The fact that these trainees acquire useful (and transferable) shipbuilding skills, which is a positive externality arising from the project but is not included on the benefit side, supports the case for a lower net cost of labour.

Estimation of benefits

The question of displacement arises to the extent that the new venture simply diverts expenditure away from other projects in the area. The geographical area chosen will influence the measure of displacement and in this case the perspective of the public sector means that any domestic tourist spending could be considered as displacement from elsewhere in the economy. Based on visitor profiles to heritage attractions approximately 50 per cent of visitors come from the domestic market with the balance from overseas. Thus we reduce the expenditure at the site by an initial 40 per cent due to displacement[17].

Offsetting factors which might generate additional expenditure are mentioned above as the additional overseas tourists who come to Ireland or extend their stay because of the Jeanie Johnston project. It is all rather conjectural as to what these proportions are, (in the absence of any meaningful survey data) but we use the findings/ assumptions of another cost-benefit study of the National Museum transfer to Collins Barracks (Office of Public Works, 1997) as a benchmark reference for our own assumptions. In that study both high and low estimates of the number of additional overseas tourists who came to Ireland because of the museum were made (a mean value of 5.8%) and an average of 12.6 per cent was estimated as having extended their stay in the country. Given Dublin's greater accessibility than Tralee, we estimate that half these percentage figures apply to the visitors to the Jeanie Johnston i.e. 2.9 per cent were truly additional and 6.3 per cent spent an extra day in the area. The mix of visitors to the Jeanie Johnston is not known but the most recent estimates of the proportionate breakdown of the 50 per cent of overseas visitors to heritage projects in Ireland is as follows:

	%
Britain	30.4
Mainland European	32.5
North American	31.8
Other Overseas	5.3

This breakdown is used to estimate the average spend of additional tourists and then used to estimate their economic impact. *All* of their spend in the country is attributed to the Jeanie Johnston. The estimated average spend was IR£359.44 at 1999 prices. Their actual expenditure at the Jeanie Johnston site is included in their total spend and thus double-counting should be avoided. Their expenditure on access fares (to Irish airlines) is also part of their economic contribution to Irish GNP and this averaged IR£86 in 1999. An average daily spend of IR£40.69 is applied to the extended stays assumed to be attributable to the project also. Appropriate multiplier values are applied to these expenditure figures using Deane and Henry's (1993 and update) estimates of 0.947 for overseas expenditure and 0.727 for international carrier receipts.

The unique nature of the Jeanie Johnston project means that during its voyage to North America, the income generated will all be equivalent to overseas tourism revenue and full additionality can be attributed to this portion of its net revenue generation in the year 2000. However, the 'trickle-down' effects of this expenditure in the form of the indirect and induced effects will not accrue to the Irish economy but rather to that of the North American economies where the ship will be berthed over several months. Consequently, a multiplier of only 0.472 is applied to the direct spending incurred on the voyage.

The sale of berths to the Irish corporate sector (for IR£120,000) is deducted from the voyage revenue flows on the basis that if it were not spent on these it would be spent elsewhere in the economy and is equivalent to domestic tourism revenues. The revenue generation at the shipyard site and visitor centre is subjected to the same treatment in terms of the application of multiplier values as the projections forward from 2001 and for the 1999 actual revenues. Table 5 summarises the various categories of expenditure and how they are dealt with using the relevant multipliers.

Table 5   Converting various categories of tourist expenditure related to the Jeanie Johnston project into GDP impacts, 1999 – 2018

Year	Expenditure Category	Adjustment Basis/Factor	Relevant GDP Multiplier
1999	Shipyard and visitor centre (vc) revenues	Overseas proportion/reduce by 40%	0.947
2000(a)	Visitor centre revenues	Overseas proportion/reduce by 40%	0.947
2000(b)	Voyage revenues	100%	0.472
2000(c)	Sale of berths to Irish corporates	Overseas proportion = 0%	0
2001 - 2018 (a)	Museum ship and vc revenues	Overseas proportion/reduce by 40%	0.947
2001 - 2018 (b)	Incremental visitors only due to Jeanie Johnston (JJ)	2.9% of overseas visitors to JJ x IR£376.40	0.947
2001 - 2018 (c)	Incremental visitors only due to JJ	As above x access costs	0.727
2001 - 2018 (d)	Incremental stay of one day due to Jeanie Johnston	6.3% of overseas visitors to JJ x IR£40.54	0.947

Source: See text

Applying the above methodology, the NPV is estimated to be IR£3.92m. and the internal rate of return is estimated at 10 per cent, well above the minimum 5 per cent reference rate. Thus we may conclude that the project should go ahead as the wider set of benefits exceeds the additional costs incurred i.e., there is a net economic benefit or gain to the economy from the investment. If we used a "shadow wage" of 100 rather than 50 per cent for the FAS/IFI trainees, the NPV would fall to IR£3.41m and the IRR to 9.1 per cent, still well above the threshold of viability.

Conclusions

While it is clearly obvious that the economic appraisal methodology is by no means an exact science, it can provide indicative insights into the feasibility or otherwise of small to medium scale tourism projects, like the Jeanie Johnston. The gap between the commercial and economic rates of return might appear excessive and, using straight commercial criteria, the project would most likely fail standard banking assessments. The market failure addressed by the public sector intervention is akin to the "finance gap" identified in the small firm sector. The capital grants and labour subsidies fulfilled a crucial role in providing the financial lubrication for the early stage development, when revenue inflows were miniscule. The early support from the corporate sector was equally critical.[18]

The positive economic appraisal rested critically on the assumptions made about the additional and extended stay tourists in the country due to the existence of the project. There is scope for a much firmer base for these assumptions through carefully designed visitor surveys, none of which were available.

The Jeanie Johnston project is an excellent example of community tourism in which the local authority and other tourism interests in Tralee initiated the process and saw it as a highly complementary project to the existing tourism infrastructure in the town. It is part of a continuum of tourism developments there which have combined over the last ten years to provide a quantum shift in its scale of tourism activity. There are intangible benefits which could not be captured in the appraisal – local pride, attractions of scale, relative authenticity – and which might outweigh any negative economic outcomes.

Nevertheless, resources are scarce and should be used as efficiently as possible. The results of the cost-benefit analysis of the Jeanie Johnston project highlighted the expectation that, for a commercially unviable project, by taking a broader and longer term perspective, it could make a positive net contribution to the economy.

Endnotes

1.   The authors wish to thank the promoters of the Jeanie Johnston project and in particular Dr Henry Lyons (Chairman) and John Griffin (Secretary) for their excellent assistance with background information and other data which was invaluable in the preparation of this paper; and to Ann Martin and Brendan Dinneen, also of the Jeanie Johnston project for helpful insights into the project's operation; finally to Declan Dineen of the National Centre for Tourism Policy Studies, University of Limerick for assistance with

some technical aspects of the paper. Data used in the paper should be read as indicative and illustrative rather than fully accurate, to preserve the confidentiality of the source.

2.   For a discussion of these concepts of deadweight and displacement in assessing the impact of small firm support systems in the Shannon region of Ireland, see Lenihan (1999) and for similar studies in Northern Ireland and of the impact of Enterprise Boards in the UK, see Hart and Scott (1994) and Monk (1991) respectively; Wanhill (1994) presents a useful framework to assess and measure these concepts for projects which attract some tourist customers.

3.   These employment estimates ignore the 30 per cent tax recycling which features in official government estimates of tourism employment. Though the net (of recycling) employment figure for 1998 is unavailable, the gross employment total of 126,000 for 1998 represented 6.2 per cent of the 1.54m. total at work.

4.   Details of the Operational Programmes for Tourism are contained in two officials publications (see Department of Transport and Tourism, 1989 and Stationery Office, 1994) and these were set in two overall Community Support Framework documents which effectively were Ireland/s national development plans (Stationery Office, 1989 and 1993) presented to the EU Commission to cover investment priority needs over the decade, 1989-99.

5.   25m ECU and over for infrastructural projects and 15m and over for productive investments.

6.   The internal rate of return can be estimated using the same data as can the benefit-cost ratio – alternative measures of the viability of the project from a commercial point of view.

7.   For more extensive treatment of this issue see the latest edition of the Treasury's "Green Book" (HMSO, 1997).

8.   Honohan (1986) gives some interesting perspectives on the pitfalls in appraising public projects, which are still pertinent today.

9.   Wanhill (1994), Johnson and Thomas (1991) and Deegan and Dineen (1992) addressed some of these issues, particularly on associated spending, in reporting the results of their empirical studies.

10.   While tourists contribute taxes through their expenditures and these are counted as part of the measurable benefits attaching to a project, these intangible costs are rarely counted on the negative impact side of tourism projects.

11.   The timing and the scale of a project can be affected also by the amount of public funding provided and partial deadweight effects can arise.

12.   This was not attempted in the present paper.

13. The requirements to ensure the ship meets appropriate safety standards as a visitor centre and the maritime standards as a sea-going vessel added to its construction costs. The need to fit out a visitor shipyard area which could be used during the construction phase, a visitor centre, shop and restaurant areas all impacted on the initial set-up costs.

Before the ship returns from its voyage, proper car and bus parking facilities will need to be in place to cater for expected visitors to the ship from 2001 onwards.

14. Trainees were drawn from both parts of the island which attracted the funding from the IFI.

15. While this is referred to as an appraisal, it is more of an evaluation of a project already up and running in which the information collected in the initial years is used as part of the overall assessment of its feasibility; one could take the view that the initial costs for a project which is already going ahead could be regarded as sunken costs and thus have no bearing on the decision to continue with the project.

16. And through a Community Employment scheme for some of the continuing operations of the project. These latter are ignored in the analysis.

17. Based on the fact that overseas visitors spend more than domestic it is assumed they account for 60 per cent of the expenditure on-site.

18. Elan Corporation, plc, one of Ireland's largest companies with extensive U.S. interests is a major sponsor of the project.

References

Deane, B., and Henry, E. (1993), "The economic impact of tourism", *Irish Banking Review,* Apr.

Department of Tourism and Transport, (1989), *Operational programme for tourism, 1989-93,* Dublin, Department of Tourism and Transport.

Deegan, J. and Dineen D. A. (1992), "Employment effects of Irish tourism projects: a microeconomic approach", in Johnson, P., and B. Thomas (eds) *Perspectives on tourism policy,* London, Manuel, 137-156

Government of Ireland, (1989), *National Development Plan, 1989-93,* Dublin, Stationery Office.

Government of Ireland, (1993), *National Development Plan, 1994-9,* Dublin, Stationery Office.

Hart, M., and Scott, R. (1994), "Measuring the effectiveness of small firm policy: some lessons from Northern Ireland", *Regional Studies,* 28.8, 849-858.

HMSO, (1997), *Appraisal and evaluation in central government, ("The Green Book"),* London, HM Treasury.

Honohan, P., (1986), "Traps in appraising public projects", *Irish Banking Review,* Spring, 28-35.

Johnson, P., and B. Thomas, (1992), *Tourism, museums and the local economy,* Aldershot, Edward Edgar.

Lenihan, H.,(1999), "An evaluation of a regional development agency's grants in terms of deadweight and displacement", *Environment and Planning C: Government and Policy,*17, 303-318.

Monk, S. (1991), "Job creation and job displacement: the impact of Enterprise Board investment on firms in the UK", *Regional Studies,*25.4, 355-362.

Office of Public Works, (1997), *Development of the national museum of Ireland at Collins Barracks, Dublin,* Cost-benefit Appraisal Report by Tourism and Leisure Partners, Office of Public Works.

Stationery Office, (1994), *Operational Programme for Tourism, 1994-9,* Dublin, Government Publications.

Wanhill, S., (1994). "The economic evaluation of publicly assisted tourism projects" in Butler, R., and D. Pearce (eds) *Change in tourism: people, places, processes,* London: Routledge, 187-207.

WTO, (2000), *Preliminary statistics,* Madrid, World Tourism Organisation.

World heritage listing and 'best intentions': A case study from Australia

Hilary du Cros and Bob McKercher

Hong Kong Polytechnic University, Hong Kong

Abstract

World Heritage properties in Australia are mostly publicly owned and the responsibility for their management usually lies with government authorities and appointed Boards. Some of these heritage places, though, are jointly managed by Indigenous communities and government agencies, such as Uluru-Kata Tjuta National Park. The travel packages associated with mass tourism to such places, however, are mainly designed and controlled by private tourism operators. Over the last 40 years, operators promoting Uluru have largely marketed it as 'Ayers Rock', a unique natural phenomenon and secular climbing experience.

The issue this paper addresses is whether the World Heritage re-listing of Uluru as a cultural landscape with high Indigenous cultural values as well as natural values has made any difference to the presentation of Uluru by both the joint managers and the tourism operators. Also, given the situation with Uluru, how is listing likely to affect the establishment of sustainable tourism in developing countries for heritage places with high cultural values for local or Indigenous communities?

Introduction

World Heritage listing is important for recognising for posterity sites and landscapes of high cultural and/or natural value. The international treaty which embodies this principle is the World Heritage Convention for the Protection of Cultural and Natural Heritage, 1972. The World Heritage list, created under the convention, is monitored by the World Heritage Centre, an arm of the United Nations Educational, Scientific and Cultural Organisation (UNESCO), based in Paris. Nominations from sovereign governments to the list are considered by the World Heritage Committee, along with a number of other related matters.

UNESCO defines cultural heritage as "monuments, buildings and sites of historical, aesthetic, archaeological, scientific, ethnological or anthropological value"(UNESCO mission statement 12/99 see UNESCO, 3/2000). It defines natural heritage value as being associated with "outstanding physical, biological and geological formations, habitats of threatened species of animals and plants and areas with scientific, conservation or aesthetic values"(UNESCO, 3/2000). A listing to recognise the above values, however, is perceived by some to have other uses beyond that of heritage conservation and promotion of scientific research. It is also sought after by governments of developing countries, that perceive it as a type of international stamp of quality for their heritage and a marketing opportunity. World heritage listed places are often marketed as primary attractions to boost tourism and economic development in these countries. For heritage managers of these sites, a listing also provides one of the few ways of attracting overseas financial aid towards the presentation and conservation of such places (e.g. through the World Monuments Fund or UNESCO itself).

But what about the impacts of World Heritage listing? Is it always positive for the management of the heritage and does it make as much difference as many people assume? This paper will examine these issues in light of a case study from a developed country, which may bring some insights to those trying to manage World Heritage listed places elsewhere for sustainability and tourism. The case study of Uluru/Ayers Rock in Central Australia is of particular interest, as it shows how a site can be listed once, then re-listed in another category. That is, the Uluru-Kata Tjuta National Park area went from being a World Heritage site of natural value, first listed in 1987, to being re-listed as a World Heritage cultural landscape in 1994 (Uluru-Kata Tjuta Board of Management and Parks Australia, 1999). A cultural landscape is a natural area or setting, often with high aesthetic value, which also has a cultural dimension to its existence. This dimension is usually both tangible (e.g. Aboriginal rock art and camping sites) and intangible (for instance, how the landscape is understood and integrated within various cultural traditions) in kind. At last count, Australia has 13 World Heritage listings. Although several others, such as Kakadu National Park have also been listed for both natural and cultural values, only Uluru has been classified as cultural landscape to fully celebrate the fact (UNESCO, 3/2000).

Kakadu, like Uluru-Kata Tjuta National Park, is also in the Northern Territory and is jointly managed by Indigenous and Commonwealth government organisations. Uluru-Kata Tjuta has been jointly managed since 1985. In this year the traditional owners, the Anangu, through the Uluru-Kata Tjuta Aboriginal Land Trust, were granted title to the park by the Labour Commonwealth government (UKTBM and Parks Australia, 1999).

The focus of this paper is on how both the tangible and intangible heritage of the Uluru-Kata Tjuta World Heritage listing were then perceived, marketed, and managed. Such an examination provides some insights into aspects of the global vs. local situation for those considering the impacts of listing on World Heritage. Some research is starting to take place into this important issue in relation to planning for sustainability, as the latter becomes a greater goal for governments and other bodies (UNESCO, 1998; Environment Australia, 1998, p.72-74, Gonzales de Remoue, 1999). Such a discussion is also of interest to those authorities in developing countries, which may be in the early stages of marketing their tangible World Heritage and have concerns about sustainability of the intangible heritage and the communities closely associated with it.

The brand: Ayers Rock or Uluru?

The relationship between tourism and cultural heritage management is one feature of this case study. Another is the nature of the relationship between the people who are the intangible heritage tradition bearers associated with the site at a local level on one hand and the tourism industry and government, which is the global promoter of that site, on the other. It is also a study of change or lack of it in how the symbolism associated with the site is being perceived, interpreted and marketed at all levels.

The question of whether it is Ayers Rock or Uluru that is being presented to tourists is at the centre of this examination of the relationship between tourism and cultural heritage management in this case study. From a tourism marketing perspective, the monolith is the key part of the listed World Heritage cultural landscape and is still mostly seen and promoted as 'Ayers Rock' a spectacular natural phenomenon. It even appears as such in what little academic tourism and leisure research has been conducted into tourist behaviour within the Park (Fielding, Pearce and Hughes, 1992). Before going into the cultural and historical reasons behind this, some discussion is needed of the advantages and disadvantages of branding tourism attractions and destinations.

Branding is a source of competitive advantage for a destination (Aaker, 1995; Bharadwaj, Varadarajan and Fahy, 1993) that allows the destination or attraction to differentiate itself from its competitors (Evans, Fox and Johnson 1995). Importantly, brands enable it to 'own' a prominent place in the consumers' mind (Ries and Trout, 1986) and in doing so, to create an emotional bond between the consumer and the destination or attraction (Rogers, 1998). Strong brands further enable a product or destination to position itself favourably in the consumer's mind and, to re-position competitors as less attractive, or inferior products (Porter, 1991). The result is that a decision to choose a less favoured destination may bring with it the associations of having made a compromise on either quality or experience.

The creation of positive, strong and enduring brand associations is a key feature of most branding strategies. In Australia, for example, the State of Queensland has branded itself as the 'Sunshine State' and supports this brand with the slogan 'Beautiful one day, Perfect the next.' The slogan builds on past and contemporary images from Australian popular culture of beaches and attractive people frolicking in the sunshine (e.g. TV soap operas that are seen both in Australia and overseas). The combined effect of the clever marketing and public perceptions (boosted by popular culture) is so effective that Queensland is now seen as the preferred sun, sand and sea holiday destination. It is also effectively pre-empting any other Australian destination from challenging for that product category.

However, attempts to re-brand or re-position products through a change of name, price or packaging may not succeed in changing the product in the eyes of the consumer and, as such, may not achieve the desired change in position (Ries and Trout, 1986). The reason is that changing a branded product's position involves changing the mindset of the consumer, a near impossible task. Ries and Trout (as cited in Pritchard, 1995, p.23), discussing the futility of trying to alter an organisation's position once it is entrenched, state that the "more money is wasted trying to change the mind of the prospect than any other endeavour in advertising. Once the mind is made up, it's almost impossible to change" (1994, p.16).

In the case of Ayers Rock vs. Uluru and the Olgas vs. Kata Tjuta, that is exactly the challenge facing the cultural heritage management camp of traditional owners and land managers of Uluru Kata Tjuta National Park. There is an existing brand of Ayers Rock and the Olgas and changing to Uluru Kata Tjuta National Park in line with current park management philosophy is still proving difficult. Even after 15 years of Indigenous local ownership and the production and implementation of three park management plans (Australian National Parks and Wildlife Service and UKTBM, 1986 and 1991; UKTBM and Parks Australia,1999), various strategies tried by the park management has failed to erode the predominance of the Ayers Rock brand over Uluru.

Why the park management would like to change the position and public perception of 'Ayers Rock', which is the current the standardised and commoditised mass tourism experience of the monolith, is that it considers it culturally insensitive (ANPWS and UKTBM, 1991 and 1999). The brand 'Uluru' would instead represent a tourism destination that emphasises the cultural and spiritual significance of the monolith within the park. It would therefore refocus attention on more specific local meanings and away from more generalised or widely held global ones in this case. Although not stated, the park management assumes that such local meanings are compatible with or at least complement nationally held non-Indigenous views of the monolith as the national icon of 'The Rock'. But, it is Ayers Rock as the natural site, though, and not Uluru as the cultural landscape, that is still the predominant meaning from popular culture that has come support and assist marketing in this case. As the tourist literature states, "its red profile is burned forever into the national consciousness" (see Central Australia Brochure by Anon.1996/97, p.9). Re-branding it as 'Uluru' will require the undoing of almost 50 years of popular cultural representations and tourism promotion and would require also changing the mindset of the millions of tourists from around the world who have visited it.

So, this attraction is considered to be well into the mature stage of its product life cycle development and it has a tourism history and pattern of use that is already well established. The first trickle of tourists to the monolith began after World War Two. By 1958 only about 3,000 people braved the nearly 500 km of dirt track from Alice Springs to 'Ayers Rock' as the main focus of attention in the area. But as the quality of the road improved, visitation increased so that by 1968 about 23,000 visitors arrived each year (Breeden, 1994). The growth in visitor numbers to visit the site demanded tourist facilities and infrastructure, and in time a ramshackle tourist precinct evolved at the base of the Rock. The spontaneous and unplanned nature of the development soon created a host of adverse environmental impacts on the fragile desert ecology and produced significant cultural impacts on the local inhabitants. Ultimately, it was felt that the quality of the tourist experience was being compromised. And so, by the late 1970s, the Commonwealth and Northern Territory governments decided to remove all tourist facilities from the Park and to relocate them in a purpose built resort community located some 20 km away. The opening of the Ayers Rock Resort complex in 1983 really heralded the beginning of the era of mass tourism at the Rock. Visitation grew from 109,000 in 1984 to 279,000 in 1993 and 334,000 by 1995/6. Projections devised by the Ayers Rock Resort Company suggest that 450,000 people a year will visit by the turn of the century (ARR, 1996).

However, the new development of Yulara was not a financial success and in 1992, the Northern Territory government unified the ownership and management of the resort under the *Ayers Rock Act*, 1992. Ayers Rock Resort today is an integrated resort village that can accommodate over 3,000 guests a night in four hotels, an apartment complex, backpackers accommodation and a large campground. It also has a wide array of retail outlets, restaurants, and its own airport and village amenities for its 900 permanent residents. Since the government has become involved, a Resort Master Plan has been developed. New facilities have been built and Yulara airport has been upgraded to handle small passenger jets (ARR, 1997). The resort is currently owned jointly by the Northern Territory Government and the private sector, with the local Aboriginal communities having the option of purchasing a 10% equity holding at some later date.

The decision to relocate all commercial tourism infrastructure outside the national park has had a profound, yet unexpected impact on the ability of the traditional owners to influence the use of the monolith. Ironically, the consequences of assuming ownership of the Rock and expelling tourism facilities from inside the Park has resulted the near total loss of the ability of the Anangu, the principal group of tradition-bearers for the area, to influence the promotional message sent to potential visitors, and therefore their expectations. The irony of the situation is that the owners of the primary attraction, that is responsible for virtually all tourism activity for some 500 km, have no real control over tourism activity in the area outside the park. The brand name Ayers Rock is almost ubiquitous at the resort and related promotions. An internet search conducted in the Spring of 1999 revealed over 700,000 matches with the term "Ayers Rock", yet showed fewer than 800 matches with the term Uluru. Both the resort complex and the airport have assumed the name Ayers Rock (Ayers Rock Resort and Ayers Rock Airport) even though both are situated in the purpose built township of Yulara. The use of the term Ayers Rock makes sound commercial sense for the tourism industry, for it reflects the commonly known name of the region. It is much easier to sell a known product than it is to have to build awareness, interest and desire to purchase an unknown product. But, it also means that, in spite of the fact that the monolith is legally called 'Uluru' and has been so for almost 15 years, most people purchasing a commercial tourism experience (full package, airfare or simply accommodation) are forced to buy an Ayers Rock branded product. More recently, some products are offered that appear to be about Uluru, but still refer to Ayers Rock in many places as well (see current Northern Territory Tourism Website 3/2000). Selling a branded product also entails selling the brand associations that accompany the product. In this case, these associations do not entail any meaningful cultural experience and the use of 'Uluru' is merely window-dressing.

It is easy to condemn the tourism industry for its failure to use the term Uluru in its promotional material properly and to promote more culturally sensitive tourism products. However, it is simply responding to consumer demand by supplying a product desired by the travelling public. The product 'Ayers Rock' with its associated features is sold because that is what is known in the marketplace. The product 'Uluru' is not sold as hard by the industry and Northern Territory government promotions, in spite of the desires of the traditional owners and managers of Uluru Kata Tjuta National Park, for the very same reasons, it is an unknown product.

Further, from a pragmatic business perspective, it is much easier to commercialise an 'Ayers Rock' experience by providing a wider array of packaged, commoditised, short duration, products that can be consumed easily, than it is to try to package intense, long duration experiences. There is the worry that beds in the resort will not be filled, costs met and profits will not be made if one concentrates on the latter type of experience. This is because the absolute size of the market mass tourism experiences is much greater than that for longer duration experiences. It is therefore not surprising then that tourism promotional material still refers to the area almost exclusively as Ayers Rock and still sells products that focus on standard Ayers Rock experiences. Over 60 inbound and domestic tourism brochures promoting more over 300 different tours were reviewed in the process of writing this paper. The oldest brochure dated from 1987, with the most current promoting the 1999/2000 season. Remarkable consistency was noted in the product offerings made among all tour operators and all tour options presented over this period. The area is referred to exclusively as Ayers Rock in most brochures, with only a small number referring to the monolith as Ayers Rock and Uluru at the same time.

Interestingly, while the authors noted a small trend in 1996 and 1997 to co-labelling the area as Ayers Rock / Uluru, a review of brochures and internet sites promoting tours in the 1999/2000 season show a shift back to the use of the name Ayers Rock. It would appear that the desire to rename the area Uluru is more a function of hope than fact.

From the tourism perspective, what does this then say about the management of the product and its place in its product life cycle? To be successful, tourism on this mass scale needs a brand that is as well-positioned and that is associated with a mature set of tourism products, such as those associated with the 'Ayers Rock' brand, and is therefore not going to want to change it overnight for economic reasons. Finally, it is important to remember that World Heritage listing itself is a type of branding, which seems to be almost ready made for tourism promoters to use as part of a marketing strategy for such sites. That 'Ayers Rock' does not seem to emphasise it as much as some other heritage tourist attractions in Australia (e.g. the South-west Tasmanian Wilderness) is a measure of how successful or mature this product has become.

The controversial tourism activity: to climb or not to climb

In addition to the name conundrum for the park managers and site owners, there is the problem of 'the climb'. The climb up the rocky face of the monolith often follows the sunrise viewing activity for the majority of tourism packages offered to and expected by tourists (Fielding et. al 1992; McKercher and du Cros, 1998). Again, tensions between global and local, tourism and heritage management, as well as colonial and post-colonial philosophies and values can be seen. Also, between measures for the protection of tangible as against intangible heritage. While the latter is acknowledged, its protection from damaging activities by Commonwealth law (DEST, 1996) in association with a World Heritage property is rarely explored. However, such definitions in relation to intangible heritage have not been really tested much until recently with the controversy over uranium mining within Kakadu. Although the 'climb', as part of the tourism experience of this World Heritage, is not seen as a 'damaging activity' as such by intangible tradition-bearers within the Anangu, it is definitely viewed in a negative light.

The degree of compulsion in the climb depends on the tour offered. Camping tours and tours targeted at the 18 to 35 market suggest that a climb is an expected activity, while other tours only encourage their clients strongly to climb. Base tours are promoted as distinctly an inferior alternative to the climb. Even some so-called ecotourist operators, which one would expect to be more culturally sensitive, refer to the monolith alternatingly as Ayers Rock then Uluru and expect their customers to climb. Once there at the start of the climb, a type of herd instinct almost takes over and some climbers feel forced to climb by the pressures of being in a group situation without many other opportunities being presented (Fielding, et. al, 1992).

Climbing remains one of the most controversial activities inside the Park. While permitted by park authorities, traditional landowners request that people not to climb, for to do so is in violation of Tjukurpa and shows disrespect for their culture. Tjukurpa is the Pitjantjatjara word for law/environmental history, knowledge, religion and morality that is the basis of Anangu values and accounts for much of their intangible heritage. In addition, as custodians of the land, they feel personally responsible for the safety of others. Whenever anyone dies or is injured climbing, Anangu are genuinely distressed (Breeden, 1994, UKTBM and Parks Australia, 1999). Since 1962, however, more than 30 people have perished on the monolith and each year another 30 or so people need to be rescued from the site (AAP, 1997).

Climbing is still permitted by the Anangu for a variety of reasons that have little to do with its cultural acceptability. Some people believe that the Aboriginal owners of Uluru - Kata Tjuta acceded to pressures from the government in the 1980s to continue to allow large scale tourism and climbing of the Rock to occur in order to obtain ownership of the land (Altman and Finlayson, 1993). Others argue that the Anangu have a strong financial interest in maintaining a high level of visitation in the Park for they are economically dependent on tourism for their livelihood. The traditional owners receive an annual rental fee from the State and 20% of all park entry fees (the rest goes towards the park's running costs). In addition, retail sales of arts and crafts provide an important source of revenue for many people (du Cros, 1996). Actions that might restrict the appeal of the Park, like the elimination of climbing, could reduce visitor numbers, and therefore, affect the major source of income for the Anangu.

In the spirit of post-colonial values, the climb is now seen as being politically incorrect, with a number of high profile people, including the former Deputy Prime Minister and leader of the conservative National Party, Tim Fischer, apologising for climbing in the past (McKay and McDonald, 1999). By the same token, if one is to believe material issued by land managers, interest in the climb is deteriorating (UKTBM and Parks Australia, 1999). However, this assertion is not verified by the fact that the climb remains the most common and central tourism activity that is promoted in virtually every tour package. So climbing remains a core feature of the commoditised tourism experience offered and tourism operators are adamant that they would never support a total ban (McKay and McDonald, 1999).

The change of legislation

Uluru-Kata Tjuta National Park is currently managed by the Uluru – Kata Tjuta Board of Management, comprising representatives of the Anangu and Parks Australia (with the Director of National Parks, a separate statutory authority, as a third wheel). Prior to the legislative change, the Board comprised six Aboriginal people nominated by the Anangu (Tjukurpa tradition bearers), the Director of National Parks, a representative of the Federal Minister for Environment, one for the Federal Minister for Tourism, and a scientist experienced in arid land ecology and management (UKTBM and Parks Australia, 1999).

This joint management arrangement between the local people and Federal government authorities appears to have worked well and in 1996 it was awarded the UNESCO Picasso Gold Award (UNESCO, 1996). This award was in recognition of its innovative use of the Indigenous intangible heritage of Tjukurpa as the ideological framework for a Western-style park management regime.

The power balance in the joint arrangement though may be tested by the recent changes to Commonwealth environmental legislation. The new *Environment Protection and Biodiversity Conservation Act*, 1999, is the result of a review of the legislative framework for environmental and heritage management (which had mainly been developed by the previous and less conservative Federal Commonwealth government). The listing of Uluru-Kata-Tjuta as a cultural landscape and the formation of the joint management arrangement were strongly promoted by the previous Labour government that lost power in 1996. At the time of writing, the Commonwealth is using recent legislation to force two of the three joint Boards of management of this type, for Uluru Kata-Tjuta, and Kakadu National Parks, respectively, to accept a Northern Territory government representative on them (Environment Australia web site 3/2000). This will probably have a greater impact on Kakadu than Uluru, given the current controversy over the Jabiluka uranium mine. However, it is possible that it could also be aimed at reducing the power of the Aboriginal tradition bearers to protect the intangible heritage associated with both parks in the face of inappropriate tourism development.

The Northern Territory government, however, presents this move as assisting its new policy of building partnerships with Aboriginal communities (Burke, 1/6/1999), while the Commonwealth is supporting it in a bid to transfer much of its current responsibility for intervening in such issues to the states. Despite the celebration of one hundred years of Federation planned for 2001, the current Liberal Coalition Commonwealth Federal government seems bent on transferring most of its obligations to the States. This is a move, which makes national policies on development and land management less effective than state ones.

The Northern Territory (State) government's record of managing Uluru as Ayers Rock-Mount Olga National Park, before Aboriginal ownership was announced in 1985, is probably not remembered positively by the Aboriginal members of the Board. It would definitely be associated with it being 'Ayers Rock and the Olgas' as a possession of the Crown, not Aboriginal people. The current NT Government's record with Indigenous people includes its unpopular efforts to repeal land rights legislation and justify the negative impacts of Mandatory Sentencing laws on Aboriginal communities. Whilst it is correct for the government to seek a partnership with the Anangu and other Indigenous communities regarding land management, the fact that it has a strong policy of promoting mining well above tourism in economic development (Burke, 1/6/1999 and the Kakadu example) is hardly encouraging. At the moment, legislation appears to be forcing a partnership, rather than inviting one, as seen below in these recent statements about the legislation in relation to the Board:

1. The Northern Territory government representative can be only added to the Board if traditional owners on the Board consent.

2. The traditional owners may not unreasonably withhold consent.

3. The Commonwealth Ombudsman will adjudicate if there is a dispute as to whether the traditional owners have unreasonably withheld consent (Environment Australia web site, 23/3/2000).

Forcing the issue like this leads to the possibility of a change back to a more paternalistic 1950s park management style, given that there are already three other government appointees of various kinds on the Board, who could possibly form a conservative faction with the State representative. How this will sit with the past Board's policy of allowing Tjukurpa to provide the guiding principles for the management of this World Heritage cultural landscape also remains to be seen. The World Heritage Committee for UNESCO may be in for some more surprises from Australia, aside from mining in Kakadu, in this troubled time of colonial and post-colonial politics. Also, if Uluru follows the example of Kakadu, its World Heritage listing could end up making very little difference to some important management decisions, such as allowing mining or insensitive tourism development within the listing boundaries.

Conclusion

So what can be learned from the Ayers Rock/Uluru case study? First, that sustainability issues relating to the management of a heritage asset can be directly and increasingly influenced by how it is branded and packaged as a tourism product as time goes on. Sustainability issues associated with local vs. global concerns are easier to deal with early in the tourism product life cycle for a World Heritage attraction and less so later on when the tourism product it inspires becomes well known and established. Such local concerns can revolve around the way intangible as well as tangible heritage is treated and included in the management philosophy of an attraction. With the global move in tourism and heritage management towards partnerships, that include all key stakeholders, the challenge of integrating the ideologies from radically different perspectives is reduced if one examines case studies like Ayers Rock/Uluru to see the patterns and trends amongst the complexity of issues. Although the picture presented by this case study may be not always as positive as the most post-colonial amongst us would like, it is important to realise that there was always the possibility of threats as well as opportunities for such a listing from the very start.

Part of the challenge of working practically with the 'best intentions' associated with making a listing into a sustainable tourism attraction is a full appreciation of the economic, political and social impacts of that ideal. A guaranteed strategy for sustainability that integrates the protection of tangible and intangible heritage values with commercial and political factors does not automatically appear out of nowhere as soon as a heritage asset is listed (or re-listed) as having World Heritage values. However, it is important to get in early (even before it is listed) to form partnerships that can regularly debate difficult issues associated with the local vs. global dichotomy (without undue political or economic pressure being put on stakeholders). Commencing the partnership process is a necessary first step towards an integrated history of managing a heritage attraction, which will then support the ideals associated with a World Heritage listing.

Uluru-Kata Tjuta National Park did not have the opportunity of forming a shared management history of this type and much of the product development on the tourism side, and management philosophy on the park management side, was established separately. It is much harder then for this heritage asset, despite being World Heritage listed, to become a sustainable tourism attraction than it would for a less well known or recently listed heritage asset that addresses this issue to become one. An attraction that properly cultivates an integrated partnership from the earliest stage of its tourism product life cycle is much more likely to work through sustainability issues than one in the mature stage of the life cycle, such as this particular case study.

References

Aaker, D. A. (1995), *Strategic Market Management*, 4th Edition, John Wiley, BrisbaneAAP (1997), Japanese tourist 30th victim of Uluru climb *The Australia* February 24, 1997.

Altman, J. C. and Finlayson, J. (1993), Aborigines, Tourism and Sustainable Development *The Journal of Tourism Studies* 4 (1), pp.38 – 48.

Anon. (1997), *Central Australia*. Brochure 1996/7.

ARR, (1996), Ayers Rock Resort Company Annual Report 1995, Ayers Rock Resort Yulara, NTARR (1997), Ayers Rock Resort Company Annual Report 1996, Ayers Rock Resort, Yulara, NT

ANPWS and Uluru-Kata Tjuta Board of Management, (1986), Uluru (Ayers Rock - Mount Olga) National Park management Plan, Uluru-Kata Tjuta Board of Management, Australian National Parks and Wildlife Service, Yulara.

Bharadwaj, S. G., Varadarajan, P. R., Fahy, J. (1993), Sustainable Competitive Advantages in Service Industries: A conceptual model and research propositions *Journal of Marketing* 57 (4), pp. 83 - 99.

Breeden, S. (1994), *Uluru: Looking After Uluru Kata Tjuta the Anangu Way* Simon and Shuster, Sydney.

Burke, D. (1999), Chief Minister's Speech to Parliament. Northern Territory Government Web site (posted 1/6/1999): http://www.nt.gov.au/foundations/speech.shtml

Department of Environment Sport and Territories (1996), *World Heritage Listing. What does it really mean?* World Heritage Unit, Department of Environment Sport and Territories, Canberra.

du Cros, H. (1996), Committing Archaeology in Australia. Unpublished Ph.D, Centre for Australian Studies, Monash University, Melbourne.

Environment Australia, (1998), Environmental Indicators for National State of the Environment Reporting: Natural and cultural heritage. Australia: State of the Environment

Environmental Indicator Report. Environment Australia, Department of Environment, Canberra.

Environment Australia (1999), The Environment Protection and Biodiversity Act, 1999: Indigenous Issues. Government Web site (posted 15/10/1999): http//www.environment.gov.au/epbc/EPBC Indigenous.htm

Evans, M. R., Fox J. B., Johnson, R. B. (1995), Identifying Competitive Strategies for Successful Tourism Development *Journal of Hospitality and Leisure Marketing* 3 (1), pp. 37 - 45.

Fielding, K. A., Pearce, P. A., Hughes, K. (1992), Climbing Ayers Rock: Relating visitor motivation, time perception and enjoyment *The Journal of Tourism Studies* 3(2), pp. 49 – 57.

Gonzales de Remoue, (1999), Peru's 'Meet the People' Tours. *UNESCO Courier* 5/6 1999:34.

McKay, S., and MacDonald, J. (1999), Fischer's Uluru view sparks row *The Age* Feb 15, 1999.

McKercher, B. and du Cros, H. (1998), I Climbed to the Top of Ayers Rock but Still Couldn't See Uluru! In Faulkner, D, Tideswell, C, and D. Weaver (eds) *Progress in Tourism and Hospitality Research 1998*, CAUTHE/BTR Canberra: 376-86.

Northern Territory Tourism, (3/2000), Official Web site: http://www.nttc.com.au

Porter, M. E. (1991), Know Your Place, *Inc.* 13 (9), pp. 90 - 95.

Pritchard, B. (1995), *Complex Marketing Made Simple*, Milner Books, Los Angeles.

Ries, A. Trout, J. (1986), *Positioning*, McGraw Hill, New York.

Rogers, D. (1998), Travel: Sun, sea and brands. *Marketing:* 17.

Uluru-Kata Tjuta Board of Management and ANPWS, (1991), Uluru (Ayers Rock - Mount Olga) National Park management Plan, Uluru-Kata Tjuta Board of Management, Australian National Parks and Wildlife Service, Yulara.

Uluru-Kata Tjuta Board of Management and Parks Australia, (1999), *Uluru-Kata Tjuta Tjukurpa Warara: Draft Plan of Management*. Uluru-Kata Tjuta Board of Management and Parks Australia, Canberra.

UNESCO, (1996), *World Heritage Newsletter No. 10, March* World Heritage Centre, UNESCO, Paris.

UNESCO, (1998), Report by the Director-General on the precise criteria for the selection of cultural spaces or forms of cultural expression that deserve to proclaimed by UNESCO to be Masterpieces of the Oral and Intangible Heritage of Humanity. 155th Session, Paris.

UNESCO, (3/2000), Official Web site: http://www.unesco.org/whc/2gift.htm

Heritage resources and tourism promotion in Nigeria: The way forward

L C Ekechukwu

University of Nigeria, Nigeria

Introduction: Nigeria - background information

Nigeria, with an area of about 923,768 square kilometres (356,669 square miles) and an estimated population of 88.5 million people, is one of most populous black nations in the world. It is located in West Africa and lies between latitudes 4^0N and 14^0N, and longitudes 3^0E and 15°E of Meridian. It is bounded in the north by the Republic of Chad and Niger, in the east by the Republic of Cameroon, in the west by Benin Republic and in the south by the Gulf of Guinea (Atlantic Ocean).

The country is endowed with accessible natural environments, which encouraged and facilitated movements and inter-group relations long before the advent of modern means of communication. There are highland areas with heights that range from 300 metres to over 600 metres above sea level. The two most important rivers in Nigeria are the Rivers Niger and the Benue. Lakes also constitute important physical features. Among the significant ones are Lake Chad, Kainji Lake, Nike Lake and Oguta Lake. Some of these lakes serve as holiday resorts while others are used for fishing and as sources of water for irrigating the land.

The mean maximum temperature is about 34.44°C in the northern area and about 30.55°C in the coastal area of the country. The mean minimum temperature is about 22.2°C over the South and 18.55°C in the North. There is a high rainfall variability throughout the country and this influences the varying types of vegetation in parts of the country. Nevertheless these many variants of vegetation can be subsumed under two broad categories, namely, forest and savannah.

Nigeria is culturally heterogeneous. About 395 languages have been identified in the country, and these have been grouped by linguists under a number of language families and sub-families. The larger linguistic and politically dominant groups include the Igbo, Yoruba, Hausa and Fulani. Other prominent but less numerous groups includes the Edo, Ibibio,

Nupe, Tiv, Efik, and Urhobo. The peoples of Nigeria have been exposed to centuries of external influences with such influences coming mainly from across the Sahara and Europe.

The country, presently, operates the presidential system of government with an Executive President as the Head of State and Government. In the present political dispensation, there are 36 states in the country.

Figure 1   Political Map of Nigeria

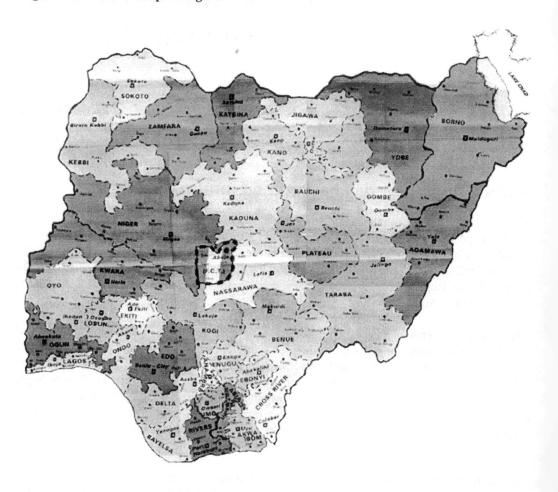

Figure 2 Nigeria – Ethnic Group

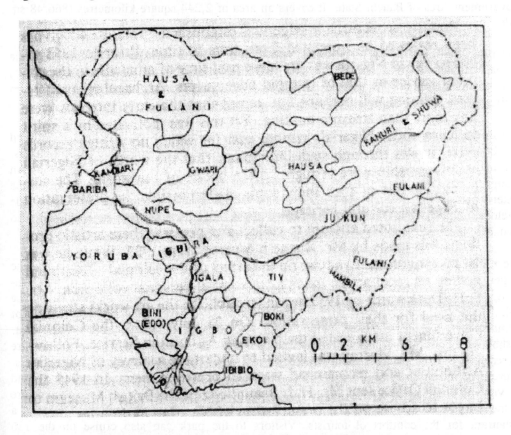

Selected tourist attraction in parts of Nigeria

Nigeria's rich heritage resources, which are both natural and cultural are important tourist attractions in the country today. These diverse tourist attractions can be found in virtually every locality in the country. Among the tourism and recreational resources in Nigeria are protected ecosystems, protected landscapes, unused lands, cultural sites and resources, to mention but a few (Ekechukwu, 1990).

The protected ecosystems in Nigeria are very often referred to as "Nature Reserves". The colonial administration promoted the creation of these nature reserves in areas referred to as buffer zones between major kingdoms. Protected ecosystems in Nigeria also include the numerous forest reserves which came into being as a result of the Forest Administration Plan formulated between 1945 and 1946 by the colonial administration. As a result of this plan, forest reserves in Nigeria were classified into four categories on the basis of use and management among which are the game reserves. These game reserves are important tourist attractions in Nigeria and they are nearly all located in the savannah zones. There are about 33 game reserves in Nigeria, most of which are, however, non-functional (Areola, 1976). The two most important game reserves are the Yankari Game Reserve in Bauchi and the Borgu, which forms part of the Kainji National Park.

The Yankari Game reserve is located in Duguri, Pali and Gwana Districts of Alkaleri Local Government Area of Bauchi State. It covers an area of 2,244 square kilometres (866.48 sq. miles) and was officially opened to the public in December 1962.

The reserve affords the visitor an opportunity to see wildlife in its natural habitats. Game animals found at the reserve include buffalos, lions, roan antelopes, elephants, hippopotamus, baboons, water and bushbucks, wester hartebeasts, etc. The Wikki Warm Spring is also located there.

The Borgu Game Reserve, which is the largest game reserve in Nigeria is located between the Kainji Lake and the Republic of Benin border. It covers an area of 3,929 sq. kilometres. The major part of the Reserve was brought under protection between 1962 and 1963. An extension was later made to the Reserve which includes a section of the lake shore on the eastern part of the Reserve. The Reserve has various species of animals, which include antelopes, hippopotamus, reindeer, bush-cows, lions, leopards, side-stripped jackal, assorted monkeys, birds and reptiles.

The Kainji Lake National Park and Dam Complex, the first national park in Nigeria and the biggest in West Africa, covers an area of 5,340.82 sq. kilometres and consists of two non-contiguous sectors. These are the Borgu and Zugurama. It is bordered in the east by the Kainji Lake and in the west by the Republic of Benin. The park contains a wide variety of animals that include elephants, hippopotamus, warthog, buffaloes, roans hartebeast, bushbucks, lions, waterbucks, red-flanked duikers, leopards, etc. The primates are represented by Red patas, Tantalus monkeys, and other species of monkeys and baboons. There is abundant bird life in the park as well. The lakeshore provides on excellent ground for viewing both local and migrating birds and reptiles. The "Olli River Lodge" in the centre of the Borgu sector of the Park, provides chalet accommodation with full facilities and a restaurant for the comfort of tourists. Visitors to the park can also cruise on the 136 kilometre long Kainji Lake.

Nigeria also has a rich store of protected landscapes. These landscapes are usually areas of exceptional scenic beauty and charm or areas of scientific importance. They are usually protected for recreational purposes and they include areas with rugged landscape, waterfalls and land-falls. In Nigeria, such areas of scenic beauty include the Ikogosi Warm Springs in Ondo State, the Warm Springs along the Benue/Gongola valleys, the Wikki Warm Spring in Bauchi, the spectacular erosion gullies in Anambra State, the Nsukka-Udi-Okigwe cuesta landscape, the Jos Plateau with its beautiful and captivating landscape and mild climate, the Birma Hills in Bauchi State, the Mambilla Plateau in Taraba State and other landscape features of exquisite beauty located in different parts of the country. A description of some description of some of these landscape features will suffice to show their tourist potential.

The Mambilla Plateau which lies to the southern tip Taraba State is noted for its rich scenic beauty and serene environment. The plateau which is over 1,830 metres above sea level, has a temperate climate with green pasture vegetation. Mambilla itself, located about 550 kilometres from Yola, forms parts of the Adamawa, Obudu, Shebshi, Alantika and Mandara Mountain Chain. The Plateau has a gently undulating topography, with beautiful green scenery which is characteristic of the temperate regions.

Some temperate plants such as Arabic coffee, tea, pear and Irish potatoes grow very well on this plateau. A beautiful resort called the Mambilla Tourist Centre is also located on the Plateau. It is situated about 1,830 metres above sea level. The ranch on the Plateau is home to more than a million cattle and is free from tse-tse fly and mosquito attacks. The Game Reserves hold various species of animals such as buffaloes, lions, hyena and elephants as well as reptile like crocodiles and alligators. There are waterfalls in the reserves and together with the numerous coffee and tea plantations on the Plateau provide important attractions for tourists.

The Ikogosi Warm Springs are located at Ikogosi about 55 kilometres from Akure, the capital of Ondo State. The warm springs roll down over a hilly landscape. From another hill flows a cold spring which joins the warm ones at a confluence and together they form a continuous stream. The entire landscape with its beautiful vegetation is rather captivating and fascinating. The immediate surrounding of the spring has tall evergreen trees which form a canopy under which visitors can relax. The springs is believed to have therapeutic effects on some diseases like rheumatism and guinea worm.

The Owu waterfall which is located about 7 kilometres from Owa Kajola in ifelodun local government area of Kwara State has been described as the highest and most spectacular natural water fall in West Africa. The fall has also been described as a "wonder in the wilderness" and is said to compare with the Niagara Falls in the U.S.A and the Victoria Falls in East Africa (GCA travels, 1994). The water of this fall, which issues from a perennial stream, cascades from a height of about 100-120 metres. At the base of the fall is a pool of almost ice-cold water that provides a most refreshing atmosphere with the luxuriant evergreen vegetation surrounding and embellishing it.

The country is also blessed with a rich store of unused lands, which include a large part of the Niger Delta and other natural environment areas with beautiful sceneries that have great potential as tourist attractions. It has been said that Nigeria has an estimated 800 kilometres of coastline with very enticing sandy beaches, with coconut groves which can be transformed into holiday resorts of international standard. Among the important sandy beaches in Nigeria is the Bar Beach located on Victoria Island in Lagos. It is one of the most pleasurable resorts in the city of Lagos, the former capital of the Federal Republic of Nigeria. At the Beach, visitors are treated to a splendid exotic view of the Atlantic Ocean. Different types of sports can be undertaken by visitors who also camp on the beach. Another important sandy beach is the one located on River Ethiope in Delta State. Along the beach are located several fishing villages that add colour to life on the beach. The Badagry Beach in Lagos is also a beautiful spot to reckon with.

The rich cultural sites and resources with which Nigeria is endowed are archaeological sites and their discoveries some of which are very famous in the world, historic towns and sites cultured festivals of several types museums and monuments of various kinds, sacred shrine and groves as well as other relics and man-made features that serves to remind us about the past and show us the present. Among the important archaeological discoveries in Nigeria are the Nok Culture, Igbo-Ukwu, Ife, and Benin. Other important archaeological discoveries have also being made at Owo, Ugwuele, Daima, the Benue Valley, Lejja and Opi in Nsukka Area, to name just a few. The terracotta figurines discovered in the Nok culture area and Ife, the bronze objects excavated from Benin, Igbo-Ukwu and the lower Niger areas have made

Nigeria a place worth visiting for culture related tourism. Among the ancient cities and towns in Nigeria are Kano, Katsina, Benin, Opobo, Calabar, Badagry and Lokoja. Most of these cities and towns still retain some important relics of the past such as ancient city walls and other architectural features inspite of the influence of modernity several museums are located in different parts of Nigeria today. Most of these are national museums, which are run by the National Commission for museums and Monuments. Other museums owned by state and local governments as well as private museums also abound in the country. The Nationals museums include those located in Lagos Benin, Enugu, Jos, Kaduna, Kano, Aba, Umuahia, Ibadan and calabar. Important national Monuments in Nigeria include the ancient city walls such as those kano and Benin, the statues of the past king and chiefs of the Niger Delta such as those of king Jaja of Opobo, Chief Oshikoya of Nembe, King Dappa Pepple of Bonny, King Nana of Itsekiri and others. Other important monuments are Chief Ogiamen's house in Benin City, Obu house at Elu Ohafia, Gidan Matama in Kano, the Rock-Paintings in Birnin Kudu in kano State, the Geji Rock Paintings in Bauchi State, the Chira Rock Paintings in the ancient city of Surame in Sokoto State as well as Chief Okoroji's house at Arochukwu, to name but a few.

An important shrine in Nigeria is the Osun Osogbo shrine located about 112 kilometres North-East of Ibadan. This shrine is the venue for the celebration of the Osun festival which is an annual festival that takes place during the month of August. People from far and near usually converge in the town during the celebration to watch the Osun worshippers descend on the banks of River Osun to offer sacrifices to the goddess of the River at the Osun Osogbo shrine. Visitors are allowed into the Osun grove, on other days, to view an assemblage of images of Yoruba gods. The Osun grove is now a national monument. Another important shrine that has helped in promote religious tourism in Nigeria is the Omukwu temple in Ohafia.

In Nigeria, there are probably as many traditional arts and crafts as there are different peoples and cultures and these artistic traditions of the Nigerian peoples are today being modified for economic reasons (Okpoko, 1990). For instance, the Annang in Akwa Ibom State produce a beautiful variety of cane and raffia crafts such as chairs, tables, baskets, bags, hats, beds and so on. In Kano, Sokoto and Bornu States skilled craftsmen produce high quality leather goods that can serve the needs of different classes of people including tourists. The Benin people of Edo State are noted for their high quality brass-works while the Nupe people are acclaimed producers of glass materials such as glass beads. The Nkwerre and Awka people in Igbo-land are acknowledged masters in blacksmithery. The Akwete, Iseyin, Okene and Aniocha (Delta State) are noted for high quality locally made textiles. Several Nigerian groups produce pottery, some engage in grass and mat-weaving while others engage in the making of varieties of jewellery as well as wood-carving. These arts and crafts represent Nigeria's legacies of a rich past.

Nigeria has abundant traditional festivals which are usually celebrated in different places at various seasons of the year, depending on the nature and purpose of such festivals. In Igboland, the most popular festival remains the New Yam Festival which is celebrated in different Igbo communities between the months of August and October each year (Okpoko, 1990). An important festival in Nigeria is the Argungu, Fishing and Cultural festival which is celebrated annually in Kebbi State. The festival has developed to an internationally accepted annual socio-cultural event attracting tourists from different parts of the world. The scenic beauty of the village and its adjacent geographical splendour and features add more to the tourist attractions of the Argungu (GCA Travels, 1994, p.116). Other fishing festivals include the Nwunyo Annual Fishing Festival at Ibi and the Njuwa Fishing Festival all in Taraba State. In addition to traditional festivals, modern festivals of Arts and Culture are now organised at National, State and Local Government levels in Nigeria today. These modern festivals take place at officially approved venues on specific dates. An example of such modern festivals in Nigeria is the Mmonwu (Masquerade) Festival instituted by the government of former Anambra State aimed at boosting tourism in the state.

Modern facilities and resorts that have been provided for the comfort of visitors and aimed at promoting tourism abound in the country today. For instance, new hotels of international standard have sprung up in different parts of the country to meet the demand in the tourist industry. Recreational facilities like swimming pools, discotheque, bars and different types of games are also provided in these hotels for the comfort of visitors. Important hotels in Nigeria include the Nicon Nuga Hilton, the Sheraton Hotels and Towers all in Abuja, the Federal Capital Territory; the L' Hotel Eko Meridien, Federal Palace Hotel, Ikoyi Hotel, Airport Hotel, Durbar Hotel, Ikeja Hilton Hotel, all in Lagos. Others are the Bagauda Lake Hotel in Kano; the Nike Lake Resort in Enugu; the Hill Station in Jos; Hamdala Hotel in Kaduna; Imo Concorde Hotel in Owerri; Shiroro Hotel in Minna; etc. In addition to hotels, there are holiday camps around some of the important tourist attractions.

Good facilities for air, water, rail and road transport are available in the country. For instance, Nigeria is served with a network of airports that operate both local and international flight services as well as good motorable roads that crisis-cross the country. The inland waterways are an important aspect of the communication system especially in the riverine areas of the country. This is in addition to the large number of ocean going vessels that enter the country's territorial waters through the Atlantic Ocean. The rail transport system in the country is also developed for mass transit of passengers.

Plate 1   Nok Style Terracotta Head from the Nok Culture

(Source: Discovering Nigeria's Past (ed.) Thubstan Shaw, Page 41)

Plate 2   Kano Museum, Gidan Makama, A National Monument

(Source: Discovering Nigeria's Past (ed.) Thubstan Shaw, Page 84)

Plate 3   Bronze Roped Vessel from Igbo-Ukwu

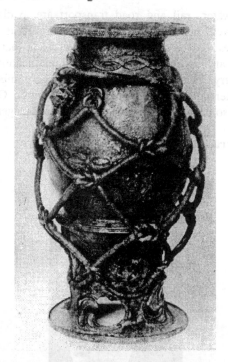

(Source: Discovering Nigeria's Past (ed.) Thubstan Shaw, Page 46)

History of tourism development in Nigeria

Tourism in Nigeria, as in other countries in the West-African sub-region, has an old beginning. It could be traced to about the 4th century A.D. when the great empires and kingdoms began to emerge in the West African Sudan. Between the 4th and 19th Century, such great empires as Ghana, Kaniaga, Mali, Songhai and Kanem-Bornu grew in succession. Within the same period, a number of forest kingdoms such as Oyo, Benin, Dahomey and Ashanti had also emerged to the south (Fage, 1969). These empires and kingdoms played a vital role in promoting pre-colonial tourism because they hosted such foreigners as scholars, adventurers, travellers and traders who also paid homage to the rulers of the places they visited. Trade objects were exchanged between the visitors and the inhabitants of the areas they visited and in addition these visitors carried home accounts and narratives about their hosts and this stimulated further interest in these exotic lands.

Books on West African History are replete with accounts of royal visits, religious pilgrimages, tributes and exchanges between one ruling dynasty and the other in pre-colonial West Africa. For example, the religious pilgrimage performed in 1324 by Mansa, Musa, the Emperor of Mali, is very significant in the history of tourism in this sub-region. The Alafin of Oyo was also known to have received gifts and tributes from Dahomey, a neighbouring kingdom, in the 18th century (see Okpoko, 1988, p.14). Portugese and Dutch traders and travellers also gave a detailed description of the walls of ancient Benin Kingdom and its inhabitants in about the 15th and 16th Century A.D. (Connah 1975, p.32).

The position of Kano as an important centre of trade, culture and learning along the transaharan trade-naute in pre-colonial Nigeria is also worthy of note in the context of the early beginnings of tourism in Nigeria.

Da Silva (1985) is of the opinion that Nigeria hosted her first European visitors in 1472 when the first batch of Portugese arrived in Lagos. Some experts and writers on tourism are of the view that the first attempt to manage Nigeria's tourism resources, especially the cultural aspect, under British Colonial administration was made with the establishment of the colonial Antiquities commission and the Federal Department of Antiquities by an Act of Parliament in 1953 (Okpoko 1988). This piece of legislation, popularly known as "Ordinance 17", was passed in parliament on the basis of a Bill introduced in the Federal House of Representatives by late Sir Abubakar Tafawa Balewa, the first Prime Minister of Independent Nigeria, then Minister of works, who saw "the urgent need to protect and preserve the history and artistic relics of the country for the benefit of the present and future generations".

In 1959, and Ad-hoc committee on tourism was inaugurated under the auspices of the Nigerian Ministry of Commerce and Industry. This Ad-hoc committee later paved the way for the establishment of the Nigerian Tourist Association, a quasi-government organisation, in 1962. This Association was charged with the responsibility of promoting a "healthy domestic tourism programme in the country and international tourism for its foreign exchange benefits" (Da Silva 1985). The efforts of this Association made possible the admission of Nigeria as a full member of the International Union of Official Travel Organisation, IOUTO, now World Tourism Organisation, WTO, in 1964. According to Okpoko (1988), no concerted effort was made to provide a programmatic government policy that would give financial and administrative support to tourism development in the country. It was not until 1975, 13 years after the establishment of the Nigeria Tourist Association, that tourism received a boost in the nation's economic planning with an allocation of 120 million by the then Military Government.

In 1976, one year later, the military administration in the country established the Nigeria Tourist Board by Decree 54. The Board was charged with the responsibility of promoting the development of tourism in Nigeria through co-ordinated researches, planning and publicity. It was specifically mandated to encourage people living in Nigeria to take their holidays locally and people from overseas to visit Nigeria; to encourage the provision and improvement of tourist amenities and facilities in Nigeria and to render financial assistance to the states in the field of tourism. In spite of the provisions of Decree 54, only a few of the tourist attractions in the country enjoyed either Federal or State government support (Olasebikan 1987, p.11). Among those attractions that received this support are the Yankari Game Reserve in Bauchi State; the Ikogosi Warm Spring in Ondo State; the Badagry Beach in Lagos State; Olumo Rock in Ogun State and Obudu Cattle Ranch in Cross River State. Following the establishment of the Nigerian Tourist Boad, most state governments inaugurated State Tourism Committees as demanded by the decree. These State Tourism Committees were mandated to take positive measures to develop the tourist potentials in their respective domains.

A number of states constituted or reconstituted their Tourism Committees and they include Lagos State in 1985, Kaduna State in 1986.

Some States such as Plateau also endeavoured to involve the private sector in tourism development. Regrettably, however, most of these efforts were geared towards hotel development as if it is the only area within the tourism sector that deserved attention. At this time also people who knew the impact of tourism on economic development were agitating for the creation of a full-blown Ministry of Tourism instead of placing it under the Ministry of Trade or Commerce, as was the arrangement in the country for a very long time.

As a result of mounting foreign-debt burden and the increasing desire to reduce the over-dependence on crude oil as the country's main source of foreign exchange, the government decided to diversify its revenue base. One of the 'preferred sector industries' for achieving this dream was tourism. In view of this and in line with the aspirations of the people, tourism was accorded a ministerial status through the creation of Ministry of Commerce and Tourism in 1985.

In 1990, the Federal Military Government launched a blue print on tourism to demonstrate its commitment to the development and promotion of tourism into an economically viable industry. The main trust of the National Tourism Policy is to generate foreign exchange, encourage even development, promote tourism-based rural enterprises, generate employment and accelerate rural-urban integration and cultural exchange (National Tourism Policy, 1990). The policy objectives were to be accomplished through broad guidelines spelt out in the blue print (see The National Tourism Policy, 1990). The strategies to be adopted as well as the institutional framework necessary for the implementation of the strategies were also made clear.

In line with the new government policy to meet the challenges of the time as well as to give a greater boost to tourism development in the country, Decree 54 was amended by Decree 81 of 1992 to give birth to the Nigerian Tourism Development Corporation, NTDC. The Nigerian Tourism Development Corporation is the apex tourism agency of the Federal Republic of Nigeria charged with the overall promotion, marketing and co-ordination of tourism activities in the country.

In realisation of the belief that tourism is an integral part of culture and also to help promote tourism at the grass-roots level, the Federal Government under President Olusegun Obasanjo, established the Ministry of Culture and Tourism in mid - 1999. To give greater dynamism to the activities of this strategic ministry, Chief Ojo Maduekwe was appointed the Minister. The new ministry is proposing a new Master Plan for the development of the country's heritage resources. As a first step, a national survey of all tourism resources in the country is being planned in order to have an inventory of these resources which is an important prelude to their development.

Although tourism development in Nigeria has undergone a gradual evolution, its impact on the economy is yet to be seen. Spirited efforts have been made by successive governments, their agencies as well as private entrepreneurs to develop Nigeria's abundant heritage resources into a viable tourism industry. Unfortunately most of these tourism development plans have hardly yielded the desired dividends due to a number of problems. One of the most crucial has been identified as the absence of a strong tourism culture among Nigerians. This situation has been blamed on the low impetus given to public education.

If the public is adequately informed about the importance of these heritage resources as ingredients for tourism development then the people will begin to patronise them and promote their use. This will eventually translate into greater economic growth as these tourism products begin to yield fruits and better national integration can be achieved when people start to see these resources as their shared heritage. The other problems has to do with the ineffectiveness of some of the legislation that gives protection to some of these heritage resources thereby making them vulnerable to man's destructive tendencies. With increasing development projects and growing urbanisation in Nigeria, for instance, most of our cultural heritage resources such as archaeological sites, sacred groves and shrines, monuments as well as ancient cities and towns which are indispensable components in our tourism development schemes, are facing serious threats. They provide the foundation upon which our cultural tourist trade could be built but this is yet to be appreciated. Again most of the Tourism Development Plans that have been launched in this country over the years may have appeared laudable and well articulated but they usually failed at the implementation stage. The failure may sometimes arise from the absence of an enabling environment for the implementation or from the absence of qualified manpower or from lack of commitment on the part of those chosen to implement the plans. It is necessary to point out also, that the immigration formalities at the borders or at the airports have sometimes posed some problems for international tourism traffic flow in this country. Recently, however, the Federal Government has taken measures to relax these entry formalities in order to eliminate the inconveniences faced by tourists to Nigeria.

Charting a new course

Looking at the problems highlighted above, it would appear that inspite of the huge reservoir of cultural and natural heritage resources available in the country, which can support a thriving tourism industry, the industry has not succeeded in achieving good results in so far as turning the economy around is concerned. In spite of the seeming odds, however, it is still possible to adopt new approaches that could ensure the systematic and sustainable development of the tourism industry in the country. These new approaches being suggested here could be incorporated in the Master Plan proposed for the country to ensure that the economic and socio-cultural values of these tourism resources are optimised.

The first approach is to make our tourism industry people-oriented in order to make them stewards of their heritage. The approach recognises the close connection between tourism development and the local population. This helps to carry them along in the process of development and ultimately encourage sustain ability. (See Arua, E. O. et al, 1999, p.4). This approach is informed by the fact that most of these attractions are located in places where these local people live, especially in the rural communities. It will, therefore, be necessary to incorporate in the Master Plan a frame work that will involve the people in the development and promotion of these tourist attractions. This could go a long way in creating awareness among the local population and help in promoting tourism at the grass roots level. To actualise this, the role of the Local Governments and their Tourism Committees as catalyst cannot be over-emphasised.

The second approach is that there should be a comprehensive inventorization of all the tourist attractions and sites in the country in order to adequately document them. In this regard, a video documentary of the selected sites and attractions will be desirable (Arua, E.O et al, 1999, p.4). In addition, brochures should be produced to complement the documentary. Such materials could be used to advertise and sell the tourist attractions locally and overseas. Also tourist offices which should be created in our foreign missions abroad should be charged with the responsibility of advertising and marketing these tourism products to potential tourists abroad. The free-listing approach should be adopted in the inventorization exercise in order to identify potential and actual attractions in the country. After free-listing, the method of rank-ordering should be used to prioritise the attractions in order to select the popular ones that should be developed before others. An environmental assessment of the selected sites and attractions will also be necessary before embarking on their development.

Another important approach to ensure sustain-ability within the industry is to initiate the process of tourism education in the country in order to inculcate tourism culture among Nigerians. To facilitate this, the Federal Ministry of Culture and Tourism along with its agencies should collaborate with researchers, institutes and departments in our tertiary institutions that specialise in tourism and related fields. The Ministry should also encourage the involvement of tertiary institutions in the country in the training of personnel for the tourism industry which is almost the exclusive preserve of the National training Scheme for Catering and Tourism Occupation. This sort of encouragement could come through affiliations with these tertiary institutions in these training programmes.

To ensure sustainability, community-oriented infrastructural facilities should also be provided in those areas where these sites and attractions are located. To promote local involvement, ancillary industries should be encouraged.

Nigeria is endowed with a rich array of tourist attractions that could be meaningfully harnessed and sold to boost the nation's economy, reduce unemployment and minimise the undue emphasis on petroleum exploitation to the consequent neglect of other sectors. To help achieve these and other objectives, the proposed master plan for tourism development in Nigeria should adopt certain approaches such as those highlighted above that could help promote as well as sustain a viable tourism industry in the country.

References

Areola, O. (1976), Recreational Landuse Nigeria, *Geographical Journal*,(NGJ),19,(2).

Arua, E. O., et al.(1999), *Cultural Tourism Masterplan for Southeast Nigeria*, University of Nigeria, Nsukka Research Team, Nsukka, Enugu State.

Discovering Nigeria's Past, Oxford University press, Ibadan, pp.27-38.

Da Silva, M. C. (1985), Opportunities for Nigeria in the Tourism industry- Public Service Lecture, Paper presented at the Nigerian Institute of International Affairs, Lagos, 2nd April.

Ekechukwu, L. C (1990), Encouraging National Development through the promotion of Tourism. The place of Archaeology, *West African Journal of Archaeology*, (WAJA), 120 pp.120-124.

Fage, J. D. (1969), *Introduction to the History of West African*, Cambridge University Press.

Federal Government of Nigeria, (1990), *National Tourism Policy, Ministry of Commerce and Tourism*, Federal Government Printer, Lagos.

G. C. A. Travels, (1994), *International Tourist Guide to Nigeria*, Format. Press Ltd., Lagos.

Okpoko, P. U. (1990), *Developing Tourism In Nigeria: The Place of Cultural Resources*, MA Dissertation, University o f Ibadan, Ibadan.

Olasebikan, D. (1987), Tourism-Historical perspective, *Sunday Times*, Lagos, Dec.13, p.11.

A tale of two world heritage cities: Old Quebec and maritime Greenwich

Graeme Evans

University of North London, UK

Melanie Smith

University of Greenwich, UK

Introduction

The following compares and considers the world heritage sites (WHS) represented by the historic quarter and fortifications of Quebec City, eastern Canada and the maritime heritage area of Greenwich, south-east London, England. These urban heritage sites were inscripted by UNESCO/ICOMOS in 1985 and 1997 respectively, and represent over 400 years of settlement and the built heritage and therefore serve as symbolic attractions in their host cities. The local and national governments and agencies responsible for both sites applied rationales for WHS designation which rested on conservation on the one hand, and tourism development on the other. These sites also share a naval and colonial 'theme', in the case of Quebec one that is also contested and re-interpreted in terms of both francophone and anglophone stages of 'ownership' and of Canadian unitary nationhood and 'hidden' First Nation history. When the British garrison finally vacated the fortifications of Quebec city in 1776 they returned to Woolwich barracks down-river from the Naval College which lies at the heart of Maritime Greenwich linking the River Thames with the National Maritime Museum, Queens House and Naval Hospital, Royal Observatory and Greenwich Royal Park. The extent to which naval/military history and power is projected in both of these heritage sites is one aspect considered in this paper (*viz* 'Heritage Britain', Quebec 'separatism'), whilst another is the contemporary image which promotes their symbolic significance as provincial capital of Quebec, and the 'Home of Time' (Greenwich meridian). The political economy surrounding their WHS status is also explored, including the extent that tourism planning has had in their development, and the distribution of conservation and management responsibilities in each case. Both sites suffer from touristic and commuter traffic, and a lack of transport planning and visitor management which limits the scope and quality of the visitor experience. As primarily 'day visit' destinations, they also suffer from negative environmental impacts but retain minimal benefits for their local communities and economies. Both locations represent long-established historic sites of the built and natural heritage - Quebec with fifteen years post-UNESCO WHS status, whilst Greenwich is a recent addition to the UNESCO list, but is presently overshadowed by the 'New Millennium Dome Experience' and other *Grand Projects* along the River Thames and adjoining areas. Lessons and experience from Old Quebec may therefore raise issues which Maritime Greenwich may wish to consider in the post-event phase of heritage and tourism development.

Historic Quebec - formation

In the fall of 1535 Jacques Cartier and his crew anchored their vessel in the Saint Charles River. More than a century later the Jesuits decided to build their first mission in the St. Lawrence river valley in the vicinity of what is now Quebec city (*trans.* 'the place where the river narrows') and Quebec city was founded by Samuel de Champlain in 1608 on the site of a former Iroquois village. Quebec is reknown as the oldest French - and uniquely the only complete fortified - city in North America, with ramparts encircling 4.5 kms. The fortifications make up the core area which was inscripted as a world heritage site by UNESCO in 1985 (ref. Map 1) having been designated a national historic monument by Canadian Heritage in 1957. The fortifications also represent over 250 years of British and French colonial history and since 1871, of Canadian military history. The star-shaped citadel located in the south of the walled city was constructed between 1820 and 1850 and today the 'Beating of the Retreat' and 'Changing of the Guard' is enacted in summertime for tourists by red-coated and bear-skin helmeted guards, reminiscent of Buckingham Palace in London. In the nineteenth century Quebec City became one of the world's leading ports with massive immigration, timber export and shipbuilding - thousands of immigrants from Britain, Ireland and France put in at Grosse Ile between 1832 and 1937 which was then Canada's main quarantine station.

In the pre-war period, the historic quarter was occupied by bourgeois/professional residents, but post-war this population declined due to suburbanisation, growth of motor car ownership and major road building; the loss of the University to the outskirts in the 1950s; and touristification of property-use (Evans 1998a), and consequent impact from tour buses and tourist/day visit activity in general. Between 1941 and 1996 the metropolitan city region's population grew by 11% whilst the old city declined by 58%. In the 1960s, the development of the area around the National Assembly just outside of the city walls (Map 1), completely transformed the cityscape which led to the elimination of many older houses. The new buildings were modern and multifunctional, containing shops, restaurants and cinemas, which in turn led to the decline in commercial streets already suffering from the new competition from suburban shopping centres. This phase of development was dominated as it was in other western cities, by private operators who had little difficulty in securing municipal approval for their plans: "In the euphoria of the 1960s, developers' plans were seen as symbols of progress" (Linteau *et al.* 1991: 401). Growth in the civil service - both provincial and federal - which increased from 15,000 to 45,000 in twenty years from the 'Quiet Revolution', brought an increase in spending power but also an imbalance between an incumbent low income, and upper income group: "a new middle class made up of government officials and academics (joined) the old elite of *notables* and merchants" (ibid.:

405). Another impact of this gentrification (which is also paralleled in Washington D.C. – Evans 2000b), was the development of modern hotels serving governmental as well as leisure (holiday, VFR) tourism activity. In the 1970s, modern development and the associated threat to the historic structures fuelled a campaign for conservation and world heritage listing, fronted by the city council and mayor, which led via the Canadian government's application, to UNESCO WHS being awarded in 1985, the only world heritage city-site in Canada: "Community groups concerned with environmental protection and historical preservation opposed large-scale demolition, (forcing) government to show concern for the quality of urban life and making an effort to preserve historic areas" (ibid.: 400).

Map 1

Since achieving world heritage site status, there has been a gradual levelling-out in the declining residential population of the inner city and old town (and an increase in property values in the historic area), including a return of a new professional class, but one which is still encroached by tourist activity and a schizophrenic existence in and out of the main tourist and summer season. In the upper old town, 45% of residents are owner-occupiers but very few of these live in detached or terraced houses, the vast majority live in apartments, whilst in the lower town, below the walled city, fewer residents own their homes and apartment living is also the norm. The lower town has continued to serve as the main utilitarian area of the inner city, with a mixed-use of offices, amenities such as libraries, railway station and cheaper shops, restaurants and hotels. Recently however, independent boutique-style hotels and restaurants have started to be developed in the lower town (with a moratorium on new hotel developments in the historic area), in contrast to the business and heritage hotels in the upper core dominated by Chateau Frontenac and high rise chain hotels, e.g. Hilton, Radisson, located in the historic and parliament zones. Average (annual) occupancy rates in the larger hotels are 65% (max. 93%), with the flagship Frontenac achieving over 90% capacity, whilst smaller establishments with 4 to 39 rooms achieve only 49% over the year (GQATCB 1999).

Profile of tourists to Quebec city and historic quarter

Quebec has a high domestic and leisure tourist profile (85%) with two thirds of Quebecois holidaying in their own province. Prior to the emergence of international travel facilitated by mass package tourism from the late-1960s, the emerging professional and middle classes pre and post-war had begun to take holidays via train, particularly to the north-east USA and Florida. With paid holidays increasing from one to two weeks after the war and subsequently up to four and five weeks, the advent of jet travel and package tours in the 1970s combined to fuel growth in Quebecois holidaying to Europe, mainly in France and Spain. The extent to which the francophone community in Quebec have *switched* from holidays in the USA and overseas is hard to measure, in particular the influence that Quebec's francophone status and "heritage" has had in encouraging domestic tourism (Hobsbawm 1990, Linteau *et al* 1991). The development of major highways from this time has certainly enabled greater intra-regional mobility and the high visitation to Quebec city by Quebecois does not in itself signify eschewing of visits elsewhere given that the travelling class and *grand tourers* (Evans 1998) take two or three holidays a year, including the ever more popular city-breaks (e.g. cultural tourism, leisure shopping, visiting friends and relatives etc.).

In terms of visitors to the historic area and the city as a whole, the next table shows the higher proportion of those originating from outside of Quebec: c.60% visiting the world heritage site, mostly for the first time, compared with 33% of 'outsiders' visiting the city region - mostly repeat visits with a high VFR element. Nonetheless, Canadians as a whole represent 53% of all visitors to Historic Quebec with the only other significant group (30%), from the USA, primarily from the north-east (e.g. Boston).

Table 1   Visitor profile of Quebec Historic Site (HNS) and City

Visitor Origins		HNS	Quebec
Metropolitan Quebec		11%	23%
Other Quebec		28%	44% (27% Montreal)
Other Canada		14%	11% (7% Ontario)
USA		30%	11% (5% Neast)
Other Francophone		9%	5% France
Other Anglophone		8%	3% Other Europe / 2% 'Other World'
Average No. of Nights		9	3.5
Group size:	Solo	15%	23%
	2/Couple	45%	46%
	3/+	40%	31%
Male/Female		49/51%	48/52% Spring
			44/56% Summer
First Visit		90%	17%

Sources: Parks Canada (1999), ZBA (1991), Breton (1995), Dion (1990)

The seasonal bias is indicated by the substantial numbers of visitors to the fortifications concentrated in the summer months (Table 2), with the city being subject to high snow (average of 380cms per year) and cold temperatures (average of -15C, dropping to -30C) between November and March. Despite this, the city and tourism bureau have promoted winter and other seasonal festivals such as the *Festival of New France* launched in August 1998, with coverage in European travel press over the last two years celebrating the Quebec winter and ice festivities and sports: "Despite the rigours of the winter climate, nothing stops the Quebeckers from enjoying this season. They have discovered how to tame winter and turn it from foe to friend" (Musée de la civilisation *Quebec Winter Carnival* www.caraval.qc.ca and see Guay 1994) In recent years these events have sustained visitor levels which have otherwise levelled out or in fact been in decline, a fate of several mature, historic tourist sites (notably those with a naval/military theme, e.g. Mary Rose, Portsmouth and Cutty Sark, Greenwich – see Table 5). Nonetheless, Historic Quebec is still one of the most visited sites in Quebec, matched, to the chagrin of the Quebec Area Tourist Bureau, by casino tourism to Montreal (2.3 million), Hull (1 million) and Charlevoix (500,000).

Table 2   Visitors to the Fortifications-De-Quebec and Artillery Park, 1995-1998

Month/Year	1995	1996	1997	1998	%
May	234669	218502	181477	208699	8%
June	510457	503004	497974	463116	18%
July	519143	482076	491718	506470	20%
August	1022799	615631	640256	736294	30%
September	500450	504303	463959	491797	19%
October	178011	172528	172528	177704	7%
Total Fortifications	**2965529**	**2491044**	**2447912**	**2584080**	Change: -13%
Artillery Park	**26677**	**19269**	**22183**	**21984**	Change: -17%

Source: Parks Canada (1999)

Notes: Les Medievales were held in 1995; Les fetes de la Nouvelle were held in 1997 and 1998
The open fortifications includes free visits (counted) whilst Artillery Park is entered by ticket.

A high proportion of visitors come to the city by car (77%), 9% by bus/coach and only 8% via airport and 5% by train. The historic area is also a popular coach trip destination for those staying outside of the city and the heritage attraction of the city is therefore a prime draw in terms of trip purpose and activity (67% of visitors to the city cited having been to the walled area during their stay) but one that is mainly perceived as a day visit destination or stop on a longer itinerary, with the deleterious environmental problems (parking, pollution, noise) and limited economic benefits arising from the classic short day trip. A typical 10 or 15 day tour from Europe of Eastern Canada and/or the USA, would spend one or two nights at the most in the city, and not necessarily in the old town - 50% of bed spaces are located to the west and in the suburbs of the city. Coaches are allowed within the walled area, even in narrow streets, and this is a common complaint of both residents and retail businesses. The seasonality of the historic area also limits the spending potential which is exacerbated by several chain stores closing out of season (for 4 to 5 months), reducing amenity for the local residents and inflating the rental/rate valuations for independent firms. Over the past year, two bookshops (one independent, one chain) have closed in the old town. Tourist shops also reflect the souvenir, fast food and mass catering establishments (larger restaurants and hotels - one quoted receiving 1,000 coach parties a week for lunch/dinner during the high season) and also the discounting of goods (e.g. clothes) as the season draws to a close, undermining traditional/indigenous and all-year round retail and catering outlets. The globalisation of tourist space is a phenomenon common to major cities, historic towns and urban heritage sites, which Edensor has identified not only as a recent development, but one which can be understood as an expansion of inscribing power through the materialisation of bourgeois ideologies since the C19th (1998: 11). Accordingly, places are now conceived not as nuclei of cultural belonging, 'foci of attachment or concern', but as "bundles of social and economic opportunity competing against one another in the open market for a share of the capital investment cake" (Kearns and Philo 1993: 12).

As well as festival and events programmes, the city has also invested in a new museum, effectively a *Grand Project* for the Quebec province and one countering the growth of cultural facilities in the main competitor Montreal (Laperriere and Latouche 1996). The *Musée de la civilisation* is a new-build attraction in the old port area of the town, conceived without a collection or specific theme, and serving as a touring and theme-exhibition centre with a strong 'edutainment' element - ten exhibits reflect various aspects of the human condition throughout history. This museum, despite its uncertain purpose and political roots (complementing the national Musée de Quebec), has proved to be successful at least in attracting visitors, drawing considerable education/school trips and extending the city's visitor amenity in the port area which itself has been undergoing gentrification and commercialisation. This includes the development of the port as a cruise ship stop, as well as tourist retail and catering, and loft-style conversions of upper floors of what were previously low-income residencies, as waterfront properties are rediscovered and repackaged in other port and waterside city locations the world over. Cruise ship visitors are of course another day visitor market (above), but at least arriving and exploring the town by foot rather than by car or coach.

Stakeholders in the Quebec historic area and tourism

Given the history of world heritage site status and the current promotion of the city as the francophone capital of an aspirational independent province ("New" France *sic*), the management, promotion and conservation of the historic quarter is of interest, not least since reconciling what are conflicting views and identities further complicates the universal tension between tourism and heritage conservation: "the complex inter-relationship between conservation and visitation that WHS status implies" (Shackley 1998: 204). In Quebec, responsibilities for different aspects of heritage and tourism are divided between several organisations with differing status and purpose. It is also important to note that there is no co-ordinating body or committee which brings these organisations together and therefore no one agency responsible for reconciling disputes or joint developments other than on an ad hoc or bilateral basis, outside of statutory responsibilities (e.g. land use planning, conservation) which even here may be shared or disputed between these bodies. This reflects the ambiguous status which world heritage site confers since UNESCO designation does not, contrary to expectations, impose a new or overarching control on site management and conservation. Whilst management planning and conservation capability is a key component of UNESCO bidding and evaluation, and once awarded, periodic ICOMOS (the technical assistance arm of UNESCO) assessment, existing state and local systems are expected to apply (e.g. land-use planning and conservation controls, transport/traffic management). In the case of the fortifications and associated sites that are managed by Parks Canada, this federal agency measures the effectiveness of its conservation role through the number of visitors (access/usage of the nation's heritage); maintaining the integrity and commemorative aspect of the site, and visitor satisfaction with their experience. Information on visitors is collected by Parks Canada through regular counting and occasional surveys which measure the first and third of these 'performance indicators'. In the latest detailed survey carried out in 1997, 91% of those interviewed considered that the site was successful in showing its national historic importance, however in terms of its commemorative and historic 'message', visitors were largely unable or unwilling to assign or answer on this aspect (only 16% responded) which sought to assess visitor's identification with French, British and industrial periods. As an indication of language groups responding to this survey, 52% were in French, but 48% in English, a proportion not of course representative of the city of Quebec or the province as a whole which is predominantly francophone (over 80%).

The next table therefore summarises the various interests and stakeholders in the Historic Quebec world heritage site and environs, revealing a complicated matrix of federal, provincial and city agencies with overlapping responsibilities in heritage protection and interpretation, as well as visitor management and marketing

Table 3   Stakeholder Analysis - Quebec Heritage Conservation and Tourism Management

Organisation	Status	Role
Parks Canada (Quebec region)	Federal Agency of Canadian Heritage Ministry	Manage and conserve Fortifications and Visitor facilities (part of World Heritage Site)
National Battlefields Commission	Federal Agency	Manages and conserves *Plains of Abraham* (part of World Heritage Site)
National Defence Commission	Federal Ministry	Manages Citadel and garrison quarters 'changing of the guard' ceremony (part of World Heritage Site)
Quebec Area Tourism Bureau	Metropolitan Agency (est. 1984) Funded: 40% local authorities (n = 13 inc.city); 35% Province; 25% private membership n = 950)	Tourism promotion and development in metropolitan Quebec region
La Ville de Quebec	City Council	Planning and city legislative authority. Tourism and Events Officer (new post) promoting festivals to spread season.
National Capital Commission	Provincial Agency	Promotion and development of Quebec as the "capital city"
Quebec Province	Provincial government	"State government", Parliament assembly building in Old Quebec vicinity (symbolic capital of New France)
Old Quebec Citizens Committee	Voluntary Residents Association	Preservation and enhancement of the historic areas of Old Quebec/WHS

In terms of the interpretation and identity projected by these agencies, this also represents a pluralist view of the history which the site (and its various components) represents, from First Nation (Native Americans), French and British colonial settlements, to "unified" (sic) Canadian, and contemporary Quebecois aspirations. This is manifested in the signage and recreations which each body managing aspects of the site promotes, from the British 'changing of the guard' at the Citadel; the re-enactment of battles on the *Plains of Abraham* (known and signed as *Battlefield Park* where First Nations fought alongside the British against the French) also the venue for the Winter Carnival; the monuments (plaques, public art, sculpture, squares) to French immigrant workers/settlers and their prospective wives in the old port (signed in French only); to the dual French and English presentation of the histories of the garrisons by Parks Canada in visitor centres and guided tours. The National Capital Commission, a latecomer to the plethora of agencies operating in the historic area, is charged with beautifying the town, parliament assembly and surrounding areas, but has extended this role to renaming streets from their catholic roots (e.g. St Pierre Rue) to celebrated Quebecois figures, and the creation of francophone parks, town squares and flags, effectively a politicisation and secularisation of the public realm. As Shackley notes: "The possession of a WHS and the development of cultural tourism can create a (spurious) image of long-term stability and the basis for establishing a national identity, or may become the focus for a new nationalism" (1998: 205). As well as widening the city's 'offer' to include business/convention trade, winter season and cultural tourists (e.g. events/festivals), the Quebec Area Tourism Bureau would rather see the conversion of squares outside of the walled city for coach and car parking, reducing traffic in the historic area, rather than self-conscious assertions of francophonie. Historic Quebec is only one of twelve districts which the Bureau promotes, and since the city council has no tourism office (until the recent appointment of a tourism and events officer within the economic development department of city hall), tourism promotion is shared (and competes) between the metropolitan region which includes winter sports and outdoor pursuits (e.g. parks and wildlife reserves), casino tourism and other historic sites outside of the city such as the basilica at St Anne de Beaupré which receives over 1.5 million visitors/pilgrims each year. On the other hand the promotion of the city and historic district to tourists looks to a wider interest group, mainly outside of the francophone world, primarily from the USA, but also from Europe, and allophone groups such as the Chinese residents in Canada (30,000 of whom live in the Quebec region). *Whose* heritage and history is being presented and interpreted (Evans 1994) is therefore arguably a function of visitor groups/ethnicity and their origin, and the politico-cultural perspective of intermediaries, as Ashworth maintains: "You cannot sell *your* heritage to tourists: you can only sell *their* heritage back to them in your locality. The unfamiliar is sellable only through the familiar" (1994: 2).

Living in the world heritage city

The role of local residents which had been largely ignored and in decline both numerically and in economic power (the middle/professional classes left to the suburbs leaving older, poorer and single parent families, and transient tourist employees), has been reasserted due to the return of a small but articulate residents group in what has been a form of gentrification of the upper old town. The Old Quebec Citizens Committee also has an interest in the conservation and promotion of the historic quarter and world heritage site, but not as a statutory body, but one literally cheek-by-jowl with the landscape and fortifications which represent the WHS itself, and the visitors who bypass their homes and the coaches who choke their streets. Resident's properties are also part of the historic site and their maintenance is therefore a responsibility which owner-occupiers bear. Their relationship with both the conserved historic area and tourists is also ambiguous, as a survey of over 700 residents revealed, below:

Table 4   Survey of Residents in Old Quebec (n=720)

Major Attractions of Life in Old Quebec	Disadvantages of Life in Old Quebec	What it means to live in a world heritage city
Historic value 20%	Parking 30%	Pride 44%
Beauty of site 18%	Lack of services 14%	Indifference 24%
Proximity of services 11%	Noise 13%	International character 11%
Atmosphere 8%	Traffic 10%	Economic benefits 5%
Proximity to St. Lawrence River 8%	Tourism 7%	Privileges 5%
Restaurants 8%	Lack of green space 7%	Recognition of beauty 3%
Lively neighbourhood 5%	Costs too high 4%	Special character 2%
Culture 5%	Presence of undesirable elements 4%	Historic value 2%

Whilst the 'historic value' and 'pride' in the built and natural heritage rank highly amongst residents, the negative impacts from tourists offsets these benefits, including the touristification and seasonality of local services (e.g. shops) and for a significant minority, indifference to world heritage site status is indicated. The 'historic value' is an attraction in itself, but this does not translate in world heritage terms (column three), where the 'international character' (i.e. from visitors, acculturation, cosmopolitan city) rather than the symbolic significance (e.g. francophone military past and capital city of *New France*) is more important to these residents as a result of WHS status and attention. This is both at odds with the politicised adoption of 'heritage' in this case and the perceived benefits which world heritage site status confers. This status is used in reference by the regional tourism bureau and some tour operators, but is a largely benign factor in the promotion and image presented for Old Quebec and by its 'keeper', Parks Canada. The 'lack of green space' cited as a disadvantage, above, might seem surprising given the green areas surrounding the fortifications and buffering town houses with the heritage site itself, however these are not public recreational spaces in the manner of local parks or play areas, and therefore access for children and for recreation (largely steep grassed areas unsuitable for games) is prohibited, with safety problems exacerbated by parking and tourist traffic through residential and historic areas.

The residents group has an increasingly vocal presence in the politics of place which is the focus of the historic zone, and one shared with local traders and business associations, particularly those whose members also reside in the historic quarter. The group has no official status however, and has no consultative place in the management of the World Heritage Site by the federal Parks Canada agency. The definition and delineation of *who* the community are also fails to reflect the displaced or those to whom heritage attaches but who may no longer be resident in the locality itself (e.g. First Nations, anglophones). Tourism and heritage development is also regrettably responsible for the enforced displacement of communities, or 'crowding out' through high land/property and tax costs and in Quebec City this included the expansion of government and major road buildings in the 1970s/1980s and the current intervention of the Capital Commission (above). Tourism promotion and development takes place in the case of Quebec, at regional, not city or historic site level and therefore Old Quebec exists as one of a range of images and products within a widening tourism profile, including other historic quarters, notably Old Montreal with whom Quebec is less able to compete, due to the latter's international city, convention facilities, airport hub and more cosmopolitan offer to tourists, both domestic and from overseas. In terms of historic towns and cities hosting major world/heritage sites, Quebec has arguably managed to reconcile a residual resident population and economy with tourism, government and other development pressures, without experiencing the extremes of say Venice or Florence, or even Bath (Gotti and van der Borg 1995). The disadvantages of living in the world heritage city have not been ameliorated however, largely due to the fragmented nature of the historic quarter's planning and management (above); the failure to integrate resident and traders input into day-to-day visitor, traffic and site management and the politicisation of the public realm, amenity and attractions in the city. The value of WHS status in this case has yet to be added to the intrinsic historic assets themselves.

A brief history of maritime Greenwich

Maritime Greenwich was designated a world heritage site in 1997. The 'Nomination for World Heritage Status' document identified the site as having "an outstanding heritage of historic buildings, monuments, and public spaces of international importance" (English Heritage 1996: 8) and "demonstrating in built and landscape form a key element of Britain's contribution to the cultural, architectural, and scientific development of Europe over five centuries" (ibid.: 10). Emphasis is placed on Greenwich's position in the history of science and astronomy, royal, and architectural history, as well as naval and maritime history. Henry VIII was born in Greenwich Palace (now the Old Royal Naval College), and his daughter Elizabeth I later knighted Sir Francis Drake there after he had circumnavigated the globe. Greenwich is also thought to be the place where Sir Walter Raleigh famously laid down his cloak so that Elizabeth could walk over a puddle. Henry VIII launched his flagship from Woolwich in 1514, the largest ship and the largest navy that England had ever had. Most of Britain's warships were produced around this stretch of the Thames until 1869. After Lord Nelson's defeat of the French at the Battle of Trafalgar in 1806, his body was carried ashore to Greenwich hospital, which is now the Royal Naval College, for a three day lying-in-state in the Painted Hall on 5th January. This ceremony took place during what was considered to be the peak of England's naval supremacy, but by 1869 the naval yards at Woolwich and Deptford were closed. The Royal Observatory was built by Charles II in 1675 and designed by Sir Christopher Wren and around 1725, John Flamsteed, the first Astronomer Royal, and the clock-maker John Harrison, who worked with Flamsteed's successor Edmund Halley, developed an advanced form of sea clock, which worked out how to find longitude at sea and improve navigation. This eventually led to the establishment of the world's prime meridian at Greenwich in 1884. The themes of maritime history and 'the Home of Time' are therefore inextricably linked, brought together in the National Maritime Museum, and Royal Observatory from where the meridian line originates (Jennings 1999).

The impact of world heritage status

World heritage site status is perceived as bringing enormous prestige, as well as impacting upon future planning decisions. Designation of a WHS tends to imply that the site both needs protection and conservation and will be subject to increased attention, usually resulting in increased publicity and higher visitor numbers (Feilden and Jokilehto 1993). But as Shackley (1998: 200) states: "It is frequently assumed that any site awarded World Heritage status will immediately receive a marked increase in visitors. However, this is not necessarily the case and visitor numbers depend on a number of factors including the way in which the site is marketed and issues connected with access". The designation of Maritime Greenwich in 1997 coincided with the designation by the UK government of the British Millennium Exhibition which was to be located on a redundant gas site on Greenwich peninsula, to the east of the Greenwich old town and Maritime area (Evans 1996a and b). The development of the 'Dome' as a year long venue for the official Millennium celebration has therefore overshadowed the world heritage award and promotion, whilst the as-yet-uncertain future of the Dome site after the year 2000, means that planning visitor and other activity in this extended riverside zone is problematic. This mega-event and the lack of co-ordination between these two developments has effectively resulted in the newly-awarded world heritage status being underplayed, allowing the imperatives of achieving 12 million visitors to the Millennium Dome exhibition to dominate the cluster of heritage attractions (CELTS 1995). The impact of the Dome 'experience' has not been the only factor in this however, since visitor access does not seem to be one of the priorities of the co-ordinators of Maritime Greenwich themselves, who seem to be largely unconcerned about the under-marketing of the heritage attractions, an attitude which is strangely at odds with the UNESCO philosophy of world heritage site management: "to preserve for the present and the future the monuments that bear witness to the creative nature of man and to make these treasures available to the widest possible public" (UNESCO 1972). In addition, one of the principal aims of the Greenwich World Heritage Site Management Plan (1997: 4) is "to increase public awareness of and interest in the World Heritage Site and promote its educational and cultural value". However, it is clear that the concept of 'promotion' in the Management Plan refers specifically to *educational* groups, rather than tourists or other visitors to Greenwich (Evans 1995).

At present, visitors seem to be largely unaware of the world heritage status of Greenwich and this is largely a result of inadequate signage in the town centre; the failure of tour guides and 'meeters and greeters' to emphasise the existence of the world heritage site; and the lack of marketing initiatives. Current marketing strategies arguably fail to do justice to the timeless qualities of Greenwich, preferring to focus most of their attention on the temporary entertainment complex that is the Dome. Not surprisingly, the London Tourist Board, English Tourist Council and British Tourist Authority have all tended to concentrate on the Millennium Dome Experience in their marketing and PR campaigns, rather than the attractions within Maritime Greenwich. The local TIC guide to Millennium Greenwich also does not place any special emphasis on the world heritage site or the maritime theme, although maritime and royal history are described briefly. The construction of the Dome is acknowledged as being 'controversial', as are the modern developments in and around Greenwich: "Ironically, just as historic Greenwich has been designated a World Heritage Site, its significance thus perceived to be on a par with the Taj Mahal, the borough is also about the become home to one of the biggest concentrations of new buildings in London"

(1999: 22 and see Edensor 1998). The WHS co-ordinator has also expressed similar concerns, lamenting the existence of eyesores in the borough which detract from the panoramic vistas of London from the hill and the 'Great Axis' as emphasised in the Royal Parks Review (DNH 1995 and see Farrell 1995).

Until recently, Greenwich suffered from an image and accessibility problem (CELTS 1995), with its key attractions showing a decline in visitors - Table 5. below. Although the volume of visits to the area is estimated at over 2 million a year (CELTS 1995) this includes weekend visits to crafts and street markets and other open attractions (Royal Park), whilst ticketed attractions have not maintained their levels of activity.

Table 5   Visitors to ticketed attractions in Greenwich (*estimates*) 1991 to 1998 (000s)

Attraction Year:	1991	1992	1993	1994	1995	1996	1997	1998	% Change 1991-1998
National Maritime Museum	600	507	505	574	609	458	476	474	-21%
Cutty Sark	408	304	262	248	234	*193*	*173*	*175*	-57%
Rangers House	18	18	19	20	9	12	9	12	-50%
Fan Museum	*8*	*8*	*8*	*8*	7	7	7	*7.5*	-6%

Note: The Maritime Museum introduced entry charges in 1984 (in 1982 there were over 1 million attendances) and tickets include visits to the Royal Observatory - 350,000 in 1988, 400,000 in 1993. Following the award of a Heritage Lottery capital grant, the Museum has expanded its gallery spaces, opened in 1999 (with fewer visitors during reconstruction), and is forecasting 750,000 visitors in 2000 (correspondence with the NMM 2000).

Sources: LTB Statistics (1998), Evans (1996b), CELTS (1995).

The designation of the WHS in 1997 has therefore given Greenwich the opportunity to enhance and reposition that image, and marketing campaigns now tend to focus on 'Historic Maritime Greenwich', or the 'Home of Time', whilst extended public transport systems have brought central London in touch via the Docklands Light Railway (Map 2) through Greenwich Town (Cutty Sark and Station) and the Jubilee Line Extension via Greenwich Peninsula 'Dome' site, in late-1999 (Evans and Shaw 1999). With less than 1% of total bed spaces in London, Greenwich is limited in terms of non-day visit activity (whilst Quebec old town has 38% of the city region's bed spaces). There is also currently some debate within the WHS co-ordination unit about the extent to which Greenwich should focus on the maritime theme in order to establish more of an identity as a maritime heritage site. This argument appears to be largely academic, as the themes of maritime history and time are clearly compatible and symbolically linked (National Maritime Museum, above). Unfortunately, the most prominent image projected of 'Greenwich' both nationally and overseas may become that of the Millennium Dome, depending, of course, on the future usage of the structure and site. In the case of the latter visitor group, from the annual summer survey of overseas visitors to London, 33% said that were aware of the Dome (versus only 12% in 1998) but only 4% were aware of Greenwich, and even of those *aware* of the Dome who intended to visit London in the year 2000 only 53% said they would actually *visit* it (LTB 1999).

Map 2

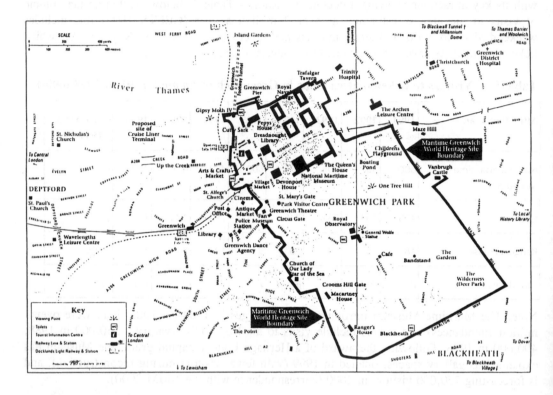

Stakeholder analysis: Maritime Greenwich

The WHS in Greenwich is located wholly within conservation areas where protection is exercised by the Borough Council (L. B. Greenwich) and is monitored by English Heritage. The public monuments and majority of town centre and residential properties are included on the 'List of Buildings of Special Architectural or Historic Interest' compiled by the Secretary of State. The Government, English Heritage and the London Borough of Greenwich therefore exercise controls over the protection and maintenance of these properties. Greenwich Park is also listed as Grade I by English Heritage, and its management is overseen by the Royal Parks Agency on behalf of the culture ministry (DCMS - below). The view over the site from the Park is also protected as a 'Strategic View', which is controlled by local planning authorities across London.

Maritime Greenwich has a WHS co-ordinator hosted by the London Borough of Greenwich, who oversees the management of the historic features, however any changes made to the existing attractions are discussed by a Steering Group which is regarded as the key management body for the site (members include representatives from the DCMS, UK

ICOMOS, English Heritage, the London Borough of Greenwich, the Greenwich Foundation, the National Maritime Museum, the University of Greenwich – Table 6. below, and a number of local organisations). The co-ordinator does not have a specific budget for managing the site, so funds are generally mobilised by the bodies who are responsible for managing each attraction. Applications for Lottery Funding and private sponsorship to support developments are common, although funding sources were temporarily exhausted as a result of the high level of funding and sponsorship required for Millennium and other year 2000 initiatives. As a consequence, some developments were postponed because of funding restrictions, such as the pier development in Cutty Sark Gardens, which is to be co-ordinated by the Greenwich Foundation. The following table shows which bodies are currently responsible for the maintenance and management of the sites which lie within the world heritage site boundary (see Map 2):

Table 6   Stakeholder analysis: Maritime Greenwich

Stakeholder	Role in World Heritage Site Management
Government Department for Culture Media and Sport (DCMS)	Identification of buildings or archaeological remains which merit listing or scheduling because of their special architectural or historic interest.
English Heritage (central government agency)	Gives advice to and monitors the effectiveness of Greenwich Council's (LBG) exercise of conservation area and listed building controls, and provision of grants for the repair and conservation of historic properties within Greenwich town centre. Advises Government in its exercise of powers to control alterations to Scheduled Ancient Monuments. Direct responsibility for the management of Ranger's House and its presentation to the public.
The London Borough of Greenwich (LBG)	Hosts Maritime Greenwich WHS co-ordinator. Powers to control changes to buildings within the site. Responsibility for local planning, transport, and highway matters, housing, education, economic development, and tourism.
The Royal Parks Agency (central government agency)	Management and care of the Royal Greenwich Park (one of nine in London – Curson and Evans 1995)
The Greenwich Hospital Trust	Ownership on behalf of the Crown of the freeholds for the Royal Naval College, the Dreadnought Seamen's Hospital, the Devonport Nurses' Home and many properties in the town.
The Greenwich Foundation	Responsibility for the Old Royal Naval College and its grounds, including the maintenance and management of the site for visitors.
The National Maritime Museum (designated National Museum)	Ownership and management of the National Maritime Museum, Queen's House, and Flamsteed House, Royal Observatory.
The Maritime Trust	Maintenance of the Cutty Sark as a museum.
The Church of England	St Alfege's Church
Private Owners	The Fan Museum, Vanburgh Castle (residential building)
The Greenwich Waterfront Development Partnership	Local regeneration agency which brings together community, business, and local and central Government interests to spearhead economic, social, and environmental programmes to stimulate the revitalisation of the area.

Source: Adapted from *Maritime Greenwich: Nomination for World Heritage Status*, English Heritage (1996 and see 1997)

Local community issues

One particular criticism of 'Maritime Greenwich' has been the perceived over-emphasis on military/naval superiority and domination (e.g. slave trade), especially in one of the Maritime Museum's permanent exhibitions which emphasises (and criticises) British colonial history and the 'greatness of Empire'. It should be noted that parts of Greenwich are some of the most deprived in the country, and that there is a diverse ethnic mix within the local area, including established and new/refugee communities (over 75% of all refugees to Britain reside in London) and the interpretation of the WHS in the twenty-first century should clearly not focus on the subjugation of minority groups. There are also fears that the regeneration process in the Borough is likely to marginalise local communities through gentrification, particularly around Greenwich and Blackheath (a process that had already impacted upon inhabitants of the Docklands a decade earlier). However, there have been several initiatives that have focused on local community issues, including education, training, and employment creation.

For instance, areas within the Borough of Greenwich (Woolwich and Deptford) are benefiting from funding received from the government's regional Single Regeneration Budget (SRB). Many of the supported projects focus on environmental improvements, the creation of new attractions and facilities, and the enhancement of employment prospects for local people. These include the *Greenwich 2000* programme, which aims to improve the economic and physical environment of the centre of Greenwich; the regeneration of derelict and industrial areas by the Greenwich Waterfront Development and Creekside Partnerships and the Greenwich Enterprise Board which provides support and assistance for people wishing to start their own business in a tourism-related area. The Borough Council has also helped to establish education and training schemes for local people, especially the young and the unemployed in deprived areas, such as the 'Meeters and Greeters' and tour guiding schemes which are being run in conjunction with local colleges. The development of tourism in the borough also seeks to help create employment in the hospitality, leisure and retail sectors, however the success of this should not be taken for granted since the impact of urban regeneration through flagship and visitor-based developments has been limited elsewhere, as Bianchini and Parkinson warn: "Experience from cities both in the USA and in western Europe suggests that cultural policy led regeneration strategies - particularly when they are focused upon city centre-based 'prestige' projects - may bring few benefits to disadvantaged social groups" (1993: 168). As the *Greenwich Sustainable Millennium Network* warned: "tourism generates little work for local people...Greenwich is a place divided by inequalities of wealth, place and power...and is in danger of becoming the pollution or asthma capital of Britain (1996). The Network, which was established in 1995 therefore focuses on community involvement in the development and regeneration of the local area addressing local concerns, such as inequality; lack of employment creation; the poor integration of the local transport infrastructure; pollution; and the potentially negative impacts from tourism development and activity. The *Cultural Plan* for the year 2000 developed by Greenwich Council (1998) also aims to involve local communities in a series of cultural events and initiatives in the Borough. In other World Heritage Cities, such as Quebec City (above), and in Edinburgh events like the International Festival have played a key role in the regeneration of the local economy, and it is hoped that some of the arts and cultural events, such as the Greenwich and Docklands International Festival may serve to promote both local pride and generate income and employment for the local area for many years to come, complementing heritage tourism activity.

The management of world heritage sites – some conclusions

UNESCO's Operational Guidelines require that all world heritage sites (WHS) have management plans. Such plans aim to ensure the preservation and conservation of sites, as well as enhancing the visitor experience, and contributing to the development of sustainable tourism. Although UNESCO and ICOMOS may provide a comprehensive set of management guidelines, it is recognised that the management of WHS requires a diversity of approaches, as emphasised by Lord Montagu of Beaulieu in a House of Lords debate in 1993: "With regard to the more general question of World Heritage Sites, they are of widely different kinds. Blenheim is, for example, a single historic site, whereas Bath is a complete city. Durham is a great cathedral in a city, whereas Stonehenge is a site set in an archaeological landscape. It is therefore impossible to lay down specific rules for WHS as different forms of approach are needed for each management plan" (Wheatley 1997). Shackley (1998: 1) also acknowledges this diversity, stating that "No two World Heritage Sites are (by definition) alike but all share common problems such as the need for a delicate balance between visitation and conservation". This highlights two of the key tensions in the management of the urban world heritage sites in Greenwich and Quebec City, as it is clear that many of the tourism development objectives could potentially create problems for the future management of their heritage attractions. They are both classic 'day visit' destinations, suffering from on the one hand negative environmental impacts as a result of considerable touristic and commuter traffic (commercial and private) and a lack of transport planning and visitor management which limits the scope and quality of the visitor experience, and on the other, minimal economic benefits for their local economies and residents. Parking and coach access are prime problems which stakeholders are unable or unwilling to address (e.g. National Capital Commission and City Hall, Quebec and Royal Parks and Borough Council, Greenwich). Large tour buses are allowed right into the centre of Quebec City (whereas most historic cities have banned these) and larger hotels, restaurants and shops do not want to lose this short-term trade. Conversely, in Greenwich, large vehicles such as lorries and coaches have been banned from the town centre, where there is limited parking provision, however the current 'dropping off' points are considered to be inconveniently located for visitors to the town centre, with "a patchy local transport infrastructure that is poorly integrated, while traffic is almost all 'through' traffic" (GSMN 1996). Both sites lack adequate accommodation provision, most acutely in Greenwich whilst Quebec's visitor catchment is widening to the suburbs and narrowing between the larger chain and independent hotels in price and occupancy rates, and together, economic leakage is high and increasing in both cases, which only a more integrated tourism, economic and heritage plan can fully address. This is not however currently facilitated by the fragmented policy and operational objectives of the various organisations and interest groups, suggesting that a cultural planning approach is needed (Evans 2000b), which of necessity would incorporate community involvement in planning and development which was largely absent in the heritage and local planning processes in both of these world heritage sites.

The ICOMOS *Principles for Sustainable Tourism* (1990) also emphasises the need for long-term planning: "The environment has an intrinsic value which outweighs its value as a tourist asset. Its enjoyment by future generations and its long term survival must not be prejudiced by short term considerations", and therefore: "The relationship between tourism and the environment must be managed so that it is sustainable in the long term". Cunliffe (1996: 266) defines 'site management' as "A comprehensive planning and management process which ensures that the conservation, enhancement, and maintenance of a heritage site is deliberately and thoughtfully designed to protect its cultural significance for present and future generations". The future management and success of the world heritage sites in Greenwich and Quebec City may therefore need to focus more overtly on the development of sustainable tourism and the creation of a lasting legacy for the local area, rather than the largely benign and passive role which the key conservation bodies currently adopt, leaving most strategic policy and planning to non-local agencies and the market. The question of responsibility for the management of sites is again emphasised by Feilden and Jokilehto (1998) and it is clear that local management control is essential for the effective management of a site and similarly, a co-ordinated approach to site management is imperative if future development and management objectives are to be compatible.

The World Heritage Convention itself (1972 and see 1985, Denhez 1997) - the supra-national guidance to which signatories such as the UK and Canada are expected to adhere (or not, which can result in sites being put on the UNESCO 'at risk' register, e.g. Jerusalem) - established a formal obligation for states to adopt a general policy which aims to give the cultural and natural heritage a function in the life of the community (Article 5a) - it is up to each Member-State however to define these 'properties of outstanding universal value' (Article 1) and there are few cases of such community planning (and management) in practice (Evans 1999), nor examples of cultural resources within which museums and heritage sites play an important part in the regeneration of communities (Newman and Maclean 1998: 149). Although the stakeholder analysis (above) indicates that there are a certain number of conflicts or tensions impacting upon the management of the two sites (for example, between those focusing on conservation issues, and those advocating tourism development), the role of the WHS agency or co-ordinator should ultimately be to maximise the benefits of WHS status whilst minimising the impacts of increasing visitor numbers. The image, promotion and interpretation of heritage in these cases also requires a more inclusive approach to their historical significance and contribution over time, including local and indigenous representation and also reflecting contemporary values and societies, rather than a fixed and arguably hegemonic version of their past and patrimony. Marx importantly distinguished between *heritage* which he saw as encompassing all historic and style periods, all social formations without exception - from *tradition*, which is only a component of the former - the "wealth of ideas consolidated in the public mind, which requires a choice, acceptance and interpretation of the heritage from the point of view of certain classes, social layers and groups" (Andra 1987: 156). The notion of 'universal patrimony' accompanying WHS status on the one hand, and the acceptance of tourism as a prime element in heritage development and resourcing (ICOMOS 1999), suggests that turning UNESCO policy into practice, as in these comparative case studies, is an imperative if 'ownership' and recognition of world heritage status is to be achieved and more universally valued.

Note: Graeme Evans gratefully acknowledges the support of the Canadian High Commission, Faculty Research Program for work carried out in Quebec.

References

Andra, I. (1987), The Dialetic of Tradition and Progress, in *Architecture and Society: In Search of Context*, Sofia, pp.156-8.

Ashworth, G. (1994), *Let's sell our heritage to tourists?*, London Council for Canadian Studies, London.

Bailey, N., Barker, A., and MacDonald, K. (1995), Greenwich Waterfront Development Partnership (GWDP) in *Partnership Agencies in British Urban Policy*, The Natural and Built Environment, Series 6, London, UCL Press Ltd.

Breton, A. (1995), *Study of the Seasonal Profile, Behaviours and Perceptions of Tourists to the Quebec City Region*, Le Groupe Leger and Leger, Office du Tourisme et des Congres de la Communaute Urbaine de Québec, December.

BTA (1999), *Millennium News - The British Tourist Authority Millennium Campaign*, 1(2)

Colin Buchanan and Partners (1994), *A Bypass for Greenwich* (Report for the London Borough of Greenwich), August.

Centre for Leisure and Tourism Studies (CELTS) (1995), *Cutty Sark 2000: Greenwich Town Centre Tourism Validation Study* (for the London Borough of Greenwich), May.

Civic Trust, (1993), *Greenwich Town Centre Action Plan,* (Report for London Borough of Greenwich, Greenwich Waterfront Development Partnership, Greenwich Town Centre Agency), February

Cunliffe, S. (1996), *Protection Through Site Management*. Proceedings of the International Conference on Tourism and Heritage Management (ICCT 1996), Yogyakarta, Indonesia.

Curson, T. and Evans, G. L. (1995), *People in the Parks - The Royal Parks in London*, CELTS for the Royal Parks Agency, London.

D'Alessandro, R. (1997), *A Leap into the New Millennium, 1997-2002 Greenwich Tourism Strategy Framework,* A Discussion Paper, London Borough of Greenwich

D'Alessandro, R. (1998), A Mean Time for Business, in *Tourism and the Millennium*, In Focus Magazine, Tourism Concern, Spring 1998.

Department of National Heritage (1995), *Royal Parks Review: Greenwich Park*, March.

Denhez, M. (1997), *The Heritage Strategy* Planning Handbook, Toronto: Dundurn Press.

Dion, W. S. (1990), *Etude sur la Visiteurs et Leurs Besoins au lieu historique national des Fortifications-de-Québec*, Québec, Parks Canada.

Dix, A. (1999), *Time to Celebrate - A Millennium Festival for the People of the London Borough of Greenwich*. Greenwich Council - Strategic Planning.

English Heritage (1993*), Time for Action: Greenwich Town Centre - A Conservation Strategy,* March, London.

English Heritage (1996*), Maritime Greenwich, Nomination for World Heritage Site Status,* English Heritage, DNH and RCHME, London.

English Heritage (1997), *Maritime Greenwich: Draft Management Plan for Consultation,* October, London

Evans, G. L. (1994), Tourism in Greater Mexico and the Indigena - Whose Culture is it Anyway? in *Tourism: State of the Art* (Seaton, A. - ed.) Chichester, Wiley Press, pp.836-847.

Evans, G. L. (1995), Tourism and Education: Core functions of Museums? in *Tourism, Culture and Participation*, Vol. I (Leslie, D. - ed.), Brighton, LSA Publication No.51, pp.157-180.

Evans, G. (1996a), The Millennium Festival and Urban Regeneration - Planning, Politics and the Party in *Managing Cultural Resources for the Tourists* (Robinson, M. and Evans, N. - eds.), Newcastle, Business Education Publishers.

Evans, G. L. (1996b), Planning for the British Millennium Festival: Establishing the Visitor Baseline and a Framework for Forecasting *Journal of Festival Management and Event Tourism* Vol.3, pp.183-196.

Evans, G. L. (1998a), *In Search of the Cultural Tourist and the Post-Modern Grand Tour,* International Sociological Association - XIV Congress, International Tourism, Montreal, July.

Evans, G. L. (1999), *Heritage Tourism: Development and Diversity* ICOMOS 12th World Congress of Conservation and Heritage: *The Wise Use of Heritage*, Mexico, October.

Evans, G .L. (2000a), The World Bank and World Heritage: Culture and Sustainable Development? *Tourism and Recreation Research*, 26(1), (forthcoming).

Evans, G. L. (2000b), *Cultural Planning: An Urban Renaissance?*, London, Routledge.

Evans, G. L. and Shaw, S. (1999), *Urban Tourism and Transport Planning: Case of the Jubilee Line Extension and East London Corridor* RGS/IBG Symposium *British Tourism: The Geographical Research Frontier*, University of Exeter, September.

Farrell, T. (1995), *London: Royal Parks Study*, 27 June, London, Terry Farrell and partners.

Feilden, B. M. and Jokilehto, J. (1993), *Management Guidelines for World Cultural Heritage Sites*, ICCROM/UNESCO/ICOMOS.

Gotti, G. and van der Borg, J. (1995), *Tourism in Heritage Cities*, Venice, CISET.

Greenwich Sustainable Millennium Network (GSMN) (1996), *Vision Greenwich* 2002, London.

GQATCB (1999), *ECHOtourism STATistics* Greater Quebec Area Tourism and Convention Bureau, July.

Guay, D. (1994), *Québec, Passion d'hiver*. Québec: Musée du Québec et Société Québec 2002, pp.142.

Hall, V. (1998), From the Inside Looking Out, in *Tourism and the Millennium*, In Focus Magazine, Tourism Concern, Spring.

Harris, B. (1996), *The Cultural Plan for the Millennium*, Greenwich Council - Strategic Planning, London.

Harvey, S. (ed.) (1997), *The Native Peoples of Quebec*, Quebec.

Hobsbawm, E. J. (1990*), Nations and Nationalism since 1780*, Cambridge University Press.

ICOMOS (1995), *Historic Cities and Sustainable Development*, Conference Papers.

ICOMOS (1999), *International Cultural Tourism Charter: Managing Tourism at Places of Heritage Significance*, 8th Draft, Paris.

Jennings, C. (1999), *Greenwich The Place Where Days Begin and End*, London, Little Brown and Co.

Johnson, N. (1995), Cast in stone: monuments, geography, and nationalism, *Environment and Planning D: Society and Space* 13(1), pp.51-56.

Laperriere, H. and Latouche, D. (1996), *So Far From Culture and So Close to Politics: The New Art Facilities in Montreal*, Culture et Ville No. 96-8, Montreal, INRS.

Laperriere, H. and Latouche, D. (1999), *Nous Sommes Tous Des Québecois: La Representation Des Regions Du Québec Dans La Capitale*. Montreal, INRS/University of Quebec in Montreal.

Linteau, P-A., Robert, J-C., Durocher, R. and Ricard, F. (1991), *Quebec since* 1930 (trans. Chodos and E. Garmaise), Toronto, J. Lorimer.

London Borough of Greenwich/Greenwich Waterfront Development Partnership (1995), *Greenwich 2000 Tourism Development* (SRB Bid Document), September.

London Borough of Greenwich/Greenwich Waterfront Development Partnership (1996), *Once in a Thousand Years: Maximising Opportunities in Greenwich* (SRB Bid), September.

London Borough of Greenwich (1997), *Unitary Development Plan Review: Greenwich into the Millennium*, October.

London Borough of Greenwich (1998), *The Greenwich Cultural Plan – A Framework for Development*, April.

London Borough of Greenwich (1999), *Millennium Greenwich*, Pitkin Unichrome Ltd.

London Tourist Board (1998), *London Tourism Statistics*, London.

London Tourist Board (1999), *Survey Among Overseas Visitors to London – Summer 1999*.

Maritime Greenwich (1997), *Draft Management Plan for Consultation*, October, London

MURSMURS (1991), *Comité Des Citoyens Du Vieux-Québec*, Vol. 2 (5): June 20, Quebec.

Newman, A., and McLean, F. (1998), Heritage Builds Communities: the application of heritage resources to the problems of social exclusion, *International Journal of Heritage Studies* 4, pp.143-153.

Parks Canada (1999), *Rapport Statistique du Parcs Canada au Québec*, Quebec.

Royal Parks Review Group (1995), *Report of the Conference on Greenwich Park*, London.

Scott, B. (1999), *Greenwich Millennium Park Project: Greenwich Gateway*. Greenwich Millennium Trust.

Shackley, M. (ed.) (1998), *Visitor Management, Case Studies from World Heritage Sites*. London, Butterworth Heinemann.

Sharples, J. (1998), *Greenwich Cultural Plan - Developing the Greenwich Millennium Celebrations,* Greenwich Council, Strategic Planning, London.

Smith, M. K. (1999), *Pre-Millennial Tension: A Missed Opportunity for Creating the Optimum Visitor Experience in Greenwich*, ATLAS Conference Paper, Munich.

The Tourism Company (1997), *Improving Visitor Management in Greenwich, Final Report,* (Report for the London Borough of Greenwich/Greenwich 2000), March.

UNESCO (1972*), Convention Concerning the Protection of the World Cultural and Natural Heritage*, Paris, UNESCO.

UNESCO (1985), *Conventions and Recommendations of UNESCO concerning the Protection of the Cultural Heritage*, Paris, UNESCO.

UNESCO (1992), *Operational Guidelines for the Implementation of the World Heritage Convention* (revised version), Paris, UNESCO.

Ville de Québec (1998), *Population Census*, Statistique Canada, Québec.

Ville de Montreal (1998), *Sondage clienteles et statistiques d'achalandage*. Rappaport final, realise par Dufresne, Dumas Mizoguchi et associes, pour le Societé de developpement de Montreal, October.

Wheatley, G. (1997), *World Heritage Sites*, London, English Heritage.

ZBA (1991), *Etude de Marche Relative aux Lieux Historiques Nationaux du District de Quebec*, Service du Canadien des Parcs Region de Québec, Québec.

Heritage and architectural preservation for tourist development: reflections on the historic Bastakia district in Dubai, UAE

Hisham S Gabr

United Arab Emirates University, Saudi Arabia

Abstract

Prospective tourism in the 21st century is evolving into an even more sophisticated and vital industry for many city economies. Some traditional forms of tourism are unchanging, others are transforming, and newer forms are emerging such as ecotourism. This paper examines heritage tourism and investigates the role of heritage revitalisation and historical preservation in the advancement of urban tourist development. Will strategies of historic renovation remain important for certain types of tourist development in the future, or will the forces of modernisation and globalisation impose upon tourism, are questions addressed in the paper. Old Bastakia District located along Dubai's creek waterfront in the United Arab Emirates is analysed from architectural and urban standpoints, and from broader heritage values and meanings. The Bastakia District is an example of old style buildings and urban fabric established along the mostly modern developed creek waterfront. The historical character of the old district is being renovated and restored for tourist purposes. The paper examines the potential effect of the restoration process and strategy on the tourist industry in the City of Dubai. Interviews with municipality and local officials were conducted to elicit goals and strategies adopted by officials in the restoration effort. The conclusions support the use of heritage preservation strategies and processes in urban tourist development. Recommendations for heritage tourism development are discussed.

Introduction

The tourist industry is widely recognised as one of the top, if not *the* top, global industries. Growing numbers of people are earning more and spending more money on travel. The economic impacts of tourism on local or regional economies are staggering, and in many cases represent a major financial resource for cities and countries. Latest figures on tourism support the booming industry. International tourist arrivals have been steadily increasing since 1950 and exceeded 500 million in 1995 (WTO 1995 cited in Williams, 1998). In some countries such as England, visitor levels to urban heritage attractions outside London have shown substantial increase, reaching 3.5 million visitors to such historic attractions as Albert Dock, Liverpool (Williams, 1998, pp.36).

Tourist development has relied upon a variety of resource types for attracting tourists. Among the conventional ones are the historically based resources, whether architectural relics or artefacts. Our attraction to the past, as Lowenthal (1993) points out, stems partly from the enjoyable link inherited between people and their precursors and descendants. This link provides a way to secure a better future. Our view of the past is a means to forge our sense of identity and an opportunity to satisfy public curiosity about cultural backgrounds. Historic buildings and environments play the role of launching one's journey to the past.

This paper addresses the role of heritage conservation and historic preservation, through building restoration and reuse for tourism development, and argues for the potential success of conservation strategies on the tourism industry.

Heritage and tourism in Cities

In spite of the growth in variety of tourism types over the past few decades, evidence suggests that cultural tourism remains one of the favourite tourism types especially within the growing public and governmental interest in global heritage conservation (Sugaya, 1997).

On a global scale, many organisations are actively taking part in saving and protecting world heritage. For one, the experience of the UNESCO's World Heritage Centre (established in 1992) in world heritage preservation cannot be understated. Figure (1) summarises the nomination process for inscribing a site on the World Heritage List. Involved in this process are the International Council on Monuments and Sites (ICOMOS) for cultural sites, and the World Conservation Union (IUCN) for natural sites. The International Centre for the Study of the Preservation and Restoration of Cultural Property (ICCROM) complements the work by providing expert advice on conservation methods and training needs. For a country to nominate one of their sites for the World Heritage List, it has to become a state party by signing the World Heritage Convention and pledging to protect its cultural and natural heritage. The World Heritage Centre, acting as co-ordinator within UNESCO, checks the state's nomination list of site or sites, passes it on to the ICOMOS and/or IUCN for technical assessment, and eventually passes it on to the World Heritage Bureau (composed of 7 members of the World Heritage Committee) to examine the evaluation and make recommendations on the nomination. Finally, the World Heritage Committee (composed of 21 representatives of the States Parties to the Convention) reviews the recommendations of the Bureau and makes the final decision on whether or not to inscribe the site on the World Heritage List. With such a procedure many natural and cultural sites across the globe are being carefully diagnosed as possessing "outstanding universal value" that warrants their conservation.

Figure 1   **The nomination process for inscribing a site on the World Heritage List (Adapted from World Heritage Review, 1997, 6, pp. 39)**

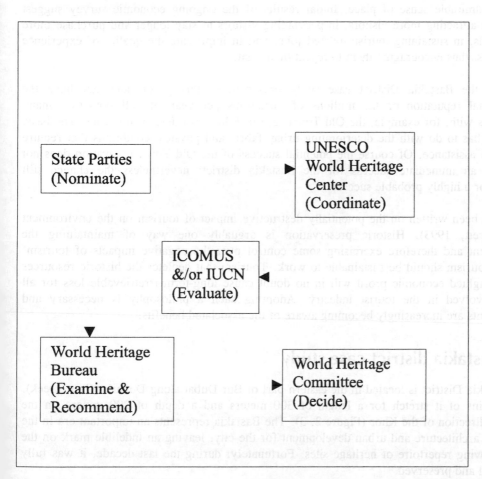

On regional and city scales, many successful case studies are reported. Edinburgh for one has recently enjoyed a successful reestablishment of its Old Town as a flourishing tourist destination while respecting the environment (Middleton and Hawkins, 1998). Prior to 1989, the value and importance of the physical fabric of Edinburgh's Old Town was unrecognised and was possibly deteriorating to the point of no return. A serious and comprehensive action plan took place to transform the Old Town back to its status as a predominant magnet for international and local tourism. The revitalisation of the Old Town relied on the ever important effect of the environment on tourism and consequently on the economy which benefits the Old Town itself. The Old Town's unique environmental character, characterised by the intermixing of living, working, and visiting activities in one area, presents itself as paramount for tourism attraction. The action plan included an organisational structure of advisory groups composed of representatives from funding agencies, local residents, local business associations, the city's tourist board and the Chamber of Commerce. Their objective was to sustain the quality of the environment, which is known to be the major factor to achieve positive visitors' perceptions of the Old Town. Several physical changes took place such as the establishment of a pedestrian environment with sufficient carrying capacity and the restoration of many buildings, which, together with an attractive promotional campaign, has transformed the Old Town into an energetic and coherent setting with an admirable sense of place. Initial results of the ongoing economic survey suggest success in attracting more visitors, in persuading visitors to stay longer and purchase more local goods, in sustaining tourism-related jobs, and in improving the quality of experience for visitors, thus encouraging them to repeat their visit.

Although the Bastakia District case study presented in this paper does not have the international reputation or the millions of visitations per year, it still possesses many similarities with, for example, the Old Town case in Edinburgh described earlier. The basic similarity has to do with the deteriorating urban fabric and physical conditions that require immediate assistance. Of course the potential success of the Old Town renovation does not guarantee an immediate success for the Bastakia district; nevertheless the chance still remains for a highly probable success.

Much has been written on the potentially destructive impact of tourism on the environment (cf. Fawcett, 1993). Historic preservation is arguably one way of maintaining the environment and therefore exercising some control over the negative impacts of tourism. Cultural tourism should be sustainable to work. Tourism that depletes the historic resources for shortsighted economic profit will in no doubt cause long-term irretrievable loss for all parties involved in the tourist industry. Adopting such a philosophy is necessary and governments are increasingly becoming aware of the associated benefits.

The Bastakia district case study

The Bastakia District is located in the eastern part of Bur Dubai along Dubai's Khor (creek). The remains of it stretch for a length of 300 meters and a depth of 200 meters on the southern direction of the Khor (Figure 2, 3). The Bastakia represents an important era in the history of architecture and urban development for the city, leaving an indelible mark on the city's growing repertoire of heritage sites. Fortunately, during the last decade, it was fully recognised and preserved.

Figure 2   The urban fabric of the Bastakia District

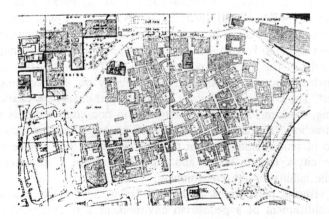

Figure 3 A recent aerial view of the Bastakia District

Architectural restoration efforts

In 1991 and under the direction of Dubai Government, the conservation movement in Dubai started to receive official attention with the establishment of the Archaeological Buildings Restoration Unit as part of Dubai Municipality. The new unit, which turned into the Historical Buildings Section in 1994, started recording and restoring buildings and architectural elements with historical value. Examples of restored buildings were Sheikh Saeed House, Al-Fahidi Fort, Al Ahmadiya School, and the Grand Souq. The Bastakia District was among the areas receiving close attention.

Later, a newly founded Committee for Preserving Urban Heritage commenced supervising new building designs in downtown area. The committee issued a handbook on traditional architectural elements of Dubai to assist designers interested in using them as precedents in their designs. This effort continues nowadays, with the close supervision and monitoring of a preservation and conservation plan in the entire Emirate of Dubai. This endeavour has been supported by increasing academic interest as evidenced in the several regional and international symposiums held over the last few years in Dubai and beyond as in the Emirate of Sharjah and the Emirate of Abu Dhabi. In Abu Dhabi, the recently established Zayed Institute for Heritage currently funds research on heritage in the UAE amongst which is architectural and urban heritage.

The conservation movement and the consequent restoration venture have no doubt provided an opportunity for changing the character of Dubai city. The modern development of Dubai has created a city with a predominantly commercial character focusing on shopping and business activities. Its annual shopping festival attracts many international tourists, and year-round business, exhibition, and conference activities attract business tourists. The city emerged as a commercial and business hub for the Gulf region and a powerful connector to East Asia. The resulting urban expression is a modern universal style, with buildings using high tech materials and reflecting a Western image. With historic parts of the city under restoration, the city is attempting to establish ties with its past heritage amidst modernisation (Figure 4). Perhaps the city can attract cultural tourists as well.

Figure 4   A newly restored house with a modern glass cladding high-rise in the background

Spatial and formal structure

Persian emigrants are credited for the founding of the Bastakia District in the early twentieth century. Influenced by the already established architectural heritage in their homeland, they brought with them new architectural forms to Dubai. The Bastakia District was characterised by a wide variety of barjeels (wind towers, or badgeer). The barjeel is a tall angular structure designed to increase air movement in the rooms below through its hollow shafts (Vine and Casey, 1989). The occupants can control this cooling effect by closing the vents of the barjeel whenever cool air is not desired (Figure 5). Barjeels differ in general appearance, height, and ornamentation, according to resident requirements and functional needs (Figure 6). A master bedroom barjeel for example would be taller and more decorative than others in the house bedroom area. Sometimes the living room barjeel may differ from the ones in the bedroom.

Figure 5   Barjeel (wind tower)

Figure 6   Barjeel (wind tower)

The Bastakia District acts as a historic resource that may have a critical part in the evolving tourist industry in Dubai. Conversely, tourism may have a critical role in the development of urban conservation and restoration of the Bastakia District and similar historical resources. Moreover, the mutual symbiosis of the two may have an everlasting impact on shaping the form and activity of the City of Dubai. These assumptions are in agreement with Ashworth and Tunbridge (1990) in their treatise of the tourist-historic city. Using their classification, Dubai would be considered, a medium-sized multifunctional city of a population around a million, and the Bastakia District as a historic resource of potential value to tourism. Additionally, the city has many non-historic resources of value to tourism and many historic resources that may not necessarily be directly associated with tourism.

The Bastakia District is being restored to act as an architectural museum, but plans are unclear so far, as to the activities to be included. The area, which is still under restoration, is open to tour guides to lead tourist groups through it. At present, the area is very rarely visited. Perhaps after complete restoration and aggressive promotional campaign, the place will receive reasonable amounts of visitors. This discussion inevitably raises the issue of authenticity of the tourism destination (MacCannell, 1973; 1976) and the interrelationship matrix between the real and staged historic resource and tourists' impression of it (Cohen, 1979). The Bastakia District is real and hopefully it can be recognised as real. If that happens to be the case, then the planner's goal is to hope for a real experience by the tourist. But can historic sites in modern cities be recognised as real? The tourist walks through the streets of the Bastakia District as if visiting an area of the past, experiencing a different world for a short time. Bastakia may present itself to the visitor as a museum of authentic historic architecture. Much of the discussion on authenticity is hypothetical and as the concept remains somewhat fuzzy in the literature, applicable data may later shed some light on such important issues.

One of the goals of the Bastakia District restoration is to reinvent the image and character of Dubai in general and to target historically sensitive and culturally sensitive tourists, quite similar to the successful case of Bradford, England. In Bradford, heritage attractions were used to establish new tourism destinations and change the industrial image of the city (a negative image in this case) to a more appealing one (Davidson and Maitland, 1997 cited in Williams, 1998). The narrow and winding streets, the solid walls with few windows and openings, the use of natural materials, the use of earth colours, the complexity of the urban skyline, the orthogonal forms of buildings, and the human scale of the site, are among the architectural attributes that make up the unique character of the Bastakia District (Figures 7, 8, 9, 10, 11).

Figure 7   Variety in building skyline, barjeels, and use of earth materials

Figure 8   Typical street alleys of the Bastakia District

Figure 9   Typical street alleys of the Bastakia District

Figure 10 Unique wood construction for a house balcony

Figure 11 House walls with minimal openings

The resulting urban fabric and architectural treatment is a reflection of the social and family needs and values. Houses were built to fit various family sizes and requirements. Few houses in the area are actually still occupied. The impact on the urban fabric is at times enhanced such as with the addition of a tree that breaks up the harshness of the materials used, and at other times deteriorated such as when TV antennas start to disturb the urban aesthetics and the homogeneity of the urban fabric (Figure 12).

Figure 12 A tree adds beauty to the urban scene, while TV antennas distract from the visual scene

Privacy, a fundamental social value in the community, is successfully manifested in the formal and spatial structure of the District. Houses are inward looking, with the least exposure to the outside. The intertwined street fabric and the small urban plazas in between, encourage social interaction without compromising privacy. Social systems and cultural factors have heavily contributed to the design and planning of the district.

Conclusion

The paper argues for the possible success of historic building preservation and restoration efforts even if occurring amidst an overwhelmingly modernised and multicultural city. By embracing the historic restoration strategy, the added valuable heritage resources would help redefine the city as a tourist destination by increasing the possibility of attracting tourists who value heritage, culture, and sustainability. These types of tourists are assumed to cause minimal negative impacts on the community because of their considerate and sensitive concerns towards local cultures. Dubai may remain a commercial and business attraction, yet its efforts for cultural revitalisation balance the image and resource structure of the growing metropolis in its competition for tourist market share. Investment in heritage preservation can in many ways lead to return in the form of increasing tourist arrivals and consequent economic benefits. Fortunately, the government is making the restoration work for ideological reasons including maintaining self-identity and historic ties rather than for mere profits. It is up to the tourism industry to make use of the historic resources.

The historic site of the Bastakia District is potentially attractive for its unique architectural character, which stands in sharp contrast to the surrounding urban modernity. The architectural character associated with the Bastakia District is part of the Gulf's regional historic character but with distinguishable local influences shown in several distinctive form variations related to Barjeels, houses, and streetscape. The experience of walking through the narrow alleys of the district is one of excitement and enjoyment, and makes one feel as if being in a different world at a different time. The sense of distinctiveness and rareness resulting from the unique architectural expression could help make the district a successful historic attraction.

Another reason for the possible success of Dubai's effort in historic revitalisation is being a manifestation of the global sustainability movement and of sustainable tourism in particular. Tourists who are becoming increasingly sensitive to the environment, natural and built, may appreciate historic revitalisation. Moreover, residents may appreciate the survival of their heritage and appreciate sensitive tourists, which would help in the host-guest relationship often encountered in the tourist industry. Some cultural tourists, one could argue, are driven to historic attractions in an appreciation of sustainability rather than as a result of pure interest in archaeology or history.

Finally, tourists' exposure to historic sites raises the awareness of cultural norms, which is suggested to contribute to better intercultural relationships. Tourists and visitors become more aware of each other, and of their cultural differences. The platform is set for beneficial cultural learning and co-operation.

Several recommendations present themselves as necessary for the success of the historic conservation of the Bastakia District and similar sites in general. Promotion of historic sites in Dubai deserves increasing realistic attention if cultural tourists are to be targeted. Already local tour operators are including the Bastakia District in their plans, even though complete restoration in not yet complete. Dubai is a fast changing city and is already a popular destination for commercial and business tourists. The tourist market of Dubai is consequently dynamic, with room for reshaping and refining, for expanding and diversifying. Much research is needed in a multitude of areas concerning Dubai's future in tourism. Although no immediate adverse effects are expected at this time, the impact of tourism on these historic sites should be continuously monitored and marketing strategies adjusted accordingly. The conservation of these historic attractions is usually the responsibility of their owners and operators, and measures should be taken to avoid resource destruction or depletion. Efficient management plans turn out to be the necessary means for achieving a reasonable balance between operation and conservation, a balance that is acceptable to all parties involved including visitors and tour operators. Innovative incentives should also advance the cause of heritage conservation, including ideas such as attractive rights of operation. Even tax relief (McDonald, 2000), which is not particularly applicable to Dubai, as it has no tax system, can generally be a useful initiative in other contexts by helping raise costs of restoring heritage buildings and sites.

In conclusion, the arguments in this paper can only be substantiated with original data. Suggestion for future research is to accumulate data on the cultural tourist market in Dubai and on the role of the historic sites in potential tourist visitation, for tourism research studies of Dubai still lags behind.

References

Ashworth, G. J. and Tunbridge, J. E. (1990). *The tourist-historic city*, Belhaven Press, London and New York.

Cohen, E. (1979), Rethinking the sociology of tourism, *Annals of Tourism Research*, 6, 18-35.

Davidson, R. and Maitland, R. (1997), *Tourism Destinations*, Hodder and Stoughton, London.

Fawcett, J. (1993), The impact of tourism on the environment, In Farmer B. and Louw H. (Editors), *Companion to Contemporary Architectural Thought*, Routledge Inc., London and New York, pp. 481-486.

Lowenthal, D. (1993), What makes the past matter? In Farmer B. and Louw H. (Editors), *Companion to Contemporary Architectural Thought*, Routledge Inc., London and New York, pp. 182-184.

MacCannell, D. (1973), Staged authenticity, *American Journal of Sociology*, 79 (3): 589-603.

MacCannell, D. (1976), *The Tourist: A New Theory of the Leisure Class*, Schocken Books, New York).

McDonald, M. (2000), Tourism, heritage, and tax relief, *Journal of Travel Research*, (38): 282-291.

Middleton, V. T. C. with Hawkins, R. (1998), *Sustainable Tourism: A Marketing Perspective*, Butterworth-Heinemann, Oxford.

Sugaya, H. B. (1997), World heritage and tourism, *World Heritage Review*, (5): 34-39.

Vine, P. and Casey, P. (1989), *Arab Gold: Heritage of the UAE,* IMMEL Publishing Ltd, London.

Williams, S. (1998), *Tourism Geography*, Routledge Contemporary Human Geography Series, London and New York.

Industrial archaeology in Basilicata (Italy): Hydroelectric power plants in the 19th and 20th centuries

Antonella Guida and Fabio Fatiguso

Università degli Studi della Basilicata, Italy

Abstract

"Tourism is one of the most important productive sectors of the general economy of our country, the natural resources are immense and the historical cultural characteristics of the "Bel Paese" are second to no other nation in the world." These brief and incontestable considerations, together with the availability of one of the most important and beautiful historical areas in Basilicata, have led to the belief that it is possible to requalify and convert Hydroelectric power plants into a cultural-tourist-reception complex for *cultural tourism*. In this way, there will also be a noticeable development in the south of Italy.

The initiative to convert the Hydroelectric power plants into a tourist reception centre is intended to meet the growing social demands of an alternative use of the area, of a new concept of ecological and cultural tourism, of free time and holidays.

These sites occupy a strategic position in the north of the region of Basilicata. The surrounding area, which is easily accessible, is also important for its historical and architectonic elements as well as being an example of the typical Lucanan countryside regarding the environmental aspects (flora, fauna and historical buildings).

The transformations that the project suggest and which need to be carried out in order to achieve an urbanistic, environmental order are of interest to a vast area.

Introduction

The object of this study is Industrial Archaeology and will be examined in four areas: processes, means, products and containers. Once a structure, belonging to the industrial cultural heritage, has been singled out, it is then advisable to ascertain the possibilities for its conservation, taking into consideration specific actions of intervention. A feasibility plan which works toward the aims that Industrial Archaeology has set for itself includes the following: prospecting, documentation, cataloguing, safeguarding, salvaging, restoration and use of the industrial cultural heritage structure. The traditional image of the region of Basilicata (Italy), seemingly far removed from the themes treated by Industrial Architecture, is linked exclusively to agricultural and animal stock raising connotations. Along with this activity, a qualified artisan and industrial production has always existed. Basilicata is a region in which the environmental, landscape and cultural heritage is still at a modest level of compromise and this heritage has the features to establish a system which has the best competitive, available and obtainable, advantages. The project for salvaging the ex-hydroelectric stations is intended to promote Basilicata as a *Green Region*. During the refurbishment interventions, particular importance has been given to the refurbishment, restoration, and utilisation of the operating systems which remain as a testimony of the conservation of the identity of these engineering works.

A new science searching for a recent past

What is industrial archaeology

It is useless to deny that ours is the era of "machine civilisation". It is therefore useful and necessary to preserve the technical, cultural and social values which have contributed to the development of human civilisation for more than a century.

It could be none other than England, the nation which, before any other, was "turned upside down" by industrial revolutions, to be, as the Anglo-Saxon world considers it to be, the homeland of *Industrial Archaeology*. This development started in the 1950s.

Industrial archaeology studies technological innovations such as: machinery, productive processes, buildings, infrastructures, company documentation and archives. It then forms an opinion based not so much on the aesthetic beauty of the work but rather on its functionality and its economic importance. It should not be forgotten that the history of industrial development is largely based on perishable materials. The buildings are therefore created with a precise intent which is limited in time. If we look at Italy, for example, every year, on average, 150 cubic metres of old industrial buildings and 300 thousand tons of equipment and machinery are dismantled.

Industrial archaeology is interested in the industrial landscape and the object of its research is industrial "monuments". This is evidently a very large field. However, the reference point we should refer to is that of capitalist production and its constitutive factors, capital and workforce. Therefore, the workman's habitation is an essential space of the workforce. Besides being the product of certain industries, the communication routes (railways, canals, roads) are the instruments of the process of the circulation of capital. The goods, which represent the end result of production are at the same time concrete objects and the manifestation of an ideology. The most important meeting place of capital and work is that of the *factory* which was invented deliberately and purely for production. It is a place where the presence of man and machinery determine and are determined by the work space. A whole series of services are connected and dependent on the factory: warehouses, storehouses, workmen's lodgings and markets, abattoirs, gas metres and so on. All of these objects make up the *"industrial monuments"*.

When they are preserved intact, they not only become excellent objects to study, but also essential reference points which help to interpret a productive past which has been reduced to ruins and deeply changed. The original shape of a factory often changes as a result of production and technological alterations.

Once it has been established what are the objects of industrial archaeology, the question of chronological limits may be asked. Since when and up until when is an object of interest? Are mediaeval ovens and buildings such as the "arsenale" in Venice examples of industrial archaeology? And if we analyse the present, should we include the atomic reactor preserved in Westinghouse in America, abandoned petrol pumps and the remains of early motorways? For some historians, the starting point dates back to the economic and social development in England during the course of the 19th century which is commonly known as the "industrial revolution".

If the problem regarding the starting point can be resolved, it is, however, much more difficult to establish limits as regards the present. It seems to be a reasonable opinion that there does not exist a finishing date for industrial archaeology. In fact, technological development continually produces waste which immediately becomes an object of historical interest. On the other hand, certain buildings which continue to carry out their original function, whether it be productive or a service, are to be considered industrial monuments. Why is the bridge of Paderno sull'Adda (Italy) which, even today, carries both rail and vehicle traffic, of industrial archaeological interest? What interests us is not the reasons connected to the loss of its functioning but because it is an example of an art of building which refers to the past and which is no longer practised.

A similar problem arises regarding the buildings whose walls are still "in use" but which now house modern plants. Here, it is more evident that the term *archaeology* refers to the container, where the contained is the result of the most sophisticated technology.

From what we have established, we can put the object of our study of industrial archaeology into four sections:

> *Processes* (ideas, know-how, projects, designs, correspondence, documentation regarding technological evolution, work cycles, patents, or rather the results of ingenuity).

> *Means* (machinery, plants, equipment, instruments, operational and controlling bodies, construction materials).

> *Products* (objects and other entities which result from productive processes and means).

> *Containers* (architectonic and structural complexes and elements which cover and protect the means and therefore the processes).

In the above mentioned structure the *human factor* is missing; processes, means, products and containers are, in fact, a direct and qualifying emission of man. They are the evident expression of man's intelligence whose immanence has no need for further explanation. In fact, its inclusion on the list would lessen its value, function, image and power of creativity.

Once a cultural and industrial element has been singled out, it is considered to be necessary to ascertain the possibilities of preserving it. The specific stages of intervention must be examined. This is an indispensable analysis which concludes in the drawing up of a *feasibility plan* in order to carry out the decisions made.

The essential functions through which one must operate in order to realise the aims of Industrial Archaeology are the following:

Prospection (identification, recognition, acquisition of the essential data to carry out the action)

Documentation (collection and cataloguing of data, iconography, critical analysis, technical analysis, historical analysis, bibliography, libraries, archives, etc.).

Filing (codification of the data collected, according to standardised procedures).

> *Safeguarding* (the actions necessary for protection, including administrative and legislative restrictions, acquisition, maintenance, etc).

> *Refurbishment* (logistical positioning, containing, arrangement, accesses, protection, financing, etc.)

> *Restoration* (technical/scientific interventions in order to guarantee the continuity of the cultural industrial property).

> *Fruition* (appropriate actions necessary to make the archeo-industrial property appealing to the public and scholars).

Industrial Archaeology is considered to be a science and the term used *to define it* is extremely problematic and in certain aspects not totally satisfying.

What counts the most, however, is the fact of establishing the importance of the culture of industrialisation: that is the complex of elements, not only objects but also ways of being and ideologies, which, by transforming, revolutionising or integrating previous systems have produced industrial civilisation. This is brought about by the study of the industrial monuments.

The reasons for protection

> *"... the conservation of monuments and of fine art productions which, despite the passing of time, are still with us today, has always been considered by our predecessors to be one of the most interesting and worthy objects of their committed attention..."*

Since the most ancient measures, the aim of the Italian legislator has been that of ensuring the existence and continuity of the patrimony, which although it is viewed as a unitary inheritance of the nation, is in reality made up of heterogenous classes of 'things'. Items of art are selected for their 'individual beauty', that is to say, objects which are able to arouse the admirer's pleasure. They are invented products of the artist whose aim is just that, to arouse pleasure. Even today, our legislation registers the 'desire of art' as a basic factor in justifying the protection of objects.

Along side this class the legislator has always juxtaposed a second category of things: "*i monumenta*" (from the Latin *moneo* = to remember, call attention, inform), those objects which are tied to civilised memory or which represent certain traces of history or which are places of collective memory. The final category of things has always been subject to protection, even if it does not enter into the ideological mechanism which connects the previously mentioned two categories, and it is that of the products of cultural material. In eighteenth century laws, this class of objects was included as being products of excavation or archaeological items of interest. However, due to the development of archaeology as a science, this class of objects also became one of those protected by the law 1089 of 1939 under the protection of cultural property.

In the 1970s TICCIH (The International Committee for the Conservation of the Industrial Heritage) was set up. It is an organisation (of which Italy is also a member) which includes 30 countries from all continents, and which under the term *Heritage* is concerned, broadly speaking, with the history of work and production. In the statute, certain criteria have been highlighted which must be taken into consideration during the studies, research, cataloguing, conservation and interpretation of the industrial patrimony. One of the first conventions took place in Milan in 1977 and, amongst other societies, SIAI, Società Italiana di Archeologia Industriale (Italian Society of Industrial Archaeology) was set up. Programmes to catalogue and survey industrial sites and monuments in Lombardia and Emilia Romagna were established. This later went on to include most of the regions in Italy.

These were also years of transformation in the industrial cities. With the abandoning of factories, there arose, in all its drama, the problem of reusing these areas.

The "derelict lands" as they are called by the English, are generally areas of large extentions of land. In Milan alone, the areas of disused land reach 3 million square metres and in Emilia almost 5 million. They are small abandoned cities within the urban makeup.

During the 1980s, local museums proliferated and collected typical, local materials such as linen, wool, sulphur salt, silk, wine etc.

In 1985 ICMAI, Istituto di Cultura Materiale e Archeologia Industriale, (Institute of Cultural Material and Industrial Archaeology) was set up. One of ICMAI's objectives was to spread the concept of a "museum system" as well as establishing the census of cultural industrial property. This was first proposed by the Ministry but is now carried out by the national commission for industrial archaeology. Industrial archaeology goes, therefore, from being a science for enthusiasts to having a supporting role for the administrations and for the protection and evaluation of "cultural industrial property".

The question of reuse

The interest in the rediscovery of the cultural and architectonic value of Industrial Archaeology has developed simultaneously with that of the reuse of these architectonic complexes, which gradually lost their role until they arrived at a point where they were emptied out.

One of the methods of the refurbishment of a "property" is that of the theory of conservational restoration. This theory receives great credit from the scientific community.

The theory of conservational restoration eliminates nothing which already exists. It intervenes constructively with new materials to save the property and safeguards the totality of the building.

It is therefore not easy to know how to intervene on buildings which inside are organised, as regards space, in two different ways. The first type offers an eventual restorer space which, although originally devised for industrial needs, once cleared of the equipment and machinery, possesses dimensions which are both usable and possibly inhabitable. The second type of space has not taken into consideration man but that of the operating of the machinery. The space, therefore, is purely connected to that of technological use.

We thus find ourselves in the condition that in order to continue to be able to use a monument it is necessary to carry out certain procedures. Not only is it necessary to insert vertical and horizontal elements capable of making the building liveable, but we are also forced to make openings, cuts and service areas. In this case, however, one works from the point of view of critical restoration rather than purely conservation restoration.

There are some cases whereby, in unusable examples of industrial archaeology, it is necessary to apply typical methods of archaeology. This is for the historical respect of the monument and follows Boito's historic attitude. In these cases the only correct procedure of restoration which allows their conservation is that of considering them to be purely archaeological excavation findings.

Realisation and projects

In this way many interventions regarding conservation and reuse have been carried out adopting different methods and 'filosophies'.

Interesting works of reuse and conservation have also been realised in Italy, such as the refurbishment of Lingotto in Turin, a project by Renzo Piano, the restoration of the iron bridge of Paderno sull'Adda, the restructuring and transformation of Mulino Stucky (Stucky Mill) in Venice into a cultural centre and hotel (Slide Venezia, Mulino Stucky) which, because of its beauty and history, is the symbol of Italian industrial archaeology. Many others are also in the stages of refurbishment today.

Many large companies have also set up or are setting up specific Museums regarding their work (the state railway, ENEL, the electricity board, the airforce, Caproni, RAI, state television, STET, FIAT, Oto Melara, etc.). There are also a large number of local museums which collect, in particular, materials connected to typical local productions.

On the basis of what has been discussed so far, it seems reasonable to establish a scale from a geographic-territorial point of view or from that of a historic-industrial one.

Industrial archaeology in Basilicata

The traditional image of the region of Basilicata would seem to be far removed from the themes treated by industrial archaeology.

Superficial opinions think of this land only in terms of agriculture and animal stock raising. However, along side these activities there has always been an artisan and skilled *industrial* production, which may not have much importance as regards quantity but it certainly has as regards quality.

Mills and pasta factories

Agriculture, together with animal stock raising, has always been one of the basic economic elements of Basilicata. Both of them have, as an end result, not only food production but also the manufacture of the vegetable fibres on the one hand, and on the other products deriving from milk and skin hides. Despite the fact that the region is mainly mountainous, the agriculture sector is pre-eminent in the cultivation of cereals. The mills also work intensely and they extend all over the region. They almost exclusively use hydraulic energy, which continued to be the main energy source even after electric energy conversion. The mills are concentrated in areas which are rich in water such as Vulture, the area of Lagonegro and Venosa.

Few of the mills have survived with time, due to the progressive modernisation of equipment (such as the modern cylinder mills of the early 20th century in Matera).

The mills often worked using a waterfall system, but there were also examples of the small tower system. *Mulino Suanno* (Suanno Mill) in Castelluccio Inferiore belongs to the first category and dates back to the end of the 18th century. It was in use up until recent times and is an example of a real industrial microsystem (2 mills, 2 spinning mills, an oil press and a hydro-electric power plant. Despite the conversion to electric energy, the horizontal wheel and much of the equipment (machinery and hoppers) have been preserved.

Besides the mills there were also some pasta factories in the region which followed on from the 19th century macaroni factories, such as those of Matera and Stigliano.

Furnaces

The use of clay as a material for construction (spread over reed frameworks or mixed with straw) dates back to recent prehistory, when groups of humans changed from being nomads to settling down. The use of the brick and the so called *pisà* (a mixture of clay and vegetable elements) were used for the walls of houses up until the Classic Age as was brick roofing which is still in use today. We should not forget the bricks, the work in clay, and the *figuli* which were protected by trademarks and commercialised all around the kingdom during the Borbon period.

Furnaces are a constant presence in the topography of the place and of the landscape, the dimensions of which vary from microplants to large brick factories. They were particularly important during the Borbon period and later during the post Unitarian period.

The *Fornace Ierace* in Potenza was fully concerned with industrial production and it is particular because it carried out the work from the beginning to the end; the extraction of the clay took place on the hill where the plants had been set up, and the primary material was transported inside by wagons which moved along a specially built railway track.

On a completely different scale are the furnaces which are still operating in the area of Lagonegro.

Spinning and woollen mills

The production of fabrics and materials (for clothes as well as for domestic use) has always flourished in Basilicata.

The main material for weaving is wool. Classic archaeology has already documented thoroughly how every house, even a small one, had space for a vertical loom. It has not been so well documented, however, how the loom and weaving arrived at industrial proportions in Basilicata. Although there are cases in the region of large fabric mills, the more common typology is that of the small spinning mill, which uses machinery operated by hydraulic energy. Only some of the mills were converted to electric energy (such as the two spinning mills on the river of S. Giovanni in Castelluccio Inferiore). The spinning mill of Ferrandina dates back to the 19th century and its external structures and tall chimney have been preserved.

Near the spinning mills were the 'gualchiere' where, once again using the water as a source of power the spinning took place. Although this operation was often carried out using rudimentary equipment, the output of the goods was high. Although the material which is manufactured on the largest scale is wool, there are also other materials produced in the textile industry such as: linen, cotton and hemp. The working of broom for the production of coarse fibres is a chapter of its own and seems to be restricted to the Albanian communities on Mount Pollino along the valley of Sarmento.

The presence of woollen mills is recorded in various parts of the region. In some cases they date back to the Borbon period and in others they date back to recent times. The area of Lagonegro and in particular Lagonegro itself have been known for some time for its production of wool, cloth and felt (used for, among other things, the characteristic cone shaped hat). The manufacture of silk finished when the breeding of silk worms was abandoned.

Amongst more minor buildings is that of the woollen mill *Guida* in Lagonegro which dates back to the end of the 19th century and is an example of the canons of modern industry. It stopped operating at the beginning of the 1960s, but until a short time ago its original machinery was preserved on site.

Printing works and paper mills

The tradition of the printing works in this small region dates back to the 18th century and since then it has continued to be a constant industry for the people of Basilicata. We cannot speak of a publishing industry but we can speak of a high and well spread craftsmanship. Besides the traditional printing works, there are present, even today, printing works which cover areas of distribution including those outside of the local area. The indication of continuity connecting the past with the present is demonstrated by those companies which started off between the end of the 19th century and the beginning of the 20th century, and which have continued, even today, to use the vintage machinery.

Continuing the discussion on paper, two paper mills of Basilicata should be pointed out, those of Avigliano and Venosa. It should be noted, however, that they only produced materials for boxes and packaging, and not for printing.

Infrastructures for trade and communication

The orographic conditions which have always had a negative effect on transport, impose on the one hand the creation of a series of local industries, whilst on the other the improvement of viability. One of the primary requests during the post Unitarian period in Basilicata was that of the creation of an infrastructure for communication. In fact, with the exception of a few parts which go back to Roman times, the road system is based on sheep tracks, which are totally inappropriate for the increasing level of traffic.

The railway network started off very slowly, in 1915, due to hundreds of technical and financial difficulties.

The section between Lagonegro-Laino Borgo is emblematic from many points of view. It is just under 40 km long and it took 20 years to build. Work began in 1909 and it was in fact inaugurated on 30 October 1929. The complex orography of the area and the numerous tectonic problems meant that experts and workmen were involved in a very difficult job of containment and consolidation (unfortunately not always effective). The great differences in height of the level of the land and the deep incisions required the planning and realisation of works of art which are, even today, one of the most eloquent examples of the techniques used for the construction of railways at the beginning of the century, due to its boldness, monumental size and the way in which it fits into the landscape.

Without doubt it is the viaducts (built in reinforced concrete, iron and a mixture of stonework and iron) which had the most impact on road communication. We should not forget the various structures along the track, from the stations to the stops; the warehouses and the fuel stations; the toilets, signal boxes, security, ovens and wells. All of these items were planned in meticulous detail.

Hydroelectric power plants

At the beginning of the 20th century, following the trend throughout the whole of the peninsula to use water resources, the Lucana Society for Hydroelectric Enterprises was set up in Basilicata, under the initiative of the engineer Simonatti.

Thus, in numerous parts of the region, the first power plants were established. They were of different sizes depending on whether they were intended as large consumer networks, to supply only to local needs, of a civil nature (public lighting) or for industry (electric energy supply to mills).

In the south western area of the region the century old tradition of using water determined the installation of many small plants in many places. Inside these plants the equipment was reduced to the minimum dispensable (one turbine, a generator, a regulator and the control board). When the size of the plant is bigger, there are large open air reservoirs or accumulation tanks at the point where water is taken up to provide energy.

There are also several examples of mills which have been converted into hydroelectric plants (Brienza and Ruvo del Monte which no longer exist, the ex mill Orofino di Episcopia, parallel to which there was also a spinning mill (now partially destroyed).

The modern power plant called Tancredi can be considered individually. It is in the area of Viggianello and was built by the Southern Hydro Electric Society. It is still operating today and uses equipment with the original machinery. It operates using a penstock which draws water from a torrent, a tributary of Mercure.

The power plant as a work of art

The first signs of hydroelectric industry in Italy are to be found in Alessandro Rossi's town of Schio. The new findings on the production and transportation of energy led to a change from mechanical transmission to electric transportation between 1887 and 1890.

Between the end of the 19th century and the First World War, the power plants devised to produce electric energy, constituted a *corpus* of buildings which are of extraordinary interest. They are interesting from a point of view regarding the history of technology as well as from an artistic-historical one. Here, we are talking about particular buildings which are interesting not just for their construction. In fact, what they produce, a transportable energy, has important effects on the localisation of industry as well as on the shape of other plants; not to mention the deep changes caused to the land by hydroelectric power stations (barrages, dams, penstocks, canalisation, etc.). With the arrival of electric energy, there was no longer the need to build 'vertical' factories. This was a forced choice because of the morphology of the land around the sources of water in the valleys and above all due to the difficulty of transporting the energy produced by a water wheel horizontally.

The electric power plants have remained more or less unchanged and this factor is indicative of an industrial culture which in many cases is intertwined with the most advanced engineering and architectural culture of the time. In this way, these power plants are distinct from most of the other architectonic structures involved in the nation's industrial take-off because the other structures underwent rapid transformations, continual restructuring and substitutions with other more up-to-date models. The Italian hydroelectric power plants have had a role which stands out in the history of electric power stations on a European scale.

In Italy 330 plants have been counted in a census, most of which belong to ENEL, the Italian electricity board, and are not operating. Others have been destroyed in wars or floods etc. If we add to these power plants the ones which are still operating today, the ones completely destroyed and those owned by third parties, we can see that the total number throughout the whole of the nation is rather high. It is enough to look at the 1960s where 43% of the nation's electricity requirements was provided by hydroelectric power plants.

The method of research and documentary material

The research into the power plants in Basilicata between the end of the 19th century and the beginning of the 20th was carried out through direct means: on site surveys as well as through a collection and subsequent revision of data and documentary sources of various types, indications taken from cartographies and finally photographic documentation. Everything was collected and filed.

All power plants, even those which no longer exist but which are however documented, have been counted and catalogued in special records.

These files along with all the material which has been collected are very important because they are proof of how man managed to use a clean source of energy without damaging or disturbing the environment. In fact, man managed to regulate and contain the water flows in the river beds by constructing a system of canalisation.

The use of water mills is very old and for centuries they have not changed the surrounding natural patrimony. If there has been any change it has been to improve the surroundings. If the water which travelled down to the sea permitted the turbines to operate without having to refer to an auxiliary source of energy and without polluting the surrounding environment, this meant that there was a guarantee for the conservation of the land as regards the landscape.

The survey of the power plants was carried out by the use of historical maps in order to locate them.

Besides the map and bibliography documentation, a detailed survey of photographs was also carried out on all the power plants. This was an exhaustive analysis of the water power plants and all of the various components connected to them.

The collection of a series of spoken reports has enabled the verification of the exact location of existing power plants as well as those of which today there is no longer any trace.

The material and information collected on the power plants has been collected in 19 files. These files have been labelled by a coloured sticker which indicates the current state of use and by a symbol which indicates the state of conservation.

Each file is made up of 4 pages (less pages for power plants which no longer exist, have been demolished or are not accessible):

- on the first page the map location is indicated on a scale of 1:25000;

- on the second page there is the information regarding the features of the water power plant and the machinery (year of construction, type of turbine, power, etc.);

- the third page reports the features of the buildings and their current condition (supporting structure, floors, roofing, etc.);

- on the fourth page we have the historical information which has been collected from the various sources previously mentioned.

- All of this is accompanied by photographs and relief designs of maps, landscapes and the relative sections of the buildings which were taken during various inspections.

The project for refurbishment

The reasons for the conservation: The area of 'Vulture' and 'Sirino-Pollino'

This research proposes something more than a simple cataloguing of 'objects' introduced to the land by man. It is, instead, an idea which coincides with a singular necessity: that of *conservation*.

In this case, regarding power plants, we wish to consider *conservation* regarding the parts connected to the historic and architectural and evolutive elements of the architecture and of the surrounding physical environment, as being a collective memory, a symbol of technological progress and development of the land. This is because we are finally heading in a direction where the *object* and *history* are moving at the same pace.

However, the treatment of the environment, the landscape and the district is, even today, difficult to approach when looking at it from the point of view of *protection* and *conservation* of the historical and architectonic elements. It is not so much a problem from the practical and operative point of view; the problem is more one of ideology and evaluation of *what* and *how* to safeguard, and what are the correct methods to adopt in order to ensure the correct action of tutelage.

This discussion of the architectonic features of the power plants takes us back to the discussion of the techniques of giving information about the 'alternative uses' of buildings which are rich in meaning and possess a particular natural beauty which should be imprinted on the collective memory.

Naturally the question of conservation is separate from the more complicated one of functional restoration. In many cases it is not possible to reinstate the original function due to economic problems as the income resulting from the production of electric energy would not be enough to cover the necessary costs of restoring the small hydroelectric power plant.

Going back to the discussion of conservation, this study has selected two geographical areas – that of VULTURE and SIRINO-POLLINO – where there are the most important power plants of naturalistic beauty in the region.

The project for the refurbishment of the hydroelectric buildings in the 'Vulture' area

Thanks to the profound reconsideration of the last few years, the cultural and environmental properties of our heritage are destined to become a strategic resource for the development of Basilicata, in addition to the ones already available.

This means that alongside the use of cultural and environmental resources there may also be 'additional' possibilities for economic and cultural growth. The connection between the refurbishment and evaluation of cultural and environmental property with that of economic development is possible through the revival of tourist interest and the appreciation of the environment and historic centres.

Within this geographic area which can be identified as the *'district of Frederick'* of VULTURE, the project of refurbishment aims at reusing the hydroelectric buildings for tourist purposes.

The three power plants are connected by 5 itineraries which may be followed on foot, by horse or by mountain bike. The itineraries wind around from the Vulture massif to the valley of Platano following the river Ofanto and offer the possibility of doing brief day trips in the area around the power plants.

The power plant of Muro Lucano (PZ)

The building is situated about one kilometre from the centre of Muro Lucano and was built in 1914 by S.L.I. (Lucana Society for Hydroelectric Enterprises). It supplied numerous parts of the region with electric energy until it was closed down in 1965 due to problems connected with the dam and the reservoir. This plant was the largest in the region.

Next to the main rectangular shaped building there was the warden's house which was demolished in 1970 and replaced with a switch box belonging to the electricity board ENEL.

The supporting structure is in brickwork of a thickness of 60cm on the ground floor and 50cm on the first.

The middle floors are made of iron I beams and small vaults. The roof of the machinery room is of 8 iron English style trusses. The layer of the roofing is made completely of slabs of bricks on which are placed flat tiles in *Marseille* style.

The main facade is subdivided into six sections by six large iron windows, typical of the style at the end of the 19th century. They have arches in scraped concrete stucco work. The northern facade has two openings, now boarded up, and a small rose window positioned high up in the centre.

The abandoned building is surrounded by thick vegetation which, in some points, is as high as the roof.

It is still possible to see the main water pipe which brought water into the building and which, once inside, splits into two pipes.

By means of an iron and small brick vault walkway which is on the south side of the building, it is possible to enter the back part of the building passing over the canal where the water from the turbines was discharged. The presence of stagnant water in the canal is due to the formation of moss and lichen on the walls. The walls are damp due to capillary ascent of the water.

Entering through the main door one finds oneself directly in the machinery room. It is still possible to see, from the spaces on the floor, where the machinery was once installed.

The capitals (in concrete in *ionic* style) of the pillars, which once held the crane, have been destroyed in some parts.

By means of an overhanging stone staircase, it is possible to go up to the room above where you will find the electric switch cabin. From an overhanging balcony (built in reinforced concrete) this room, from the south side, overlooks the machinery room. The balcony has collapsed in several areas. The balcony and the staircase were built in 1929. Originally access to the second floor was possible by the use of an iron ladder which went directly from the machinery room.

The intention of the project for the refurbishment of the ex hydroelectric building in the Vulture area is to transform the power plant of Muro Lucano into a restaurant and small hotel. This is an idea based upon the fact that the building is a few hundred metres from the entrance to the town so it could be used by both tourists and the inhabitants of the area.

The project takes into consideration conserving the large room of the building. This can be transformed into the common spaces of the restaurant and hotel which need large areas.

The small hotel will have 5 rooms on the ground floor and 5 on the first floor. To get to the first floor, the guests can either use the original stone staircase or a lift which handicapped people will also be able to use.

An iron spiral staircase leads up to another level where the restaurant, with a seating capacity of 25-30 is situated. The basement floor will house the toilets which will be accessible by means of a lift.

Outside, and on a lower level with respect to that of the entrance, there are the stables with four compartments for horses, a storehouse for hay and the necessary equipment for saddling the horses.

On the west hand side, outside, there will be a bicycle shed for mountain bikes and a storeroom for the kitchen. The latter will be connected with the kitchen via an underground tunnel.

The power plant of Pescopagano (PZ)

The building is situated approximately three kilometres from the centre of Pescopagano. Built in 1910, it operated until the end of the 1960s, when, following the disaster of Vajont Dam in 1963, it was closed down due to security problems.

It still has its original shape and its two original turbines (one is a *Francis,* the other a *Pelton)* dating from the beginning of the 20th century are still inside.

The building is divided into two sections, one of which has two floors. The supporting structure is of scabbled calcareous stone masonry of the *sacco* type. Its central part is in stones, and the thickness of the walls of the room on the ground floor is 60cm whilst that of the rooms on the first floor is 50cm.

The intermediary floor is of iron and bricks, whilst the roofing is in wood with simple trusses and hollow tiles.

The window frames, which are not present on the ground floor and have been partially destroyed on the first floor, are made of wood.

Near the building there is thick vegetation which in certain areas goes up the walls. The ground floor is divided into two rooms which are connected by means of two large archways. One of the rooms was used as a workroom and contained reserve diesel engines.

Through an opening on the west hand side it is possible to go out and go up to the first floor by means of an outside staircase. This upper level was once the lodgings of the warden and is connected to the staircase by a walkway which today has been completely destroyed.

In the project for the refurbishment of the ex hydroelectric power plants in the 'Vulture' area, the small plant of Pescopagano has been destined to become a mountain hut, as it is in a dense wood at 900m above sea level and its architectonic appearance is exactly that of a rural, mountain construction.

Through the main entrance, on the west hand side, it will be possible to gain access to the small lobby which will house the reception for receiving guests and hiring mountain bikes and horses. There will also be a bar which will have the original turbines on view.

On the upper floor, which is possible to reach by the outside staircase, there will be four bedrooms with bathrooms.

Outside, in a separate structure made of wooden and iron prefabricated panels, there will be stables for horses and a bicycle shed for mountain bikes.

The power plant of Monticchio (PZ)

The building is situated about one kilometre from the village of Monticchio Bagni and fifteen kilometres from the centre of Rionero in Vulture.

It was built in 1906 by the Lanari brothers company. It originally had two *Pelton* turbines which then became one when a second power plant was built lower down the valley at the end of the 1930s. The plant still has its original shape and produced electric energy until the end of the 1970s.

Its shape is rectangular and it has two floors. On the ground floor there were the turbines whilst on the first there was the warden's lodgings and the electricity switch cabin.

The supporting structure is of brickwork of a thickness of 50cm on the ground floor and 40cm on the first.

The intermediary floor is of iron and bricks, whilst the roofing (which today has completely collapsed following a fire) was of wood in *Lombardy* style and of a layer of flat tiles in *Marseille* style.

The external window frames are of iron with double frames made of wood and it is possible to see a few pieces of the polychrome window panes which once made the windows of the switching cabin more attractive.

The entrance to the plant is on the south side while, in order to reach the first floor, it is necessary to use the external staircase and a walkway made of iron and small brick vaults. The two entrance doors are of iron and have lunette windows. The openings are built with parapets and the frames are made of bricks.

The ground floor is split into two rooms. All of the hydroelectric equipment has been dismantled but there are still traces of it on the walls and floor. There are overhead horizontal openings like on the south side, which, once held the electric cables which led to the switching cabin on the floor above and from the inside to the outside.

In the project for the refurbishment of the ex hydroelectric plants in the 'Vulture' area, the small plant of Monticchio has been destined to become a pension, sleeping nine people, and a fast food bar.

From the main entrance on the south hand side, one enters a room on the ground floor which is on two levels. On the lower level there will be the reception for the receiving of guests and for the hiring of mountain bikes and horses, the bar and small kitchen whilst on the higher level, accessible by means of an iron spiral staircase, there will be tables.

On the first floor there will be five rooms with bathrooms. Outside in a separate structure made of prefabricated wooden and iron panels, there will be stables for horses and a bicycle shed for mountain bikes.

The project for the structural refurbishment of the ex hydroelectric power plants

During the planning stages of the structural refurbishment of the buildings, and after examining the environment, the structures, the materials and the deforming and fissuring lesions, the nature of the static problems may be defined, and it should be remembered that the principle of causality of the disintegration of the walls is regulated by an equivalence of ruins and lesions. Once one of these problems has been identified, the other one is automatically determined.

Research is then carried out to discover the causes of the problems because the ruin has not been caused by only one factor but by many different factors which have an influence in some cases individually and in others combined with other factors.

After having chosen the research to be carried out and successive results, the best techniques are chosen, taking into consideration the economic, static and aesthetic aspects of the property and the speed at which the building is being ruined. Interventions are generally divided into those regarding the building *in toto* and those which are more specific and aimed at particular parts of the building.

It has been decided to consolidate the walls by substituting the deteriorating, damaged and degraded stones and/or the unsafe walls by using the technique *scuci-cuci,* repairing the lesions with chippings of hard stone and sealing with a cement mortar. The successive consolidation of the safety of the keystones has also been planned.

The iron and wooden window frames will be recovered by means of cleaning the surfaces, disinfecting, filling in the missing parts and removing and repairing the damaged parts.

In some cases, it has been planned to consolidate the iron and brick floors by conserving the existing small vaults. Where it has been planned to consolidate the iron and brick floors by demolishing the existing small vaults, the substitution will be carried out using traditional methods.

As the buildings are in a seismic area, it has been planned to anchor the iron roof trusses to a perimeter beam in reinforced concrete. The trusses and battens will be cleaned and protected from rust.

As regards wooden roofing, it has been planned to substitute it with trusses made of lamellated wood and planks which have been treated with products against putrefaction and fire. To complete the roofing, ventilation and insulation have also been taken into consideration and will be obtained by using continuous planks, polystyrene insulation, a layer of tiles which have an anchoring system, special pieces for the highest parts and air vents which are necessary for microventilation.

Conclusion

This research has proposed making a census of these industrial monuments, because they pass by unnoticed even if time has not hidden them, so as the projects of fruition are as detailed as possible, or to concentrate on sample complexes. In this way, it will be possible to prefigure "archaeological, industrial itineraries" and "museum" institutions in which all the objects of the peasant, artisan and industrial culture of our region will find a place. This would also lead to a capillary promotion and evaluation of the historical importance of these properties.

During the refurbishment interventions, particular importance has been given to the refurbishment, restoration, and utilisation of the operating systems which remain as a testimony of the conservation of the identity of these engineering works.

To conclude, what is missing are the instruments necessary to carry out constant documentary research, field work and protective intervention. It is necessary to overcome these limits so as the cognitive aspect of industrial archaeology turns into a concrete process of acquisition, on behalf of the people, of a very significant culture.

These sites represent an under-valued resource for tourism and the tourism can provide a stimulus for the preservation of these sites.

References

Guida, A./Borelli, A. (1999), *"A new science searching for a recent past. Industrial Archaeology in Basilicata (Italy): hydroelectric power plants in the 19th and 20th centuries"*, The International Conference "Preservation of the Engineering Heritage" – Gdansk Outlook 2000.

Fatiguso, F. (1999), *"Functional adaptation of engineering heritage and preservation of its value"*, The International Conference "Preservation of the Engineering Heritage" – Gdansk Outlook 2000.

ECSC, (1996), *"Study of derelict industrial sites of the coal and steel industry."*, Gangemi Editore, Milano.

Tourism and the foreclosure of heritage: A critique of Kirschenblatt - Gimblett's 'madeness' and "hereness" of destinations

Keith Hollinshead

The University of Luton, UK

Abstract

Recently a whole profusion of new ideas have appeared in the literature of heritage tourism on the invention and manufacture of subject-peoples, subject-places, and subject-pasts notably within the splendid work of Tunbridge and Ashworth (1996), Selwyn (1996) [in drawing particularly upon the critical insights of Brown/Fees/Bowman/Edwards/Golden], and in Robinson and Boniface (1999) [in drawing especially on the diverse outlooks of Whittaker/Hollinshead/Shackley/Ireland/Ryan].

But there is a host of other emergent literature on the fabrication and production of subject-peoples, subject-places, and subject-pasts in the broader humanities which simply do not crop up in the literature of tourism studies with any degree of regularity. In this respect, one could mention the refreshingly brilliant insights of perhaps, Buck (1993), McKay (1994), Boyle (1996), Stewart (1996), Wilson (1997), Edensor (1998), et cetera. To this latter list of "cousin" treatise, must now pointedly be added the work of Kirschenblatt-Gimblett (1998) on destination development. Kirschenblatt-Gimblett is a wide-ranging transdisciplinary commentator on the manufactured *performance* of peoples, places, and pasts whose value to the literature of tourism studies has, possibly, only been fleetingly recognised there - and only in that manner, perhaps, through her occasional co-operative work with that sometime-anthropologist-of-tourism, Bruner (see in particular Bruner and Kirschenblatt-Gimblett 1996).

This chapter examines the degree to which Kirschenblatt-Gimblett's sustained work on "performativity", on "the theatricality of cultural production", and on "exhibition studies" can be used powerfully to cross-fertilise the *received* work of Tunbridge and Ashworth, of Selwyn, and of Robinson and Boniface, and others, in what could be called the mainstream literature of tourism studies and the mainstream literature of heritage-tourism studies. It probes Kirschenblatt-Gimblett's questioning the role of tourism/travel as an agent of socio-political display, and as an agent of communal consciousness. In so doing, the presentation will seek to deconstruct what she sees as the exhibitionary logic of tourism, and will thereby register a number of distilled propositions on what she simply but powerfully calls "the madeness" and "the hereness" of reality-making in tourism (or rather, in heritage-tourism).

This loose deconstruction of the invention of peoples, places, and pasts principally seeks to catalyse the following areas of meaning production:

- Institutional memory making;

- Reality and authenticity projection;

- Myth-making narratives of self;

- Myth-making narratives of other;

- The production of culture; and,

- The production of heritage ...

... via Kirschenblatt-Gimblett's multi-site critique of the objectification, the fragmentation, the contextuality, the virtuality, the theatricality, and the authorisation in and of "the madeness" and "the hereness" of different/diverse destinations.

Key terms:

Performativity	Representation
Favoured Objects	Contested Entities of Culture, Heritage, and Nature
Objectification	Evidential Literal Detail
Collaborative Imagination	The Sanitisation of Storylines
Ethnographic Marking	Repetitive Placement

Introduction: The value and timeliness of a fresh research agenda on heritage representation and control

Recently a number of major news stories have brought matters of heritage production in and around tourism to the fore in the international media. In the U.S.A., the Disney Corporation had to abandon plans to develop and manage its huge newly proposed theme park on 'American history' at Haymarket, Virginia (Hawkins and Cunningham 1996) partly in the face of strong opposition from local and national historians who felt that the interpretation of precious Civil War battlegrounds and 'Americana' storylines would undoubtedly be prostituted if entrusted to the case of such a fun - mongering and profit - oriented company (Wines 1993: A14). Also in the U.S.A., the University of Nebraska was forced to return the remains of some 1,700 'American Indians' to 15 'Native American' tribes, after its chancellor has been forced to admit that the university had over past decades handled the remains with little regard for the cultural beliefs of native populations (Marcus 1998). Meanwhile, in the Tyrolean Alps of Europe, the Italian and Austrian governments have been at loggerheads over Oetzi ('The Iceman') who seemingly perished in a snowstorm some 5,300 years ago, and whose mummified and lately - found bones are now serving Italian commercial interests in tourism at the noted expense of science and presentation, according to "competing" Austrian heritage experts (Leidig and Johnston 1998). And in Athens, the Greek government has been vitriolic in its condemnation of the apparently quixotic actions of the United Kingdom government, when the latter has continually refused to hand the Elgin marbles back to Greece from the British Museum (Kennedy 1999), yet did seemingly decide to hand an equivalent archaeological hoard (The Castor Marbles) back to Turkey (Lister 1998).

Such cases illustrate the murky realms of culture exhibitry, heritage representation, and commodified identity which Barbara Kirschenblatt - Gimblett's (1998) new University of California Press text "Destination Culture: Tourism, Museums, and Heritage seeks to investigate. Indeed, Kirschenblatt - Gimblett's examination of *what she terms museological activity,* and otherwise of *the logic of performativity* in and around tourism, promises to be a landmark study of the manufacture of travel and tourism destinations. This current paper will therefore seek to pry closely into the critical insights which Kirschenblatt - Gimblett - Professor of Performance Studies and of Hebrew and Judaic Studies at New York University, U.S.A. - attempts to bring to the study of institutionalised memory and aesthetic imperialisms of travel and tourism. That critique of the cultural dynamics she ranges across in the selection and signification of tourist destinations will be carried out via the following five steps:

- firstly, the existing but fast changing frame (or rather frames) of understanding about heritage production about and across tourism studies (into which Kirschenblatt's multi - arena work may be seen to have been pitched) will be identified: to this end, a short *deconstruction* (i.e., a brief introductory critical analysis) of this received or orthodox theoretical understanding will be provided;

- secondly, an attempt will be made to briefly make a succinct *capture* (i.e., an initial differentiation and basic characterisation) of the key contours of Kirschenblatt - Gimblett's critical commentary on heritage production;

- thirdly, a more thorough *bracketing* (i.e., a more sustained dissection) of Kirschenblatt - Gimblett's essential ideas will be provided;

- fourthly, the inter - relationships of those essential conceptual approaches will be attempted in order to determine whether there is any relevant 'order', or 'collective power' in Kirschenblatt - Gimblett's conceptual issues within "Destination Culture... ." which can be roundly presented within a fuller *contextualisation* (i.e., placed contemporaneously/situated thematically/located "atmospherically") within the existing literature on the production of heritage in and across tourism/travel; and,

- finally, an effort will be made to provide a *synthesis* between the orthodox/received literature on the representation of heritage and culture in tourism studies to determine overall the force of Kirschenblatt - Gimblett's new thinking on the signification of peoples, places, and pasts to determine whether her theoretical contributions support, augment, or even replace existing notions of 'reality', 'authenticity', and 'objectivity', et cetera, in destination projection.

Frame: The already broadening outlook on heritage production

In recent years the tourism studies literature on representation in tourism and travel has blossomed, as will be indicated in this paper by reference to three emergent commentators on the manufacture and management of culture/history/exhibited inheritances which are pitched within the field of tourism. These three texts on the cultural dynamics of tourism are, firstly, Selwyn's (1996) broad treatment of mythmaking and of culturally constructed image in travel and tourism, secondly, Tunbridge and Ashworth's (1996) examination of the symbolic value of heritage as a contested mix of resources in travel and tourism, and thirdly, Horne's (1992) critical inspection of the intelligences which are conceivably harnessed in travel and tourism to render the heritages of places enlightening or not. In selecting these three respected observers (viz.: Selwyn, Tunbridge and Ashworth, Horne) it is not meant to indicate that they are the only useful researchers on and about heritage production in the tourism/travel literature of the 1990s, it is rather to suggest that the 49 collective chapters of these three works (12 from Selwyn, plus 9 from Tunbridge/Ashworth, plus 28 from Horne) provide a reasonably wide panorama of the current state of understanding about the act of signification in and the development of heritage tourism and cultural tourism for the 1990s.

In first examining how Selwyn's work conceivably frames matters of heritage production in tourism studies, it should be noted at the outset that Selwyn is one of a legion of social scientists exploring tourism studies who build their intellectual insights around the notion of authenticity, a phenomenon that was first systematically analysed in tourism studies by Cohen (1988) only as recently as the late 1980s. But, importantly, in probing the imagined worlds of myth projection and image promotion in tourism, Selwyn (1996:19) concludes that notions of what he calls 'hot' and 'cold' authenticity are so complex that it is never possible to develop a *single* fully faithful or fully workable authentic notion of heritage/history/culture which fits what goes on in the invention of places, in the making of destinations, and in the shaping of tourism events around the world. To him, the economic, social, cultural, and political dimensions of the authenticity of peoples/places/pasts are always "creatively" harnessed in tourism and travel, particularly under the imploding playfulness of the postmodern mood or moment. What seems to matter most to Selwyn - in drawing particularly from the insights of Brown (1996: 34) within his own book, and from Frow (1991), is that the fundamental tension which informs all tourism is the quest for the authentic Self via the quest for the authentic Other (Selwyn 1996: 21; [see Hollinshead and de Burlo (2000), for a fuller treatment of *othering* in relation to the people-making, place-making, past-making agency of tourism]). To Selwyn, tourism sites and destinations have always been important 'crucibles' for the development of local/statist/nationalist *selfist* images of homeland, and for the related dialectical projectivity of and about alien/removed/distant *different* populations in their afar - land.

While Tunbridge and Ashworth (1996: backcover) also pivot their analysis of heritage dissonance on matters of authenticity (but are much less explicitly eloquent on issues of 'self' and 'other'), they are keen to examine at particular sites and destinations "whose heritage is being interpreted by whom and for what purposes?" In noting the seemingly inexorable growth of heritage itself in and through tourism, and the apparently almost infinite variety of possible pasts, they record an evidential lack of awareness of the problems of *dissonance* in cultural and heritage resource management, even though such matters of heritage dissonance "may be [frequently] interwoven in a complex cause - and - effect relationships with larger issues of disaffection" (Tunbridge and Ashworth 1996: 274). In underlining the strengths - but also a number of crippling weaknesses - of both 'inclusivist' and 'minimalist' approaches to the management of heritage dissonance in particular (and thereby to the equitous care of and over competing visions of "place" in general), Tunbridge and Ashworth (1996: 275) sardonically assert that for each and every projected place or signified destination, "only a superhuman agency [there] could adjudicate fairly between the relative significance of the ... total [local] accumulation of human culture [and received public inheritances]".

Horne is rather more judgmental than Selwyn and Tunbridge/Ashworth. While he suggests that heritage tourism in fact constitutes a huge field in which humans can search for empowering meaning and for positive self - generation, he implicitly suggests that much of the development of heritage and cultural destinations indeed constitutes a silly, deadening, depraved, and non - enlightening exhibitry (see Hollinshead's (1996/A) critique of, and glossary for, Horne's pungent commentaries). What Horne (1992: x and 382) calls for, is an end to the spiritual perils of what he styles 'civilisation packet', 'autonomic tourism', bereft of the vital ingredient of wonder, and its replacement with awe - inspiring presentations of peoples/places/pasts which can be decently and challengingly 'sight experienced' by tourists rather than merely being 'sightseen' by them. To Horne, too much of the heritage tourism of destinations, and indeed of nations, comprises a contrived inheritance, or otherwise an illusionary public culture which is not only routinely full of all sorts of silences about significant themes and events from the past, but which is rarely ever projected in ways which of refined sensibility can be arrestive or exalted of the witnessing populations or the visiting travellers (Hollinshead 1999/A). Such is the trivialising everyday sorcery of site, place and destination making in tourism, according to Horne (1992: 379).

Exhibit 1:

The loose deconstruction of culture production and heritage production: A critical analysis of received conceptions on the signification of difference and the identification of diversity in tourism studies

Area of meaning production	Field activities involved	Sample contemporary tourism studies researchers in the van of representation of difference	Sample unfolding conceptual questions and emergent research agendas in tourism studies
1 **Institutional memory making**	The manufacture, invention, and promotion of local/ state/national/ diasporic being, identity and nostalgia	To **Horne**, each modern - industrial nation state takes considerable time and effort to produce a 'national'/'certified' public -culture version of its profound and distinctive inheritances (1 > 1); to **McKay**, all manner of public sector, private sector, and special interest agencies participate in the creation, development, and furtherance of that institutional memory-making (1 > 2).	To what degree is the currently exhibited 'public culture' of a particular people/place/past legitimated via tourism?
2 **Reality and authenticity protection**	The authorised declaration and projection of 'real' and 'authentic' traditions and inheritances	To **MacCannell**, so much tourism constitutes a contemporary pilgrimage in the search for the 'real', the 'sacred', and/or the 'authentic' (2 > 1); to **Urry** such matters of authenticity can only meaningfully be explored today in relation to the processes of commoditisation and consumerism which increasingly shape cultural expression in tourism, today (2 > 2).	If authenticity is not a static property of fixed objects - (but something which can be invented or otherwise made sacred commercially - how may those processes of authentication be defined ontologically and uncovered epistemologically?
3 **Myth-making: narratives of 'self'**	The articulation of approved and supported master story- lines about self, hearth, and homeland	To **Graburn**, much of the force that drives cultural and heritage presentation in tourism is 'auratic' (i.e., an awe-inspiring imperative to display the power of 'the self' and of the assumed collective subject [the tribe/the nation] which one deems oneself to be part of (3 > 1)); to **Tunbridge and Ashworth** it is always critical to explore 'the dominant ideology thesis' of cultural heritage presentations to ascertain whether the representations being presented to visitors/tourists reflect an existing (or an aspirant) power elite keen to legitimise (or to overthrow) a dominant regime (3 > 2);	Does each tourist/traveller have multiple and conflicting 'selves' - and does the force of these hearthland or these diasporic selves alter significantly in imperative power after a given extended tour experience or a lengthy period of travel?
4 **Myth-making: narratives of 'other'**	The articulation of assumed and framed grand storylines	To **Turner**, individuals and institutions in a given 'host' society strive to identify and celebrate	Are practitioners within the tourism/travel industry conscious of the

	about others, their distant places, and their alien pasts.	themselves reflexively (i.e., differentially) against the characterisations they build up about removed/alternative/other populations (4 > 1); to **Selwyn**, contemporary global tourism is indeed organised dialectically on these axes of centre - definition (i.e., self - representation) vis - a - vis periphery - definition (i.e., other - representation) (4 > 2)	essentialisms of culture/heritage/nature which they conceivably deal in day - to - day as they project their stereotypical visions of 'Otherness' and 'difference'?
5 The production of culture and heritage	The processes of meaning and value generation in culture and heritage, and its articulation across society	To **Buck**, it is critical that tourism researchers explore the totality of production which seemingly transforms (through travel/tourism) ancient rituals and traditions into a decontextualised exotic show for the consumption of Largely unknowing tourists (5 > 1); to **Fjellman**, much of that production in travel and tourism is a purposely decontextualised mix of processes by which powerful companies and closely interlinked transnational corporations selectively reinterpret (and ultimately annihilate) 'history', 'geography', 'nature', and 'culture', et cetera, in the service of their own moneymaking and ideological collective interests (5 > 2).	What are the silences, the suppressions, and the subjugations that a given mainstream cultural storyline or a particular/embedded heritage narrative produces?
6 The production of culture and heritage	The objectifications in and about culture, and the essentialities in and about heritage within research	To **McCrone, Morris, and Kiely** received conceptions of 'Scottishness' (read: established senses of lineage and inheritance anywhere) are dynamic, and evolve in extended or unexpected directions over time (6 > 1); **Hollinshead** considers it to be important to determine whether (and, if so, how?) received notions of culture and heritage have imploded in meaning under the existential fragmentations of post-modernity (and its plausible replacement of old unitary power axes with a new pluralism of power-discourse formations (6 > 2).	Which adversarial 'corrections' or which alternative "re-interpretations" of orthodox culture/conventional inheritance are conceivably on the rise in the given place under the so-called predicaments of the postmodern mood or moment?

Key

1 > 1 = Horne 1992: 165 – 177
1 > 2 = McKay 1988
2 > 1 = MacCannell 1992: 34 & 95
2 > 2 = Urry 1990

3 > 1 = Graburn 1977
3 > 2 = Tunbridge and Ashworth 1996; 47 – 50
4 > 1 = Turner 1973
4 > 2 = Selwyn 1996:9

5 > 1 = Buck 1993:2
5 > 2 = Fjellman 1992:24
6 > 1 = McCrane, Morris, and Kiely 1995: 156 – 181
6 > 2 = Hollinshead 1997: 170 – 193

In paying particular attention to Selwyn, Tunbridge/Ashworth, and Horne, it is not intended to suggest that those are the only investigators in and around tourism studies who have probed meaning-production in the representation of culture, and in the production of heritage, natural, and human inheritances within the industry. Accordingly, Exhibit 1 is now proferred as a table which attempts to illustrate something of the range of thinking that has lately been put into such ethnological cum significatory aspects of place promotion - that is, into the exhibitory of the raw, the real, and the authentic in the literature of tourism studies within the last two decades or so. Exhibit 1 stands as an endeavour to highlight some of undulating advances which have been made in the representativity of tourism and travel, and it is girded around the following six emergent areas or consolidating arenas of meaning-production in tourism which Kirschenblatt - Gimblett's work appears to hover over and across: viz.:

- institutional memory making;

- reality and authenticity projection;

- mythmaking: narratives of self;

- mythmaking: narratives of other;

- the production of culture and heritage; and,

- the interpretation of culture and heritage.

Since Kirschenblatt - Gimblett's assault on the logic of cultural production is a very broad one, no attempt is made in Exhibit 1 to define any singular or ultra - specific subject upon which her own research agenda contributes. Instead, an attempt is made to position the received literature of McKay, MacCannell, Urry, Graburn, Turner, Buck, Fjellman, McCrane/Morris/Kiely, and Hollinshead (alongside that of Selwyn, Tunbridge and Ashworth, and Horne, of course) to which Kirschenblatt - Gimblett's own late commentaries perhaps most fittingly speak. Then a number of suggestive research questions are identified to roughly actualise (i.e., to make apparent in "real", "everyday", or quotidian" settings) the state of the art of the work of McKay, MacConnell, et al.: please refer to the end column of Exhibit 1 for those situated lines of critique. And, again, no - one should think, that the nine supplementary researchers of Exhibit 1 (i.e., McKay, MacCannell, et al.) are the only auxiliary lead international researchers in the literature of tourism studies on culture/heritage production who could have been cited here, for the Exhibit could have been alternatively drawn up utilising delineations of the work in tourism studies of Wright (1985), Cohen (1988), Bruner (1989), Greenwood (1989), Hewison (1989), Norkunas (1993), Hall (1994), Boissevain (1996), and Lanfant (1996), amongst a rich thickening stew of others.

Thus, through the likes of Selwyn, Tunbridge and Ashworth, and Horne, the fields of cultural representation and heritage production which intersect with destination projection in tourism studies, have begun recently to be theoretically fertilised. And now enter Kirschenblatt - Gimblett, with her own deeper treatment of place signification and site projection. Enter Kirschenblatt - Gimblett (1998: 221 and 272), with her critical examination of what she styles as the *madeness* of cultural and heritage places. Enter, Kirschenblatt-

Gimblett, with her incisive interrogations of the way 'the different' and 'the strange' are normalised over a people or over a past through forms of aesthetic imperialism as 'locations' are purposely turned via *the authenticity located within those very methods of staging*, per se, into newly 'unfamiliar' destinations. Enter, Kirschenblatt - Gimblett (1998: 205 and 249) at those points where aesthetics has interface with the politics and the anthropology of the tourism/travel marketplace, where that very staging (i.e., that very display of certain visions of 'peoples', 'places', and 'pasts') may be critically seen as a vital but under-examined subject for tourism studies in and of itself - constituting a cardinal matter of cognitive processes with powerful epistemological implications on and about the manufacture and projectivity of *the hereness* of those claimed/created destinations. Enter Kirschenblatt - Gimblett (1998: 194 and 205), with her trenchant exposition of the staging of or the display of authentic destinations as an immense field of *performative* reality-making - that is, of the calculated madeness of the authenticity of peoples, places, and pasts as a ubiquitous performance epistemology of imagined curatorial and representational institutional and representational agency and sectional interest. (For a previously published introductory piece on the *performative* cultural dynamics of tourism/travel, see Bruner and Kirschenblatt-Gimblett 1994)

Now having attempted to deconstruct something of the width and depth of recent progress in tourism literature on the agency of display and the power of meaning production, it is opportune to turn the limelight onto Kirschenblatt - Gimblett, herself, and to apprehend the key dimensions of her own critical attack on the logics of production as are observable within the "Destination Culture... ." manuscript.

Capture: The Kirschenblatt - Gimblett focus on 'madeness' and 'hereness'

Kirschenblatt - Gimblett's longitudinal inspection of what she calls "the shifting locus of authenticity" is, of course, not one exclusively conducted within tourism studies, itself, for her regime of interest stretches to many arenas where culture, heritage, and/or art are produced and where issue contestations have resulted where diversity is being identified/represented/portrayed. Indeed the backcover of the University of California Press paperback version of "Destination Culture... ." cites three quite different short reviews of the work which are pitched towards 'ethnography', towards 'exhibition studies', and towards 'culture and art' readerships, respectively. Yet Kirschenblatt - Gimblett is able to find commonalities of concern which stretch across these previously splintered forms or these seemingly distinct modes of cultural production, and she notes how for instance museums are today even reproducing the protocols of travel (such as Museum 'Passports') (Kirschenblatt - Gimblett 1998: 135). To her, the evidential crisis in museum identity which many commentators have observed (138) is *reflected at all sites and centres of display, exhibitry, and performance where institutions struggle today to balance their edification mission with their entertainment mission*, not readily knowing - in the Hornian sense (after Horne 1992; see, also, Hollinshead 1999/A) - how "intelligent" to render their messages and their products. To her, the special thing about tourism industry activity is the quantification and the quickness of its impetus, an aspect of destination production which can yield places like Rarotonga (capital of the Cook Islands in the South Pacific) which appear to double its inbound intake of visitors overnight to suddenly possess ten tourists for every local person

(Kirschenblatt - Gimblett 1998: 148), and also places like Hovenweep National Monument straddling the border of Utah and Colorado in the U.S.A. where visitation has been so explosive that identification of the monument's native American ruins has to be clinically removed from maps on account of the volume of visitors who nowadays are drawn then to loot or to sleep in them (Kirschenblatt - Gimblett 1998: 148).

Nonetheless, the task at hand in this critique of Kirschenblatt - Gimblett, is to capture the essence of contributions to the advance of understanding about meaning-production in and under the artifactuality of tourism and its cousin fields of diversity representation. Conceivably, this is best and simplest done through a distillation of the following six components of representational action which appear pointedly and pungently amongst and across the four parts (i.e., across the nine chapters) of "Destination Culture... .": viz., *objectification, fragmentation, contextuality, virtuality, theatricality,* and *authorisation*:

Objectification

Here, Kirschenblatt - Gimblett (1998: 18) broadly calls for more informed consciousness and sense of responsibility on the part of producers of heritage and culture about the surgical nature of their very work, and she urges displayers/exhibitors/storytellers to be much more circumspect about what she calls "the poetics of detachment", and about the selection of the represented artifacts and subjects from the overall object set by which the given theme, narrative, or site is represented. To her, only the artifacts, the tangible metonyms, are really "real". All of the rest is mimetic, is second order, and is *a representative account undeniably of our own making* (Kirschenblatt - Gimblett 1998:30; emphasis added).

Fragmentation

Here Kirschenblatt - Gimblett broadly calls for more informed consciousness and sense of responsibility on the part of agents of display/agents of difference/agents of diversity in the degree to which they themselves privilege certain *collectanea*, and thereby so frequently reify selective 'fragments' of a culture or selective 'fragments' of a narrative and not the or any larger truth. To her, "collection - driven exhibitions often suffer [in tourism and elsewhere] from ethnographic atrophy, because they tend to focus on what ... was physically detached and carried away. As a result, what one has is what one shows. Very often what is shown is the collection, whether highlights, masterpieces, or everything in it. The tendency increases for such objects to be presented as art [rather than as elements of a living culture or a throbbing cosmology]" (Kirschenblatt - Gimblett 1998: 20). And - in mirroring Fjellman's judgement on the pernicious nature of the corporatist expertise of the Disney Corporation in Florida as being self - concerned and absolutist in its exhibited storytelling (see Fjellman (1992), and Hollinshead (1998/A and 1998/B)), Kirschenblatt - Gimblett (1998: 175) considers that tourism practitioners all - too - commonly fragmentatise deliberately and inexactly towards either the attractive image or otherwise, and trivially and shamelessly so, towards the ought - to - have - been hyper - selected golden glow which they inventively wish to portray. Such is the vapid sanitisation of just for too much showing and just far too much telling in tourism (Kirschenblatt- Gimblett 1998: 173).

Contextuality

Here, Kirschenblatt - Gimblett broadly calls for more informed consciousness and sense of responsibility on the part of producers of culture - presentations and heritage - projections towards the way subjects are encapsulated, or rather more usually, the way they are decapsulated from their 'relevant', 'appropriate', or 'found' milieu. Such divorce through the decontextualisation of things, such decapitation of phenomenon, is again something which Fjellman (1992) has written acutely about in terms of the commodification of tourist sites and heritage narratives, and which Buck (1993) has commented penetratingly about in terms of the ideological baggage which can commonly accompany such context - stripping. For Kirschenblatt - Gimblett, the commonplace view that culture is itself an exceedingly durable entity is held rather too strongly even amongst what one might call 'the exhibiting professions': to her, that persistent notion of and about the 'constant' substantiality of culture and about the 'hard - wearing' substantiality of heritage almost constitutes a canon of representational logic. In Kirschenblatt - Gimblett's view, it almost constitutes an abiding outlook which posits the resiliency of culture and heritage as a block force relatively independent of environmental context, intersubjective setting, and temporal moment. And, to Kirchenblatt - Gimblett, it may be encountered by tourists and travellers, in her seasoned judgement, at storytelling site after site, at narrative interpreting destination after destination, and at icon wieding place after place in the exhibition game. Too few culture produces are skilled at distinguishing the problematics of *in situ* representation from the problematics of *in context* representation (Kirschenblatt - Gimblett 1998: 19 and 23). She would no doubt rejoice to learn that attempts are now being made in tourism studies to bring some of the close and critical decipherability of Bhabha (1994) to abstruse contexts in tourism and to vexatious travel encounters in order to probe for the presence or otherwise of all manner of ambiguous but competing cultural resonances, or to pry for all manner of possible hybrid cultural interstitialities (Hollinshead 1998/C and 1998/D).

Virtuality

Here, Kirschenblatt - Gimblett (1998: 131) broadly calls for more informed consciousness and sense of responsibility on the part of interpreters of peoples, places, and pasts to recognise how differently they mediate things when they present *virtuality* as compared to when they present *actuality* - a point which Schechner (1985: 35-116) has deliberated over at length elsewhere in a sustained critique of artifactuality which appears to be quite unknown in the literature of tourism studies. To Kirschenblatt - Gimblett, it is important for culture interpreters and for heritage signifiers to recognise that many "difficult" subjects ought still be depicted in presentations of peoples, places, and pasts even though representation of them may be exceedingly troublesome to render as 'real': to her, "realness, or the fidelity of the virtual world of the [given location], is not enough. The 'actual' must be [routinely and necessarily] exhibited alongside the 'virtual' in a [comparative] show of truth" (Kirschenblatt - Gimblett 1998: 195) under such oft - recurring circumstances, and she lauds the exhibitry of the Pilgrim Village tourist site of "Plimoth Plantation" [Plymouth, Massachusetts] for the tour de force of the marriage of its staged actuality with its staged virtuality (Kirschenblatt - Gimblett 1998: 195). To Kirschenblatt - Gimblett, it is important that the exhibiting professions do not continue to shy away from the presentation of the painful, or the atrocious merely because such 'actual' narratives are difficult to encapsulate *in the raw* or troublesome to project *in the real*: projectors of peoples, places, and pasts, must become sensible, refined, and critical projectors of virtuality when the representational going gets tough, so to speak. She therefore joins forces with Christy Coleman - supervisor of the dubious - to - some 'slave auctions' at the famed Colonial Williamsburg heritage site (Virginia, U.S.A.) who contends that only through open display and discussion, at such demanding or troublesome sites, could visitors understand, for instance, the degree of degradation a past people must have endured or otherwise come to appreciate the level of present humiliation that a population must still be suffering, today (Kirschenblatt - Gimblett 1998: 173).

Theatricality

Here, Kirschenblatt - Gimblett broadly calls for more informed consciousness and sense of responsibility on the part of site planners, operators, and programmers in the commonplace but scarcely-suspected dramaturgy of their work - that is, in the habitually denied but inexorably essential Thespian genius of their role in signifying "difference" or in projecting "diversity". By Kirschenblatt - Gimblett's (1998: 21) account, the existing curatorial conventions which have tended to drive the representation of local heritage and the presentation of local heritage privilege the endeavour to deal in 'truth' at the conceivable expense of 'understanding'. To her, such culture - communicating and heritage - hortating truthseekers classically fear "the danger that theatrical spectacle will displace [their proper goal of] scientific seriousness, [and] that the artifice of [the credited and installed drama] will overwhelm [the due decency] of ethnographic artefact and curatorial intention". In Kirschenblatt - Gimblett's judgement, many themes of place and many narratives of history need *theatricality* in and of presentation because the sites available to them (like the Museum of Sydney and the Hyde Park Barracks in New South Wales, Australia (Kirschenblatt - Gimblett 1998: 168)) are so frequently rather contained and non - evocative settings. Adopting a Barthesian stance (after Barthes 1988), she suggests that the theatrical - or rather the *performative* - is indeed required in interpretations of heritage and culture where language and metalanguage have exhausted their formal capacities, that is where things cannot be strictly or meaningfully described (Kirschenblatt - Gimblett 1998: 235). Yet, she takes pains to argue that the use of theatrical effect still must needfully be accountable, and the presenters of serious cultural events and earnest heritage representations should "try to achieve [something of] the exuberance and wide appeal of popular entertainment without exoticising performances unfamiliar to their audiences" (Kirschenblatt - Gimblett 1998: 221). And, again, one should note that Kirschenblatt - Gimblett has written weightily on this particular matter of theatrical performalivity in the tourism studies literature before (see Bruner and Kirschenblatt - Gimblett 1994).

Authorisation

Here, Kirschenblatt - Gimblett (1998:132; emphasis added) broadly calls for more responsibility on the part of its destination storytellers, its destination exhibit - designers, and its destination imagineers towards the recognition of the authorial consequences of their everyday signifying activities, warning that what may appear to be exhibited mundanely at a particular tourist locale may in fact become a larger - than - life object of reification: "what is most ordinary in the context of the [given] destination [frequently] becomes a source of [unbridled] fascination for the visitor - cows being milked on a farm, the subway in Mexico

City during rush hour, outdoor barbers in Nairobi, [and] the etiquette of bathing in Japan. Once it is [even an accidentally designated site marked, or set up] to be seen, the life becomes *a museum of itself*". It is imperative that all representators of the plain and the prosaic (and not just representators of the famously diverse and the fabulous different) become sensible to and about the inherent and the sovereign assertivity of their broadcase imagery, even where that depiction is a quotidian exhibitry of the homespun and the humble. In some circumstances that vigilant circumspection of the everyday peremptory power to authorise peoples, places, and pasts is particularly grave, however, and Kirschenblatt - Gimblett warms that few 'producers' and 'networkers' of culture and heritage proffer enough respect or humility in the presence of those traditions and social events which ought *not* be described or revealed. And, likewise, in Kirschenblatt - Gimblett's judgement, too few producers and networkers take due care to determine whether, in traditional or indigenous scenarios, they are becoming culturally aware through dialogue with *the appropriate individuals* in the population being described: the everyday determination of who is "appropriate" through descent or through other societal qualification is generally not only a complex one, it is currently a generally avoided one (or, at least, an under-recognised one) (Kirschenblatt - Gimblett 1998: 75). She also warns of the problems occasioned by those place - makers and image - mongers who all too readily cede their insider positions of cultural guardianship to outsider corporatist interests or who otherwise sell out their found powers of authorisation to the intemperate logocentrism of 'designer - label' capitalists (Kirschenblett - Gimblett 1998: 184 - 5).

The above constructions of *objectification*, *fragmentation*, *contextuality*, *virtuality*, *theatricality*, and *authorisation* stand as important conceptualisations through which Kirschenblatt - Gimblett has come to monitor meaning-production in and around the making of destinations over the last two decades around the world. While these six conceptions attest to the very potency of the right, and thus the capacity of well-situated-people, to represent things whether they recognise their supreme powers, or not, they also collectively demonstrate in misty Bhabhian half - tones of understanding [after Bhabha (1994)) that much of decipherability of "difference projection" and "diversity signification" is ineluctably cryptic and enigmatic. Such are the everyday vexations in and of the representation of populations and their places in tourism, the consciousness-industry - or, to digress, should that currently, and more fittingly be, the unconsciousness industry? Anyhow, while Kirschenblatt - Gimblett may herself note that so much cultural presentation and heritage exhibition evidently pivots upon "loud" themes of death, dissection, torture, and martyrdom, she joins MacAloon (1984) in noting that such fabulous spectacles may so often also be viewed "quietly" and less sensationally as depicting scenes of another man's simple life (Kirschenblatt - Gimblett 1998: 47 and 290).

Bracketing: Propositional knowledge on 'madeness' and 'hereness'

Having made an attempt to capture the usual but expansive manners in which Kirschenblatt - Gimblett currently approaches matters of 'madeness' and 'hereness' in the artifactuality and in the articulation of culture/heritage production, it is now salutary to hold her research agenda on site - making and destination - making up for a more rigorous and detailed analysis. To this end, an endeavour will now be take *to bracket* - after Husserl (1962: 86) -

her conceptions strictly and closely in their own terms, that is, in the conceptual schemes she herself has built up. For present purposes, this *bracketing* is Denzian in style (viz., largely after Denzin 1989: 55 - 58) constituting an intimate reading and dissection of the "Destination Culture…" manuscript. The substantialities unearthered in that attentive mining of textual meaning are now put forward in the form of thirty propositions on Kirschenblatt-Gimblett's constructions of 'madeness' and 'hereness'. They are listed within exhibits 2.1 to 2.6 in terms of their fit with or under the six previously captured constructions on cultural production and performance, viz., *objectification* (exhibit 2.1), *fragmentation* (exhibit 2.2), *contextuality* (exhibit 2.3), *virtuality* (exhibit 2.4), *theatricality* (exhibit 2.5), and *authorisation* (2.6).

Exhibit 2.1

Objectification in and of the 'madeness' and 'hereness' of places: Propositions on the representation of difference and diversity

Prognosis on objectification

The objectification and authentication of artifacts lies not so much within the objects themselves but in the methods by which they were performed, known, and therefore 'made' (196).

Proposition 1: the making of cultural and heritage objects

That the ethnographic objects of cultural and heritage tourism tend to be made and not found, becoming "ethnographic" through processes of detachment and contextualisation (3; 17 - 18;)

Proposition 2: the naturalisation of favoured objects

That in most societies, elites accumulate overtime the added power to naturalise to quintessentialise, and even to racialise people, places, and pasts. (12)

Proposition 3: the contested entities of culture, heritage, and nature

That in cultural and heritage tourism as elsewhere 'whole' or 'complete' things are not given but are constituted aggregations by certain individuals/institutions which are frequently hotly contested by other individuals/interest groups. (21)

Proposition 4: the undersuspected making and mediation of objects at events and exhibits

That administrative, organisational, and infrastructural arrangements for the management and promotion of culture heritage are *not* neutral and disinterested sites for the production of meaning, but critical and committed sites of interpretation and connotation. (204)

Proposition 5: the occasional and deliberately ambiguous objectification of things

That from time to time, objectifying agencies in cultural and heritage tourism will intentionally issue partial, negotiable, or enigmatic interpretations about peoples, places, and pasts, the labile character of which responds delicately to but differentially with various interest groups within or across a found polyvocality. (185; 195).

Source: All page numbers shown in brackets are from Kirschenblatt - Gimblett (1998), unless a separate author is shown.

Exhibit 2.2

Fragmentation in and of the 'madeness' and 'hereness' of places: propositions on the representation of difference and diversity

Prognosis on fragmentation:

Promoters and signifiers of particular cultural/heritage/natural sites and themes have available to them a boundless litany of things which they can objectivity or otherwise appropriate for a given interpreted storyline or for a particular angle of interpretation. Many of these adductable phenomena (viz., concrete items) or noumenon (viz., abstract items) are or have otherwise been deemed to be small, singular, or scanty. Each time the representer acquires (i.e., accepts or rejects a 'thing) she has climatically begun to classify and interpret a found people, place, or past, (28). Where that attentivity to detail is seen or assumed to be particularly thorough, that producer of culture/heritage/nature is deemed to operate with or by ' microveracity' (Fjellman 1992:89; see also Hollinshead 1998/B [Glossary]).

Proposition 6: the power of evidential literal detail

That the communicability and believability of presentations of culture and heritage can both be improved by the clever tactical use of apparently meticulously researched and/or apparently fastidiously reconstructed given subjects, scenes, or settings. (194)

Proposition 7: the infinity of instigation points for destination - making

That there exists an endless variety of large/small/fragmented starting points which those representing the culture, the heritage, or the nature of a location can incite, kindle, or whip up in order to turn that place, site, or setting into a significant, notable, or special 'destination'. (21)

Proposition 8: the endorsement of or by small objects

That the seeming factualness, realness, or trustworthiness of a scene, site, or subject can be vouched for through the skilled or adventitious deployment of an infinity of certain large, small, or fragmented symbolically-potent objects. (193)

Proposition 9: the unwary incorporation of error in interpretation and signification

That many presentations of a people, a place or a past in cultural tourism exhibits or in heritage tourism articulations about the distinct character of a special 'destination' are in fact founded unknowingly upon large, small or fragmentary errors of understanding which have acquired considerable value, vital force, or rich credibility over time. (8)

Proposition 10: the collaborative imagination of and about time

That frequently the producers of cultural narratives and/or heritage storylines will function associatively with site visitors to jumble up the chronology of a site or to otherwise deny due passage of time in order to collaboratively accentuate the significance of a fragmentary moment or of fragmentary moments in time because of that moment's (those moments' symbolic significance). (198)

Source: All page numbers shown in brackets are from Kirschenblatt - Gimblett (1998), unless a separate author is shown.

Exhibit 2.3

Contextuality in and of the 'madeness' and 'hereness' of places: propositions on the representation of difference and diversity

Prognosis on contextuality:

In Kirschenblatt - Gimblet's view, contextual (or in - 'context') approaches to exhibitry and representation set out a theoretical morphology of and about the subjects and objects presented for the visitor. They also "offer explanation, provide historical background, make comparisons, pose questions, and sometimes even extend to the circumstances of excavation, collection, and conservation of the objects on display. There are as many contexts for an object as there are interpretive strategies" (21). The objects themselves may be given that context via labeling, diagrams, and commentary, audio - visual explanation/brackets, educational workshops, performances, et cetera, and of course by means of the careful placement of other proximal subjects, objects, and themes (21).

Proposition 11: the strong cognitive control of and via contextualisation

That contextual approaches to the signification and/or the exhibitry of things tend to comprise modes of representation which are heavily reliant upon the say-so of classification and the know-so of taxonomic arrangement to order phenomenon and/or nonmenon in relation to one another and to the outside world, and they therefore tend to constitute modes of representation which exert rich loads of etic reasoning over those phenomenon and/or nonmenon (21 - 22).

Proposition 12: the creative - environmental character of in situ presentations

That in situ approaches to the signification and/or the exhibitry of things tend to comprise modes of representation which are heavily reliant upon the use of 'environmental' and 're-creative' displays (20).

Proposition 13: the sanitization of storylines through spectacle

That approaches to signification and/or the exhibitry of peoples/places/pasts which are heavily reliant upon 'spectacle' tend to be undeveloped in their analytical content and are also inclined to suppress profound issues of conflict and marginalisation (72).

Proposition 14: the contextual shadow over human performers

That approaches to signification and/or the exhibitry of things which are heavily reliant upon the visual appeal and the spectacular effects of 'festival' tend to objectify the human performers involved and thereby implicate them in the reductionisms and in the essentialisms being represented (72).

Proposition 15: the gradual loss of contextuality following extended performance

That long run/distended/much repeated performances of storylines tend to freeze those productions and render them canonical over time, occasioning a processual routinisation and/or trivilisation of representation which gradually can become alien to the originally important local settings and/or community contextualisations (64).

Source: All page numbers shown in brackets are from Kirschenblatt - Gimblett (1998), unless a separate author is shown.

Exhibit 2.4

Virtuality in and of the 'madeness' and 'hereness' of places: propositions on the representation of difference and diversity

Prognosis on virtuality

Kirschenblett - Gimblett reminds us that performances or presentations of culture and history can range from 'internment' (i.e., from a tomb with a view) form of exhibitry to live displays (i.e., where formal recreations generate the illusion "that the activities you watch are being done rather than represented, a practice that creates the effect of authenticity, or realness" (Kirschenblatt - Gimblett 1998: 55 and 57). The virtuality effect of performance or presentation (i.e., the degree to which it may or is taken to be 'actuality' or 'reality') may be expansively environmental (using the natural and built setting of a locale) or it may be hermetically sealed within a tightly bounded - aesthetic space (such as a proscenium stage). Hence performances and presentations can range from sensory saturating exhibitry (which engages olfactory, gustatory, auditory, tactile kinesthetic, and/or visual effects) to single - sense epiphanies (Kirschenblatt - Gimblett 1998: 58). Whatever the mode of performance or presentation, displays and exhibits can have a profound, virtual, museum effect: "not only do ordinary things become special when [paraded or put on view], but the museum experience itself becomes a model for experiencing life outside of its walls" (Kirschenblatt - Gimblett 1998: 51).

Proposition 16: the 'ethnographic' marking of reality

That certain performances and presentations of culture and heritage engender a high and everyday 'reality effect' on account of their deliberately reserved 'ethnographic' style of marking whereby the mode of exhibity/display utilised is low in theatricality but high in information. (216)

Proposition 17: the influence upon virtuality of arbitrary placement

That the arbitrary and the apparent arbitrary placement of phenomenon in performances and presentations of culture and/or heritage frequently are each deliberately utilised (by individuals/institutions who represent peoples/places/pasts as an instrument of controlled signification to effectively push their preferred interpretations about different or diverse populations, or to otherwise neutralise other interpretations. (183/4)

Proposition 18: the influence upon virtuality of repetitive placement

That the repetitive broadcast of preselected narratives or storylines about peoples/places/pasts is a deliberate practice (of individuals/institutions who represent culture or who project heritage) who seek to render some preferred interpretations of 'hereness' dominant, or otherwise to subjugate/suppress/ silence other unwanted interpretations about different or diverse populations. (183/4)

Proposition 19: the chunkable interpretive potency of 'festival'

That the highly bounded and pardonable character of festivals in time and space renders them as particularly encapsulated and powerful vehicles of virtual signification about peoples/places/pasts, especially for tourists/visitors/recreational travellers who are journeying to cultural or heritage destinations on tight schedules. (61)

Proposition 20: the stylised interpretive potency of 'folklore'

That much of the power of performances and presentations of "folklore' in the representation of cultural and heritage destinations stems from the use of precisely stylised and highly choreographed 'European' modes of production (which are generally 'selectively short', 'musically accompanied', and 'improvisation curtailed' significations of the lore of peoples/places/pasts which privilege virtuosic, athletic, dramatic, and spectacular projections) rather than distinct, stand - alone, aesthetic projections of virtuality. (62-65; 216)

Source: All page numbers shown in brackets are from Kirschenblatt - Gimblett (1998), unless a separate author is shown.

Exhibit 2.5

Theatricality in and of the 'madeness' and 'hereness' of places: propositions on the representation of difference and diversity

Prognosis on theatricality

Kirschenblatt - Gimblett (1998:3) maintains the view that expositions and representations of culture and/or heritage in tourism are fundamentally theatrical, whether they are 'in situ displays' or 'in - context' displays. To her, both in situ exhibitions and in-context significations of 'hereness' are disclosive and demonstrable in their mode of communication, and to her this highly performative aesthetic is one of intelligibility (Kirschenblatt - Gimblett 1998:3). Drawing on Heidegger (1977) and Mitchell (1989), Kirschenblatt - Gimblett (1998:4) adopts the view that expositions and representations of peoples/places/pasts are inclined to produce an effect which we subsequently call 'the real world', and this theatrical manifestation is anterior, if subsequent, to the representation. To Kirschenblatt - Gimblett, highly - artistic/highly - performative representations of culture and heritage are generally not random or intrusion-free significations of being and identity, but substantively biased and intercessive 'shaping' and 'educating' expositions.

Proposition 21: the commonplace mediation of and through art

That representation of culture and heritage at tourism destinations which are heavily reliant upon art or artistic significance tend to be 'highly mediated' rather than 'unmediated' forms of exposition. (245)

Proposition 22: the proclamatory license in and of art (as 'form' of communication)

That performances and/or presentations of culture and/or heritage have greater revelatory potency when the phenomenon on view are exhibited as 'art' rather than when they are displayed as 'artifact'. (11)

Proposition 23: the proclamatory license in and of theatre (as 'site' of communication)

That in difficult moments of contested meaning/being/identity, performances and/presentations of culture/heritage which are 'theatrical' (i.e., staged in a theatre) tend to be much more widely and acceptably received than performances and/or presentations of culture/heritage which are 'museological' (i.e., staged in a museum). (34)

Proposition 24: the objectificatory power of live exhibits

That the performance and/or presentation of 'live' exhibits tend to generate rich objectifying significations, particularly in terms of their expository capacity to turn understanding of 'people' into ethnographic 'artifacts'. (55)

Proposition 25: the illusion of the real and raw 'live' thing

That the theatricality of 'live' expositions of culture and heritage tend to create the illusory impression that the storyline/scene/setting being signified is a true, natural, and unmediated happening. (55)

Source: All page numbers shown in brackets are from Kirschenblatt - Gimblett (1998), unless a separate author is shown.

Exhibit 2.6

Authorisation in and of the 'madeness' and 'hereness' of places: propositions on the representation of difference and diversity

Prognosis on authorisation

It is the view of Kirschenblatt - Gimblett (1998:8) that most governments and cultural/heritage institutions recognise the ideological value of performances or presentations of 'hereness', and strategically try to use representations of peoples/places/pasts via forms of "tourism realism" to reflect the themes and ideas they wish to advance. But just as governments/institutions regular seek to favour some narratives and images, so they also wish to foreclose others (Kirschenblatt - Gimblett 1998:8). And governments and institutions - and even individual collectors/exhibitors/ethnographers can authorise things through their everyday/mundane activities of search, identification, and classification. Once more, it ought to be stressed that the credentialisation of the phenomenon of peoples/places/pasts is an ongoing/quotidian activity which all sorts of institutions and individuals regularly participate in consciously and/or unconsciously: the making of significant things within the cultural and heritage repertoire of destination is a matter of the petty but accumulative mobilisation of socio-political preference, and culturo-political privilege.

Proposition 26: the unavoidability of partiality in the propagation of narratives of difference

That no representations of culture and heritage even 'in situ' and/or 'mimetic' ones - are neutral: all significants of identity/being/difference are weighted towards, and thereby help authorise some images, ideas, and/or inheritances rather than towards other images, ideas, and inheritances. (2)

Proposition 27: the human entitlement for 'natural' entities

That things of culture and things of heritage are commonly found to be 'rare'/'valuable'/'important' on account of the ways in which researchers/collectors/presenters have attempted to investigate, locate, or acquire them: it is the very mustering of and classification of phenomenon and noumenon that produces and formulates so many apparently 'natural' things. (25)

Proposition 28: the authorisation of the seemingly noteworthy as 'art'

That the more singular, special, or critically different a cultural/heritage/ethnographic object is designated to be, the more likely is that assumed or certified entity to be reclassified, exhibited, and visited as a form of art, ipso facto. (25)

Proposition 29: the contained textuality of 'festival'

That representations and significations of difference and diversity which constitute arts festivals tend to be less didactic and less textual in their exposition than representations and significations of difference and diversity which constitute museum exhibitions: festival representations tend to depend more on the power of 'performance', per se, to minimise the awkwardness of discourse in 'live' settings. (61-65)

Proposition 30: the inherent conservations of 'festival' and 'carnival'

That festivals/carnivals of cultural or heritage performance tend to reinforce the status quo of articulations about a people/place/past - even when those festivals/carnivals are ostensibly 'oppositional' in intended form as intended message - because of the high degree to which dominant/mainstream values are inherently built into the organisational structure and operating decorums of that 'authorising' event. (77).

Source: All page numbers shown in brackets are from Kirschenblatt - Gimblett (1998), unless a separate author is shown.

A number of further points of clarification ought first be registered in order to aid comprehension of exhibits 2.1 to 2.6:

- firstly, Kirschenblatt - Gimblett (1998: 8) fundamentally views location - imaging and destination - making in cultural and heritage production as *a critical site* of meaning production;

- secondly, Kirschenblatt - Gimblett (1998: 7) strongly maintains that a main consequence of all the meaning - making in and of tourism and travel is that the tourism industry effectively engages in the staging of the world as *an emulatory museum of itself* - where its own images, orientations, reductionisms are privileged, mirrored, and incessantly replayed by its own actors, and agents;

- thirdly, it is through such regular incitement of those tourism industry images, orientations, and reductionisms that Kirschenblatt - Gimblett (1998: 7) suggests that tourism practitioners and exhibition display powerbrokers have a or the principal role in the conjuring up of new/refurbished/restyled *senses of 'hereness'* by which local 'locations' are converted into industry - articulated and widely - known 'destinations';

- fourthly, it is Kirschenblatt - Gimblett's (1998: 6 and 128) view that all this showing, speaking, and making of peoples, places, and pasts constitutes *an active* (i.e., a doing) *exhibitionary logic* by which museum, tourism, and other cultural/heritage displays constitute 'subjects' as being important, and classify 'objects' in time and space;

- fifthly, over the years many 'mogul' culture producers and 'baronial' heritage exhibitors in the destination - making business have recognised that there are indeed certain superb vehicles - (which as an extension of Kirschenblatt - Gimblett one could call *temples of exposition*) - for the proselytising of new/refurbished/restyled articulations of inheritance, identity, or being (Kirschenblatt - Gimblett 1998: 125) [Such temples of exposition include World Fairs, State Festivals, National Birthplace Sites, et cetera];

- sixthly, according to Kirschenblatt - Gimblett (1998: 65) much of the exhibitionary logic of the 'madeness' and 'hereness' of institutions in the business of heritage and travel is *strongly charged ideologically* whereby the performative context of destination making frequently serves as an assertive agent in contestations of territorial sovereignity, political boundedness, and language supremacy, et cetera; and,

- finally, in the cultural politics that the artifactuality of heritage tourism so frequently is, the appearance of careful 'scientific' labelling and of the privileged projection of things as, for instance, 'fine art' can serve as powerful *instruments of universalising understanding* - thereby constituting an idiom - making game of 'science' and 'truth'.

In examining the thirty propositions on 'madeness' and 'hereness' of exhibits 2.1 to 2.6, it should also be recognised that Kirschenblatt - Gimblett also offers propositional insight on how visitors to cultural tourism and/or heritage tourism sites are themselves actually inclined to interpret the projected representations of difference and diversity. If, once more, one may extend her statements in "Destination Culture... .", it ought to be recognised that:

The received experience at cultural/heritage performances and presentations

That, since no one sees 'everything' at events or exhibits which represent difference and diversity in culture and heritage, each visitor makes his/her own festival-experience/carnival-experience/show-experience (and it is therefore unwise to speak too strongly of the shared experience of all visitors) (Kirschenblatt - Gimblett 1998: 247);

The necessity for guided interpretation at representations of amorphous or inchoate subjects/objects

That, where the subject mix/object mix being performed or presented generally appears to visitors to be grotesque, rude, strange, vulgar, or nebulous, those visitors tend to require a set of guiding principles or a contextual framework to prevent that performance or presentation being interpreted as trivial or valueless (Kirschenblatt - Gimblett 1998: 23);

The immense wealth of interpretive sensation within virtual realities settings

That designers of virtual reality cultural and heritage significations and expositions may in fact harness an enormous and ever - enlarging 'arsenal' of available visceral, kinesthetic, haptic, and intimate responses on the part of visitors to 'receive' the performative presentations being conveyed, if they can immerse those visitors within that virtual encounter (Kirschenblatt - Gimblett 1998: 194);

The positive value and/or negative hindrance of conventional master - narratives on interpreted objects

That designers-of-performances/presentators-of-difference/exhibitors-of-diversity may draw upon - or may otherwise have to acknowledge - the sustained nexus between received/established/hallowed (sometimes Biblical!) narrative accounts of peoples/places/pasts and the subjects and objects which they have selected for the representation at hand;

The parallel clocks for the historical moment

That performers/presenters of cultural history or of heritage truths have routinely to heed "the shadow of time' given by at least three important clocks which the interpreting visitor is routinely cognisant about, or tuned into: (i) the stopped clock of the historical moment; (ii) the heritage clock which emanates not only from the historical 'time' being depicted, but which runs thereafter; and, (iii) the clock of the visitor's own particular travel experience of the immediate journey/immediate day/immediate vacation.

Certain other qualifying statements ought to be registered in order to conceivably round off the detailed bracketing of Kirschenblatt - Gimblett's critique of culture and heritage production as explained in exhibits 2.1 to 2.6. While in her judgement 'culture' and 'heritage' are not simply inherited things - being, instead, phenomenon which are constantly being constituted, renewed, or de-imagined (Kirschenblatt - Gimblett 1998: 242) - it is tourism itself which is the increasingly potent setting for these constitutional activities and these practices of renewal (Kirschenblatt - Gimblett 1998: 7); to her, it is tourism "which not only compresses [the culture and the heritage of] the life world, but [which] also displaces it, thereby escalating the process by which a way of life becomes heritage" (Kirschenblatt - Gimblett 1998: 7).

To Kirschenblatt - Gimblett (1998: 99 and 65) then, tourism and travel is increasingly not only the site of the representation of a received culture or heritage, it is the vehicle which nowadays activates or reactivates the given or the emergent population; and it is also the instrument by which interest groups in and across that population increasingly recognise that their claims to the past (and, *inter alia*, their claims to and for "the present' and "the future') ought to be exercised. It is her view that as the tourism industry continues its move from a product - driven to a market-led approach (Kirschenblatt - Gimblett 1998: 137), whole new sources of benefit or gain may be seen to be available to those who control it; for instance, "a place like Salem, Massachusetts, may be even more profitable as an exhibition of a mercantile centre than it [ever] was as a mercantile centre [itself]" (Kirschenblatt - Gimblett 1998: 7). In these ways, then, tourism and travel are seen by her to be important contemporary mechanisms which help accelerate the reformulation of tradition and which may help speed up the dynamic rearticulation and dearticulation of held differences in meaning, being, and identity (Kirschenblatt - Gimblett 1998: 243). Tradition has always encompassed 'change': the image-making power and ubiquity of tourism and travel seemingly now ensure that our traditions get spring-cleaned that much more frequently, speedily, and publically.

Reconnections: The elements of 'madeness' and hereness' re - assembled

Having disclosed a number of fundamental elements of Kirschenblatt - Gimblett's research agenda on 'madeness' and 'hereness', it is now helpful to re - interpret those insights collectively and to relocate them within the larger social and industrial world of tourism and travel. The intent here is to resynthesise the detailed understanding contained within and across the thirty propositions put forward within Exhibits 2.1 to 2.6, in order to reintegrate into the experience of everyday decision - making practitioner and research posts in tourism and travel. In Denzian terms, the aim is now therefore to indicate how the insights of Kirschenblatt - Gimblett conceivably fit within the interactive world of managers and developers of cultural tourism/heritage travel, or conceivably matter to those who research the cultural and heritage destinations of tourism and travel.

In attempting to reconnect or relocate Kirschenblatt - Gimblett's critique of cultural production the following matters of synthesis perhaps warrant attention:

Receiving and reconnecting 'difference'

In "Destination Culture... .", Kirschenblatt - Gimblett makes it plain that while the "other-seeking" and "encounter-craving" tourism industry *requires* the production of difference in order to inherently function (whereby successful places at promotion and projectivity reap the spillover benefits of the development and articulation of a 'positive' or a specific benefit-bestowing image (Kirschenblatt - Gimblett 1998: 152)), all too frequently those who work on matters of 'difference' and 'diversity' in tourism/travel think insufficiently about the preciousness of their own stewardship role of such matters of distinct culture and dissimilar heritage. Drawing from the judgement of (Raymond) Williams (1960: 343) that "a culture can never be reduced to its artifacts while it is being lived", she condemns the ubiquitous artifactuality of the destination makers of cultural tourism and heritage tourism. To her, their work mirrors the prosaic competence of the undertaker (who works with 'dead' exhibits) rather than it reflects the craft of the steward (who works with life-force entities, and with life-connected stimuli) (Kirschenblatt - Gimblett 1998: 165). To Kirschenblatt - Gimblett, too many managers of 'difference' and too many projectors of 'diversity' in tourism and travel rely exclusively on the mere undertaking techniques of apparent animation, and too few on the more painstaking and discerning palette of skills demanded in and of the living transmission of cultural knowledge and heritage values (Kirschenblatt - Gimblett 1998: 166). In these ways, the differences of and between places are all too readily banalized through the representational field of tourism, or rendered inconsequential in and through the everyday image - making pursuits of the representational field of travel. In Kirschenblatt - Gimblett's view, we routinely miss the very uplifting potency and the inspirational vitality that is latent at our destination sites and our tourist settings.

Reconceiving and reconnecting 'hereness'

In synthesising the significance of fuller and richer cognition about 'hereness' for tourism and travel decision - makers, the worth of Kirschenblatt - Gimblett's insights on cultural and heritage production is that she instructs everyday image - makers to be much more circumspect about the effect of their projectivity, yet still decently imaginative about its available and attainable possibilities. Too frequently, presentations of cultural differentiation and of heritage differentiation are seen to be progressivist and gloss-giving instruments of urban development (Kirschenblatt - Gimblett 1998: 155), and the common 'arbitrariness' (Kirschenblatt - Gimblett 1998: 247), or the common safe and conservative appropriateness, of such promotions of place (Kirschenblatt - Gimblett 1998: 242) is not readily identified or admitted by the so-called professionals in the field. What Kirschenblatt - Gimblett seems to praise are those projectors of 'hereness' who are decently tuned into the power of their own role in meaning-production, and who clearly self-acknowledge that they literally function within both the realm of 'the museum' and the realm of 'the theatre'. To her, lauded destination - sites like Plimoth Planation in Massachusetts, are extraordinarily powerful experiments in virtuality where the endless meaning production of and about hereness is not merely recreative and simulative, but where it is decidedly improvisational (Kirschenblatt - Gimblett 1998: 189). Culture, heritage, history are each so communicatively 'real' and "arrestive', there, that one can literally taste the 'hereness' they convey (Kirschenblatt - Gimblett 1998: 199) - and literally smell the 'whenness' of its projected authenticities, too, presumably!

Reconceiving and reconnecting 'madeness'

Kirschenblatt - Gimblett's insights on "madeness", of course, complement her intelligences on 'hereness', and work to inform decision - takers in tourism and travel (as elsewhere in the industries of projection and representation) of the inevitable problematic relationships of selected objects of display to the instruments of that act of display. To Kirschenblatt - Gimblett, all objects of received ' tradition' and of received 'inheritance' are foreign to present - day contexts of display and exposition, for each cultural performances and every heritage presentations in fact strongly mediates the message. She reminds us that 'art' can never speak for itself (Kirschenblatt - Gimblett 1998: 245). To her, the instrument of the given interface - viz., the festival, the museum exhibit, the historical village, the designed postcard - all axiomatically encode. They are all loaded "engines of meaning" (Kirschenblatt - Gimblett 1998: 157): they are all potentially powerful tools for the manufacture and/or authorisation of legitimacy (Kirschenblatt - Gimblett 1998: 242). They are potentially potent evocative and enunciatory rhetorical mechanisms of 'madeness'.

Accordingly, what Kirschenblatt - Gimblett (1998: 250) warns decision - takers involved in culture and heritage production is that they ought to be vigilant about the manner in which they might be propelling the objects of display and exhibitry "beyond contexts for which they were made". She wants such professionals to appreciate that the interpretations and significations of culture and heritage they deal in are ultimately about 'people' not 'things' (Kirschenblatt - Gimblett 1998: 159). In this regard, Kirschenblatt - Gimblett clearly seeks to underscore for such decision - takers and image - makers in tourism and travel (and beyond), the very *human agency* of their work in the 'madeness' of broader society: what counts to her is not only what represented cultural objects/heritage themes/societal secrets mean (in perhaps a one-dimensional sense), *but how and by whom they are nowadays variably made and variably shown to mean those meanings* (Kirschenblatt 1998: 254). In this sense, culture - making ought not be seen to be the exclusive preserve of the power-elite in societies - if, problematically, it even was so; culture ought not to be seen as something formally or inherently dictated to the exploited masses below, for the power-elite 'at the top' are certainly not, today, the only actual custodians of culture and heritage. Today, then, the mythmakers of tourism and the image-makers of travel not only have an immense role to play in determining which 'traditions' are to remain (and which fresh ones are to become!) durable, they also have a cardinal role to play in determining which interpretations of and about those traditions are to flower, and (more importantly!) which mix of those often-adversarial interpretations are to flickeringly, creatively, or collectively prosper.

Reconceiving and reconnecting 'destination consciousness'

Given the ubiquity of 'hereness' activities and the accumulative force of 'madeness' endeavours within tourism and travel, Kirschenblatt - Gimblett (1998: 151) considers the tourism industry to work *collaboratively* with what she calls the heritage industry: in her estimation, while the heritage industry converts locations into destinations, the tourism industry then makes them economically viable as a parodying exhibit of themselves. Sometimes, that critical and sustaining collaborative effort works to creatively conjure up 'new traditions' (Kirschenblatt - Gimblett 1998: 79 and 242), and at other times it works to reductively project or to *foreclose* 'useful' but 'troublesome' old traditions, as Kirschenblatt - Gimblett (1998: 162) - in drawing from a Reuters internet brief - maintains is the case in Burma (Myanmar), where national authorities are restrictively projecting and controlling the long - necked minority women of eastern Burma. And to Kirschenblatt - Gimblett, where such performances and presentations are only ever *virtual* without also being *actual* (and thereby connected to the raw/pulsating world!), that collaboration is only hallucinative (Kirschenblatt - Gimblett 1998: 169-7).

In these ways, then, Kirschenblatt - Gimblett (1998: 176) seeks to awaken or to reawaken decision - takers and image - producers to the seriousness of their subject as an industry of consciousness - making. She views tourism and travel as part of a repository realm for the stewardship and the creative renewal of communal imagination (Kirschenblatt - Gimblett 1998: 242). To her - as an echo of Holloway (1994: 147) - the imaginative appeal of contemporary tourism is that its purview over everything from culture and heritage to geography and nature gives it the loaded capacity to relay or manufacture a limitless array of products, themes, and images about our inheritances (Kirschenblatt - Gimblett 1998: 171). And she wants the decision-takers and the image-producers of tourism and travel to be just so much more attentive to the inherently performative dynamics of their projections, and to the human and societal values they help either circulate or deny. And that is not just a matter of responsibly selecting this or that cultural narrative or this or that heritage storyline: to her, in seconding the judgement of Peter Sellars (Director of the 1990 Los Angeles Festival), it is also vitally a matter of responsibly knowing how much about any - theme/any - image/any - narrative to explain, and how much to leave to each visitor's own untreated but open powers of perception (Kirschenblatt - Gimblett 1998: 237). Kirschenblatt-Gimblett is considerably concerned about whether the producers of culture and heritage "shows" ever ask just how much informative 'talk' should accompany 'the dance' being exhibited? And just how 'old' or 'relevant' should that actualising or virtualising talk be? Thus, she constantly questions whether the tourism industry is itself currently no more than a tarted - up museum of old consciousnesses (Kirschenblatt - Gimblett 1998: 176), compromising a tired old realm where ancient and ethnocentric ideas of 'difference' and 'diversity' merely gain their cosmetic afterlife?

Endnote: Relocation of Kirschenblatt - Gimblett's insights on 'the consciousness industry' within tourism studies

The last task in this deconstructive or textual dissection of the intelligences within "Destination Culture... ." is to relocate or recontextualise Kirschenblatt - Gimblett's conceptions within the literature of present-day tourism/travel studies. To that end, it is important to restate that while "Destination Culture... ." is clearly not just a text about tourism and travel, per se, but a more extensive one about exhibition studies (and, perhaps, a deeper one about ethnological artifactuality), the work comprises a much needed testimony to the mediating power of tourism and travel in our post-industrial and increasingly diasporic age. While some of the writing in "Destination Culture... ." may be somewhat obtuse and rather thin on its background reasoning in places - particularly with regard to her discussions of 'techniques of familiarisation' and of '[Barthesian] gratuitous meaning' Kirschenblatt - Gimblett 1998: 235), for instance, it is otherwise a sustained inspection of the increasingly *professionalised* power of the place - makers and image - merchants of tourism and travel (Kirschenblatt - Gimblett 1998: 119) as brokers of peoples/places/pasts as the cultural tourism and heritage tourism both seemingly grow exponentially around the world. And to Kirschenblatt - Gimblett, this professionalised power is particularly pungent in Australia and New Zealand where so much of her later ruminations on culture production and heritage manufacture seem to have been catalysed (Kirschenblatt - Gimblett 1998: 140 - 1), distant from her own Swedish roots and North American hearth.

So, to recap, how does Kirschenblatt - Gimblett singly advance the literature of tourism studies in her 1998 University of California publication? Or, otherwise, how has she shifted our received understanding of the cultural and political dynamism which may or may not be enwrapped within tourism and travel? In response to these related questions, one might suggest that, after Kirschenblatt - Gimblett 1990s regime of work:

- matters of authenticity ought in tourism no longer be exclusively about what Stuart Hall (1981: 237) called 'self - enclosed' approaches to representation where meanings are hunted down *ahistorically* within what is assumed to be fixed and frozen cultural forms. After Kirschenblatt - Gimblett - and in the light of the thirty propositions of Exhibits 2.1 to 2.6 - what now counts is not so much what qualifies as the 'authentic', per se, but how each or any claim to authenticity is an almost Bhabhian representational social drama of constituted, of reconstituted, or of deconstituted display - though Bhabha's own ideas on the emergent "new sense" and on "the fantasmatics" of cultural exposition (from such as Bhabha 1994) does not seem to be known to Kirschenblatt - Gimblett, herself. Nonetheless, what is now seen to be of import in the slowly-developing cultural studies and political studies literature on tourism and travel after Kirschenblatt - Gimblett, is whether or not the given locale, narrative, or object being representated 'authentically' is detached from its accepted (?) and/or its appropriate (?) context, and how theatrically it is accorded performative power as variously a traditional, a commodified, or another meaning which shows/which speaks/or which acts as a shaper of our local inheritances;

- matters of cultural production ought in tourism no longer just be assumed to be about the classifying/labelling/signposting of things as carried out in dominant, privileged, or lead museologically settings (and then more or less blindly be followed elsewhere across the tourism and travel industry). After Kirschenblatt - Gimblett - and the thirty propositions on representational power - it should be easier for more observers to critically recognise the enormous power of all levels or corners of the tourism/travel industry as a potential realm of not just destination - making, but of *culture and society construction*. As art - historian

Gambrich (1988: 124) pointedly put it - cited in Kirschenblatt - Gimblett (1998: 137) - any single windowdresser anywhere at any interpreted site or exposition can in fact spotlight a new/a different/an alternative angle of understanding about the stories being featured there. Hence, 'madeness' in art, in tourism, or in any heavily representational field, is not the rare and restricted privilege of that field"s cultural or political 'aristocracy', it is also in fact manifestly there within the small bailiwicks of each and every large and small signifying agent. And those apparently piecemeal and everyday small-fare articulations can indeed add up noticeably and loudly. The madenesses accumulate and the herenesses aggregate over time.

And, finally, that:

- matters of cultural mobilisation ought to be more prominently expected to exist within the high local selectivity involved in the development and promotion of culture in tourism, where that cultural choice is newly understood to be deeply politicized. Thereby, the performance and the presentations of culture and heritage ought to be seen much more commonly critically as important instruments for the mobilisation of interest groups, particularly of non-materialist identities and of anationalist streams of consciousness. After Kirschenblatt - Gimblett, hopefully more researchers in tourism studies will be inspired to trace how various populations have negotiated their local, regional, or national identifications, guiding them between contesting political representations. After Kirschenblatt-Gimblett, hopefully more political scientists in tourism will be encouraged to probe how the apparent proprietary cultural/heritage rights of indigenous populations or subnational groups have been appropriated by 'the nation' itself, something that Hall (1994) and Hollinshead (2000) have been pointedly calling for at the turn of the century. And hopefully, other investigators in tourism studies will gain confidence to delve into the endless future - looking and normativist pronouncements of public agencies and large corporations in tourism to determine whether their pluralist-*sounding* discourse is bona fide, or whether it stands as nothing more than the vacant multiculturalist rhetoric of sectional interests, unsupported by any grounded positively-discriminating action.

"Destination Culture... ." is therefore a timely work for the adolescent transdisciplinary field of tourism studies. As the demand for cultural tourism and heritage tourism visitation appears to be steadily upgrading from the 'been - there - done - that' accumulative type of *site visit* to the more engaged and arrestive *experiential visit*, and as exhibiting managements increasingly adapt new forms of market - driven museology to replace hackneyed, product - driven approaches, it is rather valuable to have Kirschenblatt - Gimblett's widely-situated ethnology of the agency of display to serve as a primer for further inquiry into the industry's sometimes confirmative and sometimes inventive socio-political intercessions in culture and heritage.

Perhaps, in the fluidity of contemporary life, and given the more resonant nomadic lifestyles and nomadic thoughtlines of our time (Deleuze and Quattari: 1987), we are going to increasingly value tourism and travels as our educative self - formative metaphors for living (Featherstone 1995: 127). Accordingly, we must become more proven at investigating the exhibitorial epistemologies and the performance pedagogues of this massive and globe-consuming self-consciousness industry. If tourism and travel do indeed increasingly and quintessentially serve to constitute our vehicles of *public* collective remembering and our mechanisms of *public* self-understanding, the field of tourism studies must become much more circumspect, critical, and competent in determining who did what to which cultural narrative, and who felt what about which heritage image. To repeat, the makings of "here", and the manufacturings of "there" are not random. Certain somebodies - not nobody - in the past imagined our inheritances for us, and certain other somebodies are remodelling those inheritances up or down right now within specific, celebrated, public, mediated after-stories, new-stories, and instead-stories. Such conscious and unconscious mediators are inevitably fabricating old and new after-lives at this very moment, for iconographies are routinely reconfigured for each sub-cultural group, within each society, and across each continent. The makers of precious, local, myth and the shapers of proud, local, destinations are doing it for their own posthumous future, and kindly for what they think ought to be our ensuing future, too. We must all therefore learn to be much more alert to the quiet, everyday and everyplace recompositions of our consciousnesses, certain of which are nowadays accelerating in number and reach owing to either the gravitational pull of "official", box-seat, statist forms of societal imagineering via local/regional/nationalist tourism development, or otherwise to the gravitational pull of "corporatist", product-tied forms of societal imagineering via tourism globalising styles of tourism promotion. As consumers of both sorts of intercessionary narrtives, we must learn to watch out for the added value and the divisive value at our colisseums of culture and to be wary of the added glitter and the divisive glitter at our hyper-sites of heritage! Such is the kind of iconological awarenesses that Kirschenblatt-Gimblett has tried to cultivate within us. In "Destination Culture... .", our Professor-of-the-Performative from New York has simply reminded us that mythmaking is almost the oldest profession in the world. She implicitly reminds us that we can now get "it" - whether we want it or not - in handy, and ubiquitous chunks of corporate intelligence, or we can vote for more taxes for tourism, and get it courtesy of "the state". And she explicitly reveals how we ubiquitously prostitute our inheritances and ourselves through the way we make, bake, fake and take our places.

Acknowledgements

An early version of this paper first appeared in **Cultural Dynamics**. Cultural Dynamics is an international peer review journal produced by Sage Publications (London), and is devoted to the interdisciplinary study of processes, changes, evolutions, and histories of knowledge, and of social and cultural phenomena.

References

Barthes, R. (1977), The Third Meaning: Research Notes on Some Eisenstein Stills. In *Image - Music - Text*, comp. and trans. S. Heath. New York. Hill and Wang. pp. 52 - 68.

Bhabha, H. (1994), *The Location of Culture*. London. Routledge.

Boissevain, J. (1996), *Coping with Tourists: European Reactions to Mass Tourism*. Oxford. Berghahn.

Brown, D. (1996), Genuine Fakes. In *The Tourist Image: Myths and Mythmaking in Tourism*, T. Selwyn, ed.. Chichester, England. John Wiley. pp. 33 - 48.

Bruner, E. (1989), Cannibals, Tourists and Ethnographers. *Cultural Anthropology*. 4:4.

Bruner, E., and B. Kirschenblatt - Gimblett (1994), Maasai on the Lawn: Tourist Realism in East Africa. *Cultural Anthropology*. 9:4. pp. 435 - 470.

Buck, E. (1993), *Paradise Remade: The Politics of Culture and History in Hawaii*. Philadelphia. Temple University Press.

Cohen, E. (1988), Authenticity and Commoditisation in Tourism. *Annals of Tourism Research* 15. pp. 371 - 86.

Deleuze, G. and Guattari, F. (1987) *A Thousand Plateaus: Capitalism and Schizophrenia*. Minneapolis, Minnesota University Press.

Edensor, T. (1998), *Tourists at the Taj: Performance and Meaning at a Symbolic Site*. London. Routledge.

Featherstone, M. (1995), *Undoing Culture: Globalisation, Postmodernity and Identity*. London. Sage.

Fjellman, S. (1992), *Vinyl Leaves: Walt Disney World and America*. Boulder, Colorado. Westview Press.

Frow, J. (1991), Tourism and the Semantics of Nostalgia. *October*. 57. pp. 121 - 151.

Graburn, N. (1977) The Museum and the Visitor Experience. In *The Visitor and the Museum*. L. Draper, ed. Berkeley, California. Lowie Museum. [for Museum educators: American Association of Museums].

Greenwood, D. (1989), Culture by the Pound: An Anthropological Perspective on Tourism as Cultural Commoditisation. In *Hosts and Quests: The Anthropology of Tourism*, V. Smith, ed. Philadelphia. University of Philadelphia Press. 2nd edition.

Hall, S. (1981), Notes on Deconstructing 'the Popular'. In *People's History and Socialist Theory*, R. Samuel, ed.. London. Routledge and Kegan Paul.

Hall, C.M. (1994), *Tourism and Politics: Policy, Power and Place*. Chichester, England. John Wiley.

Hawkins, D. and J. Cunningham (1996), It is 'Never - Never Land' When Interest Groups Prevail. In *Practicing Responsible Tourism: International Case Studies in Tourism Planning, Policy and Development*, L. C. Harrison and W. Husbands, eds. New York. John Wiley and Sons. pp. 350 - 365.

Heidegger, M. (1977), The Age of the World Picture. In *The Question Concerning Technology and Other Essays*. Trans. William Lovitt. New York. Harper and Row. pp. 115 - 54.

Hewison, R. (1989), *The Heritage Industry: Britain in a Climate of Decline*. London. Methuen.

Hollinshead, K. (1997) Heritage Tourism under Postmodernity: Truth and the Past. In *The Tourist Experience: A New Introduction*, C. Ryan, ed. London. Cassell. pp.170-193.

Hollinshead, K. (1998/A), Cross - Referential Marketing Across Walt Disney's 'World': Corporate Power and the Imagineering of Nation and Culture. *Tourism Analysis*. 2. pp. 217 - 228.

Hollinshead, K. (1998/B), Disney and Commodity Aesthetics: A Critique of Fjellman's Analysis of 'Distory and the Historicide of the Past. *Current Issues in Tourism*. 1:1 pp. 58 - 119.

Hollinshead, K. (1998/C) Tourism, Hybridity and Ambiguity: The Relevance of Bhabha's 'Third Space" Cultures. *Journal of Leisure Research*. Special Issue on Race, Ethnicity and Leisure. 30. 1. pp. 121 - 156.

Hollinshead, K. (1998/D) Tourism and the Restless Peoples: A Dialectical Inspection of Bhabha's Halfway Populations. Tourism, Culture and Communication. 1:1.

Hollinshead, K. (1999) Tourism as Public Culture: Horne's Ideological Commentary on the Legerdemain of Tourism. *International Journal of Tourism Research*. I. 267-292.

Hollinshead, K. (2000), The Disregard for Dialectics: The Nonchalant Neglect of Political Science in Tourism Studies. *Current Issues in Tourism*.

Hollinshead, K. and de Burlo, C. (2000), *Journeys into Otherness: The Representation of Difference and Identity in Tourism*. Clevedon, England. Channel View Publications.

Holloway, C. (1994), *The Business of Tourism*. London. Pitman. 4th eds.

Horne, D. (1992), *The Intelligent Tourist*. McMahon's Point, N.S.W., Australia. Margaret Gee Publishing.

Husserl, E. (1962), *Ideas: General Introduction to Pure Phenomenology*. New York. Collier. [First Published in 1913].

Kennedy, M. (1999), Greek Team Puts Marbles Under Microscope. *The Guardian*. London. 29th Oct.

Kirschenblatt - Gimblett, B. (1998), *Destination Culture*. Berkeley, Ca. University of California Press.

Lanfant, M - F. (1966), International Tourism, Internationalisation, and the Challenge to Identity. In *International Tourism: Identity and Change*, M-F. Lanfant, J. B. Allcock, and E. M. Bruner, eds. London. Sage. pp. 24 - 43.

Leidig, M. and Johnston, B. (1998), Iceman Oetzi Still in a Storm. Weekly Telegraph (*The Daily Telegraph*: London). Issue No. 350. p. 14.

Lister, D. (1998) Britain to Hand Historic Marbles Back to Turkey. *The Independent* (of London). 13th July.

MacAloon, J .J. (1984), Olympic Games and the Theory of Spectacle in Modern Societies. In *Rite, Drama, Festival, Spectacle: Rehearsals Toward a Theory of Cultural Performance*, J .J. McAloon, ed. Philadelphia. I.S.H.I. pp. 241 - 280.

MacCannell, D. (1992), *Empty Meeting Grounds*. London. Routledge.

McKay, I. (1994), The Quest for the Folk: Antimodernism and Cultural Selection in Twentieth Century Nova Scotia. Montreal. McGill-Queens University Press.

Marcus, J. (1998), Indian Tribes Given Bones for Reburial. *Times Higher Education Supplement*. 25th September.

McCrane, D., M. Morris and D. Kiely (1995), *Scotland - The Brand: The Making of Scottish Heritage*. Edinburgh, Scotland. Edinburgh University Press.

McKay, I. (1988), Twilight at Peggy's Cove; Towards a Genealogy of 'Maritimicity' in Nova Scotia. *Borderlines*. Summer. pp. 29 - 37.

Mitchell, T. (1989), The World as Exhibition. *Comparative Studies in Society and History*. 31. 2. p. 225.

Norkunas, M. K. (1993), *The Politics of Public Memory: Tourism, History, and Ethnicity in Monterey, California*. Albany, N. York. State University of New York.

Robinson, M. and Boniface, P. *Tourism and Cultural Conflicts*. Wallingford, Oxon. CAB International.

Selwyn, T. ed. (1996), *The Tourist Image: Myths and Mythmaking in Tourism*. Chichester, England. John Wiley.

Schechner, R. (1985), *Between Theatre and Anthropology*. Philadelphia. University of Pennsylvania Press.

Tunbridge, J. E., and G. J. Ashworth, eds. (1996), *Dissonant Heritage: The Management of the Past as a Resource in Conflict*. Chichester, England. John Wiley.

Stewart, K. (1996), *A Space on the Side of the Road: Cultural Poetics in an "Other" America*. Princeton. Princeton University Press.

Turner, V. (1973) The Centre Out There: Pilgrim's Goal. *History of Religions*. 12: pp. 191 - 230.

Urry, J. (1990), *The Tourist Gaze: Leisure and Travel in Contemporary Societies*. London. Sage.

Williams, R. (1960) *Culture and Society: 1790 - 1950*. New York. Anchor Books.

Wilson, C. (1997) *The Myth of Santa Fe: Creating a Modern Regional Tradition*. Albuquerque. University of New Mexico Press.

Wright, P. (1985) *On Living in an Old Country*. London. Verso.

Professional volunteer management at a World Heritage Site: Reconciling both visitors' and volunteers' needs

Kirsten Holmes

Sheffield University, UK

Caroline MacFarlane

The National Trust, UK

Introduction

One of the most remarkable places in Europe (Parry, 2000)

Fountains Abbey and Studley Royal is one of the largest National Trust properties, and the second most visited pay-for-entry NT property with around 200,000 (NT) paying visitors each year. The estate has also been awarded UNESCO World Heritage status in recognition of its many important aspects. The estate comprises the ruins of the Cistercian monastery of Fountains Abbey, the Elizabethan Fountains Hall, Studley Royal water garden, the High Victorian church of St Mary, designed by William Burges, and the medieval deer park of Studley Royal, with over 500 deer. The estate is self-financing, which means that visitor numbers are crucial, both paying visitors and those who sign up for membership at the estate.

Volunteers have been involved at Fountains Abbey with increasing importance since the National Trust took over the estate in 1983 and there are now approximately 250 regular estate volunteers and 350 estate conservation volunteers each year working on a range of activities, from giving guided tours of the abbey to playing the organ in St Mary's Church. As such there is a very good chance that the visitors will come into contact with the volunteers at some part of their visit.

For museums and heritage attractions the most effective form of advertising is word-of-mouth recommendation (Davies, 1994), and the most elusive market is the repeat visitor market. However repeat visiting is very important as the museum or attraction relies on visitors, both through admission charges or secondary spend in the shop or restaurant. Moreover the National Trust seeks to encourage visitors to take up membership, rather than pay admission each visit, and if the visitor joins at a property, the property will receive some of that income. As Fountains Abbey does not receive any funds centrally from the National Trust this is the only way they can benefit financially from membership.

While access to the abbey ruins, the water gardens and the Elizabethan Fountains Hall is by admission charge, there is no charge to the deer park or the church, both of which are stewarded. There is a large visitor centre, with a car park, shop and restaurant. In the deer park there is a tea room next to a second car park. There are toilets at the visitor centre, near the abbey and at the tea room. There are three entrances to the estate via the visitor centre, the deer park or next to Fountains Hall.

Many of the voluntary activities at Fountains Abbey are likely to bring the volunteers into contact with the visitors, such as the stewarding at events, but on a more regular basis there are 4 room stewards on duty each day, two at St Mary's Church and two at Fountains Hall. There are three guided tours, two of the abbey and one of the water gardens, and between 2 and 6 estate wardens on duty each day. As the purpose of this study was to assess the impact volunteers could have on the visitor experience the volunteer interviews were limited to estate wardens, room stewards and tour guides as they had the greatest likelihood of interacting with the visitors.

Both volunteers and visitors were interviewed to find out their own motivations and how interaction with each other can impact on the experiences of both, whether it is a volunteer answering questions for the visitor, or a visitor stopping to chat with a volunteer. With such a large number of volunteers covering such a large range of activities, and with Fountains Abbeys' dependence on both visitors *per se* and a favourable word-of-mouth recommendation, how can these volunteers be managed in a professional manner to provide a quality customer care service to the visitors? Moreover how can this management approach also continue to foster the friendly nature of the volunteers?

This paper examines the importance of the volunteers to the visitors' experiences at Fountains Abbey. It will report on how the estate has, since becoming a National Trust property, developed a management programme to incorporate the diverse motivations of their volunteers. The estate has sought to reconcile the need to provide a professional level of service to meet their visitors' needs, while meeting the needs of an essentially leisure-seeking volunteer work-force.

Volunteering with the National Trust

The National Trust estimate that there are 35, 000 volunteers working with the Trust each year (The National Trust, 1998). Moreover the Trust is committed to working with volunteers as part of its National Strategic Plan, and introduced a new policy on volunteering in 1999 (National Trust, 1999). This policy states that the National Trust as an organisation is committed to the voluntary principle as it is one of the organisation's greatest strengths and without their active participation, the organisation would be unable to prosper. The National Trust Policy on Volunteering covers all the points of good volunteer management practice. It clearly covers the purpose of volunteers, recruitment and selection, training and development, support and recognition and management and communication, including insurance. However the National Trust policy states that the volunteer role is a gift relationship and that no enforceable obligation, contractual or otherwise can be imposed, although there is a presumption of mutual support and reliability. Reciprocal expectations are acknowledged.

National Trust volunteers are awarded with a discount card after 50 hours of service in any one year. The card is valid for a year and gives the holder free entry to any Trust property or free entry to a friend if the holder is already a Trust member, and a discount in National Trust shops and cafes. Moreover all staff and volunteers responsible for volunteers are encouraged to ensure appropriate acknowledgement on a regular basis (National Trust, 1999). The Fountains Abbey estate provides its own volunteer handbook, as not only does it have a large number of volunteers but is also self-governing.

While the National Trust policy advocates a structured approach to volunteer management, there are clearly differences between recommended policy and the actual procedures at the National Trust properties studied, however as the case studies show these differences are not necessarily detrimental to the volunteer experience.

The National Trust Survey 1997

The National Trust conducted a national survey of its staff and volunteers in 1997 (Davis Smith and Chambers, 1997). The survey found that National trust volunteers are predominantly older and retired. 56% of volunteers were aged over 60 years; and 82% were permanently retired, while only 18% of respondents were aged under 45 years. 71 of respondents were members of the National Trust. Over three-quarters of volunteers, 77%, are based at a National Trust property and 71% work at either National Trust houses or gardens.

The volunteers are very committed to their activities, with 59% volunteering once a week or more, 48% having volunteered for 5 years or more and 39% travelling over ten miles each way to the place where they volunteer.

The respondents listed the three main benefits of their voluntary activities as:

- I really enjoy it.

- I meet people and make friends through it.

- It gives me a sense of personal achievement.

Volunteers commented that the main drawbacks of volunteering for the National Trust were lack of communication, especially between staff and volunteers, lack of information and that they would welcome more training. Studies conducted by the authors at other heritage sites suggest that these drawbacks are commonly experienced by volunteers.

Management of volunteers at Fountains Abbey

Without the volunteers Fountains Abbey estate would not be able to open all the buildings it currently does, nor offer such a varied events programme, as volunteers not only organise events such as wildlife trails, Easter egg rolling and church services in the Abbey, but also steward at concerts and plays. The volunteers contribute approximately 1500 hours per month, while staff spend only 63 hours supervising the volunteers. Indeed the estate estimates that the volunteer input is worth around £92, 000 per annum (based on £4 per volunteer hour. The volunteer contribution therefore represents a major net gain for the estate.

The volunteer programme at Fountains Abbey follows both the National Trust policy (National Trust, 1999) and accepted procedure on good volunteer management practice (Millar, 1991; Kuyper, 1993; McCurley and Lynch, 1998). The volunteers are managed by a paid volunteer co-ordinator, with two semi-voluntary assistant volunteer co-ordinators, who both receive a stipend. The volunteers have a line manager for each volunteer group, they are able to claim their expenses and they are given induction training, including health and safety. Moreover each volunteer is provided with a volunteer handbook covering all the health and safety procedures for the estate. The volunteers are eligible for the National Trust discount card and can claim travel expenses in mileage.

Research methodology

35 volunteers and 59 visitors were interviewed at Fountains Abbey between June and August 1998. The interview days included days during school term, during the school holidays and at weekends, to try and glean as varied a cross-section of both visitors and volunteers as possible. By interviewing visitors and volunteers on the same day as each other it was hoped that any interaction the visitors had with volunteers would be with those volunteers who were interviewed.

Visitors were questioned as they arrived at the visitor centre, they were given a second questionnaire to return after their visit and were telephoned 6-8 weeks after their visit to find out what their memories were and whether they had any plans to make a repeat visit.

The questions included in the survey were both closed and open, so generated a mixture of quantitative and qualitative data. The survey results were analysed using SPSS v6.1 and content analysis.

The volunteers

The profile of volunteers at Fountains Abbey very much reflects the National Trust norm in the survey above. 81% of respondents were retired, and 74% were aged over 60 years, with no respondents aged under 45 years. As in the survey above the volunteers were very committed to their work, with 54% having volunteered for more than 5 years. While 30% of volunteers help out each week, a greater proportion, 48%, help out each fortnight. This reflects the fact that only a few volunteers are required each day, compared to the large number who offer their services, with two stewards for Fountains Hall and St Mary's Church, and three daily tours, two of the Abbey and one of the Water Gardens. 82% of the volunteers were members of the National Trust.

The respondents further commitment was shown by the 64% of who had volunteered elsewhere, while 32% had helped at another heritage site. These included stewarding at Skipton Church, conservation at Brimham Rocks, guiding at Treasurer's House, York and stewarding at Newby Hall. 22% of the volunteers interviewed at Fountains Abbey described themselves as estate wardens, 44% as stewards and 35% as tour guides.

The volunteers were very highly educated, with 29% holding a degree, and a further 12% holding a postgraduate qualification.

The visitors

The visitors were mostly either on a day trip, with 48%, or on holiday, 33%. They were visiting most commonly with their partner, 48%, or with their family, 29%. A very large proportion of visitors, 71%, were making a repeat visit, and the visitors were also experienced heritage visitors, with 48% having visited 6 or more similar attractions in the past 12 months, and for only 5% of visitors was Fountains Abbey their only heritage visit of the year. This high incidence of heritage visiting was supported by the 60% of visitors who were members of the National Trust.

The visitors were also very highly educated with 16% holding a degree but a further 26% holding a postgraduate qualification. However, the visitors tended to be younger than the volunteers, with 37% aged between 25 and 54 years, a reflection of the proportion of visitors who had come with their families. As a result of the lower age range of visitors 63% were working fulltime.

It is significant that while the volunteers and visitors represented different generations, they also had many characteristics in common. Both groups were regular heritage consumers. The volunteers demonstrated a considerable commitment to the Abbey and heritage in general through their incidence of heritage volunteering elsewhere. The visitors were mostly repeat visitors and had recently visited many other heritage sites as well as belonging to the National Trust. Moreover both groups were very highly educated, as previous studies show would be expected from heritage consumers (Merriman, 1991; McIntosh, 1997).

Future volunteers are likely to be recruited from visitors, so visitors could be considered to be volunteers-in-waiting, waiting for when they have the time to commit to such a venture, such as retirement. In turn volunteers could be considered to be super-visitors, visitors who are extremely committed to their chosen heritage attraction to the point where they have become both an interface between the regular visitors and the attraction by working as tour guides or stewards, or even by becoming a part of the attraction itself, if working as demonstrators or interpreters.

Volunteers on management

Good volunteer management is more than simply a means to an end. Volunteers are often, as at Fountains Abbey, experienced people who can tell whether they are being managed properly or not.

> *The place is very well run, though I suspect we're moving into a situation where there's more usage of the site than the guides can relate to.*

Good management demonstrates how the organisation views the volunteers as much as reward schemes and travel expenses.

> *There's very good liaison in some things between the estate and if you suggest something. I'm talking about [The Education Gallery] because I set up games down there.*

The interviews with the volunteers above show how committed volunteers can be and what contribution they can make in hours and financial savings. In return the motivation of the volunteer must be taken into account. For the volunteers who have chosen to give tours or steward buildings at Fountains the opportunity to meet other people was not surprisingly an important motivator,

> *I'm retired so it's a place to meet people and be part of the world.*

And an absence of this could lead to unhappy volunteers,

> *You're rather isolated from the other volunteers, I had hoped to meet people.*

With volunteers involved in the service delivery process unhappy volunteers could lead to unhappy visitors.

Training volunteers is also important, particularly if they are being involved in customer oriented roles, as at Fountains Abbey,

> *I was trained initially and then follow up courses if there's a new procedure. It's very good here, I must say, keeping everything on the ball.*

[Training consisted of] *10 weeks of indoor and around the estate study. How to treat visitors, being aware of their needs.*

[Training involved] *A one morning session with a mixture of volunteers and paid staff. This was excellent but is no longer part of the training, but should be.*

By inducting both the volunteers and staff together Fountains was demonstrating the equal importance of both, and building a team culture from the start. A major source of volunteer problems can be tensions between volunteers and paid staff (Hooper-Greenhill and Chadwick, 1985; Millar, 1991) and this approach sought to alleviate this. Training for front-of-house volunteers at Fountains Abbey includes an in-house variant of the English Tourist Board's Welcome-Host customer care package, a one-day course teaching participants a greater awareness of customer needs.

Volunteer motivation

The large proportion of retired volunteers is reflected in the reasons volunteers gave for choosing to volunteer in the first place.

A friend knew I was retiring and asked me.

I'm retired and my wife wanted me out of the house.

After retirement seeking outdoors voluntary activities.

I'm retired so I've plenty of time and it seemed a nice thing to do – meeting people and something different.

I'm retired so it's a nice place to meet people and be part of the world.

The volunteers were looking for leisure activities to keep them occupied in retirement, which may serve as a substitute for attributes they no longer have access to since giving up paid work, such as the regular social contact with volunteers or a purpose and structure to their day.

Volunteers on visitors

Interaction with the visitors is the primary function of the tour guides and room stewards, and a major part of the estate wardens' role (they also report on the condition of the estate).

As I walk about the estate I pass the time of day with visitors and try to answer any of their questions.

There's a lot of chatting with visitors and answering questions.

Not surprisingly then this opportunity to meet and talk with the visitors is a source of great satisfaction to the volunteers who have chosen to undertake this role.

> *You enjoy meeting people, you're able to give the visitors more interest in the place they're visiting.*

> *Meet all sorts of people, proving what history there is when people say it's just a load of old stones.*

> *By far and away the greatest interest is the actual guiding and the meeting of people who want to know something about the place.*

Volunteers were asked to rate the main reason why they continued to volunteer at Fountains and 50% rated 'Opportunity to talk to visitors'.

Visitor feedback

> *Most* [of the visitors] *appreciate a chat, once the initial reserve has been overcome.*

95% of the volunteers have received some feedback from the visitors. This could be in the form of comments at the time.

> *I hear from many people who have been many times who tell me at the end of the tour that they have learned more in this one visit than they've ever learned previously and they'll be coming back and I always tell them to go with another guide because the other guides all have a different viewpoint of the facets of the abbey than the one I perceive.*

> *Some people say they remember me.*

Or letters sent after the visit

> *Letters over the years from people who have enjoyed it. I've hear from people who've been many times.*

64% of volunteers had met the same visitors more than once, which given that these visitors could be visiting on any day of the year and the volunteers do not work every day is quite an achievement.

The volunteers are aware of the role they play in creating the visitor experience:

> *We're trying to sell it, visitors feel it when you enjoy it yourself, you transmit enthusiasm.*

Committed volunteers?

The input volunteers have to the successful running of the estate has already highlighted the importance of fostering committed volunteers. The length of service given by the volunteers at Fountains has been noted above but what is it that prompts volunteers to come to the estate for each duty they have signed up to?

Commitment, knowing I'll give pleasure.

A combination of visitor interaction and the atmosphere and beauty of the estate.

I have a moral obligation to come, except if illness prevents. It's nice if visitors ask questions, as they are enjoying it if they're interested.

The place and the people.

Visitors on volunteers

Nearly a third of respondents, 31%, spoke to the stewards during their visit, whether on a guided tour, a warden in the deer park or a steward in either Fountains Hall or St Mary's Church. Given the size of the estate and that there are only a small number of volunteers on duty each day there is a considerable amount of interaction between the visitors and the volunteers.

They bring the place alive.

The human touch makes a place seem more friendly.

Although one visitor suggested the estate introduced,

A roving guide within the abbey precincts to answer questions would be an asset.

This would be rather like the estate wardens in the deer park and would fulfil a similar function.

Repeat visiting

The visitors were contacted by telephone between 6-8 weeks after their visit to find out what they could remember of their visit and whether they had any intention to make a repeat visit. While not all the visitors had spoken to stewards during their visit, for those that had their encounters with volunteers were clearly memorable.

...the person who did the tour was certainly very enthusiastic and knew her stuff...we found it very interesting, we had been before but we hadn't been on one of these, escorted as it were, tour round the abbey ... pointing out the details.

We asked directions for the deer park and the steward was very helpful.

It was a pleasant walk with a guide, talking to someone who knew what they were talking about.

Two of the visitors expressed an intention to make a repeat visit,

Next summer we plan to go for a picnic.

We'll probably do it again as it was a really nice day out and we didn't get to see all of it.

Yet more significantly ten out of twelve of the respondents said that they had recommended their visit to their friends or family

I mention it to everyone, you see, I say it's beautiful, you've got to go.

We have [mentioned it] *to family and friends, when people ask where we went on our holidays, where we went and what we saw, and they've said they'll have to go there as it sounds so nice.*

Hosts and guests

During the 18th and 19th centuries owners of private collections or country houses opened their doors to visitors, literally acting as hosts to the guests in their house (Mandler, 1997). Today at Fountains Abbey the volunteers, as super-visitors are acting as hosts for the visitors, their guests, at Fountains Abbey. As both groups have similar interests and share characteristics, and the volunteers do not gain financially from the guests, their host-guest relationship is less likely to be affected by the negative factors associated with host-guest encounters both between Western tourists and local residents of less developed countries and the 19th century country house owners and their visitors (Smith, 1978; Pearce, 1982). There is no asymmetry between the host's knowledge and the guest's status, nor is there any significant cultural distance between the participants. Country house hosts and guests in the 21st century both have a degree of knowledge and experience with heritage and the host-guest encounter is a mutually beneficial experience.

They [the visitors] *often provide facts of which I* [a volunteer] *was unaware*

Conclusions

In tune with volunteering with the National Trust, volunteering at Fountains Abbey is largely a leisure activity to be pursued in retirement, which offers social opportunities with people who share similar interests, and may replace the regular contact with colleagues that retired people no longer have access to. In other words volunteering at Fountains is a

Day out in a nice place, meeting people.

Both the volunteers and the visitors shared similar characteristics and were regular heritage consumers. However the generational difference between the two groups suggests that the visitors could indeed be volunteers-in-waiting, while the volunteers are super-visitors, who have made a step up from simply visiting to becoming a part of the attraction where they offer their services.

The volunteers involved in front-of-house roles at Fountains Abbey are purposefully seeking social interaction. While not all of the visitors experienced interaction with the volunteers during their visit, for those visitors who did interact with the volunteers this not only improved their experience at the estate but their memories of their visit indicate that the volunteer role does have a lasting impact. The encounters between front-of-house volunteers and visitors at Fountains Abbey is a host-guest encounter which is a direct descendant of the tradition of country house owners opening their houses to the public in the 18th and 19th centuries.

It is the visitors memories that will ultimately inform their decision either to recommend the visit by word of mouth or to make a repeat visit (Kawashima, 1993). Both word of mouth recommendation and repeat visiting are the most important market, and the most difficult to influence through marketing. Therefore any role the front-of-house volunteers have in this process is extremely valuable.

In this context it is very important to manage the volunteers in a way that will make them feel a valued member of the organisation. This can be achieved through effective communication between both staff and volunteers and the organisation and volunteers. Effective communication may seem obvious but it is so often overlooked by organisations that involve volunteers, and can be difficult to achieve especially if the volunteers do not come in regularly. Moreover at Fountains the estate is so large that volunteers do not always sign in at the same gate so information is sent by post to make sure that everyone is aware of changes. It is also very important to offer volunteers out-of-pocket expenses, and while this is National Trust policy research by the authors at other site found that this is not always the case. Paying volunteers their expenses is important so that they are not left out-of-pocket but it is also indicative of the management attitude towards their volunteers, that they are not simply free labour. Indeed offering expenses may not be as costly as some organisations may think as 40% of volunteers at Fountains do not even claim their expenses, as they feel it is another way of supporting the property.

Large numbers of hours are given freely and I imagine they couldn't manage without us. I think the Trust knows that and appreciates it.

If volunteers feel valued by management they will feel committed to the attraction where they are helping and they will want the attraction to be successful and they will want the visitors to leave with a good impression of the attraction. Volunteers are not only valuable workforce but also a powerful marketing tool.

Useful further research would be to follow up the visitors a year later to see if their repeat visiting intentions bore fruit.

References

Davies, S. (1994), By Popular Demand: A Strategic Analysis of the Market Potential for Museums and Arts Galleries in the UK, Museums and Galleries Commission: London.

Davis Smith, J. and Chambers, D. (1997), Volunteering with the National Trust: Survey Report, The National Centre for Volunteering: 1997.

Hooper-Greenhill, E. and Chadwick, A. (1985), Volunteers in Museums and Galleries: a Discussion of Some of the Issues, Museums Journal 84 (4): 177-8.

Kawashima, N. (1998), Knowing the Public: A Review of Museum Marketing Literature and Research, Museum Management and Curatorship 17 (1): 21-39.

Kuyper, J. (1993), Volunteer Programme Administration: A Handbook for Museums and Other Cultural Institutions, American Council for the Arts: Washington.

Mandler, P. (1997), *The Fall and Rise of the Country House*, Yale University Press: Yale.

McCurley, R. and Lynch, S. (1998), *Essential Volunteer Management,* 2nd Edition, Directory of Social Change: London.

McIntosh, Alison (1997*), The Experiences and Benefits gained by Tourists Visiting Socio-Industrial Heritage Attractions*, PhD Thesis, St Margaret's College, Edinburgh.

Merriman, Nick (1991), *Beyond the Glass Case,* Leicester University Press: Leicester.

Millar, S. (1991), *Volunteers in Museums and Heritage Organisations: Policy, Planning and Management*, HMSO: London.

The National Trust (1998), *Volunteering with the National Trust: summary of the findings of the 1997 survey*, The National Trust: Cirencester.

National Trust (1999), *Policy on Volunteering*, The National Trust: Cirencester.

Parry, J. (Ed.) (2000), *The National Trust Handbook for Members and Visitors 2000*, The National Trust: Bromley, Kent.

Pearce, P. (1982), *The Social Psychology of Tourist Behaviour*. International Series in Experimental Social Psychology, Pergamon Press.

Smith, V. (Ed.) (1978), *Hosts and Guests: the Anthropology of Tourism*, Basil Blackwell: Oxford.

A clash of cultures: Using tourism as a means of preserving industrial heritage in outback Australia

Christine Landorf

University of South Australia, Australia

Introduction

The motives for interest in industrial heritage have been diverse – interest, pride or concern to promote as aspect of current industrial culture, a desire to celebrate achievement, an interest in innovation and ingenuity, or an effort to compensate for irreparable loss. As the management of industrial heritage becomes more professional it is important not to lose that diversity of motive and of uses which has been a key to its vitality, and gives it a secure place in the current expansion of heritage culture (Alfrey and Putnam, 1992).

Mining is an industry of violence in terms of both the physical and the political landscape that it creates, occupies and ultimately relinquishes. A mined landscape will leave patterns of often brutal economic rationalism and social expedience but these patterns tell a story of human endeavour rich in memory and cultural uniqueness worthy of recovery. In terms of the physical, in Australia mining has tended to occur in fragile environments remote from mainstream European settlement. As a finite economic activity involving the harvesting of non-renewable resources, issues of sustainable development, social amenity and sensitivity toward indigenous concepts of spiritual attachment have historically not been high priorities for those involved in the industry. The understanding of mining as a finite activity also leads to different notions of what it is to be a community. Townships either become camps for transient, mainly male, workers or temporary dormitories for dislocated families, families without a sense of permanence, and without a sense of permanence there can be no sense of place and no sense of belonging. In relation to the political, the inherently dangerous and physical nature of the work leads to pronounced distinctions between management and the 'daily paid' contract miner. As a result, since the turn of the century in Australia, mining has had a strong association with the rise of unionism and the constant threat of death or disablement, coupled with job insecurity, hard physical labour and harsh living conditions has led to prolonged and violent industrial clashes.

Broken Hill is a mining community of 23,000 people in arid central Australia that has witnessed much of the physical and political violence discussed above. The city was established around the Line of Lode orebody in 1883 and has contributed greatly to the industrial growth and technological advancement of mining in Australia since then. There have been over 700 deaths on the mines and a series of protracted strikes that have, together with the harsh environment, helped colour the development of a unique community. The working life of the mines is now estimated to be less that ten years and alternative uses for the Line of Lode are being developed along the 7.3 kilometre industrial site unique in its scale, historical complexity and cultural heritage value. In a significant gesture to the community of Broken Hill and the nation, the one remaining company has donated the various surface workings to the city for development as a tourism, education and research facility. The site consists of head frames, tailings dams, mullock heaps, open cuts, and associated buildings and equipment. The site also spans all stages of production from the late 19th century South Mine, through the 1930s crusher, mill and administration building at the Zinc Corporation, to the 1950s change house at North Broken Hill.

This paper will initially establish the unique character of Broken Hill under three headings - the physical, the political and the socio-cultural. The paper will then outline the development of the Broken Hill Line of Lode Project with an emphasis on the long term strategic management and feasibility of the operation. The paper will also discuss the cultural consequences of tourism for a community with a proud and independent industrial heritage. The paper will consider whether the project represents the recovery of a site of national significance, or the morphosis of a powerful industrial community into a tourist theme park with a self-image based on historical, and largely absent, meaning. To draw on Alfrey and Putnam, the project will ultimately be judged as either a celebration of achievement or merely an effort to compensate for an irreparable loss.

The physical setting: Dust, disease, death and disablement

The district surrounding Broken Hill had been an area of known mineral wealth for ten years when Charles Rasp first pegged a series of mining leases in 1883. It was not until 1885 that what was initially thought to be a tin deposit, was found to be the rich silver chloride orebody of the Line of Lode. The Broken Hill Proprietary Company Limited (BHP) was officially registered on 10th August 1885 and full scale production begun soon after (Blainey, 1968 and Woodward, 1965). The success of the BHP mine encouraged the opening of other mines nearby leading to a rapid increase in population. By 1886 the population stood at around 8,000 growing to almost 20,000 by 1890. Many settlers of this period drifted in from the surrounding Barrier Ranges where nearly 300 claims had been pegged over 5,000 square kilometres with limited success. A large proportion of also moved from the South Australian copper fields of Burra, Moonta and Kadina (Turner, 1983).

Broken Hill is some 500 kilometres from the nearest state capital, Adelaide, and over 1,100 kilometres from Sydney. The city sits in the Barrier Ranges approximately 300 metres above sea level. The surrounding landscape is characterised by undulating hills rising above extensive low-lying plains. The climate is semi arid with warm to hot summers (average maximum of 32°C) and cool winters (average maximum of 19°C). Rainfall is erratic with a yearly average of 240 millimetres. Annual falls as low as 57 millimetres have been recorded and in the drought period 1940-1944 the annual average was only 142 millimetres (Solomon,

1988). With a highest recorded temperature of 46.6°C and a lowest of -2.8°C (Turner, 1983), the climate could be described as harsh adding much to the hardships of the early community.

The orebody originally contained over 200 million tonnes of high grade lead-silver-zinc ore, had a continuous length of 7.3 kilometres (km), maximum width of 250 metres and maximum vertical extent of 850 metres (Turner, 1983). A longitudinal section through the deposit reveals a distinct boomerang shape inclining away from the surface at either end (Woodward, 1965). The central section was clearly visible above ground level and was described in 1885 as resembled '. . . part of an old broken blunt tooth saw' (Blainey, 1968). Whilst early operations largely removed this surface section it has been replaced by the residue dumps and mullock heaps which still dominate the city skyline. Current activities are limited to the deeper south-western end of the orebody at levels in excess of 1,500 metres.

The original natural vegetation surrounding Broken Hill consisted of low and sparse native trees and shrubs. With the rapid growth in population and early development of smelting operations, the local natural environment was heavily utilised for fuel, grazing of stock and as a source of timber underground. Even though the last of the smelting operations were removed to the coastal city of Port Pirie in 1898, the local environment continued to be used for fuel and the pasturing of horses, cattle, sheep and goats for domestic use. This meant that by the 1930s the landscape was barren and the city was suffering severe dust storms and soil erosion. In 1936 one of the mining companies, the Zinc Corporation, initiated the fencing and re-planting of sections immediately surrounding the city (Woodward, 1965). These regeneration areas effectively reduced the incidence of severe dust storms and improved the micro-climate and visual amenity of the city. It was also the start of a paternalistic relationship between the mining companies and the community that had until then been largely in conflict over industrial conditions and community welfare.

Water shortages and inadequate sanitation also threatened the early community's health, as did apathy brought about by the sense of impermanence attached to the early mining community. Between 1886 and 1890 the mortality rate in Broken Hill was almost twice that of the state of New South Wales. The serious health problems continued well into the 20th century with cases of typhoid, scarlet fever and diphtheria recorded as late as 1943 (Solomon, 1988). Initial attempts to legislate for a private water supplier failed with accusations at the time of corruption and speculation being levelled at the State Government. A reservoir was completed in 1891 at Stephen's Creek, 16 km to the north east of the city. This was followed in 1915 by the opening of a second reservoir at Umberumberka, 31 km to the north west. Both reservoirs had small catchment areas and this, combined with the low and uncertain rainfall and high level of evaporation, meant that additional shipments of water were required until 1952 when a 100 km pipeline to the Menindie lake system was completed (Solomon, 1988). The Broken Hill Water Supply and Sewerage Act, 1938, established the Broken Hill Water Board and provided for the introduction of sewerage and stormwater systems (Latona Masterman, 1987).

There have been a total of 754 deaths recorded since 1885 along the Line of Lode (Kenny, 1979). They were usually violent and often marked by the courage of others either trying to save mates or recover their bodies but the physical danger was not confined to the mine lease and many deaths from lung diseases remain unrecorded. Lead poisoning was a constant threat until water based drilling techniques and the flotation process of minerals extraction became common practice in the 1940s. A decrease in lung disease followed the findings of the Technical Commission of Inquiry established to investigate working conditions during the 1919-20 strike. Several Acts of parliament followed placing considerable moral and financial obligation on the companies to provide safe working conditions.

The industrial setting: Political struggle

Significant industrial relations developments were made in Broken Hill around the turn of the century and trade unionism developed as a strong force in the city, a combination of the isolation and the dangerous nature of the working conditions. The militancy and success of the union movement in Broken Hill is best captured by Donald Horne (1968) who commented in 1964 that '. . . Broken Hill is run by its trade unions and as far as Broken Hill is concerned the Barrier Industrial Council is stronger than the state of New South Wales.' Blainey (1968) also suggests the strength of the union movement came as a result of there being up to eleven operating mines on the Lode at the turn of the century resulting in a lack of employer unity. Strikers at one mine were often supported by working men at another thus allowing the striking miners to hold out for longer periods than was usual in the industry at the time.

Protracted strikes occurred in 1892, 1909 and 1919-20. In 1916 employees won the right to a forty-four hour working week in a Federal Court award designed to maintain metals production during the First World War. The award was for a period of three years and in 1919 severe unrest resulted in productive operations ceasing along the Line of Lode for eighteen months. In September, 1920 the Commonwealth Court of Conciliation and Arbitration issued a new award which included a thirty-five hour underground working week, compensation for workers suffering from lung related diseases and a limitation on the type of work conducted on night shift. This was a landmark agreement of national significance in terms of working conditions and is a talked about with a degree of pride by the community. The union also won the right to compulsory unionism and to have union dues collected by employers. In 1925 the employers and the unions won the right to negotiate outside of the National wage fixation system when provision was made for the payment of a lead bonus profit sharing incentive for employees (Woodward, 1965).

The socio-cultural setting: The birth and death of cultural identity

The city plan is set out in two slightly offset grid patterns bisected by the mining precinct. Other irregularities in the grid relate to the Silverton and Tarrawingee rail lines, both important to the city's early survival. This was noted in the Line of Lode Identification Study (Austral Archaeology, 1994) as '. . . a unique example of town planning strategies' as it follows the shifting orientation of the Line of Lode and supply routes rather than the more usual compass points of the time. It also locates the mining operations as the undeniable heart of the township upon which all else depends for survival. This can be considered further as an expression of the powerful and dominant nature of the mining industry over the lighter and subservient domestic environment.

Many of the major public and religious buildings, and a number of substantial hotels were erected in the 1890s and 1900s. The majority of the population however remained housed in tents or iron clad, dirt floored timber frame dwellings, many of which remain in use today with minor modifications. The uncertain extent of the mineral deposit slowed development and improvement in housing standards and the city's amenities. It was not until 1936 that a detailed investigation of the ore reserves was undertaken and a minimum of twenty-five years production forecast. This prompted re-building of the surface workings at the Zinc Corporation, Limited and North Broken Hill Pty. Ltd as production was expanded.

Whilst wage rates were relatively high in Broken Hill, the companies knew that living conditions had to be improved if they were to attract the 1,000 additional employees necessary to expand production. In common with the rest of Australia, the shortage of labour and materials during World War Two had meant that very few houses had been built between 1939 and 1945. This had been compounded by the financial institution's unwillingness to finance housing loans in mining communities (Broken Hill Cooperative Societies Association, 1943). From 1940, the Zinc Corporation and North Broken Hill instigated a number of terminating and permanent housing societies to provide finance to employees at rates as low as 2%. A total of 1,900 houses had been financed through the societies by 1981 (Australian Mining and Smelting, 1981). During this period the companies also constructed houses for senior managers that tended to be larger and more refined in appearance than the workers cottages. They were also grouped in small enclaves or suburbs on the mining leases which tended to emphasise the divide that had existed between management and working class in the city since 1885 (Latona Masterman, 1987).

The companies assumed much of the responsibility for promoting civic pride in the post-War period. A number of building inspectors were employed by the companies to provided technical assistance in association with dwelling construction as many of the employees undertook the unskilled labour themselves (The Conveyor, 1961). A free nursery for employees was provided to encourage tree planting. House and garden competitions were sponsored and amenities such as sports ovals, lakes, parks, a swimming pool and bowling greens were also provided during the 1950s and 1960s. This paternalistic approach united the community at the same time as it emphasised the social structure mentioned above.

The later half of the 19th century witnessed the construction of a number of significant Government buildings including the Crystal Street Railway Station, Broken Hill Civic Centre, Broken Hill City Council Administration Building and the State Government Offices. These all have a corporate international character not totally keeping with the existing built environment but none are located on Argent Street where the main Civic Group of heritage buildings are located. Residential architecture has also adopted the styles of the larger urban centres to the south. Again, the majority of new dwellings are located on the city outskirts in North Broken Hill and do not impact unduly on the existing residential character of the city. The later half of the 19th century also witnessed an increase in unemployment, a decline in total population, and an increase in the proportion of the population over sixty (Turner, 1983 and Broken Hill City Council, 1993). Only one mine now remains fully operational employing fewer than 500 people. The population has correspondingly declined from a high of 33,000 in 1952 to less than 23,000 today and the power that once saw Broken Hill celebrated as the bastion of unionism in Australia, has dwindled to near insignificance.

The Line of Lode Project

In 1992, with only 15 years of production remaining, the two companies still in operation, Normandy Poseidon Pty Ltd and Pasminco Mining, offered to lease the non-working surface infrastructure along the Line of Lode to the community for development as an educational and tourism centre. The Normandy Poseidon operations have since been taken over by Pasminco who remains committed to the development of the Project. The Project objectives are to:

1. Provide public access to the Line of Lode and interpretative facilities.

2. Provide a mechanism to conserve, maintain and re-use items of cultural significance.

3. Establish an Australian Mining Centre.

4. Enhance Broken Hill as a regional centre.

The Line of Lode Identification Study (1994) describes the Line of Lode as culturally significant for historical, technical, social and architectural reasons. Its association with several of Australia's largest industrial companies, the rise of unionism and a number of technological innovations, make it a significant contributor to the modern identity of Australia. The built environment is also considered to provide excellent examples of architectural styles from the utilitarian turn of the century structures at the South Mine, to Art Deco at the Zinc Mine and structural concrete at the North Mine.

The actual Line of Lode Project is a 7.3 km long industrial site consisting of underground mines, tailings dams, mullock heaps, open cuts, and associated buildings and equipment from over one hundred years of continuous production. The Project starts at the former Zinc Corporation. The site includes a concentration mill, administration building, headframe, winder and crusher house and demonstrates the evolution of three phases of mining activity in the 1900s, 1930s and 1950s. A national mining museum is proposed for the site. The South and Central Mines contain some of the oldest surviving remains on the Line of Lode. They collectively demonstrate a sequence of mining activities on a restricted site from the 1880s to the 1960s. The site has also been the centre of the later zinc recovery operations most evident in the Kintore open cut. The South and Central mines will form the basis of a heritage walk. The North Mine is the third major site along the precinct. Buildings include an administration block, headframe, crusher house, mill and changehouse that uses a butterfly wing concrete frame structure unique for the period. The heavier pieces of plant and equipment and the educational facilities are to be located at the North Mine. Significant ruins are also evident along the entire length of the precinct and are most obvious in the remains of the Broken Hill Proprietary Company Limited concentration mill fronting on to the central business area of the city. The ruins form an important background to the overall interpretation of the site as does the whole of the city which is considered part of a greater 'living museum' of industrial heritage and cultural significance (Latona Masterman, 1987).

Project feasibility and management

The Broken Hill City Council commissioned a report on the heritage significance of the mine precincts in 1994, the Line of Lode Identification Study, and a Feasibility Report and Study in 1995. The Identification Study (1994) suggests that cultural significance refers to a wide range of qualities - historical, social, aesthetic, archaeological, architectural, scientific and technological - that make some places especially important to a community. Understanding and articulating those qualities is the first step in the process of managing cultural heritage, determining appropriate uses and interpretations for the sites is the next step to ensure that they remain protected and embraced as an integral part of the history of a community. The Identification Study concludes that, whilst individual features could be singled out as representative examples of different aspects of the mining industry, they lose their interpretive value when removed from the overall context. The Line of Lode, in its present form, is not only evidence of the economic and technological development of mining over a 110 year period, it is evidence of work practices, social structures, political struggles, working and living conditions that have helped form the national character of modern Australia.

The Feasibility Report (1995) defined the Project objectives and key issues as follows:

- regional issues - the extreme climatic characteristics should be considered as a major driver in the Project design and management

- transport - improvements in air and rail services would be required for viability

- marketing - the Project should be developed in terms of outback imagery and pioneering spirit to take advantage of a broader market base

- mining - the history and international significance of the city should be emphasised

- environment - there are legal issues associated with the contaminated nature of the site and the management of mining leases

- safety - there are also legal issues associated with health and safety on the site

- social and cultural - the Project would create employment and a sense of community;

- financial - tax exempt status and sponsorship should be sought

- government - funding should be sought to support the initial Project establishment

- legal - an incorporated association structure, merchandising agreements and adequate public liability insurance would be required

- heritage - conservation should be minimal so as to retain the existing decaying character.

The Feasibility Report went on to assess the site in terms of development potential, site constraints, project weaknesses and threats. The Report concludes the following:

- a major strength is the relationship to the outback and the existing city infrastructure

- weaknesses include the negative environmental image of mining and the climatic extremes, and the lack of quality conference facilities and resort style accommodation

- the unique scale, completeness and variety of the mining precinct and city together with the proposed educational/research facilities offer a significant opportunity, whilst

- threats include competition from similar heritage sites and possible service reductions.

The follow-up Feasibility Study (1995) estimated an initial capital subsidy of AU$360,000 would be required to establish the necessary safety levels and management structures in the first year of operation. The Study estimated a visitation scenario of 24,000 in the first year based on the same number of visits to the Broken Hill City Art Gallery. Using an annual growth rate of approximately three percent, the Project was estimated to break even after six years. An additional AU$18.8m would then be required for further staged developments including a national mining museum, operating plant tour, educational facility and virtual mining experience, heritage walk, miners memorial and visitors centre. The city has been attracting visitors for a number of years so demographic characteristics and visitation estimates are based on reliable historical data. Growth and visitation patterns are also based on reliable data for the state of New South Wales (NSW Department of Public Works, 1995). In September 1998, the Deputy Prime Minister announced a Federal Government grant to the Line of Lode Project of AU$4.625 million that will be used to construct the Line of Lode Miners Memorial and the Miners Memorial Visitors Centre. The grant will also be used to implement a restoration program and heritage walk at the South Mine. The incorporated association legal structure and associated legal frameworks have already been established and building work is due to commence on the Miners Memorial and Visitors Centre in April.

Conclusion: The inevitability of the loss of meaning

In his essay 'Semiology and the Urban', Roland Barthes (1997) discusses the semantics of the city, the signifying nature of urban space. He argues that modern planning calls into conflict the semantic nature of our cities bought about by their respective histories, and the functional requirements of modern living. He considers the following:

> *The city is a discourse and this discourse is truly a language: the city speaks to its inhabitants, we speak our city, the city where we are, simply by living in it, by wandering through it, by looking at it. Still the problem is to bring an expression like 'the language of the city' out of the purely metaphorical stage.*

Barthes uses the objective reality of a street map and the correlating signification or meaning given to an urban space by its inhabitants. A map might show two neighbourhoods adjoining each other in geographical terms and yet both neighbourhoods might be seen as '. . . radically separated in the image of the city.' This is the danger for Broken Hill. The city has for so long held an image of itself full of meaning, an image relating to industrial struggle and physical labour, a meaning that did not need to be imparted to the visitor because it was an image founded on functionality, community and the immediate need for survival. Now, also for reasons of functionality, that image needs to be conveyed to visitors, to tourists, to people 'from away' and yet that image will shortly be a purely historical one, one that no longer exists as a functional part of the city.

Barthes contends that the city centre in most cases does not constitute the peak of any particular activity rather it is an empty 'focal point' for the image that a community develops of itself. He uses the example of Tokyo where the city's image of itself is tied inextricably to the Imperial Palace and yet it is an empty centre, not reflecting or connected to the complex urban life of greater Tokyo. Barthes argues that it is possible for meaning to exist in concert with changes necessitated by more functional needs.

By contrast, the centre of Broken Hill has until now been the Line of Lode, the economic, industrial and social heart of the city and a centre that was full of life and connection to the daily activities of the community. The Line of Lode Project is intended for the use of people 'from away' and not by the city inhabitants and as such, the centre will no longer be connected to the community with the same force as before. Whilst tourism will provide some form of economic activity that may sustain the physical city, the identity and social structure that is so inter-woven with the history of the place will surely die or at least, cease to actively live. It will instead be frozen at a variety of instances in time to feed the ' . . . the public's nostalgia for escaping into the recent past' (Palmer and Neaverson, 1998, see also Urry, 1998). That frozen history will be subject to a further level of interpretation that will limit its inclusivity and capacity to capture the city's social structures and evolution (Hayden, 1995, Loomba, 1998). As such, it can be argued that it is inevitable that Broken Hill will lose the meaning that made it the community that it is and hence the tourist attraction that it has been to date. The question that remains to be answered is whether Broken Hill will become a city with an 'empty focal point' as argued by Barthes (1997), or the placeless postmodern Euro-Disney described by Jameson (1997) and Urry (1998).

References

Alfrey, J. and Putnam, T. (1992), *The Industrial Heritage: managing resources and uses,* Routledge, London.

Austral Archaeology (1994), *Broken Hill Line of Lode Identification Study,* unpublished report, Sydney.

Australian Mining and Smelting Ltd. (1981), *The Zinc Corporation limited, New Broken Hill Consolidated Limited and The Southern Power Corporation Pty Limited Operations Handbook,* Hyde Park Press, Adelaide.

Barthes, R., 'Semiology and the Urban', in Leach, N. (ed) (1997), *Rethinking Architecture: a critical reader in cultural theory,* Routledge, London.

Blainey, G. (1968), *The Rise of Broken Hill,* Griffin Press, Netley, South Australia.

Broken Hill Cooperative Housing Societies Association (1943), *Report on Housing in Broken Hill,* unpublished report, Broken Hill.

Broken Hill City Council Community Services Department (1993), *Broken Hill: a basic profile,* Broken Hill City Council, Broken Hill.

Hayden, D. (1995), *The Power of Place: urban landscapes as public history,* The MIT Press, Cambridge, Mass.

Horne, D. (1968), *The Lucky Country,* Penguin Books, Ringwood, Victoria.

Jameson, F., 'The Constraints of Postmodernism', in Leach, N. (ed) (1997), *Rethinking Architecture: a critical reader in cultural theory,* Routledge, London.

Kenny, D. J. (1979), *An Account of the Men Killed on the Line of Lode and Surrounding Mines from 1885,* unpublished report, Broken Hill.

Latona Masterman and Associates (1987), *A Tale of Tin and Silver: Broken Hill Heritage Study,* unpublished report, Sydney.

Loomba, A. (1998), *Colonialism/Postcolonialism,* Routledge, London.

New South Wales Department of Public Works (1995), *Feasibility Report* and *Feasibility Study,* unpublished reports, Sydney.

Palmer, M. and Neaverson, P. (1998), *Industrial Archaeology: principles and practice,* Routedge, London.

Solomon, R. J. (1988), *The Richest Lode: Broken Hill 1883-1988,* Hale and Iremonger, Sydney.

The Conveyor (August 1961), 'Home Owners Receive their Title Deeds', p. 13.

Turner, B. and Associates (1983), *Broken Hill Strategy Report,* Griffin Press, Netley, South Australia.

Urry, J. (1995), *Consuming Places,* Routledge, London.

Woodward, O. H. (1965), *A Review of the Broken Hill Lead-Silver-Zinc Industry,* West Publishing, Sydney.

World heritage sites: Current issues and future implications

Anna Leask

Napier University, UK

Alan Fyall

Bournemouth University, UK

Abstract

This paper critically explores the process and implications of obtaining World Heritage Site designation status. With a focus on sites within the United Kingdom, it explores the current process of inscription and seeks to identify the appeal of this UNESCO award for both visitors and managers.

After a brief review of the World Heritage Convention and Listing process, the paper investigates the current and future policy of the Department for Culture, Media and Sport in short-listing candidates for nomination to the World Heritage Bureau. Particular reference is made to the potential effects of the Bureau's Global Strategy Resolution 1999. The paper synthesises the outcomes of in-depth interviews, correspondence and site visits with key personnel at the Maritime Greenwich World Heritage Site in London and utilises this site as a case study to discuss the implications for a site with World Heritage Site status.

Not only does the paper address the current implications of either having or not having the award, but it projects into the future to investigate the implications and responsibilities for sites with award status in the new millennium. The paper concludes with a set of recommendations for sites wishing to pursue the goal of World Heritage Site designation in the next decade.

Introduction

The World Heritage Convention, whose full title is "The Convention Concerning the Protection of World Cultural and Natural Heritage", was adopted by UNESCO in 1972. A total of 158 countries are now party to the Convention, which enlists the nations of the world to "recognise, inventory, and protect unique and irreplaceable properties of universal value" (ICOMOS, 1999). The Convention provides a permanent legal, administrative and financial framework for international co-operation in safeguarding humankind's cultural and natural heritage. On signing the Convention, each State Party pledges to conserve those cultural and natural sites within it's borders that are recognised by the World Heritage Convention (WHC) as being of 'outstanding universal value' (Cleere, 1998). In return the international community helps to protect the World Heritage Sites (WHS), via payments made to the World Heritage Fund and the exchange of conservation expertise and advice. The Convention established the World Heritage List (WHL), which contains only those cultural, natural or mixed sites that are deemed to have met the specific criteria defined by the WHC. State Parties nominate sites which they feel meet the criteria to the WHC, who take advice from experts before agreeing to inscribe a site onto the List or not. WHS, which include outstanding attractions such as the Taj Mahal, Grand Canyon and Petra, frequently act as magnets for tourists and often represent national icons. The sites, which link the past to the future on a continuum, require effective management to ensure they are preserved for the future, whilst allowing access to present generations.

This paper investigates the process of obtaining WHS status within the UK, with particular reference to the implications of new WHC and UK government policies and changes. It then utilises a case study approach to identify the effects of WHS status on Maritime Greenwich, the key issues in their management plan and its implementation. It then concludes with a set of recommendations for sites wishing to pursue the goal of WHS status, with particular reference to the WHC Global Strategy.

Introduction to the World Heritage Convention

The process of gaining WHS status is demonstrated in Figure 1, which seeks to highlight the range of bodies and stages involved. The inscription process is long, taking on average 18 months from nomination to inscription, in addition to the required procedures within the State Party prior to nomination. It is resource intensive, with input from the site, local and national governments, development agencies, conservation bodies and the panel of experts sent to evaluate the nomination. A condition of nomination is the preparation of a management plan for the site, detailing the boundaries, land use, conservation, utilities, community development, tourism and overall co-ordinating plans. This plan should adhere to the operational guidelines of the Convention, working to protect, conserve and present the heritage of the site, and provide a framework for the various stakeholders to observe. The whole process relies heavily on government involvement and support and is thus open to political and ideological influence (Byrne,1999). The process does allow for nominations to be amended during the application process, usually in line with feedback from ICOMOS or IUCN experts. It is usual to withdraw a nomination prior to WHC consideration if the experts appear likely to recommend refusing inscription. The Committee may also recommend that a nomination is deferred, usually as a result of the need for policy clarification or research, for example, to identify the criteria for cultural landscapes as a type of WHS. In this situation the site may have to wait until the guidelines are produced and then be re-nominated in light of these.

Figure 1   World Heritage List Cycle

WORLD HERITAGE LIST
Cycle for processing cultural and natural nominations from the UK

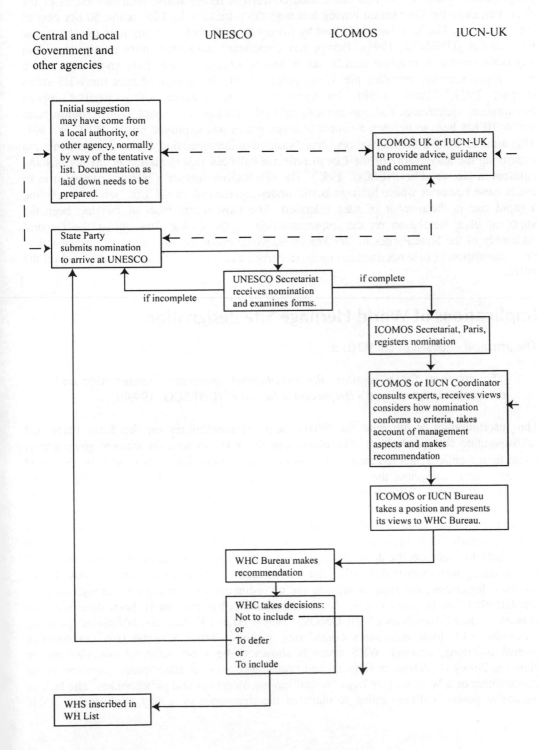

The WHL began in 1978 with the first twelve inscriptions, with the UK's first WHS being inscribed in 1986. There are now a total of 630 sites inscribed, representing 118 countries, with a record number of 48 having been added at the last WHC meeting in 1999. The geographical spread of the sites has caused concern in recent years, with two thirds of the State Parties to the Convention having less than three sites on the List, while 50 per cent of the sites on the List have been inscribed by twenty State Parties, who continue to submit new nominations (UNESCO, 1999). Europe has consistently submitted more nominations than any other continent, demonstrated by the wealth of sites in France, Italy and Spain, which has led to discussion regarding the role of politics in the designation of sites for WHS status (Byrne, 1999; Cleere, 1998). Furthermore, a predominance of western European monumental architecture and bias towards cultural sites has been noted. The response from the WHB has been to develop a Global Strategy which was approved by the WHC in 1994. This aims to address the imbalances, thus "sustaining the reputation of the Convention...and improving the universality of the List to reflect a balanced representation of all regions and cultures in the world" (UNESCO, 1997). The key features include a number of measures to assist those countries whose heritage is still under-represented on the List, whilst preventing a rapid rise in the number of sites inscribed. The most recent facet of this has been the approval of a Resolution on the implementation of the Global Strategy at the General Assembly of the State Parties in October 1999, which encourages a voluntary suspension of the presentation of new nominations by State Parties that are already well-represented on the WHL.

Implications of World Heritage Site designation

The principal intention of the WHL is:

> "To ensure as far as possible, the identification, protection, conservation and presentation of the World's irreplaceable heritage" (UNESCO, 1999b)

The inscription of a site onto the WHL incurs responsibilities on the State Party and corresponding site stakeholders. The obligations the WHC impose on national governments relate to authenticity, management, education and protection. While these may be delegated to state or local authorities the obligations remain, at an international level, with the national government. When a WHS is inscribed a number of stakeholders will act as signatories to the Convention on behalf of the State Party. This does not necessarily attribute any legislative powers upon the management body, but may encourage the imposition of domestic legislation to regulate and control WHS within their jurisdiction. In fact, the only State Party to enact specific domestic legislation setting out the powers and responsibilities of the national government is Australia. The United States of America has limited provision of domestic legislation, referring mainly to the co-ordination of nominations, though they do stipulate that "no property can be nominated unless it has previously been determined to possess national significance" (ICOMOS, 1999). The UK has no additional planning provision, with local authorities considering planning issues via standard development control functions, although WHS status is shown to be a *key material consideration* in Planning Policy Guidelines in England and Wales. The range of stakeholders involved in the management of a WHS may be huge, with disparate objectives and philosophies. The lack of legislative power is disappointing to many of the signatories as it may allow unfavourable developments or discourage new proposals, allowing them only to fit in with existing, broad based planning frameworks.

Despite the paucity of conclusive research, there are a number of perceived and actual benefits to a site obtaining WHS status. Being listed "enhances a property's attractiveness to tourists" (ICOMOS, 1999) and it is often assumed that inscription will lead to increased visitor numbers. Depending on the site concerned and the existing pressure from visitors this could be taken as an advantage or disadvantage. As long as no resulting impacts prejudice the resource itself, the additional earnings may be favourable and assist with conservation. Many sites may benefit from improved marketing activity too, through the activities of the WHS management body.

Another benefit is the required preparation of a management plan specific to the WHS and its buffer zone. These set the framework for the stakeholders to work within, which otherwise would be unlikely to exist, partly due to the large number of bodies involved. The concern of the managing bodies must be to ensure that the authenticity of the site is maintained and that proper management plans are adhered to, in line with those submitted to the Convention. Many WHS still lack a management plan, as the condition of nomination was not introduced until 1995, though this is a point that the World Heritage Centre is keen to remedy. This can be a problem particularly in less developed countries where expertise and resources may be limited. The implications of WHS status on a site with no management plan are varied, with an increase in visitor numbers perhaps leading to an increased need for visitor services and interpretation. It is important that these sites adhere to the level of management detailed in the original nomination, though again no legislative procedure ensures this. Even simply the nomination of a property can revitalise existing organisations or stimulate new approaches.

A significant advantage for many WHS is that inscription brings access to the World Heritage Fund (WHF), which provides limited funds to support equipment and personnel for conservation projects, training and studies at sites. This tends to be directed towards poorly resourced WHS and those in danger from threats to the site itself, for example the uranium mining at Kakadu National Park in Australia. However, no funding is available to assist the nomination process itself, which can be resource intensive, with the estimated cost of preparing a management plan standing at £100,000 (Byrne, 2000).

One disadvantage to the process might be the subsequent withdrawal or rejection of a site by the WHC. This could limit any future partnership success due to disagreement over the way forward and/or the generation of frustration, distrust and conflict between stakeholders. If it is thought that a WHS may be deteriorating, due to visitor pressure or industrial activity for example, then the WHC may place that site on the Properties in Danger List. This entails various investigations into the issues and may assist in the imposition of management plans in the area. The final fallback situation remains the threat of removal from the WHL where a site is deemed to no longer meet the criteria.

In many instances, there is a low level of economic exploitation at world heritage sites; this despite the preponderance of world heritage sites in the imaging and promotion of nation states. However, there is a gradual move towards the commercialisation and optimisation of yield management at sites. How one maintains the authenticity of the site is hence of growing interest to site managers (Garrod and Fyall, 2000). Further disadvantages incurred in WHS inscription should be limited by the provision of an appropriate management plan. However, the vast resources required to compile and implement the plan can prove prohibitive, as can the time it takes to complete the process. The time-scale involved in the UK and within the World Heritage Centre is lengthy and often results in a change of personnel and/or administrative procedures during the nomination process. This can, and frequently does, impact on the stakeholders. On occasion, priorities, boundaries and policies may change during preparation of the nomination and management plan as a consequence of time delays which often lead to re-negotiation and further discussion. These minor disadvantages apart, Shackley (1998) contends that designation represents a key opportunity to further the development and implementation of protection and conservation measures; the benefits of WHS designation status appearing to outweigh the drawbacks.

UK world heritage sites

The State Party in the UK is the government, which nominates properties from Scotland, England, Wales and Northern Ireland. To date the UK has 18 listed sites, of which sixteen are on the British Isles (see Figure 2) with 2, Gough Island and Henderson Island, being overseas territories. Only four sites are designated as 'natural sites', which mirrors the overall imbalance between cultural and natural designated sites around the world. The UK ratified the Convention in 1984, with a surge of nominations in 1986, which resulted in the inscription of seven sites, including Ironbridge Gorge and St Kilda. A further seven sites were inscribed in the next two years, though several more were nominated but withdrew prior to the Committee meeting. No UK sites were inscribed between 1988 and 1995, due to a brief period in time when the UK remained a State Party to the Convention, despite having withdrawn from UNESCO. The incumbent government felt that there were sufficient statutory controls in place within the UK to regulate development which weakened the necessity for UNESCO guidelines. The government also felt that the UK would become a net-loser in terms of conservation funding due to the WHC's support of poorer nations. Despite this, the UK remained a State Party, continued its financial contributions to the World Heritage Fund and successfully nominated two further sites in 1995. After gaining power in 1997, New Labour promptly rejoined UNESCO, with Maritime Greenwich inscribed in 1997 and the Heart of Neolithic Orkney joining the List in December 1999. They also announced their intention to produce a new Tentative List which details the properties identified as those for nomination to the WHC over the next decade.

Figure 2 UK World Heritage Sites

The Heart of Neolithic Orkney

St. Kilda ○

○ Natural Site
● Cultural Site

Edinburgh
Old and
New Town

Giants
Causeway ○

Hadrian's Wall ●

Durham Castle ●
and Cathedral

Fountains Abbey ●

Edward I ●
Castle Towns

Ironbridge Gorge ●

Blenheim Palace ●

Tower of London ● Canterbury
Cathedral
Bath ●

Westminster
Palace

Maritime
Greenwich

Stonehenge
and Avebury

The UK tentative list

As stated, properties can only be nominated by State Parties from an identified Tentative List. The first UK Tentative List was prepared by The Department of the Environment in

1985, following representation from ICOMOS (UK), English Heritage, the Scottish and Welsh Offices, the Department of the Environment (Northern Ireland) and the Foreign and Commonwealth Office. A total of 36 sites were selected, of which 23 were nominated for inscription. A total of eighteen of these are now inscribed on the WHL with the remainder either rejected, deferred or withdrawn. Although no recipe for success exists, the quality of the site's presentation has been said to play a significant part (Pocock, 1997), with recent nominations from the UK, such as the Heart of Neolithic Orkney, being extremely detailed and methodical. Furthermore, Pocock (1997) suggests that the pattern of inscription within the UK is more about the cultural background of the people who select the sites, rather than the worthiness of the actual sites themselves. This could only be as a result of the process involved in the preparation of the Tentative Lists.

Consultation on the contents of the second list began in 1997, led by the Department for Culture, Media and Sport (DCMS). This involved a wide range of stakeholders, including Historic Scotland, English Heritage, Cadw and the Northern Ireland Environmental and Heritage Service. A number of sites were chosen through a relatively informal system within these organisations prior to them being forwarded to the DCMS. The DCMS then issued a draft Tentative List for public consultation, with a clear statement that those sites representing areas currently under-represented on the WHL, such as cultural landscapes and industrialisation, were those deemed most likely to succeed.

The draft list contained 32 sites, which was reduced to 25 after consultation, including three overseas territories. Published in June 1999 the full Tentative List of the United Kingdom of Great Britain and Northern Ireland detailed the sites which are to be nominated to the WHC over the next 10 years. The list is heavily biased in favour of examples of cultural landscapes such as the Lake District, natural sites such as the Cairngorms, sites of industrialisation such as New Lanark, and sites which reflect Britain's global influence such as Shakespeare's Stratford. Basic information on each site is listed, including the criteria under which it might be inscribed, the boundaries of the site and a justification of its perceived 'outstanding universal value' (Cleere, 1998). It also attempts to remedy the historical imbalance of sites within the UK, with two-fifths of the nominees to be found outside England. Four sites have now been identified as the first to be nominated up until 2000 but, as yet, no further sites have been prioritised for nomination thereafter.

The UK has adopted a highly targeted strategy in its attempt to gain greater representation for its sites on the WHL. In addition, the UK has closely considered the resource implications of WHS designation status for each site. Where possible, it has identified sites with existing or realistic prospects of creating a management body. To appear on the Tentative List, each site was required to demonstrate its suitability for nomination in a combination of both formal and informal settings. Although investment at this stage is not high, in order to progress preparation of the nomination document and management plan, a pre-requisite to nomination to the WHC, considerable expense is required with no guarantee of success. In many instances the question as to who will co-ordinate and pay for this process is difficult to answer. This is particularly the case where there is no obvious owner such as the Forth Rail Bridge or Lake District. This issue is particularly acute in developing countries or in situations where it is UNESCO itself who has identified a potential site for WHS status and where there is no clear accountability as to who funds the nomination.

One factor which appears to have been ignored is that of the WHB's Global Strategy. It is not referred to at any point in the consultation or Tentative List publication process. The UK is one of the 21 State Parties listed as having nine or more properties on the WHL, and is one of the thirteen of these that achieved successful nominations in 1999. The DCMS has submitted nominations for Blaenavon and the Town of St George, Bermuda for consideration by the WHC in 2000, with nomination of New Lanark and the Dorset and East Devon Coast planned for the 2001 cycle, in spite of the Resolution agreed in October 1999 at the WHC. It would appear that the DCMS has no intention of voluntarily suspending nomination from the UK State Party.

Case study

The process of obtaining WHS designation status within the UK can best be explained via a case study. With its' unique place in history at the dawning of the new millennium, Maritime Greenwich has been chosen by the authors as a suitable case within the UK to explain the following issues relating to WHS designation; the process of inscription, issues specific to the implementation of the management plan, implications for the site of WHS designation and the means by which effective collaboration among stakeholder partners is maintained. In addition, Maritime Greenwich serves as a suitable vehicle to explore the overall appeal of designation status for sites in the future, and issues surrounding the recent policy announcement encouraging 'voluntary suspension' suggested by UNESCO.

Maritime Greenwich

Inscribed in 1997, Greenwich was included on the original Tentative List of 1986 and was selected for nomination as part of the rolling programme of site selection by the then Department of National Heritage (DNH) in 1996. The three bodies involved in preparation of the nomination were DNH, the Royal Commission on the Historical Monuments in England (RCHME) and English Heritage (EH), with EH being the principal lead body in terms of preparation of the nomination document and liaison with UNESCO. According to Byrne (1999), the catalyst for inscription was that Greenwich represented a 'set of scientific values and historical facts within a cultural landscape whose time had come'; a view seemingly shared by UNESCO:

> *'The public and private buildings and the Royal Park at Greenwich form an exceptional ensemble that bears witness to human artistic and scientific endeavour of the highest quality, to European architecture at an important stage of its evolution, and to the creation of a landscape that integrates nature and culture in a harmonious whole'* (UNESCO, 1997).

In many instances, the Greenwich application was quite straight forward and not particularly resource intensive. The two principal thrusts of the application centred around the background historical research to the site, much of which was already completed, and the preparation of illustrative materials which was conducted by the RCHME. Once the application was deemed to have met the criteria laid down by UNESCO it was very much a case of 'wait and see' as the general consensus among the authors of the nomination document was one of quiet confidence. Only limited feedback was received throughout the process, relating mainly to the need for greater attention to be applied to the 'cultural landscape' aspects of the site. Although the advice from the expert adviser was deemed to be somewhat vague, principally due to the lack of clarification from UNESCO on 'cultural landscapes', this issue was addressed within the nomination document and added to the richness of the application. One area that was slightly problematical was that of the 'buffer zone'. Whilst boundary decisions were self-selecting, definition of the 'buffer zone' proved difficult with management issues not identified as part of the process (Byrne, 1999). Since inscription however, the extent to which the site has been viewed and managed as a single entity and the means by which 'multifarious bodies and interests have been brought together under a coherent regime and programme' has been highly beneficial (Byrne, 1999).

The management plan for Maritime Greenwich was not submitted as part of the nomination, mainly due to the recency of this as a condition of nomination. However, it was swiftly prepared following inscription, at a cost of approximately £45,000 (Byrne, 2000). The plan sets out programmes and projects for the effective administration of the site, with the appointment of a site based co-ordinator reinforcing the perception of the site as a single entity and a steering group representing the interests of the stakeholders. One of the strengths of the plan is the extent to which significant consensus has been achieved to date among these stakeholders. The steering group has managed to foster a strong working relationship with a single vision for the future development of the Maritime Greenwich site, with financial contributions from six members; Greenwich Hospital, the Greenwich Foundation, the University of Greenwich, the National Maritime Museum, Greenwich Council and the Greenwich Development Agency. A combination of domain consensus and like-minded members has contributed to the success of the group, something that has not been so easy to foster in other sites with designation status across the country (Belcher, 2000).

Although only limited research has been conducted to date on the implications of WHS status, there is widespread belief that the accolade has generated significant levels of civic pride and a sense of achievement within the area (Byrne, 2000). Furthermore it has represented a particular reference point and a source of recognition for the London Borough and has undoubtedly contributed to a new air of confidence. Although work has recently been conducted on the tourism effects of the Millennium Dome on the area, a suitable methodology to gauge the impact of WHS status has proved elusive. This said, it is perhaps too early to conduct such an investigation in Greenwich. Notwithstanding, it is believed that designation status, coupled with the 'millennium factor' has contributed much 'goodwill' and 'value added contributions' to Greenwich. A future audit of such activity is being considered by the WHS co-ordinator for the site. Where inscription has been viewed very positively is in the extent to which it has served as a catalyst for the long-term management of the site. By bringing together numerous disparate parties under one common domain, Byrne (1999) hopes that WHS status will lead to "better concern and care for the sites and monuments" and "encourage a greater knowledge and appreciation of the value of the heritage and an understanding of the position of the national heritage in an international context".

One of the challenges facing Greenwich is its' ability to promote the benefits of the site to both a local and international audience. To some extent, it is believed that the full potential of the site with its WHS designation status has yet to be tapped, although this is believed to not be uncommon to many sites (Byrne, 2000). Greenwich has arguably adopted a very pragmatic focus in its early years and has concentrated its efforts on the maintenance and protection of its built and cultural heritage, rather than communicate the worth and benefits to be derived from WHS designation status. Those involved with the site at close hand are very conscious not to "over cook" the site and are eager to mitigate any future conflict between the resident population and visitors from home and abroad (Belcher, 2000). Much work has been conducted with local schools and the local communities in an attempt to engender local interest and involvement with the site. In addition, much time has been taken in deciding how Greenwich can/should incorporate the UNESCO logo in its visitor management and street furniture initiatives. However, the promotion to a wider audience as to what WHS designation means for the site in a global context and how the site is to develop with its accolade from UNESCO has yet to be launched. This is of significance for the attraction of overseas tourists as it is widely regarded that the general levels of awareness of sites with designation status among overseas visitors is much higher than for domestic visitors (Byrne, 2000). Although Greenwich is renowned around the world for its Observatory and Maritime heritage the accolade of WHS status is less recognised.

With regard to the future role of WHS designation status and the proposed change of policy by UNESCO, those individuals behind the inscription of Maritime Greenwich foresee little change. It is difficult to foresee a situation whereby a State Party will unilaterally withdraw sites from the inscription process. Within the UK it is widely believed that the depth and rigour applied to the inscription process ensures that only sites of 'outstanding universal value' are nominated. Additionally, support from central government, particularly in the form of the appointment of a World Heritage and International Policy Co-ordinator, is testament to the fact that the UK will continue to submit sites for inscription and seek to maintain its share of sites with designation status.

Although the above does nothing to address the issue of too many sites, the perceived worth of the UNESCO award stands, although the benefits are difficult to quantify. This said, Greenwich is undoubtedly a site worthy of WHS designation status and is using the accolade wisely in its attempt to underline its' global significance, at the same time as managing its' long-term care and enhancement for both local residents and domestic and international tourists alike.

Future implications from a United Kingdom perspective

Within the UK the DCMS has demonstrated a clear targeted strategy in identifying sites which they feel meet the criteria set by UNESCO; notably to redress the balance of the types of sites on the WHL. In their attempt to obtain more widespread recognition of sites in the UK, the DCMS strategy may unfold if UNESCO enforce their strategy of improving the representation of cultural heritage on the WHL towards non-European cultures. While the Resolution is inviting voluntary suspension of nominations, it will be interesting to see their response should none of the well-represented State Parties practice this. In this scenario it will be interesting to see whether UNESCO reject worthy sites, purely on the basis of their location and type, rather than merit. This will be particularly so with regard to sites in France, Italy and Spain; countries which continue to nominate sites in spite of their recognised domination, though naturally they might subscribe to the voluntary suspension of nominations. The decision by DCMS to enter two of its previously deferred sites, New Lanark (a 2000 nomination) and the Lake District, as cultural landscapes may also represent tactical moves towards the selection of new types of site that are currently under-represented on the List, which may perhaps assist their nomination, in broadening the type of site, regardless of their location.

Serious concern has been voiced as to the total number of world heritage sites that UNESCO can justifiably inscribe (Pocock, 1997). In addition, and by definition of the criteria for inscription, ultimately the time will come when State Parties no longer have any sites to nominate and, via UNESCO's Global Strategy, the WHL will be deemed complete. This is certainly true for the UK where at some point all appropriate sites will have been through the process, either successfully or unsuccessfully, and there will no longer be any sites that meet the appropriate credentials for inscription. In this instance, the limited resources available should be channelled into existing sites, to raise the quality of the current provision, rather than diminish the value of world heritage sites per se. With this in mind, it is necessary for the DCMS to set clear parameters and redress the balance of sites within the UK through a co-ordinated approach and prioritisation of future nominations. It also raises the issue as to the perceived worth of remaining parts of UNESCO once a State Party has achieved its 'quota' of sites. An alternative approach would be for UNESCO to set a more rigorous selection process with more tightly defined criteria, perhaps with existing sites re-evaluated against them (Byrne, 1999). The potential difficulty in this approach would be the cost-barrier to less developed State Parties. While the threat of being taken off the WHL exists, this has never occurred in practice, perhaps now is the time to exercise this option where a WHS is clearly not upholding its responsibilities. One final approach could be to set up a legislative structure that acts to safeguard the inscribed sites in a more effective manner, allowing stakeholders to ensure that threats to the WHS are removed. This would raise the awareness and effectiveness of the designation, which could in turn attract further resources to the sites and develop the quality of the conservation.

Conclusions and recommendations

Future policy for sites with WHS designation status in the UK will continue to lie with the DCMS, as advised by Historic Scotland, English Heritage, CADW, Northern Ireland Environmental and Heritage Service, the Foreign Office and the Home Secretary. The combination of a rather informal, then increasingly formal process of site proposition and nomination appears to suit the UK, in that it achieves broad representation. What remains to be seen is how successful the UK's strategy of targeting nominations to identifiable gaps in the WHL is likely to be, particularly in light of the Global Strategy. The DCMS has to take a decision as to their future policy on nominations, though it would be difficult to see them withhold their current prioritised nominees. New Lanark in particular would be disappointed if their nomination was held back in 2000, since they were on both UK Tentative Lists and were only deferred due to a lack of clarity on the UNESCO criteria for industrial sites. To refuse them nomination at this stage would be most unfortunate, and yet UNESCO has a valid point too, in that the WHL is not fully representative of the world's heritage in its current form.

While it is a difficult situation, those sites already on the Tentative List must now concentrate on the effective preparation of their nomination and management plan proposals, in order to be considered seriously by UNESCO. They will not necessarily be involved in the decision-making process regarding voluntary suspension and so should concentrate on preparing their nominations. For some sites this should not present insurmountable difficulties, e.g. New Lanark, where geographic and management boundaries are clear. For others, this may create problems where there is no obvious management structure or political will to succeed e.g. Lake District. English Heritage are keen to adopt a mentoring role for future nominees, though limited funding is available and relies on contributions from stakeholders (Byrne, 2000). This role may involve the dissemination of best practice from previously successful sites, for example the soon to be formed Westminster Steering Group. Nonetheless, it is essential that all sites resolve any outstanding disputes prior to nomination to the WHC and present quality nominations. In particular the issue of the statutory planning importance of WHS status requires clarification, as does the provision of funding. For those sites that have not made it onto the Tentative List in this Review, the time to commence lobbying must be now. Due to the time the process takes, it is perhaps in this instance where the newly formed Scottish Parliament and Welsh Assembly are to play a far greater role in the process.

Irrespective of the political agenda, further research is required into the implications of WHS status; not only to more accurately measure the costs and benefits of inscription but to assist in the formation of future nominations. It is essential that the management bodies at the sites and the corresponding State Parties learn from the actions of the WHC, noting the criteria on which nominated sites are rejected or approved. If lessons are learned then future nominations can be tailored to suit the Committee's perceived priorities. However, these priorities are prone to change in response to the type of nominations it receives and the potential for political influences. The success of the Global Strategy may also influence this, in that a large influx of nominations from previously under-represented State Parties might prevent the inscription of those from more established ones. In this situation it will be interesting to see how the WHC manages selection, either by large increases to the WHL or by limiting those from existing State Parties through deferral or refusal. Both of these options could undermine the philosophy of the WHL. For example, too many sites will detract from the significance of those on the List, while refusing some sites on the basis of geography alone may restrict the inscription of sites that meet the criteria of 'outstanding universal value' (ICOMOS, 1999).

In conclusion, the new millennium will see many sites from around the world seek nomination for WHS designation status in their attempt to experience the prestige that WHS endorsement undoubtedly brings with it. The effectiveness of the new Global Strategy Resolution will dictate the future inscription of new sites and the form of the WHL. It is worth noting that the gratuitous recruitment of additional sites may just demean the ideal of WHS status. Too many sites and insufficient funds may serve as the catalyst for change and the gradual dilution of all that UNESCO set out to achieve.

References

Arnold, J. E. (1998), Letter to Historic Scotland, *New Lanark*, Scotland.

Belcher, Geoffrey (2000), Interview, *Maritime Greenwich*, London.

Byrne, Alan (1999), Interview, *English Heritage*, London.

Byrne, Alan (2000), Interview, *English Heritage*, London.

Cleere, Henry (1998), Europe's Cultural Heritage from a World Perspective. In ICOMOS UK Conference *Sustaining The Cultural Heritage of Europe*, London.

Department for Culture, Media and Sport (1998), *Consultation Paper On A New UK Tentative List of Future Nominations*, DCMS, London.

Department for Culture, Media and Sport (1999), *World Heritage Sites - The Tentative List of The UK of Great Britain and Northern Ireland*, DCMS, London.

Garrod, B. and A. Fyall (2000), Managing Heritage Tourism: A Delphi Study, *Annals of Tourism Research*, 27.

Gillon, Jack (1996), Edinburgh's World Heritage Site, *The Scottish Planner* (September): 6-7.

Gillon, Jack (1999), Interview. *City of Edinburgh Council*, Edinburgh, Scotland.

ICOMOS (1997), *World Heritage List: Cycle For Processing Cultural Nominations From UK*. London, ICOMOS.

ICOMOS (1999), *Tourism at World Heritage Cultural Sites*. Washington, World Tourism Organisation.

Pocock, Douglas (1997), The UK World Heritage, *Geography* 82 (4): 380-385.

Shackley, Myra (1998), *Visitor Management: Case Studies From World Heritage Sites*, Butterworth-Heinemann, Oxford.

Stovel, Herb (1996), Evaluation Visit to Edinburgh, *ICOMOS Canada Bulletin* 5 (3): 31-36.

UNESCO (1995), *World Heritage Committee Report*. UNESCO, Paris.

UNESCO (1997), *World Heritage Committee Report*. UNESCO, Paris.

UNESCO (1999a), *Interview Held At The World Heritage Centre*, Paris.

UNESCO (1999b), *Operational Guidelines For The Implementation Of The World Heritage Convention (WHC-99/2)*. UNESCO, Paris.

Kakadu: Managing sustainable tourism in a World Heritage Site

Ian Moffatt

University of Stirling, UK

Abstract

Kakadu is a World Heritage site located some 270kms East of Darwin in the north of the Northern Territory, Australia. As a World Heritage site Kakadu has experienced a growth in tourism from 45,000 in 1980 to over 220,000 in 1992. Like other world heritage sites Kakadu is becoming more popular as a tourist destination. The popularity of the site brings with it problems which need to be addressed to ensure that the world site is conserved for future generations benefit. This paper has two purposes, namely, to describe the impact of tourists on the physical and cultural landscapes of the Kakadu; and then to examine the ways in which prescriptive management plans have been developed to ensure that this unique landscape, together with its indigenous peoples culture, can continue to be developed in a sustainable manner.

First, the physical setting of Kakadu National Park is described. It is against this backcloth that the aboriginal peoples have evolved a unique way of surviving and living in an often harsh environment. Next, this important cultural landscape, which has been occupied for over 40,000 years, is described. In this section the conflicting demands of tourism and other economic activities are described. This then leads into a discussion of the ways in which tourism is managed in this World Heritage site. Finally, some of the lessons gained from this study are discussed as a contribution to the sustainable management of this and other World Heritage sites.

Introduction

Kakadu is a World Heritage site located in the north of the Northern Territory, Australia some 270kms East of Darwin. This area is a beautiful region in the wet/dry tropics and is the cultural heart of the Aboriginal traditional owners of the area. Like many other world heritage sites, the landscape and its peoples has become an area of interest to scientists, anthropologists – as well as a destination for an increasing number of tourists. The purpose of this paper is to examine the ways in which tourism can be managed so that the site can be developed in a sustainable manner for the benefit of current and future generations without damaging the cultural and physical landscapes of the region. Kakadu is one of only seventeen world sites listed for both natural and cultural landscapes and if we are to manage sustainable tourism in this and similar destinations then we have been to appreciate the physical and cultural factors which have been created and are still moulding this unique region.

In the following section the physical setting of Kakadu is described. In section four the conflicting demands of tourism and other economic activities upon the lives and landscapes of Kakadu are described. This then leads into a discussion of the ways in which tourism is managed in this World Heritage site. Finally, some of the lessons gained from this study are discussed as a contribution to the sustainable management of this and other World Heritage sites.

The physical setting

Geologically the Kakadu national park, covering some 19,804 square kilometres, is composed of very ancient as well as young rock formations. In the East of the area, the region is dominated by the Arnhem plateau – a high, deeply dissected sandstone ridge which runs from the north-east to the south-west of the region. This ridge is a noticeable geological feature but is part of the more general Precambrian geological formation known as the Pine Creek geosynclines. The rocks of these geosynclines include granitic intrusions, gabbro and a series of metamorphosed sandstones, which compose the Arnhem plateau itself. The rocks have been dated as some 2,470 million years old (BP Before Present). This area is tectonically stable and if sedimentary rocks were laid down during the development of this area, which is very likely, no evidence of such periods of sedimentation are recorded in the geological record. There is, however, evidence of marine deposits associated with the movement of the Australian plate. This tectonic activity witnessed the Indian subcontinent breaking away from Gondwanaland resulting in the late Cretaceous marine transgression (circa 50 million years BP).

Figure 1   A cross section through the Arnhem plateau

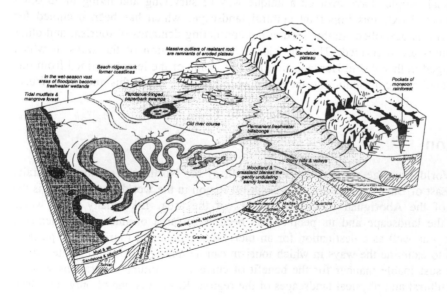

After the withdrawal of the Late Cretaceous Sea the old rocks were re-worked and fresh deposits were laid down during the Tertiary period. By the Quaternary period, some 2 million years ago, the main features include the deeply dissected Arnhem plateau; the lower lying re-exhumed hills of metamorphic rocks located in the south of the region; the lowland plains and incised rivers systems draining to the north and the geologically recent developments in the extensive coastal riverine plains. The latter have been extensively studied over the last ten years (Woodroffe 1988; Woodrooffe and Mulrennan, 1992).

The melting of the ice caps in Northern and Southern hemisphere in the Quaternary saw the beginning of a rise in global sea-level some 14 000 BP and the sea level slowly rose from some 150m below its present level. At this time the northern continental shelf of Australia was 300km north and Australia and New Guinea were one land mass. Between 6800 and 5300 BP there was a widespread development of mangroves and the development of the "Big Swamp" which has eventually resulted in the patterns of sedimentation and vegetation development we witness today in the coastal plains.

The coastal plains and riverine systems consist of a saline estuarine funnel at the marine margin. This area then gives way to mudflats and creeks. The entire river system has been further divided into three regions into three regions namely the sinuous meandering region near to the coast; a cuspate meandering section and an intermittently inundated main river channels found upstream (Woodroofe, 1988). Most of this area is flooded for up to four months during the wet season. The lower lying areas can be inundated for as long as nine months creating semi-permanent billabongs and backwater swamps.

Whilst the soils of the floodplains appear dark in colour they are not nutrient rich and many early European explorers, viewing the luxuriant vegetation cover in the Wet season, were misled to believe that agriculture, including rice cultivation, could be successfully practised in the area. They were wrong. The soils of most of the region, outwith the floodplains are hard, infertile, acidic red laterites. Soils are virtually absent on the sandstone plateau and where pockets of soil do occur they are skeletal veneers of sand rarely more that 150cm deep.

Despite the poor pedalogical conditions the vegetation of Kakadu is one of the most floristically rich areas of Australia. It has been estimated that there are over 1682 species, including 96 naturalised alien species. This rich biodiversity has adapted to the underlying geology, soil complexes and landforms inland from the coastal margins. The flood plains adjacent to the present day coastlines are also rich in freshwater and tidal flat species including mangroves, remnants of the monsoon forests. Further inland the wetlands give way to the ubiquitous eucalyptus-dominated open forests and woodland formations.

In the eucalyptus woodlands and the forests of Kakadu is a unique assemblage of animals and, like the flora, represents one of the most diverse in Australia. Recent estimates have noted that are fifty different fish species; over 120 reptiles and amphibians; over 60 species of mammals; over 1000 species of termites and 300 species of ants plus tens of thousands of other invertebrates. There are over 280 species of birds recorded in Kakadu, representing one third of all the bird species in Australia (Press et al, 1995). Included amongst the bird life are the magpie geese and the large Jabiru stork. Often these and other species can be seen at tourist locations such as Yellow Waters and many other tourists actually come to view the birdlife as one of the attractions of their visit. Another attraction is the presence of alligators in the fresh water rivers and the salt water crocodile which inhabit the coastal and estarine areas of the East and South Alligator Rivers and the flood plains in the north of the park. Some of the animal species are found nowhere else in the world. Together the flora and fauna of Kakadu provide an important biological reserve and gene pool of plants and animals; they also represent one of the main reasons for tourists coming to the park together with the attraction of viewing the rock art and bushwalking and scenic driving (Knapman, 1990). It is against this changing physical landscape that the indigenous Aboriginal populations have developed a unique way of life in this harsh and yet beautiful landscape.

The cultural landscape

The first people to live in this area are unknown. It is speculated that seafarers from the Indonesian archipelago first came to the land; reliable thermoluminesence and opticoluminesence dating of artefacts found in the rock caves in the Northern coastal area of the park have been dated as between 40,000-60,000 years BP (Roberts et al, 1990). These dates would indicate that the area has been home of non-aboriginal (Predominantly European) influence in the region (Stanner, 1965).

One of the major cultural features of this area is the beautiful rock art caves and rock shelters found within the region. These rock art express scenes of hunting; the sightings of European ships; as well as a rich diversity of flora and fauna and religious icons. One of the major tourist attractions is to visit several sites to see these ancient art forms which are still practised today by some Aboriginal peoples. Another feature which tourists find interesting is the use of timber and reeds to make up weapons and baskets used for hunting and carrying. Bush tucker visits are also popular amongst some tourists as well as Aboriginal artwork, which can be seen at the Science Museum in Darwin and is a traditional skill still practised by Aborigines in the villages and schools in Kakadu. It should be noted that the cultural artefacts are not some monument to past ancestors but are an integral part of the cultural and belief system of many contemporary Aborigines.

To many Aboriginal people their traditional way of life is intimately associated with changes in the weather patterns. To non-Aborigines the area is characterised by a Wet/Dry season. The precipitation is very high with 1460 mm being the mean annual rainfall in Jabber, 1971-1994. This high rainfall begins in September and rapidly builds up with the monsoonal rains in November to March. The rainfall then subsides and the Dry season commences May to September. The temperature is uniformly high about 30-35 degrees Celsius throughout the year with an extremely high humidity during the wet season and very dry conditions in the winter months (June to September). The vegetation cover dries out during the year. This natural drying is also accompanied by burning the bush so that the extensive cattle ranching and animals can take green picking i.e. new plant growth as food supply. In the past, as well as today, the Aboriginal populations also burn bush but their fires are less extensive and localised (Head et al, 1992). These small scale bush fires also allow Aboriginal peoples to hunt small animals escaping the fires. Whilst many non-Aboriginal people perceive this area as dominated by a Wet/Dry season some Aboriginal calendars subdivide the seasons into 12 sub-units – illustrating the fine distinctions that Aboriginal peoples, living in close proximity to nature, actually use (Figure 2).

Figure 2   Aboriginal and non-Aboriginal classification of the seasons in Kakadu

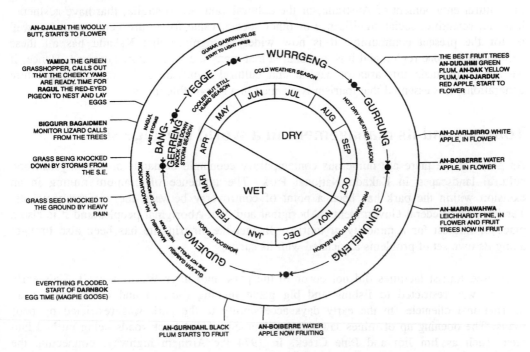

During the European colonisation of the Top End water buffalo were initially introduced to feed the garrison in the Coburg Peninsula. Today these large animals are feral. These large ruminants are hard hoofed and these, together with the cattle industry, are causing much damage in water holes and in trampling the wetlands. The native Australian fauna are soft hoofed animals and have a less heavy "footprint" on the landscape. Other damage to the landscape is the result of saltwater intrusion into the wetlands and the increasing use of four wheel drive vehicles which are essential for motorised transport in the bush especially in the Wet season. Furthermore, the increase in tourists is causing damage to the flora and fauna and some rock areas.

The hunting of feral buffalo, during the dry season, employed both non-Aboriginal and Aboriginal peoples. The biggest impact on the Aborigines cultural landscape is the sporadic development of mining for gold, platinum, palladium at Coronation Hill and uranium at Rum Jungle, Coronation Hill and especially at Ranger Uranium mine. The latter mine is located within an excision in the national Park and was only allowed to be developed after a protracted period of negotiations culminating in the environment impact analysis named after the chairperson- the Fox Report (Fox et al, 1997; Buckley 1989). It should be noted that aboriginal peoples do not traditionally mine for mineral resources such activity is damaging their land and also offends religious sensibilities of some Aborigines who view mining as damage to the scared land sites.

The changes to the physical and cultural landscape have resulted in the harsh beauty of the Kakadu area. The waterfowl and wetlands of Kakadu were recognised as sites of international importance in the Ramsar Convention. This unique region is officially recognised by being included in the Register of the National Estate kept by the Australian Heritage Commission. The National estate is defined as those places, being components of the natural environment of Australia, or the cultural value of Australia, that have aesthetic, historic, scientific, social significance or other special value for future generations, as well as for the present community. It is now widely recognised that Kakadu has all these components in one region and it is to this area that many tourist are now attracted. Hence, if we are to maintain this area of natural and cultural significance for current and future generations, it is essential that tourism is planned in a sustainable manner.

Tourism and its management in a world heritage site

As noted above there are numerous contemporary economic demands on the physical and cultural landscaped in Kakadu National Park. The influence of uranium mining in an excision within the park has been a point of controversy between the environmentalists, Territory and Federal Governments, Aboriginal and Non-Aboriginal peoples and it is also a place of interest for a minority of tourists. In fact the airstrip site has been also brought along its own set of problems associated with its success.

Organised tourist facilities did not occur in the park until after World War II. This early tourism was restricted to fishing and big game hunting (buffalo and crocodile) for an international clientele. In the early days accessibility to the park was restricted by poor roads. The opening up of mines saw the development of dirt track roads being pushed into areas such as Jim Jim and Pine Creek. In 1974 the Arnhem highway, connecting the townships of Jabiru to Pine Creek, was built as the first sealed road known as the Kakadu highway. This development of mining roads also paved the way for tourists. By 1987 tourism in Australia was the largest and fastest growing industry with a turnover if 12 billion dollars, employing some 40,000 people. In the case of the Northern Territory alone it provided some 3000 jobs in a population of 150,000 people of which only 75,000 people lived in the Top End i.e. the Northern part of the Northern Territory.

Tourism has grown substantially over the years rising from some 45,000 per year in 1980 to 220,000 in 1992 (Figure 3). Often the international tourists visits Kakadu as part of their "Australian experience". Flights to Darwin's new airport en route to Sydney, Melbourne or other Australian destinations disembark people to take in a short visit to Kakadu. Some of these short visits can be taken by coach along the Arnhem highway and then east to Jabiru. Domestic tourists and visitors both from within the Northern Territory or from inter-state destinations visit Kakadu on vacation. The pattern of tourists to the park has varied between years and during different seasons. In the 1980s most visitors, approximately 80%, were domestic tourists. Yet, by April 1993 64% of then visitors were international although by June of that year (the winter) the number of international tourists had fallen to less than 28%.

Figure 3   The growth of Tourists to Kakadu, 1982-1993

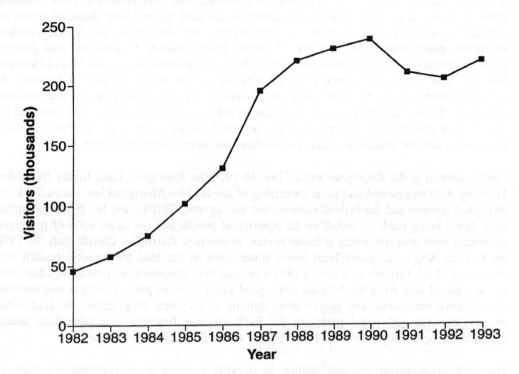

There is little doubt that tourism has been adverse effect on the Park. It is true that such impacts are less damaging than say the Ranger Uranium mining in an excision surrounded by the Park (Buckley, 1989); or the infestation of the water ways by Mimosa pigra and other weeds; and the damage done by feral animals. Nevertheless, tourists do damage the park, in particular the use of four wheel drives are often essential for travelling in this part of the outback. Yet, paradoxically, 95% of the visitors to the Park come mainly to see wildlife and rock art rather than visits to the Ranger mine which is often included on their itinerary (Allen and Harris, 1087).

Similarly, the indigenous Aboriginal people originally claimed that tourists often viewed them as "Living Exhibits" rather than individuals and communities attempting to follow their own chosen lifestyle. This lifestyle includes very close contact with the changing environment and its use of the flora and fauna that provides much of the life support for many of these contemporary aboriginal groups. Yet, commercial and recreational fishing has seen foods such as Barramundi decline. In the period 1972 to 1985 the number of commercial hundred meter net days (hmd) had declined from 34.9kg/hmd to 9.4kg/hmd. Furthermore, the increasing number of tourists entering the park has occasionally led to strained relationships between aboriginal peoples and the non-aboriginals.

It would be wrong to suggest that all aborigines are against tourism. In fact many Aboriginal people see tourism as a way of educating non-aboriginal people about a way of life which is less materialistic and more social than "western lifestyles" (Coombs, 1990). Nevertheless, to most Aboriginal peoples land is central to their lifestyle and many of the areas of tourist interest, such as the beautiful rock art at Norlangie or Ubirr, are part of the Aborigines living and cultural heritage. The latter site has recorded over 1741 visitors in 1984 including some 37 in one day. Over 60% of all visitors to the park go to Ubirr. Such an influx of tourists is putting strains on both the environment and the social life of the resident aboriginal populations. With the rise of nature based tourism (eco-tourist) and general growing awareness of green issues and cultural heritage appreciation Kakadu World Heritage Site will face a major challenge from the forecast growth in the number of tourists. At present tourism, alongside other users, is potentially damaging the physical and cultural landscape. These conflicting claims on the use of the land is recognised and are managed by use of Park management schemes but this inevitably leads to complex community based discussions with the traditional owners of the land and other interested parties.

Land is central to the Aboriginal way of life. In 1976 the Aboriginal Land Rights (Northern Territory Act) was passed and some ownership of the land by Aboriginal land councils, local aboriginal peoples and the Federal Government was agreed. This act has led to several major land claims being made on behalf of the Aboriginal people and the entire suite of problems associated with property rights is under review of the new Australian Constitution. In 1978 the Kakadu Aboriginal Land Trust leased three areas of the land for the use, benefit and enjoyment of all Australians. Later in 1991 a revised land agreement was made together with a new lease of land from the Jabiluka Aboriginal Land Trust to provide for the maintenance of traditional occupation and usage rights; training employment programmes for traditional owners; benefits and rental payments for Park use and finally a commitment to world standard management procedures. It is the latter that will be examined below.

The park management schemes attempt to provide a range of recreational activities in Kakadu whilst providing for protection and appreciation of the cultural and natural assets. As Wellings notes, it is imperative that visitor use of the Park is planned and organised and not allowed to develop incrementally in an uncontrolled and overtly market driven fashion (Wellings 1995, 262). One way of achieving these aims is to develop land use management zoning to minimise the possibility of damage to the cultural and physical landscape. Four such zone are used: Intensive; Intermediate; Minimum; Wilderness and a fifth zone is used for research purposes at Kapalga – which is adjacent to the World Heritage site. These five zones are used to guide tourists through the Park and to minimise the impact on the Aboriginal peoples culture as well as the physical landscapes in and adjacent to the park.

The areas of intensive use are located at Coonida and Yellow Water en route to Nourlangie Rock – famous for its rock art – and to the hotel accommodation at Jabiru. The areas of intermediate use are located as a 40 km band either side of the Kakadu Highway and lying south of the Arnhem Highway. Two other areas of intermediate use are the Wildman River in the west and the Magela Creek complex in the north east of the park. These areas of intensive and intermediate use are unsurprisingly the regions where tourist activities are having the highest impact. The Minimum Management and Wilderness zones are located in the west and south-east sections of the Park. Both of these areas are subject to little formal management; the first area has been deliberately chosen by the park management team to safeguard other areas, whilst the southern area has access difficulties for tourists or other potential isers. The fifth zone is used exclusively for scientific research at Kapalga Research area located in the north of the National park between the West and South Alligator Rivers.

This zone has been used for vegetation and fauna studies as well as for experiments with different fire management regimes (Figure 4).

Figure 4   Management Zones in Kakadu National Park (After Wellings 1995 p265)

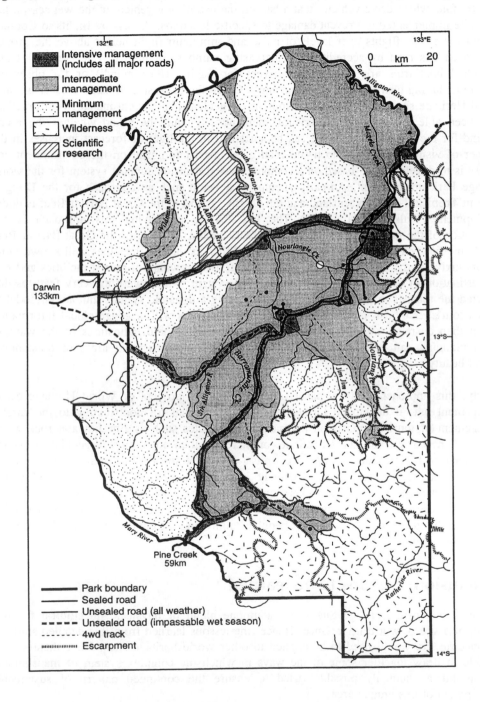

Despite the Park management plans tourism still puts pressures on the cultural and physical landscape. In 1993, for example, over 175 tour companies operated visits to the park. Twenty-two percent were based in the Northern Territory. Almost all of these tours access the Park by road in the dry season. Some areas such as Jim Jim falls are so heavily used-even by four wheel drive vehicles that a ban on the use of any vehicle in the wet season has had to be implemented to prevent damage to specific locations. Access by flights to Cooinda airstrip for scenic flights over levels of noise and minimum flight height above the ground have to be observed by accredited but increasing numbers of both private companies and individual boat trips are made on the rivers for fishing (Barramundi) or for observing wildlife including bird and crocodile watching. Given the interest in Kakadu park as a major World Heritage site and as a focus for tourism, it is clear that current management practices have been able to cope with the visitors demands. It could be asked whether the rising demand for the Kakadu experience can be sustained in the light of forecast increases in the number of visitors. One way to try to reduce the tourist footprint on the environment and culture is to develop plans based on a computer based decision support system for the world heritage Park management. An early attempt to develop such an approach for the Douglas Shire in Tropical North Queensland and the Cairns section of the Great Barrier Reef is under development (Walker et al, 1997) The key feature underlying this approach is the recognition of the fact that areas of remote beauty such as Kakadu or the Great Barrier Reef are often "discovered" by the tourist industry and then as the area becomes well known more visitors arrive at the destination. This can result in overcrowding of tourist facilities and / or the destination of the natural beauty and cultural system, which were the very features that attracted the tourists in the first place. By integrating a dynamic system simulation model to predict tourist numbers and probable environment impacts with a geographical information system then current, ongoing research is able to provide some indications of the ways in which planning can help reduce the adverse impacts of tourism in areas of outstanding natural beauty.

Clearly, this approach is not a panacea to the complex process of World Heritage estate management but, if developed further, it has the potential for contributing to the careful management of tourist impacts on the most popular sites such as Jim Jim and rock art at Ubirri. If the current pressures continue, or increase, then other more draconian measures would have to be introduced, such as permits to visit the site i.e. restricting the number of visitors per day to this area; or , alternatively, increasing the cost of the visits – which would probably disadvantage the backpackers and campers as well as those on low incomes. Clearly, the use of a decision support system can help in the complex process of managing Kakadu so that tourism, the indigenous peoples culture and the environment can develop in a sustainable manner.

Conclusion: Lessons to be learned

Kakadu – a World Heritage Site – has a unique blend of physical and cultural features making it a site of world importance. Hence, the lessons learned from this detailed study of this specific site would need to be applied to other world heritage sites. Nevertheless, it is possible to draw together some of the ways in which the complex system of management has, as far as humanly possible, tried to ensure the continued pattern of sustainable development of this unique area.

At present the management of tourism as part of the use of World Heritage site shows the interplay of political, economic, social and environmental interests. The fact the site is defined as a place of global significance is also political statement. The political aspects include the joint management agreements between the local Aboriginal peoples and the Northern Land Councils and the Federal and Northern Territory Government. The social and economic aspects of the management plans ensures that the traditional owners of the land can continue to develop their own unique way of life whilst still embracing some aspects of Western economic development. The sensitive management of these interactions is important and points a way forward for the other First nation peoples. The designation of world heritage status means that environmental groups and environmental organisations, such as the departments of the Commonwealth Scientific and Industrial Organisation (CSIRO) and the Commission of the Northern Territory (CCNT), have an interest in seeing that the environment is not damaged by unsustainable developments in tourism and other contemporary activities.

Currently the management of the park has been able to cope with the demands of tourism. Yet, there are signs that some areas of the park are becoming too popular and bans or permits to visit the area are being considered as in other heavily used national parks. It has been suggested that the development of the CSIRO tourist model, with suitable parameter changes, may be a useful way managing the full suite of tourist demand increases and puts further stresses and strains on this unique landscape.

Given the long time range of human residence in Kakadu it is clear that tourism is a relatively new additional pressure that this world heritage site faces – especially one which has outstanding physical and cultural features in the one location. The management plans which have been developed for managing the growing number of tourists, as part of the general economic activity which flourishes in the Park, have been successful. It is to be hoped that further improvements in the ways in which tourists are integrated into life of the region via the joint management agreements will also be successful so that the changing patterns of development can be sustained well beyond the 21st century.

References

Allen, L. and Harris, C. (1987), *Kakadu: Our Land, Our heritage*. Weldons press, McMahons Point, NSW.

Buckley, R. (1989), Precision in Environmental impact prediction: First national environmental audit. Resources and Environmental Studies, 2, pp.1-73. Centre for Resources and Environmental Studies, Australian National University, Canberra.

Coombs, H. C. (1990), *The Return to Scarcity: Strategies for an Economic Future*, Cambridge University Press, Cambridge.

Fox, R. W., Kelleher, G. G. and Kerr, C. B. (1997). *Ranger Uranium Environmental Inquiry* AGPS, Canberra.

Knapman, B. (1990). Tourist in Kakadu National park: Some results from a visitor survey. North Australian Research Unit (NARU), Australian National University, Darwin.

Moffatt, I. and Webb, A. (Editors.)(1992), *Conservation and Development in North Australia* (ANU, Darwin).

Moffatt, I (1996), *Sustainable Development: Principles, Analysis and Policies*. Parthenon Press, Carnforth and New York.

Head, L. M., O'Neil, A. L., Marthick, J. K. and Fullager, R. L. K. (1992), A comparison of Aboriginal and pastoral fires in the north-west Northern Territory, in Moffatt, I and Webb, A. (Editors.) *Conservation and Development in North Australia* pp.130-144.

Press, T., Lea, D. Webb, A and Graham, A. (Editors) (1995), *Kakadu: Natural and Cultural Heritage and Management* (ANC, Darwin).

Roberts, R,. Jones, R. and Smith, M. (1990), Thermouluminesence dating of a 50,000 year old human occupation site in Northern Australia. *Nature*, 345, pp153-6.

Stanner, W. (1965), Aboriginal territorial organisation: estate, range, domain and regime. *Oceania*, 36,pp.1-26.

Walker, P. A., Grenier, R. McDonald, D. and Lyne, V. (1997), Benefits and impacts of tourism: A systems Thinking Approach. In McDonald D A and McAleer M (Eds.) *MODSIM 97 International Congress on Modelling and Simulation*. University of Tasmania, Tasmania, Volume 2 pp. 502-507.

Wellings, P. (1995). Management considerations. Press, T. Lea, D. Webb, A. and Graham, A (Editors) (1995). *Kakadu: Natural and Cultural Heritage and Management* (ANC, Darwin), pp.238-270.

Woodrooffe, C. (1998), Changing mangrove and wetland habitats over the last 8000 years, northern Australia and South East Asia. In Wade – Marshall, D and Loveday, P (Editors)

Northern Australia: Progress and Prospects, (Volume II) pp.1-33 Floodplains Research North Australian Research Unit (NARU), Australian National University, Darwin.

Woodroffe, C. and Mulrennan, M. (1992). The past, present and future extent of tidal influence in Northern Territory coastal wetlands. In Moffatt, I and Webb, A. (Editors) *Conservation and Development in North Australia,* pp.83-104.

History, heritage, and economic development: The American Civil War and heritage tourism in Kentucky

William H Mulligan[1]

Murray State University, USA

Introduction

Brent and Mulligan (1998) have observed that "Since 1992 a concerted effort has been made to preserve, manage, and interpret America's Civil War historical and cultural resources." This effort has involved a federal agency, the American Battlefield Protection Program; a number of State Historic Preservation Offices; and, most importantly, people in communities with Civil War sites who have built support within their communities and made the program succeed.

The American Civil War (1861-1865) stands as one of the great watersheds in American history. In nearly every high school and university it neatly divides the national history survey course into two parts. The pervasiveness of The War as part of American life and culture is perhaps best illustrated by the many names, (including in some sections of the country, simply, still, "The War") it has accumulated over the years.

Originally called the War of 1861 by many – following the model of the War of 1812 – its subsequent designation as "The Civil War" was actually meant to soften its earlier designation by the ultimate victors as "The War of the Rebellion" or "War of the Southern Rebellion." But even that softer name has had its critics and many Southern partisans, rejecting "Civil War", have moved away from the fairly contemporary "War for Southern Independence" and now prefer the somewhat more neutral "War between the States." Among the more militant, or less reconstructed, Southerners "The War of Northern Aggression" has a strong constituency. I have been verbally assaulted at speaking engagements for referring to the conflict as the Civil War by such folks. They are not kidding around, there is a seriousness to their refusal to accept any name for the conflict that casts a negative light, however dim, on the motivations of their ancestors, real or spiritual. For many "The Cause" has never died and the dream of an independent Southern nation lives, although relatively few publicly discuss the desire that this nation be white and Protestant, although even that idea has a militant constituency. And, none of this debate over what to call The War attracts nearly the heat and enthusiasm as debates over displaying or flying "The Flag," a.k.a. the Confederate battle flag, never actually an official flag of the Confederate states, but now THE symbol of The Cause. The current focus, as this is written, for this ongoing controversy is the state of South Carolina and the issue of flying "the flag" over its state capitol. The War, as William Faulkner said of history generally in the South, is neither over nor really past for many. This presents both opportunities and potential pitfalls for those seeking to use the historical and cultural legacy of the War, particularly sites associated with it, in heritage tourism programs.

My personal favourite among the many names for the war has long been "The Late Unpleasantness," especially popular among ladies of a certain age and social class in the South since shortly after the event. It seems to capture the essence of The War, and war in general, and its ultimate lack of real glamour.

Despite its extreme unpleasantness, interest in our Civil War has been a recurring factor in American life since the guns fell silent in 1865. Reunions of Confederate and Federal veterans were regular events in the last decades of the nineteenth century and the early decades of the twentieth until the number of veterans reached a point at which there were simply not enough around and those who were around were not mobile enough to sustain such events. Dramatic pictures of group handshakes across walls and barricades at critical, and especially vicious, sites of fighting during the War became recurring symbols of a nation reunited and of enemies reconciled. Organised efforts to preserve at least part of key battlefields in large part an outgrowth of these reunions, date from the 1890s, and have gained momentum in recent years for other reasons entirely.

Both sides in the late unpleasantness had "alumni" groups – the Grand Army of the Republic, a powerful force in northern and national politics throughout the balance of the nineteenth century, and the Confederate Veterans Association and, most interestingly, the United Daughters of the Confederacy, being the most significant. The male groups survive today as successor organisations: Sons of Confederate Veterans and Sons of Union Veterans, with "son" understood as "descendant." The United Daughters endure. Festooning battlefields, cemeteries, and courthouse squares with monuments was an early form of commemoration of the conflict in which the United Daughters played a leading role, especially, but not exclusively, in the South.[2] Commemorating the War and its participants, interestingly, was perhaps more important in the South, the ostensible losers, than in the North and certainly a more persistent effort there. This may be the one conflict in world history in which the winners have not controlled the writing of its history and the understanding subsequent generations have had of the conflict. (Pressly, 1965; Cullen, 1995) There is not time here to go into the complexities of the historiography of the American Civil War, but such a study is needed given the tremendous volume of work that has appeared since Pressly. (1965) This peculiar aspect of the historiography of The War - the strong influence of the Southern perspective - has had a lasting impact on site interpretation and preservation efforts.

The level of scholarly, and especially popular, interest in the War has waxed and waned over the years, but has never completely disappeared. (Pressly, 1965; Cullen, 1995) The centennial observance of the War in the early 1960s was one high point of popular interest. In recent years, due to a significant degree to the Ken Burns public television documentary, "The Civil War," (still, nearly ten years later, available on home video), the United States has been in a period of rising interest in its Civil War that does not seem to have crested yet. Interest today is not confined to the United States, but exists in other countries as well. There are Confederate societies and commemorations in Brazil, where some Southerners fled with their slaves as the war was ending. More interesting perhaps is the interest in the war in Germany, Britain, and as far away as Australia where there are organised reenactor groups and "re-enactments" of battles.

In the US there are a number of glossy, colour magazines devoted to The War; specialised publishing houses which churn out books; a monthly newspaper, *The Civil War News*, as well as periodicals for re-enactors; artists who specialise in Civil War prints, which sell at handsome prices; tours and river boat cruises with Civil War themes; a wide variety of theme merchandise; and many other aspects of a Civil War industry, including re-enactments of battles, "living histories," and numerous other events, including lectures. The last category, re-enactments and other events, is at the heart of a growing sector of the heritage tourism industry in the U. S. focused on The War.

As part of this renewed interest in the Civil War there have been increased, almost unprecedented, efforts to preserve Civil War battlefields and sites by state and local governments and private organisations. One purpose of these preservation efforts, almost always the major purpose, is to interpret the sites for visitors, both local residents and tourists.

There has also been a significant increase in the last decade in visitation at Civil War battlefields and sites across the country. Since many battlefields are in rural areas this has presented a set of challenges to go along with the opportunities. (Kennedy and Porter, 1994) One early and continuing effort to promote Civil War site tourism nationally, while also establishing some minimal standards for interpretation, is the Civil War Discovery Trail begun by the Civil War Trust in 1995. The first edition of *The Civil Wear Discovery Trail Official Guidebook* (1995) has already been updated twice. (Brasleton, 1996, 1998) and has grown from "more than 300" sites in 16 states to nearly 500 in 28 states. The first edition had 99 pages and was published by the Civil War Trust itself. The third edition was over 300 pages and was published by Macmillan. The Discovery Trail has a website (www.CivilWar.org) and through a "corporate partnership" with Cracker Barrel restaurants distributes a large format, multicolour map nationally.

The current effort at preserving and interpreting Civil War sites and marketing them as part of tourism development efforts, especially as it is being done in the Commonwealth of Kentucky is the focus of this essay.[3]

Preservation of battlefields nationally - background

While a number of military parks were established at Civil War battlefields in the 1890s and several battlefields and historic sites related to the Civil War were added to the National Park system in subsequent years, the current battlefield and sites preservation activity is more directly an outgrowth of controversy over development on part of the battlefield at Manassas Virginia in the 1980 than to any long-term plan. (Gossett, 1998; Boge and Boge, 1993; Zenzen, 1998) The ultimate settlement of the controversy at Manassas was so costly for the federal government that Congress instructed the National Park Service (NPS) to survey Civil War battlefields nationally, evaluate the risks they faced, and make recommendations for their preservation. NPS had become the custodian of the nation's battlefield parks in the 1930s when they were transferred from the war department. None of these national military parks and battlefields are in Kentucky, although one, Fort Donelson in Dover, Tennessee is within a few miles of the border and the birthplace of Abraham Lincoln is a National Historic Site.

One result of the Manassas controversy and the resultant survey is the American Battlefield Protection Program (ABPP), an ongoing federal program within the National Park Service. Gossett (1998) discusses the background for the formation of ABPP and its program. ABPP awards grants to encourage and assist local efforts to identify and preserve battlefields, hosts a bi-annual battlefield preservation conference, and generally serves as a clearing house for information among interested groups nationally. The national survey of battlefields conducted by ABPP has been significant not only for its results, but because of the process it followed, which involved state historic preservation programs and community-level organisations as well as individual citizens. (Civil War Sites Advisory Committee, 1993, 1998, 1999)

The National Park Service maintains a regular, statutory relationship with fifty nine State Historic Preservation Offices (SHPO) under the National Historic Preservation Act of 1966.[4] In conducting the survey of battlefields the NPS worked with the SHPO in each state. A number of SHPO maintained an interest in the identification of Civil war sites after the completion of the survey and several established commissions to continue the work of identifying and preserving Civil War sites. While Kentucky did not establish a separate Civil War sites commission, the Kentucky Heritage Council, the SHPO, did dedicate one staff position to working with Civil War sites in the Commonwealth and took a leadership role in both preservation and interpretation efforts. This commitment served as a catalyst for the development of a number of grass roots organisations, several of which are direct outgrowths of community meetings held during the original ABPP survey. In fact nearly all of the new Civil War preservation groups in the state trace their origin in some way to the work of the Heritage Council.

Kentucky civil war preservation efforts - background

Kentucky occupied an ambiguous position during the early days of the Civil War and its position only became more ambiguous as the War unfolded. Kentucky was a slave state with a strong attachment to the Union that was deeply rooted in its political tradition. Henry Clay, the dominant politician in the Commonwealth during the first half of the nineteenth century, was a strong supporter of the Union and of slavery. He was the central figure in a series of compromises that temporarily resolved conflict between the two major sections of the country. His influence continued after his death and Kentucky Senator John J. Crittenden attempted to effect a compromise to preserve the Union after the first group of states had seceded. Although the large majority of Kentuckians who fought in the War fought for the

Union, conflict between the Commonwealth's political leaders and the Lincoln administration were constant. The Emancipation Proclamation was a major source of conflict, as was the enlistment of African Americans into the Union army after 1863. Kentuckians deeply resented and strongly protested the enlistment of their slaves into the Union army - and the provision of freedom for such troops and their families. Such protests, and the continuation of slavery in Kentucky during the War, raised questions about the loyalty of Kentucky to the Union cause both in Washington and among Union commanders on the scene. Open support for the Confederacy in western Kentucky, combined with these protests, led Union troops in Kentucky to deal with a civilian population as if it were disloyal. This, of course, further worsened the situation. (Mulligan, 1998b, 1998c)

Kentucky was a significant theatre of activity during the War, beginning in the fall of 1861 when Confederate troops moved into the state and established a defensive line along the Kentucky-Tennessee border. This led to a large scale Union military presence in the state. The Battle of Mill Springs in January 1862 was the result of Confederate efforts to extend this line further into Kentucky. Union success here was one of few such early victories by Union forces.

The largest and most significant battle fought on Kentucky soil during the war was the Battle of Perryville in October 1862. A large Confederate force under Gen. Braxton Bragg invaded Kentucky in expectation receiving of massive popular support. Not only did the support fail to materialise, but the Confederate plan to link Bragg's army with Kirby Smith's never came together, and Bragg was defeated by Gen. Don Carlos Buell and forced to retreat in disarray.

Much of the action in Kentucky involved Confederate cavalry raids on Union communications and transportation lines, led most notably by John Hunt Morgan and Nathan Bedford Forrest. The state was an important location for Union supply and transportation operations, including Louisville, Paducah, Columbus, and Camp Nelson in Jessamine County. The last was a major site for recruiting and training African American troops, as well as being a major Quartermaster Corps facility. Other sites across the state saw skirmishes and small battles or were the site of recruiting and training troops or garrisons posted to protect communications and transportation.

Prior to 1990 there was little organised effort to identify and preserve these sites, let alone use them as a base for tourism. The Commonwealth had established three state parks with a connection to the Civil War. The Confederate fortifications erected at Columbus in far western Kentucky as part of the Confederate defence line of 1861, and subsequently the site of a major Union installation, were added to the nascent state park system in 1934. Just under one thousand acres of land at Perryville has been a state historic site since 1910, as is the Jefferson Davis monument at Fairview his birthplace. The Davis monument was partially funded by the state after World War I and was dedicated in 1924.

A one Acre local park in Nancy marked the spot where Confederate General Zollicoffer's body had been propped against a tree after he was killed during the Battle of Mill Springs. Several monuments were erected in the park by Confederate veterans early in the twentieth century. Scattered sites across the state were marked with state historic highway markers, but nothing beyond that was done. All of these markers are brief, and many were very vague. "Near here, Nathan Bedford Forrest and his troops camped in the fall of 1864." Little, if any, effort was made to set aside the sites of skirmishes or battles other than Perryville. The Hunt-Morgan House, Mary Todd Lincoln House, and Ashland, the Henry Clay Estate, all in Lexington, and several other historic houses were exceptions to the lack of effort to preserve Civil war sites, but they were valued more for their architecture and association with great families or prominent individuals than their role in the War. The National Park Service had responsibility for Abraham Lincoln's birthplace, but other Lincoln sites in Kentucky were held privately until the last few years. The Lincoln birthplace, oddly, has an orientation film that never mentions that he was president or that there was a Civil War. Its major interpretive feature is a nature walk that focuses on the natural world of pioneers during the period of Lincoln's youth. Why the birthplace of this one young pioneer is a National Historic Site is not really addressed in the orientation film or most of the site interpretation.

Almost no effort was made to protect the sites of Union supply depots or other bases. In Paducah, the site of Fort Anderson, not only a significant Union strong point throughout the War, but the focal point of the Battle of Paducah in which the 8th U. S. Coloured Heavy Artillery distinguished itself, was destroyed first for a marine hospital and later for a convention hotel. There is no interpretation of the Union occupation of Columbus at the park or the recruitment of large numbers of African American troops there. (This last will be addressed with two interpretive signs that are ready to be installed.)

Although nearly three of four Kentuckians who had fought during the War had fought for the Union, the overwhelming majority of the monuments erected in Kentucky to the War and those who fought it honoured the Confederacy and Confederates, 55 of 62. (Brent 1997) The state established a Confederate veterans home at Pewee Valley, near Louisville, paid Confederate veterans' pensions, and set aside state funds to maintain several Confederate cemeteries. Much of the very limited state preservation effort and the interpretation of Civil War sites in Kentucky prior to 1990 reflected this retroactive allegiance to the Confederacy. In a very real sense, Kentucky had joined the Southern cause after the war was over and the history it presented at its Civil War sites reflected history as its presenters wished it had been, not as it actually had been.

Kentucky civil war preservation efforts - the 1990s

One indication of the level of activity in Kentucky to identify Civil War sites and interpret them for visitors is the increase in the number of sites listed on the Civil War Discovery Trail from 24 in the first edition in 1995 to 50 in the third edition in 1998. Many of these sites, the 24 as well as the 50, had no organisation concerned with their preservation and interpretation before the ABPP survey in 1992. A second indication of the scope of what has been done in Kentucky since 1992 is the amount of money spent on Civil war sites preservation and the development of interpretive programs – at least $10,390,487.

What exactly has been done? The answer, of course, is a great many things in a great many places, literally from one corner of the Commonwealth to the other. From the banks of the Mississippi to the mountains of Appalachia. Brent (1998) discusses the development of the Kentucky program in some detail. Rather than discuss each project or repeat all of what has already been published, I would like to focus on several general principles that have guided efforts in Kentucky in this area and then discuss several projects I have been personally involved with in some detail.

One general principle that has been applied in Kentucky with great success is decentralisation. While the Kentucky Heritage Council has provided leadership and served as a clearing house for information and technical assistance, local groups have taken primary responsibility for individual sites, except for a very small number that are state or federal properties. Local initiative in developing goals, establishing priorities, and in implementing programs has fostered broad based support.

A second general principle has been co-operation and the development of co-operative relationships whenever possible. Kentucky was among seven states that worked actively with the National Park Service to develop a common promotional strategy for Civil War sites in the lower Mississippi Valley. Kentucky's delegation included representatives of the SHPO, the State Department of Travel Development, Murray State University, the state historical society, and a major site. The first three played a major role in the task force's work over a two year period and Kentucky sites were well represented on the promotional brochure that resulted. (Calcote, 1998).

A joint project involving the Kentucky Heritage Council and the Illinois SHPO has identified sites on both sides of the Ohio River border between the two states and is moving ahead with common interpretive signage and promotional brochures. (Thompson, 1998)

Within state government a number of agencies with responsibilities for different aspects of heritage tourism have co-operated in publishing *Kentucky's Civil War Heritage Trail*, which was timed to coincide with an article on Kentucky Civil War sites in a major regional magazine, *Southern Living*. More than 100,000 booklets were distributed within a few months to individuals who returned a coupon or called a toll-free number. No single agency could have brought together the resources, both human and financial, to have accomplished this in the time that was available after the opportunity became known. Since that time, a Civil War heritage theme tour has been a regular aspect of the state's travel development publications and promotions.

A third general principle has been the use of a broad range of federal, state, and local sources of funding, particularly the use of federal and state funds to supplement local funds. The Kentucky Heritage Council has used its federal "survey and planning" grants program to fund site identification, archaeology, the development of preservation and interpretive plans, and other preliminary or early stage work in the development of sites. These grants require 40 percent local cost sharing and help stimulate local support and involvement. The Kentucky Humanities Council has funded the development of interpretive materials and programs at a number of sites. The state has also appropriated funds directly and allocated funds from a cultural bond issue to Civil War projects. With one exception these have been to state-owned properties, but have been large amounts, approximately $3,360,000 in total. Kentucky has also used federal highway funds, through the ISTEA and TEA-21 programs, for Civil War site preservation and interpretation. Seven sites received more than $.5 million through the ISTEA program alone. The American Battlefield Protection Program, the Civil War Trust and the Association for the Preservation of Civil War Sites (now merged as the

Civil War Heritage Trust) have also provided substantial funding for Kentucky Civil War sites. (Brent, 1999)

Finally, in Kentucky, we established the Kentucky Civil War Sites Association in 1995 to promote co-operation, information sharing, and co-ordination among the Civil War sites in the state. The Association is in the process of being formally incorporated to better carry out this mission.

The specific projects I have been most involved with are illustrative of how these basic principles have operated in practice. Two of our larger Civil War projects are at Columbus-Belmont State Park and in McLean County focused on the Battle of Sacramento. Both are in small, rural, economically depressed counties, which is a factor in how we have approached them. (Mulligan, 1998a)

Columbus-Belmont State Park background

Columbus, Kentucky was an important port on the Mississippi River and the northern terminus of the Mobile and Ohio Railroad when the Civil War began. At the beginning of September 1861 Confederate General Leonidas Polk occupied Columbus and began erecting extensive fortifications to defend the Mississippi River. Polk's move prompted Federal General U. S. Grant to occupy Paducah and Smithland on the Ohio River to protect Federal control of the Ohio River and its tributaries, the Tennessee and Cumberland rivers.

In November 1861, Grant led a detachment of troops from Fort Defiance at Cairo, Illinois against a small Confederate camp at Belmont, Missouri -- directly across the river from Columbus. He was forced to withdraw in some haste after overrunning the Confederate camp when the guns from Columbus opened fire on his troops. Polk had 143 cannon at Columbus. Grant returned to Paducah and in late January 1862 began his campaign against Forts Henry and Donelson, which eventually led to Union control of the Mississippi Valley, and was a keystone of Union victory.

When Fort Donelson fell in early February 1862 the Confederate position at Columbus was seen as indefensible - especially after an epidemic all but wiped out the garrison at Camp Beauregard, part of its outer defences, - and the fortifications were abandoned at the very end of February. When Union forces arrived to attack the fort on March 1 they found it abandoned and occupied it without a struggle. The "Gibraltar of the West" fell without a struggle or the loss of a single life. For the rest of the War it was a Union garrison in the very pro-Confederate Purchase region of Kentucky and Tennessee. During this period of occupation, it was a gathering point for African Americans fleeing slavery, known at the time as contrabands, and a major recruiting point for African American troops, some of whom garrisoned the site. Columbus was second only to Fort Nelson as a recruiting site for African American troops in Kentucky.

Shortly after the war the fort was abandoned and allowed to return to its natural state – earthworks eroded, trees and other vegetation grew up, the river shifted -- the Fort is on the cutbank side of the river, unfortunately for its preservation. In 1867 the cannon were shipped out and all surplus property dispersed. At some point the cemetery was consolidated with the national cemetery at Mound City and all the bodies moved. Massive flooding in 1927 led to the relocation of the city of Columbus and the loss of nearly every antebellum building – one of the exceptions being a small frame house on the bluff used as a hospital after the battle. In 1934 much, probably most, of the Fort became part of the Kentucky State Park system and the CCC "restored" the surviving earthworks and made other improvements to the Park.

Our work

Early in 1994 I was invited to serve on a Taskforce on the future of Columbus-Belmont State Park, being in the midst of a survey of Civil War sites in the Purchase region of Kentucky at the time. As I sat in the Taskforce meetings several ideas emerged about how Murray State and our public history program could become involved. Our direct involvement with the Park begins from this point. The planning committee is an example of interagency cooperation within the state involving not only Parks but the Heritage Council, Travel Development, Murray State University, and National Park Service personnel.

In the fall of 1994 my museum studies course used the Park as a laboratory. One group took up the redesign of the small museum in the Park - located in the surviving antebellum building, another developing an interpretive program for the earthworks. Working with the existing collection and space, applying the what they were learning in the course the museum group developed a 96-page report that got down to the level of how many 2 x 4 s would be needed for the panels. The earthworks group took a more general approach, but had several ideas that we have subsequently developed – restoring a portion, at least of the earthworks to an appearance closer to that when they were in use stationing costumed interpreters in the earthworks area.

These reports were given to the State Parks Department and to the Taskforce. We then obtained a grant from the Kentucky Humanities Council (with additional funding from the Kentucky Parks Department) to develop characters for a first person interpretation program that would use Murray State graduate students and summer youth program participants from Hickman County for implementation.

For a year two graduate students (Chamonie Miller and Robyn Warren) worked on the development of these characters. When we began we had several types in mind – a Confederate and a Union soldier, male and female slaves, townsmen and women, and an African American soldier. In the course of our research we added another type – an observer of the battle. We researched various accounts of the Battle of Belmont with special attention to primary sources – first person accounts – and other materials by people who were in Columbus during the War.

We ended up developing four characters:

- Sally Law, an upper class woman from Memphis, who observed the Battle of Belmont from a riverboat and went ashore to help care for wounded soldiers;

- Robert Hancock Wood, a Confederate captain from Bolivar, Tennessee who fought in the battle;

- William, Wood's personal slave servant who accompanied him to Columbus; and

- Chauncey Cooke, a sixteen-year-old Union private from Wisconsin who served on garrison duty in Columbus.

While we were developing the characters two things happened that impacted the project. First, we worked with the Park to obtain a grant from Americorps. An Americorps team then restored a section of the earthworks by removing the vegetation that had grown up over the years. The second was that Congress played with the federal budget, you will recall those exciting days. The first of these developments was positive - we had an excellent setting for our military characters; the second was very damaging - Hickman County was cut from 50 plus summer youth workers to 4. We were not going to be able to implement our program as we had intended. We did not give up, but after some consideration presented three of the characters during Hickman County Civil War Days at Columbus-Belmont State Park in October 1996 and have presented them each year since then.

Undergraduate students and an alumnus from our masters program interpreted Sally Law, Chauncey Cooke, and Robert Hancock Wood. They used the material we had collected and created a character. Each prepared a 5 to 8 minute monologue for the opening ceremony of the event and a number of other stories and background information so that they could meet and interact with visitors on Saturday for a six-hour period when walking tours of the park were offered. Each character had a station appropriate to their story where they met groups and casual visitors throughout the day. Visitor reaction was overwhelmingly positive, as was that of event organisers. What was a vague idea to many because they had no experience with first-person interpretation became clear and they got excited. Each year we refine what we do - not only the script, but the props and locations.

We have just completed two interpretive signs on African Americans at Columbus during the War. This was funded by the Kentucky African American Heritage Commission. We will soon have a brochure on this aspect of the park's history as well.

Currently, we are working with the Park to develop a seventeen-station interpretive walking tour. As we can identify funding we will be adding all-weather interpretive signs for each station.

McLean County - background

Civil War events in McLean County, particularly the Battle of Sacramento, are broadly related to those in Columbus, but that was not a factor in our involvement. When Polk occupied Columbus, the Confederate Army established a defensive line across southern Kentucky from Columbus through Bowling Green to the Cumberland Gap, with a small jog down into Tennessee for Forts Henry and Donelson. In preparing to defend Bowling Green, Confederate forces seized Lock and Dams 3 and 4 on the Green River and heavily damaged Number 3 to prevent Union forces from using the river to attack their position in what became the "Confederate capitol" of Kentucky. The Union responded quickly sending 10,000 troops under Gen. Thomas L. Crittenden, a member of a very prominent Kentucky family, to occupy Calhoun and protect Lock and Dam Number 2. This all took place in

September and October 1861. The Green River was strategically important to both sides for reasons there isn't time to go into now, but which we develop in the National Register nomination and the driving tours.

Both sides patrolled the territory between Bowling Green and Calhoun to keep an eye on one another's movements. In December, at Sacramento, about ten miles south of Calhoun, a Union scouting patrol, about 180 men, under eighteen-year-old Major Eli Murray was surprised by a Confederate patrol of about 300 led by then Col. Nathan Bedford Forrest. The engagement that followed ranged over several miles after an initial skirmish as the Confederates pursued the withdrawing Union troops part way back to Calhoun - but not so close as to encounter the large relief party Crittenden dispatched.

The Battle of Sacramento is not a major engagement, fewer than 500 men combined on both sides were involved. It is, however, representative of the small, random skirmishes between patrolling forces that characterise most of the military action in western Kentucky. It is also important for several other reasons, but primarily as Forrest's first combat action. At Sacramento he displays many of the tactics and personality traits that helped him succeed during the war and which became the basis for his enduring popularity in western Kentucky and Tennessee.

McLean County - our work

Our involvement in McLean County begins differently from our involvement at Columbus - there is no park or publicly-owned site, yet, in McLean County. It began with a National Register nomination for the battlefield at Sacramento and developing two driving tours, one related to the Battle of Sacramento, the other to the impact of the Civil War on the county generally. Joe Brent of the Kentucky Heritage Council and I met with county Judge/Executive Larry Whitaker about Civil War sites in the county. We were concerned with how they might be interpreted and developed as part of an effort to increase tourism in the county and increase local awareness of the county's history. We agreed to focus initially on a National Register nomination for the battlefield at Sacramento, if the site could be identified precisely enough and had sufficient "integrity," and two driving tours. The driving tours would bring the entire county into the project.

Simultaneously, a community group developed a plan to hold a re-enactment at the battlefield, which has greatly increased interest and awareness of the county's Civil War history. The re-enactment has been a great success and the battlefield is currently protected from development because it is in an agricultural set aside program. The county has the right of first refusal to purchase it should it ever be put on the market.

Jarrod Smith, then a graduate student at Murray State, did most of the research and met with many local historians to identify sites. The first tour, the battle tour (or the "red tour" because we used red dots to mark the sites on the county road map while were developing it), has ten sites and can be begun from either Greenville, the seat of Muhlenberg County, or Calhoun, the seat of McLean County. Forrest assembled his troops at the courthouse in Greenville the morning of the skirmish and proceeded toward Sacramento. We have identified several sites where he met with scouts and a remarkable young woman, Molly Morehead, who warned him of the exact location of Union troops. The tour also includes

Garst's Pond where the first shots were exchanged - Forrest himself fired the first shot; the battlefield; and several sites along the route the engagement followed as Union troops withdrew until it reaches Calhoun where it includes the Lock and Dam and Crittenden's headquarters. The tour brochure explains not only what happened at each stop, but also why it is significant. In the future we plan to have all-weather interpretive signs at each stop.

The second tour follows a similar approach with less thematic unity. It includes a number of cemeteries - using graves and tombstones to focus on themes important to the Civil War and to McLean County, such as the Orphan Brigade, family division, four African American veterans, etc. An good example is the Hackett family plot in the cemetery in Livermore. The Union and Confederate veterans from the family are buried at opposite sides of the large plot from one another. The tour also includes the site of a Union recruiting and training camp; the home of Sue Monday, a guerrilla executed late in the War; and the site of the Battle of Panther Creek just over the county line in Daviess County. The main focus is on the extent to which the War permeated the experience of people in a small rural county. This tour has yet to be put up.

The re-enactment of the Battle of Sacramento has been held annually to larger crowds each year. The re-enactment involves more re-enactors than the battle did troops. It is entirely a locally organised event and has brought together people from all sections of the county. Neighbouring counties are developing driving tours that can link with the Battle Tour. One of my graduate students is developing a driving tour for Civil War sites in Muhlenberg County, for example.

Plans are well along for a Civil War museum in two historic buildings in Calhoun. We've worked with the local committee in planning and designing the museum. I am in the process of developing community-based plans for the long-term preservation and interpretation of the battlefield at Sacramento and the site of Camp Calhoun.

When we started this project McLean County was 120th out of the 120 counties in Kentucky in tourism activity and there was a bill in the legislature to eliminate the county. Our work primarily served to energise local efforts and provide advice and technical support. Tourism revenue in McLean County has risen, as has its ranking into the mid 90s.

Conclusion

During the last eight years Kentucky has invested a large amount of money and a great deal of time and energy in its Civil War sites. Long forgotten and neglected sites have been rediscovered and identified. Known sites have received renewed attention and appreciation. The state government has joined with citizen groups across the state in this effort. More importantly, these sites are now recognised as resources, valued assets to their community. School children visit them as part of their education, bringing history closer to home and helping implement the state's ambitious educational reform program. Residents learn new things about their community's past and come together to develop its future. Tourists come to the sites. Each site has seen a steady increase in visitation. In Kentucky we have also pursued a large vision of what should be preserved and interpreted. Our concern has not been battlefields, but all sites that figured in the War. One of the most powerful and important sites in the state, Camp Nelson in Jessamine County, never saw combat action.

Yet, it was a major supply depot. More importantly it was one of the largest centres for the recruitment of African American troops and the site of a large community of former slaves. Camp Nelson brings people into contact with an important, and often neglected aspect of the war. Columbus is in the same category, a site that saw little if any combat, but which makes important aspects of the war tangible for visitors.

While there is still work to do identifying and defining sites, our greatest emphasis now is on improving the interpretation at each site, offering visitors a richer experience, and developing thematic tours that will link the individual sites so that those visiting them will see and understand how they fit into the larger conflict.

Endnotes

1. William H. Mulligan, Jr., Ph.D. is Associate Professor of History and Director of the Forrest C. Pogue Public History Institute, Murray State University. He is currently president of the Kentucky Civil War Sites Association and Vice President of the Kentucky Association of Museums, among other professional activities. Address: Department of History, 6B Faculty Hall, Murray State University, Murray, KY 42071-3341 USA, ☎270/762-6571, bill.mulligan@murraystate.edu.

    He wishes to acknowledge the support of the Department of History and the College of Humanistic Studies, Murray State University and a number of governmental agencies for his work with Kentucky's Civil War sites: the Kentucky Heritage Council (especially David Morgan), the Kentucky African American Heritage Commission, the Kentucky Humanities Council, the Kentucky State Parks Department, the McLean County (KY) Fiscal Court, Columbus-Belmont State Park, and the American Battlefield Protection Program, National Park Service.

    He also wishes to acknowledge the many individuals with whom he has worked and who have shaped his understanding of the Civil War and site preservation and interpretation: Connie Alexander, Maryann Andrus, Sharon A. Calcote, Mark Christ, Tom Fugate, Leslie Jill Gordon, the late Dan Kidd, Sue Knost, Cindy Lynch, Steve McBride, Bill Neikirk, Greg Pruitt, John Y. Simon, Connie Slaughter, Debby Spencer, Bill Stevens, Fred Wilhite, Larry B. Whitaker, and most of all Joe Brent, collaborator and friend, who has shown the way for Civil War preservation efforts in Kentucky. Further, he wishes to acknowledge the work of his undergraduate and graduate students since 1993 on various Civil War preservation and interpretation projects: Nathanael Bazzell, Andrea Askew Bonk, Chamonie S. Miller, Darian Mock, Jay Poston, Jared Smith, Robert N. Superchi, Robyn Warren, and Jerry T. Wooten.

2. For purposes of this paper, the South is best understood as those states that seceded from the Union.

3. Kentucky like Virginia, from which it developed, Pennsylvania, and Massachusetts is officially a Commonwealth. In practice there is no difference between a Commonwealth and a State.

4.   There are "State Historic Preservation Offices in the District of Columbia, Guam, Puerto Rico, and other U. S. territories and possessions, hence the number is larger than the number of states.

References

Altogether Fitting and Proper: Saving America's Battlefields (1997), *CRM* 20, no. 5.

Andrus, Patrick W. (1992), *National Register Bulletin 40: Guidelines for Identifying, Evaluating, and Registering America's Historic Battlefields,* Washington, DC: Government Printing Office.

Battlefield Update. American Battlefield Protection Program, National Park Service (1990-date).

Boge, George and Margie Holder, Boge (1993), *Paving over the Past: A History and Guide to Civil War Battlefield Preservation,* Washington, DC: Island Press.

Braselton, Susan Collier, et al., eds. (1996), *Official Guide to the Civil War Discovery Trail,* [second edition]. New York: Macmillan Travel.

Braselton, Susan Collier, ed. (1998), *Official Guide to the Civil War Discovery Trail,* third edition. New York: Macmillan Travel.

Brent, Joseph E. (1997), Civil War Monuments in Kentucky, 1861-1935. Multiple Property Documentation Form, Kentucky Heritage Council, Frankfort.

Brent, Joseph E. (1998), Preserving Kentucky's Civil War Sites: Grassroots Efforts and Statewide Leadership, *George Wright Society Forum* 15 (2): 70-79.

Brent, Joseph E. (1999), Kentucky Civil War Sites Preservation Program 1999: A Status Report. Unpublished, in possession of author.

Brent, Joseph E. and William H. Mulligan, Jr. (1998), Introduction: Sacred Ground: Preserving America's Civil War Heritage, *George Wright Society Forum* 15 (2): 57-60.

Calcote, Sharon A. (1998), Thousand -Mile Front: Civil War in the Lower Mississippi Valley, *George Wright Society Forum,* 15 (3): 56-60.

The Civil War Discovery Trail Official Guidebook (1995), Washington, DC: The Civil War Trust.

Civil War Sites Advisory Commission (1993), *Report on the Nation's Civil War Battlefields,* Washington, DC: Civil War Sites Advisory Commission, National Park Service.

Civil War Sites Advisory Commission (1998), *Report on the Nation's Civil War Battlefields: Technical Volume II: Battle Summaries,* revised edition. Washington, DC: Civil War Sites Advisory Commission, National Park Service.

Civil War Sites Advisory Commission (1999), *Report on the Nation's Civil War Battlefields: Technical Volume I: Appendices,* revised edition. Washington, DC: Civil War Sites Advisory Commission, National Park Service.

Cullen, Jim (1995), *The Civil War in Popular Culture.* Washington, DC: Smithsonian Institution Press.

Gossett, Tanya M. (1998), The American Battlefield Protection Program: Forging Partnerships at Historic Battlefields, *George Wright Society Forum*, 15 (2): 61-69.

Kennedy, Frances H. (1990), *The Civil War Battlefield Guide.* Boston: Houghton Mifflin.

Kentucky's Civil War Heritage Trail (no date), [Frankfort: Kentucky Heritage Council.]

Kennedy, Frances H. and Douglas R. Porter (1994), *Dollar$ and Sense of Battlefield Preservation: The Economic Benefits of Protecting Civil War Battlefields: A Handbook for Community Leaders,* Washington, DC: The Preservation Press.

Mulligan, William H., Jr. (1998a), Interpretation and Preservation of Civil War Sites: Two Case Studies from West Kentucky, *George Wright Society Forum,* 15 (3): 69-74.

Mulligan, William H., Jr. (1998b), Surrounded by 'Secesh': The Union Army in Far Western Kentucky, 1862-1868" at The 135 Anniversary Northeast Civil War Conference: *Bridging the Gap. A 21st Century Perspective on the Civil War* Sponsored by The Capital District Civil War Round Table, the New York State Archives and Records Administration, and the New York State Division of Military & Naval Affairs, November 5-7, 1998.

Mulligan, William H., Jr. (1998c), The Civil War in Far Western Kentucky: Union Occupation in a Pro-Confederate Union State," at On the Margins of the War, sponsored by Cumberland County Historical Society and Dickinson College, Carlisle, PA, August 14-16, 1998.

Mulligan, William H., Jr. (1996b), Presenting the Civil War to the Public: Interpretation Initiatives at Columbus-Belmont State Park and Sacramento, Kentucky, at the Ohio Valley History Conference, Bowling Green, KY, October 18-19, 1996.

Mulligan, William H., Jr. (1995), McLean County during the Civil War: Developing Heritage Tourism at Preserving Real Places, Kentucky Heritage Council Conference, Lexington, KY, September 2 1-23, 1995.

Pressly, Thomas J. (1965), *Americans Interpret Their Civil War.* New York: The Free Press.

Thompson, Stephen A., Bilateral Resource Management and Development: The Illinois-Kentucky Civil War Heritage Trail, *George Wright Society Forum*, 15 (3): 61-68.

Thousand-Mile Front: Civil War in the Lower Mississippi Valley (no date), [National Park Service].

Zenzen, Joan M., (1998), Battling for Manassas: The Fifty-Year Preservation Struggle at Manassas National Battlefield. University Park, PA: The Pennsylvania State University Press.

Heritage tourism and English national identity

Catherine Palmer

University of Brighton, UK

Introduction

Theoretical concepts of nationalism and nationness are well developed and extensive (see Gellner, 1983; Smith, 1986, 1991; Anderson, 1991). Increasingly, however, the focus of attention has shifted towards an examination of the specific social processes that enable nations to continue and which legitimate their existence in the eyes of their citizens. As McCrone (1992: 195) argues "the question to ask is not how best do cultural forms reflect an essential national identity, but how do cultural forms actually help to construct and shape identity". The research under discussion here was intended to address just such an issue by investigating the influence of heritage tourism on the creation and maintenance of English national identity (Palmer, 1999). While it is accepted that Great Britain comprises a number of distinctive nations, regions and ethnic groups for example, England, Scotland, Northern Ireland, Wales, the Isle of Man, the Channel Islands and Cornwall. It was not the intention to examine each of these inter-related, yet at the same time separate identities. This would have been neither practicable nor achievable. As such, this study concentrated on one of these, that of English identity.

The theoretical framework for this study lies primarily within that concerned with the birth of nations, nationalism and the emergence of national consciousness. Although this field provides a rich source of material for discussion and debate it also raises as many questions as it does answers. Indeed, questions of identity and belonging rarely, if ever, produce answers that can be applied to all people and to all situations. As Dawson (1997: 328) illustrates by reference to Great Britain, "more than ever, it is misleading to suggest there is, if there ever was, such a thing as a single British character or personality, rather than a variety of welcomingly different and potentially collaborative cultural identities". Despite this Horne (1984: 165) is right when he states "nationality can be one of the principle colourings of the tourist vision". The focus of attention here thus rests upon an examination of the foundations upon which this 'vision' is based, so that a better understanding can be gained of both the components of identity, and the social processes by which these are communicated and maintained. This investigation focuses upon three sites Battle Abbey, Hever Castle and Chartwell.

Battle Abbey was chosen because the Battle of Hastings represents the last time England was invaded. The date 1066 and the battle associated with it are consistently referred to as "the origin of a nation", in both books, documentaries and tourist promotions (see Phillips, 1989; Hastings Borough Council, 1997; Starkey, 1998). Hever Castle's inclusion was based upon its association with the Tudor period generally, and with the romance between Anne Boleyn and Henry V111 in particular. People and events underpinning the castle's guide book description as "a treasured part of Britain's heritage". Moreover, the Tudor period is often taken to be the start of modern England (Elton, 1974). Thus notions of what it means to be English, conceptions of a national identity, are often rooted in Tudor times (Storry and Childs, 1997). Finally, Chartwell was chosen because of its association with recent history, with World War Two and Winston Churchill "the greatest living Englishman" (National Trust, 1992). An event and a person intimately bound up with notions of patriotism and the foundations upon which such a sentiment is based. If men and women were prepared to die for their country then there must have been some understanding of what it was they were trying to protect. It is the implications of all these issues, as regards the maintenance and communication of a sense of national identity, that is of interest here.

As previously stated, a national identity is not reducible to a single element, it is invariably a combination of elements such as, culture, political affiliation, language, sport and religion and the relative importance of each will not be the same for all. Moreover, interpretations of identity are affected by such as personal experiences, age, gender and race (Dimbleby, 1995; Norton, 1997; Eade, 1997). Nationness is thus a frequently contested concept since multiple definitions and interpretations can and do exist (see England, my England 1998). As Hall illustrates:

> ......*identities are constructed through, not outside, difference......every identity has at its 'margin', an excess, something more......(national) unity...is not a natural, but a constructed form of closure, every identity naming has its necessary, even if silenced and unspoken other, that which it 'lacks'* (1996:4,5).

Consequently, the sense of Englishness under investigation represents more *a process of closure*, the point at which alternative, contested definitions of identity are excluded, than it does a unified whole. It is about one particular articulation of nationness, that of heritage tourism. This is not meant to imply that nationness is fixed and immovable, as all cultures interpret their past in the light of current pre-occupations, values and beliefs. This is an articulation limited to a specific time and space. It is how one industry chooses to interpret Englishness in the late twentieth century. However, before detailing the specific research methods employed and their key findings it is first necessary to examine some of the ways in which a sense of nationness can be communicated and understood.

From theory to practice

Theories of nationalism and national identity are not only many and varied but, for most people complex arguments that do not feature as part of their everyday lives. Moreover, whilst the views of scholars such as Gellner (1983), Smith (1983, 1986) and Anderson (1991) highlight the main structural changes behind the emergence of nations, nationalism and identity they fall short of examining the many ways in which a sense of nationness is maintained everyday (Schlesinger, 1987). Indeed, Breuilly (1985: 70) argues that the crucial point is how one moves forward from this understanding of the structural changes that allowed the idea of a cultural community to emerge, towards an understanding of how individuals came to be *consciously* aware of the cultural community. In other words how people, both individually and collectively, come to understand and to feel part of a particular national identity (see Palmer, 1998a). What is it that happens at the level of the ordinary, the everyday, that allows people to keep in touch with their roots, either consciously or unconsciously? For Walker Connor (1993) the answer lies in an understanding of the psychological components of nationhood. What he refers to as the "....distinction between reason and the emotional essence of the nation...." (1993:382). According to Connor (1993) an emotional, non-rational, attachment to the nation is primarily based upon a sense of consanguinity whereby the nation is conceived of as a kinship group founded upon a unique and separate line of descent. What is important here, however, is not whether a nation's origins are *actually* unique, but rather the existence of an *intuitive conviction* that it is unique:

> The sense of unique descent, of course, need not, and *in nearly all* cases *will not*, accord with factual history. Nearly all nations are the variegated offspring of numerous ethnic strains. It is not chronological or factual history that is the key to the nation, but sentient or felt history (Connor, 1993: 382).

Thus, for Connor, debates about the origin of nations do not on their own explain why people continue to feel attachment to a particular group of people. What is missing is an understanding of the subconscious, psycho-emotional aspects of nationness that underpin and help to weld together the more tangible elements of culture, territory, language and religion. In other words the feeling that *we* are a nation, that *we* belong together, that *we* are all related in some way, intuitively rather than genetically. It is this psychological component that enables the link between theories of nations and nationalism and the practical experience of nationness to be made.

Banal nationalism

A sense of belonging and attachment to a particular culture, a particular identity is most frequently experienced in the context of rather mundane circumstances. "How to evaluate your neighbour's work in making a wheelbarrow; where, and in which tidal conditions, to fish...Mundane they maybe, but...each such commonplace event is a metaphorical statement of the culture in which it occurs" (Cohen, 1982: 6). This mundane reminding is referred to by Michael Billig (1995: 6) as Banal Nationalism '...the ideological habits which enable the established nations of the West to be reproduced'. It is something that happens all day, everyday and it may often go unnoticed as its seeming inoccuousness does not mark it for special attention.

According to Billig (1995) for the man or woman in the street nationalism happens in times of war, in times of crisis, when groups, individuals or countries are threatened in some way and it is characterised by overt nationalistic rhetoric, such as that employed by heads of state. However, a sense of communal understanding between a nation and its people is not only triggered in response to a crisis but also by certain events or ceremonies of significance. These events may be national, local or individual, they may be party political or sports related, religious or constitutional, royal or musical. When they emerge they are often accompanied by a specific type of rhetoric that highlights the importance of what is happening. For example, Wheatcroft (1994: 8) refers to the waving of the Union Jack and the singing of hymns such as I vow to thee my Country and Jerusalem at the Last Night of the Proms concert in London as "...an expression of simple patriotism...". However, Billig (1995) argues that awareness of the nation is not something reserved for state or official occasions as there is a continual reminding, or what he refers to as a 'flagging' of nationhood on a daily basis. For example, via the political rhetoric of governments and the sports pages of daily newspapers. Indeed, almost anything, from Levi jeans to the weather forecast can be used to "flag" the nation to its own citizens and to those of other nations. As Billig (1995) argues flags are unmindful reminders of a national identity they are the embodied habits of social life, the places we live, the way we live and the unconsciously held thoughts of home that we take with us wherever we go.

Symbols of nationness

Billig's concept of banal nationalism is relevant to tourism since touristic activities are in themselves mundane, routine habits of life that are taken for granted by individuals in the industrialised world. Moreover, given the fact that for Great Britain the most predominant form of tourism is that associated with the heritage (ETB/BTA, 1996/7) then it is important to consider the ways in which heritage tourism can be said to flag the nation daily.

The link between heritage and national identity is well documented (Walsh, 1992; Ashworth and Larkham, 1994; Palmer, 1998b). However, a nation's history, or heritage is only one of the elements that combine to form a national identity. Others include language, political affiliation, race and religion. Yet the tourism industry has been criticised for selecting and promoting certain aspects of the past as if they were "a unified phenomenon representative of *the* nation" (Walsh, 1992: 178 emphasis added). Hence, words such as historic, nostalgia and heritage are frequently seen on tourist brochures. Likewise, landscapes, castles, country houses and their associated paraphernalia of everyday life are presented as embodying the essence of nationhood. As Rowlands (1996) illustrates landscapes, objects, images and words can elicit forms of remembering that emphasise continuity and tradition. The nation's cultural heritage thus provides visitors with both a physical and an experiential link with the wider nation and its people.

The desire to better understand how such a link is both created and communicated underpinned the research methods upon which this study is based. It was thus important to consider not only how individuals, as tourists and employees, related to and understood the sites - the social mechanisms by which identity was conveyed. But also what aspects of Englishness were represented by the sites. As Hewison (1997:15) illustrates "culture puts the flesh on the bones of national identity....". Consequently, any study of the ways in which a nation's cultural heritage underpins national identity cannot ignore the fact that cultural icons, practices and artefacts have a symbolic, as well as a physical function (see Malinowski, 1944). As Geertz's understanding of the concept of culture illustrates:

> the concept of culture I espouse....is essentially a semiotic one. Believing with Max Weber, that man is an animal suspended in webs of significance he himself has spun, I take culture to be these webs, and the analysis of it to be therefore

not an experimental science in search of law but an interpretive one in search of meaning (1973:5).

Geertz's definition is important here because it further highlights the experiential, rather than the deterministic component of culture. In other words *what it feels like* to belong to a culture. Moreover, there is a boundary to this sense of belonging, a point at which the individual becomes aware of another culture, another way of behaving, of there being an us and a them (see Barth, 1969). "Thus we might conclude that one of the primary experiential senses of culture is that it is *our* culture, and that it differs from others" (Cohen, 1982: 5). Recognition of *our* culture is thus a recognition of ourselves as an identity, as a separate ethnic group, region, tribe or nation. Hence symbolic representations of a culture are central to its perpetuation because they remind individuals of the foundations upon which their sense of belonging is based. Thus what is important is not only the symbolic content of the sites, but the extent to which the memories evoked enable individual's to link their own personal memories to those of the wider nation. To recognise the individual and the collective as being part of an integrated whole. As Rowlands (1994: 130) has also argued "for cultural heritage to be significant it must therefore be unifying and transcendent and be constitutive of personal and group identity".

Methodological context

As the primary focus of the study is the cultural representation of nationness, the symbolic display of 'ourselves', this involves analysing the ways in which individuals both related to and with the cultural locations, practices and artefacts on view. As Geertz (1973:17) states "behaviour must be attended to, and with some exactness, because it is through the flow of behaviour - or, more precisely, social action - that cultural forms find articulation".

The overall aim, then, is to employ a range of methods that enable the researcher to reconstruct patterns of common-sense thinking by searching for underlying themes. Hence the methods are not designed to reveal divisions between different groups of respondents but rather to uncover the thought processes behind visitor reactions to each site. A similar strategy was employed by Billig (1992:19) in his study of attitudes towards the British Royal Family, where he argues that "ideology is to be found in those patterns of common-sense thinking which cut across class, age and gender distinctions. This means looking for commonalities in what is said...(and)....in what is not said". Furthermore, Geertz (1973:24) states that, "the whole point of a semiotic approach to culture is.....to aid us in gaining access to the conceptual world in which our subjects live....". As such, a key feature of the research methods is the identification and analysis of the structures of signification inherent in the three sites under investigation. Battle Abbey, Hever Castle and Chartwell represent specific social settings within which individuals interact with themselves and with others. It is through the observation and recording of such interactions that the visitors 'conceptual world' is to be accessed.

Ethnographic methods

While the participation in, and the recording of the social settings in which people live is a key principle of ethnographic research, it was important not to lose sight of the need to remain objective throughout the period of investigation. Bearing this in mind triangulation, or multiple methods (see Denzin, 1970, 1998) was necessary if reliable information was to be gathered for analysis. As Hammersley and Atkinson illustrate:

> ....*data-source triangulation involves the comparison of data relating to the same phenomenon but deriving from different phases of the fieldwork.....This is very time consuming but, besides providing a validity check, it also gives added depth to the description of the social meanings involved in a setting* (1983:198).

Overall, then, this study was designed around four interdependent methods of data collection. This illicited a rich and varied amount of information, thus enabling a more in-depth analysis to be carried out than would have been the case had fewer methods been employed.

1. The review and analysis of books, documents, guides and other relevant published and unpublished material relating to the three sites.

2. Tape recorded interviews with key people for example, employees, managers, members of related associations and relevant individuals from the organisations that owned two of the sites, English Heritage and the National Trust.

3. Participant, covert, observation of visitors on a number of different occasions/times with written notes being made of behaviour and conversations.

4. Tape recorded interviews with a random selection of visitors at each site. Every tenth person or group was approached and a total of 200 people were interviewed overall.

The interviews with key people and tourists were based upon set themes that had emerged from the review and analysis stage. Thus the same questions were not asked at each site. Moreover, the interviews with the tourists, and where appropriate with the key people, were conducted along the line of conversations. The intention here was to put people at their ease and so increase the possibility of obtaining information that may more readily indicate underlying feelings, assumptions and beliefs. Cohen provides an apt illustration of the way in which these interviews were conducted:

> *the proper ethnographic interview is a conversation in which ethnographers risk the appearance of naivety and ignorance in order continually to satisfy themselves that they have understood what is being said...the conversations...are instruments...for stripping away the ballasts of expectation and assumption....* (1984:226).

The only site where employee interviews did not take place was Hever Castle. This was at the express wish of the Managing Director, who felt that staff were too busy and that such a process would interfere with and detract from their duties.

The visitor observations were conducted on a covert, participatory basis whereby the researcher observed visitor's behaviour and noted down comments that were made by them as they went around each site. However, this inevitably meant that the researcher was aware of her own reactions to the sites, not merely those of the visitors themselves. Such a situation has to be acknowledged and dealt with as it is an issue that relates directly to the validity and reliability of results. Adler and Adler (1998) state that the type of measures that can be taken to address such issues include: using multiple observers, conducting observations systematically and repeatedly over varying conditions and combining observation with other research methods. Whilst the former activity was not possible given the nature of the research, the latter two activities were undertaken. As previously mentioned the observations took place in a variety of locations and at differing times (weekends/ weekdays, mornings/ afternoons and different months depending upon seasonal opening times). Likewise, the observations were combined with the interviews involving both tourists and key people, resulting in a triangulation of methods that enhanced consistency and validity. Moreover, this was not a controlled laboratory experiment, but rather a sustained investigation into the activities, motivations and feelings of individuals within specific social settings. As Geertz illustrates:

> ...*ethnography is thick description....Doing ethnography is like trying to read (in the sense of "construct a reading of") a manuscript - foreign, faded, full of ellipses, incoherencies, suspicious emendations, and tendentious commentaries, but written not in conventionalised graphs of sound but in transient examples of shaped behaviour.* (1973:9-10)

In the light of the above discussion some of the key findings from the research will now be examined.

Experiencing Englishness

In all three of the sites the language and symbolism of nationness was found to be central to the way in which identity and belonging was both constructed and communicated. Constant references in the tourist literature to the fact that Battle Abbey represented the "origin of the nation", that Hever Castle was "a treasured part of Britain's heritage" and that Churchill was "the greatest living Englishman" triggered speculative reverie about the nation, about the elements upon which its identity is based and about the individuals relationship with the nation. As such, the three sites are communicating, or rather telling stories about the nation that can be handed down to descendants of the national line. They thus operate rather in the manner described by Byng-Hall in his discussion of the therapeutic importance of family stories, myths and legends:

> *family stories can give a feeling of continuity, of how the past led to the present, of rootedness and family tradition, and so help to make sense of a complicated and fraught family life in the present....it is not so much the story itself as the story-line which matters most, the family ethos which it transmits* (1990: 216, 220).

The key point here is the underlying tug of the communal heart strings, what has previously been referred to as the creation of a "psycho-emotional bond" (Connor, 1993), that all the sites rely upon to attract tourists. It is the communication of such a 'bond', through guides and brochures that enables visitors to the sites to get in touch with the soul and the spirit of the nation, its beliefs and values. The three sites not only communicate the relationship between the nation and its citizens, but also the foundations upon which this relationship is based.

Battle Abbey and the date 1066 represent the nations historic roots. Indeed, the date 1066, more than any other perhaps, is remembered because it marks the point at which the unbroken tradition that underpins the nations existence is understood to have begun. The Norman Conquest took the main political, social, cultural, religious and economic structures of Anglo-Saxon England and revolutionised them. William the Conqueror became King of all the land sweeping away the rule of multiple kinship. This new nation-state based on a feudal system of land tenure under the ultimate control of one king provided the basis for the way in which the country is governed today (see Douglas, 1964; Loyn, 1991). It matters not that in other centuries outside influences helped to shape the nation, or that not all subsequent kings of England have been native to this country. What does matter is that this date marks the last time the country was invaded, the last time this country's institutions and way of life were forcefully altered. This is why the date of 1066 and the Battle of Hastings is referred to as the origin of the English *as a nation*.

Hever Castle likewise exemplifies the nation's roots, both historic and religious. The castle's importance as regards English and British history is highlighted by the current guide book which describes it as "...a treasured part of Britain's heritage" (Hever Castle, 1995: 11). Although the castle has had a variety of owners, it is the Boleyn family that are the most significant. Hever is thus treasured for its part as a backdrop to the relationship between Henry VIII and Anne Boleyn. It was Henry VIII's push to divorce Anne that provided the catalyst for the break with the Catholic Church in Rome and the establishment of the Protestant Faith as the 'official' religion of England. Hever Castle is thus a physical reminder of the birth of the nation's 'Official Faith'.

In addition, Hever presents a dual nationality in its juxtaposition of images that have both masculine and feminine connotations. For example, although Hever is referred to as a castle, it is not a 'true' castle in the mould of a Warwick or a Leeds which were built both as fortresses and as places in which to live. Indeed, the main part of Hever Castle is quite small and is in effect a protective wall for the house that lies behind it. Hever thus resembles more a fortified manor house than a place from which invaders can be repelled. As an early guide to the castle states, Hever is a "castle in miniature"....a "castle-ette" of the feminine gender" (Hever Castle and Gardens, 1972: 17). In a sense, then, the castle is a medieval facade, an illusion of strength that masks a soft inner core. As the above quote states it is a feminine rather than a masculine structure. Moreover, the word castle signifies the nation as ancient, powerful, majestic, strong and enduring, all characteristics that are essentially masculine. Yet in being described as feminine rather than masculine and as a castle-ette rather than a true castle this highlights the nation's alter ego. Hever Castle is the nation as a feminine construct. This is why it is described above as a facade, because its supposedly strong outer masculine shell hides an inner feminine core, a home, a place of women and domestic life. This is the nation as a feminine entity, homely, domestic, a mother.

Attached to the medieval structure of Hever is a Tudor-style village that was added at the beginning of the twentieth century by the castle's then owner William Waldorf Astor. In 1963 the village was converted into more than a dozen self-contained and separate cottages and flats to resemble "....a real village of small individual dwellings" (Hever Castle and Gardens, 1963: 2). The Tudor Village's contribution to the national imagination is its personification of an idealised village community. Indeed, Strathern (1982) states that the village concept can reflect and magnify notions of kinship, belonging and class, both of the village itself and of the wider society of which it is a part. As such, she argues, the idea of village-ness can often command a powerful emotional commitment to the existence of both a core of "real villagers" and of "real" village concerns. Thus, the Tudor Village reflects those aspects of the nation based upon an idealised vision of what village life represents, a sense of community and tradition (see Childs, 1997).

Chartwell is significant because of its owner Sir Winston Churchill. All that Chartwell represents is based entirely around the character of the man whose home it was and the time in history when he came to prominence. The sense of certainty that Churchill epitomised during the Second World War is re-created in the house by both tangible and intangible means. The whole atmosphere infers that Churchill still lives at Chartwell. There are fresh flowers in the rooms, up-to-date daily newspapers, glasses of whisky on tables and cigars in ashtrays. In the Drawing Room the chairs appear recently vacated, with the cushions naturally dented. In the Dining Room the table is laid out for a family tea with real scones, cake and jam. This enhances the feel of the house as a lived-in family home. This is not an empty house, a museum or a mausoleum, this is a living house intended to evoke memories and feelings. As one visitor commented, "well yes, it made me think in a way how lucky I was to be a child old enough during the war to realise what was going on, yes, you know, it does bring it all home to you".

What are 'brought home' are not only memories of the time, but memories of the man and what he represented. As Walden (1998: 3) states Churchill personifies the unique characteristics of the nation at its very best. Characteristics based upon those of the man whose 'finest hour' saved the legacy of 1066, the legacy of a nation unconquered and inviolate namely, indomitable courage, defiance, endurance, love of freedom and determination. As the journalist Keith Waterhouse (1997: 12) illustrates "...if you wanted it (Englishness) in one word it would be an abstract one: bloodymindedness".

In terms of the interviews and observations these revealed interesting insights into the ways in which individuals related to and understood the sense of nationness on display. Attachment to the nation was triggered in relation to the memories evoked by the times and events depicted. This emotional recognition occurred from within the imagination, which is important because it enabled people to visualise themselves as a part of their history. In this way visitors were able to both feel and experience their roots, their sense of belonging. As the following illustrates:

Chartwell

> Man 1- *you can really get a feel for those days here. I can remember what my friends and I were up to when the war ended.*

> Man 2- *Yes, I was in France, a bit older than you and he was thought of as like a God, you know.*

> Man 1 - *Yes. I can remember sitting listening to his speeches on the wireless. We were all mesmerised. I couldn't wait to join up. A bit too late though.*

Battle Abbey

> Man - *I tried to look across the fields and picture it, yeah like you do, and you think, you seem to think more deeply about how they lived in those times and exactly what they had to endure their suffering and what have you...*

Furthermore, this feeling of attachment reminded visitors about themselves and 'their' nation. These remindings were familiar to them both as individuals and as a collective national entity. In other words these are *our* cultural and historic roots, *our* way of life. Recognition of *our* roots was based upon the visitor's identification with key aspects of the sites and their contents. The contents and artefacts were variously described as cosy, warm and homely. Safe and comforting in their familiarity. Hever *Woman* - "It's really livable this room, cosy not imposing". *Man* -"Very comfortable you could live here all right". Similarly:

Chartwell

> Woman 1 - *(About the display china) - oh, look, beautiful.*

> Woman 2 - *Yes, gosh.*

> Woman 3 - *Can you imagine using them for your coffee?*

> Woman 1 - *Oh yes, a bit thin*

These familiar triggers of nationness are primarily concerned with communicating a sense of kinship that links the visitors into the ancestral line of descent that connects the us of the present to the us of the past. As Connor (1993) states felt kinship ties link individuals to the fully extended, national, family. Thus individuals recognise themselves and their ancestors as being related in someway. This is *my* history, these are *my* people, *my* kith and kin. As the following illustrates:

Hever Castle

> Woman 1- *Very interesting, all those wives and many rooms to see and pictures.*

> Woman 2 - *It's very interesting this history, isn't it? It gives you a sense of yourself, you know, like tracing your family tree. My Albert was always interested in history.*

> Woman 3- *Yes, it is, isn't it? My brother traced our family once, took a long time though.*

Moreover, as Connor (1993) argues the key to the nation is sentient, or felt history, rather than chronological history. This is illustrated by a comment from one of the custodians at Battle Abbey:

> *oh yes I think all of us custodians we, you know, it becomes part of your blood. If you're away from it and you're at a different site you think no, my monuments Battle Abbey or whatever, but yeah it does become part of you....the historical feel...it's lovely getting out in the grounds and walking around seeing that lovely roof vaulting and all the rest of it, yeah, it does give you a lot... .*

The above discussion highlights the main representative themes to emerge from the research undertaken at the three sites. These themes can be viewed diagrammatically as a family tree depicting the kinship links between the generations.

Figure 1   Kinship Diagram

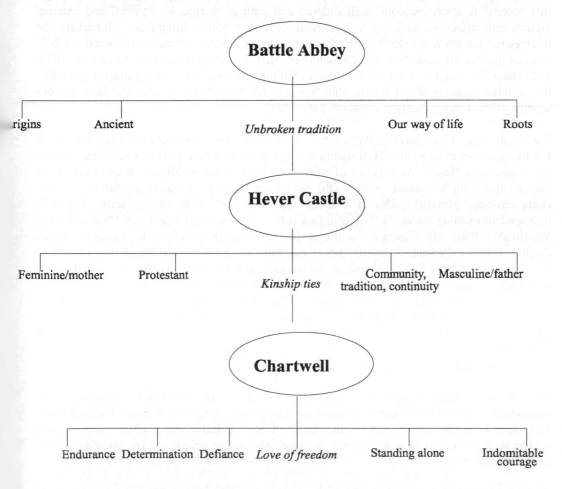

The presentation of these themes as a family tree is intentional as this illustrates the generational links between each site. Moreover, this tree operates in a similar way to the more usual family tree. Which depicts not only a family's descendants, but also the era to which each belonged and its associated social, moral, political and economic values and beliefs. Each site thus symbolises aspects of the nation relating to the particular period represented. These various national pasts join and intermingle to form a legacy that evolves down through the ages and into the present. The present takes on this legacy, which it too develops in accordance with its own circumstances, and then hands down to the generation that follows. This generational intermingling of past and present represents one of the ways in which a national identity evolves. As Hewison illustrates:

> *within a cat's cradle of dynamic forces, between the counterbalances of solid and fluid, chaos and order, inner and outer, dark and light, physical and spiritual, national and emotional, abstract and concrete, idealist and realist, male and female, the symbolic elements that constitute the particularities of a culture are shaped* (1997: 17).

In referring to the development of identity as an evolutionary process this is not to imply that this process is always smooth, well ordered and without disruption. Internal and external factors can affect it, such as wars, invasions and political instability. Moreover, the interrelated themes highlighted by the kinship diagram represent clusters of sacred symbols guiding individuals towards an understanding of what the nation stands for. As Geertz (1973: 408) states the analysis of culture involves a searching out of clusters of significant symbols - the material vehicles of perception, emotion and understanding. So what do these various aspects of the kinship diagram say about the nation?

The main symbolic message is highlighted in the connecting links between each site in the kinship diagram namely, unbroken tradition, kinship ties and love of freedom. These present the nation as a family. As a group of relations with a common history, a common set of values and beliefs handed from each generation and as possessing common, basic characteristics. Moreover, this is a family that is 'free'. Free in the sense that it is independent of other nations and free in that it has remained inviolate since 1066. As Peter Vansittart (1998: 84) illustrates in his review of English history "the much-trumpeted English love of freedom....usually meant not individual liberty but resolution to defend national independence". This is one of the reasons why Chartwell is the focus of patriotic reveration, because it reminds visitors of Churchill's determination to protect this freedom from outside interference. He is seen as a guardian of the unbroken tradition that enables the nation to *imagine* its evolution as being somehow independent of outside forces. Even though this is obviously not the case, the important point is that it is *perceived to be so*. As Connor (1993: 377) states "a subconscious belief in the groups separate origin and evolution is an important ingredient of national psychology".

Overall, then, these three sites communicate different yet interlinked components of nationness. While these elements combine to create what is termed a gaze of Englishness, they also illustrate one of the issues discussed in the Introduction. That such a gaze represents a process of closure, the point at which alternative definitions are excluded, rather than a unified whole.

Conclusion

The above discussion has outlined the theoretical and methodological principles underpinning the study outlined in the Introduction. In this respect the findings from each of the three sites illustrate some of the mechanisms and the processes by which attachment to the nation is promoted and reinforced by the heritage industry. In the language of heritage tourism the three sites claim to symbolize fundamental aspects of English nationalism. Battle Abbey is *our* way of life, Hever Castle is *our* ancestral line and Chartwell is Churchill, *our* honorary relative. The sites thus present the nation as a family. As a group of relations with a common history, a common set of values and beliefs and as possessing common basic characteristics. It is these felt kinship ties that are said to bind individuals to the wider nation. It is upon this basis that Battle Abbey, Hever Castle and Chartwell are described as flags of identity, as important co-communicators of Billig's (1995) concept of banal nationalism. The routine habits of everyday life that serve to flag the homeland to its citizens and to those of other nations.

However, one of the interesting issues to emerge from this study is the extent to which the heritage industry's concept of Englishness is based upon a view of identity as being essentially primordial in character. That there are fixed and unchanging aspects of the nation's identity that can be handed down from one generation to the next. When in reality identity is highly contingent and contested. Thus the kinship diagram is merely representative of one part of the total national tree. Other, related parts exist that reveal different, but complimentary evolutionary stages to those depicted here. For example, there will be elements of the tree relating to the political, religious and linguistic components of the nation's identity and these can be linked into the total tree as appropriate. These various intermingling parts of the national tree operate rather like a kaleidoscope whose multi-coloured 'chips' are formed and re-formed into a variety of different, yet complimentary, structures. As Geertz illustrates:

> *...the chips of the kaleidoscope, are images drawn from myth, ritual, magic, and empirical lore...Such images are inevitably embodied in larger structures - in myths, ceremonies, folk taxonomies, and so on - for, as in a kaleidoscope, one always sees the chips distributed in some pattern, however ill-formed or irregular. But, as in a kaleidoscope, they are detachable from these structures and arrangeable into different ones of a similar sort* (1973: 352-3).

Battle Abbey, Hever Castle and Chartwell thus symbolise one version of the nation's identity, one 'chip' in the total kaleidoscope of differing interpretations and understandings of nationness that comprise today's multi-cultural world. This is why these sites will resonate with some people, but not with all the people. Others will resonate with alternative, but complimentary 'chips' from within the total kaleidoscope of identity.

More generally, this discussion highlights the relevance and applicability of ethnography, not only in terms of tourism research, but also in relation to the analysis and interpretation of human behaviour in specific social settings. Such analysis is necessary if social scientists are to expand their knowledge of the individual and collective world and to formulate theoretical approaches and hypotheses as a result. In terms of tourism there are a wide, and often complex array of social settings and interactions to be studied. For example, between the tourist and the local population, between an individual tourist and groups of other tourists and between the tourist and the environment in which he/she finds themself. Indeed, a series of television programmes in 1998 covertly observed different nationalities of tourists with the aim of uncovering the 'truth' behind the national stereotype (The Tourist Trap, 1998). While these programmes claimed to be anthropologically based and despite the many methodological questions they generated, the series did uncover some interesting insights into group behaviour. All of the above research potentialities provide opportunities to analyse the underlying meanings behind how and why people behave as they do. A better understanding of such issues can only contribute towards a more thorough appreciation of the differences between ourselves as individuals and ourselves as groups of people or nations. The ethnographic principles and findings outlined here thus offer a rich and diverse method of investigation.

References

Adler, P. A. and Adler, P. (1998), Observational Techniques, in Denzin, K. and Lincoln, Y. (Editors), *Collecting and Interpreting Qualitative Materials*, Sage, London, pp. 79-109.

Anderson, B. (1991), *Imagined Communities: Reflections on the Origin and Spread of Nationalism* (2nd ed.), Verso, London.

Ashworth, G. J. and Larkham, P. J. (Editors), (1994), *Building a New Heritage. Tourism, culture and identity in the new Europe*, Routledge, London.

Barth, F. (Editor), (1969), *Ethnic Groups and Boundaries,* Allen and Unwin, London.

Billig, M. (1992), *Talking of the Royal Family.* Routledge, London.

Billig, M. (1995), *Banal Nationalism.* Sage, London.

Breuilly, J. (1985), Reflections of Nationalism, *Philosophy of the Social Sciences*, 15, (1), pp. 65-75.

Byng-Hall, J. (1990), The power of family myths, in *The Myths We Live By*, Samuel, R. and Thompson, P. (Editors), Routledge, London, pp. 216-224.

Childs, P. (1997), Place and environment: nation and region, in Storry, M. and Childs, P. (Editors) *British Cultural Identities*, Routledge, London, pp. 43-83.

Cohen, A. P. (1982), Belonging: the experience of culture, in Cohen, A.P. (Editor), *Belonging. Identity and Social Organisation in British Rural Communities*, Manchester University Press, pp. 1-17.

Cohen, A. P. (1984), Informants, in Ellen, R.F. (Editor), *Ethnographic Research: A Guide to General Conduct. (Research Methods in Social Anthropology 1)*, Academic Press, London, pp.223-229.

Connor, W. (1993), Beyond Reason: the nature of the ethnonational bond, *Ethnic and Racial Studies*, 16, (3), pp. 373-89.

Dawson, R. (1997), Conclusion: present and future Britain, in Storry, M. and Childs, P. (Editors) *British Cultural Identities*, Routledge, London, pp. 315-334.

Denzin, N. K. (1970), The Research Art in Sociology: A Theoretical Introduction to Sociological Methods, Butterworth, London.

Denzin, N. K. (1998), Introduction. in Denzin, K. and Lincoln, Y. (Editors), Collecting and Interpreting Qualitative Materials, Sage, London, pp. 1-34.

Dimbleby, D. (1995), *The Disunited Kingdom*. BBC Radio 4. (A series of five weekly programmes beginning 23rd September).

Douglas, C. (1964,) William the Conqueror. The Norman Impact Upon England, Eyre and Spottiswood, London.

Eade, J. (1997), Identity, Nation and Religion. Educated young Bangladeshi Muslims in London's East End, in Eade, J. (Editor) Living the Global City, Routledge, London, pp. 146-62.

Elton, G. R. (1974), England under the Tudors, (2nd ed.), Methuen, London.

England, My England, (1998), Channel 4 TV, 26th April.

ETB/BTA, (1996/7), Insights. Marketing Intelligence Service, Volume 8, London.

Gellner, E. (1983), *Nations and Nationalism*, Blackwell, Oxford.

Geertz, C. (1973), *The Interpretation of Cultures*, Basic Books, New York.

Hall, S. (1996), Introduction, who needs 'identity'?, in Hall, S. and du Guy, P. (Editors) *Questions of Cultural Identity*, Sage, London, pp. 1-17.

Hammersley, M. and Atkinson, P. (1983), *Ethnography. Principles in Practice*, Routledge, London.

Hastings Borough Council, (1997), *Short Breaks and Holidays in Battle, Bexhill, Hastings, Pevensey and Rye*, Promotional booklet.

Hever Castle and Gardens (1963), Tourist Guide.

Hever Castle and Gardens (1972), Promotional Tourist Brochure. Jarrold and Sons, Norwich.

Hever Castle (1995), Promotional Tourist Brochure, Edenbridge.

Hewison, R. (1997), *Culture and Consensus. England, art and politics since 1940,* Methuen, London.

Horne, D. (1984), *The Great Museum: The Re-presentation of History*, Pluto, London.

Loyn, H. R. (1991), *Anglo-Saxon England and the Norman Conquest, (2nd ed.), Longman, London.*

Malinowski, B. (1944), *A Scientific Theory of Culture and Other Essays*, Oxford University Press.

McCrone, D. (1992), *Understanding Scotland: The Sociology of a Stateless Nation*, Routledge, London.

National Trust (1992), *An Introduction to Chartwell Kent*, National Trust Enterprises, London.

Norton, C. (1997), Youth rallies to English flag, *The Sunday Times*, 21st September, p. 11.

Palmer, C. (1998a), From Theory To Practice. Experiencing the Nation in Everyday Life, *Journal of Material Culture*, 3, (2), pp. 175-199.

Palmer, C. (1998b), Tourism and the Symbols of Identity, *Tourism Management*, 20, (3), pp. 313-321.

Palmer, C. (1999), *Heritage Tourism and English National Identity*, Unpublished PhD Thesis, University of North London.

Phillips, M. (1989), *1066 Origin of a Nation*, (3rd ed.), Michael Phillips, Bexhill on Sea.

Rowlands, M. (1994), The politics of identity in archaeology, in Bond, G and Gilliam, A. (Editors), *Social Construction of the Past: representation as power*, Routledge, London, pp. 129-143.

Rowlands, M. (1996), Memory, Sacrifice and the Nation, *New Formations*, 30, pp. 8-17.

Schlesinger, P. (1987), On national identity: some conceptions and misconceptions criticised, *Social Science Information*, 26, (2), pp. 219-64.

Smith, A. D. (1983), *Theories of Nationalism*, (2nd ed.), Duckworth, London.

Smith, A. D. (1986), *Ethnic Origin of Nations*, Blackwell, Oxford.

Smith, A. D. (1991) *National Identity*, Penguin, London.

Starkey, D. (1998), *Henry VIII*, Channel 4 Television, 29th March.

Storry, M. and Childs, P. (1997), Introduction, in Storry, M. and Childs, P. (Editors) *British Cultural Identities*, Routledge, London, pp. 1-40.

Strathern, M. (1982), The village as an idea: constructs of village-ness in Elmdon, Essex, in Cohen, A. P. (Editor), *Belonging. Identity and social organisation in British rural cultures,* Manchester University Press, pp 247-277.

The Tourist Trap, (1998), Channel 4 Television. (A series of weekly programmes beginning).

Vansittart, P. (1998), *In Memory of Engl*and, John Murray, London.

Walden, B. (1998), *Walden on Heroes*, BBC Learning Support, London.

Walsh, K. (1992), *The Representation of the Past. Museums and heritage in the post-modern world,* Routledge, London.

Waterhouse, K. (1997), And now England for the English, *Daily Mail*, 21st July, p. 12.

Wheatcroft, G. (1994), Why nostalgia can be such a potent force for good, *Daily Mail*, Saturday, 10th September, pp. 8-9.

Resolving the conflicts between preservation, car management and accessibility

Keith D Parsons

University of Central Lancashire, UK

Abstract

This paper seeks to address two of the themes of the conference. It is primarily concerned with World Heritage Sites and tourism, but it also makes reference to the relationships between tourism and heritage.

The focus of heritage management has shifted over the last few decades. In the 1970s it was about conserving the physical resource whereas in the 1980s it was about balancing visitor numbers and the revenue they provided against conservation issues. The focus over the last decade of the 20th century has been about managing stakeholders' interests in, and managing access to, the heritage. This paper assumes that, in the early years of the new century, stakeholders' interests will still be important but will be balanced against environmental issues. Whereas in the 1990s Heritage Management focused on the human dimension, this paper examines the premise that conserving the physical resource will return to prominence, but this will be in tandem with environmental issues and balanced against visitor expectations.

The net result of the shift in focus in heritage management is that many heritage sites have essentially become tourist destinations and need to be carefully managed on both a strategic and operational level. Some sites are now such popular destinations that they are victims of their own success. This is especially true of World Heritage Sites. This popularity has implications in terms of the impact of so many visitors on the *spirit of the place* and in terms of their impact on the local environment.

Most visitors to heritage sites arrive in their own vehicles and increasingly the greatest challenges at such "honeypots" is the management of the car. At several major heritage sites across the world, various schemes have been tried that range from relocating car parks and closing roads to the clearance of the settlements that develop at the sites. In Britain too solutions to these problems are now being proposed and trialed.

Management of the car removes one set of problems whilst introducing another set of issues. Access and facilities for disabled people at heritage attractions has become an increasingly important aspect of the management of stakeholders' interests and visitors' expectations. This has been fuelled in some instances by anti-discrimination legislation. Making heritage sites "accessible" involves finding a balance between access and preservation. Another balance needs to be struck if the managing the car is to be achieved, without precluding disabled people from heritage sites.

This paper discusses these general issues and reports on the efforts being made to resolve the conflict between accessibility, preservation and managing the car. It includes a consideration of a UK World Heritage Site. The site in question is actually a series of sites, namely the thirteenth century castles of Edward I, in North Wales.

It would appear that managing the car, without compromising access for disabled people, is becoming an issue at popular World Heritage sites. At less popular sites, however, the priorities have been: first to provide good access to the site by car and then to address access for disabled people. Currently, car management does not appear to be a priority at less popular sites.

Introduction

This paper begins with a discussion of the philosophy of conservation and the question of why we conserve historic buildings and monuments. The priorities and the focus of managing our cultural heritage are then considered. The impact of tourism on heritage sites and the environment is also addressed before two particular issues are discussed in more detail: car management and access for disabled people. The paper seeks to establish whether a balance can be achieved between these two issues. Various initiatives and examples are considered and an evaluation of the World Heritage castles of Edward I in Wales is included before some conclusions are drawn.

The philosophy of heritage conservation

The conservation of heritage buildings in the UK is usually concerned with what are called "scheduled monuments" or "listed buildings".

In England and Wales, listed buildings are protected under listed building control. (HMSO 1990) For a building to be *listed* it needs to satisfy certain criteria. These criteria are described in Planning Policy Guidance Note 15 [PPG 15] and can be summarised as architectural or historical value and age or rarity.(DOE/DNH 1994)

Ancient monuments are protected under separate scheduled monument legislation.(HMSO 1979) The legislation relating to ancient monuments predates the statutory controls on listed buildings by 60 years and the two codes have never been combined. This results in some historic buildings being both scheduled as ancient monuments and listed as buildings of special architectural or historical interest. The idea of separate designations of historic buildings and ancient monuments would seem strange outside the UK, elsewhere there is

usually one statutory system of control and no distinction is made betw
monument or building.(Ross 1996)

World Heritage designation is conferred by the World Heritage Committee
United Nations Educational Scientific and Cultural Organisation under a c
(UNESCO 1972). World Heritage site designation does not provide any formal legal
protection but it does bestow international prestige and it is presumed that, by nominating a
site for designation, a country is explicitly stating its commitment to conserving the
site.(Wheatley 1996) There are three types of (World Heritage) cultural site: monuments,
groups of buildings and sites. World Heritage sites in England and Wales are normally
scheduled monuments, but sometimes they may be listed buildings; although they may be
both.

Appreciating the statutory background is one thing, but the concept of heritage conservation
can not be understood fully, however, without making reference to philosophical issues such
as: why is conservation important?

In England and Wales buildings are listed: "Because we want to identify and protect our
heritage."(DNH 1994) What heritage actually is could be debated at great length, but to put
it simply it has been equated with the term patrimony, as used in France, i.e. those things
that are inherited and provide cultural identity and continuity, or a link with the
past.(Brisbane and Wood 1996) Historic buildings obviously form an important part of this
heritage and it has been claimed that: "Left to itself…heritage…would gradually disappear
through natural decay, and without study it would become meaningless."(Brisbane and
Wood 1996 p15) This echoes the sentiments expressed in William Morris's Manifesto for
The Society for the Protection of Ancient Buildings [SPAB].(Morris 1877) Morris said: "We
are only trustees for those that come after us."

An attempt has been made previously, to summarise the motives for conserving historic
buildings by synthesising the reasons that are advanced, by various commentators. These
reasons can be summarised as:

- to act as custodians of the built heritage for future generations

- to conserve buildings of architectural merit and/or the work of a famous architect

- to conserve evidence of social history/ordinary people's lives

- to conserve the character and appearance of the built environment

- to provide stability and continuity

- to enhance tourism potential

- to encourage economic regeneration

- to provide accommodation economically

- to conserve the energy embodied within an existing building (Parsons 2000).

It would depend on the nature of the site in question whether all these reasons were applicable to a particular World Heritage Site. Certainly it has been found (Parsons 2000) that some reasons for conservation are more important than others. Stewardship or custodianship of the built heritage was found to be the most important reason, closely followed by conserving works of architectural merit, evidence of social history and the character and appearance of the built environment. It is suggested that these reasons for conservation would all apply to World Heritage Sites. Providing stability and continuity, enhancing tourism and encouraging economic regeneration were found to be the next most important reasons for building conservation. The first two reasons in this group seem to be appropriate to World Heritage Sites, whereas the latter would only apply to some sites. The final two reasons (economic accommodation and conserving embodied energy) were considered to be the least important reasons for conserving historic buildings. These reasons are unlikely to be relevant to a World Heritage Site, especially if the site in question is a scheduled monument.

The intention of the World Heritage List is to create an inventory of the 'works of man' (sic) that is comprehensive, representative and coherent, but the key point is that sites must be internationally important: they must be "of outstanding universal value from the point of view of history, art or science."(Wheatley 1996) This could be interpreted as a summary of the reasons for conservation.

The shifting focus of heritage management

Management in the field of heritage and conservation is about resolving conflicts. It is about achieving a balance between access and conservation. It is also a mixture between education and tourism and conservation and marketing. Heritage Managers manage the actual heritage resources and manage access to these resources. They also perform a traditional management function within the organisation where they work.(Hall and McArthur 1998)

The focus of heritage management has shifted over the last few decades. In the 1970s conserving the physical resource was paramount. The duty of stewardship fell to curators and other such professionals. Hence these professionals saw themselves as the gate-keepers and saw the visiting public as *the problem*. Access always came second to the needs of conservation, although special arrangements could be made for scholars.

In the 1980s government grants for heritage and conservation were reduced. Visitors then became a source of revenue, through admission charges and through retail and catering outlets at heritage sites. The focus shifted to achieving a balance between visitors and the revenue they provided on the one hand and conservation issues on the other.(Yale 1997) The focus over the last decade of the 20th century has been about managing stakeholders' interests in, and managing access to, the heritage.

The shift in focus has been from a 'one-dimensional outlook' (that concentrated on managing the resource) to a 'multidimensional outlook' that considered the human dimension. In many ways the human dimension overshadowed the conservation of the heritage resource itself.

The human dimension is about addressing stakeholders' concerns. It is about balancing the needs of visitors and the local community. As such it is about issues like visitor impact, sustainability and who owns heritage? (or at least who are the stakeholders?) (Hall and McArthur 1998).

Any consideration of the impact of visitors on the sites themselves and on the local community necessarily raises environmental issues. Therefore, this paper assumes that, in the early years of the new century, stakeholders' interests will still be important but they will be balanced against environmental issues. Whereas in the 1990s Heritage Management focused on the human dimension, this paper examines the premise that conserving the physical resource will return to prominence, but this will be in tandem with environmental issues and balanced against visitor expectations.

The impact of heritage tourism

The net result of the shift in focus in heritage management is that many heritage sites have essentially become tourist destinations and need to be carefully managed on both a strategic and operational level. Certainly, heritage attractions have become the backbone of the tourist industry. The travel business and the hospitality trade forms the infrastructure of tourism but the 'real attractions' are heritage attractions (Yale 1997).

Some sites are now such popular destinations that they are victims of their own success. This is especially true of World Heritage Sites. This popularity has implications in terms of the impact on the '*spirit of the place*' and on the local environment.

That visitors impact on the *spirit of the place* is well documented. What the *spirit of the place* actually is, is harder to establish. Take the example of Mont-St-Michel. This island sanctuary on the coast of Normandy has been described as "a marvel of the western world" by the Michelin Guide. In high season it receives 9000 vehicles a day which spoil the view and the steep narrow streets become crowded with tourists (Huw Davies 1999). Whatever the *spirit of the place* is, mass tourism of this volume is bound to have a significant impact on it.

According to Mariana Mould, an historian in Lima, the 'lost city' of Machu Picchu, in the Peruvian Andes "...is a place where the Inca spirit remains...The mystique of Machu Picchu is in its remoteness." The ruined site is only accessible by foot or by an old bus; even so visitor numbers are already counted in thousands. There are proposals to 'improve access' to the site by constructing a cable car, extending the existing hotel on the site and building a multi-storey shopping complex. The cable car would carry 400 people an hour and quadruple the number of tourists. The cable car pylons and terminal building along with the hotel extension and the shopping complex will have such a profound impact on the environment, that will effectively destroy the *spirit of the place* (Rhodes 1999). Machu Picchu is an of example how popularity can lead to conflict between the commercial pressures of tourism and conservation (both in terms of cultural heritage and the environment).

According to the above point of view, the impact that tourism has on the *spirit of the place* is linked to its impact on the environment. Certainly the environmental impact of tourism, when it is introduced in urban revitalisation and regeneration programmes, has been highlighted.(Tiesdell et al 1996) Concerns have been raised about the sustainability of tourism in relation to the historic built environment. The specific concerns that have been highlighted are: the pressure on the infrastructure and support services in the locality and the issue of traffic congestion and pollution.

It would appear, from the above, that the *spirit of the place* can be equated to ideas such as sense of place, ambience and special character (Tiesdell et al 1996), continuity or collective memory (Rossi 1989) and a sense of identity (Lowenthal 1985). Certainly, in commenting on the development proposals described above, Patricia Barnett of Tourism Concern says: "Machu Picchu is atmospheric, very, very powerful: this induces a semi-panic in me. If they can do that to Machu Picchu, there will be nowhere sacred in the world."(Keenan 1999)

The following definition is offered: the *spirit of the place* is a feeling that can be experienced through exposure to the historic environment. This feeling can be very powerful emotionally, indeed almost religious in nature. The strength of feeling experienced will obviously depend on the monument in question. Lowenthal (1985) suggests, that one of the levels on which we make sense of the past is psychological and that perception is important to this process. We can assume, therefore, that the strength of feeling will also depend on a person's experience and emotional nature. It has also been demonstrated that the perception of how significant a monument is, to an individual or to a group in society, is influenced by cultural or ethnic background. (Hall and McArthur 1998) It follows then that the strength of feeling induced by the *spirit of the place* depends on three factors: the ancient monument or historic environment in question; the nature of the individual; and cultural/ethnic background. There is a fourth factor, however, since the *spirit of the place* is affected by the volume of tourists and the number of cars.

World Heritage Sites are victims of their own success and the greatest challenge facing these "honeypots", in Heritage Management terms, is managing this popularity in order to achieve a balance between stakeholders' interests, access and visitor amenities and conservation or preservation. How to manage the car is a key element of this challenge, because car usage both impinges on the *spirit of the place* and has an environmental impact.

Managing the car

Stonehenge has been attracting visitors some time. It has been described variously as an astronomical calendar, a druid temple or some sort of funerary monument; but other than knowing that it was some sort of cult centre, its function remains a mystery.(Honour and Fleming 1999) Although the car park is some distance away, the site is bounded by busy main roads, which impact on the *spirit of the place*. Paying visitors approach the monument via an underpass under one of the roads, although some visitors literally take their lives in their hands and cross the road itself, in order to avoid paying.(Wheatley 1997) Ambitious plans were announced in 1999 to close one of the roads and submerge it in a tunnel.(Huw Davies 1999) It was hoped that the car park would be re-sited so that people could approach the site 'more atmospherically'.(Yale 1997)

Similar initiatives are already being implemented at other World Heritage sites. At the Pont du Gard near Nimes in the South of France, work began in September 1998. The car parks adjacent to the structure have already been closed along with the road for a distance of 500 meters from the bridge. A new car park, which will be obscured by mature trees and dry stone walls, is being constructed behind a new visitor's centre. Other schemes include: clearing away a settlement at the base of Uluru (or Ayres Rock) in Australia and closing roads around the Boyne Valley in Ireland. In 2001 work will commence at Mont-St-Michel, where the car park will be relocated a mile away and the causeway will be replaced by a light footbridge, along which visitors will have to walk.(Huw Davies 1999)

Car Management schemes of this scale are not cheap. The Pont du Gard scheme is costing £17m and the Mont-St-Michel scheme is estimated to cost £57m. There are smaller scale schemes, however! For example, in the UK the National Trust has deliberately omitted to provide car parks at two of its properties. Visitors to Prior Park Landscape Garden, on the outskirts of Bath, are encouraged to use the city's park and ride to get into the city and then catch a bus to the site. Visitors to 20 Forthlin Road, Liverpool (the boyhood home of Sir Paul McCartney) are advised that they must arrive by shuttle bus. The buses leave from either the Albert Dock or Speke Hall (another National Trust property in the city).(National Trust 2000) Providing a car park at Prior Park would have added to the traffic congestion in Bath and allowing visitors to arrive by car at 20 Forthlin Road would have caused serious congestion in the road and significantly increased the impact on the lives of local residents.

Although the term World Heritage Site may conjure up an image of a particular building or monument, the reality is more diverse. Historic towns or historic quarters have also been designated as World Heritage Sites. Car management in these situations is a complex matter. Car management at World Heritage sites that essentially comprise individual structures might be considered as the resolution of *static conflicts*. Car management at World Heritage designated Historic cities or quarters, on the other hand, might be considered as the resolution of *dynamic conflicts*. To treat a city or quarter in the same way as a monument, in static terms, would be to fossilise it and turn it into a museum exhibit. This will only be appropriate if preservation is our aim, rather than conservation.

In considering *dynamic conflicts*, like car management in historic towns, it should be remembered that heritage should not be an obstruction to development, rather a determining factor in the process. It is also recognised as important to involve the community in the planning of all aspects of conservation work.(OWHC 1996)

The city of Bath is one example. Although the city stands on the site of a Roman settlement its significance is as an 18th century planned town, with classical buildings and landscaping combined in harmony. The city contains 4900 listed buildings, but its townscape was drastically altered in the inter-war period, when its coherence was lost in order to accommodate the motor car. In developing an approach to traffic management there has been an attempt to recognise the need to balance the interests of: residents, pedestrians, other road users and the business community. The initial study used "perception studies" as well as statistics gathered from surveys. The perception studies included individual interviews and focus group discussions. The findings suggested an integrated approach to traffic management and recommendations were made in respect of several generalised areas: area traffic calming, removal of on-street parking, restrictions on access, paved surfaces, street furniture, signing and additional park and ride facilities.(OWHC 1996)

Another World Heritage historic city is the Medina (or traditional Islamic City) of Tunis. This is very different from Bath in that its significance is in the distinctive nature the settlement patterns and the intricate web of circulation routes that have both evolved over 1000 years. The city was left to decay during the colonial period of the 19th century. The traffic management policy for this city is aimed at resolving the conflict between improving accessibility and protecting traditional spaces and movement patterns. The arrival of the car constitutes the greatest threat to the survival of the Medina, a problem it shares with other traditional Arab cities. New roads have been introduced which have had considerable impact on the existing structure and patterns of circulation. New nodes and transport hubs have also developed, which have further altered the traditional flows of goods and people. The idea 'improving access by car' is no longer considered to be a universally desirable goal. This would involve further intervention in the guise of road widening. The preferred option is to relegate heavy traffic flows to the periphery and provide parking at 'transfer points' to the pedestrian system.(OWHC 1996)

Traffic management measures are also being considered at the Acropolis in Athens. This site has been all but surrounded by busy streets. There is a plan to close some of these roads and create a traffic free archaeological park in the centre of the city. This will provide pedestrian links between the Acropolis and other classical ruins and "create the atmosphere of Ancient Athens in the heart of the modern city".(Pringle 2000)

Access for disabled people

Whilst such schemes are highly laudable in terms of minimising the impact on the *spirit of the place* and on the environment, there is a particular problem in terms of access and stakeholder issues. Initiatives aimed managing the car may be appropriate for able-bodied people, but some people are not so mobile. People with mobility impairments can not necessarily walk a mile or so, from a re-sited car park to a heritage attraction, however atmospheric the approach and environs may have become. These people need to be considered in such schemes, otherwise a whole section of society will effectively be excluded from heritage sites. This is another dimension of the challenge; achieving car management that is socially inclusive, means managing the car without excluding disabled people.

"Access for the disabled" and "disabled access" may be phrases that are commonly used, but neither of them are appropriate. "The disabled" is a particularly unhelpful term, since it implies that we are referring to an homogeneous group with specialist requirements rather than a disparate group of people with a wide range of needs. It is difficult to agree on a definition of disabled people. For many people the phrase conjures up images of wheelchair users. Some definitions may include people who rely on 'props' to aid mobility, such as walking sticks, crutches or zimmer frames, i.e., "ambulant disabled people". However, there are many people for whom mobility is not a problem, but they are still handicapped socially or in terms of employment, through impaired sight or hearing, for example. It is important to consider the needs of all groups of disabled people.

Attitudes towards disability are changing: "People still think of disability negatively, seeing what is wrong with the individual, rather than the built environment."(Watt 1997) Disabled people reject this view. Many are more likely to believe that: "My body makes me disabled, the environment makes me handicapped."(Ferguson 1988 p.165)

This view defines disabled people in terms of the 'social model' of disability.(Holmes-Siedle 1996) The emphasis in this model is on trying to encourage society to change itself, rather than expecting disabled people to adapt to 'hostile' environments. Car management schemes could potentially introduce new barriers for disabled people, which would be a retrograde step.

There is a relatively large proportion of the UK population that is disabled and, paradoxically, this is partly due to the advances in medical science. Life expectancy has also increased and the UK's population is ageing. It was stated recently that pensioners represented 40% of the population.(CIRIA 1996) Such figures do not include pregnant women, parents with prams or temporarily disabled people - who may be recovering from sporting or motoring accidents. If all those people who would benefit, from so called special provisions, were included it is likely that the total would be at least 65% of the population.(Parsons 1999)

The term *universal accessibility* has been coined because, rather than catering for a minority with special needs, this approach benefits the majority of society.(Hellman 1990) Recently the concept has become known as *inclusive design*.(Paton 1998) The concept emphasises that the built environment should be designed in such a way that all users, regardless of any disability, should be able to use it. The specific problems we are interested in this paper is how to manage the car at heritage sites, without compromising the principles of inclusive design.

"Society is now committed to providing equal opportunities for disabled people in employment, social and leisure activity. This commitment is expressed through Part M of the Building Regulations; also through the criteria of National Lottery funding, which place a high priority on accessibility for disabled people in building related projects"(Cullingworth 1998) The introduction of the Disability Discrimination Act 1995 has also added to the statutory anti-discrimination armoury. Under this Act a Heritage Attraction is classed as service provision and it is illegal for service providers to discriminate on the grounds of disability. The various provisions of this Act are being brought into force incrementally. We can see that it is not appropriate to ignore the needs of mobility impaired people.

Inclusive design refers to access and facilities for everyone whatever their special needs. This paper, however, is concerned with the impact of car management schemes at World Heritage Sites. As such it concentrates on access i.e., approaching and entering a site. Also, it focuses on mobility impaired people, because it has been assumed that they will be most affected by the impact of car management schemes.

PPG 15 states that: "Disabled people should have dignified easy access to and within historic buildings."(DOE/DNH 1994) If heritage buildings and sites are to be made accessible, it is important to emphasise equal treatment rather than special treatment. "Dignified access" means ensuring integrated access and circulation and independent movement. 'Integrated access' describes a situation where everyone uses the same access arrangements, as opposed to one where there are separate arrangements for disabled people. "Independent movement means freedom from being carried or having to rely on assistance to move or find the way."(Foster 1995)

The properties that the National Trust owns in England and Wales are likely to fall into the category of cultural monuments and some are designated as World Heritage Sites. The Trust sets out its policy towards disabled visitors in Leaflet Number 4.(National Trust 1996) It has a policy of *access for all* and at various properties there are ramps, lifts and stair climbing machines. Wheelchairs are available for loan at some sites: powered ones for outdoor use (to see the gardens) and manual ones for indoor use. The Trust assumes that if they concentrate on: "Easing access for severely disabled people, including wheelchair users...it usually follows that more ambulant visitors will also have a comfortable visit."(National Trust 1996)

According to Historic Scotland, ensuring full access to heritage sites necessitates finding imaginative solutions that do not diminish the significance of the monument.(Young and Urquhart 1996) In other words poorly considered provisions for access to sites can impact on the *spirit of the place*. The problem is that, even if we focus on visitors with mobility impairments, disabled visitors all have different needs and each historic site is different. This makes it difficult to provide prescriptive solutions that will cover every situation. With this in mind, Young and Urquhart (1996) recommend the use of a site assessment methodology. This helps determine the existing level of accessibility and highlight where adjustments are required. The methodology is similar to the systematic methodology that should be used in assessing access and facilities in buildings, namely an access audit.

In terms of access and approach to a heritage site the following aspects need to be assessed: car parking and setting down points, site entrances and entrance gates, surface finishes, changes in level, physical features/barriers, site information, site facilities and staff (disability) awareness.

Balancing traffic management and access for disabled people

Originally in the Stonehenge scheme it was hoped that there would be 'environmentally friendly vehicles' for less mobile visitors.(Yale 1997) The Mont-St-Michel scheme allows for residents vehicles and service vehicles (Huw Davies 1999), this could presumably include provision for mobility impaired disabled people.

As described above, electric wheel chairs are provided for disabled people to borrow and make use of at National Trust properties. This idea could be adopted to help in terms of access to sites where the car park has been re-sited, assuming that the surface finishes are appropriate.

The castles and town walls of King Edward in North Wales are included on the list of World Heritage sites as a joint entry. This includes the four great castles of Conwy, Caernarfon, Beaumaris and Harlech. They were commissioned in the late thirteenth century by the English King Edward I and built by James of Saint George d'Esparanche, the foremost military engineer of his day. This massive construction programme was part of the King's campaign to subdue the Welsh, with a ring of iron fortresses unsurpassed in Europe.(castlewales website 1999)

These castles with their fortified towns are examples of bastides. Edward I was responsible for a total of 10 bastides in Wales, in total, although only the four named above, constitute the World Heritage site. The establishment of bastides followed three principles: first they were new planned towns; second they were built on the gridiron pattern; and lastly settlers were induced by the grant of a house within the walls and farming land nearby. In the case of the Welsh bastides, the settlers were mostly English.(Morris 1994)

This paper considers how the issues of car management and access for disabled people have been considered at three of these locations: Conwy, Caernarfon and Beaumaris. The findings are based on observations from site visits and telephone conversations with the custodians. For the purpose of this discussion, consideration of access have been focused on approaching and entering each site. The castles are all in the care of Cadw: Welsh Historic Monuments. Cadw is in the process of developing guidance on access for disabled people. Presently wheelchair users are admitted free, along with a companion, at all Cadw properties.

Conwy Castle is a magnificent eight towered structure sitting on a crag overlooking the Conwy estuary. The North Wales coastal traffic used to cross the river on a road bridge (dwarfing the adjacent historic suspension bridge by Telford), thunder past the walls of the castle at the foot of the crag and plough through the town. This situation has been radically altered since the A55 was diverted through a road tunnel under the river, to by-pass the town. Conwy is now relatively peaceful, partly pedestrianised and the *spirit of the place* is more evident, however, visitor numbers at the castle have not been affected. There are no car parks visible on approaching the castle from across the river, or from the town. There is one large car park outside the town walls and a smaller one almost adjacent to the castle. The small car park is screened from view behind buildings. One of these buildings is the castle entrance, which also houses a shop and an exhibition. This building is fully accessible from the small car park. Castle visitors cross the road to the castle using a concrete footbridge. This route provides level access until visitors cross the road and have to tackle the steep path to the castle gate. The topography is the problem here, depending on the level of mobility impairment.

Cadw owns another property in the town: an Elizabethan town house called Plas Mawr. The street outside is pedestrianised but setting down is possible, 50 yards away in a small square. The main entrance is stepped, but the original entrance is up a side street and this is accessible to mobility impaired people. Efforts have been made in terms of car management at Conwy. This has not been at the expense of access for the disabled, but the access situation does need addressing at the castle and Plas Mawr is a long way from the setting down point.

Caernarfon is also a walled castle town. The castle itself is one of the most impressive architecturally in Wales and was modelled on Constantinople.(Huw Davies 1997) It is situated at the western end of the Menai Straits, on the south bank, adjacent to the quayside of Caernarfon's small harbour. The town square has been pedestrianised which has removed some car parking. There is a large car park below the castle walls on the quayside, but there are categorically no plans to remove this facility; it is not considered to be a problem. Entrance to the castle is on the opposite side, away from the car park. There is no setting down point and access is via concrete steps, slabs and then a wooden bridge. At Caernarfon some traffic management in the form of pedestrianisation has been introduced by the Local Authority, but both car management and access for disabled visitors have still to be addressed by Cadw.

Beaumaris was the last and largest of castles of Edward I and was probably the most sophisticated example of medieval military engineering in Britain. It is built on a flat site, close to the north bank of the Menai Straits, at the eastern end. A large car park is provided over the road on the green, about a 100 yards from the castle entrance. Visitors have to cross a road, then enter the castle via a footpath and a bridge. The castle is fully accessible to mobility impaired visitors, despite being built back in the 13th century. At Beaumaris there has been no attempt to address the issue of car management, but fortuitously access is not a problem.

From these examples, it would seem that the priorities have been: first to provide good access to the site by car and then to address access for disabled people. Managing the car does not seem to be considered a high priority at these particular Welsh sites, at present, but perhaps this is because the visitor numbers are not as great as at some of the other World Heritage sites described above.

Conclusion

Managing the car is becoming an issue at some of the most popular World Heritage sites, because of the effect of the car on the *spirit of the place* and on the environment. There are ways of improving the situation without compromising access for disabled people. It would appear that at the Welsh castle sites, however, the priorities have been to provide good access to the site by car and then to address access for disabled people. Currently, car management does not appear to be a priority at less popular sites.

References

Brisbane, M. and Wood, J.(1996), *A Future For Our Past?* English Heritage, London.

castlewales website (1999), Welsh Castles of Edward. http//w.w.w.castlewales.com/edwrdcas. html (22/11/99).

CIRIA. (1996), *Buildings For All To Use*. Construction Industry Research and Information Association, London 1996[13].

Cullingworth, R. (1998), Opening doors to disabled people. *Chartered Surveyor Monthly*, January 1998.

Department of National Heritage.(1994), *What Listing Means: A Guide for Owners and Occupiers*. DNH, London.

Department of the Environment/Department of National Heritage. (1994), Planning Policy Guidance Note 15 (PPG 15) *Planning and the Historic Environment*. HMSO, London.

Ferguson, R. (1988), Environmental Design for Disabled Persons - in Brown, R. Quality of Life for Handicapped People. Croom Helm, London.

Foster, L. (1995), Access to Historic Properties: A Look Forward. *Journal of Architectural Conservation* No. 3 November 1995.

Hall, C. M. and McArthur, S. (1998), *Integrated Heritage Management*. The Stationery Office, London.

Hellman, L. (1990), Redesigning Approaches. *Building Design*. 16 March 1990.

HMSO. (1979), *Ancient Monuments and Archaeological Areas Act*. London.

HMSO. (1990), *Planning (Listed Buildings and Conservation Areas) Act 1990*, London.

Holmes-Siedle, J. (1996), *Barrier-Free Design*. Architectural Press, Oxford.

Honour, H. and Fleming, J. (1999), *A World History of Art*. Lawrence King Publishing, London.

Huw Davies, G. (1997), Romancing the stones. *Sunday Times*. 24 August 1997.

Huw Davies, G. (1999), Can Mont-St-Michel go from this to this? *The Times Weekend* Saturday June 5, 1999.

Keenan, S. (1999), Machu Picchu by Cable Car. *The Times Weekend* Saturday July 3, 1999.

Lowenthal, D (1985), *The Past is a Foreign Country*. Cambridge University Press, Cambridge.

Morris, A. E. J. (1994), *History of Urban Form: before the Industrial Revolution*. 3rd ed. Addison Wesley Longman Harlow, Essex.

Morris, W. (1877), *The Society for the Protection of Ancient Buildings: Manifesto*. SPAB, London.

National Trust. (1996), *The National Trust and Disabled Visitors*. National Trust Leaflet Number 4, London 1991 (revised 1996).

National Trust. (2000), *Handbook for Members and Visitors 2000*. The national trust, Bromley, Kent.

Organisation of World Heritage Cities. (1996), *World Heritage Cities Management Guide*. Organisation of World Heritage Cities.

Parsons, K. (1999*), The Conservation of Historic Buildings as Contemporary Workplaces*. Unpublished thesis, University of Central Lancashire, Preston.

Parsons, K. (2000), Sustainability and the Reasons for Building Conservation. Brandon, P. Lombardi, P. and Perera, S. (eds.) *Cities and Sustainability: Sustaining Our Cultural Heritage* (Conference Proceedings). University of Moratuwa, Sri Lanka ISBN 955-9027-09-3.

Paton, T. (1998), Glossary of terms - Special report: Access. *Chartered Surveyor Monthly* January 1998.

Pringle, J. Retracing ancient footsteps on the Acropolis. *The Times*. Saturday January 15, 2000.

Rhodes, T. (1999), Tourist Tide Threatens Magic City of the Incas. *Sunday Times* 20 June 1999.

Ross, M.(1996), *Planning and the Heritage: Policy and Procedures*. 2nd Ed. Spon, London.

Rossi, A. (1989), *The Architecture of the City*. MIT Press, Cambridge, Massachusetts.

Tiesdell, S. Oc, T. and Heath, T. (1996), *Revitalising Historic Urban Quarters*. Architectural Press, Oxford.

United Nations Educational Scientific and Cultural Organisation (UNESCO) (1972), *International Convention for the Protection of World Cultural and Natural Heritage*.

Watt, J. (1997), Open To All. *Perspectives* 30 August/September 1997.

Wheatley, G. (1996), *World Heritage Sites*. English Heritage, London.

Yale, P. (1997), *From Tourist Attractions to Heritage Tourism*. 2nd ed. Elm.

Young, V. and Urquhart, D. (1996), *Access to the Built Heritage*. Technical Advice Note 7, Historic Scotland, Edinburgh.

The Turks and Caicos National Museum: A case study of the role of a museum in a country developing tourism

Nigel Sadler

Turks and Caicos National Museum, British West Indies

Introduction

Tourism is soon to be the world's largest industry but tourism and its global influence are not fully understood. The airlines, hotels, tour operators, travel agents and tourist attractions are all an integral part of the tourist industry but their roles and those of governments, tourist boards, tourist sites, heritage interpreters and tourist themselves are still unclear. For example are tourists there to enjoy the culture or to demand entertainment and encourage a new indigenous culture, especially one that entertains and does not offend.

The Turks and Caicos Islands lie at the south-eastern end of the Bahamas and consist of over 40 Cays (see map 1), of which 8 are inhabited. They claim to have some of the World's best beaches and diving sites, are beautiful by nature and was the landfall of Christopher Columbus, thus using heritage to capture tourism. The regional trend in the Caribbean is the "growing dependence of more islands on tourism as the engine of economic growth" (Strategic Plan for 1998-2001, 1998, p8). How is this to affect the Turks and Caicos Islands and the stakeholders in tourism, most notably the National Museum?

Map 1   Location of the Turks and Caicos Islands

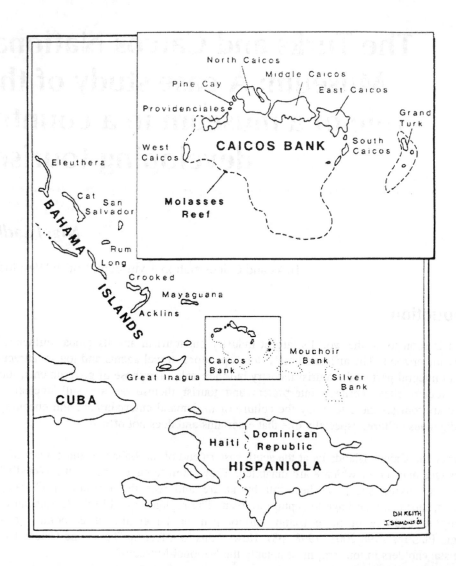

Map 1. The Turks and Caicos Islands lie SE of the Bahamas and North of Hispaniola. They are made up of two banks, the Caicos Bank and Turk Bank. Providenciales has the largest population amongst the Caicos Islands whilst Grand Turk has the largest population amongst the Turk Islands.

Who are tourists?

To understand how a museum works within tourism we must at first understand the tourist. Tourists generally suffer from escapism and don't want to experience the humdrum of everyday life when on holiday especially the deprivations of the local inhabitants. For example most Caribbean countries suffer from water shortages and it is estimated that a tourist uses 6 times as much water as a local resident (Pattullo, 1999, P32). How can we expect tourists who are used to having non-stop running water to live in an environment where water is such a precious commodity? Museums can explain why there are these shortages (the geology, the weather patterns etc.) but are not in a position to make tourists ration their water use.

Tourists gain their first impressions about a destination through guidebooks, which can create or kill a place. It is often the understanding and research of one person, a very subjective and biased view but in many cases is all that the tourist will go on. In the case of the Lonely Planet guide to the Bahamas, Grand Turk is described as the only negative aspect of the area, albeit the museum gained high praise. This stemmed from the writer's apparent alienation of the locals on his visit rather than the local's general attitude towards tourists. It is unclear how these negative comments have affected tourism to Grand Turk.

There is also the issue of the manner of the holiday the tourist is after. A look at some of the glossy magazines which list 'new' destinations clearly show the direction tourism is taking. The January 2000 issue of "Travel and Leisure" details a cruise around the western Caribbean. At no time does the article actually mention the Caribbean culture – aboard the ship there are opera performances, recording of TV game shows, a whole range of sports, shopping, restaurants and a Mardi Gras themed street fair on one of the promenades. It is the true cultural Island.

Tourism in the Turks and Caicos Islands

Development of tourism in the Turks and Caicos Islands

The Turks and Caicos Islands still benefit, or suffer, from the fact that they are little known with some tourists visiting as the Islands have "not been discovered" by the tourist market or to "visit strange lands for status reasons" (Boniface and Fowler, 1996, p13). It hasn't suffered from the over development that has occurred elsewhere in the Caribbean but by coming, tourists have the potential to send the Islands on a downward spiral. Tourists are seen to have money, therefore more must be attracted and soon before you know it the country no longer maintains its cultural identity.

Tourism really began on the Turks and Caicos Islands in the 1960s when they faced an economic crisis. As Sadler (1997) records "The Islands had arrived at a crossroads, with the wealth and uncertainty of the salt industry behind them: the future seemed to lie in the exploitation of tourism, and, to a lesser extent, development of the fisheries and financial Industries. The 60s and 70s were largely devoted to exploring other courses for economic self sufficiency".

The 1966 development plan was aimed at introducing the basic infrastructure required for the tourist development of the Islands. The plan came to little and various other experts came to the Islands to try and identify the way forward. Since 1968 tourism has been part of Providenciales economy. Prior to this most islanders were subsistence farmers and fishermen living within extended families. As the tourism industry grew the move from peasant agriculture to wage labour eroded the extended family and changed family dynamics.

Tourism provided a means where the locals had options – they could continue to work the fields or sea, or alternatively seek employment to gain wages to purchase goods, especially those being imported to cater for the growing tourist market and expatriate communities (Weis, 1988).

Since the 1960s some of the smaller cays have been developed as private resorts/retirement homes, most notably Pine Cay and Parrot Cay. These plans have not been restricted to the past. Today Cotton Cay is under 'threat' of development of a private hotel and golf complex.

The last detailed plan for tourism was the Strategic Plan for 1998-2001. It recorded that the broad objectives for tourism development were "to promote tourism in such a way as to contribute towards employment in TCI and to achieve real income growth with minimal environmental degradation". It also recorded that "the outlook is for continued growth in both tourism and offshore business activity, although tourism sector performance will continue to be sensitive to the threat of hurricanes". The Tourist Board clearly see the preservation of natural, cultural and built environment as a necessity for developing tourism as well as maximising *"the economic benefits to all Turks and Caicos Islanders"* and whatever development takes place must be to the highest quality and sustainable (Strategic Plan for 1998-2001, 1998). It shows awareness of the different rates of development between the Islands, most notably Providenciales and Grand Turk and the need for a more balanced growth that favours all the Islands.

As they do not have the skills internally, tourism on the Islands relies on outside intervention to succeed and this means many stakeholders in tourism are not indigenous to the Turks and Caicos Islands. The hotels are owned by multi national companies or individuals who have come from outside the Islands, the dive shops are generally owned and managed by people who have come off Island and people writing strategies and policies are often relying on outside specialists. The museum is no different as the reasoning behind the foundation of the museum came from outsiders, the Director is English, the Manager American, albeit that 7 of the 9 trustees are Turks and Caicos Islanders. It is no wonder that many of the local people do not feel any ownership of the tourism issue and are sometimes hostile to development.

The Islands are politically stable which helps guarantee the safety and comfort of the visitors. However, recent demonstrations against development (in this instance the closure of access to a beach) can show that the local population want a voice and will protest to get it. "This latest protest underscores citizens disgust at the authorities for not protecting and acting in the best interests of the people" (Turks and Caicos Weekly News, Jan14-20th 2000).

Tourist statistics for the Turks and Caicos Islands

Since 1982 the number of tourists has risen from by over 900% (see table 1). The biggest single rise occurred in 1985 with a 68.6% increase as a result of the opening of the Club Med Hotel in 1984. In 1999 the majority of the tourists were from the United States (88%) whilst those coming from Europe totalled 10.7%. 97% entered the Islands on Providenciales, whilst 2.5% entered on Grand Turk. 71% of the visitors came on holiday whilst 5.1% came for the diving and 19.3% came on business, with 73.8% staying a week or less. Probably the most important single figure is that 70.6% (85 387) were on a repeat visit which meant that they must have enjoyed their previous visit(s).

As the number of tourists to the Islands increase the number of "tourist attractions" must also increase. The museum is just a part of this, along with duty free shopping, souvenir shops, restaurants, bars and heritage sites. New proposals are looking into a "tourist centre" on Grand Turk, possibly converting the old prison, and the museum is likely to have a central role in this.

Year	Tourists to Turks and Caicos Islands	% Increase	Tourists to Grand Turk (Port of Entry)	Museum Visitors (paying)
1982	13 343	—	—	—
1983	14 216	6.5	—	—
1984	17 291	21.6	—	—
1985	29 148	68.6	—	—
1986	35 418	21.5	—	—
1987	36 657	3.5	—	—
1988	47 079	28.4	—	—
1989	48 709	3.5	—	—
1990	48 756	0.1	6858	—
1991	54 419	11.6	5709	No Data
1992	52 379	-3.7	3701	Incomplete Data
1993	67 303	28.5	6409	1635
1994	71 655	6.5	5037	1835
1995	78 957	10.2	4729	1942
1996	87 794	11.2	3539	2115
1997	93 011	5.9	3490	1914
1998	110 855	19.2	5390	1858
1999	120 898	9.0	3028	2027

Table 1: The number of tourists to the Turks and Caicos Islands and the visitors to the Turks and Caicos National Museum (statistics supplied by the Turks and Caicos Tourist Board and the National Museum). The number of tourists to Grand Turk are those who first arrive on the Islands at Grand Turk and do not include those who have day trips from Providenciales or first arrive on Providenciales and then take internal flights. There are no exact figures for the total number of tourists to Grand Turk.

The tourism infrastructure on the Turks and Caicos Islands

Tourism is in fact the modern form of colonisation. Destinations try to adapt to the suit the tourists whilst the tourist travel with cultural baggage, ranging from their education to personal experiences. Cultural 'Islands' abound in the holiday destination (Boniface & Fowler, 1996, p 17) and amongst these are Club Med. They are similar the world over and offer the same experience no matter where.

Club Med was the first real big hotel to come to the Islands, opening on Providenciales on December 22nd 1984, covering 70 acres and provided over 576 beds. The British government put up $10.3 million for the development of the infra structure, including a new 7 600 feet runway and terminal at the airport to cater for the new tourists, and 17 miles of paved roads (Sadler, 1997) to help entice the multi national company here. Today it is an all-inclusive resort and the tourists get the 'Club Med experience' rather than the Turks and Caicos experience. The tourist will visit and say that they have seen The Turks and Caicos Islands, yet never venture away from the holiday compound or away from the guided tours.

For most of the first half of the 20th century there were no hotels on Grand Turk. The government changed this when they converted a private residence into the Turks Head Inn, complete with room for 14 guests. It remained in government hands for three years and was then sold to a commercial operator. Today there are 113 rooms on Grand Turk, albeit looking at increasing this to 200, compared to 15000 on Providenciales. However on Grand Turk it has been common that at least one hotel, or part of one, has been closed during the main tourist season which means the number of available rooms is less than the 113.

Like elsewhere in the Caribbean air transport is a major issue. American Airlines appear to dominate the Caribbean skies and in 1991 half of all seats on planes belonged to American Airlines (Patullo 1999). This affects the Turks and Caicos Islands as American Airlines have a virtual monopoly between Miami and Providenciales, creating high prices compared to the actual distance travelled. This situation means that tourism is at the whim of the Airline. They dictate prices, flight times and routes and do not fly to the nation's capital, a bone of contention on Grand Turk, suggesting they will only do so when there are 200 hotel rooms. This fails to take into consideration the local residents who travel on business to Miami and those who visit family members – it is based on tourism alone. Many believe they should be at least a weekly service between Miami and Grand Turk. However, "hopes have grown that TWA will begin regular scheduled flights to Florida to give American Airlines some competition" (Turks and Caicos Free Press, Feb 4-10, 2000) and new carriers coming to the Islands is seen as positive as "it does mean increased tourism for the Island" (ibid).

To attract tourists a modern infrastructure is needed. This tourism led development should also benefit those locals who live near to the resorts as they will use the roads and benefit from service provision. However, the benefits are restricted and create uneven provision not only on individual Islands but also between Islands.

Changing fortunes of the islands

Whilst Grand Turk, the political, and historically economic capital appears in decline the annual growth rate in GDP for the Turks and Caicos Islands as a whole is 7.9% over the last decade, mostly centred on Providenciales. Businesses are moving to Providenciales leading to a declining population on and a feeling of depression on Grand Turk whilst the residents watch a booming economy on Providenciales. The booming economy creates a hidden problem for heritage. The need for rapid development can see planning permissions being flaunted and a misunderstanding of what preserving heritage means.

Few studies have been undertaken on the Islands to see what the impact of tourism has been on the residents. One of the most detailed to date has been Weis's (1988) assessment of the changing family dynamics that looked at the decline of the extended family. If her findings are correct it clearly indicates that the cultural identity of the Islanders is being lost forever.

It has been argued that tourism is one cause for a declining Belonger population (Weis, 1988) through emigration and a lower child birth rate. The movement to wage earning saw many emigrate and as one islander said recently "those with get up and go have got up and gone". Of course much of this paid work is in the tourist trade or work that links with tourism, such as building a better infra structure. People on the impoverished Islands have gone in search of work on Providenciales where the tourist trade rules. Alternatively they have sought their fortunes in America. Those who have stayed have fewer children, as they are no longer productive members of the family but a cash burden - the more children the more income that had to be earned to feed them. The aspirations of the children and youth have also changed. The old family ties are lost whilst money becomes the goal. We must ask if tourism is benefiting the average local or exploiting them.

It is clear that the Islands have been influenced greatly by western beliefs, from the colonial ties through to Cable TV today. This reflects in everyday life. It is difficult to comprehend a community that looks longingly to America, especially Miami, as its role model and aspires to have the American way of life based upon the consumables imported, yet insist on keeping their laid back attitude that seems to encompass the whole Caribbean.

The Turks and Caicos National Museum

The museum history

The Museum's mission statement declares that:

> *The Turks and Caicos National Museum is a not for profit organisation aimed at recording, interpreting, preserving and celebrating the history of the Turks and Caicos Islands and its people.*

It was the discovery and eventual scientific recovery of the Molasses Reef Shipwreck between 1982 and 1986 that instigated the development of the museum, which opened in November 1991. Up until this date, archaeological finds had been taken to the USA for conservation and added to American museum collections. This was not a state of affairs that the Molasses Reef Shipwreck excavation team found acceptable and wanted to return the items to where they belonged: The Turks and Caicos Islands. After several meetings with local residents a building was donated and funds found to establish a museum that would tell the history of the Islands.

In 1996 a building was opened behind the museum so that scientific research could be undertaken on Grand Turk in up to date laboratories. Now most material from archaeological excavations no longer has to be taken off the Islands for conservation and are added to the museum collection after being recorded.

The museum's collection and displays

Unfortunately, the nature of the Turks and Caicos Islands: high humidity and temperature, salt content in the air and small population means that there is little evidence of human occupation. What there was has either decayed or been taken off the Islands. This limits the objects available for collection and by removing an item from its context, both physical and cultural, the museum is required to provide some form of interpretation.

The museum is slowly and steadily building up a collection. This has been hindered by the fact that during the 19th and early 20th century private collectors removed items, mostly Lucayan material. These collections have generally ended up in American museums, where most sit in the stores, only being viewed by the occasional academic researcher. One of these institutions, The Smithsonian, mission is the "increase and diffusion of knowledge" (Smithsonian, February 2000) and declares its interest in getting more of its collections out to the wider public through touring exhibitions and "affiliating with other museums and depositing with them portions of our collections" (Lawrence M Small, secretary of the Smithsonian).

By displaying objects museums can deliberately or accidentally create cultural clashes by the choice and interpretation of artefacts. They can dictate the viewer's physical and emotional responses by the context of an object by itself or in conjunction with other artefacts. It can dictate whose history we interpret and display. This situation is made worse when there has only been a limited amount of research undertaken on material held by the Turks and Caicos National Museum. For example recent archaeological work on Lucayan sites has seen some reinterpretation and has led to a new gallery solely on the Lucayans.

There is also the issue of how museums interpret objects from another cultural viewpoint. Just by using historical sources it will bias the interpretation as all records are subjective, for example how much information was written down by slaves and not the slave owners or white colonialists? We have to consider whom the exhibition is for. The tourists who bring their own cultural baggage and own ideas, or the locals who have their own understanding of their history. The museum must show no bias and present the known facts, but this is easier said than done. In the case of slavery the museum has avoided this sensitive subject, not because it wants to (or as some locals see it as deliberately not touching on a negative colonial aspect) but because there is little evidence and anything the museum did would be tokenism. However, the museum is researching this topic at present and a gallery on slavery is proposed for 2002/2003.

The museum has also been developed by American specialist and therefore appeals more to the tourist market. There is a lot of text but it must be remembered that many locals only have rudimentary English skills and will possibly be put off as they see the museum as not theirs but the intellectual tourists. This is not true! On top of this is the clash between entertainment and education. For many years museums have been viewed as educational establishments. They are now becoming part of the entertainment world and losing their important education role. Museums should be able to educate and entertain and the National Museum's traditional approach i.e. objects in cases and text panels appear to do this without the gimmicks.

The museum's role

What role does a museum have in tourism? As a case study the Turks and Caicos National Museum offers some individual examples of what it is to be a "tourist attraction". Museums in the Caribbean range from basic to modern, with the Turks and Caicos National Museum being one of the better ones, described as "This little gem" in the Lonely Planet Guide (Baker, 1998). Destinations have to provide a variety of attractions that are parallel or better than other Caribbean resorts competing for the same tourists. They can all offer excellent turquoise waters, sun and sandy beaches but the islands must create and maintain their separate identity. It is no good if all cater for the nightclubers, the cruise ship clientele, or the get way from it all posses. It is therefore the role of such institutions as museums to provide a unique tourist attraction and to assist in encouraging the preservation of other heritage sites.

The museum is here to represent the past, present and future residents and to act as an attraction for the locals as well as the tourists. It therefore has many competing roles. However, because of its newness the local population has yet to gain ownership. This situation is perhaps made worse by the feeling that the museum is here for tourists only and therefore has little relevance to locals. This is not true but is a difficult perception to break.

The museum's prime role is to preserve the human artefacts and items from the natural world. It interprets the Island's history for residents and tourists and helps the country keep its own identity and not be engulfed by what the tourist wants or expects to see or before it is subsumed by the American Culture. The Museum also acts as an advisor to local people and government of the importance of the history of the Islands as well as to tourists who visit the museum on their role, for example environmental issues such as the removal of coral.

The museum has made in clear from the beginning that it has no official ties to government. This allows it to be autonomous but it works closely with government departments, most notably the National Trust, Education Department, Coastal Resources and the Ministry of Tourism. By remaining separate it has a reputation of getting things done: The government is perceived as being slow.

The Strategic plan for tourism (1998) records that the private sector will *"provide sound advice, expertise and support when required"*. This assumes that it will be the Ministry of Tourism or the Tourist Board that will seek the assistance when they feel it is needed. Maybe though the museum's role is to provide the assistance when it feels it is needed and not requested. The Strategic Plan (1998) then states that the private sector must also *"ensure as far as possible the advancement of indigenous interests"*

The museum shop

The shop is one way that the museum makes money and stocks books on the natural and human history of the Turks and Caicos Islands and the Caribbean in general. There are also the obligatory postcards, T-shirts and posters. The shop does not try to compete with the few local craft shops supplying the tourist market but it does sell baskets and paintings made by residents and model boats made by inmates at Her Majesties Prison. It may not be much but the museum tries to put some money back into the local economy but there is a shortage of locally manufactured products that can be sold.

Another one of the shop's roles is education. This includes several books on the effect of Tourism in the Caribbean. Of course few tourists notice these but some local government officials have been given copies to aid their understanding of the Caribbean issues.

Heritage interpretation

The museum can not be seen as the only place where the history of the Islands can be told. Each historic building, archaeological site and the site of the industrial production, most notably the salinas, all play a part. Proposals at present include joint projects between the museum and the National Trust to set up interpretation centres on Providenciales, Middle Caicos and Salt Cay to act as education centres for the locals as well as tourist attractions. The museum also provides published material on the areas history for consumption both on and off the Islands, most notably through the *Astrolabe* pages in the "Times of the Islands Publication", and has instigated a publishing programme in 2000.

The museum also helps to safeguard historic remains. Shipwrecks often bring to mind sunken treasure and in the recent past many have been pilfered directly by treasure hunters or indirectly by tourists who want to take away momentos. Unscientific "recovery" of objects means that valuable information is lost and the item loses its historic value. The museum can educate the local people, especially those who dive, to help safeguard the national archaeological treasures as well as explaining in the museum why it is wrong to take items from wrecks.

The museum also tries to influence how the tourist trade interprets the heritage. How often in the Caribbean are we faced with a "pirate crew" giving a tour of the shoreline and telling stories of days of yore when pirates roamed these waters. At best the stereotypical image (eye patch, hat with skull and cross bones etc) is portrayed but it often ignores the true story of piracy on the sea, the dangers and risks past travellers faced and the fate of the pirates. The real story is fascinating but maybe the operators don't have the time or inclination to learn it. The museum's role is to provide the "storyboard" of facts and present them to the tourist and maybe at the same time to encourage those involved with the tourists and locals to learn the history and pass it on when interacting with tourists. Does authenticity have to suffer? Does life have to be sanitised? Does culture have to be compromised? The Museum does not believe so.

The Christopher Columbus dilemma

Throughout the world places try to identify themselves with historic people, especially those with tourist appeal. The Caribbean is no different and here the claim has major world importance - Christopher Columbus' first landfall. Many Islands claim as fact that their Island was the first Landfall but without proof. The Turks and Caicos Islands have one of these claims and Columbus' records fit the Islands well (better than other claimants). The museum's role is to try and get those involved in tourism not to state this as fact but tell the true story – no one country will ever be able to prove that Columbus landed on their patch of sand!

The museum can not censor the affect of Columbus' discovery of the Americas. Westerners see that Columbus' discovery was a major historical event benefiting Europe and today's white Americans. However, how many reflect on the negative aspects – the enslaving and in most cases annihilation of the local indigenous people, the destruction of the indigenous peoples way of life and the need for large numbers of slaves from Africa to farm and exploit the land in later years. This global history, and its interpretation has "high political, ethnic and financial stakes" (Boniface & Fowler, 1996, p27) and it is this struggle for the heritage "truth" which influences tourism. The 500th anniversary of Columbus's journey to the Americas in 1992 was a major tourist opportunity and everybody who could claim some connection to Columbus did so.

The museum visitor

The museum has to be aware of the different ways tourists and locals perceive and experience the museum. For example, locals normally have a sense of ownership: it is their museum, their history, and even though they might not visit the museum themselves they still take pride in its existence. In the Turks and Caicos Islands the division line becomes even more confused because of the mix of residents and their division by Islands.

The population of around 20 000 is spread over 8 islands and the residents include Belongers and expatriates. Belongers are people who were born on the Islands or have been granted Belonger status because of their work. Most of the Belongers are Black and appear to have direct lines back to the slave history of the Islands. These make up an estimated 6 500 of the population. The Expatriates consist of many groups. The largest sub group are the Haitian, both legal and illegal immigrants. They make up the under class who carry out a large percentage of the menial work. Other expatriates include those who have set up homes, and/or businesses and retiring Americans who move to the Islands because of cheap land and the weather (many move here seasonally to escape cold winters). Also being a Crown Colony there are British expatriates on the Islands in positions within the Governor's office and government departments.

It is clear from the visitor numbers that many of the adult Belongers do not visit the museum, whilst the children come as part of school groups or on their own, usually to sit in an air conditioned building. It is because of this apathy that most locals see the museum as only being here for the tourist.

Tourism does not have to be a necessary evil. Without tourists the museum would probably not survive financial – they pay admission and they buy goods from the museum shop. Without the European and American expatriates the museum would also suffer – they bring their visiting friends and many are members of the museum, providing an annual contribution to keep the museum running. However, a main goal of the museum has to be to preserve the heritage of the Islands. The museum clearly understands that by preserving the heritage it would create more of a pull for the tourists, especially through the uniqueness of some of the collections. The museum houses the oldest European shipwreck discovered in the Americas and has one of only two Lucayan Indian paddles to have been found. All of these things should be of interest to the local population as well as the tourist.

Most tourist are from the Western World and are part of a museum culture – they know (or think they do) what the role of a museum is. The museum has to educate the local population, many of whom believe its only role is for tourism, into understanding the role of the museum before they visit. These barriers have to be broken down and the specific needs of the residents have to be identified and met – the museum must build bridges (Dodd and Sandell, 1998). Audience development is a necessity to meet the changing social, political and economic pressures on the Islands. The museum has to illustrate its social significance but at the same time it must be remembered that the museum can not be everything to everyone.

In the first decade of opening the museum, quite rightly, was interested in putting itself on a firm footing financially. This meant that all records kept had financial implications. Unfortunately, only paying visitors were recorded (see table 1) and then were assessed by the income taken per month. Statistical breakdowns of changing visitor numbers, the percentage of paying (mainly tourists) and non paying (mainly residents) were not made.

The cruise ship dilemma

Much has been written about the phenomena of the Caribbean Cruise Ship experience. The infrequent liners that stop off at Turks and Caicos Islands contain from 400 to over 1000 passengers. They unload the passengers who want to have a "cultural experience". The following is a personal account of a visit by a ship in February 2000 to Grand Turk. Their first views are of a working dock and to get into town tourists either hire a taxi or walk the three miles. Unfortunately, the taxi drivers are disgruntled as the tourists have been told that the fare is half of what it should be by the tour operators. The resentment by the taxi drivers is not towards the tourist but the operators, but it is the tourist that they have contact with and their resentment will show through. It is maybe for this reason one guide book called the locals sullen (Baker 1998 p 450), whereas in fact they are usually friendly and helpful if treated properly, like most people.

In the end the tourists arrive in town looking for the tourist shops, come to the museum door but do not enter as there is a charge, and return to the boat probably somewhat disillusioned by their experience. This is not the fault of the Island but the tour operators that do not know the destination properly. It is also the fault of the tourist – a glimpse of life on several Islands for a few hours at a time is not a "cultural experience". The museum can do little to change the expectations of the tourist as they are in the building for less than an hour. It is interesting that those who complained at having to pay an admission charge decided not to go around the museum but still wanted to buy the postcard, map and T shirt from the museum shop to say that they had done the Grand Turk experience.

Conclusion

Some see tourism as neo-colonialism (Boniface and Fowler, 1996). However does the visitor's patronage of an area give them rights over that area? Can they dictate the heritage story that is told, should it be sanitised, trivialised or made more exciting for the pleasure of the tourist? Is heritage a commodity that can be sold or reinterpreted to please the visitor? Many people will argue that a place is not just the physical landscape, but how that landscape has changed through the cultural development. Intellectual colonialism through the interpretation of a place can dictate what the tourist may wish to see or is shown and maybe not what is real. There is often no single history for an area and many seek ownership of part of that history, often neglecting the overall picture so we must ask whose history do we show. We can't alienate the local population to satisfy the needs of the tourist whom, through their own backgrounds, take sides. As Weis (1988, p18) puts it "Perhaps tourism is destroying a culture unnecessarily. Why should a host country transform itself to the visitor's ideal? After all, tourists are only visiting and the residents must live on the Island". However, at the present time 'outsiders' may be the only ones who value the Islands' history and culture.

Therefore should we be celebrating the fact that tourism is developing the Islands? The answer has to be a reserved yes. The Islands have no natural resources and therefore rely on the service industries. They are famed for their off shore financial services but the international stance against this could see its collapse. This means the Islands have to develop tourism. At present it appears that the government, although making mistakes like all governments are prone to, are learning lessons from the other Caribbean Islands. They are restricting all-inclusive hotels on Providenciales realising that this prevents money going into the local economy, they have forbidden private ownership of any beaches and there are strict building regulations. The museum is only a small part in all of this. It acts as an advisor when required, it acts as a tourist attraction and it acts as an education establishment for the Belongers to gain a sense of ownership of their history before the physical remnants, such as buildings, are removed forever.

The museum can be a major player in the development of the Islands. A working party set up in January 2000 to rejuvenate Grand Turk saw that heritage would play a part (although not specifically stating the museum) and that Government and Tourism would be the life-blood for Grand Turk. It is hoped that the Museum can provide the assistance required enabling the Turks and Caicos Islanders to make wise choices. As Weis (1988) wrote "May they always have the power to determine their own development".

References

Baker, Christopher, (1998), *Bahamas, Turks and Caicos*, Lonely planet publications, Australia, (pages 442-497).

Boniface, Priscilla and Fowler, Peter J. (1996), *Heritage and Tourism*, Routledge, London.

Dodd, Jocely and Sandell, Richard (1998), *Building Bridges*, Museums and Galleries Commission, London.

Pattullo, Polly (1999), *Last Resorts. The Cost of Tourism in the Caribbean*, Ian Randle Publishers, Jamaica.

Sadler, H. E. (1997), *Turks Islands Landfall*, United Cooperative Printers Ltd. Jamaica.

Weis, Mary Francis (1988), *The Impact of Tourism upon the extended Matrifocal Family in the Turks and Caicos Islands*, Denison University Honors Project, Department of Sociology/Anthropology.

Unpublished material

A Strategic Plan for 1998-2001. TCI Tourism Into the 21st Century, Aubrey Armstrong Management Associates, August 1998.

Grand Turk Revitalisation Strategy (proposal), January 12, 2000.

Tourist Statistics supplied by the Turks and Caicos Tourist Board.

Magazines and newspapers

Smithsonian, P14, February 2000.

Travel and Leisure, January 2000, American Express Publishing Corporation.

Turks and Caicos Free Press, Vol 10 Number 5, Feb 4-10, 2000.

Turks and Caicos Weekly News, Vol 14 No 2 Jan14-20th 2000.

Further Information on the Museum

Museum website: www.tcmuseum.org

Astrolabe in *Times of the Islands*, The International Magazine of the Turks and Caicos Islands, published quarterly.

Positioning Castlefield Urban Heritage Park in day trip product space using multidimensional scaling analysis

Peter Schofield

University of Salford, UK

Abstract

A desired positioning for a tourist destination is one that clearly distinguishes its image from that of its competitors on attributes that are considered to be important; effective positioning will insulate the 'product' from competition and enhance its market performance. The paper examines the position of Castlefield Urban Heritage Park in Manchester relative to other day trip destinations in consumers' perceptual space. A multidimensional scaling analysis using SPSS ALSCAL procedure was employed to derive the structure of the consumers' psychological dimensions of the relevant day trip tourist destinations.

The 'stimulus set' was comprised of the subjects' most preferred 'evoked set' (Howard and Sheth, 1969) destinations for day trips, i.e, those places they intended to visit over the next year. Subjects were asked to rate the 'proximity' of all possible pairs of destinations on a seven-point scale ranging from one ('very similar') to seven ('very different') by making a total of 78 pairwise judgements. The resultant 'dissimilarity' matrix produced a 'simple space map' the dimensions of which reflect the subjects' normal implicit criteria in making their judgements rather than distinguishing between the destinations on the basis of *a priori* specified attributes which could represent constructs they may not normally use.

Three dimensions were identified: heritage – excitement; urban location – rural location; and 'new' tourism – traditional tourism. The spatial configuration of the destinations in this product space highlighted a number of important issues for positioning Castlefield. The existence of object clusters in both two- and three-dimensional configurations indicates that the experience which is sought by day trip tourists can potentially be satisfied by a number of alternative and directly competing destinations. This suggests that product differentiation is an important strategic priority in this marketplace. The implications for product augmentation, new product development and the creation and transmission of appropriate promotional images are discussed.

Introduction

The importance of tourist images of destinations in the decision-making process is widely recognised and there is a general consensus that it is probably the image of a place rather than the factual information that has most influence on destination choice (Mayo, 1973; La Page and Cormier, 1977; Goodrich, 1978; Dilley, 1986; Stabler, 1988; Gartner, 1989; Woodside and Lysonski, 1989; Um and Crompton, 1990; Ahmed, 1991). Um and Crompton, (1990) argue that the image of a place, to a greater or lesser extent, is derived from attitudes towards a destination's perceived attributes. Smith (1989: 35) defines an attitude as 'a predisposition of an individual to act or otherwise respond to an object or stimulus. It is not the actual response, but rather the tendency towards a consistent response'.

Attitudes have been one of the most popular variables used in the consumer behaviour field to try to predict consumer choice behaviour, usually within an expectancy-value framework based on Fishbein and Ajzen's (1975) model of reasoned action. Within this context, an individual's attitude toward an object is conceptualised as a composite of his/her evaluation of that object in terms of attaining certain goals, weighted by the relative importance or saliency of the goals. The model has received considerable empirical support both generally (Glassman and Fitzhenry, 1976; Bowman and Fishbein, 1978; Ryan and Bonfield, 1980; McCarty, 1981; Kantola, Syme and Campbell, 1982; Warshaw, Calantone and Joyce, 1986; Sheppard, Hartwick and Warshaw, 1988) and within the leisure and tourism literature (Scott, Schewe and Frederick, 1978; Young and Kent, 1985; Cable et al., 1987; Tourism Canada, 1988; Saleh and Ryan, 1992; Sternquist-Witter, B., 1985). The original expectancy-value model (Fishbein, 1967) describes a predicted relationship between the attractiveness of some object or action, Aj, and two variables: Bij, 'belief' about whether a particular object or action (j) possesses a given quality (I); and Vi, 'value' placed on the desirability of the ith quality, to predict the attitude or opinion a person holds about a particular choice.

During the destination choice process, a consumer will typically evaluate not just one brand, but a number of brands in his/her 'evoked' set' (Howard and Sheth, 1969) or salient brand set – the subset of brands that the consumer considers buying out of the set s/he is aware of . The concept is captured by the 'multi-brand, multi-attribute expectancy-value model' in which a number of brands are competitively rated across the same set of attributes. In considering a range of alternative destinations, the consumer does not consider every possibility, however, only those destinations which they are aware about and/or which have some appeal to either the individual or the family or social group to which the individual belongs. Scott, Schewe and Frederick (1978) therefore postulate that if this is so, then a 'proportionality of product knowledge' exists. This concept can then be incorporated into the multi-brand, multi-attribute model to produce the formula given in Figure 1.

Figure 1   An Expectancy-Value Multi-Brand, Multi-Attribute Model

$$BIij = Aij \sum_{j=1}^{m} \sum_{k=1}^{n} (Bijk\ Vik\ PPKij)$$

Where: i   =   Consumer

j   =   Brand or product

k   =   Attribute or product characteristic

n   =   Number of attributes

m   =   Number of brands/ products

BIij   =   Consumer i's behavioural intention toward brand j

Aij   =   A unidimensional measure of consumer i's attitude toward brand j

Bijk =   The strength of consumer i's belief that attribute k is possessed by brand j

Vik   =   The degree to which attribute k is desired by consumer I

PPKij =   Proportional product knowledge of consumer i for brand j

(Adapted from Scott et al, 1978)

On the supply side, the consumer decision making process is also influenced by competition between destinations in the form of new product development and augmentation and through the creation and transmission of the 'official' images of place. As a preparatory step towards product development, new product planning, diversification and differentiation, market structuring and positioning analysis are key considerations. Market structure analysis, introduced by Myers and Tauber (1977), determines the competitive relationships between brands in a product class whereas positioning analysis establishes the perceptual differences between the brands in a product class and their relationship with consumer preferences (Dolnicar et al, 1999). This type of analysis can assist in the identification of the competitive strengths and weaknesses of the brands, from the consumer perspective (Urban and Hauser, 1993). The focus of this paper is on product positioning analysis using the expectancy-value, multi-brand, multi-attribute model as a conceptual framework. The model was employed to structure an analysis of consumer attitudes toward Castlefield Urban Heritage Park, Manchester's premier heritage visitor attraction, and to establish its position in the mind of the consumer relative to competitive destinations.

Methodology

This piece of research was part of a larger project on day trip tourism involving a more comprehensive analysis of Castlefield which is perceived by consumers as a day trip destination (Schofield, 1997). The project included a timed sequence of four successive surveys using the *same* sample of respondents. Repeated access to this sample was required because of the cumulative nature of both the questionnaire designs and the information required. Freely elicited data from the first questionnaire was incorporated into an attitude construct and a day trip destination preference grid in the second questionnaire. The subjects were asked to rate each attribute in the construct in terms of its importance for a day trip.

They were then asked to rate Castlefield Urban Heritage Park in Manchester (after visiting the destination) on each attribute in terms of how much or how little of each item the destination had. A third survey was used to assess the stability of subjects' mental categorisation of day trip destinations over time, and the validity of the 'evoked set' concept (Howard and Sheth, 1969) within this context (in terms of actual visitation or otherwise during the year after they were elicited during the first survey). Finally, an analysis of the results from the second questionnaire formed the basis of the MDS similarity/ dissimilarity scales presented to respondents in the fourth questionnaire. Sample stability was, therefore, critical for this process. The selection of the sample was also influenced by such practical considerations as the length and complexity of the questionnaires and the amount of detailed information required from the respondents. In order to satisfy these specific requirements, the sample consisted of undergraduates studying at Salford University (n = 320).

For the purpose of this research, it was important to consider the structure of competitive elements in the marketplace, i.e. determine the consumers' preferred destinations in the day trip market. Castlefield's position in n-dimensional day trip product space could then be determined using a multidimensional scaling perceptual mapping technique.

The structure of competitive elements

Woodside and Sherell (1977) and Thompson and Cooper (1979) demonstrated empirically the existence of a strong link between destinations most memorable in consumers' minds (measured by unaided awareness questioning) as places to visit, and the intention of actually visiting them. Following a procedure established by Woodside and Sherell (1977), the day trip 'evoked sets' of 320 subjects were established by asking them to list those destinations they intended to visit in the next 12 months. The subjects were then asked to rank the 12 most frequently listed 'evoked set' destinations together with Castlefield in order of preference for a day trip. The results are given in Table 1.

The subjects' preferred day trip destinations represent different types and scales of attraction ranging from London through Granada Studios Tour to Old Trafford – Manchester United's football ground. Alton Towers, London and Blackpool are the most preferred destinations with mean scores of 3.58, 3.96 and 5.17 respectively. By contrast, Castlefield is the least preferred destination with a mean score of 10.82. Given that the subjects' overall impression of Castlefield, after a visit to the destination, was positive (Schofield, 1997), these results demonstrate both the limitations of examining one destination in isolation and the importance of conducting a comparative analysis. Table 1 also shows the frequency with which each destination was ranked first and, therefore, provides a further measure of relative preference which highlights many of the features discussed above. Alton Towers, London and Blackpool were ranked first by 29.40%, 16.70% and 15.00% of all respondents, respectively. By comparison, Albert Dock, Camelot and Castlefield were not ranked first by any respondents.

In order to determine the reliability of the 'preference' data, a measure of the consistency of responses was obtained by comparing the correlation between respondents' highest ranked 'evoked set' destinations and the rank order of the 'preferred' destinations (Table 2). A Spearman Rank correlation coefficient of +0.75 was obtained which indicates a high level of agreement between the 'evoked' and 'preferred' data sets, particularly given that the results were derived from an unaided, free-elicitation technique and an aided direct ranking method, respectively. Only Manchester City Centre and York show marked differences in their rank order between the two sets.

The significance of 'primary images' of destinations in the destination choice process is supported by the data in Table 3 which displays a relatively high level of repeat visitation to the 'preferred' destinations. The high level of previous visits by subjects to their 'evoked set' destinations (88.12%) has been reported elsewhere (Schofield, 1997). Castlefield is ranked first in Table 3 because of the subjects' visit to the destination, and Manchester City Centre achieves second rank (above Blackpool, London and Alton Towers) by virtue of its proximity to the institution where the subjects were based. It is notable that except for the last three ranked places, almost half of all respondents had previously visited each 'preferred' destination. Even the lowest ranked destination was visited by over one third of all respondents. This relatively high level of first hand experience of the destinations is also significant in terms of the ability of the subjects to differentiate between them on the grounds of similarity based on 'primary' rather than 'secondary' images.

Table 1   Mean Scores and Rank Order of Subjects' 'Preferred'* Destinations

Rank	Destination	Mean	Std Dev	Std Err	FRF	%
1	Alton Towers	3.577	2.876	0.168	86	29
2	London	3.956	2.799	0.164	49	17
3	Blackpool	5.174	3.523	0.206	44	15
4	Lake District	5.669	3.129	0.183	21	7
5	Granada Studios	6.174	3.042	0.178	22	8
6	York	7.263	3.192	0.186	6	2
7	Albert Dock	7.427	3.027	0.177	-	-
8	Old Trafford	7.662	4.311	0.252	41	14
9	North Wales	7.945	3.359	0.196	10	3
10	Manchester	8.157	3.421	0.200	4	1
11	Chester	8.478	3.430	0.200	8	8
12	Camelot	8.604	3.032	0.177	-	-
13	**Castlefield**	**10.823**	**1.992**	**0.166**	-	-

n = 293

*N.B. Respondents were asked to rank the 12 most frequently mentioned 'evoked set' destinations and Castlefield (for comparative purposes) in order of preference for a visit on a day trip.

FRF = First Rank Frequency (number of times the destination was ranked first, i.e., was the most preferred destination).

Table 2   Spearman Rank Correlation Between All Subjects' Highest Ranked 'Evoked Set' and 'Preferred' Destinations

Destination	'Evoked Set' Rank	'Preferred' Destination Rank	d	d^2
Blackpool	1	3	-2	4
Alton Towers	2	1	+1	1
London	3	2	+1	1
Manchester	4	10	-6	36
Granada Studios	5	5	-	-
Lake District	6	4	+2	4
Albert Dock	7	7	-	-
Old Trafford	8	8	-	-
North Wales	9	9	-	-
Chester	10	11	-1	1
York	11	6	+5	25
Camelot	12	12	-	-
Castlefield *	-	13	-	-

n = 293 R = +0.75
Castlefield was excluded from the analysis because it was not listed in subjects' 'evoked sets'.

Table 3   Subjects' Previous Visits to the 'Preferred' Destinations in Rank Order of All (Total) Subjects' Previous Visits

Destination	Male		Female		Total	
	T	%	T	%	T	%
Castlefield	109	100.0	138	100.0	247	100.0
Manchester	109	100.0	135	97.83	244	98.79
Blackpool	98	89.91	119	86.23	217	87.85
London	100	91.73	108	78.26	208	84.21
Alton Towers	95	87.16	103	74.64	198	80.16
Lake District	82	75.23	94	68.12	176	71.26
North Wales	79	72.48	78	56.52	157	63.56
York	56	51.38	69	50.00	125	50.61
Chester	54	49.54	66	47.83	120	48.58
Albert Dock	52	47.71	64	46.38	116	46.96
Granada Studios	45	41.28	48	34.78	93	37.65
Camelot	39	35.78	52	37.68	91	36.84
Old Trafford	50	45.87	33	23.91	83	33.60

N = 247
Males: 109
Females: 138

Multidimensional scaling analysis and day trip tourism 'product' positioning

Product positioning is a key element of competitive marketing strategy. It has been conceptualised in various ways by both practitioners and academics (Haahti, 1986). Within a tourism marketing context, the notion of positioning recognises that consumers evaluate and make purchase decisions based on images of destination attributes. Each destination in a set of competitive offerings is thought of as occupying a certain position in a visitor's or potential visitor's 'perceptual space' which can be determined through the employment of perceptual mapping techniques.

Ahmed (1991: 318) defines positioning as

> *detecting or developing product attributes which are expected to establish a competitive advantage and may, therefore, be transformed into valuable arguments and appeals in advertising. Thus, a product's position is the result of a complex set of consumer perceptions, impressions, and feelings which tourists as consumers have for the product(s) as compared with competing product(s).*

Consequently, there are two components to perceptual mapping. First, the identification of product attributes which are determinant in influencing customer choice. These have been reported elsewhere (Schofield, 1999). Second, the determination of a product's position in the mind of the consumer relative to competing products, or in other words, the 'psychological distance' (degree of similarity/ dissimilarity) that exists between the products.

A multidimensional scaling (MDS) analysis program was used to identify subjects' perceptions of the similarity/dissimilarity between the twelve most 'preferred' day trip destinations together with Castlefield. The resultant grouping of the destinations into clusters on the basis of their similarity enabled judgements to be made concerning the critical attributes of destination choice. This, in turn, permitted an analysis of the degree of image separation of the destinations as a basis for 'product differentiation' (Kotler et al, 1999) to distinguish Castlefield from competitor's 'products'.

The subjects were asked to provide a 'direct' estimate of the degree of similarity/ dissimilarity between the 'objects' (destinations in the stimulus set). This was operationalised by asking the respondents to rate the 'proximity' of all possible pairs of destinations on a seven-point scale ranging from one ('very similar') to seven ('very different') by making a total of 78 pairwise judgements. In this application, given that a large rating means that the objects are 'very different', the 'proximities' will be referred to as 'dissimilarities' (Kruscal and Wish, 1978). The premise underlying this type of scaling is that the respondents' judgements are useful indices of perceptual structure. The criteria by which the overall dissimilarity of the destinations in each pair was to be judged was therefore left to individual subjects. As a result, the 'dissimilarity' matrix, therefore, produced a 'simple space map' the dimensions of which reflect the respondents' normal implicit criteria in making their judgements. They are, therefore, more salient to the respondent than *a priori* specified attributes which could represent constructs they may not normally use.

A square symmetric data matrix (13 x 13) was constructed using the mean values from 293 respondents' 'dissimilarity' ratings on the 78 stimulus pairs. A 'classical MDS' (CMDS) analysis (Norusis, 1987) was then performed on the matrix using the SPSS ALSCAL (alternating least squares scaling) procedure (Takane, Young and de Leeuw, 1977). In MDS, the number of stimuli places a limit on the number of dimensions which can be extracted and too few stimuli may lead to unstable solutions or the obscuring of subtle dimensions which may differentiate between the destinations. According to Kruscal and Wish (1978: 34) 'the number of stimuli minus one should be at least four times as great as the dimensionality'. Moreover, empirical support for this rule of thumb exists mostly for situations where the dimensions are less than or equal to three. Consequently, a minimum of nine stimuli are desirable for a two dimensional solution and a minimum of 13 are required for a three-dimensional solution. Therefore, given a stimulus set comprised of 13 destinations (which represents the lower limit for a three-dimensional solution), both two- and three-dimensional solutions were sought (see Figure 2). This approach conforms to Shepard's (1962: 130) recommendation to 'always try for a solution in a space of three, or preferably fewer dimensions where the spatial structure of the entire configuration can be seen and interpreted directly'. Young's 's-stress' formula, Kruscal's stress formula (1: 0.20664) and the squared correlation coefficient (+0.72831) all indicated a good fit between the model and the data.

Figure 2   Stimulus Co-ordinates for the two-Dimensional Solution

Stimulus Number	Stimulus Name	Dimensional 1	Dimensional 2
1	ALBERT	+0.8554	+0.9836
2	ALTONTOW	-1.4094	-0.8752
3	BLAKPOOL	-1.0893	-0.6643
4	CAMELOT	-0.8271	-1.1447
5	CASTLE	+1.0873	+0.5078
6	CHESTER	+1.4891	-0.0738
7	GRANADA	-1.2044	+0.0541
8	LAKES	+1.1181	-1.2747
9	LONDON	-0.6849	+1.2487
10	MANCITY	-0.3792	+1.1969
11	NORWALES	+1.1041	-1.1774
12	OLDTRAF	-1.1213	+1.1561
13	YORK	+1.0617	+0.0628

Results and discussion

The two-dimensional solution

Figure 3 displays the stimulus configuration derived from the co-ordinates of the two-dimensional solution. It shows the relative locations of the 12 'preferred' destinations together with Castlefield. The set of relative distances between the points is 'the most basic significant information in the solution' (Coxon, 1982: 93). As a result, the destinations that are perceived to be similar are represented by points that are in close proximity whereas the destinations which are perceived as being dissimilar are represented by points that are far apart.

The interpretation of the 'dimensions' of the configuration is the traditional approach in MDS although Guttman (1965) argued that a 'neighbourhood' or 'pattern' approach to interpretation is preferable. In contrast with the dimensional approach, the focus of the neighbourhood approach is primarily on the small distances or large similarities. Kruscal and Wish (1978) recommend that a combination of the two approaches should be used in decoding MDS configurations. Given the pattern described by the objects in two-dimensional space (Figure 3), both dimensional and neighbourhood approaches were employed to interpret the 'hidden structure' in the data. Information about the destinations obtained independently of the scaling itself, such as the variables and factors of importance in the day trip decision choice process and the respondents' attitude, preference and visitation data relating to the stimulus set were employed to decipher the configuration. In other words, an 'external method of interpretation' (Coxon, 1982: 95) was used.

The overall configuration of the objects in Figure 3 can be described in Guttman's (1968) terminology as a 'circumplex' or circular arrangement of points. Within this structure there appear to be four groups of destinations. First, the 'circumplex' is divided into the left and right sides of the plot on the basis of dimension one. Second, both sides of the structure contain two groups of destinations which are distinguishable in terms of their relative positions on dimension two. Dimension one is longer and differentiates more effectively between the destinations (as a whole group) than dimension two.

Figure 3   Stimulus configuration (simple Space Map) Derived from the Co-ordinates of the Two-Dimensional Solution

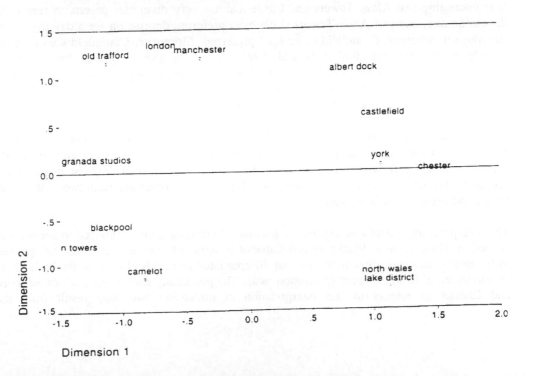

Predictably, Blackpool, Alton Towers and Camelot are perceived as being similar destinations. London, Manchester City Centre and, to a lesser extent, Old Trafford are also considered to be similar. These two groups are separated by a 'sparsely populated region' (Coxon, 1982: 100) where Granada Studios is located. It appears to be more closely related to the first cluster on the basis of both dimensions one and two, although there is also a clear differentiation from the first cluster on dimension two.

North Wales and the Lake District are perceived as being the most similar destinations within the stimulus set. They form a distinct cluster which is differentiated from Alton Towers, Blackpool and Camelot on dimension one and from Albert Dock, Castlefield, York and Chester on dimension two. Albert Dock, Castlefield, York and Chester appear to be a relatively homogeneous sub-group in relation to dimension one, and relatively heterogeneous on the basis of dimension two (in terms of distinguishing between the individual destinations).

Interpreting the dimensions

The cognitive process of naming the dimensions involved first, establishing the bi-polarity of these higher order organising constructs (by comparing the co-ordinates of the objects) and, second, determining the properties which these points share. Chester, the Lake District and North Wales have the highest positive co-ordinates on dimension one. However, it should be noted that Castlefield and York also have relatively high positive co-ordinates. By contrast, Alton Towers, Granada Studios, Old Trafford and Blackpool have the highest negative co-ordinates. The former group could be characterised as 'interesting', 'scenic' 'educational', 'heritage' attractions whereas, the latter could be described by the words 'fun', 'enjoyment' and 'excitement'. These terms were used by the respondents to describe what they were looking for on a day trip.

It is interesting that Alton Towers and Castlefield are very dissimilar objects in respect to dimension one, and that Alton Towers is the most preferred destination for a day trip in the stimulus set, whereas, Castlefield is the least preferred. Moreover, Castlefield's weaknesses include 'excitement' and 'fun' (Schofield, 1997). All of the above suggests that dimension one could represent one or any combination of the labels 'interesting', 'scenic' 'educational' or 'heritage'. Notably, 'interesting' and 'fun' were the freely elicited words that were listed most frequently by subjects to describe what they were looking for on a day trip.

London, Manchester, Old Trafford and Albert Dock have the highest positive co-ordinates for dimension two. These destinations are either cities or city-based tourist attractions. By contrast, the Lake District, North Wales and Camelot have both the highest negative co-ordinates and rural characteristics in common. This indicates that dimension two is spatial in nature and relates to 'urban location'.

This interpretation would also explain the position of Granada Studios referred to above. It is related to Alton Towers, Blackpool and Camelot in terms of 'excitement'/ 'fun' as opposed to 'interest'/'heritage' (dimension one) but differentiated from this cluster on the basis of its 'urban location' in Manchester (dimension two). The potentially anomalous position of York and Chester in respect to this interpretation of dimension two may result from the respondents' perception of these objects as comparatively smaller centres than the cities where the other urban-based attractions are located.

The three-dimensional solution

In an effort to gain a further understanding of the constructs underpinning the spatial configuration of the stimulus set, the model was directed to fit the data in three dimensions. The iteration history, Kruscal's (1964) stress formula 1 (1: 0.11890) and the squared correlation coefficient (RSQ) between the data and the distances (+0.87408) all indicate that a good fit exists between the model and the data. A comparison of the s-stress, Kruscal's stress 'formula 1' and the RSQ values for the two- and three-dimensional solutions with those obtained from the four-, five- and six-dimensional solutions (Table 11.17) shows that although the addition of further dimensions does improve the goodness-of-fit, the degree of improvement in the fit tapers off with the addition of the fourth and subsequent dimensions. This also indicates that the three-dimensional space is the most appropriate for this 'relatedness data' (Kruscal and Wish, 1978: 37).

The stimulus co-ordinates for the three-dimensional solution are given in Figure 4 and the plot of the relative positions of the objects derived from the co-ordinates is given in Figure 5. The addition of the third dimension has refined the configuration of objects which emerged from the two-dimensional solution. This has facilitated the identification of five clusters which, in certain cases, appeared as loosely connected larger groups of objects in two-dimensional space. For example, Chester and York have relatively high negative co-ordinates on dimension three compared with Castlefield and Albert Dock which have high positive co-ordinates. As a result, the two pairs of objects are more easily distinguishable on the basis of this dimension. Chester and York are perceived to be similar on all three dimensions, although they are least similar on the third dimension, and Castlefield is considered to be most similar to Albert Dock on all three dimensions.

It is interesting to note the position of Granada Studios relative to Castlefield and Albert Dock. Granada Studios is perceived as being similar to Blackpool, Camelot and Alton Towers on dimension one, and shares positive co-ordinates with these destinations on dimension three. However, it is perceived as being more similar to Castlefield and Albert Dock on dimension three, and is in closer proximity to these destinations and to Chester, York and Old Trafford on dimension two. As a result, it occupies a relatively unique position within the stimulus set, although it is clearly related to Castlefield and Albert Dock on the basis of dimensions two and three.

The additional dimension has confirmed the association between North Wales and the Lake District which are perceived as being 'very' similar destinations on the basis of all three dimensions. By comparison, Blackpool, Alton Towers and Camelot are perceived to be 'relatively' similar on all three dimensions. Within this cluster, Alton Towers and Blackpool are perceived to be most similar on dimension one, whilst Alton Towers and Camelot are most similar on dimensions two and three.

The final cluster comprises London, Manchester City Centre and Old Trafford. London is perceived to be closer to Old Trafford than Manchester City Centre on dimension one, although London and Manchester City Centre are perceived to be closer to each other than to

Old Trafford on the basis of dimensions two and three. Further, Old Trafford is clearly differentiated from the other two destinations on dimension three.

Figure 4   Stimulus Co-ordinates for the Three-Dimensional Solution

Stimulus Number	Stimulus Name	Dimension 1	Dimension 2	Dimension 3
1	ALBERT	+0.4094	-0.5849	+1.5122
2	ALTONTOW	-1.6844	+0.9562	+0.0990
3	BLAKPOOL	-1.3089	+0.6387	+0.0195
4	CAMELOT	-1.0027	+1.2792	+0.1322
5	CASTLE	+0.8871	-0.5554	+1.1799
6	CHESTER	+1.7815	-0.1654	-0.1799
7	GRANADA	-1.3711	-0.1227	+0.6401
8	LAKES	+1.3906	+1.4436	-0.2887
9	LONDON	-0.6472	-1.5742	-0.5285
10	MANCITY	-0.3567	-1.4834	-0.3309
11	NORWALES	+1.4129	-1.2624	-0.4183
12	OLDTRAF	-0.8068	-0.8405	-1.7451
13	YORK	+1.2964	-0.2535	-0.0917

Figure 5   Stimulus Configuration (Simple Space Map) Derived from the Co-ordinates of the Three-Dimensional Solution

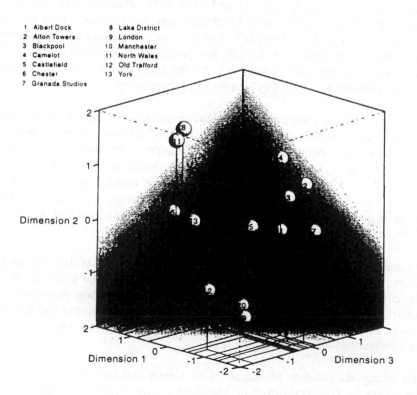

1	Albert Dock	8	Lake District
2	Alton Towers	9	London
3	Blackpool	10	Manchester
4	Camelot	11	North Wales
5	Castlefield	12	Old Trafford
6	Chester	13	York
7	Granada Studios		

Interpreting the dimensions

The three-dimensional configuration also provides a new perspective on the interpretation of the dimensions. The position of Chester, the Lake District, North Wales and York relative to Castlefield and Albert Dock on dimension one, in comparison with the configuration of these objects in two-dimensional space, indicates that this dimension relates to 'scenic interest' or 'heritage' rather than more generally 'interesting'.

A comparison of Figures 2 and 4 and Figures 3 and 5 shows that the polarity of dimension two has been reversed, although it appears to have retained its spatial characteristics. As a result, the high positive co-ordinates for the Lake District, Camelot and North Wales and the high negative co-ordinates for London, Manchester and, to a lesser extent, Old Trafford, indicate that dimension two relates to 'rural location'.

The nature of dimension three is difficult to interpret because of the absence of a prominent thread which links the objects with the highest co-ordinates. Albert Dock and Castlefield have the highest positive co-ordinates for dimension three and only Old Trafford has high negative co-ordinates. Moreover, there are a range of different types of attractions occupying the lower and middle ground of both the positive, but particularly the negative sections of the construct. Given the configuration of these destinations, it is possible that the dimension relates to either new types of attraction and forms of tourism as opposed to more traditional pursuits, or to 'special interest' tourism compared with recreation that has more general appeal. Albert Dock, Castlefield and Granada Studios are 'new tourism' attractions (Poon, 1993). They are 'manufactured' visitor attractions and tourism is their *raison d'etre*. By comparison, Old Trafford, London, Manchester City Centre, North Wales and the Lake District are more traditional visitor destinations which owe their existence to a wider range of factors.

Albert Dock and Castlefield are similar in terms of their museum/ heritage special interest and Granada Studios has a Coronation Street/media theme special interest. By comparison, the objects with negative co-ordinates have a much broader base of interest. In many cases this relates to size of the destinations, for example, London or Chester. Old Trafford's high negative co-ordinates on dimension three may, however, represent a problem for the 'special interest' interpretation. Arguably, the attraction of Old Trafford is a special interest in Manchester United and/ or football. On this basis, the 'new tourism' (as opposed to a more traditional tourism) interpretation of dimension three would appear to be less problematic than the 'special interest' label.

It should be noted that Old Trafford is a special case in relation to the other objects in the stimulus set. Feedback obtained from subjects during the debrief indicated that the attraction of Old Trafford was the football match as opposed to the museum and guided tours of the ground. It is therefore, an ephemeral visitor attraction by comparison with the other destinations. This does not, however, adversely affect the 'new tourism' interpretation of dimension three.

A 'neighbourhood' interpretation of the object clusters, and in particular, the position of Granada Studios relative to Castlefield and Albert Dock in the three-dimensional stimulus configuration, also supports the 'new tourism' 'dimensional' interpretation. In comparison with the clusters of more traditional tourist attractions, Granada Studios, Castlefield and Albert Dock represent 'new tourism' destinations. This could also indicate that the attraction of these places is 'different' or 'a change from the usual' - freely-elicited terms used by respondents (see Chapter 8) because 'new tourists' are more discerning visitors in search of a different experience whilst demanding quality, choice and value for money (Poon, 1993).

Positioning Castlefield's tourism 'product'

The objective of a positioning strategy is to create an appropriate concept in the mind of the consumer with competitive products as an explicit or implicit frame of reference. A desired positioning is one that clearly distinguishes a destination's image from its competitors on 'product' attributes that are considered to be important (Moutinho, 1987). Moreover, effective positioning will insulate the 'product' from competition and enhance its market performance (Park, Jaworski and MacInnis, 1986).

The results of the MDS analysis together with the evidence presented elsewhere have highlighted a number of important implications for positioning Castlefield relative to perceived competitive offerings. Clearly, all of the 'preferred' destinations represent a significant threat on the basis that the majority of potential visitors are likely to patronise a variety of different destinations which offer a wide range of perceived benefits. However, the spatial configuration of objects in the three-dimensional solution suggests that Castlefield is positioned against, and in direct competition with Albert Dock because it is perceived to be similar on all three dimensions.

The three-dimensional MDS solution indicates that 'heritage', 'urban location' and 'new tourism' are Castlefield's key constructs. Clearly, the destination has a comparative advantage in 'industrial' heritage, the 'unique selling proposition' that the official promotional literature attempts to exploit. This reflects a typical 'product-orientation' rooted in supply side considerations. The evidence presented here and elsewhere (Schofield, 1997), however, suggests that the extant 'single-benefit positioning' (Kotler and Armstrong, 1994) strategy may not be the most viable option given the wide range of variables which have a greater influence on the respondents, and 'new tourists' generally, in their choice of day trip destination. This finding is supported by empirical evidence from a wide range of heritage attractions (see Herbert, 1995). Moreover, since many people do not travel alone to tourist attractions, destinations which offer many benefits are more capable of satisfying the range of preferences that are found even within small groups of visitors.

Castlefield could differentiate its 'product' and gain a competitive advantage by combining the destination's unique heritage resources with its other strengths (attributes which are both important and believed to be part of its 'product'). The strengths include such perceived benefits as its varied, high quality attractions and facilities, value for money, atmosphere and a convenient location. By comparison, Castlefield's weaknesses, namely the perceived absence of 'nightlife', 'shopping', 'excitement' and 'fun' at the destination, and their influence on its current position must also be given careful consideration. The destination's position on dimension one relative to Albert Dock and in relation to destinations such as Alton Towers and Blackpool which have perceived benefits that include 'fun', 'enjoyment' and 'excitement', is interesting in this respect.

Conclusions

The identification of a number of object clusters in day trip product space together with the interpretation of the two- and three-dimensional configurations indicates that the experience which is sought by day trip tourists can potentially be satisfied by a number of alternative and directly competing destinations. In turn, this suggests both that product differentiation is an important strategic priority in this marketplace, and that a clear and simple message must be created and transmitted to the relevant target markets. The effectiveness of a destination's image in terms of developing a predisposition to visit the place, will depend on its ease of recognition and a minimum of dissonance with the pre-existing prejudices of the consumer in addition to highlighting the benefits which are important from the consumer perspective.

Given the research findings, the aforementioned considerations and the image of Castlefield in relation to Manchester's overall brand values, the most viable strategy for the destination is 'triple-benefit positioning' (Kotler et al, 1999) with a focus on quality, value and choice within the context of its heritage resources. This could potentially position Castlefield more effectively as a distinct and valued place in the mind of the consumer. Additional benefits from this strategic orientation include the avoidance of conflict which typically arises over the issue of whether to project a specific or a general image, and because the strategy is based on consumer perceptions, there is less risk of a discrepancy between the image projected by the agents responsible for marketing the destination and that received by prospective consumers.

Fallon (1989) refers to the process of identifying the 'essence' of a product and effectively communicating it as 'building bridges'. This term seems appropriate to Castlefield, where some of the most prominent visual features of the site are the Victorian railway and canal bridges. Indeed, the logo of the Castlefield Management Company is a canal bridge. Use of the term 'building bridges' in this context is, however, somewhat ironic given the considerable gap between contemporary visitor needs and the supply of facilities, resulting from the destination's overall 'product-orientation' and the lack of both a research-based strategy and a heritage interpretation plan for the site.

References

Ahmed, Z.U. (1991), The influence of the components of a state's tourist image on product positioning strategy, *Tourism Management*, December, pp. 331-355.

Bowman, C. H. and Fishbein, M. (1978), Understanding public reactions to energy proposals: an application of the Fishbein model, *Journal of Applied Social Psychology*, Vol. 8 (October – December), pp. 319-340.

Cable, T. Knudson, D. M., Udd, E. and Stewart, D. J. (1987), Attitude changes as a result of exposure to interpretive messages, *Journal of Park and Recreation Administration*, Vol. 5, pp. 47-60.

Child, D. (1970), *The Essentials of Factor Analysis*, Holt, Rinehart and Winston, London.

Coxon, A. P. M. (1982), *The User's Guide To Multidimensional Scaling*, Chauser Press, London.

Dilley, R. (1986), *Tourist brochures and tourist images*, The Canadian Geographer, 30 (1), pp. 59-65.

Dolnicar, S., Grabler, K and Mazanec, J. A. (1999*), A Tale of three cities: perceptual charting for analysing destination images*, A. G. Woodside et al (Editors) Consumer Psychology of Tourism, Hospitality and Leisure, CABI, Oxford, pp. 39-62.

Fallon, P. (1989), cited in J. M. Collins, Image and advertising, *Harvard Business Review*, Jan - Feb, pp. 93-97.

Fishbein, M. (1967), A consideration of beliefs, and their role in attitude measurement, M. A. Fishbein (Editor) *Readings in Attitude Theory and Measurement*, John Wiley, New York, pp. 257-266.

Fishbein, M. and Ajzen, I. (1975), *Belief, Attitude, Intention, Behaviour: An Introduction to Theory and Research*, Reading, Addison-Wesley, Reading, MA.

Gartner, W. C. (1989), Tourism image: attribute measurement of state tourism products using multi-dimensional scaling techniques, *Journal of Travel Research*, Vol. 28 (2): 16-20.

Glassman, M. and Fitzhenry, N. (1976), Fishbein's subjective norm: theoretical considerations and empirical evidence, *Advances in Consumer Research*, Vol. 3, Association for Consumer Research, Ann Arbor, MI., pp. 477-484.

Goodrich, J. N. (1978), The relationship between preference for and perception of vacation destinations: application of a choice model, *Journal of Travel Research*, Vol. 17 (2): pp. 8-13.

Guttman, L. (1965), *The structure of interrelations among intelligence texts, Proceedings of the 1964 Invitational Conference on Testing Problems*, Education Testing Service, Princeton, pp. 25-36.

Guttman, L. (1968), *A general non-metric technique for finding the smallest co-ordinate space for a configuration of points*, Psychometrica, Vol. 33 (4): 469-506.

Haahti, A. J. (1986), Finland's competitive positioning as a destination, *Annals of Tourism Research*, Vol. 13, pp. 11-26.

Herbert, D. T. (Editor) (1995), *Heritage, Tourism and Society*, Belhaven, London.

Hoffman, D. L. and Perreault, W. D. (1987), *Consumer preference and perception*, F. W. Young (Editor) Multidimensional Scaling: History, Theory and Applications, Erlbaum, New Jersey.

Howard, J. A. and Sheth, J. N. (1969), *The Theory of Buyer Behaviour*, Wiley, New York.

Kantola, S. J., Syme, G. J. and Campbell, N. A. (1982), The role of individual differences and external variables in a test of the sufficiency of Fishbein's model to explain behavioural intentions to conserve water, *Journal of Applied Social Psychology*, Vol. 12 (January – February), pp. 70-83.

Kaiser, H. F. (1974), An index of factorial simplicity, *Psychometrica*, Vol. 39, pp. 31-36.

Kotler, P., Armstrong, G., Saunders, J. and Wong, V. (1999), *Principles of Marketing*, Prentice Hall, London.

Kruscal, J. B. (1964), Multidimensional scaling by optimising goodness-of-fit to a nonmetric hypothesis, *Psychometrika*, Vol. 29 (1): 1-28.

Kruscal, J. B. and Wish, M. (1978), *Multidimensional Scaling*, Sage University Paper Series on Quantitative Applications in the Social Sciences, 7-11. Sage Publications, Beverley Hills.

La Page, W. F. and Cormier, P. L. (1977), Images of camping - barriers to participation, *Journal of Travel Research*, Vol. 15 (4): 21-25.

Mayo, E .J. (1973), *Regional images and regional travel behaviour*, Proceedings of the Travel Research Association 4th Annual Conference, August 12-15, Salt Lake City, Utah, pp. 211-218.

McCarty, D. (1981), Changing contraceptive usage intentions: a test of the Fishbein model of intention, *Journal of Applied Social Psychology*, Vol. 11 (May – June), pp. 192 – 211.

Moutinho, L. (1987), Consumer behaviour in tourism, *European Journal of Marketing*, Vol. 21 (1): 34-39.

Myers, J. H. and Tauber, E. (1977), *Market Structure Analysis*, American Marketing Association, Chicago.

Park, C. W. Jaworski, B. J. and MacInnis, D. J. (1986), Strategic brand concept-image management, *Journal of Marketing*, Vol. 50 (October), pp. 135-145.

Phelps, A. (1986), *Holiday destination image - the problem of assessment: an example developed in Menorca,* Tourism Management, Vol. 7 (3): 168-180.

Pizam, A. Neuman, Y. Reichel, A. (1978), Dimensions of tourist satisfaction with a destination area, *Annals of Tourism Research*, Vol. 5 (3): 314-322.

Poon, A. (1993), *Tourism, Technology and Competitive Strategies*, Wallingford, Oxford, CAB International.

Reilly, M. D. (1990), Free elicitation of descriptive adjectives for tourism image assessment, *Journal of Travel Research*, Vol. 28 (Spring) pp 21-26.

Ryan, M. and Bonfield, E. H. (1980), Fishbein's intention model: a test of external and pragmatic validity, *Journal of Marketing*, Vol. 44 (Spring), pp. 82-95.

Saleh, F. and Ryan, C. (1992), Client perception of hotels – a multi-attribute approach, *Tourism Management*, Vol. 13 (2): 163-168.

Schofield, P. (1997), *Tourist destination images: a cognitive-behavioural approach to the study of day trip tourism and the strategic marketing of Castlefield Urban Heritage Park*, Unpublished Doctoral Dissertation, University of Manchester.

Schofield, P. (1999), *Deciphering day trip destination choice using a tourist expectation/satisfaction construct: a comparative analysis of scale construction techniques*, Woodside, A. and Mazanec, J. (Editors) Consumer Psychology of Travel, Hospitality and Leisure CAB International, London.

Scott, D. R., Schewe, C. D. and Frederick, D. G. (1978), A multi-brand/multi-attribute model of tourist state choice, *Journal of Travel Research*, Vol. 17 (1): 23-29.

Shepard, R. N. (1962), The analysis of proximities: multidimensional scaling with an unknown distance function I and II, *Psychometrica*, Vol. 27 (1): 125-139 and 219-246.

Sheppard, B. H., Hartwick, J. and Warshaw, P. R. (1988), The theory of reasoned action: a meta-analysis of past research with recommendations for modifications and future research, *Journal of Consumer Research*, Vol. 15 (December), pp. 325-343.

Smith, S. L. J. (1989), *Tourism Analysis*: A Handbook, Longman, London.

Stabler, M. J. (1988), *The image of destination regions: theoretical and empirical aspects*, Goodall, B. and Ashworth, G. (Editors) Marketing in the Tourism Industry, Croom Helm, Beckenham, UK.

Sternquist-Witter, B. (1985), Attitudes about a resort area: a comparison of tourists and local retailers, *Journal of Travel Research*, Vol. 24 (1): 14-19.

Thompson, J. R. and Cooper, P. D. Dimension (1979), Additional evidence on the limited size of evoked and inept sets of travel destinations, *Journal of Travel Research*, Vol. 18, pp. 23-25.

Tourism Canada (1988), *Pleasure Travel Markets to North America - Switzerland, Hong Kong, Singapore – Highlights* Report, March, Prepared by Market Facts of Canada, Tourism Canada, Ottawa, Ontario.

Um, S. and Crompton, J. L. (1990), Attitude determinants in pleasure travel destination choice, *Annals of Tourism Research*, Vol. 17 (2): 432-448.

Urban, G. L. and Hauser, J. R. (1993), *Design and marketing of New Products*, 2nd Edition, Prentice-Hall, Englewood Cliffs, New Jersey.

Warshaw, R., Calantone, R. and Joyce, M. (1986), A field application of the Fishbein and Ajzen intention model, *Journal of Social Psychology*, Vol. 126 (February), pp. 135-136.

Wilson, D. T., Mathews, H. L. and Harvey, J. W. (1975), An empirical test of the Fishbein intention model, *Journal of Consumer Research*, Vol. 1 (March), pp. 39-48.

Woodside, A. G. and Lysonski, S. (1989), A general model of traveller destination choice, *Journal of Travel Research*, Vol. 27 (4): 8-14.

Woodside, A. G. and Sherell, D. (1977), Travellers' evoked, inept, and inert sets of vacation destinations, *Journal of Travel Research*, Vol. 16 (4): 14-18.

Yi, Y. (1990), A critical review of consumer satisfaction, V. A. Zeithaml (Editor) *Review of Marketing*, American Marketing Association.

Young, R. A. and Kent, A. (1985), Using the theory of reasoned action to improve the understanding of recreation behaviour, *Journal of Leisure Research*, Vol. 17, pp. 90-106.

Young, F. W. and Harris, D. F. (1994), Multidimensional Scaling, M.J. Norusis, SPSS Professional Statistics 6.1, SPSS Inc., Chicago, pp. 155-222.

The road to world heritage site designation: Derwent Valley Mills, a work in progress

Karen A Smith

University of Greenwich, UK

Introduction

Tourism plays an important role in World Heritage Sites and this paper considers how individual sites attempt to attain this much coveted status. Whilst the formal process for evaluating World Heritage nominations is clearly set out; what is less evident is how a site becomes a candidate for nomination. This process will be appraised by examining the recent review of the United Kingdom's 'tentative list' of potential nominations to UNESCO (The United Nations Educational, Scientific and Cultural Organisation). In response to a perceived dominance on the World Heritage List of cultural sites and sites focusing on palaces, cathedrals and historic towns in Western Europe (Department of Culture, Media and Sport, 1999c; UNESCO, 1999a), the review emphasised a number of themes. One of the key themes identified was industrial heritage, and the significance of this refocusing will be discussed. The process of nomination, described by Shackley (1998) as complex, lengthy and expensive, is reviewed from the perspective of one applicant: the industrial heritage site of Derwent Valley Mills, in Derbyshire, UK. This includes a consideration of the motivations for seeking designation, the potential impacts of inscription, the application process, and the stakeholders involved.

World heritage sites

The *Convention for the Protection of the World's Cultural and Natural Heritage* was formerly adopted by UNESCO in 1972. The *Convention* embodies the view that "parts of the cultural or natural heritage are of outstanding interest and therefore need to be preserved as part of the world heritage of mankind as a whole" (UNESCO, 1972:1). UNESCO and those State Parties (i.e. countries) that have ratified the *Convention*, currently 158 nations, thus seek to identify, protect and preserve cultural and natural heritage sites that are of 'outstanding universal value'. The mechanism for this is the World Heritage List. There are currently 630 sites across 118 state parties inscribed on the World Heritage List (UNESCO, 1999c); of these, 480 are cultural, 128 natural and 22 are mixed properties, also known as cultural landscapes. The *Convention* sets out definitions of the categories (see UNESCO, 1972: Articles 1 and 2) and criteria for the inclusion of sites on the World Heritage List is presented in subsequent *Operational Guidelines* (for example, see UNESCO, 1996b: paragraphs 24 and 44).

Inclusion on the World Heritage List is essentially honorific and the existing rights and obligations of owners and planning authorities are unaffected (DCMS, 1998a). Inscription brings both benefits and responsibilities, including: "[a]...duty of protection and a management programme which is subject to monitoring" (Pocock, 1997b:383), whilst resulting in no guarantee of extra funding (Shackley, 1998). Nevertheless, World Heritage status is a highly sought-after and coveted prize (Drost, 1996), particularly because of the potential for tourism. Although the correlation between World Heritage status and visitor numbers is not straight forward as many sites are already popular tourist destinations before designation (Drost, 1996), in general, the status and publicity generated by inscription leads to an increase in visitors (Shackley, 1998).

The designation process

The process of obtaining World Heritage Status is described by Shackley (1998) as complex, lengthy and expensive. Figure 1 illustrates the formal nomination process. Individual sites are nominated through their 'State Party'. The application is submitted to the UNESCO who co-ordinate their World Heritage activities through the World Heritage Centre, created in 1992. Applications are passed to the International Council on Monuments and Sites (ICOMOS) and/or the World Conservation Union (IUCN), the non-governmental organisations who act as UNESCO's technical advisors on cultural and natural sites respectively. It is ICOMOS and IUCN who visit the sites and evaluate the application, including assessing whether the site is of 'outstanding universal value'. Their technical report is then evaluated by the World Heritage Bureau, a seven member executive body made up of representatives of the full World Heritage Committee. The Bureau either make a recommendation on the site or seeks further information from the State Party. The final decision is made by the World Heritage Committee, composed of twenty-one representatives from State Parties who have ratified the Convention. They have three options: inscribe the site; defer the decision pending further information; or refuse the inscription. The process from nomination through evaluation to decision-making, takes at least a year and a half. Nominations have to be with UNESCO by 1st July each year and a final decision is usually made a year and a half later at the annual meeting of the World Heritage Committee each December.

Figure 1   Nominating Procedure for World Heritage Status

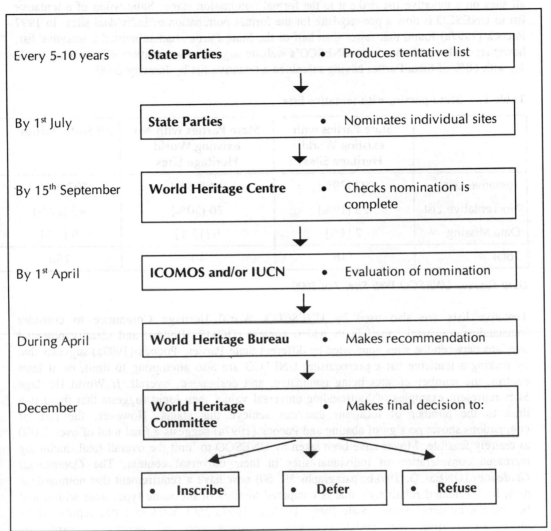

| Every 5-10 years | **State Parties** | • Produces tentative list |

| By 1ˢᵗ July | **State Parties** | • Nominates individual sites |

| By 15ᵗʰ September | **World Heritage Centre** | • Checks nomination is complete |

| By 1ˢᵗ April | **ICOMOS and/or IUCN** | • Evaluation of nomination |

| During April | **World Heritage Bureau** | • Makes recommendation |

| December | **World Heritage Committee** | • Makes final decision to: |

• **Inscribe**   • **Defer**   • **Refuse**

After: UNESCO (1999b)

Whilst the procedure following nomination is clearly set out, what is less evident is the process *before* formal nomination. This will form the focus of this paper, and will be illustrated by examination of the case of a current potential nominee: Derwent Valley Mills, in Derbyshire, UK.

Tentative lists

Article 11 (1) of the *World Heritage Convention* established the requirement for State Parties to prepare and submit an 'inventory of property', referred to as a 'tentative list' in the *Operational Guidelines*, to the World Heritage Committee (UNESCO, 1996a). Tentative lists are seen as a 'plan of action' for the next five to ten years and include details of sites to be considered for nomination, although, as will be illustrated using the case of the UK, not all sites on a tentative list make it to the formal nomination stage. Submission of a tentative list to UNESCO is now a pre-requisite for the formal nomination of individual sites. In 1997 Pocock (1997a) found that fewer than half of the State Parties had submitted a tentative list, however, analysis of data from UNESCO's website suggests the situation is improving (table 1), with 68% of State Parties having submitted a tentative list by January 2000.

Table 1   State parties with tentative lists

	State Parties with existing World Heritage Sites	State Parties with No existing World Heritage Sites	All State Parties
Tentative List	93 [79%]	14 [35%]	107 [68%]
No Tentative List	23 [19%]	20 [50%]	43 [27%]
Data Missing	2 [2%]	6 [15%]	8 [5%]
Total	118	40	158

Data Source: UNESCO Web Site, Jan 2000

Tentative lists are also used by UNESCO's World Heritage Committee to consider 'outstanding universal value' in its widest context (DCMS, 1999b), and identify potential overlaps between the sites nominated by different State Parties. Pocock (1997a) suggests that by making a tentative list a prerequisite, UNESCO are also attempting to limit, or at least control, the number of sites being nominated, and designated, overall. If World Heritage Sites represent examples of 'outstanding universal value' then logic suggests that there is a limit to the number of locations that can achieve this status. However, the rate of nominations shows no sign of abating and Pocock (1997a) suggests a final total of over 1,000 as entirely feasible. Moves have been taken by UNESCO to limit the overall total, including increased consideration of individual sites in their universal context. The *Operational Guidelines* (UNESCO, 1996b: paragraphs 59, 60) now have a requirement that nominations must be 'evaluated relatively', that is compared to sites of the same type, both within and beyond the borders of their State Party. Pocock (1997a:266) notes that this represents "a move away from the initial emphasis on uniqueness of heritage towards its representativeness".

World heritage sites in the UK

The United Kingdom ratified the World Heritage Convention in 1984, and although it withdrew from UNESCO in 1985, non-membership does not prevent the nomination of sites for World Heritage Status (Shackley, 1998). The election of the current Labour government signalled a renewed interest in World Heritage and in 1997 the Government rejoined UNESCO (UNESCO, 1997a), affirmed its commitment to the World Heritage Convention and announced a review of the UK's tentative list of sites (DCMS, 1998a). The first UK tentative list was submitted in 1986 and included thirty-six sites. Of the thirty UK-based properties, eighteen have been successfully inscribed as World Heritage Sites, the latest being 'The Heart of Neolithic Orkney' in late 1999. This paper will focus on UK-based sites although it is important to note that the UK also acts as State Party for its territories, for example, Henderson Island in the South Pacific and Gough Island Wildlife Reserve in the South Atlantic.

The Department of Culture, Media and Sport (DCMS) is the government department responsible for World Heritage Sites in the UK. DCMS (1999b) stress that the tentative list is an indication of the Government's intentions concerning nominations and a site's inclusion does not automatically mean that it will be nominated. In his 1997b review of World Heritage Sites in the UK, Pocock tracked the subsequent history of the 30 UK sites on the 1985 tentative list. Updating this information (table 2), of the thirty initial sites, fifteen have been successfully inscribed (including Studley Royal Park and Fountains Abbey Ruins which was not on the original list); three were nominated and rejected; the decision was deferred on four sites; and twelve were formally withdrawn, at different stages of the process.

Table 2   UK tentative list of world heritage sites, 1985, showing subsequent history of each site

Site	Type of site	Nominated	Accepted	Rejected	Deferred	Withdrawn
Castles and Town Walls of King Edward I in Gwynedd	C	1986	1986			
Durham Cathedral and Castle	C	1986	1986			
Giant's Causeway and Causeway Coast	N	1986	1986			
Ironbridge Gorge	C	1986	1986			
St Kilda	N	1986	1986			
Stonehenge, Avebury and Associated Sites	C	1986	1986			
Studley Royal Park and Fountains Abbey Ruins[1]	C	1986	1986			
Lough Erne Ecclesiastical Sites	C	1987			1987	
New Lanark	C	1987				1988
St David's Close and Bishop's Palace	C	1987		1987		1992
Blenheim Palace	C	1987	1987			
City of Bath	C	1987	1987			
Hadrian's Wall Roman Military Zone	C	1987	1987			
Westminster Palace and Abbey, St Margaret's Church	C	1987	1987			
Lake District[2]	N	1987 1989			1989	1992
Historic Cambridge Colleges	C	1988		1988		1992
Mainland Orkney Archaeological Sites	C	1988			1988	
Menai and Conway Suspension Bridges	C	1988				1988
Navan Fort	C	1988			1988	1992
SS Gt Britain and Western Docks, Bristol	C	1988				1988
Canterbury Cathedral, St Augustine's Abbey, St Margaret's Church	C	1988	1988			
Tower of London	C	1988	1988			
Edinburgh Old and New Towns	C	1995	1995			
Maritime Greenwich	C	1997	1997			
Careleon Legionary Fortress	C					1992
Chatsworth	C					1992
Cregnesh, Isle of Man	C					1992
Lacock	C					1992
St Patrick's Isle, Isle of Man	C					1990
Stourhead	C					1992
The Wash and North Norfolk Coast	N					1994

[1] not included on original 1985 Tentative List.
[2] included on 1985 Tentative List as a natural site; initially nominated in 1987 as a 'mixed site', resubmitted and rejected as cultural site in 1989
After Pocock (1997:382, table 1); Additional data: UNESCO (1997b)

Revision of the UK tentative list

The UK tentative list has recently gone through a major review. This began in October 1997 when DCMS announced the review, sought nominations, and set up a committee, under the Chair of English Heritage, comprising experts in built and natural heritage to advise on potential sites in England, the Overseas Territories and Crown Dependencies (DCMS, 1998a). Scotland, Wales and Northern Ireland made their own arrangements for the review, however there was close liaison to ensure an integrated proposal for the UK as a whole (DCMS, 1998b; 1999c).

In August 1998, DCMS began a period of public consultation with the publication of *UNESCO World Heritage Sites: a consultation paper on a new United Kingdom tentative list of future nominations* (DCMS, 1998b). The thirty-two sites discussed in the Consultation Review were the result of a consideration of a much larger number of proposals from a range of sources including private and public organisations and individuals, as well as by members of the Review Committees themselves. For example, the *Consultation Paper* (DCMS, 1998b) lists 121 English sites considered for inclusion, of which only fourteen made the final public consultation process.

The aim of the public consultation was to obtain views on the thirty-two 'front-runners', partly to seek comments on those selected and also to judge whether there had been any important omissions (DCMS, 1998a). Comments were particularly sought on the "...significance of the sites proposed and on the practical inclusions on the list" (DCMS, 1998b:6). The consultation process aimed to include the views of a wide range of stakeholders. The full consultation document was published both on paper and on the DCMS website. The document was sent to all local authorities, the owners and managers of proposed sites, and heritage and conservation bodies (DCMS, 1999a). Views were also sought from local communities: those living and working in or near the proposed sites. The two month consultation period ended on 30th October 1998; overall 500 organisations and individuals were involved and over 420 responses were received (DCMS, 1999a). The formal announcement of the new UK tentative list was made on 6th April 1999 (DCMS, 1999a) and submitted to UNESCO in June of the same year (DCMS, 1999b). A further review of the list is planned for five years' time (DCMS, 1999a).

Identification of world heritage themes

As with World Heritage Sites across the world, in the UK and its territories, cultural rather than natural inscriptions dominate (see table 2). Of the current eighteen UK sites, only four are natural, of which two are in overseas territories; the remaining fourteen sites are all UK-based cultural inscriptions. The tentative list review identified eleven key cultural themes amongst the current inscriptions:

- prehistoric ceremonial monuments;

- impact of the Roman Empire;

- origins of Christianity and the development and transmission of medieval culture;

- Gothic ecclesiastical architecture;

- development of medieval fortification;

- urban planning and development;

- public buildings;

- great houses;

- planned landscapes and gardens;

- industrial revolution; and

- Britain's global influence.

The review judged the spread of current UK designations and sought to identify categories where the UK's cultural heritage is under-represented in terms of World Heritage Sites (DCMS, 1998b). At a global level UNESCO and ICOMOS have identified that certain 'European' types of cultural property are disproportionately represented on the List (ICOMOS, 2000). The DCMS review thus placed the UK in the wider context of Western Europe and identified that some themes, for example, great country houses and palaces, cathedrals and historic towns, are adequately represented at present, if not within the UK at least within Western European cultural sites. Compilation of the tentative list therefore focused on the remaining cultural categories (DCMS, 1998b): Christian origins and the development and transfer of learning and culture, planned landscapes and gardens, and in particular the UK's industrial heritage and global influence; together with natural sites and cultural landscapes.

In presenting the final list, DCMS (1999c) acknowledged the selectivity of the process and discussed the criteria on which the tentative list sites were selected. These factors included: meeting the UNESCO World Heritage criteria; identifying sites in which the UK has made outstanding contributions to the world's heritage, and those themes and regions which are currently under-represented; practical and resource considerations, including designations that can be achieved within the timescale of the next decade; and due to the importance of "positive management and co-ordination to achieve the appropriate balance between conservation, access, the interests of the local community and economic benefit" (DCMS, 1999c:8), a requirement that each site has a body which either has or will take responsibility for the nomination and management of the site.

Of the thirty-two sites considered in the Consultation Review, the themes of industrialisation and Britain's global influence dominated, with nine and seven sites respectively. This paper will focus on the first of these two themes: industrial heritage.

Industrial heritage

The preservation and an appreciation of the value of industrial heritage has been a theme of increasing importance within both the heritage sector in general (for example see Ball and Stobart, 1996; Edwards and Llurdés, 1996; Palmer and Neaverson, 1994; Rudd and Davis, 1998) and in terms of World Heritage.

In 1994 a meeting of the World Heritage Committee considered a 'Global Strategy' for World Heritage to "ensure that the List reflects the world's cultural and natural diversity of outstanding universal value" (UNESCO, 1999a:1). A key issue under discussion was how the concept of cultural heritage had developed in meaning, depth and extent since the World Heritage Convention had first been ratified in 1972. Two key intentions were identified at the meeting:

> *"...rectification of the imbalances on the List between regions of the world, types of monument, and periods, and at the same time a move away from a purely architectural view of the cultural heritage of humanity towards one which was much more anthropological, multi-functional, and universal."* (World Heritage Committee, 1994:4)

A thematic approach to world heritage was therefore proposed in order to consider this wider notion of cultural heritage: "only by means of this thematic approach would it be possible to appreciate cultural properties in their full range of functions and meanings" (World Heritage Committee, 1994:6). The implementation of this strategy is evident on the World Heritage Centre website which includes lists of heritage sites by themes, including: cultural landscapes, hominid sites, rock art sites, industrial heritage, and urban sites, primarily historic cities and towns. However, a recent paper by ICOMOS (2000) suggests that the latest inscriptions have not yet made a significant impact on the imbalance of types of cultural properties with cultural landscapes, industrial heritage and the heritage of the twentieth century still disproportionaly under-represented. Although strategically World Heritage has broaden its definition of cultural heritage, in terms of inscribed sites, an 'elitist' approach to cultural heritage still remains.

One of the key themes identified in the *Global Strategy* was 'evidence of technological evolution' (UNESCO, 1999a), i.e. industrial heritage. The process of industrialisation can have a tremendous impact on both landscapes and peoples. Recognition of industrial heritage is particularly important because industrialisation implies change, much of which is ongoing: "rapid technological advances and the striping of certain deposits [has] rendered most industrial sites obsolete" (UNESCO, 2000:1). World Heritage inscription has thus been used to preserve examples of mines, factories, transportation and engineering, usually within their wider landscape context as it is the interaction between the various elements that makes an industrial landscape valuable (Palmer and Neaverson, 1994:188):

> *"A textile mill, for example, can only function with a supply of raw materials, a power source, means of production, a workforce and a system of distribution to its market."*

Currently twenty-five World Heritage Sites are grouped under the industrial heritage theme (UNESCO, 2000); twenty of which are located in Europe (see table 3). However, some of these sites were inscribed principally for reasons other than their technological significance (Cleere, 1999), often on the basis of their aesthetic appeal. For example, a number of the historic towns, including Kutná Hora in the Czech Republic and Røros in Norway, were nominated primarily because of their architecture and town plans.

Table 3   Industrial world heritage sites, by year of inscription

Year of inscription	Site, State Party
1978	Wieliczka Salt Mine, Poland
1980	Historic Town of Ouro Preto, Brazil
	Røros, Norway
1982	Royal Saltworks of Arc-et-Senans, France
1985	Old Town of Segovia and its Aqueduct, Spain
	Pont du Gard (Roman Aqueduct), France
1986	Ironbridge Gorge, UK
1988	Historic Town of Guanajuato and Adjacent Mines, Mexico
1992	Mines of Rammelsberg and Historic Town of Goslar, Germany
1993	Banska Stiavnica, Slovakia
	Engelsberg Ironworks, Sweden
	Historic Centre of Zacatecas, Mexico
1994	Völklingen Ironworks, Germany
1995	Crespi d'Adda, Italy
	Kutná Hora: Historical Town Centre with the Church of St Barbara and the Cathedral of Our Lady at Sedlec, Czech Republic
1996	Canal du Midi, France
	Verla Groundwood and Board Mill, Finland
1997	City of Potosi, Bolivia
	Hallstatt-Dachstein Salzkammergut Cultural Landscape, Austria
	Las Médulas, Spain
	Mill Network at Kinderdijk-Elshout, Netherlands
1998	Ir.D.F. Woudagemaal (D.F. Wouda Steam Pumping Station), Netherlands
	Semmering Railway, Austria
	The Four Lifts on the Canal du Centre and their Environs, La Louvière and Le Roeulx (Hainault), Belgium
1999	Darjeeling Himalayan Railway, India

After: UNESCO (2000)

To address the under-representation of industrial heritage identified in the *Global Strategy*, UNESCO sought the assistance of The International Committee for the Conservation of the

Industrial Heritage (TICCIH), in preparing authoritative studies of different sectors of industrial heritage to aid in evaluating world heritage nominations. To date, studies of historic bridges, canals, railways and 'company towns' have been completed, with those on food, non-ferrous mining, coal mines, and textiles currently in progress (ICOMOS, 2000).

As has been discussed above, Britain's fundamental global role in industrialisation was a key theme identified in the tentative list review as under-represented in World Heritage designations. Currently Ironbridge Gorge, one of the first wave of UK sites inscribed in 1986, is the only illustration of the importance of the UK as the 'birthplace' of the industrial revolution. Further sub-division of the industrialisation theme recognised five key areas within which outstandingly representative sites could be identified:

- industrialisation of processing and manufacture;

- developments in inland transport;

- prowess in generating;

- using power, virtuosity in civil engineering; and

- innovation in telecommunications

The consultative review considered a range of sites, ultimately identifying nine across the first four sub-divisions. No site was recommended which the review committee considered represented the twentieth century innovation in telecommunications, and this was left for consideration in future reviews of the tentative list (DCMS, 1998b). The two Welsh, three Scottish, and four English sites identified as outstanding examples of industrialisation are shown in table 4, along with the industrialisation sub-divisions they represent, and the wider UNESCO cultural criteria they characterise.

Table 4   World heritage assessment of united kingdom industrial sites

	Blaenavon Industrial Landscape, Wales [1]	Cornish Mining Industry, England	*Dallas Dhu Distillery, Scotland* [2]	Derwent Valley Mills, England	Forth Fail Bridge, Scotland	Manchester (Ancoats, Castlefield & Worsley), England	New Lanark, Scotland	The Great Western Railway: Paddington-Bristol (selected parts), England	Pont-Cysyllte Aqueduct, Wales	Saltaire, England [3]
INDUSTRIAL SUB-THEME										
1. Industrialisation of process and manufacturing	✓	✓	✓	✓		✓				
2. Developments in inland transport								✓	✓	
3. Prowess in generating and using power	✓	✓		✓		✓				
4. Virtuosity in civil engineering	✓				✓			✓	✓	
5. Innovation in telecommunications										
UNESCO CULTURAL CRITERIA										
i. Represent a masterpiece of human creative genius	✓			✓			✓	✓		
ii. Exhibit an important interchange of human values on development in architecture or technology, monumental arts, town planning or landscape design	✓	✓	✓	✓	✓	✓	✓	✓	✓	✓
iii. Bear a unique or at least exceptional testimony to a cultural tradition or to a civilisation	✓	✓	✓	✓	✓					✓
iv. Be an outstanding example of a type of building or architecture or technological assemblage or landscape which illustrates (a) significant stage(s) in human history	✓	✓	✓	✓			✓	✓	✓	✓
v. Be an outstanding example of a traditional human settlement or land use which is representation of a culture	✓									
vi. Be directly or tangibly associated with events or living tradition, with ideas, or with beliefs, with artistic and literary works of outstanding universal significance			✓				✓			

[1] Names used are those adopted in the final Tentative List
[2] Dallas Dhu Distillery was on the Consultative List but not selected for the Final Tentative List
[3] Saltaire was added to the Final Tentative List but was not on the Consultative List

After: DCMS (1998b;1999c)

Following public consultation, the thirty-two sites in the tentative review were reduced to twenty-five, including three in overseas territories. Twenty-three of the sites had been included in the consultation document; Saltaire and Shakespeare's Stratford were additions from the consultative process. These are the sites that the UK will nominate to UNESCO for consideration as World Heritage Sites over the next five to ten years. However, the UK have not followed UNESCO's guidelines that the order in which properties are to be presented for inscription should ideally be indicated (UNESCO, 1996b). Apart from the submission of Blaenavon Industrial Landscape, Wales and the Town of St. George, Bermuda in 1999, and the potential year 2000 nominations of New Lanark, and Dorset and East Devon Coast, no indication was included in the *Tentative List* on the order of future nominations (DCMS, 1999c):

> *"This will depend on detailed discussions with the owners and local authorities concerned, in particular about the need to comply with UNESCO's very stringent management requirements."* (DCMS, 1999a:2)

Industrial sites still dominate on the final tentative list and included all those in the consultative document, with the exception of Dallas Dhu Distillery, plus Saltaire in Bradford. This paper will now consider one of these sites in more detail, Derwent Valley Mills, and review the World Heritage nomination process from the point of view of this single applicant.

Derwent Valley Mills proposed world heritage site

The East Midlands site of the Derwent Valley Mills in Derbyshire is one of the nine sites included on the UK tentative list under the theme of 'industrialisation'. The proposed World Heritage Site is a narrow linear area based on the early mill complexes along a twenty-four kilometre stretch of the lower Derwent Valley. The site focuses on the development of the textile factory system in the 18th century, pioneered in the Derwent Valley. As presented in the *Tentative List* (DCMS, 1999c:28):

> *"...the textile factory system...witnessed innovations in the harnessing of power, the marshalling and housing of the labour force and, above all, in the scale and structure of manufacturing buildings. Over the following century it was to transform economies and landscapes far beyond the Derwent Valley itself."*

The site includes developments from two centuries of the textile industry from the early 18th to early 20th centuries, and illustrates two key industrialisation events: the introduction of water powered silk throwing, and the application of water power to cotton spinning (DCMS, 1999c). From Sir Richard Arkwright's 18th century mills and associated workers' housing at Cromford in the north, the site stretches down the lower Derwent Valley to include mills at Belper (housing the Derwent Valley Visitor Centre), Milford, Darley Abbey, and finally Derby Silk Mill at the southern boundary of the proposed site. Whilst the mills are the prime focus of the site, justification for designation goes beyond the mills themselves and encompasses the associated domestic dwellings and transportation systems. The site is presented as the 'Cradle of the Industrial Revolution':

"The Derwent Valley as a whole exhibits all the characteristics of early industrialisation, including a transport system comprising roads, canal and railways." (DCMS, 1998b: paragraph 56)

Derwent Valley Mills is submitted as representing three of UNESCO's cultural criteria: ii, iii and iv (see table 4). It is presented as an important site because of its technical innovation: the application of water power to silk throwing at Derby and then cotton spinning at Cromford; and the buildings and landscapes associated with these developments. Comparisons with other sites are made through the repercussions of the technological techniques developed in the Derwent Valley; for example, Palmer and Neaverson (1994) estimate that over 200 mills in the UK, from the Midlands to central Scotland, were licensed to use the machines developed at Arkwright's Derwent mills. The *Tentative List* document draws strong links with other textile mill sites, emphasising the role of the mills at Cromford and Belper as 'pioneering precursors' (DCMS, 1999c) to the developments at New Lanark, Scotland in the late 18th century, and later developments at Saltaire, Bradford; both sites are also on the *Tentative List*. Comparisons are also drawn with international examples such as Kromford, Ratingen in Germany, and Slater's Mill, Pawtuket in the USA; again emphasising that these sites are later developments after the original Derwent Valley model.

The initial idea for World Heritage Status was first put forward in the mid-1980s by His Grace the Duke of Devonshire during his time as President of The Arkwright Society, the charitable trust owning Sir Richard Arkwright's Mill at Cromford. The concept was enthusiastically embraced by the local authorities in the area: Derbyshire County Council, Derbyshire Dales District Council and Amber Valley Borough Council. However, the UK's withdrawal from UNESCO in 1985 meant that these bodies saw little success of designation and although the proposal was discussed and conservation of individual areas within the site continued, little action was taken to formally develop the world heritage idea. Independently of this, The International Committee for the Conservation of the Industrial Heritage (TICCIH) were preparing a global list of important industrial heritage sites, recognising the Derwent Valley's world-wide importance. Election of a Labour government in 1997 and their re-prioritising of UNESCO and world heritage provided the stimulus for the formal consideration of a bid from the Derwent Valley to be included on the *Tentative List*. This lobbying period and inclusion on the *Tentative List* in April 1999 refocused efforts on the formal proposal and the associated supporting evidence and consultation required.

Motivations for seeking world heritage status and the potential impacts

The motivations for seeking World Heritage Status for the Derwent Valley Mills are two-fold: global recognition of the importance of the site, and the potential for economic benefits to the area, principally through tourism and inward investment. As noted by The Arkwright Society (1999:13) in relation to their site at Cromford: "Inscription by UNESCO as a World Heritage site would be the ultimate confirmation of Cromford's place in the cultural history of the world". Although World Heritage status brings no direct funding from UNESCO, designation acts as an important recognition of world importance when competing for funds from elsewhere. As noted by Barry Joyce, Senior Conservation and Design Officer for Derbyshire County Council, World Heritage Status can act "as an engine for conservation". Preservation of the Derwent Valley Mills has been a recent development; the principle site at Cromford was only rescued from destruction by The Arkwright Society in 1979, and it is only more recently that the other mills have been valued for their heritage. Designation would therefore bring both universal recognition of the status of the site and acknowledgement of the importance of preserving these examples of industrial heritage.

The potential economic benefits to the area from designation are also key; these are likely to come from two sources: increased tourism to the site itself and the surrounding area, and general inward investment to the region from companies wanting to be associated with an environmentally attractive, and internationally recognised, location. This is summed up by Derbyshire County Council's Leader Martin Doughty, quoted in a statement released following the *Tentative List* announcement:

> "*Quite apart from the obvious conservation benefits, the potential to boost the county's economy is huge. If the area ultimately gains World Heritage status, it will be thrown into the international spotlight with a massive increase in tourism trade and visitor-related employment.*" (Derbyshire County Council, 1999:1)

Tourism already plays an important role in the local economy of the Derwent Valley and it is judged likely that World Heritage Status would increase interest and visits to the site. Whilst this may have positive economic benefits, there is concern about the potential impact on an already overburdened transport systems. The A6, a major link route, runs up the Derwent Valley along the length of the proposed site; this road is already overloaded and particularly congested during the summer months with existing visitors heading up the valley towards the resort of Matlock Bath, just outside the proposed boundaries of the site, and beyond into the Peak District National Park. Concerns are such that sustainable transport is a key theme of the designation, and the bid includes proposals for schemes to ensure that the majority of projected visitors travel by public transport within the site, including buses, rail, cyclepaths and walking routes. An essential component of this is the utilisation of the Derby to Matlock railway line which also runs the length of the site; sections are included as part of the World Heritage designation, for example, George Stephenson's railway bridge at Ambergate, whilst elsewhere the railway acts as a boundary to the site. By providing the stimulus for improving rail services and ticketing along the line, for example, by increasing the frequency of trains, it is hoped that World Heritage status will bring benefits to the wider community for whom transport in general is a major concern.

Stakeholders involved in the Derwent Valley Mills world heritage bid

The majority of World Heritage Sites are owned and managed by a range of individuals and organisations; for example, over thirty organisations are responsible for the management of Hadrian's Wall World Heritage Site (Turley, 1998). This means that "...co-operation among a wide variety of owners and agencies is required" (Pocock, 1997b:384). The Derwent Valley Mills site is no exception and the preparation of the bid involves stakeholders from the public, private and voluntary sectors. In the *Tentative List* document, DCMS (1999c) stressed the requirement that successful sites should have a single body undertaking the crucial management and co-ordination role, both pre-and post-designation. The Derwent Valley Mills nomination bid is being managed in such a way. A Working Group made up of representatives from the planning departments of the local councils, English Heritage and The Arkwright Society, deals with technical and logistical matters. A larger Steering Committee is concerned with the wider political and strategic issues and includes elected members from local authorities, and representatives from DCMS, ICOMOS, and private sector sponsors. This remainder of this paper will provide an overview of the *main* stakeholders in the project and discuss the process of public consultation being undertaken.

Ultimately, the bid to UNESCO is made by the UK government, through DCMS. However, in practical terms, the preparation of the bid at the local level is co-ordinated by Derbyshire County Council. Local government bodies play perhaps the key role in the preparation of the nomination and in co-ordinating the subsequent management, if the bid is successful. The proposed boundaries of the site are included in the jurisdiction of four second-tier local authorities: Amber Valley District Council, Derbyshire Dales District Council, Derby City Council, and Erewash Borough Council, although the latter includes only a small area. To date, most of the work involved in the bid preparation has been through the planning departments of these authorities; each authority has a seat on the Working Group and is responsible for developments in their areas, for example, identification of the buffer zone around the main site. Local authorities are also involved in the ownership and management of elements of the proposed site, including some of its constitute attractions, as part of a strategy identified by Ball and Stobart (1996:28-29) of harnessing tourism for the "generation of real environmental improvement... [including] re-using industrial infrastructure as tourist attractions". For example, Jeddiah Strutt's North Mill at Belper houses the Derwent Valley Visitor Centre, operated by a charitable trust supported by Amber Valley District Council.

The key voluntary sector organisation is The Arkwright Society, a registered charity run by a small professional paid staff and supported by volunteers. The Society owns and manages one of the key components of the wider Derwent Valley site: Sir Richard Arkwright's Mill at Cromford. Established in 1771, it was the world's first successful water powered cotton spinning mill. The mill had fallen into disrepair after a series of industrial uses, the last being a chemical colour works. In the summer of 1979 the Arkwright Society, then a small civic society, purchased the major part of the Cromford Mill site and began an extensive programme of ongoing restoration and regeneration. Although preservation of the mill was initially motivated by its value in heritage terms, it was clear that visitor admissions alone would be unlikely to sustain the site (The Arkwright Society, 1999), particularly through the costly restoration period. The Society therefore followed a strategy of partnership and Cromford Mill is now a multi-use site, drawing rental income from a range of tenants including the Derbyshire Probation Service, reflecting their aim to have a social as well as economic role in the local community. Public access to the site began on very limited scale in 1980 and gradually further sections of the site have been renovated and opened.

English Heritage acts as advisors to DCMS on the proposed World Heritage sites in England and is also involved in the preparation of the bids from individual sites. English Heritage also provides a networking link to other sites submitting proposals; in particular, Derwent Valley Mills has developed links with Saltaire, who also share the same consultants. These consultants are from Sheffield Hallam University's School of Urban and Regional Studies and have been employed with money from a variety of sources including English Heritage, Derbyshire County Council, Derby City Council, Derbyshire Dales District Council, Amber Valley District Council and South Derbyshire Chamber of Commerce. The consultants are involved working on preparing both the nomination documents and management plan, the latter being a requirement for inscription (DCMS, 1999c; Shackley, 1998; UNESCO, 1996b).

As noted above, inclusion of the UK *Tentative List* does not imply any timetable for nomination. The two 1999 nominations included the Welsh industrial heritage site Blaenavon Industrial Landscape. With Scottish and Welsh devolution both Blaenavon and New Lanark in Scotland, which the *Tentative List* indicated would be proposed in 2000, were politically important sites to nominate first. Since publication of the *Tentative List*, DCMS has revised its approach and currently the June 2000 submission will include three sites grouped together under the theme 'heritage of the textile industry': New Lanark, Saltaire, and Derwent Valley Mills. Although each site will be nominated separately, they will be presented together as illustrating the development of the textile industry in Britain and the progression of the factory system from Arkwright's early mills in the Derwent Valley, through Robert Owen's mill settlement at New Lanark, to Titus Salt's later developments at Saltaire. Although the Derwent Valley Mills team have developed links with Saltaire through their common consultants and English Heritage, links with New Lanark are less strong as they operate within a different political system, i.e. a devolved Scotland with Historic Scotland rather than English Heritage as a key stakeholder. Other networking opportunities have been afford through membership of groups such as UK Local Authorities World Heritage Sites Forum, and TICCIH.

Beyond these core stakeholders, other are involved in the project; some of which have particular importance in terms of the regional political recognition of the bid. For example, the Regional Director of East Midlands CBI sits on the Steering Committee, and South Derbyshire Chamber of Commerce have contributed to the cost of the project consultants, a recognition of the perceived economic benefits World Heritage Status may bring to the wider area.

Whilst these are the key bodies involved in developing the nomination bid, as work has progressed, there has been a period of consultation with the wider local community. This is in line with UNESCO, who's *Operational Guidelines* (1996b: paragraph 14) stress the importance of involving local people in the nomination process in order to "make them feel a shared responsibility with the State Party in the maintenance of the site". This process has involved both the 'public' and other identifiable local stakeholders. For example: the Working Group have consulted the twelve parish councils within whose boundaries the proposed site lies; and a special meeting has been held with forty principal land and building owners in the area. Public awareness of the project has been raised in a number of ways. Locally-based financial institution, The Derbyshire Building Society, have sponsored both mobile displays for a touring public exhibition, and accompanying leaflets, available in local buildings such as libraries and the individual attractions within the site. Subsequently, a number of public consultation events have been held: a public evening event at the University of Derby which attracted 250 participants, and four public consultation days in February 2000, spread around the local area, each involving drop-in surgeries throughout the day and a public meeting in the evening with representatives of the Working Group. Interest and support from the local media was particularly strong around the time of the *Tentative List* publication, with headlines such as 'Glories of our industrial past deserve world status: Stonehenge, the Taj Mahal, the Great Wall of China and...Cromford Mill!' (Derby Evening Telegraph, 1999).

Conclusions

As more sites across the globe seek World Heritage status, it is important to understand the processes that both state parties and individuals sites have to undergo to obtain this coveted accolade. This paper has focused on the procedure *before* formal nomination, namely the preparation of a tentative list and the stakeholders involved in preparing an individual nomination bid.

Although more state parties are producing tentative list documents, the shift in nominations considered necessary by UNESCO, both in terms of regions of the world and types of sites, is not yet evident at the inscription stage. Nevertheless, the UK provides a useful case study of the impact of guidelines such as UNESCO's *Global Strategy* at the individual state party level. Comparison of the UK's two tentative lists indicates a clear re-focusing of priorities, incorporating a widening of the notion of 'heritage'. This has been illustrated here by discussion of the importance of 'industrial heritage'; all but absent from the original 1985 selection, this theme dominates the revised 1999 list. Both industrial heritage and 'Britain's global influence' are themes in which the UK can clearly demonstrate 'uniqueness'; in particular, it signals a move away from sites and themes which are more 'common' across Western Europe in general, for example historic cities, cathedrals and palaces, towards a focus on less elitist forms of cultural heritage. The outcomes of the current nominee Blaenavon Industrial Landscape, and the forthcoming 'textile' sites, will determine how successful this refocusing has been in the context of the wider global World Heritage arena.

Examination of one of these forthcoming candidates, Derwent Valley Mills, has illustrated the range of stakeholders involved in preparing a world heritage nomination. The initial impetus came from a key voluntary sector organisation managing one of the attractions within the proposed site, and although representatives of the public, private and voluntary sectors are involved, it is the public sector that have taken the lead in co-ordinating the bid. Significantly, at this initial preparation stage, it is representatives of the local authority planning departments rather than, for example, tourism, who have been at the forefront of the nomination process. This further emphasises that the motivation for, and potential impact of, designation is a regional economic issue rather than solely a tourism concern. Nevertheless, tourism is an important consideration and if increased tourism is to be a successful outcome of the designation then it is significant that the motivational factors identified fit with several of the elements identified by Rudd and Davis (1998) as characteristic of a successful industrial heritage tourism site; namely that sites are in an area of positive economic growth, have well-structured transport systems, and existing accommodations. The case study has also illustrated the gradual widening of stakeholders involved in the nomination bid. From an initial public-voluntary sector ownership, private sector support has been drawn, through both sponsorship and expertise, including representatives on the strategic Steering Group. Informing the local community and seeking feedback through a public consultation programme is also crucial, particularly in terms of the accountability of local authorities.

Derwent Valley Mills is very much a 'work in progress'; the fate of its nomination over the next two years will go some way to illustrating the success, or otherwise, of the UK and UNESCO's reconsideration of what 'heritage' of 'outstanding universal value' really entails.

Acknowledgements

The author gratefully acknowledges the assistance of Katy Damiral and Chris Charlton from The Arkwright Society, and Barry Joyce of Derbyshire County Council; however, the views expressed are the responsibility of the author alone, as are any inaccuracies.

References

Arkwright Society, The (1999), *The Cromford Mills: a major heritage site*, The Arkwright Society, Cromford.

Ball, R. and Stobart, J. (1996), 'Promoting the industrial heritage dimensions in Midlands tourism: a critical analysis of local policy attitudes and approaches' in Robinson, M. *et al* (Eds) *Managing Cultural Resources for the Tourist*, Business Education Publishers Ltd, Sunderland, pp.21-38.

Cleere, H. (1999), 'Putting industry on the World Heritage List' *TICCIH Bulletin*. 6 Autumn, [Online: http://www.museu.mnactec.com/TICCIH].

DCMS (1998a), 'Chris Smith launches consultation on proposed UK World Heritage Sites for the new millennium' *DCMS News Release*, 207/98, 21 August.

DCMS (1998b), *UNESCO World Heritage Sites: a consultation paper on a new United Kingdom tentative list of future nominations*, Department of Culture, Media and Sport, London.

DCMS (1999a), 'Chris Smith announces final UK nominations for World Heritage Status' *DCMS News Release*, 86/99, 6 April.

DCMS (1999b) 'Chris Smith announces formal publication of list of potential World Heritage Site nominations' *DCMS News Release*, 209/99, 30 July.

DCMS (1999c), *World Heritage Sites: the tentative list of the United Kingdom of Great Britain and Northern Ireland*, DCMS, London.

Derby Evening Telegraph (1999), 'Glories of our industrial past deserve world status: Stonehenge, the Taj Mahal, the Great Wall of China and...Cromford Mill!' *Derby Evening Telegraph*, 9 April. [Online: http://www.thisisderbyshire.co.uk]

Derbyshire County Council (1999), 'Another step towards world heritage accolade' *News from Derbyshire County Council*, 6 August.

Drost, A. (1996), 'Developing sustainable tourism for World Heritage Sites' *Annals of Tourism Research*, 23 (2): 279-292.

Edwards, J .A. and Llurdés, J. C. (1996), 'Mines and quarries: industrial heritage tourism' *Annals of Tourism Research*, 23 (2): 341-363.

ICOMOS (2000), *Proposals for Achieving a More Representative Sample of the Cultural Heritage on the World Heritage List*, ICOMOS, Paris.

Palmer, M. and Neaverson, P. (1994), *Industry in the Landscape, 1700-1900*, Routledge, London.

Pocock, D. (1997a), 'Some reflections on World Heritage' *Area*, 29 (3): 260-268.

Pocock, D. (1997b), 'The UK World Heritage' *Geography*, 357, pp.380-384.

Rudd, M. A. and Davis, J. A. (1998), 'Industrial heritage tourism at the Bingham Canyon Copper Mine' *Journal of Travel Research*, 36, pp.85-89.

Shackley, M. (1998) (Ed) *Visitor Management: case studies from World Heritage Sites*, Butterworth-Heinemann, Oxford.

Turley, S. (1998), 'Hadrian's Wall (UK): managing the visitor experience at the Roman Frontier' in Shackley, M. (Ed) *Visitor Management: case studies from World Heritage Sites*, Butterworth-Heinemann, Oxford, pp.100-120.

UNESCO (1972), *Convention for the Protection of the World's Cultural and Natural Heritage*, UNESCO, Paris.

UNESCO (1996a), *Information Document: Glossary of World Heritage Terms*, WHC-96/CONF.201/INF.21, World Heritage Centre, Paris.

UNESCO (1996b), *Operational Guidelines for the Implementation of the World Heritage Convention*, World Heritage Centre, Paris.

UNESCO (1997a), 'Director-General welcomes United Kingdom's decision to rejoin UNESCO' *UNESCO Press Release*, 97-71, 14 May.

UNESCO (1997b), *World Heritage Committee Paper*. WHC-97/CONF.208/9, UNESCO, Paris.

UNESCO (1999a), *Global Strategy*, UNESCO, Paris, [Online: http://www.unesco.org/whc/nwhc/pages/doc/dc_p7a.htm].

UNESCO (1999b), *Nominating Procedure*, UNESCO, Paris, [Online: http://www.unesco.org/whc/nwhc/pages/doc/dc_p8a.htm].

UNESCO (1999c), *The World Heritage List*, UNESCO, Paris, [Online: http://www.unesco.org/whc/ heritage.htm].

UNESCO (2000), *Industrial Heritage*, UNESCO, Paris, [Online: http://www.unesco.org/whc/nwhc/ pages/doc/mainf3.htm].

World Heritage Committee (1994), *Convention Concerning the Protection of the World Cultural and Natural Heritage*. 18th session. 12-17 November. whc-94/conf.003/inf.6, UNESCO, Paris.

Museums: Theme parks of the third Millennium?

John Swarbrooke

Sheffield Hallam University, UK

Introduction

The suggestion that museums might become the theme parks of the third Millennium would probably be enough to cause apoplexy at most meetings of museum professionals. Surely, they would argue, museums and theme parks are like 'chalk and cheese', two polarised opposites. Their objectives vary dramatically, don't they, and they look different, don't they? And obviously people choose to visit them, for very different reasons, don't they?

Yet, at the same time, museums appear to be becoming more like theme parks in some ways. They are deliberately - and expensively - endeavouring to become more entertaining places, although they may not appreciate the use of this term. They are also, increasingly, focusing on income generation, marketing, branding and sponsorship. Cafés and shops are becoming major 'profit centres' to be nurtured and given attention as if they were priceless artefacts, which, of course, they are to the museum accountant.

Furthermore, major exhibitions are now hyped and promoted as if they were the latest theme park 'white knuckle ride'.

In this paper the author suggests that if this trend continues, museums will simply become part of the leisure industry, competing with theme parks and shopping malls.

His argued that this would be a great pity, because it would damage their ability to perform their unique function, as intermediaries between the people of today and the world of yesterday, stimulating critical evaluation of past events.

However, this paper does not argue for a return to the 'good old days' of formal museums and exhibits imprisoned behind glass.

Instead the author argues that we need a new more radical vision for our museums, differentiating them from both theme parks and the traditional old museum. This way they will have a valuable and distinctive purpose in the new century. Otherwise, they may simply become, either, the theme parks, or the dinosaurs, of the third Millennium.

This paper is clearly subjective and provocative, with the author seeking to ask questions and challenge some conventional wisdoms. If this brief paper stimulates debate and argument, then it will have achieved its aim.

The diversity of museums

At the beginning of this paper it is important to recognise that the Museums sector is a very diverse field. Figure 1 seeks to illustrate the scale of this diversity.

Figure 1   The Diversity of the Museums Sector

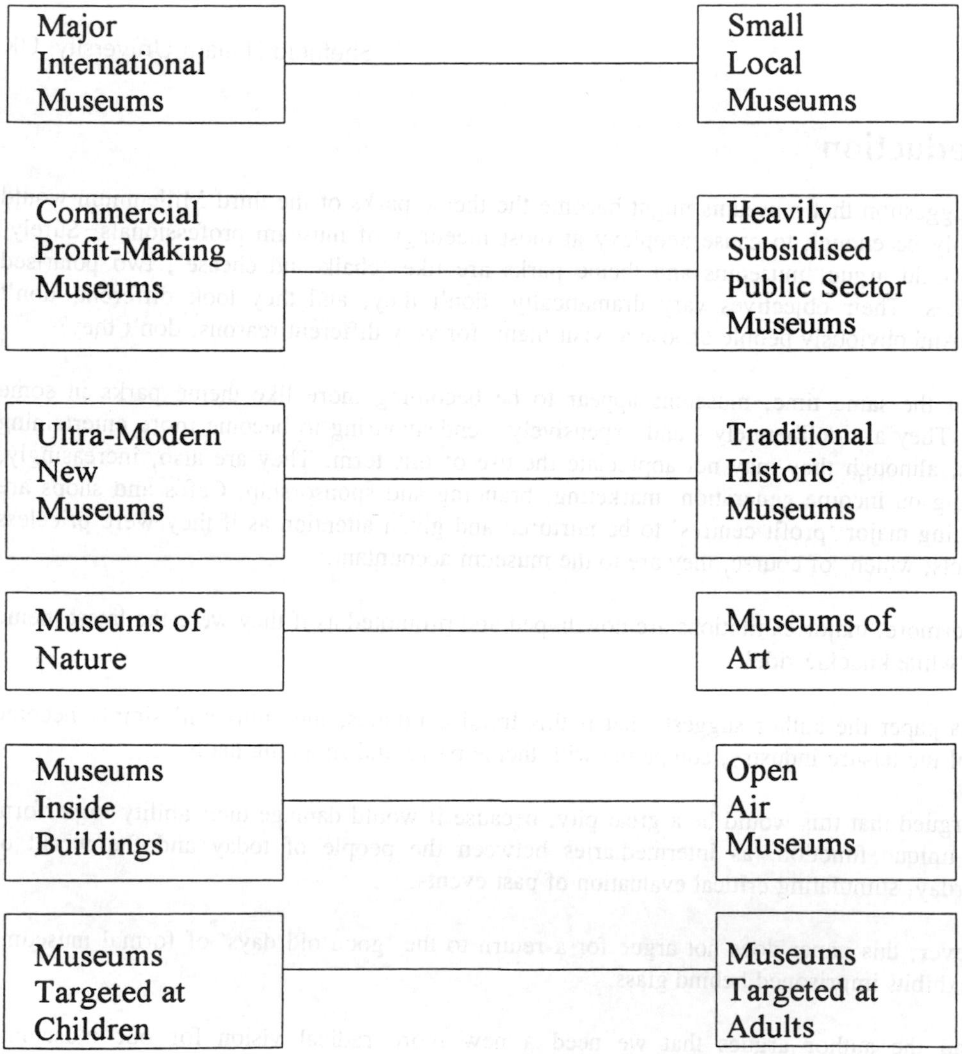

Major International Museums	Small Local Museums
Commercial Profit-Making Museums	Heavily Subsidised Public Sector Museums
Ultra-Modern New Museums	Traditional Historic Museums
Museums of Nature	Museums of Art
Museums Inside Buildings	Open Air Museums
Museums Targeted at Children	Museums Targeted at Adults

While not comprehensive, this diagram clearly shows that there are many different types of museums.

In view of this diversity, the author recognises that this paper will, of necessity, take a generalised view of the sector as a whole. There may be many exceptions, therefore, that prove, or do not prove, the rule!

Perhaps the critique presented in this paper is most appropriate to larger, public and voluntary sector museums, but it hopefully says something of relevance to most types of museum.

While largely based on experience in the UK and the USA this paper will hopefully be of interest to museum professionals and tourism specialists from around the world.

The changing world of museums

To the ordinary person in the street, museums have changed dramatically in recent years, in many countries around the world. Dark decor, glass cases, and 'do not touch' signs have often now been replaced by bright interiors, open plan design and invitations to touch and 'interact' with exhibits.

Likewise, the old kiosk selling guide books and postcards is now likely to be a large themed retailed outlet, full of a bewildering range of merchandise.

Where, yesterday, visitors might be pleased to be able to buy a cup of tea and a cake, today's customer may well be invited to buy a salad of warm goats cheese drizzled with balsamic vinegar, washed down with a glass of Chilean Chardonnay.

This is clearly a very simplistic picture; reality is much more complex. There are still many little visited, old fashioned museums, but the overall trend is clear.

It is now time for us to look at the reasons behind this trend, the reasons why museums are now apparently becoming increasingly part of the mainstream leisure industry.

External pressures and internal change

The changing nature of museums has been the result of the interaction of two sets of forces, namely external pressures and internal change with the museums sector itself. This interaction has often been the cause of friction and tension.

The external pressures in museums in many countries in recent years have been numerous and powerful. The most important ones are illustrated in Figure 2.

Figure 2   External Pressures on Museums

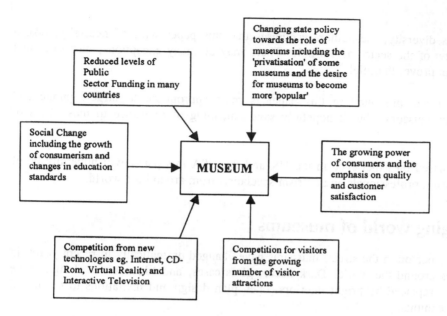

However, there has also been a sea of change within the museum world itself, some of which has been voluntary, while some has been the result of the external pressures noted in Figure 3.

The author has endeavoured to identify some of the main internal changes seen in the museum sector in recent years, in Figure 3.

Figure 3   Internal Change within the Museum sector

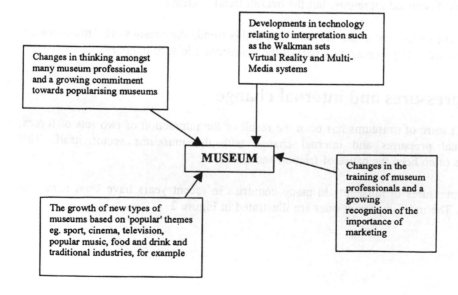

Museums and tourism - old enemies, new friends?

Not very long ago museum professionals and the tourism industry viewed each other suspiciously across a sea of mutual distrust and ignorance. Today, while still uneasy bed fellows at times, these two worlds have discovered that they can be of great assistance to each other.

Tourism planners have identified the potential value of museums as catalysts for the development of tourism in a region. Museums have often been seen as the grain of sand across which the pearl of tourism and economic development can grow.

The idea that museums bring tourism and tourism brings economic development has stimulated a range of new museum projects in recent years, including:

- The creation of the National Centre for Popular Music and the;

- Earth Centre in South Yorkshire, UK;

- The Guggenheim Museum, Bilbao, Spain;

- The new heritage centres that have been developed in many small;

- Towns in Ireland; and,

- The ecomusées based on traditional but declining industries in France.

At the same time museums have been encouraged to see tourism as an opportunity to attract more visitors and increase their income.

There has also been a coming together of museums and other types of tourist or visitor attractions too.

Museums have learnt lessons in marketing from theme parks and other attractions which are targeted clearly at the mass tourism markets. At the same time, tourist attractions have sought to develop the educational side and conservation dimension of their product to attract school groups and adults who want to learn something new from their leisure experience.

The distinction between museums and tourist or visitor attractions, in general, is thus becoming more blurred.

In the minds of many customers, museums are now competing directly with theme parks and leisure shopping malls for their leisure time and disposable income.

There is still a hard-core of museum 'addicts' who are not easily tempted by the other types of attractions, but these are greatly outnumbered by the vast armies of tourists which many museums are wishing to attract. They can only achieve this aim, they appear to think, by becoming more like mainstream tourist attractions.

The positive dimension of the museum world today

The changes which have taken place in the museum world have, undoubtedly, been beneficial in a number of ways. They have allowed museums to increase their visitor numbers and income. At the same time, they have greatly enhanced the quality of experience for most of their visitors.

The sector is clearly thriving with new museums opening all the time, albeit often only with the aid of substantial public funds. Nevertheless the variety of museums available is greater than ever, as is the diversity of themes featured in museums.

Museums have helped many places become established on the tourism map and have undoubtedly, therefore, contributed to the generation of new jobs and new income within their host community.

However, it is now time for us to turn our attention to the developments in the museums sector about which the author is concerned.

The negative dimension of the museums world today

The author has a number of concerns about current trends in the museums sector. Some of these are illustrated in Figure 4 and will be discussed later in this section.

Figure 4   The Negative Dimension of the Museums World Today

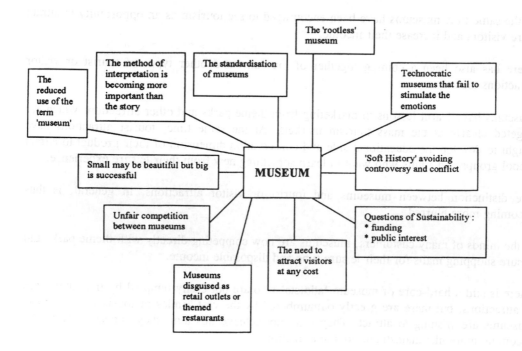

The method of interpretation is becoming more important than the story

The author is seriously concerned that the balance in museums has moved too far away from the artefacts and the stories they tell towards the methods of interpreting the objects and their stories.

Museum marketing often focuses upon the medium rather than the message. The terms 'interactive' and 'hands on' cry out from leaflets. We are not really encouraged to ask what we will be interacting with or what we will have our hands on!

Several anecdotes based on real conversations between the author and his nine year old son will suffice to illustrate the point the author is making.

Author:	*'Would you like to go to 'X' museum'*
Son:	*'Is that the one with the computer you can play on'*
Author:	*'Did you enjoy going to 'Y' museum*
Son:	*'No, there were not enough buttons to press or things to touch'*
Author:	*'Do you remember the 'Z' museum'*
Son:	*'Yes, that's the one where the IMAX cinema was closed for repairs!'*

Given that many museums want and need to attract families and young people, such comments are very important.

The author believes that the emphasis on modern, high tech- expensive- methods of interpretation brings three main problems, as follows

Firstly, it makes it very difficult for small, less well-funded museums to compete, or even survive. This is a pity because in countries like the UK it is the diversity of the museums sector which is one of its strengths. Visitors often enjoy small, specialist, private museums just as much as the famous 'flagship' museums.

Secondly, it can mean that visitors tend to remember the technology not the story. There is no doubt that imaginative interpretation can help communicate stories to visitors better than written labels on glass cases. But the author believes that this benefit can be exaggerated. Visitors often remember just a few, often trivial, pieces of information after they have been exposed to interactive interpretation at museums.

Thirdly, the constant evolution of technologies can quickly make today's 'state of the art' system outdated by tomorrow. This can be very expensive and it is a phenomenon with which theme parts are familiar in relation to their 'white knuckle rides'.

The standardisation of museums

Throughout history, museums have tended to be very clearly differentiated from each other. Indeed their appeal to visitors and their value to scholars has lay in their individuality.

Museums are understandably very different to each other because, of course, they:

- Are located in different geographical areas;

- Have different themes;

- Are managed separately by people and organisations with;

- Different priorities and objectives;

- Have different histories, cultures, and traditions; and,

- Have different collections and artefacts and exhibitions.

However, it is the author's contention that current trends in the museums sector are slowly leading to greater homogenisation amongst museums, particularly amongst the larger institutions. This homogenisation is particularly evident in the way artefacts are displayed, methods of interpretation, and the design of retail and catering outlets, for example.

The reasons for this slow standardisation are undoubtedly many and varied but they probably include the following:

(i)   The fact that museum professionals today have more opportunity than ever before to meet each other and travel to see museums in different countries;

(ii)   The role of consultants who tend to work in a number of countries and take their ideas with them;

(iii) The desire of many museum professionals to emulate the success of museums elsewhere. Having features in your museum which are also found in highly reputed museums appears to be thought to bestow status on a museum as well as increasing the chance of achieving success; and,

(iv)   An apparent belief amongst many managers of museums that there are certain things the modern visitor expects to find at all 'good quality' museums. It seems to be thought that failure to provide these things will result in competitive disadvantage.

This process of homogenisation brings two main problems, namely:

- The emphasis on copying existing approaches can lead to a;

- Reduction in innovation and new ideas; and,

- It can make life a little boring for the avid museum visitor.

The 'Rootless' Museum

Many of today's museums appear to be rather 'rootless', in other words there appears to be no real reason for their location in a particular place, while, often they are also managed by organisations which are not directly accountable to the local population. Both of these characteristics are at odds with the concept of sustainable development, and raise both ethical questions and concerns about the long-term viability of such museums.

This phenomenon of the 'rootless' museum has been seen clearly in the UK. The availability of Millennium Commission and National Lottery funding has encouraged local councils and voluntary organisations to try to come up with imaginative projects, while museums have also been seen as away of achieving regional development or urban regeneration. This has led to 'museums' being built with specialist themes that often do not seem to have a great deal in common with their location.

This 'rootlessness' would not be a problem for theme parks or shopping malls but it is for museums. Museums have traditionally usually told the story of a region's history or at least an aspect of it; and they were usually part of the public sector, accountable, at least in theory, to the local community.

The author strongly believes that the commercial failure of many new museums, in the UK for example, may well be partly due to their lack of roots and the fact that the community often feels no sense of ownership or loyalty in relation to them.

Technocracy versus emotion

Many modern museums have been designed by specialists keen to demonstrate their skills at creating innovative new museums, utilising the latest technologies.

However, the author believes that most of these museums are rather cold and sterile. This may be in keeping with the fashionable design concepts of our time but it means they may lack emotional appeal. They often fail to stir the imagination of the visitor and engage them in an emotional experience.

This is hard to forgive because museums are often concerned with history and the lives of human beings, and surely nothing can be more emotional than the lives of people, their loves and fears, triumphs and disasters.

'Soft' history - the avoidance of controversy and conflict

The museum of today wants to attract and satisfy a wide variety of markets as well as gaining substantial sponsorship income.

These aims are not easy to reconcile to the mission of many museums to present as complete a view of history as possible, as objectively as possible.

Museums cannot afford to offend visitors or potential sponsors. This can lead to the avoidance of controversial subjects, such as slavery, hunting, religion or abortion, for example. Many museums, for the same reason, tend to play down conflict within societies such as conflicts between ethnic communities or between social classes. Where such issues are tackled, they are often dealt with in a gentle way so as not to upset the visitor. This is, it could be argued, a betrayal of the role of museums to endeavour to tell a story, no matter how painful it is.

Questions of sustainability

There are serious question marks over the long-term future of certain modern museums, due to the following criticisms:

(i)   Some museums, it is felt, were forced to over-estimate their potential visitor numbers to persuade funding bodies to give them the money they required. Expenditure plans can be based, therefore, on unrealistically high income, figures which can lead to either closure or some organisation having to subsidise the museum, permanently;

(ii) The fashion cycle in the museums world, seems to be shortening, just as it is in the theme park sector. This means there is a need for continual investment which may not be available to many museums;

(iii) It also often appears that some museums do not spend enough money or effort on marketing and marketing research, and are not utilising the latest marketing techniques, such as relationship market; and,

(iv) Many museums now rely on either public sector subsidies, voluntary sector funding or private sponsorship. None of these sources is secure and guaranteed and any reduction in any of these income sources could be catastrophic for the museum.

It is particularly important that museums do not fail because this can create derelict sites and can harm the image of the place in which the museum is located.

The need to attract visitors at any cost

The need for museums to meet their visitor numbers and income targets can lead to some museums becoming involved in questionable activities that do not relate to their mission.

For example, the author remembers an industrial heritage attraction that was proud of its authenticity and its refusal to compromise its standards. However, when funding was cut this museum hosted a dinosaur exhibition which had absolutely nothing to do with the site. Such short-term crisis measures may well harm the integrity of the museum.

For those attractions where visitor numbers are very important they can be tempted to make offers to attract visitors which may cost more money than they generate.

Museums disguised as shopping malls and themed restaurants

Many major museums today seem to be as much shopping malls and themed restaurants as they are museums. Often museums now allow visitors to use their shops or cafés without even requiring the customer to visit the actual museum. This approach may well make visiting the museum appear as a rather marginal activity.

The author recently visited a museum and observed a small number of visitors. The results make interesting reading. One visitor spent thirty minutes looking around the museum, twenty-five minutes in the shop, and forty minutes in the café, while another saw the museum was rather busy and went straight to the shop, bought several postcards, and left! The third visitor arrived half an hour before the museum closed and chose to spend this time in the shop rather than the museum, even though entry to the museum was free.

No-one denies the importance of income from retailing and catering for museums, but we must try to get the balance right between these activities and the central purpose of the museums.

Unfair competition between museums

The museums sector appears increasingly to be the scene of competition which is simply not fair. Some major museums make no charge for entry in spite of having excellent collections and offering a first class experience. Other museums, without the benefits of subsidies or sponsorship are forced to charge for admission and to ask for more money than visitors may feel the quality of the visit merits.

We are not used to getting a Porsche for free while being asked to pay £20,000 for a Lada, yet that is what happens in the museum field, thanks to the rather confusing and apparently unfair system of subsidies seen in many countries.

Small is beautiful but big is successful

Many small museums, with important collections and knowledgeable and enthusiastic staff, are finding it increasingly difficult to compete against the 'mega-museums'. They cannot afford the 'blockbuster' high profile exhibitions or the latest interactive technologies. They cannot afford to spend heavily on marketing or fund regular refurbishments. As time goes on these smaller museums may begin to close in significant numbers, leaving the museum world a poorer place and reducing choice for the museum-visiting public.

The reduced use of the term 'museum'

Today more and more museums are being opened but fewer and fewer of them appear to be being given the name 'museum'. It is as if the word now carries some form of stigma! Instead we have 'heritage experiences', the 'X, Y,Z story', 'Centres of ABC' etc.

Indeed many operators of what appear to be museums appear to now go out of their way to insist that their 'attraction' is not a 'museum'. This devalues the idea of museums and is not at all helpful. And, as we know from some well publicised example, in the UK particularly, avoiding the word 'museum' does not guarantee success!

Summary

In the preceding section, the author has made a number of criticisms and voiced some concerns over the current situation in the museum sector. He recognises that these views have been highly subjective and that they do not relate to all museums. Nevertheless, it is the author's opinion that the issues raised in this paper threaten the long-term sustainability of museums as a whole.

However, there is no suggestion that we should seek to return to the 'old days' of elitist attitudes and dusty, uninspiring museums.

Instead, the author would like to see a new approach to museums, building on the strengths of some of today's best museums.

Towards a new vision for museums

If museums are going to flourish and fulfil a valuable role in our world, we need perhaps to develop a new vision of their form and purpose. This will mean being willing to tackle conventional wisdoms and take difficult decisions.

The author has the following suggestions that he believes might help create a vibrant, sustainable future for museums.

1. *Complete the Democratisation of Museums* so that everyone feels a sense of ownership in relation to them, and everyone sees them as things which are relevant to their lives.

This means:

   - Testing local public opinion before museum themes are decided; and,

   - Allowing local people to influence how artefacts are presented and stories interpreted for the visitor.

     This may well go against the views of museum professionals but it is morally right and may well be the only way of guaranteeing the sustainability of museums.

2. *Make Museums More Sustainable, Challenging and Memorable.* This should be achieved according to the author not just by using exciting technologies but also by encouraging the consideration of controversial issues and conflict. Visitors should constantly be forced to question their prejudices and stereotyping of different groups.

3. *Museums should be made Warmer and more Human.* This means, amongst other things, putting a greater emphasis on human beings, as interpreters of history. This does not just mean using actors and guides, but also using volunteers from local communities coming in to just tell stories and share their life experiences with visitors. Or local people could tell visitors what they think of particular works of art in their local museum.

4. *Rejecting the Idea that Museums are just Concerned with the Past.* Museums will increase their appeal and fulfil a more valuable role if they recognise that they should not just be concerned with the past. Museums should not only tell us where we come from but also where we re now and where we might go in the future.

5. *Recognising that Museums do not have to be located in Buildings called Museums.* Museums do not have to be separate buildings, or even buildings at all. For example, we can have:

   - Mobile museums which travel around bringing history to the people; this would simply be an extension of the service some museums already offer to schools, for example. But this service could also visit factories and housing estates;

   - Museums in other buildings such as supermarkets, schools, and transport terminii; and,

   - 'Virtual museums', utilising virtual reality technologies to create highly interactive 'virtual museums' which offer a vivid experience for the visitor. These museums could be enjoyed anytime by anyone, wherever they live. Virtual Reality could even be used to allow individuals to create their own 'virtual musuems' in the comfort of their own homes.

6. *The '24 Hour Museum'* The idea of 24 hour cities is growing, where services are available 24 hours a day, such as shops and even libraries in some countries. Why not museums? Who says people will only want to visit a museum between 10.00 and 18.00. The experiment with overnight 'sleep ins' for children at the Natural History Museum in London is an interesting example of this idea.

7. *Enhance the diversity of Museums* by seeking consciously to:

   - Constantly innovate in the design and choice of themes in museums;

   - Rather than simply copying what has worked elsewhere; and,

   - Encouraging the development of quality, highly individual, museums, looking at unusual subjects. Novel themes and enthusiastic, museum curators can provide a memorable experience for tourists.

8. *Tighten the rules for the funding of new museums* to make sure they will meet the needs of society as a whole and that they will be accountable to the community, if they want to benefit from public funding.

9. *Mounting a Marketing Campaign* designed to establish a positive, modern clear image for the word 'Museum'.

Conclusions

The author believes that museums are in danger of losing sight of their unique mission and losing their way. They need to demonstrate they have confidence in an up-dated concept of museums rather than in trying to make people believe they are now simply leisure or tourist attractions.

Museums have a unique role to play in our society which is conserving artefacts that represent our past, interpreting heritage for today's population and stimulating interest in this heritage.

However, if museums are to fulfil this role, they must become more accessible to the whole population.

There is absolutely nothing wrong with museums adopting the latest technologies and thinking from the leisure industry providing they adapt them to help them further the unique mission of museums.

However, museums need to recognise that they are fundamentally different to other leisure attractions. Museums are concerned with both the past and the future as well as with today, while most leisure attractions are focused on the present only.

Museums must recognise their unique role, be proud of it, and endeavour to meet the challenges of new technologies and social change to ensure that they will continue to play a valuable role in society, in the years to come.

If they fail to meet these challenges, the author fears that museums may well become the theme parks, or even worse, the dinosaurs of the third Millennium.

References

Ashworth, G. and Larkham, P. J. (1994), *Building a New Heritage*. Routledge, London.

Boniface, P. (1995). *Managing Quality Cultural Tourism*. Routledge, London.

Hewison, R. (1987), *The Heritage Industry: Britain in a Climate of Decline*. Methuen, London.

Middleton, V. T. C. (1990), *New Visions for Independent Museums in the UK*. Association of Independent Museums, Chichester.

Prentice, R. (1993), *Tourism and Heritage Attractions*. Routledge, London.

Robinson, M. Evans, N. and Callaghan, P. (eds) (1996), *Tourism and Culture. Conference Proceedings*. 4 Volumes. Business Education Publishers, Sunderland.

Swarbrooke, J. (1995), *The Development and Management of Visitor Attractions*. Butterworth-Heinneman, Oxford.

Urry, J. (1990), *The Tourist Gaze : Leisure and Travel in Contemporary Societies*. Sage, London

What price heritage? An Anglo-American discussion of public ownership

J V Thomas

Oxford Brookes University, UK

Abstract

This paper is concerned with the management of heritage sites in public ownership. Theoretical concepts of public goods are reviewed, in particular the circumstances in which charging for public goods would deliver optimal allocation. Empirical work undertaken in the United Kingdom and the United States is presented and this sheds light on how the directors of heritage sites view their management task in the context of decreasing state funding. A range of approaches to charging is discussed and these approaches are shown to be consistent with public goods theory. However, some heritage sites are also shown to charge 'what the market will bear': this leads to a discussion of the role of the market for private benefit (admission to a site) and the problematic area of resource allocation for public benefits.

Introduction

Tourism is a phenomenon of global importance. A curiosity to see different places, peoples and customs is an important human characteristic to which the travel and tourism industry has been very responsive. Increasing disposable income, free time, and technology have combined to encourage the opening up of sacred places to tourist inspection. Whereas countries offer similar provision for tourists in terms of accommodation and other tourist facilities, each place also offers an unique experience. For many countries it is their heritage sites which lie at the heart of their tourist industry. This is as true for a developed country such as the United Kingdom as for developing countries such as Cambodia, Burma or Jordan.

Heritage has been defined as 'monuments, groups of buildings and moveable cultural property' which illustrate a 'unique artistic achievement and meet the test of authenticity' (UNESCO 1972). For the purposes of this paper heritage sites include museums, art galleries, historic buildings and other sites which form part of the cityscape of a tourist city.

As heritage sites have become an important part of the tourism industry, and tourists, through admission charges, have come to be regarded as a source of revenue, there is a growing need to understand the relationship between tourism and heritage. This paper will concentrate on one aspect of heritage management, namely that of charging for admission to heritage sites in public ownership. The importance of this topic lies, on the one hand, in the perceived problem of charging *at all* for access to heritage and, on the other, in the financial contribution which visitors might make - hence its relevance to decision-makers in the developed and developing world.

Research methodology

Whereas other researchers have investigated pricing policies [Fyall and Garrod (1998) in the heritage industry in general; and Rogers (1995) in tourist attractions] with the aid of questionnaires, a qualitative approach was deemed to be appropriate for this project. This was because charging for admission to heritage sites in public ownership has become a contentious issue in museum circles for many years (Great Britain 1989). The incoming Labour government in the United Kingdom in 1997 pledged to restore free admission to the London-based National Museums, but three years later the charges are still in place and remain a topic of critical comment in the leader columns of the broadsheet newspapers (see The Independent 1999; The Guardian 2000). On the one hand the politicians and newspaper journalists believe that admission should be free, while economists argue for the introduction of admission charges as a means of introducing accountability and a visitor orientation in this seemingly conservative sector (Peacock 1998). Because of this very public discussion the author wanted to capture the meaning of 'public ownership' for those who manage our heritage, to explore their understanding and to understand their perspective. A pre-structured questionnaire cannot adequately capture this information, but a qualitative study can make a contribution to this understanding.

There were several choices to be made before undertaking this project. **The respondent** - As this paper is concerned with the establishment of contemporary practice and decision making process the target respondent had to be the *site director*. Only this person would have the responsibility and authority to discuss the fundamental question of charging for admission to heritage in public ownership. Twenty three interviews were conducted, thirteen at sites which offered free admission and ten at sites which charged for admission (see Table 1). It is the preoccupation of the heritage site directors which dictates the structure and content reported of this paper *viz.* the dilemma of charging for public goods; how to implement charges; and ways of ensuring equity of access. The author also wanted to explore the extent to which the market could allocate resources to heritage. This was dealt with by discussing what a 'sustainable' price (admission charge) might be. (A 'sustainable' price would be one which ensured that the site could be handed on to future generations through adequate funding raised by the market mechanism).

A cross-cultural approach: A cross-cultural comparison with the United States was deemed to be appropriate on three counts. (i) In both the United Kingdom and the United States there had been two decades or so of a philosophy of less government, lower taxation and less central government grant aid to arts and culture. It was felt that examining the management of heritage sites in a changing environment could therefore be enhanced by comparing responses across the two cultures which had apparently undergone a similar transformation. (ii) It was also thought at the outset that a sophisticated approach to pricing would be observed in the United States, as a 'free market' approach had been the guiding philosophy in that country in many spheres of life. (iii) The choice of the United States was supported on a historical basis by the work of Ridley (1987), Cummings and Katz (1987) and Minihan (1977), and by Bromwich (1994)'s comparative study of the museum sector in the United Kingdom and France which concluded that there were few parallels in the system or the sector.

Choice of heritage site: This was intended to reflect a range of responses, from free sites, to sites with high charges. Where there were several sites with little reason for choosing one over another, then random sampling was employed. Some sites were included on the recommendation of other site directors in order to illuminate contextual issues. A cluster of sites in the City of Oxford was chosen in order to explore the link between charging for admission and congestion at the site and in the City in general.

Analysis: Open coding was used for the interview transcripts [see Miles and Huberman (1984); Glaser and Strauss (1967); Strauss and Corbin (1990)]. Other sources of information such as annual reports, private documents and working papers, and visits as a typical tourist, were also included in the analysis. [Triangulation has been highlighted as being an important aspect of qualitative research (Burgess 1984; Yin 1989; Denzin and Lincoln 1994)]. The qualitative approach adopted here opened the way for understanding the processes involved in decision making not just the outcomes (Burgess 1984; Hammersley 1990; Emerson 1983).

The theoretical concepts

This section presents a review of the theoretical concepts that underpin the public funding of heritage. The vast literature on the workings of the market, shows the conditions under which the market mechanism will deliver a pareto optimal solution to resource allocation [see for example, Ng (1983); Boadway and Bruce (1984)]. Such a paradigm is not encountered in the real world, and pareto optimal allocation is generally regarded as being the yardstick against which deviations can be measured. These deviations or sources of market failure address the following overlapping issues:

- property rights,

- unpriced resources or thin markets,

- positive and negative externalities,

- high transaction costs which discourage market exchanges,

- myopia, uncertainty and risk aversion resulting in a concentration on individual rather than society's well being, and

- public goods.

All of these are relevant to heritage. As Johnson and Thomas (1994:182) point out a market for all kinds of heritage would fail on the grounds of links with future generations; and a market for buildings which are part of cityscapes would fail because there is a lack of property rights attached to them. They also note that heritage is generally regarded as being a public good;

Public goods theory is discussed here extends to include merit goods, impure public goods, and club good theory. These approaches, whilst being based on the recognition of the special characteristics of public goods, question whether the concept of a public good is necessarily inconsistent with a 'user pays' approach, and if not, the conditions under which charging for public goods may be efficient (in an economic sense).

The development of the literature on public goods is well documented in Oakland (1988). The traditional way of characterising public goods is by supply. That is, public goods are described as being non-rivalrous, non-excludable, and indivisible, so that a good is a public good if providing it for anyone means that it can be costlessly provided for all. It then follows that as no one can be excluded, or should be excluded, a consumer would not freely pay for such a good. The market would not supply such a good, and this is the reason why governments intervene in the market for goods with public characteristics.

If instead of conceptualising public goods by their supply characteristics, they are examined for the `utility' they confer on individuals, then alternative paradigms come into play. Some public goods may be regarded as merit goods. Merit goods are said to exist because of information asymmetry between governments and individuals. This information concerns the social benefits of the goods, of which individuals would not be aware because of ignorance, uncertainty or irrationality. Merit goods are therefore those goods which a paternalistic state wishes to impose on its citizens. State provision of merit goods implies free admission, although state supplied merit goods may exist alongside similar privately supplied goods for example state and private provision of education or health services.

Duffy (1992) argues that *national* museums are merit goods. He shows how consumption externalities associated with national museums, (education, research, national identity and prestige) depend on public access, which he asserts should be measured not merely in terms of opportunity but in terms of outcome. Not so much that the museum *may* be visited, but that it is visited, so that on grounds of consumption externalities, national museums as merit goods, should be provided by the state and be free of charge.

If public-type goods are again analysed on the grounds of the *utility* they confer and it can be shown that there is both private and public benefit then, in these cases, it is argued that user charges are efficient and consistent with pareto optimal approaches. These are the so-called impure public goods. Ng (1983) shows how goods which have high setting-up and transaction costs may be provided by the state, although it could be argued that the benefits are almost entirely private. The free availability of goods which confer private benefits results in such management responses as queuing, quotas, any kind of dispersal in time or place, or user charges. User charges would generally be set to cover the variable costs of the visit, although in theory, an appropriate user charge would cover marginal costs, with the fixed costs met out of taxation.

Buchanan (1965) argued that where a public good gives rise to problems of congestion, its non-rival property is in doubt, the marginal cost is no longer zero, and therefore public good optimality rules no longer apply. Congestion has been shown by Oakland (1972; 1987) to impose significant welfare losses. Congestion as Sandler (1987) points out, can refer to technical congestion, that is, the number of visitors, but more generally congestion refers to the loss of ambience. The ability to control entry and the possibility of congestion are explain why charges are made for concerts, opera, and the theatre, but not for visiting museums, which are seldom congested. However, museums may charge for special exhibitions, which are assumed to attract a crowd (congestion). [Where congestion is a problem, goods with public-type characteristics may be provided as club goods, either collectively or privately. But clubs are too far removed from the world of heritage management in practice and so will not be developed further.]

The concepts of the market and of public goods has been shown to be useful in the discussion of heritage sites. From the merit good argument, which demands state provision and free access, to the identification of impure public goods, and congestion costs, it has been shown that (a) state provision is not the only possible mode of delivery for public goods; and (b) state provision is not incompatible with a 'user pays' policy. If perceptual barriers have been breached and charging for admission to heritage is regarded as appropriate in some circumstances, what other considerations might be taken into account? An obvious starting point is the tension between revenue generation and the desirability of access. This has been discussed widely (Great Britain 1989; Robinson 1994; Clarke 1991; Griffiths 1994) as has asking for voluntary donations rather than charging for admission (Rados 1981; Robinson 1994). In addition, the valuation of free resources has been explored in numerous willingness-to-pay studies, some of which address heritage sites (Thomas 1992; Thomas 1993; Willis 1994). These then are the models which may inform decision makers at heritage sites.

The research findings

In the public sector there are museums and art galleries, historic houses and other sites which form part of the cityscape in a historic city. Not all heritage sites in the public sector are free but a higher proportion of British sites offer free admission than their American counterparts. In the United States the national museums are free, but in the United Kingdom they now charge for admission. In the United Kingdom other museums and galleries are owned and operated by public bodies (universities, city authorities) and are likely to be free. In the United States, although the same pattern is seen, the non-profit model is more usual. Overall there is less public ownership in the United States than in the United Kingdom. The range of admission charges is wider in the United` Kingdom than in the United States (see Table 1)

Table 1   Type of heritage site and range of charging responses

Type of Site	Number of sites offering free admission	Number of sites charging for admission	Range of Charges* (£1 - $1.50)
American Sites			
National Museum	3 sites	1 site	$2 (£1.33)
Historic House		1 site	$3 (£2)
Art Museum		1 site (voluntary donation)	$3 (£2)
British Sites			
National Art Gallery/National Museum	1 site	2 charging sites 1 (voluntary donation)	£3.50 - £4 £3.50
London Art Gallery	1 site		
Regional Art Gallery	3 sites		
Museums attached to a university	5 sites		
Historic Building as part of a cityscape (Oxford)		3 sites	50p- £2
Historic Botanical Garden (Oxford)		1 site	£1.50
Total number of sites	**13 free sites**	**10 charging for admission**	

*The charges shown in the table are those prevailing in the early 1990s when the bulk of the research was being carried out. These figures have not been updated because they are presented to support the arguments presented in this paper rather than being of importance themselves. The relevant exchange rate was £1 = $1.50

The charging dilemma. - According to respondents there are two unresolved issues at the heart of the charging dilemma. The first concerns the special situation of the *national* collections in the cultural life of the nation, and the second is the perceived appropriateness of a 'public goods model' for these sites. Site directors interviewed stressed the importance of the national collections beyond their role as the flagships of the nation's culture. Their contribution to academic research, scholarship and their role as a resource to be drawn upon by government and other interested bodies, is what they said makes them different. Such responsibilities are associated with high fixed costs (salaries, conservation work, and the maintenance of the buildings in which these collections are housed). The public, though, is only aware of the public face of the institution, and it was said that this could be 'dangerous' when a museum or gallery charges an admission fee. As a director commented *'the public thinks the fee pays for everything'*. In reality the entrance charge usually covers the extra cost of the visitor. The conservation work, education, research, maintenance of buildings etc. which are the primary concerns and tasks of museum staff, are not covered by these charges, and in the view of the director quoted above, never could be.

The tenuous nature of the link between charging and covering all the costs associated with a national museum and gallery makes the setting of an appropriate admission charge problematic. As one American site director said *'less than $5 is a gesture, as you move to $6.50 it becomes a fee'*. (This was an interesting comment as Table 1 indicates that no publicly owned American site charged even $5.)

One site director where admission charges had been discussed, accepted and were awaiting introduction, reflected on the possible halving of the number of admissions, and a possible halving of the trading account if this policy was put in place. With a present attendance figure of 1.8 million and a trading account yielding around £60,000 per annum, he explained that charging for admission would make good economic sense, but his concern was that his particular heritage site played a pivotal role in the economic regeneration of the city.

At another site, the director argued that if visitors paid they would expect to be entertained.

A prime example of the 'public good' model is the Smithsonian Institution in the US. Supported directly by Congress, and not subject to a decreasing budgetary allocation in the 1980s, the Smithsonian Institution is devoted to research as well as being the cultural flagship of the nation, and a huge tourist attraction. Even the modest donation boxes placed in 1993 in the entrance halls of the museum sites, were said to have been placed with one eye on Congress, in the hope that these would be seen as a spirit of self-help, and would not upset the paternalistic instincts of congressional leaders towards the institution.

The national museums and galleries in the UK have moved a long way from this traditional public good model with the highest admission charges of all (see Table 1). This accounts for the debate over charging for admission to national museums in the British press, by members of the government and by economists.

Implementation: making the decision - Unswerving adherence to a public good model has at many sites been superseded by a pragmatic approach in the face of decreasing state funding. Many free sites have already taken a decision to charge, a decision dictated by the financial position of the institution. Strategic decisions of this kind are usually taken at the highest level, with the technicalities of what to charge being taken at a lower managerial level. For some sites included in the study, it was the appointment of a new director which 'allowed' a site to charge. A new director was able to insist on major changes, and charging for admission would be an example of such a change.

In the United Kingdom difficulties of balancing the budget have been tackled by other means before introducing charging for admission. For instance at one of the national museums a cost cutting exercise of leaving academic posts vacant and boosting the retail arm of the museum had been undertaken. At the same time, the decision to introduce an admission charge had already been taken by the Board of Trustees and only awaited an appropriate time for its introduction, which was defined as `failing to balance the budget'.

The reasons given for charging are either financial as discussed above, or to control access. As one respondent said *'it's one part of the revenue mix, all go up and down, but not in tandem, and we hope to smooth the curves'*. Charging for special exhibitions means that popular exhibitions can be balanced with the more esoteric, and so produce an overall profit. Another site charged for admission because local authority involvement had been made on the basis of a projected rate of return on an investment.

At a university botanic garden which lay directly on the tourist route in the town, the pressure of 60,000 visitors a month was reduced to 15,000 by introducing an admission charge during the problematic months of July and August only. Other site directors reported that they would like to charge the groups of overseas teenagers which were deposited at the museums on rainy summer afternoons, with little preparation for their visit or interest on their part, except that these sites had a policy of free admission for all. Overall, revenue from admissions is viewed as a useful management tool, both in funding the site and in controlling access.

Establishing an appropriate charge - the British way: Charging is practised as an art governed by certain rules of thumb. For example, paying to go to a museum is deemed to be more acceptable than paying to enter an art gallery, and `follow my leader' tactics abound. For example, a director commented *'we can't charge if other nationals are free'*, and another said *'if the XXX Museum charged we would follow suit.'*

In the United Kingdom it is at least as important to compensate for inflation, as it is to keep in line with one's competitors. Inflationary pressures result in an annual or bi-annual review of charges in the UK, which contrasts with the American sites which charged for admission which had not reviewed their charges since the inception of the charge (3 years and 5 years earlier respectively).

In general, charges for admission to sites in public ownership are very modest. In a busy tourist town (Oxford UK), site directors questioned professional tour guides about the prices of other sites around the town, and adjusted their prices accordingly (being, they said, prepared to lower prices if advised to do so!). Local authority sites charged what surveys revealed residents would be willing to pay. (In one town this was £1, in another town it was £1.40.) £1.50 was collected by volunteers at a botanical garden and split on a 50/50 basis between the site and a horticultural project in the developing world. For the most part, site directors acknowledged that a £2 charge was the lowest it was feasible to collect, - a £1 charge would mean a loss if the cost of collecting, and possible VAT, had to be taken into account. However, in the situation referred to above where the charge was £1, the collector of the fee had to achieve twice his weekly wage in order to break-even and keep his job.

The London-based national museums have moved ahead of other public sector sites in charging terms. The museum directors who took part in the study were chosen because they had had been responsible for initiating admission charges at their site and claimed these based on *'what the market will bear'*. One national museum which had closed for re-furbishment, on re-opening, based its admission charge to reflect the new 'product' on offer.

Establishing an appropriate charge - the American way: The situation in the US is not dissimilar. A successful introduction of an admission charge was described as being *'a modest charge, well announced in advance'*. The price of other leisure time activities is seen as the base line, and this can embrace the cost of admission to Disney or local cultural sites, or the cost of going to the movies. Charging for sites which are part of the US National Park Service (NPS) was introduced in 1985 as 'a means of relieving the taxpayer burden and requiring the user to pay more than the non-user'. But charging is *not* to be linked to anything in particular, site directors can chose the amount to charge, and as monies so collected are returned to the US Treasury for cross-subsidisation, there is little incentive at the local level for introducing anything more than a nominal charge. The NPS site included in the research, charged $2 for admission, contributing $32,000 to the Treasury, and receiving $60,000 from this communal pool. There was no basis for evaluating whether this was an appropriate exchange.

To charge or not to charge - the voluntary donation. There are several reasons why site directors opt for voluntary donations rather than charging for admission. Voluntary donations are regarded by site directors as less painful than charging, allowing visitors to refuse or to pay less, and are thought to be appropriate in circumstances where there are many free sites in the vicinity. On a pragmatic note, a voluntary donation is not counted as earned income and therefore not top-sliced by the central administration of some American universities. For these museums, a voluntary donation rather than a charge makes good sense.

Other sites asked for voluntary donations from visitors at the end of their visit. One British site asked for a £2 donation to be dedicated to providing access and toilets for the disabled, - the average donation received was 8p.

Another respondent said that suggesting an appropriate amount was essential as people *'don't know what to give'.....'the amount may not be what they would pull out of their pockets'*. The suggested amount was seen as a useful way of suggesting the 'value in the market place'. One site which had recently raised its suggested voluntary donation from £3 to £3.50, found that the increase in revenue was more than could be accounted for by the difference in the two prices. The general expectation was that the visitor would pay the amount that was suggested, although it was also felt that the nature of the voluntary donation was an opportunity for visitors to give *more* than the stated amount, something not likely to happen with an admission charge.

Dealing with equity of access. This is undertaken by defining target groups for concessionary prices, and defining an appropriate level of concession. This is far more developed in the United Kingdom than in the United States.

In the United Kingdom, typical target groups are children, families, senior citizens, students, the unemployed and the disabled. As far as the level of concession is concerned, the overall trend is to offer half price admission to children, the other groups are offered admission at either half price or a little more than half price. Families are offered a family ticket for two adults and two children, at the price of two adults and one child. The reason for having a family ticket is explained by one museum director ... *'this is not a local drop-in museums, our repeat visitors are families who have travelled some distance'*.

Concessionary charges are related to two factors, the first is the perceived ability to pay, and the second is the responsibility for the education of the young. The importance of latter point is well illustrated by one of the leading British national art galleries. Their dilemma is that 50% of their visitors are from overseas, and despite the trustees having no qualms over charging overseas visitors *per se, these* overseas visitors are under 25 years old. The trustees conclude that the overriding responsibility is to grant access to the young regardless of nationality or ability to pay.

Equity of access is also dealt with by offering limited free access. One free day a week used to be the norm for the national museums in London. Directors noted the congestion on the free day, when tour operators deliberately chose the free day to bring overseas tourists to the site. This pattern was subsequently changed, and free access was available on a daily basis, from 4.30pm to 6 pm.

For one American site where charges had recently been introduced, there was as yet no free admission, but should this be needed in the future, the director reported that he would take the usual American route of seeking corporate sponsorship to cover operating costs.

In the UK, sites which regard themselves as making a contribution to their town, offer free admission to local people. Where sites have developed 'Friends', they are given free admission, and university members have free admission for sites in university control.

Can the market mechanism allocate resources to heritage to ensure that these sites are passed on to future generations? Few directors were able to discuss the question concerning a 'sustainable' price, either because the site was free or because the respondent did not have full financial responsibility for the site. One of the national museums had, however, used a 'sustainable' price as one of the possible charging scenarios when its admission charge was first decided upon. Despite the potentially infinite resources which could be spent on conservation and acquisition, this director quoted £15/£16 per head as an appropriate figure, adding that this was clearly not feasible. Three other museum directors suggested that for their site a sustainable price would be in the £3 - £6.50 range. Not only did they all say that these prices were not feasible, but continued the extrapolation by saying that should state support be cut, the real alternative was closure.

Summary - Overall, the reasons why charging is resisted by museum professionals in national museums and galleries and other publicly owned sites in both the United States and the United Kingdom relate to the theoretical concepts of public goods. These are (a) an abiding ideal of public goods being supported by the state, so that 'the only barrier (to entry) should be interest'; (b) the importance of externalities - that the site serves the interest of the wider community; (c) concern for equity of access and how to deal with those whom they wish to encourage.

Where there is a problem of congestion, charges are imposed but this too is consistent with public goods theory.

Charging for admission is also resisted when there is (a) no financial pressure to raise extra revenue or (b) when the admission charge goes into a central fund. Charging for admission is said by those who do *not* charge, to bring problems in its wake namely, (a) that paying customers will want to be entertained and (b) that there is a correlation between charging and a drop in spending on retail and catering.

When charges have been introduced what approaches have been taken? By imposing a modest charge (more of a gesture than a fee); by asking for a voluntary donation; by basing the charge on a willingness to pay study (although this was regarded as a market research exercise rather than a model of the 'value' of a resource); or with reference to the price of other leisure activities. Equity of access has been dealt with through the reduction of fees and free admission at certain times; but charges have also been imposed at the level that the market would bear.

The research findings show that the reasons for charging for admission at heritage sites in public ownership in the United States and the United Kingdom are a mixture of financial and political factors. That is, the financial situation of the site in question and its ability to attract paying visitors on the one hand, and the political decisions taken at the site level, or at national and local government level on the other.

Discussion

Heritage site directors rehearse the concept of public goods and the discussion of charging for admission in their institution. Both of these reveal approaches consistent with economic theory. The public goods model is seen to be uppermost in the heritage directors' minds. The positive externalities associated with heritage are widely recognised. These include a pivotal role in the economic regeneration of an inner city area; an aesthetic role as part of the cityscape of an historic town, as well as the perceived benefits to those who visit the site. The merit good argument is evoked particularly in relation to access for the young. Charging to deal with congestion (numbers of people and loss of ambience) is prevalent in an historic city and consistent with economic theory.

Charging because of a financial shortfall is not consistent with economic theory as such, but may be viewed as the catalyst which changes the perception of heritage from public good to impure public good, - in other words a recognition of both the public and private benefit of heritage. In this scenario the appropriate charge would be based on marginal costs with the government meeting the fixed costs out of taxation. (It is unclear whether conservation, research, maintenance of the building etc would be defined as fixed costs.) In practice as the sample showed, admission charges are often set to cover the additional cost of the visitor; this is a pragmatic solution, the identification of other costs being a time-consuming process.

Whereas other authors have decried the lack of experience and sophistication in price setting in many sectors of the tourism industry [Rogers (1995); Fyall and Garrod (1998)] others suggest that it is the lack of a group approach to this process which is a key problem (Fyall and Garrod 1998). This latter argument is supported by the very different approach of the London-based national museums which have all charged for admission at a market rate.

This paper has demonstrated the dual problem facing those responsible for the financial health of heritage - problems of implementation and the market model itself. A major policy change such as initiating a charge may be implemented without the wholehearted agreement of decision makers, resulting in many decision makers displaying an ambivalence towards charging in principle and practice. Equally, establishing an appropriate charge is not an easy task, the guidelines drawn from economic theory are difficult and/or costly to implement in the real world, and the public/private benefits of heritage and its intertemporal nature makes this task even more difficult.

Once a charge is introduced, a heritage site become part of the heritage industry, a site open for business, a product with a price label attached, to be judged by the consumer on the basis of value for money. The tourism industry is a fragmented, competitive one and entering the industry can only result in pricing levels which reflect market conditions rather than the resource base. [This point is also raised by Fyall and Garrod (1998).] Heritage sites can never be regarded simply as a product in the market place. In addition to the imperative of passing on our heritage to future generations, heritage sites confer wider benefits on society which are regarded as both private and public. Charging for admission creates a market for the *private* benefit only. With the public goods model being out of political favour and charging for admission creating a market for private benefit, it is important to ascertain what other sources of revenue heritage sites may draw upon to ensure their sustainability. In effect, the search must be for a third way of resource allocation and the establishment of a range of different markets to ensure sustainability.

References

Boadway, R. and Bruce, N. (1984), *Welfare Economics*. Oxford Blackwell.

Bromwich, J. (1994), *A Comparison of the Marketing Approaches adopted by a Sample of French and English Museums and Sites*. Department of Business Studies Occasional Paper New Series, No 2, London Guildhall University.

Buchanan, J. (1965), 'An economic theory of clubs', *Economica*, 32,pp 1-14.

Burgess, R. G. (1984), 'Evaluating Field Studies' in R.G. Burgess *In The Field*. Hemel Hempstead, George Allen and Unwin.

Clarke, R. (1991), 'Government Policy and Art Museums in the UK' in M. Feldstein (ed) *The Economics of Art Museums*. Chicago and London, University of Chicago Press.

Cummings Jnr, M. C. and Katz, R. S. (eds) (1987), *The Patron State, Government and the Arts in Europe, North American and Japan*. Oxford, Oxford University Press.

Denzin, N. K. and Lincoln, Y. S. (1994), *Handbook of Qualitative Research*. London, Sage.

Duffy, C. T. (1992), 'The Rationale for Public Funding of a National Museum', in Towse, R. and Khakee, A. (eds) *Cultural Economics*. Berlin, Springer Verlag.

Emerson, R. M. (ed) (1983), *Contemporary Field Research*. Boston, Little Brown and Co.

Fyall, A. and Garrod, B. (1998), 'Heritage Tourism at what price*?' Managing Leisure*, vol 3, pp 213-228.

Glaser, B. G. and Strauss, A. L. (1967), *The Discovery of Grounded Research*. London, Weidenfeld and Nicolson.

Great Britain (1989), House of Commons, *Should Museums Charge? Some Case Studies*. First Report of the Education, Science and Arts Committee. London. HMSO.

Griffiths, B.(1994), 'Financial Management' in R. Harrison (ed) (1994) *Manual of Heritage Management*, Oxford, Butterworth Heinemann in association with AIM.

Guardian The (2000), *Ban the Cash Registers. Museum charges ought to be scrapped*. 9th February 2000.

Hammersley, M. (1990), *The Dilemma of Qualitative Method. Herbert Blumer and the Chicago Tradition*. London, Routledge.

Independent The (1999), *An Artless Response* 5th December 1999.

Johnson, P. and Thomas, B.(1994), 'Heritage as Business' D. T. Herbert (ed) (1994) *Heritage, Tourism and Society*, London, Mansell.

Miles, M. B. and Huberman, A. M. (1984), *Qualitative Data Analysis: A Sourcebook of New Methods*. Beverley Hills Ca, Sage Publications.

Minihan, J. O. (1977), *The Nationalisation of Culture. The Development of State Subsidies to the Arts in G. B.* London, Hamish Hamilton.

Ng, Y-K. (1983), *Welfare Economics: Introduction and Development of Basic Concepts.* Basingstoke, Macmillan.

Oakland, W. H. (1988), 'The Theory of Public Goods' in A. J. Auerbach and M. Feldstein (eds) (1988) *Handbook of Public Economics.* Vol II, Amsterdam, North Holland.

Peacock, A. (1998), 'The Economist and Heritage Policy' in A Peacock (ed) *Does the Past have a Future?* Reading 47. London. The Institute of Economic Affairs.

Rados D. L. (1981) *Marketing for Non-Profit Organisations* Boston Ma. Auburn House Publishing

Ridley, F .F. (1987), 'Tradition, Change and Crisis in Great Britain' in M. C. Cummings Jnr, and R. S. Katz (eds) (1987) *The Patron State, Government and the Arts in Europe, North American and Japan.* Oxford, Oxford University Press.

Robinson, K. (1994), 'Selling the Heritage Product' in Harrison R. (ed) *(1994) Manual of Heritage Management.* Butterworth Heinemann in assoc, AIM.

Rogers, H. A. (1995), 'Pricing Policies in Tourist Attractions' *Tourism Management* 16 (3): 217-224.

Sandler, T. (1987). 'On optimal prices and animal consumers in congested markets', *Economic Inquiry*, vol 25, iss 4 Oct 1987, pp 715-722.

Strauss, A. L. and Corbin, J. (1990), *Basics of Qualitative Research: Grounded Theory Procedures and Techniques.* London, Sage Publications.

Thomas, J. V. (1992), *'Tourism and the Environment: an Exploration of the Willingness to Pay of the Average Visitor'.* Paper published in the proceedings of the 'Tourism in Europe: the 1992 Conference', University of Durham, July 1992.

Thomas, J. V. (1993), *'Magdalen Bridge is falling down, falling down, falling down'.* Paper published in the proceedings of the 'Values and the Environment' conference, University of Surrey 23/24 Sept. 1993.

UNESCO (1972), *Convention Concerning the Protection of the World Cultural Heritage, Paris UNESCO.*

Willis, K. G. (1994), 'Paying for Heritage. What price for Durham Cathedral?' *Journal of Environmental Planning and Management* vol 37, pp 267-278.

Yin, R. K. (1989), Case Study Research: Design and Methods. London, Sage.

Theorising heritage tourism: A review

Steve Watson

Hull University Scarborough Campus, UK

Introduction

As Hall (1994) has stated, tourism and heritage are inextricably linked. They have a reciprocal significance, heritage bolstering the tourism industry and tourism providing a justification for the preservation of heritage assets. There is a problem, however, when confronting the growing literature on the subject, is the sizeable gap between much of its theory and practice. Whilst common in other spheres of activity, the effect is exaggerated in heritage tourism by an antipathy towards the idea and practice of heritage in much of the broader theoretical material, especially the social and cultural aetiologies and history. On the other hand, the development within museology and interpretation of specialised technical knowledge and the desire of practitioners simply to "get on with it" are further expressions of the same dichotomy. The result is an effective operational literature with manuals on interpretation, visitor management, and marketing (Harrison, Ed. 1994), and another literature replete with social theory and critical analysis in which these same activities are subjected to relentless deconstruction (Walsh, 1992; Brett, 1996)

The twain have occasionally met. Interpretation, for example, has been subjected to a rigorous and informative critical analysis that has placed critics with practitioners in the hope that something will happen (Uzzell, Ed., 1989). But it is still possible to attend conferences and read papers that are technically sophisticated and professionally orientated but essentially atheoretical (Moscardo, 1996). It is precisely this theoretical deficit that has fuelled the antipathy mentioned above.

Jenkins (1999) has articulated the challenge of 'bridging the great divide' between tourism academics and practitioners and suggests ways of facilitating an effective 'cross-over'. His very practical solutions provide ways of connecting practitioners with academics who might bring some benefit in terms of overview or specialist knowledge. But this is the practitioner connecting with the scholar and not the theoretical debate. The latter will have left on the bookshelves for fear of seeming 'too academic'.

The purpose of this paper is to explore the possibility of an effective theorisation of heritage tourism, one that the scholar *can* take out into the world, but which also responds to the theoretical critique that is, after all, an essential purpose of the academy. From an examination of the present theoretical debate an attempt will be made to evaluate the extent to which heritage tourism can be more effectively theorised and the ways in which this process might have already begun. It will be suggested, ultimately, that there is scope for developing theory around consumer rather than supplier dynamics and around the concept of 'place', as one which admits a more inclusive approach to both the consumption and supply of heritage than has been the case hitherto.

Antiheritage animus

Lowenthal has coined the term 'antiheritage animus' (Lowenthal, 1998, 100) for the corpus of theoretical opposition to the concept of heritage and its uses, and has distilled much of what has been expressed over the last ten or fifteen years. 'Heritage', Lowenthal states, 'is vilified as selfish and chauvinistic, nostalgic and escapist, trivial and sterile, ignorant and anachronistic. Intricacy is simplified, the diverse made uniform, the exotic turned insipid' (1998, p.88). He goes on to identify six basic elements wherein heritage is variously assailed as:

- destructively chauvinistic,

- elitist,

- incoherent,

- eclectic,

- commercially debased, and

- 'bad' historically.

We might add to this the idea of society beset with an enervating nostalgia which he has explored in more detail elsewhere (1985, pp.4-13) and to which others have contributed. More might also be said about the alleged social structural role of heritage as an hegemonic project to maintain and advance the interests of dominant classes and postmodern analyses which draw attention to the shallowness and evanescence of much that constitutes 'brown sign' heritage. These elements of antiheritage will be explored in more detail below.

Two important texts from the 1980s set the scene for the growth of antiheritage: The first was Patrick Wright's *On Living in an Old Country* (1985), an incisive and astringent account of the cultural context of the rapidly growing interest in heritage. As such it has hardly been bettered. Less effective, but better known and more influential in the debate that followed was Hewison's *The Heritage Industry* (1987), with its particular position on heritage as debased history, biased in favour of the values of the dominant class and ultimately entropic.

Two anthologies on museology from the end of the 1980s have also been significant and influential: Vergo (Ed. 1988) and Lumley (Ed. 1988) did much to stimulate debate around the nature and essential purpose of museum collection and display. Contributors variously examine the transformations of museums into attractions, the nature of the artefactual display and question the status of interpretation as a *fully achieved* account of the past.

What then is the current status of theory in heritage tourism? Can it be taken seriously as anything other than an object of critical analysis? Are the consumers of heritage the willing dupes of cynical commercialism or the unselfconscious victims of a hegemonic project bent on perpetuating existing power relations within society?

The elements of antiheritage

Heritage seems often to have been in thrall to politics and there is perhaps an inevitability about its use to support ideological movements, powerful interests and indeed their opposing factions. Thus the production of heritage is always in jeopardy of appropriation by one or other political agenda. It also risks falling foul of other, perhaps less powerful, ideologies of identity, race, gender or class.

The concept of 'dissonant heritage' was developed by Tunbridge and Ashworth (1995) in order to analyse the potential conflicts between different versions of the past. Dubin's recent account of museum displays as the site of cultural contests is a compelling analysis of power of interpretation and its essential contestability (Dubin, 1999).

Culture war may be a significant contemporary phenomenon but it is not necessary to heritage tourism that it should be attached to any particular political agenda. Heritage may be used for these purposes, but so might any other cultural production from rewritten history to popular music. Clearly a plurality of meanings can be attached to the past and elucidated as such. Once this is admitted heritage interpretation can be construed either as a political tightrope with only the prospect of falling off sooner or later, or as an opportunity for using interpretative processes to explore different, even competing accounts. The accusation of chauvinism in heritage is just one side of the coin and it is at least possible that interpretation may be placed in the service of genuine debate. Whilst a postmodernist perspective might suggest that a plurality of meaning can never transcend a state of free-floating signification. (Rojek, 1993, pp.132 and 168.) the empirical realities of Dubin's analysis suggest that the deracinated view of heritage such analyses imply, may be difficult to sustain.

There has always been a whiff of elitism about the heritage industry, something that has not been lost on its critics. Both Mellor (1991, pp.98) and Lowenthal (1998, pp.48-52) make the point that the historical experience of women, children and a variety of ethnic groups is not well represented in what is received through the production of heritage. In the terms of a class-based analysis Mellor mentions the 'cult of the country house' and associates this with the ascendancy of the National Trust and the Laura Ashley style of interior décor and clothing. (Mellor, 1991, p.97)

Walsh supports this view:

> *There is no doubt that it is the country house which for many people symbolises the idea of the 'heritage' in Britain or, more specifically, England.. It is this type of heritage which should be defined as state heritage, and is clearly a part of a wider hegemonic struggle on the part of the traditional conservatives to maintain their position in British society.* (Walsh, 1992, p.75)

Corner and Harvey (1991) refer to a broadening of the definition of heritage to include the industrial past to which a much higher proportion of the visitors can relate, but which is also, ultimately, hegemonic. As Wright put it, 'purged of political tension it becomes a unifying spectacle, the settling of all disputes,' (Wright, 1985, p.69) particularly where a deeper analysis might reveal conflicts and ideas which challenge prevailing beliefs about the national past and its social and economic corollaries. The move away from representing a national history to the vernacular and the social is, therefore, the production of a past that is complete, or frozen over with nothing to reveal the historical context of the present or how the conditions of the present came to be.

For Urry (1990) the broadening of that which constitutes heritage is connected with a changed perception of history with a movement away from national versions of it to the proliferation of vernacular alternatives representing social, economic, populist, ethnic and industrial images. There is also an associated tendency to contemporise history, to bring it right up to date or at least until the last decade or so. To explain this phenomenon, he invokes a postmodern disdain for elitism. This has resulted in a shift from 'aura to nostalgia' so that anything old is interesting and as interesting as anything else that is old (Urry, 1990, pp.129-130).

The charge of elitism is perhaps the easiest to make against heritage and the counter argument is well rehearsed. Lowenthal elsewhere counters it by reference to Samuel's argument (1994) that much of the heart and soul of the conservation movement and its heritage corollaries have populist, even working class origins. There is certainly a discernible radicalism here that contradicts the charge that heritage is dominated by the cult of the country house and even the National Trust, has radical origins (Mandler, 1997, pp.171-2).

Related to the broadening of what constitutes heritage is the 'leisurisation' of the past, the past as fun, as excitement, as interesting technology, quaintness or engaging style. The results are industrial heritage, folk museums and museums with an emphasis on machinery and paraphernalia, the factory, the household and the community. Add to this the development of interactive displays and the use of spectacle and we are close to a contemporary account of what constitutes the heritage industry. But this is the past in the service of commerce, and commercial debasement is probably the most frequently expressed criticism of heritage. It is also brings on charges of inauthenticity - the real being sacrificed for the spectacular, the arresting imagery of contemporary display methods or a good story. As Lowenthal states, there is nothing new in any of this 'what *is* novel is the mistaken notion that such abuses are new and hence intolerable'(Lowenthal, 1998, p.101). Such charges might also be made against many other cultural productions, and frequently are, from the

BBC to the programming of theatres, the point being that commercial debasement is an artefact of market demand and while the commodification of heritage may be a fact, it is not a necessary condition. Heritage can exist without commerce and perhaps more of it should. Goodey (1998) makes the point well, that peoples' heritage goes on regardless of 'official recognition' which simply adds layers to personal understandings.

Ironically, heritage is as much at risk of commercial debasement from its traditional guardians in the public sector as it is from the private sector. (Rojek, 1993, pp.146-152) Museums are under the pressure of income generation as subsidies subside and local authorities look to heritage tourism as an economic lifeline and so are probably more culpable than any other actor or sector, however misplaced this faith in the commercial viability of heritage tourism may be ultimately. (Craik, 1997).

Of any of Lowenthal's elements of antiheritage, the charges of incoherence and eclecticism are closest to the postmodern perspective. Heritage is thus seen as trivialised by an endless eclecticism that will admit anything, and as devalued by duplication. As Goodey states, 'because everyone and everything has a history, this is potentially a good thing, but it does mean that any professional or authoritative sorting of items or events has long been discarded' (Goodey, 1998, p. 200).

This dedifferentiation (Urry, 1990, pp.82-103) creates a melting pot of heritage, consumed by the 'post-tourist' Feifer (1985) with an ironic consciousness, both knowing and playful. The National Trust may thus present Calke Abbey and the birthplace of Paul McCartney, and the post-tourist consumes them as part of the shallow multiplicity of the tourist experience (Rojek, 1993, pp.174-9).

The rejection of structure in postmodern theory dispels the notion of heritage as an hegemonic project and the antiheritage animus is found here in the denial of meaning in the relationship between past and present and the fugitive nature of authenticity. It has thus been replaced by superficial and evanescent meaning, wherein all manner of objects can be represented and consumed together in a chaotic mixture, the mixture itself being of more interest than its constituent parts. Herein lies the incoherence and eclecticism to which Lowenthal refers.

It seems inevitable that a commercialised heritage will be an incoherent jumble. After all we rather expect our supermarkets to contain a varied and eclectic stock and would shop elsewhere if it were otherwise. It seems unreasonable to expect a commodified heritage industry to be anything other than eclectic. Thus, once commercialism is admitted then so, inevitably, is the customer's (and therefore the marketer's) need for choice and diversification. Incoherence is only another way of describing the swirling eclecticism of the heritage industry and is not necessarily problematic, unless judged by the standards of history. Giving the consumer of heritage some credit in being able to discriminate and re-differentiate that which the industry has dedifferentiated would dispel much of the conceit of the postmodernists, that they have successfully theorised the contemporary perception and consumption of cultural products.

This conceit finds its ultimate expression in notions of simulacra as ultra replicas of supposed scenes from the past and of hyper-reality as the perceptual framework through which these are consumed. The Jorvik Centre at York and Beamish Open Air Museum in Durham are often quoted as examples of these phenomena. This is surprising. At the Jorvik Centre the display is accessed in a 'time car' that not only conveys the tourist past a series of motionless mannequins, but speaks to them with the voice of Magnus Magnusson!

Nor should we under estimate the capacity of the consumer or indeed members of staff to subvert such formats for comedic effect. "Hurry up, get in that carriage," yelled the train driver at Beamish. "I can be as rude as I like, I've been dead for nearly two hundred years." A visitor asked an 'eighteenth century farmer' if he would turn to dust if he left the theme park. "I hope not", he laughed, "I have to drive home after this" (author's notes).

A lack of research evokes personal observation and anecdote. But it seems reasonable to ask how useful the concepts of postmoderism are in understanding the ways in which the past is being received at Jorvik, Beamish and similar places. The staff and the visitors at Beamish seem more than willing to play with the *idea* of the past and it relationship with the present, and to use irony and a certain native humour to reveal what scholars have agonised endlessly over, that an authentic past can never be known, only played at. The artefacts create the conditions for this to be achieved, but the result is not a fugal wander through a recreated past. It is rather, a playful engagement with *pastness*, not so much as the ironic, knowing, post-tourist, but within a more genuine framework for learning that has begun to be theorised within the context of tourism (Mitchell, 1998). The material at Beamish looks real, because most of it is. At Jorvik it is meant to look real, but how else should it look? This may be a society toying with its past, it may be the past in the guise of an imaginary friend, it may be a manifestation of the loss of aura formerly associated with the objects of the past. The sinister fakery of postmodernism is harder to find.

Perhaps the most compelling criticism applied to the themed attractions is, as Urry has said of industrial heritage, that their version of the past is heavily dependent on, and therefore distorted by, an emphasis on the visual. Thus, they tend towards the marginalisation and trivialisation of social experience (Urry, 1990, p.112; 1995, p.161). But distortion comes in many forms and cannot be applied uniquely to the heritage industry in its commercial guise. Museum collections and art galleries often represent the discrimination of Victorian benefactors, contemporary budget limitations and legal constraints on disposal. Archaeological collections represent the availability of sites for excavation. English Heritage castles seem to represent a category which survived Cromwell's demolition teams, but not well enough for subsequent habitation, and for its monastic portfolio it is forever indebted to Henry VIII. To speak of the visual distortion of the heritage industry against this background seems somewhat captious.

Perhaps it should be left to historians to decide what is authentic. It might be safer, however, to let them decide what is history. Heritage in the service of identity, ideology or commerce, heritage as a colourful chaos of shallow meanings and stereotypical images; all of this tends to the view that heritage is 'bad' history. 'The crux of most aspersions against heritage is that it undermines 'real' history, defiling the pristine record that is our rightful legacy' (Lowenthal, 1998, p.102). Wright sees heritage as an extraction and an abstraction of history. History becomes "the historical," a gloss, an "impression of pastness" redeployed as a new kind of cultural product (1985, p.69). In fact, he rarely uses the word heritage, preferring 'historicity' to denote the process he describes.

The problem here is that the epistemological status of history itself remains unchallenged, which is odd, as historians themselves have clearly given it a great deal of thought over a long period of time (Marwick, 1989; Carr, 1987). Nowadays it seems almost too obvious to say that history is what historians write about rather than what took place in any absolute sense. And so its distinctness from heritage is expressed in terms of method and objectives. Lowenthal resolves the issue with what is clearly meant to be a revelatory conclusion that history and heritage are separate categories with different purposes, precepts and methods. To castigate heritage as "bad history" is therefore unnecessary and pointless. Heritage is no usurper of the past after all, but simply another use of it, neither plausible not testable, but a declaration of faith, not susceptible to the validations of the historical method (Lowenthal, 1998, p.121).

None of this is new. The same argument was advanced previously by Schouten:

Heritage is not the same as history. Heritage is History processed through mythology, ideology, nationalism, local pride, romantic ideas or just plain marketing, into a commodity (Schouten, 1995, p.21).

Plumb (cited Wright, 1985) made exactly the same point over 30 years ago. But this is dangerous ground, not least because there is displayed here an unquestioning faith in the methods of history. It is worth considering that a jury was asked to decide what is history in the case of David Irvine and the facts of the Holocaust.

As Maleuvre has stated:

Since the past does not belong to the past but to the present, the historian who searches for an authentic relation to the past searches in vain. For if the past only comes to be in the act of being handed down, the very act of receiving the past is nevertheless a betrayal of its actual nature: to treat the past as past is a perversion of the fact the past once took place as a present (Maleuvre, 1999, p.272)

Lowenthal might have attempted to save history from heritage, but his argument does not save heritage from its critics. Lowenthal simply 'owns up' for heritage. It does not matter that it has no veracity, or method; it does not matter that it is biased, for in a sense it is meant to be. But as in so many aspects of antiheritage it simply need not be the case that heritage is framed in this way. In fact it may well be susceptible to a critical reading of its visual narrative, as Brett (1996) has suggested. It is not a necessary condition of heritage that it is devoid of substance and it might be better seen as simply another means of receiving the past, a medium through which history might be conveyed or a taste for it given. Its potential for learning may not yet be fully realised, and Brett's concept of it as a kind of popular history that is susceptible to critical analysis is useful. Wright, however, warns that any such attempt would have to compete with the existing baggage of received wisdom, tradition and ideology (Wright, p.142), but given the cultural significance of heritage tourism then such an attempt might well be justified. A perception of heritage as applied history has also been developed recently in the context of a programme development project in higher education (Ditchfield, 1998). This welcome initiative might go some way to reconcile history and heritage studies within the academy.

The restoration of heritage

How does heritage tourism fare after the barrage of the antiheritage animus? While it seems clear that each of the points of criticism examined above contains some measure of justification it has been demonstrated that a reasonable defence of it can still be mounted. Even Wright provides a caveat to his criticism of the industry when he asks "whether all those millions can really be mistaken in their enthusiasms" (Wright, p.80).

There are two further lines of counter argument to antiheritage as a whole. The first is its homogenisation of heritage, the second is its almost exclusive concern with the supply side of heritage.

Lowenthal is as guilty as anyone in homogenising heritage. Is it really all the same, the theme park and the museum, the stately home and prehistoric henge? Their coalescence in a postmodern pottage and the proliferation of brown signs does not mean that heritage *is* all the same. Can it never be the case that some heritage attractions do pay due respect to history? And what of the unsacrilised, the site that has not yet, or never will, become a 'sight', but which still attracts the poet, the tourist as seeker of the sublime or the wanderer? Surely these does not deserve the basilisk glare of the antiheritage animus.

What seems clear from this brief survey of antiheritage that is that much of it is directed at the supply side of the heritage industry, especially (but not exclusively) the more commercial aspects of it. Few critics seem willing to berate 'those millions' for supporting the commodification and appropriation upon which it seems to depend, still fewer to point an accusing finger of false consciousness or gullibility at those who queue at its turnstiles. This would, after all, smack of elitism, albeit of a different kind to that for which the industry has been criticised. It is all the more difficult to sustain such a critique when the consumption of heritage is apparently biased towards the middle classes (Herbert et al., Eds., 1989; Light and Prentice, 1994) and towards a particular version of this that depends on the possession of cultural capital, the wherewithal for consuming and appreciating heritage (see Munt, 1994, for a review of these arguments).

Clearly the consumers of heritage have been neglected by the critics of heritage and it is also clear that much of the critique would be weakened by an attempt to address them. It is to consumers of heritage that we must therefore turn in order to pursue the development of theory.

The consumption of heritage

Good quality academic research on consumers' views of heritage has begun to develop. The pioneering work of Herbert et al (1989) and Merriman (1989 and 1991) have made significant though essentially exploratory contributions. The latter, especially, has made a decisive attempt to theorise museum visiting by moving beyond existing psycho-social explanations and class-based social structural analysis to a synthesis based on the concept of 'leisure opportunity'. This is an amalgam of ideas about socialisation within a socially determined framework of expectation and class conditioned behavioural norms. He has also concluded that the material culture represented in museum displays is only part of a broader narrative that also includes memory and imagination.

Outside the museum Herbert et al. focused on heritage sites and while most of the effort was directed at profiling visitors in socio-demographic terms there was an attempt to explore motivational issues, the weakness here being a (purely intentional) focus on operational marketing.

What is clear from these studies is that there are levels of meaning and significance attached to the consumption of heritage that must be acknowledged even by its most ardent critics and whilst popularity is not in itself a reason for approbation it does imply a need for explanation.

More recent studies support this conclusion. For example, Fyfe and Ross (1996) theorised the structuring of the museum visitors' gaze and found that subjects are able to construct themselves in terms of a museum discourse within the socio-physical space that they represent. Johnstone has looked at the way museums can display more than artefactual history and make links with personal histories by providing 'substitute heirlooms' with 'emotional resonance'. Curators of social history collections should, therefore, provide displays which are informed by the memories that condition the visitors' gaze.

Prentice et al. have examined the perception of 'beneficial experience' as a key component of visitor motivation at an industrial heritage park. A conclusion was that segmentation based on this can not only be used for marketing and promotional purposes but also to measure the effectiveness of interpretation, especially where personal interest in local history may be a variable (Prentice, et al., 1998) There is evidence then, that visitors vary in the ways in which they receive and consume heritage. Similar research by McIntosh and Prentice (1999) has examined the concept of authenticity in the light of visitors' own responses to heritage attractions and the diversity shown within these. The cognitive processes at work and the particular notion of 'insightfulness' as an expression of the way that visitors encode their consumption of the display through the meanings they attach to them has been discussed by Moscardo (1996). The challenge, according to Moscardo, is to encompass what is essentially behavioural, cognitive research into a coherent theoretical framework.

This is more than nostalgia, it is the beginning of a discourse between the subject and the past that is facilitated by the museum. Thus what is revealed is a far more positive picture of heritage than its critics would hitherto allow, and which finds resonance in theories of cultural tourism which place emphasis on self-realisation, education and what might be classed broadly as individuated fulfilment rather than collective consumption.

The fundamental question that lies at the heart of whether heritage is worth understanding beyond its commercial guise is whether there a genuine sense of something that is evoked when people meet and interact with the relics of the past? It is possible that such responses can be deconstructed to other components of meaning and that they have a significance only as cultural objects. If, however, there were a genuine sense of engagement with the past this would be a thing that is worthy of investigation, explanation and theorisation *for its own sake*. These early studies suggest that such enquiry might well be worthwhile.

Potential for the development of theory

If heritage tourism is to be effectively theorised it needs to be able to address the theoretical critique which has developed over the last fifteen years and which is summarised in this paper. It should also be able to provide a frame of reference for practitioners, if not always to inform their actions then certainly to explain them and to differentiate them in some way.

Whilst it is unlikely that antiheritage represents a paradigm in the Kuhnian sense it may still require a 'scientific revolution' to move things forward and to demonstrate that antiheritage theory does not address the questions and issues currently being raised. It seems clear, therefore, that any new theoretical development must be epistemologically robust: it must express knowledge of its theoretical contexts, influences and origins. It must be self-conscious and it must self consciously address antiheritage theory and avoid the problems of technical neutrality.

It should also address the meaning of heritage from the point of view of the consumer, the richness of which perspective is implied by the studies referred to above. It is simply not enough to offer critiques of commodified supply side of heritage, its consumption must also be theorised and supported by empirical research. A basis for this would be the exploration of engagement with the past as a category of human behaviour that is worthy of academic curiosity.

In encompassing the consumption of heritage, theory must also be able to differentiate between different qualities of heritage production and should, as Brett has suggested, introduce critical analysis into the popular forum in which much of this production is represented. It should be able to inform and evaluate the work of the practitioner in the presentation of politics, plurality and dissonance. It should make the practitioner self-conscious about these issues and others that are significant: that interpretation at a technical level is not fully accomplished as a means of communicating ideas about the past, that the decontextualised object has little value and that the past is not complete and frozen over, but active in the present.

The extent to which existing theoretical developments satisfy these conditions is difficult to establish. Interpretative theory provides a useful context for looking at consumer perspectives, but this is not the whole story. What is needed is a theorisation which encompasses the societal context of interpretation and explains the social construction of that which is susceptible to interpretation. Established tourism theory provides a basis: the MacCannellian tourist in a futile search for authenticity (MacCannell, 1999), Cohen's typology of tourist experience (Cohen, 1979) and Fiefer's ubiquitous post-tourist, taking it all with a pinch of salt. Within heritage tourism there is a recent and therefore necessarily limited empiricism.

It is clear that a number of authors over the last ten years have not only sought to add their weight to the critique of heritage but have also sought solutions which go at least some way to responding to the conditions outlined above. Brett's solution of developing a critical analysis within heritage as a popular version of history may be an uphill struggle for reasons given earlier, but there is scope for exploring such an idea through the visual narrative of the display.

Another possibility, which appears to be developing a certain impetus, is the idea of 'place'. Wright raised it when he attempted to extend the inclusivity of his concept of "Deep England" (pp.86-87). It resonates with Walsh's view that heritage may find some meaning if it is democratised, if it acts to reconnect the past to the present and if it does so through a re-investment of value in the 'local' (Walsh, 1992, Ch.7).

It also finds expression in the recent theories of interpretation which stress the significance of 'place' and the need for a theory-driven approach to it (Stewart and Kirby, 1998; Stewart, Hayward, Devlin and Kirby, 1998). It can be found in the work of Britton (1991) in a spatial version of cultural capital, that is, 'real' cultural capital. Ashworth has set it within a planning context that is at once aware of the requirements of consumers and sensitive to the sense of place held by host communities and their assertion of local place identity (Ashworth, 1994, pp.15-22). "The heritage on display", Goodey asserts, "has not been fully reviewed by its communities..." (Goodey, 1998, pp. 201)

Previous studies have been concerned with the commodification of place as part of the production of tourism and its political context (Hall, 1994, Ch.7). But recent research provides a new orientation to this issue in the ways that local people might interpret their place for tourists (McDonald, 1997) and in using this invested sense of place as an inclusive device for community development and social inclusion (Russell, 1997; Newman and Mclean, 1998). Some of the practical issues of planning and management are discussed by Hall and McArthur (1998, Ch.4). The *Local Heritage Initiative* in the UK is a response to these movements and the provision of Lottery grant support to local groups in order to preserve and present aspects of their heritage of place is of interest within this developing perspective. There is a clear agenda here for research in establishing the conditions necessary within individual communities for such schemes to be successful.

It is also significant that MacCannell has turned his attention to the matter of place. He tells of a lesson long learnt, that 'heritage is not what the dead did and thought, it is more their manner of speaking to the living' (MacCannell, 1998, p.352). He goes on to make a distinction between the global industry and its presentation of dreamworks, and the local presentation of minor places. Thus the stewards of minor places should be local people, who 'should be crawling all over the place with the tourists, speaking about the significance of history and heritage for them and making the tourists aware of contested heritage'. The minor place should also be presented in a way that goes beyond the visual and indeed the other senses and engages 'vision, integrity, honesty and sympathetic understanding', and in which mere sightseeing is placed in the service of something more profound (pp.360-361). It is perhaps fitting that such a significant theoretical development should find a spokesman in one of tourism theory's earliest and most influential exponents.

Conclusion

Emerging ideas provide opportunities to review the theorisation of heritage tourism. The inhibiting effects of the antiheritage animus highlighted by Lowenthal have been explored and the validity of the individual elements within the critique have been evaluated. The critique of heritage is a compelling one and it potentially adds value to the practice of heritage tourism by elucidating social and cultural influences and issues that form the context for its production. Neglecting these issues leads to precisely those misdemeanours for which the producers of heritage have been arraigned and which by extension and unfairly have tainted all that passes for heritage.

The development of theory in heritage tourism must move on, however, to emerent forms of heritage tourism which are not addressed by the antiheritage critique. Of particular importance are the concept of local place, in opposition to the touristic space created by the commercial sector and the role of local people in realising the cultural capital such places contain. Their role in interpreting heritage assets for visitors and the sense of place and of identity that such inclusive practices imply for them, are all fertile areas for a new theorisation of heritage tourism that has already begun. Thus, might develop a new theoretical paradigm where *touring the past* might be explored in all its manifestations from the avowedly commercial to the genuinely communal, and which also encompasses the diverse perceptions and understandings of those who find a genuine wonderment and awe in such activity.

References

Ashworth, G. J. (1994), From History to Heritage - From Heritage to Identity, In Search of Concepts and Models in Ashworth, G.J. and Larkham, P.J. (Editors) *Building a New Heritage, Tourism, Culture and Identity in the New Europe*, Routledge, London.

Brett, D. (1996), *The Construction of Heritage*, Cork University Press.

Britton, S. (1991), Tourism, Capital and Place: Towards a Critical Geography of Tourism, *Environment and Planning D: Society and Space*, 9, pp 451-78.

Carr, E. H. (1987), *What is History*, Second Edn., Penguin Books, London.

Cohen, E. (1979), A Phenomenology of Tourist Experiences, *Sociology*, 13, pp.179-201.

Corner, J. and Harvey, S. (Editors) (1991), *Enterprise and Heritage: Crosscurrents of National Culture*, Routledge, London.

Craik, J. (1997), The Culture of Tourism, in Rojek, C. and Urry, J. *Touring Cultures: Transformations of Travel and Theory,* Routledge, London.

Ditchfield, S. (1998), *Foreword*, in Arnold, J. Davies, K. and Ditchfield, S., *History and Heritage: Consuming the Past in Contemporary Culture*, Donhead, Shaftesbury.

Dubin, S.C. (1999), *Displays of Power, Memory and Amnesia in the American Museum*, New York University Press.

Feifer, M. (1985), *Going Places*, Macmillan, London.

Johnstone, C. (1998), Your Granny Had One of Those! How Visitors Use Museum Collections, in Arnold, J. Davies, K. and Ditchfield, S., *History and Heritage: Consuming the Past in Contemporary Culture*, Donhead, Shaftesbury.

Goodey, B. (1998), New Britain, New Heritage: the Consumption of Heritage Culture, *International Journal of Heritage Studies*, 3&4, pp, 197-205.

Hall, C. M. (1994), *Tourism and Politics: Policy, Power and Place*, John Wiley and Sons, Chichester.

Hall, C. M. and McArthur, S. (1998), *Integrated Heritage Management*, The Stationery Office, London.

Harrison, R. (Editor) (1994), *Manual of Heritage Management*, London, Butterworth Heinemann.

Herbert, D., Prentice, R. C. and Thomas, C. J. (Editors)(1989), *Heritage Sites: Strategies for Marketing and Development*, Ashgate, Aldershot.

Hewison, R. (1987), *The Heritage Industry*, Methuen, London.

Jenkins, C. L. (1999), Tourism Academics and Tourism Practitioners, Bridging the Great Divide, in Pearce, D. G. and Butler, R. W. (Editors), *Contemporary Issues in Tourism Development* Routledge, London.

Light, D. and Prentice, R. C. (1994), Who Consumes the Heritage Product? Implications for European Heritage Tourism, in Ashworth, G. J. and Larkham, P. J. (Editors) *Building a New Heritage, Tourism, Culture and Identity in the New Europe*, Routledge, London.

Lowenthal, D. (1985), *The Past is a Foreign Country*, Cambridge University Press.

Lowenthal, D. (1998), *The Heritage Crusade and the Spoils of History*, Cambridge University Press.

Lumley, P. (1988), *The Museum Time Machine*, Routledge, London.

MacCannell, D. (1998), Making Minor Places, Dilemmas in Modern Tourism, in Fladmark, J. M., *In Search of Heritage As Pilgrim or Tourist?* Shaftesbury, Donhead.

MacCannell, D. (1999), *The Tourist, A New Theory of the Leisure Class*, University of California Press.

MacDonald, S. (1997), A People's Story, Heritage, Identity and Authenticity, in Rojek, C. and Urry, J. *Touring Cultures: Transformations of Travel and Theory*, Routledge, London.

MacDonald, S. and Fyfe, G. (Editors) (1996), *Theorising Museums*, Blackwell, Oxford.

McIntosh, A. J. and Prentice, R. C. (1999), Affirming Authenticity, Consuming Cultural Heritage, *Annals of Tourism Research*, 26 (3): 589-612.

Mandler, P. (1997), *The Rise and Fall of the Stately Home*, Yale University Press, London.

Marwick, A. (1989), *The Nature of History*, Third Edn., Macmillan, Basingstoke.

Mellor, A. (1991), Enterprise and Heritage in the Dock, in Corner, J. and Harvey, S. (Editors) *Enterprise and Heritage: Crosscurrents of National Culture*, Routledge, London.

Merriman, N. (1989), Museum Visiting as a Cultural Phenomenon, in Vergo, P. (Editor), *The New Museology*, Reaktion Books, London.

Merriman, N. (1991), Beyond the Glass Case: *The Past, The Heritage and the Public in Britain*, Leicester University Press.

Mitchell, R. D. (1998), Learning Through Play and Pleasure Travel: Using play Literature to Enhance Research into Touristic Learning, *Current Issues in Tourism*, 1 (2).

Moscardo, G. (1996), Mindful Visitors: Heritage and Tourism, *Annals of Tourism Research*, 23, (2), pp.376-397.

Munt, I. (1994), The 'Other' Postmodern Tourism: Culture, Travel and the New Middle Classes, *Theory, Culture and Society*, 11, pp.101-123.

Newman, A. and McClean, F. (1998), Heritage Builds Communities: the Application of Heritage Resources to the Problems of Social Exclusion, *International Journal of Heritage Studies*, 3&4, pp.143-153.

Prentice, R. C., Witt, S .F. and Hamer, C. (1998), Tourism as Experience, the Case of Heritage Parks, *Annals of Tourism Research*, 25 (1): 1-24.

Rojek, C. (1993), *Ways of Escape, Modern Transformations in Leisure and Travel*, Macmillan, Basingstoke.

Russell, J. (1997), Towards More Inclusive, Vital Models of Heritage: An Australian Perspective, *International Journal of Heritage Studies*, 3 (2): 71-80.

Samuel, R. (1994), *Theatres of Memory*, Verso, London.

Schouten, F. F. J. (1995), Heritage as Historical Reality, in Herbert, D. T., *Heritage, Tourism and Society*, Pinter, London.

Stewart, E. and Kirby, V. (1998). Interpretive Evaluation: Towards a Place Approach, *International Journal of Heritage Studies*, 4 (1): 30-44.

Stewart, E. J., Hayward, B. M. and Devlin, P. J. (1998), The "Place" of Interpretation, *Tourism Management*, 9 (3): 257-266.

Tunbridge, J. E. and Ashworth, G. J. (1995), *Dissonant Heritage,* John Wiley and Sons, London.

Urry, J. (1990), *The Tourist Gaze*, Sage, London.

Urry, J. (1995), *Consuming Places*, Routledge, London.

Uzzell, D. (ed.) (1989), *Heritage Interpretation, Vols. 1 and 2*, London: Belhaven.

Vergo, P. (Editor) (1988), *The New Museology*, Reaktion Books. London.

Walsh, K. (1992), *The Representation of the Past, Museums and Heritage in the Post-Moderne World*, Routledge, London.

Wright, P. (1985), *On Living in an Old Country*, Verso, London.